(ex•ploring)

SERIES

1. To investigate in a systematic way: examine. 2. To search into or range over for the purpose of discovery.

Microsoft® Office

Word 2007

COMPREHENSIVE

Robert T. Grauer

Michelle Hulett | Keith Mulbery

PEARSON

Prentice Hall

**Upper Saddle River
New Jersey 07458**

Library of Congress Cataloging-in-Publication Data

Grauer, Robert T., 1945–
  Microsoft Office Word 2007/Robert T. Grauer, Michelle Hulett, Keith Mulbery.—Comprehensive.
    p. cm. —(Exploring series)
  ISBN-13: 978-0-13-232852-4
  ISBN-10: 0-13-232852-6
  1. Microsoft Word. 2. Word processing. I. Hulett, Michelle J. II. Mulbery, Keith. III. Title.
  Z52.5.M52G7483 2007
  005.52—dc2

                                                                                        2007015469

Vice President and Publisher: Natalie E. Anderson
Associate VP/ Executive Acquisitions Editor, Print: Stephanie Wall
Executive Acquisitions Editor, Media: Richard Keaveny
Sr. Acquisitions Editor: Melissa Sabella
Product Development Manager: Eileen Bien Calabro
Sr. Editorial Project Manager/Development: Eileen Clark
Editorial Project Manager/Assistant Editor: Jenelle J. Woodrup
Market Development Editor: Claire Hunter
Editorial Assistant: Rebecca Knauer
Executive Producer: Lisa Strite
Content Development Manager: Cathi Profitko
Project Manager, Media: Ashley Lulling
Director of Marketing: Margaret Waples
Sr. Marketing Manager: Scott Davidson
Sr. Sales Associate: Rebecca Scott
Sr. Managing Editor: Cynthia Zonneveld
Associate Managing Editor: Camille Trentacoste
Production Project Manager: Lynne Breitfeller
Senior Operations Supervisor: Nick Sklitsis
Design Director: Maria Lange
Art Director/Interior and Cover Design: Blair Brown
Cover Illustration/Photo: Courtesy of Getty Images/Laurent Hamels
Composition: GGS Book Services
Project Management: GGS Book Services
Project Manager: Kevin Bradley
Production Editors: Blair Woodcock and Andrea Shearer
Cover Printer: Phoenix Color
Printer/Binder: Banta/Menasha

10 9 8 7 6 5 4 3 2
ISBN-13: 978-0-13-232852-4
ISBN-10: 0-13-232852-6

Dedications

To Marion—my wife, my lover, and my best friend.

Robert Grauer

I would like to dedicate this book to the memory of my grandmother,
Effie Burrell Marcum. Her love, encouragement, and belief in my abilities got me to this
point and help me endure every day. And also to John. 143

Michelle Hulett

I would like to dedicate this book to my family and close friends who provided a
strong community of emotional support and patience as I completed my doctorate program
and worked on this edition of the Exploring series.

Keith Mulbery

About the Authors

Dr. Robert T. Grauer

Dr. Robert T. Grauer is an Associate Professor in the Department of Computer Information Systems at the University of Miami, where he has been honored with the Outstanding Teacher Award in the School of Business. He is the vision behind the Exploring Series, which is about to sell its 3 millionth copy.

Dr. Grauer has written more than 50 books on programming and information systems. His work has been translated into three foreign languages and is used in all aspects of higher education at both national and international levels.

Dr. Grauer also has been a consultant to several major corporations including IBM and American Express. He received his Ph.D. in operations research in 1972 from the Polytechnic Institute of Brooklyn.

Michelle Hulett

Michelle Hulett received a B.S. degree in CIS from the University of Arkansas and a M.B.A. from Missouri State University. She has worked for various organizations as a programmer, network administrator, computer literacy coordinator, and educator. She currently teaches computer literacy and Web design classes at Missouri State University.

When not teaching or writing, she enjoys flower gardening, traveling (Alaska and Hawaii are favorites), hiking, canoeing, and camping with her husband, John, and dog, Dakota.

Dr. Keith Mulbery

Dr. Keith Mulbery is an Associate Professor in the Information Systems and Technology Department at Utah Valley State College, where he teaches computer applications, programming, and MIS classes. He has written more than 15 software textbooks and business communication test banks. In January 2001, he received the Utah Valley State College Board of Trustees Award of Excellence for authoring *MOUS Essentials Word 2000*. In addition to his series editor and authoring experience, he also served as a developmental editor on two word processing textbooks. In 2007, he received the UVSC School of Technology and Computing Scholar Award.

He received his B.S. and M.Ed. (majoring in Business Education) from Southwestern Oklahoma State University and earned his Ph.D. in Education with an emphasis in Business Information Systems at Utah State University in 2006. His dissertation topic was computer-assisted instruction using TAIT to supplement traditional instruction in basic computer proficiency courses.

Linda Ericksen, Office Fundamentals Chapter

Linda Ericksen is Associate Professor of Software Engineering at the University of Advancing Technology in Tempe, Arizona. She is the author of over 20 college-level computer text books on topics ranging from the Internet through many software applications, writing for major publishers such as Que, Addison-Wesley, and Course Technology. She was also the author of her own popular series for Prentice Hall, the Quick Simple Series, which featured Microsoft Office 2000.

Brief Contents

Contents

CHAPTER ONE | Office Fundamentals: Using Word, Excel, Access, and PowerPoint   1

Microsoft Office Word 2007

CHAPTER ONE | Microsoft Word: What Will Word Processing Do for Me?   69

CHAPTER TWO | Gaining Proficiency: Editing and Formatting   131

CHAPTER THREE | Enhancing a Document: Tables and Graphics 195

CHAPTER FOUR | Share, Compare, and Document: Workgroups, Collaboration, and References   249

CHAPTER FIVE | Productivity Tools: Templates, Themes, and Mail Merge 311

CHAPTER SIX | Desktop Publishing: Creating a Newsletter, Using Graphic Design, and Linking Objects 361

CHAPTER SEVEN | The Advanced User: Forms, Document Security, and Macros 417

CHAPTER EIGHT | Word and the Internet: Web Pages, XML, and Blogs   471

Acknowledgments

The success of the Exploring series is attributed to contributions from numerous individuals. First and foremost, our heartfelt appreciation to Melissa Sabella, senior acquisitions editor, for providing new leadership and direction to capitalize on the strength and tradition of the Exploring series while implementing innovative ideas into the Exploring Office 2007 edition. Scott Davidson, senior marketing manager, was an invaluable addition to the team who believes in the mission of this series passionately and did an amazing job communicating its message.

During the first few months of the project, Eileen Clark, senior editorial project manager, kept the team focused on the vision, pedagogy, and voice that has been the driving force behind the success of the Exploring series. Claire Hunter, market development editor, facilitated communication between the editorial team and the reviewers to ensure that this edition meets the changing needs of computer professors and students at the collegiate level. Keith Mulbery gave up many nights and weekends (including Thanksgiving) to jump in and help out with anything that was asked of him, including assisting with topical organization, reviewing and revising content, capturing screenshots, and ensuring chapter manuscripts adhered to series guidelines.

Jenelle Woodrup, editorial project manager/assistant editor, masterfully managed the flow of manuscript files among the authors, editorial team, and production to ensure timely publication of the series. Laura Town, developmental editor, provided an objective perspective in reviewing the content and organization of selected chapters. Eileen Calabro, product development manager, facilitated communication among the editorial team, authors, and production during a transitional stage. The team at GGS worked through software delays, style changes, and anything else we threw at them to bring the whole thing together. Art director Blair Brown's conversations with students and professors across the country yielded a design that addressed the realities of today's students with function and style.

A special thanks to the following for the use of their work in the PowerPoint section of the text: Cameron Martin, Ph.D., Assistant to the President, Utah Valley State College, for the use of the Institutional Policies and Procedures Approval Process flowchart; Nick Finner, Paralegal Studies, Utah Valley State College, for the use of his research relating to the elderly population residing in the prisons of Utah; Ryan Phillips, Xeric Landscape and Design (XericUtah.com), for sharing Xeric's concepts for creating beautiful, drought-tolerant landscapes and for the photographs illustrating these concepts; Jo Porter, Photographer, Mapleton, Utah, for allowing the use of her beautiful engagement and wedding photographs; and David and Ali Valeti for the photographs of their baby and their family.

The following organizations and individuals generously provided data and structure from their organizational databases: Replacements, Ltd., Shweta Ponnappa, JC Raulston Arboretum at North Carolina State University, and Valerie Tyson. We deeply appreciate the ability to give students a feel for "real" data.

The new members of the Exploring author team would like to especially thank Bob Grauer for his vision in developing Exploring and his leadership in creating this highly successful series.

Maryann Barber would like to thank Bob Grauer for a wonderful collaboration and providing the opportunities through which so much of her life has changed.

The Exploring team would like to especially thank the following instructors who drew on their experience in the classroom and their software expertise to give us daily advice on how to improve this book. Their impact can be seen on every page:

Barbara Stover, Marion Technical College

Bob McCloud, Sacred Heart University

Cassie Georgetti, Florida Technical College

Dana Johnson, North Dakota State University

Jackie Lamoureux, Central New Mexico Community College

Jim Pepe, Bentley College

Judy Brown, The University of Memphis

Lancie Anthony Affonso, College of Charleston

Mimi Duncan, University of Missouri – St. Louis

Minnie Proctor, Indian River Community College

Richard Albright, Goldey-Beacom College

We also want to acknowledge all the reviewers of the Exploring 2007 series. Their valuable comments and constructive criticism greatly improved this edition:

Aaron Schorr
Fashion Institute of Technology

Alicia Stonesifer
La Salle University

Allen Alexander, Delaware
Tech & Community College

Amy Williams, Abraham
Baldwin Agriculture College

Annie Brown
Hawaii Community College

Barbara Cierny
Harper College

Barbara Hearn
Community College of Philadelphia

Barbara Meguro
University of Hawaii at Hilo

Bette Pitts
South Plains College

Beverly Fite
Amarillo College

Bill Wagner
Villanova

Brandi N. Guidry
University of Louisiana at Lafayette

Brian Powell
West Virginia University – Morgantown
Campus

Carl Farrell
Hawaii Pacific University

Carl Penzuil
Ithaca College

Carole Bagley;
University of St. Thomas

Catherine Hain
Central New Mexico CC

Charles Edwards
University of Texas of the Permian Basin

Christine L. Moore
College of Charleston

David Barnes
Penn State Altoona

David Childress;
Ashland Community College

David Law, Alfred
State College

Dennis Chalupa
Houston Baptist

Diane Stark
Phoenix College

Dianna Patterson
Texarkana College

Dianne Ross
University of Louisiana at Lafayette

Dr. Behrooz Saghafi
Chicago State University

Dr. Gladys Swindler
Fort Hays State University

Dr. Joe Teng
Barry University

Dr. Karen Nantz
Eastern Illinois University.

Duane D. Lintner
Amarillo College

Elizabeth Edmiston
North Carolina Central University

Erhan Uskup
Houston Community College

Fred Hills, McClellan
Community College

Gary R. Armstrong
Shippensburg University of Pennsylvania

Glenna Vanderhoof
Missouri State

Gregg Asher
Minnesota State University, Mankato

Hong K. Sung
University of Central Oklahoma

Hyekyung Clark
Central New Mexico CC

J Patrick Fenton
West Valley College

Jana Carver
Amarillo College

Jane Cheng
Bloomfield College

Janos T. Fustos
Metropolitan State College of Denver

Jeffrey A Hassett
University of Utah

Jennifer Pickle
Amarillo College

Jerry Kolata
New England Institute of Technology

Jesse Day
South Plains College

John Arehart
Longwood University

John Lee Reardon
University of Hawaii, Manoa

Joshua Mindel
San Francisco State University

Karen Wisniewski
County College of Morris

Karl Smart
Central Michigan University

Kathryn L. Hatch
University of Arizona

Krista Terry
Radford University

Laura McManamon
University of Dayton

Laura Reid
University of Western Ontario

Linda Johnsonius
Murray State University

Lori Kelley
Madison Area Technical College

Lucy Parker,
California State University, Northridge

Lynda Henrie
LDS Business College

Malia Young
Utah State University

Margie Martyn
Baldwin Wallace

Marianne Trudgeon
Fanshawe College

Marilyn Hibbert
Salt Lake Community College

Marjean Lake
LDS Business College

Mark Olaveson
Brigham Young University

Nancy Sardone
Seton Hall University

Patricia Joseph
Slippery Rock University.

Patrick Hogan
Cape Fear Community College

Paula F. Bell
Lock Haven University of Pennsylvania

Paulette Comet
Community College of Baltimore County,
Catonsville

Pratap Kotala
North Dakota State University

Richard Blamer
John Carroll University

Richard Herschel
St. Joseph's University

Richard Hewer
Ferris State University

Robert Gordon
Hofstra University

Robert Marmelstein
East Stroudsburg University

Robert Stumbur
Northern Alberta Institute of Technology

Roberta I. Hollen
University of Central Oklahoma

Roland Moreira
South Plains College

Ron Murch
University of Calgary

Rory J. de Simone
University of Florida

Ruth Neal
Navarro College

Sandra M. Brown
Finger Lakes Community College

Sharon Mulroney
Mount Royal College

Stephen E. Lunce
Midwestern State University

Steve Schwarz
Raritan Valley Community College

Steven Choy
University of Calgary

Susan Byrne
St. Clair College

Thomas Setaro
Brookdale Community College

Todd McLeod
Fresno City College

Vickie Pickett
Midland College

Vipul Gupta
St Joseph's University

Vivek Shah
Texas State University - San Marcos

Wei-Lun Chuang
Utah State University

William Dorin
Indiana University Northwest

Finally, we wish to acknowledge reviewers of previous editions of the Exploring series—we wouldn't have made it to the 7th edition without you:

Alan Moltz
Naugatuck Valley Technical Community
College

Alok Charturvedi
Purdue University

Antonio Vargas
El Paso Community College

Barbara Sherman
Buffalo State College

Bill Daley
University of Oregon

Bill Morse
DeVry Institute of Technology

Bonnie Homan
San Francisco State University

Carl M. Briggs
Indiana University School of Business

Carlotta Eaton
Radford University

Carolyn DiLeo
Westchester Community College

Cody Copeland
Johnson County Community College

Connie Wells
Georgia State University

Daniela Marghitu
Auburn University

David B. Meinert
Southwest Missouri State University

David Douglas
University of Arkansas

David Langley
University of Oregon

David Rinehard
Lansing Community College

David Weiner
University of San Francisco

Dean Combellick
Scottsdale Community College

Delores Pusins
Hillsborough Community College

Don Belle
Central Piedmont Community College

Douglas Cross
Clackamas Community College

Ernie Ivey
Polk Community College

Gale E. Rand
College Misericordia

Helen Stoloff
Hudson Valley Community College

Herach Safarian
College of the Canyons

Jack Zeller
Kirkwood Community College

James Franck
College of St. Scholastica

James Gips
Boston College

Jane King
Everett Community College

Janis Cox
Tri-County Technical College

Jerry Chin
Southwest Missouri State University

Jill Chapnick
Florida International University

Jim Pruitt
Central Washington University

John Lesson
University of Central Florida

John Shepherd
Duquesne University

Judith M. Fitspatrick
Gulf Coast Community College

Judith Rice
Santa Fe Community College

Judy Dolan
Palomar College

Karen Tracey
Central Connecticut State University

Kevin Pauli
University of Nebraska

Kim Montney
Kellogg Community College

Kimberly Chambers
Scottsdale Community College

Larry S. Corman
Fort Lewis College

Lynn Band
Middlesex Community College

Margaret Thomas
Ohio University

Marguerite Nedreberg
Youngstown State University

Marilyn Salas
Scottsdale Community College

Martin Crossland
Southwest Missouri State University

Mary McKenry Percival
University of Miami

Michael Hassett
Fort Hayes State University

Michael Stewardson
San Jacinto College – North

Midge Gerber
Southwestern Oklahoma State University

Mike Hearn
Community College of Philadelphia

Mike Kelly
Community College of Rhode Island

Mike Thomas
Indiana University School of Business

Paul E. Daurelle
Western Piedmont Community College

Ranette Halverson
Midwestern State University

Raymond Frost
Central Connecticut State University

Robert Spear, Prince
George's Community College

Rose M. Laird
Northern Virginia Community College

Sally Visci
Lorain County Community College

Shawna DePlonty
Sault College of Applied Arts and Technology

Stuart P. Brian
Holy Family College

Susan Fry
Boise State Universtiy

Suzanne Tomlinson
Iowa State University

Vernon Griffin
Austin Community College

Wallace John Whistance-Smith
Ryerson Polytechnic University

Walter Johnson
Community College of Philadelphia

Wanda D. Heller
Seminole Community College

We very much appreciate the following individuals for painstakingly checking every step and every explanation for technical accuracy, while dealing with an entirely new software application:

Barbara Waxer

Bill Daley

Beverly Fite

Dawn Wood

Denise Askew

Elizabeth Lockley

James Reidel

Janet Pickard

Janice Snyder

Jeremy Harris

John Griffin

Joyce Neilsen

LeeAnn Bates

Mara Zebest

Mary E. Pascarella

Michael Meyers

Sue McCrory

The Exploring Series

Exploring has been Prentice Hall's most successful Office Application series of the past 15 years. For Office 2007 Exploring has undergone the most extensive changes in its history, so that it can truly move today's student "beyond the point and click."

The goal of Exploring has always been to teach more than just the steps to accomplish a task – the series provides the theoretical foundation necessary for a student to understand when and why to apply a skill. This way, students achieve a broader understanding of Office.

Today's students are changing and Exploring has evolved with them. Prentice Hall traveled to college campuses across the country and spoke directly to students to determine how they study and prepare for class. We also spoke with hundreds of professors about the best ways to administer materials to such a diverse body of students.

Here is what we learned

Students go to college now with a different set of skills than they did 5 years ago. The new edition of Exploring moves students beyond the basics of the software at a faster pace, without sacrificing coverage of the fundamental skills that everybody needs to know. This ensures that students will be engaged from Chapter 1 to the end of the book.

Students have diverse career goals. With this in mind, we broadened the examples in the text (and the accompanying Instructor Resources) to include the health sciences, hospitality, urban planning, business and more. Exploring will be relevant to every student in the course.

Students read, prepare and study differently than they used to. Rather than reading a book cover to cover students want to easily identify what they need to know, and then learn it efficiently. We have added key features that will bring students into the content and make the text easy to use such as objective mapping, pull quotes, and key terms in the margins.

Moving students beyond the point and click

All of these additions mean students will be more engaged, achieve a higher level of understanding, and successfully complete this course. In addition to the experience and expertise of the series creator and author Robert T. Grauer we have assembled a tremendously talented team of supporting authors to assist with this critical revision. Each of them is equally dedicated to the Exploring mission of **moving students beyond the point and click.**

Key Features of the Office 2007 revision include

- **New** **Office Fundamentals Chapter** efficiently covers skills common among all applications like save, print, and bold to avoid repetition in each Office application's first chapter, along with coverage of problem solving skills to prepare students to apply what they learn in any situation.

- **New** **Moving Beyond the Basics** introduces advanced skills earlier because students are learning basic skills faster.

- **White Pages/Yellow Pages clearly** distinguish the theory (white pages) from the skills covered in the Hands-On exercises (yellow pages) so students always know what they are supposed to be doing.

- **New** **Objective Mapping** enables students to skip the skills and concepts they know, and quickly find those they don't, by scanning the chapter opener page for the page numbers of the material they need.

- **New** **Pull Quotes** entice students into the theory by highlighting the most interesting points.

- **New** **Conceptual Animations** connect the theory with the skills, by illustrating tough to understand concepts with interactive multimedia

- **New** **More End of Chapter Exercises** offer instructors more options for assessment. Each chapter has approximately 12–15 exercises ranging from Multiple Choice questions to open-ended projects.

- **New** **More Levels of End of Chapter Exercises,** including new Mid-Level Exercises tell students what to do, but not how to do it, and Capstone Exercises cover all of the skills within each chapter.

- **New** **Mini Cases with Rubrics** are open ended exercises that guide both instructors and students to a solution with a specific rubric for each mini case.

Instructor and Student Resources

Instructor Chapter Reference Cards

A four page color card for every chapter that includes a:

- *Concept Summary* that outlines the KEY objectives to cover in class with tips on where students get stuck as well as how to get them un-stuck. It helps bridge the gap between the instructor and student when discussing more difficult topics.

- *Case Study Lecture Demonstration Document* which provides instructors with a lecture sample based on the chapter opening case that will guide students to critically use the skills covered in the chapter, with examples of other ways the skills can be applied.

The Enhanced Instructor's Resource Center on CD-ROM includes:

- **Additional Capstone Production Tests** allow instructors to assess all the skills in a chapter with a single project.

- **Mini Case Rubrics** in Microsoft® Word format enable instructors to customize the assignment for their class.

- **PowerPoint® Presentations** for each chapter with notes included for online students

- **Lesson Plans** that provide a detailed blueprint for an instructor to achieve chapter learning objectives and outcomes.

- **Student Data Files**

- **Annotated Solution Files**

- **Complete Test Bank**

- **Test Gen Software with QuizMaster**

TestGen is a test generator program that lets you view and easily edit testbank questions, transfer them to tests, and print in a variety of formats suitable to your teaching situation. The program also offers many options for organizing and displaying testbanks and tests. A random number test generator enables you to create multiple versions of an exam.

QuizMaster, also included in this package, allows students to take tests created with TestGen on a local area network. The QuizMaster Utility built into TestGen lets instructors view student records and print a variety of reports. Building tests is easy with Test-Gen, and exams can be easily uploaded into WebCT, BlackBoard, and CourseCompass.

Prentice Hall's Companion Web Site

www.prenhall.com/exploring offers expanded IT resources and downloadable supplements. This site also includes an online study guide for student self-study.

Online Course Cartridges

Flexible, robust and customizable content is available for all major online course platforms that include everything instructors need in one place.
www.prenhall.com/webct
www.prenhall.com/blackboard
www.coursecompass.com

my**it**lab for Microsoft Office 2007, is a solution designed by professors that allows you to easily deliver Office courses with defensible assessment and outcomes-based training.

The new *Exploring Office 2007* System will seamlessly integrate online assessment and training with the new my**it**lab for Microsoft Office 2007!

Integrated Assessment and Training

To fully integrate the new my**it**lab into the *Exploring Office 2007* System we built my**it**lab assessment and training directly from the *Exploring* instructional content. No longer is the technology just mapped to your textbook.

This 1:1 content relationship between the *Exploring* text and my**it**lab means that your online assessment and training will work with your textbook to move your students beyond the point and click.

Advanced Reporting

With my**it**lab you will get advanced reporting capabilities including a detailed student click stream. This ability to see exactly what actions your students took on a test, click-by-click, provides you with true defensible grading.

In addition, myitlab for Office 2007 will feature. . .

Project-based assessment: Test students on Exploring projects, or break down assignments into individual Office application skills.

Outcomes-based training: Students train on what they don't know without having to relearn skills they already know.

Optimal performance and uptime: Provided by a world-class hosting environment.

Dedicated student and instructor support: Professional tech support is available by phone and email when you need it.

No installation required! my**it**lab runs entirely from the Web.

And much more!

www.prenhall.com/myitlab

Visual Walk-Through

Office Fundamentals Chapter

efficiently covers skills common among all applications like save, print, and bold to avoid repetition in each 1st application chapter.

---

chapter 1 | Office Fundamentals

Using Word, Excel, Access, and PowerPoint

**bjectives**

After you read this chapter you will be able to:

1. Identify common interface components (page 4).
2. Use Office 2007 Help (page 10).
3. Open a file (page 18).
4. Save a file (page 21).
5. Print a document (page 24).
6. Select text to edit (page 31).
7. Insert text and change to the Overtype mode (page 32).
8. Move and copy text (page 34).
9. Find, replace, and go to text (page 36).
10. Use the Undo and Redo commands (page 39).
11. Use language tools (page 39).
12. Apply font attributes (page 43).
13. Copy formats with the Format Painter (page 47).

Hands-On Exercises

Exercises	Skills Covered
1. IDENTIFYING PROGRAM INTERFACE COMPONENTS AND USING HELP (page 12)	• Use PowerPoint's Office Button, Get Help in a Dialog Box, and Use the Zoom Slider • Use Excel's Ribbon, Get Help from an Enhanced ScreenTip, and Use the Zoom Dialog Box • Search Help in Access • Use Word's Status Bar • Search Help and Print a Help Topic
2. PERFORMING UNIVERSAL TASKS (page 28) Open: chap1_ho2_sample.docx Save as: chap1_ho2_solution.docx	• Open a File and Save it with a Different Name • Use Print Preview and Select Options • Print a Document
3. PERFORMING BASIC TASKS (page 48) Open: chap1_ho3_internet.docx Save as: chap_ho3_internet_solution.docx	• Cut, Copy, Paste, and Undo • Find and Replace Text • Check Spelling • Choose Synonyms and Use Thesaurus • Use the Research Tool • Apply Font Attributes • Use Format Painter

Microsoft Office 2007 Software Office Fundamentals   1

chapter 3 | **Access**

Customize, Analyze, and Summarize Query Data

Creating and Using Queries to Make Decisions

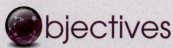bjectives

After you read this chapter you will be able to:

1. Understand the order of precedence (**page 679**).
2. Create a calculated field in a query (**page 679**).
3. Create expressions with the Expression Builder (**page 679**).
4. Create and edit Access functions (**page 690**).
5. Perform date arithmetic (**page 694**).
6. Create and work with data aggregates (**page 704**).

Hands-On Exercises

Exercises	Skills Covered
1. **CALCULATED QUERY FIELDS (PAGE 683)** **Open:** chap3_ho1-3_realestate.accdb **Save:** chap3_ho1-3_realestate_solution.accdb **Back up as:** chap3_ho1_realestate_solution.accdb	• Copy a Database and Start the Query • Select the Fields, Save, and Open the Query • Create a Calculated Field and Run the Query • Verify the Calculated Results • Recover from a Common Error
2. **EXPRESSION BUILDER, FUNCTIONS, AND DATE ARITHMETIC (page 695)** **Open:** chap3_ho1-3_realestate.accdb (from Exercise 1) **Save:** chap3_ho1-3_realestate_solution.accdb (additional modifications) **Back up as:** chap3_ho2_realestate_solution.accdb	• Create a Select Query • Use the Expression Builder • Create Calculations Using Input Stored in a Different Query or Table • Edit Expressions Using the Expression Builder • Use Functions • Work with Date Arithmetic
3. **DATA AGGREGATES (page 707)** **Open:** chap3_ho1-3_realestate.accdb (from Exercise 2) **Save:** chap3_ho1-3_realestate_solution.accdb (additional modifications)	• Add a Total Row • Create a Totals Query Based on a Select Query • Add Fields to the Design Grid • Add Grouping Options and Specify Summary Statistics

Access 2007

677

Objective Mapping

allows students to skip the skills and concepts they know and quickly find those they don't by scanning the chapter opening page for the page numbers of the material they need.

Case Study

begins each chapter to provide an effective overview of what students can accomplish by completing the chapter.

CASE STUDY

West Transylvania College Athletic Department

The athletic department of West Transylvania College has reached a fork in the road. A significant alumni contingent insists that the college upgrade its athletic program from NCAA Division II to Division I. This process will involve adding sports, funding athletic scholarships, expanding staff, and coordinating a variety of fundraising activities.

Tom Hunt, the athletic director, wants to determine if the funding support is available both inside and outside the college to accomplish this goal. You are helping Tom prepare the five-year projected budget based on current budget figures. The plan is to increase revenues at a rate of 10% per year for five years while handling an estimated 8% increase in expenses over the same five-year period. Tom feels that a 10% increase in revenue versus an 8% increase in expenses should make the upgrade viable. Tom wants to examine how increased alumni giving, increases in college fees, and grant monies will increase the revenue flow. The Transylvania College's Athletic Committee and its Alumni Association Board of Directors want Tom to present an analysis of funding and expenses to determine if the move to NCAA Division I is feasible. As Tom's student assistant this year, it is your responsibility to help him with special projects. Tom prepared the basic projected budget spreadsheet and has asked you to finish it for him.

Case Study

Your Assignment

- Read the chapter carefully and pay close attention to mathematical operations, formulas, and functions.
- Open *chap2_case_athletics*, which contains the partially completed, projected budget spreadsheet.
- Study the structure of the worksheet to determine what type of formulas you need to complete the financial calculations. Identify how you would perform calculations if you were using a calculator and make a list of formulas using regular language to determine if the financial goals will be met. As you read the chapter, identify formulas and functions that will help you complete the financial analysis. You will insert formulas in the revenue and expenditures sections for column C. Use appropriate cell references in formulas. Do not enter constant values within a formula; instead enter the 10% and 8% increases in an input area. Use appropriate functions for column totals in both the revenue and expenditures sections. Insert formulas for the Net Operating Margin and Net Margin rows. Copy the formulas.
- Review the spreadsheet and identify weaknesses in the formatting. Use your knowledge of good formatting design to improve the appearance of the spreadsheet so that it will be attractive to the Athletic Committee and the alumni board. You will format cells as currency with 0 decimals and widen columns as needed. Merge and center the title and use an attractive fill color. Emphasize the totals and margin rows with borders. Enter your name and current date. Create a custom footer that includes a page number and your instructor's name. Print the worksheet as displayed and again with cell formulas displayed. Save the workbook as **chap2_case_athletics_solution**.

Key Terms

are called out in the margins of the chapter so students can more effectively study definitions.

Pull Quotes

entice students into the theory by highlighting the most interesting points.

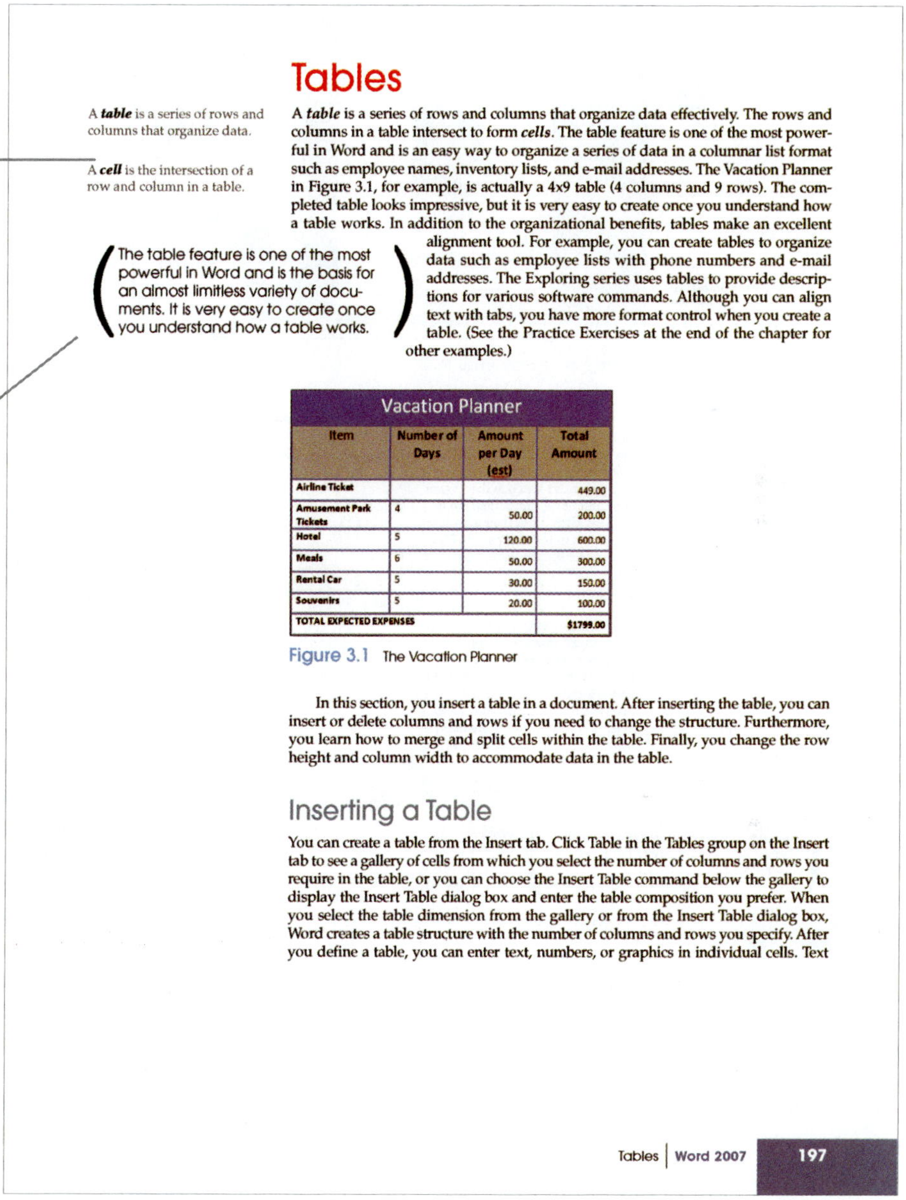

Tables

A **table** is a series of rows and columns that organize data.

A **cell** is the intersection of a row and column in a table.

The table feature is one of the most powerful in Word and is the basis for an almost limitless variety of documents. It is very easy to create once you understand how a table works.

A *table* is a series of rows and columns that organize data effectively. The rows and columns in a table intersect to form *cells*. The table feature is one of the most powerful in Word and is an easy way to organize a series of data in a columnar list format such as employee names, inventory lists, and e-mail addresses. The Vacation Planner in Figure 3.1, for example, is actually a 4x9 table (4 columns and 9 rows). The completed table looks impressive, but it is very easy to create once you understand how a table works. In addition to the organizational benefits, tables make an excellent alignment tool. For example, you can create tables to organize data such as employee lists with phone numbers and e-mail addresses. The Exploring series uses tables to provide descriptions for various software commands. Although you can align text with tabs, you have more format control when you create a table. (See the Practice Exercises at the end of the chapter for other examples.)

Vacation Planner

Item	Number of Days	Amount per Day (est)	Total Amount
Airline Ticket			449.00
Amusement Park Tickets	4	50.00	200.00
Hotel	5	120.00	600.00
Meals	6	50.00	300.00
Rental Car	5	30.00	150.00
Souvenirs	5	20.00	100.00
TOTAL EXPECTED EXPENSES			$1799.00

Figure 3.1 The Vacation Planner

In this section, you insert a table in a document. After inserting the table, you can insert or delete columns and rows if you need to change the structure. Furthermore, you learn how to merge and split cells within the table. Finally, you change the row height and column width to accommodate data in the table.

Inserting a Table

You can create a table from the Insert tab. Click Table in the Tables group on the Insert tab to see a gallery of cells from which you select the number of columns and rows you require in the table, or you can choose the Insert Table command below the gallery to display the Insert Table dialog box and enter the table composition you prefer. When you select the table dimension from the gallery or from the Insert Table dialog box, Word creates a table structure with the number of columns and rows you specify. After you define a table, you can enter text, numbers, or graphics in individual cells. Text

Keyword for search

Collections to be searched

Type of clips to be included in results

Search results

Link to Microsoft Clip Organizer

Link to more clips online

CIS 101 Review Session

Test #2

Monday

7pm

Glass 102

Figure 3.18 The Clip Art Task Pane

White Pages/ Yellow Pages

clearly distinguishes the theory (white pages) from the skills covered in the Hands-On exercises (yellow pages) so students always know what they are supposed to be doing.

You can access the Microsoft Clip Organizer (to view the various collections) by clicking Organize clips at the bottom of the Clip Art task pane. You also can access the Clip Organizer when you are not using Word; click the Start button on the taskbar, click All Programs, Micros... Clip Organizer. Once in the Organi... ous collections, reorganize the exis... add new clips (with their associated... the bottom of the task pane in Figur... and tips for finding more relevant c...

Insert a Picture

In addition to the collection of clip... you also can insert your own pictur... ital camera attached to your compu... Word. After you save the picture to... on the Insert tab to locate and inser... opens so that you can navigate to t... insert the picture, there are many c... mands are discussed in the next sec...

Formatting a Grap...

Remember that graphical elements should enhance a document, not overpower it.

When you inse... fined size. For... very large and... resized. Most t... within the do...

220   CHAPTER 3 | Enhancing a Document

Step 2
Move and Resize the Clip Art Object

Refer to Figure 3.24 as you complete Step 2.

a. Click once on the clip art object to select it. Click Text Wrapping in the Arrange group on the Picture Tools Format tab to display the text wrapping options and then select Square as shown in Figure 3.24.

You must change the layout in order to move and size the object.

b. Click Position in the Arrange group, and then click More Layout Options. Click the Picture Position tab in the Advanced Layout dialog box, if necessary, then click Alignment in the *Horizontal* section. Click the Alignment drop-down arrow and select Right. Deselect the Allow overlap check box in the *Options* section. Click OK.

c. Click Crop in the Size group, then hold your mouse over the sizing handles and notice how the pointer changes to angular shapes. Click the bottom center handle and drag it up. Drag the side handles inward to remove excess space surrounding the graphical object.

d. Click the Shape Height box in the Size group and type 2.77.

Notice the width is changed automatically to retain the proportion.

e. Save the document.

Click to select Square Text Wrapping style

Point to Sizing handles

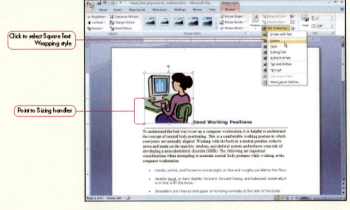

Figure 3.24 Formatting Clip Art

Step 3
Create a WordArt Object

Refer to Figure 3.25 as you complete Step 3.

a. Press Ctrl+End to move to the end of the document. Click the Insert tab and then click WordArt in the Text group to display the WordArt gallery.

b. Click WordArt Style 28 on the bottom row of the gallery.

The Edit WordArt Text dialog box displays, as shown in Figure 3.25.

228   CHAPTER 3 | Enhancing a Document

Summary

1. **Create a presentation using a template.** Using a template saves you a great deal of time and enables you to create a more professional presentation. Templates incorporate a theme, a layout, and content that can be modified. You can use templates that are installed when Microsoft Office is installed, or you can download templates from Microsoft Office Online. Microsoft is constantly adding templates to the online site for your use.

2. **Modify a template.** In addition to changing the content of a template, you can modify the structure and design. The structure is modified by changing the layout of a slide. To change the layout, drag placeholders to new locations or resize placeholders. You can even add placeholders so that elements such as logos can be included.

3. **Create a presentation in Outline view.** When you use a storyboard to determine your content, you create a basic outline. Then you can enter your presentation in Outline view, which enables you to concentrate on the content of the presentation. Using Outline view keeps you from getting buried in design issues at the cost of your content. It also saves you time because you can enter the information without having to move from placeholder to placeholder.

4. **Modify an outline structure.** Because the Outline view gives you a global view of the presentation, it helps you see the underlying structure of the presentation. You are able to see where content needs to be strengthened, or where the flow of information needs to be revised. If you find a slide with content that would be presented better in another location in the slide show, you can use the Collapse and Expand features to easily move it. By collapsing the slide content, you can drag it to a new location and then expand it. To move individual bullet points, cut and paste the bullet point or drag-and-drop it.

5. **Print an outline.** When you present, using the outline version of your slide show as a reference is a boon. No matter how well you know your information, it is easy to forget to present some information when facing an audience. While you would print speaker's notes if you have many details, you can print the outline as a quick reference. The outline can be printed in either the collapsed or the expanded form, giving you far fewer pages to shuffle in front of an audience than printing speaker's notes would.

6. **Import an outline.** You do not need to re-enter information from an outline created in Microsoft Word or another word processor. You can use the Open feature to import any outline that has been saved in a format that PowerPoint can read. In addition to a Word outline, you can use the common generic formats Rich Text Format and Plain Text Format.

7. **Add existing content to a presentation.** After you spend time creating the slides in a slide show, you may find that slides in the slide show would be appropriate in another show at a later date. Any slide you create can be reused in another presentation, thereby saving you considerable time and effort. You simply open the Reuse Slides pane, locate the slide show with the slide you need, and then click on the thumbnail of the slide to insert a copy of it in the new slide show.

8. **Examine slide show design principles.** With a basic understanding of slide show design principles you can create presentations that reflect your personality in a professional way. The goal of applying these principles is to create a slide show that focuses the audience on the message of the slide without being distracted by clutter or unreadable text.

9. **Apply and modify a design theme.** PowerPoint provides you with themes to help you create a clean, professional look for your presentation. Once a theme is applied you can modify the theme by changing the color scheme, the font scheme, the effects scheme, or the background style.

10. **Insert a header or footer.** Identifying information can be included in a header or footer. You may, for example, wish to include the group to whom you are presenting, or the location of the presentation, or a copyright notation for original work. You can apply footers to slides, handouts, and Notes pages. Headers may be applied to handouts and Notes pages.

Summary

links directly back to the objectives so students can more effectively study and locate the concepts that they need to focus on.

More End of Chapter Exercises with New Levels of Assessment

offer instructors more options for assessment. Each chapter has approximately 12-15 projects per chapter ranging from multiple choice to open-ended projects.

Practice Exercises

reinforce skills learned in the chapter with specific directions on what to do and how to do it.

New Mid-Level Exercises

assess the skills learned in the chapter by directing the students on what to do but not how to do it.

New Capstone Exercises

cover all of the skills with in each chapter without telling students how to perform the skills.

Mini Cases with Rubrics

are open ended exercises that guide both instructors and students to a solution with a specific rubric for each Mini Case.

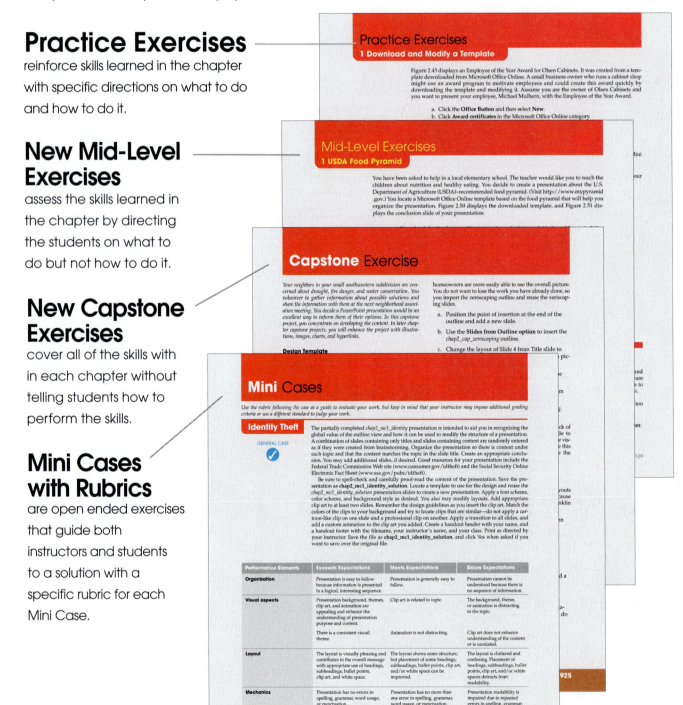

Using Word, Excel, Access, and PowerPoint

bjectives

After you read this chapter, you will be able to:

1. Identify common interface components **(page 4)**.
2. Use Office 2007 Help **(page 10)**.
3. Open a file **(page 18)**.
4. Save a file **(page 21)**.
5. Print a document **(page 24)**.
6. Select text to edit **(page 31)**.
7. Insert text and change to the Overtype mode **(page 32)**.
8. Move and copy text **(page 34)**.
9. Find, replace, and go to text **(page 36)**.
10. Use the Undo and Redo commands **(page 39)**.
11. Use language tools **(page 39)**.
12. Apply font attributes **(page 43)**.
13. Copy formats with the Format Painter **(page 47)**.

Hands-On Exercises

Exercises	Skills Covered
1. IDENTIFYING PROGRAM INTERFACE COMPONENTS AND USING HELP (page 12)	• Use PowerPoint's Office Button, Get Help in a Dialog Box, and Use the Zoom Slider • Use Excel's Ribbon, Get Help from an Enhanced ScreenTip, and Use the Zoom Dialog Box • Search Help in Access • Use Word's Status Bar • Search Help and Print a Help Topic
2. PERFORMING UNIVERSAL TASKS (page 28) Open: chap1_ho2_sample.docx Save as: chap1_ho2_solution.docx	• Open a File and Save It with a Different Name • Use Print Preview and Select Options • Print a Document
3. PERFORMING BASIC TASKS (page 48) Open: chap1_ho3_internet.docx Save as: chap_ho3_internet_solution.docx	• Cut, Copy, Paste, and Undo • Find and Replace Text • Check Spelling • Choose Synonyms and Use Thesaurus • Use the Research Tool • Apply Font Attributes • Use Format Painter

CASE STUDY

Color Theory Design

Natalie Trevino's first job after finishing her interior design degree is with Color Theory Design of San Diego. Her new supervisor has asked her to review a letter written to an important client and to make any changes or corrections she thinks will improve it. Even though Natalie has used word processing software in the past, she is unfamiliar with Microsoft Office 2007. She needs to get up to speed with Word 2007 so that she can open the letter, edit the content, format the appearance, re-save the file, and print the client letter. Natalie wants to successfully complete this important first task, plus she wants to become familiar with all of Office 2007 because she realizes that her new employer, CTD, makes extensive use of all the Office products.

Case Study

In addition, Natalie needs to improve the appearance of an Excel workbook by applying font attributes, correcting spelling errors, changing the zoom magnification, and printing the worksheet. Finally, Natalie needs to modify a short PowerPoint presentation that features supplemental design information for CTD's important client.

Your Assignment

- Read the chapter and open the existing client letter, *chap1_case_design*.
- Edit the letter by inserting and overtyping text and moving existing text to improve the letter's readability.
- Find and replace text that you want to update.
- Check the spelling and improve the vocabulary by using the thesaurus.
- Modify the letter's appearance by applying font attributes.
- Save the file as **chap1_case_design_solution**, print preview, and print a copy of the letter.
- Open the *chap1_case_bid* workbook in Excel, apply bold and blue font color to the column headings, spell-check the worksheet, change the zoom to 125%, print preview, and print the workbook. Save the workbook as **chap1_case_bid_solution**.
- Open the *chap1_case_design* presentation in PowerPoint, spell-check the presentation, format text, and save it as **chap1_case_design_solution**.

Microsoft Office 2007 Software

(Which software application should you choose? You have to start with an analysis of the output required.)

Microsoft Office 2007 is composed of several software applications, of which the primary components are Word, Excel, PowerPoint, and Access. These programs are powerful tools that can be used to increase productivity in creating, editing, saving, and printing files. Each program is a specialized and sophisticated program, so it is necessary to use the correct one to successfully complete a task, much like using the correct tool in the physical world. For example, you use a hammer, not a screwdriver, to pound a nail into the wall. Using the correct tool gets the job done correctly and efficiently the first time; using the wrong tool may require redoing the task, thus wasting time. Likewise, you should use the most appropriate software application to create and work with computer data.

Choosing the appropriate application to use in a situation seems easy to the beginner. If you need to create a letter, you type the letter in Word. However, as situations increase in complexity, so does the need to think through using each application. For example, you can create an address book of names and addresses in Word to create form letters; you can create an address list in Excel and then use spreadsheet commands to manipulate the data; further, you can store addresses in an Access database table and then use database capabilities to manipulate the data. Which software application should you choose? You have to start with an analysis of the output required. If you only want a form letter as the final product, then you might use Word; however, if you want to spot customer trends with the data and provide detailed reports, you would use Access. Table 1.1 describes the main characteristics of the four primary programs in Microsoft Office 2007 to help you decide which program to use for particular tasks.

Table 1.1 Office Products

Office 2007 Product	Application Characteristics
Word 2007	Word processing software is used with text to create, edit, and format documents such as letters, memos, reports, brochures, resumes, and flyers.
Excel 2007	Spreadsheet software is used to store quantitative data and to perform accurate and rapid calculations with results ranging from simple budgets to financial analyses and statistical analyses.
PowerPoint 2007	Presentation graphics software is used to create slide shows for presentation by a speaker, to be published as part of a Web site, or to run as a stand-alone application on a computer kiosk.
Access 2007	Relational database software is used to store data and convert it into information. Database software is used primarily for decision-making by businesses that compile data from multiple records stored in tables to produce informative reports.

Word processing software is used primarily with text to create, edit, and format documents.

Spreadsheet software is used primarily with numbers to create worksheets.

Presentation graphics software is used primarily to create electronic slide shows.

Relational database software is used to store data and convert it into information.

In this section, you explore the common interface among the programs. You learn the names of the interface elements. In addition, you learn how to use Help to get assistance in using the software.

Identifying Common Interface Components

A ***user interface*** is the meeting point between computer software and the person using it.

A ***user interface*** is the meeting point between computer software and the person using it and provides the means for a person to communicate with a software program. Word, Excel, PowerPoint, and Access share the overall Microsoft Office 2007 interface. This interface is made up of three main sections of the screen display shown in Figure 1.1.

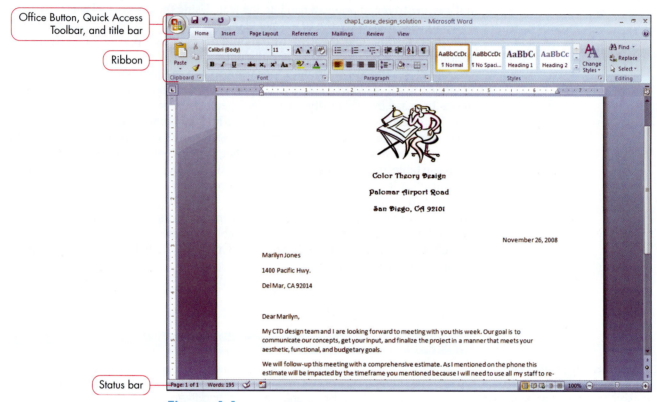

Figure 1.1 Office 2007 Interface

Use the Office Button and Quick Access Toolbar

The first section of the Office 2007 interface contains three distinct items: the Microsoft Office Button (referred to as Office Button in the Exploring series), Quick Access Toolbar, and the title bar. These three items are located at the top of the interface for quick access and reference. The following paragraphs explain each item.

Click the ***Office Button*** to display the Office menu.

The ***Office menu*** contains commands that work with an entire file or with the program.

The ***Office Button*** is an icon that, when clicked, displays the ***Office menu***, a list of commands that you can perform on the entire file or for the specific Office program. For example, when you want to perform a task that involves the entire document, such as saving, printing, or sharing a file with others, you use the commands on the Office menu. You also use the Office menu commands to work with the entire program, such as customizing program settings or exiting from the program. Some commands on the Office menu perform a default action when you click them, such as Save—the file open in the active window is saved. However, other commands open a submenu when you point to or click the command. Figure 1.2 displays the Office menu in Access 2007.

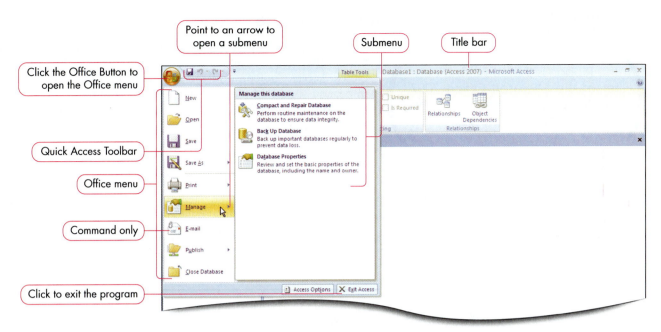

Figure 1.2   Access Office Menu

TIP   Displaying the Office Menu from the Keyboard

If you prefer to use a keyboard shortcut to display the Office menu instead of clicking the Office Button, press Alt+F.

The **Quick Access Toolbar** contains buttons for frequently used commands.

The second item at the top of the window is the **Quick Access Toolbar**, which contains buttons for frequently used commands, such as saving a file or undoing an action. This toolbar keeps buttons for common tasks on the screen at all times, enabling you to be more productive in using these frequently used commands.

TIP   Customizing the Quick Access Toolbar

As you become more familiar with Microsoft Office 2007, you might find that you need quick access to additional commands, such as Print Preview or Spelling & Grammar. You can easily customize the Quick Access Toolbar by clicking the Customize Quick Access Toolbar drop-down arrow on the right end of the toolbar and adding command buttons from the list that displays. You also can customize the toolbar by changing where it displays. If you want it closer to the document window, you can move the toolbar below the Ribbon.

A **title bar** displays the program name and file name at the top of a window.

The third item at the top of the screen is the **title bar**, which displays the name of the open program and the file name at the top of a window. For example, in Figure 1.1, *chap1_case_design_solution* is the name of a document, and *Microsoft Word* is the name of the program. In Figure 1.2, *Database1* is the name of the file, and *Microsoft Access* is the name of the program.

The **Ribbon** is a large strip of visual commands that enables you to perform tasks.

> The Ribbon is the command center of the Microsoft Office 2007 interface, providing access to the functionality of the programs.

Familiarize Yourself with the Ribbon

The second section of the Office 2007 interface is the **Ribbon**, a large strip of visual commands that displays across the screen below the Office Button, Quick Access Toolbar, and the title bar. The Ribbon is the most important section of the interface: It is the command center of the Microsoft Office 2007 interface, providing access to the functionality of the programs (see Figure 1.3).

Figure 1.3   The Ribbon

The Ribbon has three main components: tabs, groups, and commands. The following list describes each component.

Tabs, which look like folder tabs, divide the Ribbon into task-oriented categories.

- **Tabs**, which look like folder tabs, divide the Ribbon into task-oriented sections. For example, the Ribbon in Word contains these tabs: Home, Insert, Page Layout, Reference, Mailings, Review, and View. When you click the Home tab, you see a set of core commands for that program. When you click the Insert tab, you see a set of commands that enable you to insert objects, such as tables, clip art, headers, page numbers, etc.

Groups organize similar commands together within each tab.

- **Groups** organize related commands together on each tab. For example, the Home tab in Word contains these groups: Clipboard, Font, Paragraph, Styles, and Editing. These groups help organize related commands together so that you can find them easily. For example, the Font group contains font-related commands, such as Font, Font Size, Bold, Italic, Underline, Highlighter, and Font Color.

A **command** is a visual icon in each group that you click to perform a task.

- **Commands** are specific tasks performed. Commands appear as visual icons or buttons within the groups on the Ribbon. The icons are designed to provide a visual clue of the purpose of the command. For example, the Bold command looks like a bolded B in the Font group on the Home tab. You simply click the desired command to perform the respective task.

The Ribbon has the same basic design—tabs, groups, and commands—across all Microsoft Office 2007 applications. When you first start using an Office 2007 application, you use the Home tab most often. The groups of commands on the Home tab are designed to get you started using the software. For example, the Home tab contains commands to help you create, edit, and format a document in Word, a worksheet in Excel, and a presentation in PowerPoint. In Access, the Home tab contains groups of commands to insert, delete, and edit records in a database table. While three of the four applications contain an Insert tab, the specific groups and commands differ by application. Regardless of the application, however, the Insert tab contains commands to *insert something*, whether it is a page number in Word, a column chart in Excel, or a shape in PowerPoint. One of the best ways to develop an understanding of the Ribbon is to study its structure in each application. As you explore each program, you will notice the similarities in how commands are grouped on tabs, and you will notice the differences specific to each application.

TIP   Hiding the Ribbon

If you are creating a large document or worksheet, you might find that the Ribbon takes up too much of the screen display. Microsoft enables you to temporarily hide a large portion of the Ribbon. Double-click the active tab, such as Home, to hide all the groups and commands, greatly reducing the size of the Ribbon. When you want to display the entire Ribbon, double-click the active tab. You also can press **Ctrl+F1** to minimize and maximize the Ribbon.

The Ribbon provides an extensive sets of commands that you use when creating and editing documents, worksheets, slides, tables, or other items. Figure 1.4 points out other important components of the Ribbon.

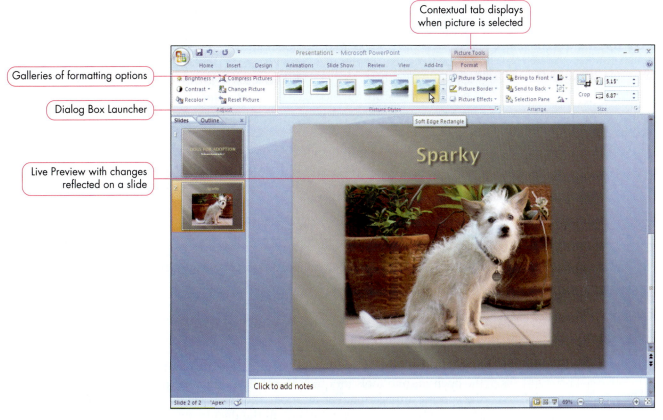

Figure 1.4   PowerPoint with Ribbon

A *dialog box* is a window that provides options related to a group of commands.

A *Dialog Box Launcher* is a small icon that, when clicked, opens a related dialog box.

A *gallery* is a set of options that appears as thumbnail graphics.

Live Preview provides a preview of the results for gallery options.

Figure 1.4 shows examples of four other components of the Ribbon. These components include a Dialog Box Launcher, a gallery, Live Preview, and a contextual tab. The following list describes each component:

- A *Dialog Box Launcher* is a small icon located on the right side of some group names that you click to open a related *dialog box*, which is a window that provides options related to a group of commands.

- A *gallery* is a set of options that appear as thumbnail graphics that visually represent the option results. For example, if you create a chart in Excel, a gallery of chart formatting options provides numerous choices for formatting the chart.

- *Live Preview* works with the galleries, providing a preview of the results of formatting in the document. As you move your mouse pointer over the gallery thumbnails, you see how each formatting option affects the selected item in your document, worksheet, or presentation. This feature increases productivity because you see the results immediately. If you do not like the results, keep moving the mouse pointer over other gallery options until you find a result you like.

A ***contextual tab*** is a tab that provides specialized commands that display only when the object they affect is selected.

- A ***contextual tab*** provides specialized commands that display only when the object they affect is selected. For example, if you insert a picture on a slide, PowerPoint displays a contextual tab on the Ribbon with commands specifically related to the selected image. When you click outside the picture to deselect it, the contextual tab disappears.

A ***Key Tip*** is the letter or number that displays over each feature on the Ribbon and Quick Access Toolbar and is the keyboard equivalent that you press.

TIP   Using Keyboard Shortcuts

Many people who have used previous Office products like to use the keyboard to initiate commands. Microsoft Office 2007 makes it possible for you to continue to use keyboard shortcuts for commands on the Ribbon. Simply press Alt on the keyboard to display the Ribbon and Quick Access Toolbar with shortcuts called Key Tips. A Key Tip is the letter or number that displays over each feature on the Ribbon or Quick Access Toolbar and is the keyboard equivalent that you press. Notice the Key Tips that display in Figure 1.5 as a result of pressing Alt on the keyboard. Other keyboard shortcuts, such as Ctrl+C to copy text, remain the same from previous versions of Microsoft Office.

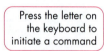
Press the letter on the keyboard to initiate a command

Figure 1.5   Key Tips Displayed for Ribbon and Quick Access Toolbar

Use the Status Bar

The **status bar** displays below the document and provides information about the open file and buttons for quick access.

The third major section of the Office 2007 user interface is the status bar. The ***status bar*** displays at the bottom of the program window and contains information about the open file and tools for quick access. The status bar contains details for the file in the specific application. For example, the Word status bar shows the current page, total number of pages, total words in the document, and proofreading status. The PowerPoint status bar shows the slide number, total slides in the presentation, and the applied theme. The Excel status bar provides general instructions and displays the average, count, and sum of values for selected cells. In each program, the status bar also includes View commands from the View tab for quick access. You can use the View commands to change the way the document, worksheet, or presentation displays onscreen. Table 1.2 describes the main characteristics of each Word 2007 view.

Table 1.2 Word Document Views

View Option	Characteristics
Print Layout	Displays the document as it will appear when printed.
Full Screen Reading	Displays the document on the entire screen to make reading long documents easier. To remove Full Screen Reading, press the Esc key on the keyboard.
Web Page	Displays the document as it would look as a Web page.
Outline	Displays the document as an outline.
Draft	Displays the document for quick editing without additional elements such as headers or footers.

The ***Zoom slider*** enables you to increase or decrease the magnification of the file onscreen.

The ***Zoom slider***, located on the right edge of the status bar, enables you to drag the slide control to change the magnification of the current document, worksheet, or presentation. You can change the display to zoom in on the file to get a close up view, or you can zoom out to get an overview of the file. To use the Zoom slider, click and drag the slider control to the right to increase the zoom or to the left to decrease the zoom. If you want to set a specific zoom, such as 78%, you can type the precise value in the Zoom dialog box when you click Zoom on the View tab. Figure 1.6 shows the Zoom dialog box and the elements on Word's status bar. The Zoom dialog box in Excel and PowerPoint looks similar to the Word Zoom dialog box, but it contains fewer options in the other programs.

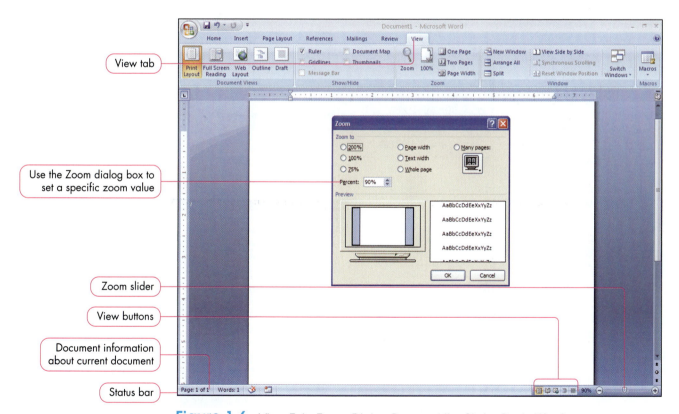

Figure 1.6 View Tab, Zoom Dialog Box, and the Status Bar in Word

Using Office 2007 Help

Help is always available when you use any Office 2007 program.

Have you ever started a project such as assembling an entertainment center and had to abandon it because you had no way to get help when you got stuck? Microsoft Office includes features that keep this type of scenario from happening when you use Word, Excel, Access, or PowerPoint. In fact, several methods are available to locate help when you need assistance performing tasks. Help is always available when you use any Office 2007 program. Help files reside on your computer when you install Microsoft Office, and Microsoft provides additional help files on its Web site. If you link to Microsoft Office Online, you not only have access to help files for all applications, you also have access to up-to-date products, files, and graphics to help you complete projects.

Use Office 2007 Help

To access Help, press F1 on the keyboard or click the Help button on the right edge of the Ribbon shown in Figure 1.7. If you know the topic you want help with, such as printing, you can type the key term in the Search box to display help files on that topic. Help also displays general topics in the lower part of the Help window that are links to further information. To display a table of contents for the Help files, click the Show Table of Contents button, and after locating the desired help topic, you can print the information for future reference by clicking the Print button. Figure 1.7 shows these elements in Excel Help.

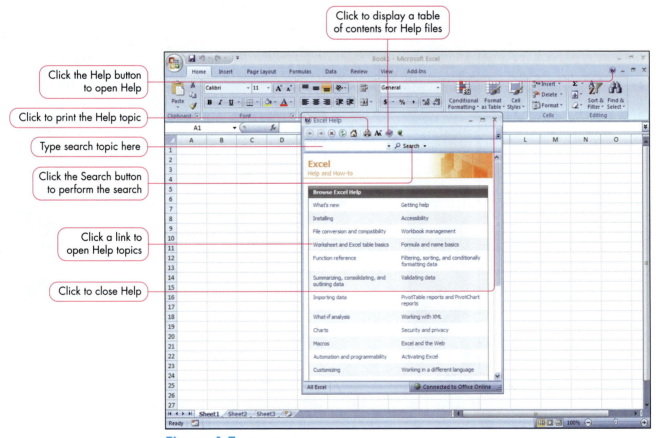

Figure 1.7 Excel Help

Use Enhanced ScreenTips

An ***Enhanced ScreenTip*** displays the name and brief description of a command when you rest the pointer on a command.

Another method for getting help is to use the Office 2007 Enhanced ScreenTips. An ***Enhanced ScreenTip*** displays when you rest the mouse pointer on a command. Notice in Figure 1.8 that the Enhanced ScreenTip provides the command name, a brief description of the command, and a link for additional help. To get help on the specific command, keep the pointer resting on the command and press F1 if the Enhanced ScreenTip displays a Help icon. The advantage of this method is that you do not have to find the correct information yourself because the Enhanced ScreenTip help is context sensitive.

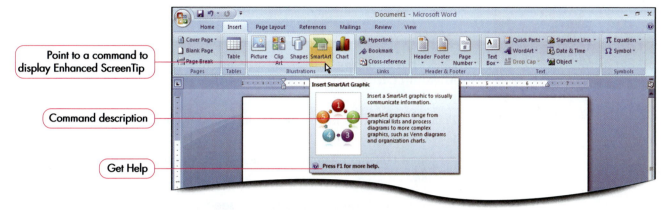

Point to a command to display Enhanced ScreenTip

Command description

Get Help

Figure 1.8 Enhanced ScreenTip

Get Help with Dialog Boxes

As you work within a dialog box, you might need help with some of the numerous options contained in that dialog box, but you do not want to close the dialog box to get assistance. For example, if you open the Insert Picture dialog box and want help with inserting files, click the Help button located on the title bar of the dialog box to display help for the dialog box. Figure 1.9 shows the Insert Picture dialog box with Help displayed.

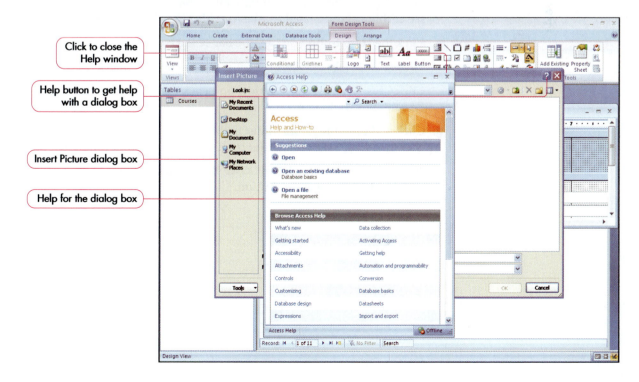

Click to close the Help window

Help button to get help with a dialog box

Insert Picture dialog box

Help for the dialog box

Figure 1.9 Help with Dialog Boxes

Hands-On Exercises

1 | Identifying Program Interface Components and Using Help

Skills covered: 1. Use PowerPoint's Office Button, Get Help in a Dialog Box, and Use the Zoom Slider **2.** Use Excel's Ribbon, Get Help from an Enhanced ScreenTip, and Use the Zoom Dialog Box **3.** Search Help in Access **4.** Use Word's Status Bar **5.** Search Help and Print a Help Topic

Step 1
Use PowerPoint's Office Button, Get Help in a Dialog Box, and Use the Zoom Slider

Refer to Figure 1.10 as you complete Step 1.

a. Click **Start** to display the Start menu. Click (or point to) **All Programs**, click **Microsoft Office**, then click **Microsoft Office PowerPoint 2007** to start the program.

b. Point to and rest the mouse on the Office Button, and then do the same to the Quick Access Toolbar.

As you rest the mouse pointer on each object, you see an Enhanced ScreenTip for that object.

TROUBLESHOOTING: If you do not see the Enhanced ScreenTip, keep the mouse pointer on the object a little longer.

c. Click the **Office Button** and slowly move your mouse down the list of menu options, pointing to the arrow after any command name that has one.

The Office menu displays, and as you move the mouse down the list, submenus display for menu options that have an arrow.

d. Select **New**.

The New Presentation dialog box displays. Depending on how Microsoft Office 2007 was installed, your screen may vary. If Microsoft Office 2007 was fully installed, you should see a thumbnail to create a Blank Presentation, and you may see additional thumbnails in the *Recently Used Templates* section of the dialog box.

e. Click the **Help button** on the title bar of the New Presentation dialog box.

PowerPoint Help displays the topic *Create a new file from a template.*

f. Click **Close** on the Help Window and click the **Cancel** button in the New Presentation dialog box.

g. Click and drag the **Zoom slider** to the right to increase the magnification. Then click and drag the **Zoom slider** back to the center point for a 100% zoom.

h. To exit PowerPoint, click the **Office Button** to display the Office menu, and then click the **Exit PowerPoint button**.

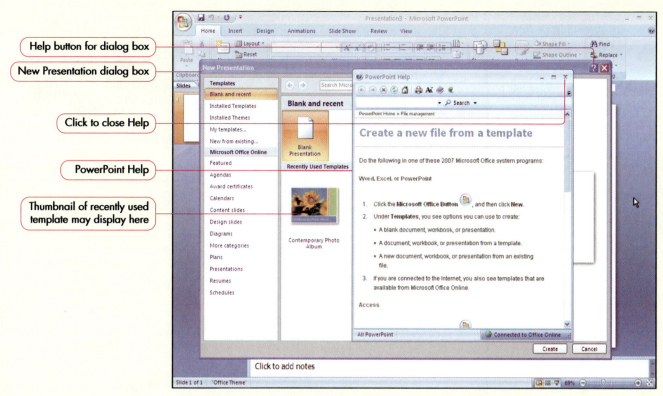

Help button for dialog box

New Presentation dialog box

Click to close Help

PowerPoint Help

Thumbnail of recently used template may display here

Figure 1.10 PowerPoint Help for New Presentations Dialog Box

Step 2
Use Excel's Ribbon, Get Help from an Enhanced ScreenTip, and Use the Zoom Dialog Box

Refer to Figure 1.11 as you complete Step 2.

a. Click **Start** to display the Start menu. Click (or point to) **All Programs**, click **Microsoft Office**, then click **Microsoft Office Excel 2007** to open the program.

b. Click the **Insert tab** on the Ribbon.

The Insert tab contains groups of commands for inserting objects, such as tables, illustrations, charts, links, and text.

c. Rest the mouse on **Hyperlink** in the Links group on the Insert tab.

The Enhanced ScreenTip for Hyperlinks displays. Notice the Enhanced ScreenTip contains a Help icon.

d. Press **F1** on the keyboard.

Excel Help displays the *Create or remove a hyperlink* Help topic.

TROUBLESHOOTING: If you are not connected to the Internet, you might not see the context-sensitive help.

e. Click the **Close button** on the Help window.

f. Click the **View tab** on the Ribbon and click **Zoom** in the Zoom group.

The Zoom dialog box appears so that you can change the zoom percentage.

g. Click the **200%** option and click **OK**.

The worksheet is now magnified to 200% of its regular size.

h. Click **Zoom** in the Zoom group on the View tab, click the **100%** option, and click **OK**.

The worksheet is now restored to 100%.

i. To exit Excel, click the **Office Button** to display the Office menu, and then click the **Exit Excel button**.

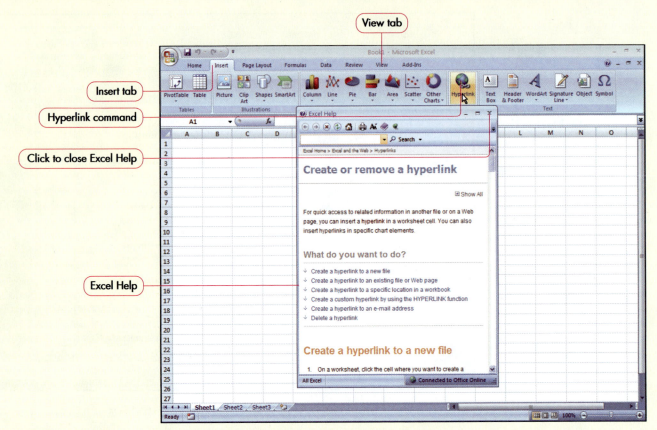

Figure 1.11 Excel Ribbon with Help

Refer to Figure 1.12 as you complete Step 3.

a. Click **Start** to display the Start menu. Click (or point to) **All Programs**, click **Microsoft Office**, then click **Microsoft Office Access 2007** to start the program.

Access opens and displays the Getting Started with Microsoft Access screen.

TROUBLESHOOTING: If you are not familiar with Access, just use the opening screen that displays and continue with the exercise.

b. Press **F1** on the keyboard.

Access Help displays.

c. Type **table** in the Search box in the Access Help window.

d. Click the **Search** button.

Access displays help topics.

e. Click the topic **Create a table in a database**.

The help topic displays.

f. Click the **Close** button on the Access Help window.

Access Help closes.

g. To exit Access, click the **Office Button** to display the Office menu, and then click the **Exit Access button**.

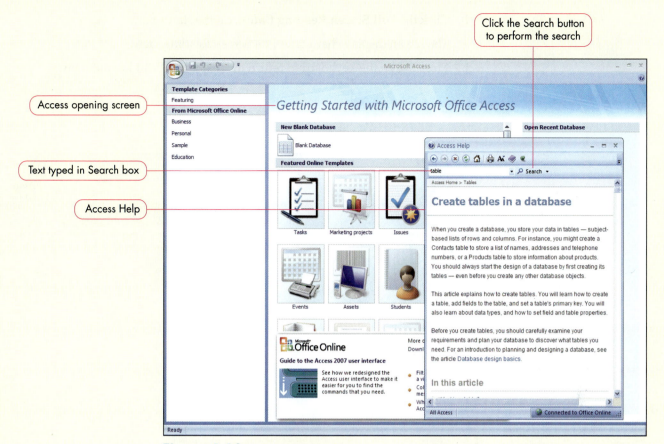

Click the Search button to perform the search

Access opening screen

Text typed in Search box

Access Help

Figure 1.12 Access Help

Refer to Figure 1.13 as you complete Step 4.

a. Click **Start** to display the Start menu. Click (or point to) **All Programs**, click **Microsoft Office**, then click **Microsoft Office Word 2007** to start the program.

Word opens with a blank document ready for you to start typing.

b. Type your first name.

Your first name displays in the document window.

c. Point your mouse to the **Zoom slider** on the status bar.

d. Click and drag the **Zoom slider** to the right to increase the magnification.

The document with your first name increases in size onscreen.

e. Click and drag the slider control to the left to decrease the magnification.

The document with your first name decreases in size.

f. Click and drag the **Zoom slider** back to the center.

The document returns to 100% magnification.

g. Slowly point the mouse to the buttons on the status bar.

A ScreenTip displays the names of the buttons.

h. Click the **Full Screen Reading button** on the status bar.

The screen display changes to Full Screen Reading view.

i. Press **Esc** on the keyboard to return the display to Print Layout view.

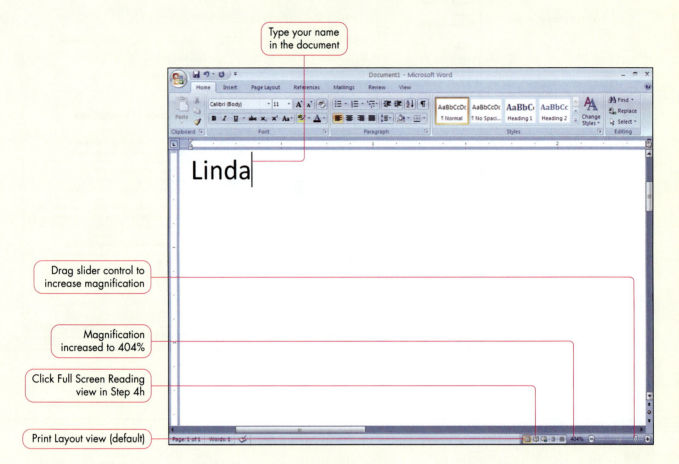

Figure 1.13 The Word Status Bar

Step 5
Search Help and Print a Help Topic

Refer to Figure 1.14 as you complete Step 5.

a. With Word open on the screen, press **F1** on the keyboard.

Word Help displays.

b. Type **zoom** in the Search box in the Word Help window.

c. Click the **Search** button.

Word Help displays related topics.

d. Click the topic **Zoom in or out of a document, presentation, or worksheet**.

The help topic displays.

TROUBLESHOOTING: If you do not have a printer that is ready to print, skip Step 5e and continue with the exercise.

e. Turn on the attached printer, be sure it has paper, and then click the Word Help **Print** button.

The Help topic prints on the attached printer.

f. Click the **Show Table of Contents** button on the Word Help toolbar.

The Table of Contents pane displays on the left side of the Word Help dialog box so that you can click popular Help topics, such as *What's new*. You can click a closed book icon to see specific topics to click for additional information, and you can click an open book icon to close the main Help topic.

g. Click the **Close** button on Word Help.

Word Help closes.

h. To exit Word, click the **Office Button** to display the Office menu, and then click the **Exit Word button**.

A warning appears stating that you have not saved changes to your document.

i. Click **No** in the Word warning box.

You exit Word without saving the document.

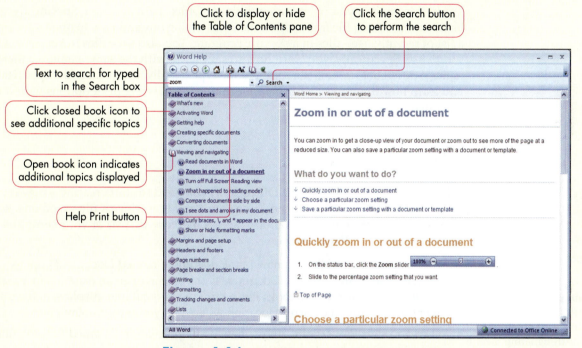

Figure 1.14 Word Help

Universal Tasks

Today, storing large amounts of information on a computer is taken for granted, but in reality, computers would not have become very important if you could not save and re-use the files you create.

One of the most useful and important aspects of using computers is the ability to save and re-use information. For example, you can store letters, reports, budgets, presentations, and databases as files to reopen and use at some time in the future. Today, storing large amounts of information on a computer is taken for granted, but in reality, computers would not have become very important if you could not save and re-use the files you create.

Three fundamental tasks are so important for productivity that they are considered universal to most every computer program, including Office 2007:

* opening files that have been saved

* saving files you create

* printing files

In this section, you open a file within an Office 2007 program. Specifically, you learn how to open a file from within the Open dialog box and how to open a file from a list of recently used files in a specific program. You also save files to keep them for future use. Specifically, you learn how to save a file with the same name, a different name, a different location, or a different file type. Finally, you print a file. Specifically, you learn how to preview a file before printing it and select print options within the Print dialog box.

Opening a File

When you start any program in Office 2007, you need to start creating a new file or open an existing one. You use the Open command to retrieve a file saved on a storage device and place it in the random access memory (RAM) of your computer so you can work on it. For example:

The *insertion point* is the blinking vertical line in the document, cell, slide show, or database table designating the current location where text you type displays.

* When you start Word 2007, a new blank document named Document1 opens. You can either start typing in Document1, or you can open an existing document. The *insertion point*, which looks like a blinking vertical line, displays in the document designating the current location where text you type displays.

* When you start PowerPoint 2007, a new blank presentation named Presentation1 opens. You can either start creating a new slide for the blank presentation, or you can open an existing presentation.

* When you start Excel 2007, a new blank workbook named Book1 opens. You can either start inputting labels and values into Book1, or you can open an existing workbook.

* When you start Access 2007—unlike Word, PowerPoint, and Excel—a new blank database is not created automatically for you. In order to get started using Access, you must create and name a database first or open an existing database.

Open a File Using the Open Dialog Box

Opening a file in any of the Office 2007 applications is an easy process: Use the Open command from the Office menu and specify the file to open. However, locating the file to open can be difficult at times because you might not know where the file you want to use is located. You can open files stored on your computer or on a remote computer that you have access to. Further, files are saved in folders, and you might need to look for files located within folders or subfolders. The Open dialog box, shown in Figure 1.15, contains many features designed for file management; however, two features are designed specifically to help you locate files.

- **Look in**—provides a hierarchical view of the structure of folders and subfolders on your computer or on any computer network you are attached to. Move up or down in the structure to find a specific location or folder and then click the desired location to select it. The file list in the center of the dialog box displays the subfolders and files saved in the location you select. Table 1.3 lists and describes the toolbar buttons.

- **My Places bar**—provides a list of shortcut links to specific folders on your computer and locations on a computer network that you are attached to. Click a link to select it, and the file list changes to display subfolders and files in that location.

Table 1.3 Toolbar Buttons

Buttons	Characteristics
Previous Folder	Returns to the previous folder you viewed.
Up One Level	Moves up one level in the folder structure from the current folder.
Delete	Deletes the selected file or selected folder.
Create New Folder	Creates a new folder within the current folder.
Views	Changes the way the list of folders and files displays in the File list.

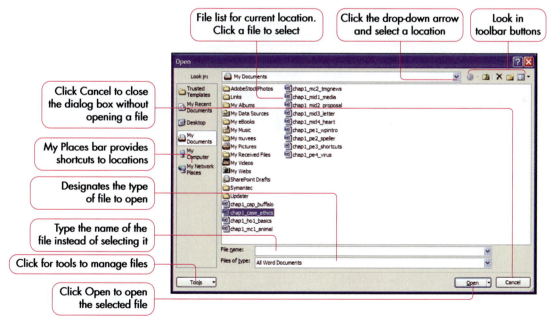

Figure 1.15 Open Dialog Box in Word

After you locate and select the file, click the Open button in the dialog box to display the file on the screen. However, if, for example, you work as part of a workgroup that shares files with each other, you might find the need to open files in a more specialized way. Microsoft Office programs provide several options for opening files when you click the drop-down arrow on the Open button. For example, if you want to keep the original file intact, you might open the file as a copy of the original. Table 1.4 describes the Open options.

Table 1.4 Open Options

Open Options	Characteristics
Open	Opens the selected file with the ability to read and write (edit).
Open Read-Only	Opens the selected file with the ability to read the contents but prevents you from changing or editing it.
Open as Copy	Opens the selected file as a copy of the original so that if you edit the file, the original remains unchanged.
Open in Browser	Opens the selected file in a Web browser.
Open with Transform	Opens a file and provides the ability to transform it into another type of document, such as an HTML document.
Open and Repair	Opens the selected file and attempts to repair any damage. If you have difficulty opening a file, try to open it by selecting Open and Repair.

Open Files Using the Recent Documents List

Office 2007 provides a quick method for accessing files you used recently. The Recent Documents list displays when the Office menu opens and provides a list of links to the last few files you used. The list changes as you work in the application to reflect only the most recent files. Figure 1.16 shows the Office menu with the Recent Documents list.

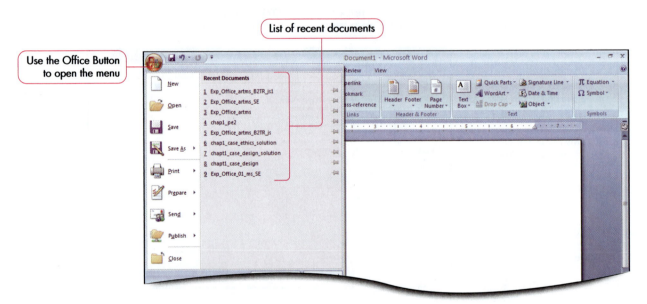

Figure 1.16 The Recent Documents List

TIP   Keeping Files on the Recent Documents List

As you use the Office application and open several files, the list of Recent Documents changes; however, you can designate files to keep displayed on the Recent Documents list at all times. Notice the icon of the pushpin that displays immediately following each file name on the Recent Documents list. Just as you use pushpins to post an important notice in the real world, you use pushpins here to designate important files that you want easy access to. To pin a specific file to the Recent Documents list, click the icon of a gray pushpin. The shape of the pin changes as if pushed in, and the color of the pin changes to green designating that the file is pinned permanently on the list. However, if later you decide to remove the file from the list, you can unpin it by simply clicking the green pushpin, changing the icon back to gray, and the file will disappear from the list over time. Notice the Recent Documents list with both gray and green pushpins in Figure 1.17.

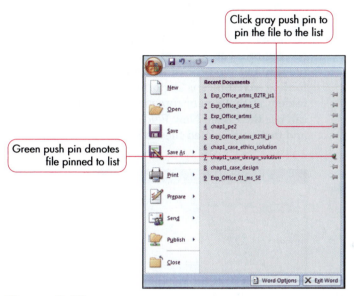

Click gray push pin to pin the file to the list

Green push pin denotes file pinned to list

Figure 1.17 The Recent Documents List

Saving a File

As you work with any Office 2007 application and create files, you will need to save them for future use. While you are working on a file, it is stored in the temporary memory or RAM of your computer. When you save a file, the contents of the file stored in RAM are saved to the hard drive of your computer or to a storage device such as a flash drive. As you create, edit, and format a complex file such as a report, slide show, or budget, you should consider saving several versions of it as you work. For example, you might number versions or use the date in the file name to designate each version. Using this method enables you to revert to a previous version of the document if necessary. To save a file you create in Word, PowerPoint, or Excel, click the Office Button to display the Office menu. Office provides two commands that work similarly: Save and Save As. Table 1.5 describes the characteristics of these two commands.

> As you create, edit, and format a complex file such as a report, slide show, or budget, you should consider saving several versions of it as you work.

Table 1.5 Save Options

Command	Characteristics
Save	Saves the open document: • If this is the first time the document is being saved, Office 2007 opens the Save As dialog box so that you can name the file. • If this document was saved previously, the document is automatically saved using the original file name.
Save As	Opens the Save As dialog box: • If this is the first time the document is being saved, use the Save As dialog box to name the file. • If this document was saved previously, use this option to save the file with a new name, in a new location, or as a new file type preserving the original file with its original name.

When you select the Save As command, the Save As dialog box appears (see Figure 1.18). Notice that saving and opening files are related, that the Save As dialog box looks very similar to the Open dialog box that you saw in Figure 1.15. The dialog box requires you to specify the drive or folder in which to store the file, the name of the file, and the type of file you wish the file to be saved as. Additionally, because finding saved files is important, you should always group related files together in folders, so that you or someone else can find them in a location that makes sense. You can use the Create New Folder button in the dialog box to create and name a folder, and then save related files to it.

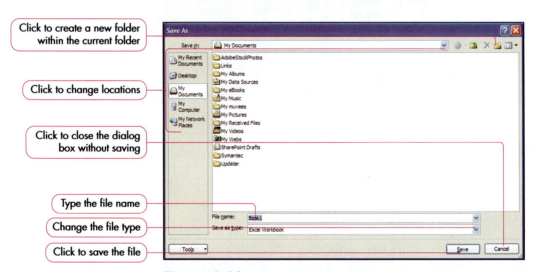

Figure 1.18 Save As Dialog Box in Excel

All subsequent executions of the Save command save the file under the assigned name, replacing the previously saved version with the new version. Pressing Ctrl+S is another way to activate the Save command. If you want to change the name of the file, use the Save As command. Word, PowerPoint, and Excel use the same basic process for saving files, which include the following options:

• naming and saving a previously unsaved file

• saving an updated file with the same name and replacing the original file with the updated one

• saving an updated file with a different name or in a different location to keep the original intact

• saving the file in a different file format

A *macro* is a small program that automates tasks in a file.

A *virus checker* is software that scans files for a hidden program that can damage your computer.

Office 2007 saves files in a different format from previous versions of the software. Office now makes use of XML formats for files created in Word, PowerPoint, and Excel. For example, in previous versions of Word, all documents were saved with the three-letter extension .doc. Now Word saves default documents with the four-letter extension .docx. The new XML format makes use of file compression to save storage space for the user. The files are compressed automatically when saved and uncompressed when opened. Another important feature is that the XML format makes using the files you create in Office 2007 easier to open in other software. This increased portability of files is a major benefit in any workplace that might have numerous applications to deal with. The new file format also differentiates between files that contain *macros*, which are small programs that automate tasks in a file, and those that do not. This specification of files that contain macros enables a virus checker to rigorously check for damaging programs hidden in files. A *virus checker* is software that scans files for a hidden program that can damage your computer. Table 1.6 lists the file formats with the four-letter extension for Word, PowerPoint, and Excel, and a five-letter extension for Access.

A *template* is a file that contains formatting and design elements.

Table 1.6 Word, PowerPoint, Excel, and Access File Extensions

File Format	Characteristics
Word	.docx—default document format .docm—a document that contains macros .dotx—a template without macros (a template is a file that contains formatting and design elements) .dotm—a template with macros
PowerPoint	.pptx—default presentation format .pptm—a presentation that contains macros .potx—a template .potm—a template with macros .ppam—an add-in that contains macros .ppsx—a slide show .ppsm—a slide show with macros .sldx—a slide saved independently of a presentation .sldm—a slide saved independently of a presentation that contains a macro .thmx—a theme used to format a slide
Excel	.xlsx—default workbook .xlsm—a workbook with macros .xltx—a template .xltm—a template with a macro .xlsb—non-XML binary workbook—for previous versions of the software .xlam—an add-in that contains macros
Access	.accdb—default database

Access 2007 saves data differently from Word, PowerPoint, and Excel. When you start Access, which is a relational database, you must create a database and define at least one table for your data. Then as you work, your data is stored automatically. This powerful software enables multiple users access to up-to-date data. The concepts of saving, opening, and printing remain the same, but the process of how data is saved is unique to this powerful environment.

A **shortcut menu** displays when you right-click the mouse on an object and provides a list of commands pertaining to the object you clicked.

TIP Changing the Display of the My Places Bar

Sometimes finding saved files can be a time-consuming chore. To help you quickly locate files, Office 2007 provides options for changing the display of the My Places bar. In Word, PowerPoint, Excel, and Access, you can create shortcuts to folders where you store commonly used files and add them to the My Places bar. From the Open or Save As dialog box, select the location in the Look in list you want to add to the bar. With the desired location selected, point to an empty space below the existing shortcuts on the My Places bar. Right-click the mouse to display a shortcut menu, which displays when you right-click the mouse on an object and provides a list of commands pertaining to the object you clicked. From the shortcut menu, choose Add (folder name)—the folder name is the name of the location you selected in the Look in box. The new shortcut is added to the bottom of the My Places bar. Notice the shortcut menu in Figure 1.19, which also provides options to change the order of added shortcuts or remove an unwanted shortcut. However, you can only remove the shortcuts that you add to the bar; the default shortcuts cannot be removed.

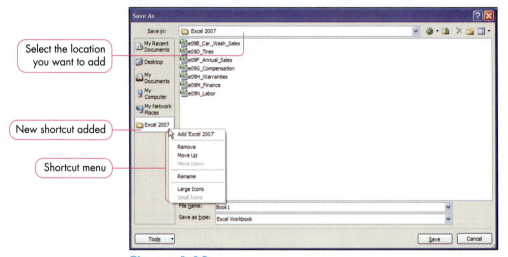

Figure 1.19 Save As Dialog Box with New Shortcut Added to My Places Bar

Printing a Document

As you work with Office 2007 applications, you will need to print hard copies of documents, such as letters to mail, presentation notes to distribute to accompany a slide show, budget spreadsheets to distribute at a staff meeting, or database summary reports to submit. Office provides flexibility so that you can preview the document before you send it to the printer; you also can select from numerous print options, such as changing the number of copies printed; or you can simply and quickly print the current document on the default printer.

Preview Before You Print

It is highly recommended that you preview your document before you print because Print Preview displays all the document elements, such as graphics and formatting, as they will appear when printed on paper. Previewing the document first enables you to make any changes that you need to make without wasting paper. Previewing documents uses the same method in all Office 2007 applications, that is, point to the arrow next to the Print command on the Office menu and select Print Preview to display the current document, worksheet, presentation, or database table in the Print Preview window. Figure 1.20 shows the Print Preview window in Word 2007.

> It is highly recommended that you preview your document before you print because Print Preview displays all the document elements, such as graphics and formatting, as they will appear when printed on paper.

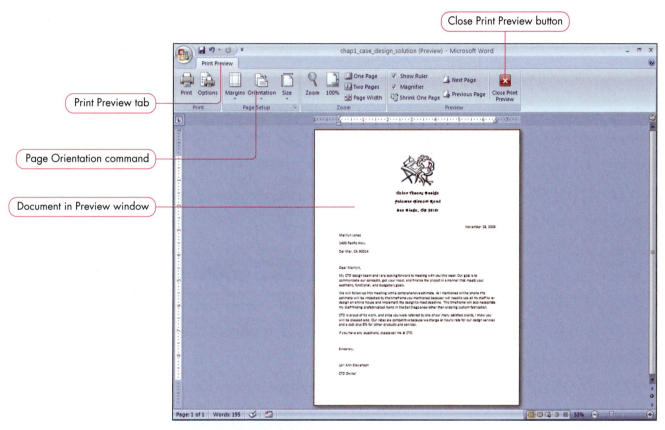

Close Print Preview button

Print Preview tab

Page Orientation command

Document in Preview window

Figure 1.20 Print Preview Window

As you preview the document, you can get a closer look at the results by changing the zoom. Notice that the mouse pointer displays in the Preview window as a magnifying glass with a plus sign, so that you can simply click in the document to increase the zoom. Once clicked, the plus sign changes to a minus sign, enabling you to click in the document again to decrease the zoom. You also can use the Zoom group on the Print Preview tab or the Zoom slider on the status bar to change the view of the document.

Portrait orientation is longer than it is wide—like the portrait of a person.

Landscape orientation is wider than it is long, resembling a landscape scene.

Other options on the Print Preview tab change depending on the application that you are using. For example, you might want to change the orientation to switch from portrait to landscape. Refer to Figure 1.20. **Portrait orientation** is longer than it is wide, like the portrait of a person; whereas, **landscape orientation** is wider than it is long, resembling a landscape scene. You also can change the size of the paper or other options from the Print Preview tab.

If you need to edit the document before printing, close the Print Preview window and return to the document. However, if you are satisfied with the document and want to print, click Print in the Print group on the Print Preview tab. The Print dialog box displays. Figure 1.21 shows Word's Print dialog box.

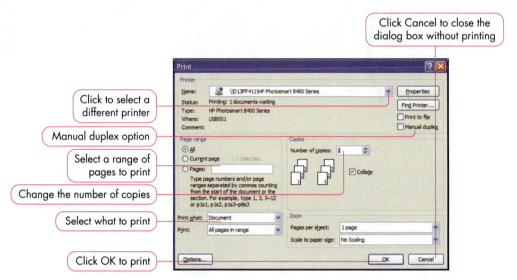

Figure 1.21 Print Dialog Box

The Print dialog box provides numerous options for selecting the correct printer, selecting what to print, and selecting how to print. Table 1.7 describes several important and often-used features of the Print dialog box.

Table 1.7 Print Dialog Box

Print Option	Characteristics
All	Select to print all the pages in the file.
Current page/slide	Select to print only the page or slide with the insertion point. This is a handy feature when you notice an error in a file, and you only want to reprint the corrected page.
Pages	Select to print only specific pages in a document. You must specify page numbers in the text box.
Number of Copies	Change the number of copies printed from the default 1 to the number desired.
Collate	Click if you are printing multiple copies of a multi-page file, and you want to print an entire first copy before printing an entire second copy, and so forth.
Print what	Select from options on what to print, varying with each application.
Selection	Select to print only selected text or objects in an Excel worksheet.
Active sheet(s)	Select to print only the active worksheet(s) in Excel.
Entire workbook	Select to print all worksheets in the Excel workbook.

As you work with other Office 2007 applications, you will notice that the main print options remain unchanged; however, the details vary based on the specific task of the application. For example, the *Print what* option in PowerPoint includes options such as printing the slide, printing handouts, printing notes, or printing an outline of the presentation.

A ***duplex printer*** prints on both sides of the page.

A ***manual duplex*** operation allows you to print on both sides of the paper by printing first on one side and then on the other.

TIP   Printing on Both Sides of the Paper

Duplex printers print on both sides of the page. However, if you do not have a duplex printer, you can still print on two sides of the paper by performing a manual duplex operation, which prints on both sides of the paper by printing first on one side, and then on the other. To perform a manual duplex print job in Word 2007, select the Manual duplex option in the Print dialog box. Refer to Figure 1.21. With this option selected, Word prints all pages that display on one side of the paper first, then prompts you to turn the pages over and place them back in the printer tray. The print job continues by printing all the pages that appear on the other side of the paper.

Print Without Previewing the File

If you want to print a file without previewing the results, select Print from the Office menu, and the Print dialog box displays. You can still make changes in the Print dialog box, or just immediately send the print job to the printer. However, if you just want to print quickly, Office 2007 provides a quick print option that enables you to send the current file to the default printer without opening the Print dialog box. This is a handy feature to use if you have only one printer attached and you want to print the current file without changing any print options. You have two ways to quick print:

- Select Quick Print from the Office menu.
- Customize the Quick Access toolbar to add the Print icon. Click the icon to print the current file without opening the Print dialog box.

Hands-On Exercises

2 | Performing Universal Tasks

Skills covered: 1. Open a File and Save It with a Different Name **2.** Use Print Preview and Select Options **3.** Print a Document

Step 1

Open a File and Save It with a Different Name

Refer to Figure 1.22 as you complete Step 1.

a. Start Word, click the **Office Button** to display the Office menu, and then select **Open**.

The Open dialog box displays.

b. If necessary, click the **File Type List** button to locate the files for this textbook to find *chap1_ho2_sample*.

TROUBLESHOOTING: If you have trouble finding the files that accompany this text, you may want to ask your instructor where they are located.

c. Select the file and click **Open**.

The document displays on the screen.

d. Click the **Office Button,** and then select **Save As** on the Office menu.

The Save As dialog box displays.

e. In the *File name* box, type **chap1_ho2_solution**.

f. Check the location listed in the **Save in** box. If you need to change locations to save your files, use the **Save in drop-down arrow** to select the correct location.

g. Make sure that the *Save as type* option is Word Document.

TROUBLESHOOTING: Be sure that you click the **Save As** command rather than pointing to the arrow after the command, and be sure that Word Document is specified in the Save as type box.

h. Click the **Save** button in the dialog box to save the file under the new name.

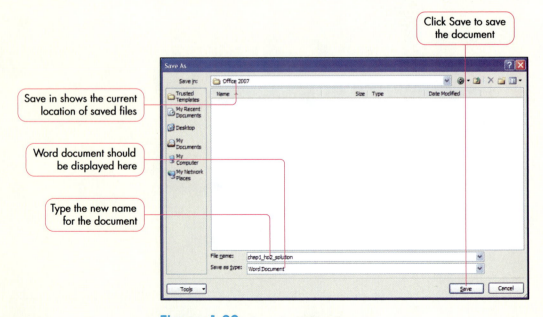

Click Save to save the document

Save in shows the current location of saved files

Word document should be displayed here

Type the new name for the document

Figure 1.22 Save As Dialog Box

Step 2

Use Print Preview and Select Options

Refer to Figure 1.23 as you complete Step 2.

a. With the document displayed on the screen, click the **Office Button** and point to the arrow following **Print** on the Office menu.

The Print submenu displays.

b. Select **Print Preview**.

The document displays in the Print Preview window.

c. Point the magnifying glass mouse pointer in the document and click the mouse once.

TROUBLESHOOTING: If you do not see the magnifying glass pointer, point the mouse in the document and keep it still for a moment.

The document magnification increases.

d. Point the magnifying glass mouse pointer in the document and click the mouse again.

The document magnification decreases.

e. Click **Orientation** in the Page Setup group on the Print Preview tab.

The orientation options display.

f. Click **Landscape**.

The document orientation changes to landscape.

g. Click **Orientation** a second time, and then choose **Portrait**.

The document returns to portrait orientation.

h. Click the **Close Print Preview** button on the Print Preview tab.

i. The Print Preview window closes.

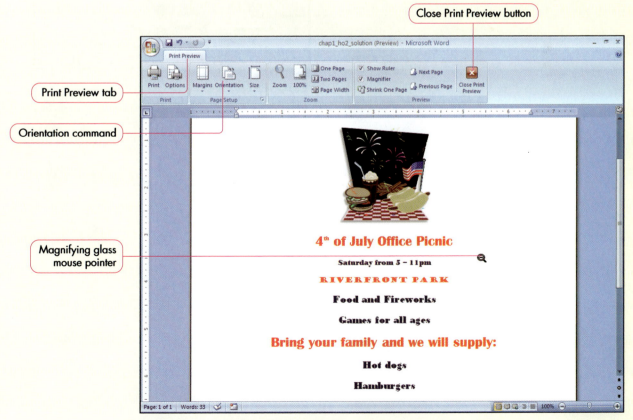

Figure 1.23 Print Preview

Refer to Figure 1.24 as you complete Step 3.

a. Click the **Office Button,** and then point to the arrow next to **Print** on the Office menu.

The print options display.

b. Select **Print**.

The Print dialog box displays.

TROUBLESHOOTING: Be sure that your printer is turned on and has paper loaded.

c. If necessary, select the correct printer in the **Name box** by clicking the drop-down arrow and selecting from the resulting list.

d. Click **OK**.

The Word document prints on the selected printer.

e. To exit Word, click the **Office Button,** and then click the **Exit Word button**.

f. If prompted to save the file, choose **No**.

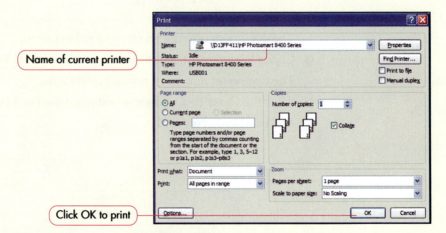

Figure 1.24 The Print Dialog Box

Basic Tasks

Many of the operations you perform in one Office program are the same or similar in all Office applications. These tasks are referred to as basic tasks and include such operations as inserting and typing over, copying and moving items, finding and replacing text, undoing and redoing commands, checking spelling and grammar, using the thesaurus, and using formatting tools. Once you learn the underlying concepts of these operations, you can apply them in different applications.

Most basic tasks in Word fall into two categories:

- editing a document
- formatting a document

Most successful writers use many word processing features to revise and edit documents, and most would agree that the revision process takes more time than the initial writing process. Errors such as spelling and grammar need to be eliminated to produce error-free writing. However, to turn a rough draft into a finished document, such as a report for a class or for a business, requires writers to revise and edit several times by adding text, removing text, replacing text, and moving text around to make the meaning clearer. Writers also improve their writing using tools to conduct research to make the information accurate and to find the most appropriate word using the thesaurus. Modern word processing applications such as Word 2007 provide these tools and more to aid the writer.

> Most successful writers use many word processing features to revise and edit documents, and most would agree that the revision process takes more time than the initial writing process.

The second category of basic tasks is formatting text in a document. Formatting text includes changing the type, the size, and appearance of text. You might want to apply formatting to simply improve the look of a document, or you might want to emphasize particular aspects of your message. Remember that a poorly formatted document or workbook probably will not be read. So whether you are creating your résumé or the income statement for a corporation's annual report, how the output looks is important. Office 2007 provides many tools for formatting documents, but in this section, you will start by learning to apply font attributes and copy those to other locations in the document.

In this section, you learn to perform basic tasks in Office 2007, using Word 2007 as the model. As you progress in learning other Office programs such as PowerPoint, Excel, and Access, you will apply the same principles in other applications.

Selecting Text to Edit

Most editing processes involve identifying the text that the writer wants to work with. For example, to specify which text to edit, you must select it. The most common method used to select text is to use the mouse. Point to one end of the text you want to select (either the beginning or end) and click-and-drag over the text. The selected text displays highlighted with a light blue background so that it stands out from other text and is ready for you to work with. The *Mini toolbar* displays when you select text in Word, Excel, and PowerPoint. It displays above the selected text as semitransparent and remains semitransparent until you point to it. Often-used commands from the Clipboard, Font, and Paragraph groups on the Home tab are repeated on the Mini toolbar for quick access. Figure 1.25 shows selected text with the Mini toolbar fully displayed in the document.

The *Mini toolbar* displays above the selected text as semitransparent and repeats often-used commands.

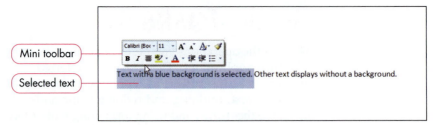

Figure 1.25 Selected Text

Sometimes you want to select only one word or character, and trying to drag over it to select it can be frustrating. Table 1.8 describes other methods used to select text.

Table 1.8 Easy Text Selection in Word

Outcome Desired	Method
Select a word	Double-click the word.
One line of text	Point the mouse to the left of the line, and when the mouse pointer changes to a right-pointing arrow, click the mouse.
A sentence	Hold down Ctrl and click in the sentence to select.
A paragraph	Triple-click the mouse in the paragraph.
One character to the left of the insertion point	Hold down Shift and press the left arrow key.
One character to the right of the insertion point	Hold down Shift and press the right arrow key.

TIP Selecting Large Amounts of Text

As you edit documents, you might need to select a large portion of a document. However, as you click-and-drag over the text, you might have trouble stopping the selection at the desired location because the document scrolls by too quickly. This is actually a handy feature in Word 2007 that scrolls through the document when you drag the mouse pointer at the edge of the document window.

To select a large portion of a document, click the insertion point at the beginning of the desired selection. Then move the display to the end of the selection using the scroll bar at the right edge of the window. Scrolling leaves the insertion point where you placed it. When you reach the end of the text you want to select, hold down Shift and click the mouse. The entire body of text is selected.

Inserting Text and Changing to the Overtype Mode

Insert is adding text in a document.

As you create and edit documents using Word, you will need to *insert* text, which is adding text in a document. To insert or add text, point and click the mouse in the location where the text should display. With the insertion point in the location to insert the text, simply start typing. Any existing text moves to the right, making room for the new inserted text. At times, you might need to add a large amount of text in a document, and you might want to replace or type over existing text instead of inserting text. This task can be accomplished two ways:

- Select the text to replace and start typing. The new text replaces the selected text.

Overtype mode replaces the existing text with text you type character by character.

- Switch to *Overtype mode*, which replaces the existing text with text you type character by character. To change to Overtype mode, select the Word Options button on the Office menu. Select the option Use Overtype Mode in the Editing Options section of the Advanced tab. Later, if you want to return to Insert mode, repeat these steps to deselect the overtype mode option. Figure 1.26 shows the Word Options dialog box.

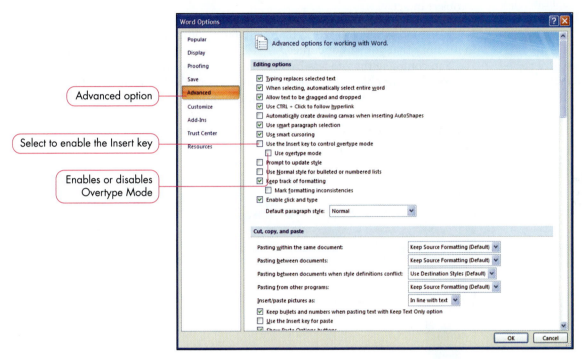

Figure 1.26 The Word Options Dialog Box

TIP Using the Insert Key on the Keyboard

If you find that you need to switch between Insert and Overtype mode often, you can enable Insert on the keyboard by clicking the Word Options button on the Office menu. Select the option Use the Insert Key to Control Overtype Mode in the Editing Options section on the Advanced tab. Refer to Figure 1.26. You can now use Insert on the keyboard to switch between the two modes, and this option stays in effect until you go back to the Word Options dialog box and deselect it.

Moving and Copying Text

As you revise a document, you might find that you need to move text from one location to another to improve the readability of the content. To move text, you must cut the selected text from its original location and then place it in the new location by pasting it there. To duplicate text, you must copy the selected text in its original location and then paste the duplicate in the desired location. To decide whether you should use the Cut or Copy command in the Clipboard group on the Home tab to perform the task, you must notice the difference in the results of each command:

Cut removes the original text or object from its current location.

Copy makes a duplicate copy of the text or object, leaving the original intact.

Paste places the cut or copied text or object in the new location.

- **Cut** removes the selected original text or object from its current location.
- **Copy** makes a duplicate copy of the text or object, leaving the original text or object intact.

Keep in mind while you work, that by default, Office 2007 retains only the last item in memory that you cut or copied.

You complete the process by invoking the Paste command. **Paste** places the cut or copied text or object in the new location. Notice the Paste Options button displays along with the pasted text. You can simply ignore the Paste Options button, and it will disappear from the display, or you can click the drop-down arrow on the button and select a formatting option to change the display of the text you pasted. Figure 1.27 shows the options available.

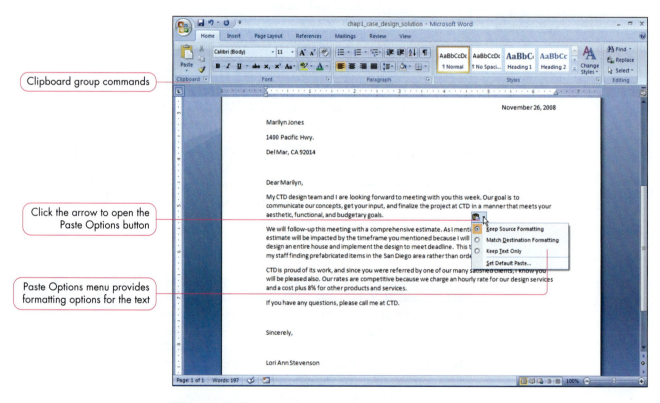

Clipboard group commands

Click the arrow to open the Paste Options button

Paste Options menu provides formatting options for the text

Figure 1.27 Text Pasted in the Document

You can use alternative methods instead of using the commands located on the Home tab to cut, copy, and paste text. Office 2007 provides the following shortcuts:

- After selecting text, point back to the selected text and right-click the mouse. The shortcut menu displays, allowing you to choose Cut or Copy. Move the insertion point to the desired location, right-click the mouse again, and choose Paste from the shortcut menu.

- After selecting text, use the keyboard shortcut combinations Ctrl+C to copy or Ctrl+X to cut text. Move the insertion point to the new location and press Ctrl+V to paste. These keyboard shortcuts work in most Windows applications, so they can be very useful.

- After selecting text, you can move it a short distance in the document by dragging to the new location. Point to the selected text, hold down the left mouse button, and then drag to the desired location. While you are dragging the mouse, the pointer changes to a left-pointing arrow with a box attached to it. Release the mouse button when you have placed the insertion point in the desired location, and the text displays in the new location.

Use the Office Clipboard

The ***Clipboard*** is a memory location that holds up to 24 items for you to paste into the current document, another file, or another application.

Office 2007 provides an option that enables you to cut or copy multiple items to the ***Clipboard***, which is a memory location that holds up to 24 items for you to paste into the current file, another file, or another application. The Clipboard stays active only while you are using one of the Office 2007 applications. When you exit from all Office 2007 applications, all items on the Clipboard are deleted. To accumulate items on the Clipboard, you must first display it by clicking the Dialog Box Launcher in the Clipboard group on the Home tab. When the Clipboard pane is open on the screen, its memory location is active, and the Clipboard accumulates all items you cut or copy up to the maximum 24. To paste an item from the Clipboard, point to it, click the resulting drop-down arrow, and choose Paste. To change how the Clipboard functions, use the Options button shown in Figure 1.28. One of the most important options allows the Clipboard to accumulate items even when it is not open on the screen. To activate the Clipboard so that it works in the background, click the Options button in the Clipboard, and then select Collect without Showing Office Clipboard.

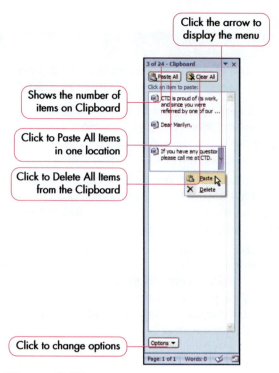

Figure 1.28 Clipboard

Finding, Replacing, and Going to Text

You can waste a great deal of time slowly scrolling through a document trying to locate text or other items. Office 2007 provides features that speed up editing by automatically finding text and objects in a document, thus making you more productive. Office 2007 provides the following three related operations that all use the Find and Replace dialog box:

Find locates a word or group of words in a document.

Replace not only finds text, it replaces a word or group of words with other text.

Go To moves the insertion point to a specific location in the document.

- The *Find* command enables you to locate a word or group of words in a document quickly.

- The *Replace* command not only finds text quickly, it replaces a word or group of words with other text.

- The *Go To* command moves the insertion point to a specific location in the document.

Find Text

To locate text in an Office file, choose the Find command in the Editing group on the Home tab and type the text you want to locate in the resulting dialog box, as shown in Figure 1.29. After you type the text to locate, you can find the next instance after the insertion point and work through the file until you find the instance of the text you were looking for. Alternatively, you can find all instances of the text in the file at one time. If you decide to find every instance at once, the Office application temporarily highlights each one, and the text stays highlighted until you perform another operation in the file.

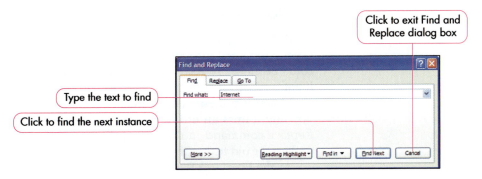

Figure 1.29 Find Tab of the Find and Replace Dialog Box

Sometimes, temporarily highlighting all instances of text is not sufficient to help you edit the text you find. If you want Word to find all instances of specific text in a document and keep the highlighting from disappearing until you want it to, you can use the Reading Highlight option in the Find dialog box. One nice feature of this option is that even though the text remains highlighted on the screen, the document prints normally without highlighting. Figure 1.30 shows the Find and Replace dialog box with the Reading Highlight options that you use to highlight or remove the highlight from a document.

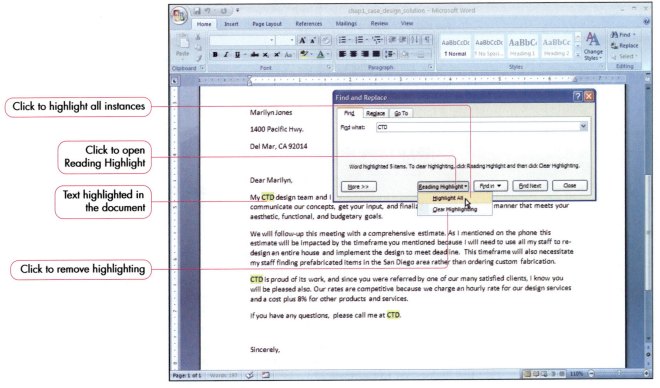

Figure 1.30 Find and Replace Dialog Box with Highlighting Options

Replace Text

While revising a file, you might realize that you have used an incorrect term and need to replace it throughout the entire file. Alternatively, you might realize that you could be more productive by re-using a letter or report that you polished and saved if you replace the previous client's or corporation's name with a new one. While you could perform these tasks manually, it would not be worth the time involved, and you might miss an instance of the old text, which could prove embarrassing. The Replace command in the Editing group on the Home tab can quickly and easily replace the old text with the new text throughout an entire file.

In the Find and Replace dialog box, first type the text to find, using the same process you used with the Find command. Second, type the text to replace the existing text with. Third, specify how you want Word to perform the operation. You can either replace each instance of the text individually, which can be time-consuming but allows you to decide whether to replace each instance one at a time, or you can replace every instance of the text in the document all at once. Word (but not the other Office applications) also provides options in the dialog box that help you replace only the correct text in the document. Click the More button to display these options. The most important one is the Find whole words only option. This option forces the application to find only complete words, not text that is part of other words. For instance, if you are searching for the word *off* to replace with other text, you would not want Word to replace the *off* in *office* with other text. Figure 1.31 shows these options along with the options for replacing text.

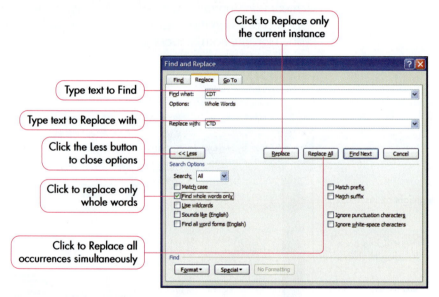

Figure 1.31 Find and Replace Dialog Box

Go Directly to a Location in a File

If you are editing a long document and want to move within it quickly, you can use the Go To command by clicking the down arrow on the Find command in the Editing group on the Home tab rather than slowly scrolling through an entire document or workbook. For example, if you want to move the insertion point to page 40 in a 200-page document, choose the Go To command and type 40 in the *Enter page number* text box. Notice the list of objects you can choose from in the Go to what section of the dialog box in Figure 1.32.

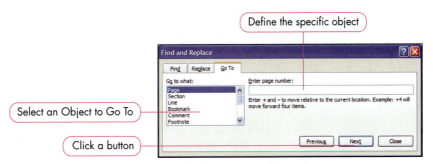

Define the specific object

Select an Object to Go To

Click a button

Figure 1.32 Go To Tab of the Find and Replace Dialog Box

Using the Undo and Redo Commands

The **Undo** command cancels your last one or more operations.

The **Redo** command reinstates or reverses an action performed by the Undo command.

As you create and edit files, you may perform an operation by mistake or simply change your mind about an edit you make. Office applications provide the **Undo** command, which can cancel your previous operation or even your last few operations. After using Undo to reverse an action or operation, you might decide that you want to use the **Redo** command to reinstate or reverse the action taken by the Undo command.

To undo the last action you performed, click Undo on the Quick Access Toolbar. For example, if you deleted text by mistake, immediately click Undo to restore it. If, however, you deleted some text and then performed several other operations, you can find the correct action to undo, with the understanding that all actions after that one will also be undone. To review a list of the last few actions you performed, click the Undo drop-down arrow and select the desired one from the list—Undo highlights all actions in the list down to that item and will undo all of the highlighted actions. Figure 1.33 shows a list of recent actions in PowerPoint. To reinstate or reverse an action as a result of using the Undo command, click Redo on the Quick Access Toolbar.

The **Repeat** command repeats only the last action you performed.

The **Repeat** command provides limited use because it repeats only the last action you performed. To repeat the last action, click Repeat on the Quick Access Toolbar. If the Office application is able to repeat your last action, the results will display in the document. Note that the Repeat command is replaced with the Redo command after you use the Undo command. For example, Figure 1.33 shows the Redo command after the Undo command has been used, and Figure 1.34 shows the Repeat command when Undo has not been used.

Click Redo to reverse an Undo command action.

Click the Undo list to find the first action to undo

Click Undo to undo the last action

Figure 1.33 Undo and Redo Buttons

Using Language Tools

Documents, spreadsheets, and presentations represent the author, so remember that errors in writing can keep people from getting a desired job, or once on the job, can keep them from getting a desired promotion. To avoid holding yourself back, you should polish your final documents before submitting them electronically or as a hard copy. Office 2007 provides built-in proofing tools to help you fix spelling and grammar errors and help you locate the correct word or information.

Check Spelling and Grammar Automatically

By default, Office applications check spelling as you type and flag potential spelling errors by underlining them with a red wavy line. Word also flags potential grammar errors by underlining them with a green wavy line. You can fix these errors as you enter text, or you can ignore the errors and fix them all at once.

To fix spelling errors as you type, simply move the insertion point to a red wavy underlined word and correct the spelling yourself. If you spell the word correctly, the red wavy underline disappears. However, if you need help figuring out the correct spelling for the flagged word, then point to the error and right-click the mouse. The shortcut menu displays with possible corrections for the error. If you find the correction on the shortcut menu, click it to replace the word in the document. To fix grammar errors, follow the same process, but when the shortcut menu displays, you can choose to view more information to see rules that apply to the potential error. Notice the errors flagged in Figure 1.34. Note that the Mini toolbar also displays automatically.

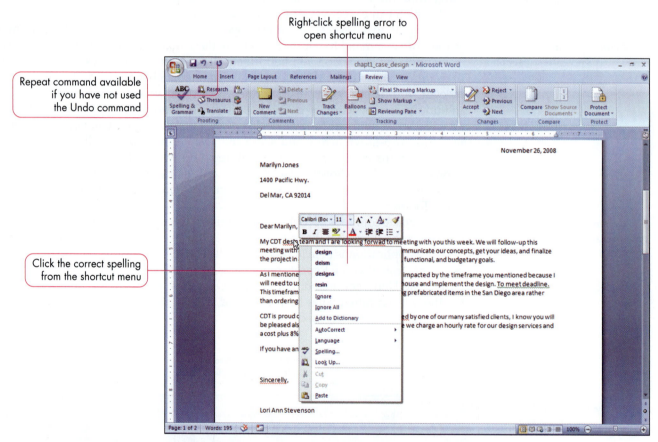

Figure 1.34 Automatic Spell and Grammar Check

Check Spelling and Grammar at Once

Some people prefer to wait until they complete typing the entire document and then check spelling and grammar at once. To check for errors, click Spelling & Grammar in Word (Spelling in Excel or PowerPoint) in the Proofing group on the Review tab. As the checking proceeds through the file and detects any spelling or grammar errors, it displays the Spelling dialog box if you are using Excel or PowerPoint, or the Spelling and Grammar dialog box in Word. You can either correct or ignore the changes that the Spelling checker proposes to your document. For example, Figure 1.35 shows the Spelling and Grammar dialog box with a misspelled word in the top section and Word's suggestions in the bottom section. Select the correction from the list and change the current instance, or you can change all instances of the error throughout the document. However, sometimes the flagged word might be a specialized term or a person's name, so if the flagged word is not a spelling error, you can ignore it once in the current document or throughout the entire document; further, you could add the word to the spell-check list so that it never flags that spelling again.

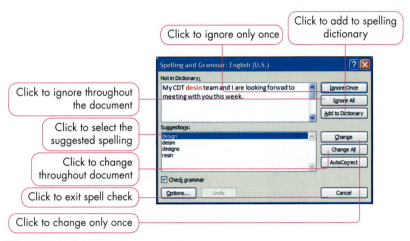

Figure 1.35 Spelling and Grammar Dialog Box

TIP   Proofreading Your Document

The spelling and grammar checks available in Word provide great help improving your documents. However, you should not forget that you still have to proofread your document to ensure that the writing is clear, appropriate for the intended audience, and makes sense.

Use the Thesaurus

As you edit a document, spreadsheet, or presentation, you might want to improve your writing by finding a better or different word for a particular situation. For example, say you are stuck and cannot think of a better word for *big*, and you would like to find an alternative word that means the same. Word, Excel, and PowerPoint provide a built-in thesaurus, which is an electronic version of a book of synonyms. Synonyms are different words with the same or similar meaning, and antonyms are words with the opposite meaning.

The easiest method for accessing the Thesaurus is to point to the word in the file that you want to find an alternative for and right-click the mouse. When the shortcut menu displays, point to Synonyms, and the program displays a list of alternatives. Notice the shortcut menu and list of synonyms in Figure 1.36. To select one of the alternative words on the list, click it, and the word you select replaces the original word. If you do not see an alternative on the list that you want to use and you want to investigate further, click Thesaurus on the shortcut menu to open the full Thesaurus.

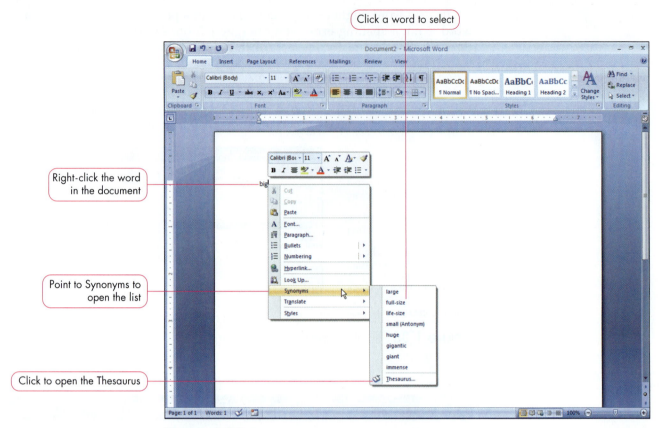

Figure 1.36 Shortcut Menu with Synonyms

An alternative method for opening the full Thesaurus is to place the insertion point in the word you want to look up, and then click the Thesaurus command in the Proofing group on the Review tab. The Thesaurus opens with alternatives for the selected word. You can use one of the words presented in the pane, or you can look up additional words. If you do not find the word you want, use the Search option to find more alternatives. Figure 1.37 shows the Thesaurus.

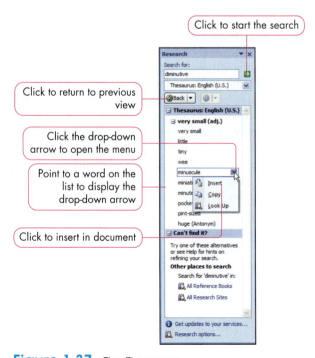

Figure 1.37 The Thesaurus

Conduct Research

As you work in Word, Excel, or PowerPoint, you might need to find the definition of a word or look up an item in the encyclopedia to include accurate information. Office 2007 provides quick access to research tools. To access research tools, click the Research button in the Proofing group on the Review tab. Notice in Figure 1.38 that you can specify what you want to research and specify where to Search. Using this feature, you can choose from reference books, research sites, and business and financial sites.

Figure 1.38 Research Task Pane

> ((( )))
> ### TIP Avoiding Plagiarism
>
> If you use the research feature in Office to find information in an encyclopedia or in other locations to help you create your document, then you need to credit the source of that information. Avoid the problem of plagiarism, which is borrowing other people's words or ideas, by citing all sources that you use. You might want to check with your instructor for the exact format for citing sources.

Applying Font Attributes

> Taking the time to format text helps the reader find important information in the document by making it stand out and helps the reader understand the message by emphasizing key items.

After you have edited a document, you might want to improve its visual appeal by formatting the text. *Formatting text* changes an individual letter, a word, or a body of selected text. Taking the time to format text helps the reader find important information in the document by making it stand out and helps the reader understand the message by emphasizing key items. You can format the text in the document by changing the following font attributes:

Formatting text changes an individual letter, a word, or a body of selected text.

- font face or size
- font attributes such as bold, underline, or italic
- font color

The Font group on the Home tab—available in Word, Excel, PowerPoint, and Access—provides many formatting options, and Office provides two methods for applying these font attributes:

- Choose the font attributes first, and then type the text. The text displays in the document with the formatting.
- Type the text, select the text to format, and choose the font attributes. The selected text displays with the formatting.

You can apply more than one attribute to text, so you can select one or more attributes either all at once or at any time. Also, it is easy to see which attributes you have applied to text in the document. Select the formatted text and look at the commands in the Font group on the Home tab. The commands in effect display with a gold background. See Figure 1.39. To remove an effect from text, select it and click the command. The gold background disappears for attributes that are no longer in effect.

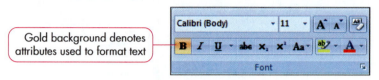

Gold background denotes attributes used to format text

Figure 1.39 Font Group of the Home tab

Change the Font

A **font** is a named set of characters with the same design.

> Remember that more is not always better when applied to fonts, so limit the number of font changes in your document.

A **font** is a named set of characters with the same design, and Office 2007 provides many built-in fonts for you to choose from. Remember that more is not always better when applied to fonts, so limit the number of font changes in your document. Additionally, the choice of a font should depend on the intent of the document and should never overpower the message. For example, using a fancy or highly stylized font that may be difficult to read for a client letter might seem odd to the person receiving it and overpower the intended message.

One powerful feature of Office 2007 that can help you decide how a font will look in your document is Live Preview. First, select the existing text, and then click the drop-down arrow on the Font list in the Font group on the Home tab. As you point to a font name in the list, Live Preview changes the selected text in the document to that font. Figure 1.40 shows the selected text displaying in a different font as a result of Live Preview.

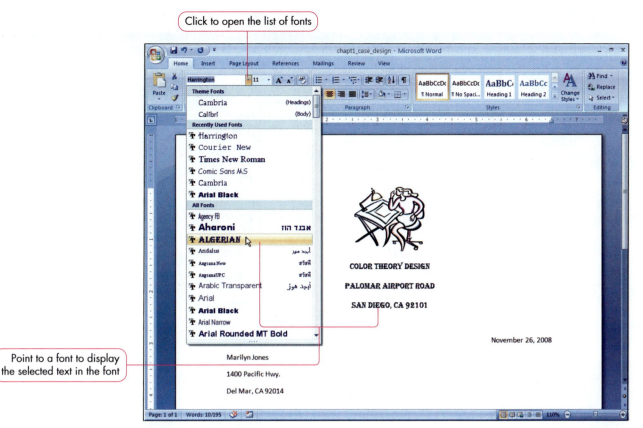

Figure 1.40 Font List

Change the Font Size, Color, and Attributes

Besides changing the font, you also can change the size, color, and other attributes of text in a document. Because these formatting operations are used so frequently, Office places many of these commands in several places for easy access:

- in the Font group on the Home tab
- on the Mini toolbar
- in the Font dialog box

Table 1.9 describes the commands that display in the Font group of the Home tab and in the Font dialog box.

Table 1.9 Font Commands

Command	Description	Example
Font	Enables you to designate the font.	Arial Comic Sans MS
Font Size	Enables you to designate an exact font size.	Size 8 Size 18
Grow Font	Each time you click the command, the selected text increases one size.	A A
Shrink Font	Each time you click the command, the selected text decreases one size.	B B
Clear Formatting	Removes all formatting from the selected text.	Formatted Cleared
Bold	Makes the text darker than the surrounding text.	**Bold**
Italic	Places the selected text in italic, that is, slants the letters to the right.	*Italic*
Underline	Places a line under the text. Click the drop-down arrow to change the underline style.	Underline
Strikethrough	Draws a line through the middle of the text.	~~Strikethrough~~
Subscript	Places selected text below the baseline.	Sub$_{script}$
Superscript	Places selected text above the line of letters.	Super^{script}
Change Case	Changes the case of the selected text. Click the drop-down arrow to select the desired case.	lowercase UPPERCASE
Text Highlight Color	Makes selected text look like it was highlighted with a marker pen. Click the drop-down arrow to change color and other options.	Highlighted
Font Color	Changes the color of selected text. Click the drop-down arrow to change colors.	Font Color

If you have several formatting changes to make, click the Dialog Box Launcher in the Font group on the Home tab to display the Font dialog box. The Font dialog box is handy because all the formatting features display in one location, and it provides additional options such as changing the underline color. Figure 1.41 shows the Font dialog box in Word.

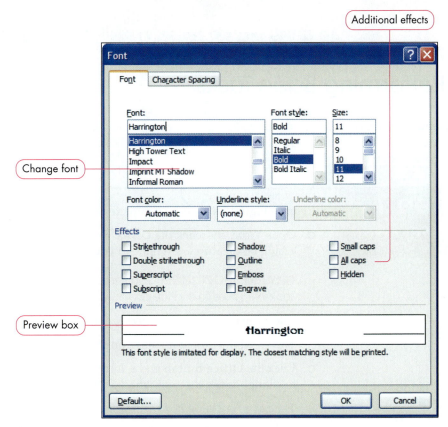

Figure 1.41 Font Dialog Box

Copying Formats with the Format Painter

After formatting text in one part of a document, you might want to apply that same formatting to other text in a different location in the document. You could try to remember all the formatting options you selected, but that process would be time-consuming and could produce inconsistent results. Office 2007 provides a shortcut method called the *Format Painter*, which copies the formatting of text from one location to another.

The **Format Painter** copies the formatting of text from one location to another.

Select the formatted text you want to copy and click the Format Painter in the Clipboard group on the Home tab to copy the format. Single-click the command to turn it on to copy formatting to one location—the option turns off automatically after one copy—or double-click the command to turn it on for unlimited format copying—you must press Esc on the keyboard to turn it off.

Hands-On Exercises

3 | Performing Basic Tasks

Skills covered: 1. Cut, Copy, Paste, and Undo **2.** Find and Replace Text **3.** Check Spelling **4.** Choose Synonyms and Use Thesaurus **5.** Use the Research Tool **6.** Apply Font Attributes **7.** Use Format Painter

---

Step 1 Cut, Copy, Paste, and Undo	Refer to Figure 1.42 as you complete Steps 1 and 2.

a. Open Word and click the **Office Button**, click **Open**, and then using the Open dialog box features, navigate to your classroom file location.

> **TROUBLESHOOTING:** If you have trouble finding the file, remember to use the Look in feature to find the correct location.

b. Select the file *chap1_ho3_internet* and click the **Open** button.

The Word document displays on the screen.

c. Click the **Office Button** and select **Save As**. If necessary, use the **Look in** feature to change to the location where you save files.

The Save As dialog box displays.

d. Type the new file name, **chap1_ho3_internet_solution**, be sure that *Word Document* displays in the *Save as type* box, and click **Save**.

The file is saved with the new name.

e. Click to place the insertion point at the beginning of the second sentence in the first paragraph. Type **These developments brought together**, and then press **Spacebar**.

The text moves to the right, making room for the new inserted text.

f. Press and hold down **Ctrl** as you click this sentence below the heading The World Wide Web: *The Netscape browser led in user share until Microsoft Internet Explorer took the lead in 1999.*

g. Click **Cut** in the Clipboard group on the Home tab.

The text disappears from the document.

h. Move the insertion point to the end of the last paragraph and click **Paste** in the Clipboard group on the Home tab.

The text displays in the new location.

i. Reselect the sentence you just moved and click **Copy** in the Clipboard group on the Home tab.

j. Move the insertion point to the end of the first paragraph beginning *The idea* and click the right mouse button.

The shortcut menu displays.

k. Select **Paste** from the shortcut menu.

The text remains in the original position and is copied to the second location.

l. Click **Undo** on the Quick Access Toolbar to undo the last paste.

Refer to Figure 1.42 to complete Step 2.

a. Press **Ctrl + Home** to move the insertion point to the beginning of the document. Click **Replace** in the Editing group on the Home tab.

The Find and Replace dialog box displays.

b. Type **Internet** in the *Find what* box and type **World Wide Web** in the *Replace with* box.

c. Click the **Replace All** button. Click **OK** to close the information box that informs you that Word has made seven replacements. Click **Close** to close the Find and Replace dialog box.

All instances of Internet have been replaced with World Wide Web in the document.

d. Click **Undo** on the Quick Access Toolbar.

All instances of *World Wide Web* have changed back to *Internet* in the document.

e. Click **Replace** in the Editing group on the Home tab.

The Find and Replace dialog box displays with the text you typed still in the boxes.

f. Click the **Find Next** button.

The first instance of the text *Internet* is highlighted.

g. Click the **Replace** button.

The first instance of Internet is replaced with World Wide Web, and the next instance of Internet is highlighted.

h. Click the **Find Next** button.

The highlight moves to the next instance of Internet without changing the previous one.

i. Click the **Close** button to close the Find and Replace dialog box.

The Find and Replace dialog box closes.

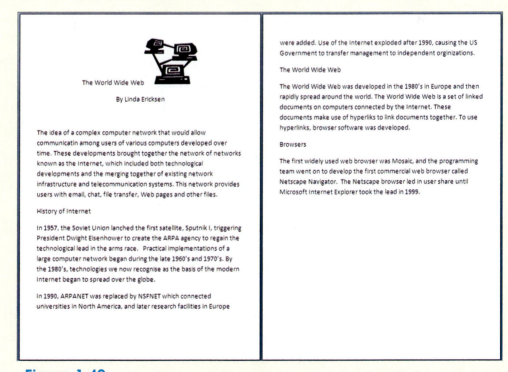

Figure 1.42 Edited Document (Shown in Full Screen Reading View)

Step 3
Check Spelling

Refer to Figure 1.43 as you complete Steps 3–5.

a. Right-click the first word in the document that displays with the red wavy underline: *communicatin*.

> **TROUBLESHOOTING:** If the first word highlighted is the author's last name, ignore it for now. The name is spelled correctly, but if it is not listed in the spell check, then Word flags it.

The shortcut menu displays with correct alternatives.

b. Click **communication** to replace the misspelled word in the document.

The incorrect spelling is replaced, and the red wavy underline disappears.

c. Click the **Review tab**, and then click **Spelling & Grammar** in the Proofing group.

The Spelling and Grammar dialog box opens with the first detected error displayed.

d. Move through the document selecting the correct word from the suggestions provided and choosing to **Change** the errors.

e. Click **OK** to close the Spelling and Grammar checker when the process is complete.

Step 4
Choose Synonyms and Use Thesaurus

a. Place the insertion point in the word **complex** in the first sentence and right-click the mouse.

The shortcut menu displays.

b. Point to **Synonyms** on the shortcut menu.

The list of alternative words displays.

c. Click the alternative word **multifaceted**.

The new word replaces the word *complex* in the document.

d. Click in the word you just replaced, *multifaceted*, and click the **Thesaurus** button on the Review tab.

The Thesaurus displays with alternatives for **multifaceted**.

e. Scroll down the list and point to the word *comprehensive*.

A box displays around the word with a drop-down arrow on the right.

f. Click the drop-down arrow to display the menu and click **Insert**.

The word *comprehensive* replaces the word in the document.

Step 5
Use the Research Tool

Refer to Figure 1.43 to complete Step 5.

a. Place the insertion point in the Search for text box and type **browser**.

b. Click the drop-down arrow on the **Reference** list, which currently displays the Thesaurus.

The list of reference sites displays.

c. Click **Encarta Encyclopedia: English (North American)** option.

A definition of the browser displays in the results box.

d. Click the **Close** button on the Research title bar.

The Research pane closes.

The World Wide Web

By Linda Ericksen

The idea of a comprehensive computer network that would allow communication among users of various computers developed over time. These developments brought together the network of networks known as the Internet, which included both technological developments and the merging together of existing network infrastructure and telecommunication systems. This network provides users with email, chat, file transfer, Web pages and other files.

History of Internet

In 1957, the Soviet Union launched the first satellite, Sputnik I, triggering President Dwight Eisenhower to create the ARPA agency to regain the technological lead in the arms race. Practical implementations of a large computer network began during the late 1960's and 1970's. By the 1980's, technologies we now recognize as the basis of the modern Internet began to spread over the globe.

In 1990, ARPANET was replaced by NSFNET which connected universities in North America, and later research facilities in Europe

were added. Use of the Internet exploded after 1990, causing the US Government to transfer management to independent organizations.

The World Wide Web

The World Wide Web was developed in the 1980's in Europe and then rapidly spread around the world. The World Wide Web is a set of linked documents on computers connected by the Internet. These documents make use of hyperlinks to link documents together. To use hyperlinks, browser software was developed.

Browsers

The first widely used web browser was Mosaic, and the programming team went on to develop the first commercial web browser called Netscape Navigator. The Netscape browser led in user share until Microsoft Internet Explorer took the lead in 1999.

Figure 1.43 Language Tools Improved the Document

Step 6
Apply Font Attributes

Refer to Figure 1.44 as you complete Steps 6 and 7.

a. Select the title of the document.

The Mini toolbar displays.

b. Click **Bold** on the Mini toolbar, and then click outside the title.

TROUBLESHOOTING: If the Mini toolbar is hard to read, remember to point to it to make it display fully.

The text changes to boldface.

c. Select the title again and click the drop-down arrow on the **Font** command in the Font group on the Home tab.

The list of fonts displays.

d. Point to font names on the list.

Live Preview changes the font of the selected sentence to display the fonts you point to.

e. Scroll down, and then select the **Lucinda Bright** font by clicking on the name.

The title changes to the new font.

f. With the title still selected, click the drop-down arrow on the **Font Size** command and select **16**.

The title changes to font size 16.

g. Select the byline that contains the author's name and click the **Underline** command, the **Italic** command, and the **Shrink Font** command once. All are located in the Font group on the Home tab.

The author's byline displays underlined, in italic, and one font size smaller.

h. Select the first heading *History of Internet* and click the **Font Color** down arrow command in the Font group on the Home tab. When the colors display, under Standard Colors, choose **Purple**, and then click outside the selected text.

The heading displays in purple.

i. Select the heading you just formatted as purple text and click **Bold**.

Refer to Figure 1.44 to complete Step 7.

a. Click the **Format Painter** command in the Clipboard group on the Home tab.

The pointer changes to a small paintbrush.

b. Select the second unformatted heading and repeat the process to format the third unformatted heading.

The Format Painter formats that heading as purple and bold and automatically turns off.

c. Press **Ctrl** while you click the last sentence in the document and click the **Dialog Box Launcher** in the Font group.

d. Select **Bold** in the Font style box and **Double strikethrough** in the *Effects* section of the dialog box, then click **OK**.

e. Click outside the selected sentence to remove the selection and view the effects, and then click back in the formatted text.

The sentence displays bold with two lines through the text. The Bold command in the Font group on the Home tab displays with a gold background.

f. Select the same sentence again, click **Bold** in the Font group on the Home tab, and then click outside the sentence.

The Bold format has been removed from the text.

g. Click **Save** on the Quick Access Toolbar.

The document is saved under the same name.

h. To exit Word, click the **Office Button**, and then click the **Exit Word** button.

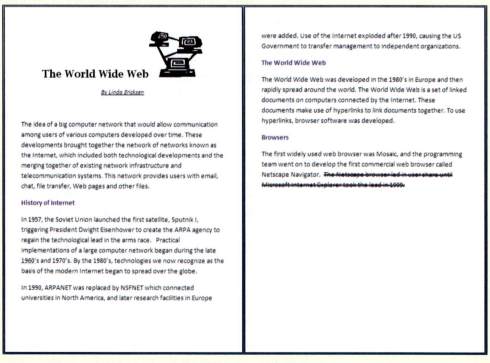

Figure 1.44 Formatted Document

Summary

1. **Identify common interface components.** You learned to identify and use the common elements of the Office 2007 interface and apply them in Word, PowerPoint, Excel, and Access. The top of the application window contains the Office Button that, when clicked, displays the Office menu. The Quick Access Toolbar provides commonly used commands, such as Save and Undo. The primary command center is the Ribbon, which contains tabs to organize major tasks. Each tab contains groups of related commands. The bottom of the window contains a status bar that gives general information, view options, and the Zoom slider.

2. **Use Office 2007 Help.** When you need help to continue working with Office 2007, you can use the Help feature from your computer or get help at Microsoft Office Online. You can position the mouse pointer on a command to see an Enhanced ScreenTip. You can click some Enhanced ScreenTips to display help. You can often get context-sensitive help by clicking Help within dialog boxes.

3. **Open a file.** To retrieve a file you have previously saved, you use the Open command. When you open a file, it is copied into RAM so that you can view and work on it.

4. **Save a file.** As you create and edit documents, you should save your work for future use. Use the Save or Save As command to save a file for the first time, giving it a name and location. To continue saving changes to the same file name, use Save. To assign a new name, location, or file type, use Save As.

5. **Print a document.** Producing a perfect hard copy of the document is an important task, and you can make it easier by previewing, selecting options, and printing. You can select the printer, how many copies to print, and the pages you want to print. In addition, each program has specific print options.

6. **Select text to edit.** In order to edit text, you have to identify the body of text you want to work with by selecting it first. You can select text by using the mouse.

7. **Insert text and change to the Overtype mode.** To edit text in the document, you need to be able to insert text and to replace text by typing over it. The Insert mode inserts text without deleting existing text. The Overtype mode types over existing text as you type.

8. **Move and copy text.** You can move text from one location to another to achieve a better flow in a document, worksheet, or presentation. You can use the Copy command to duplicate data in one location and use the Paste command to place the duplicate in another location.

9. **Find, replace, and go to text.** Another editing feature that can save you time is to find text by searching for it or going directly to a specific element in the document. You can also replace text that needs updating.

10. **Use the Undo and Redo commands.** If you make a mistake and want to undo it, you can easily remedy it by using the Undo feature. Likewise, to save time, you can repeat the last action with the Redo command.

11. **Use language tools.** Office 2007 provides tools to help you create and edit error-free documents. You can use the spelling check and grammar check, the built-in thesaurus, and even conduct research all from your Word document. You can check spelling and conduct research in Excel and PowerPoint as well.

12. **Apply font attributes.** Applying font formats can help make the message clearer. For example, you can select a different font to achieve a different look. In addition, you can adjust the font size and change the font color of text. Other font attributes include bold, underline, and italic.

13. **Copy formats with the Format Painter.** You might want to copy the format of text to another location or to several locations in the document. You can easily accomplish that with the Format Painter.

Key Terms

Multiple Choice

1. Software that is used primarily with text to create, edit, and format documents is known as:

   (a) Electronic spreadsheet software

   (b) Word processing software

   (c) Presentation graphics software

   (d) Relational database software

2. Which Office feature displays when you rest the mouse pointer on a command?

   (a) The Ribbon

   (b) The status bar

   (c) An Enhanced ScreenTip

   (d) A dialog box

3. What is the name of the blinking vertical line in a document that designates the current location in the document?

   (a) A command

   (b) Overtype mode

   (c) Insert mode

   (d) Insertion point

4. If you wanted to locate every instance of text in a document and have it temporarily highlighted, which command would you use?

   (a) Find

   (b) Replace

   (c) Go To

   (d) Spell Check

5. The meeting point between computer software and the person using it is known as:

   (a) A file

   (b) Software

   (c) A template

   (d) An interface

6. Which of the following is true about the Office Ribbon?

   (a) The Ribbon displays at the bottom of the screen.

   (b) The Ribbon is only available in the Word 2007 application.

   (c) The Ribbon is the main component of the Office 2007 interface.

   (d) The Ribbon cannot be used for selecting commands.

7. Which element of the Ribbon looks like folder tabs and provides commands that are task oriented?

   (a) Groups

   (b) Tabs

   (c) Status bar

   (d) Galleries

8. Which Office 2007 element provides commands that work with an entire document or file and displays by default in the title bar?

   (a) Galleries

   (b) Ribbon

   (c) Office Button

   (d) Groups

9. If you needed the entire screen to read a document, which document view would you use?

   (a) Outline view

   (b) Draft view

   (c) Print Layout

   (d) Full Screen Reading

10. The default four-letter extension for Word documents that do not contain macros is:

    (a) .docx

    (b) .pptx

    (c) .xlsx

    (d) .dotm

11. Before you can cut or copy text, you must first do which one of the following?

    (a) Preview the document.

    (b) Save the document.

    (c) Select the text.

    (d) Undo the previous command.

12. What is the name of the memory location that holds up to twenty-four items for you to paste into the current document, another document, or another application?

    (a) My Places bar

    (b) My Documents

    (c) Ribbon

    (d) Clipboard

Multiple Choice Continued...

13. Word flags misspelled words by marking them with which one of the following?

(a) A green wavy underline

(b) Boldfacing them

(c) A red wavy underline

(d) A double-underline in black

14. Which of the following displays when you select text in a document?

(a) The Mini toolbar

(b) The Quick Access Toolbar

(c) A shortcut menu

(d) The Ribbon

15. Formatting text allows you to change which of the following text attributes?

(a) The font

(b) The font size

(c) The font type

(d) All of the above

Practice Exercises

1 Using Help and Print Preview in Access 2007

a. Open Access. Click the **Office Button**, and then select **Open**. Use the Look in feature to find the *chap1_pe1* database, and then click **Open**.

b. At the right side of the Ribbon, click the **Help** button. In the Help window, type **table** in the **Type words to search for** box. Click the **Search** button.

c. Click the topic *Create a Table*. Browse the content of the Help window, and then click the **Close** button in the Help window.

d. Double-click the **Courses table** in the left pane. The table opens in Datasheet view.

e. Click the **Office Button**, point to the arrow after the **Print** command, and select **Print Preview** to open the Print Preview window with the Courses table displayed.

f. Point the mouse pointer on the table and click to magnify the display. Compare your screen to Figure 1.45.

g. Click the **Close Print Preview** button on the Print Preview tab.

h. Click the **Office Button**, and then click the **Exit Access button**.

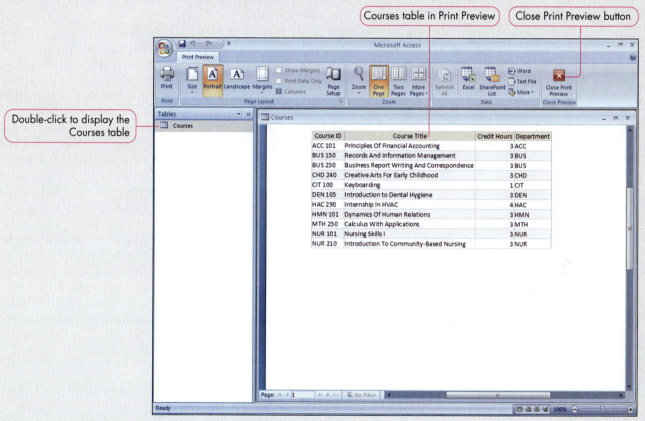

Figure 1.45 Access Print Preview

...continued on Next Page

As part of your Introduction to Computers course, you have prepared an oral report on phishing. You want to provide class members with a handout that summarizes the main points of your report. This handout is in the rough stages, so you need to edit it, and you also realize that you can format some of the text to emphasize the main points.

a. Start Word. Click the **Office Button,** and then select **Open**. Use the *Look in* feature to find the *chap1_pe2* document, and then click **Open**.

b. Click the **Office Button,** and then select **Save As**. In the *File name* box, type the document name, **chap1_pe2_solution**, be sure that Word document displays in the *Save as type* box, and use the *Look in* option to move to the location where you save your class files. Click **Save**.

c. In the document, click after the word Name and type **your name**.

d. Select your name, and then click **Bold** and **Italic** on the Mini toolbar—remember to point to the Mini toolbar to make it display fully. Your name displays in bold and italic.

e. Move the insertion point immediately before the title of the document and click the **Replace** button in the Editing group on the Home tab.

f. In the *Find what* box of the Find and Replace dialog box, type **internet**.

g. In the *Replace with* box of the Find and Replace dialog box, type **email**.

h. Click the **Replace All** button to have Word replace the text. Click **OK**, and then click **Close** to close the dialog boxes.

i. To format the title of the document, first select it, and then click the **Font arrow** in the Font group on the Home tab to display the available fonts.

j. Scroll down and choose the **Impact** font if you have it; otherwise, use one that is available.

k. Place the insertion point in the word *Phishng*. Right-click the word, and then click **Phishing** from the shortcut menu.

l. To emphasize important text in the list, double-click the first **NOT** to select it.

m. Click the **Font Color** arrow and select Red, and then click **Bold** in the Font group on the Home tab to apply bold to the text.

n. With the first instance of NOT selected, double-click **Format Painter** in the Clipboard group on the Home tab.

o. Double-click the second and then the third instance of **NOT** in the list, and then press **Esc** on the keyboard to turn off the Format Painter.

p. Compare your document to Figure 1.46. Save by clicking **Save** on the Quick Access Toolbar. Close the document and exit Word or proceed to the next step to preview and print the document.

...continued on Next Page

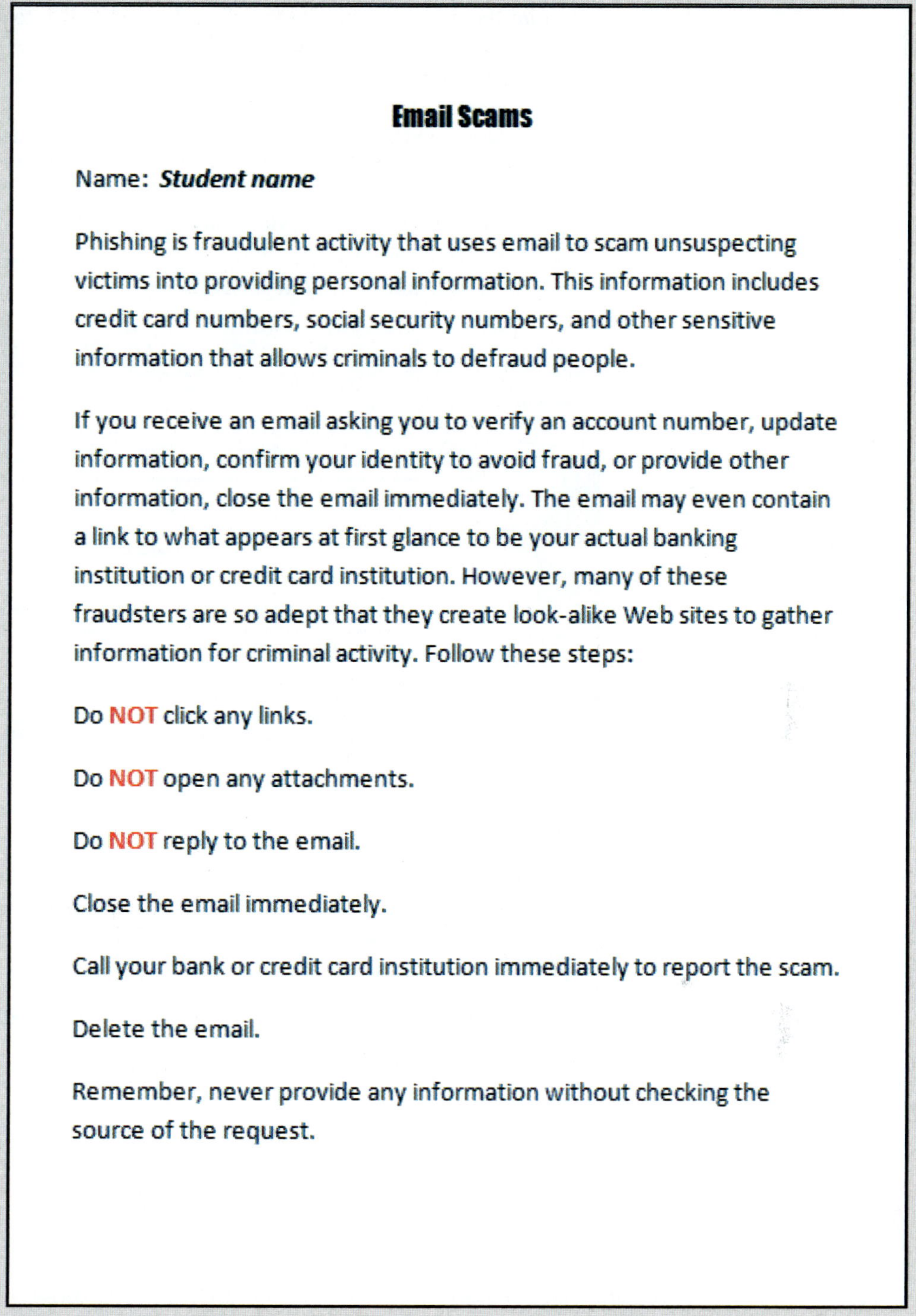

Email Scams

Name: *Student name*

Phishing is fraudulent activity that uses email to scam unsuspecting victims into providing personal information. This information includes credit card numbers, social security numbers, and other sensitive information that allows criminals to defraud people.

If you receive an email asking you to verify an account number, update information, confirm your identity to avoid fraud, or provide other information, close the email immediately. The email may even contain a link to what appears at first glance to be your actual banking institution or credit card institution. However, many of these fraudsters are so adept that they create look-alike Web sites to gather information for criminal activity. Follow these steps:

Do **NOT** click any links.

Do **NOT** open any attachments.

Do **NOT** reply to the email.

Close the email immediately.

Call your bank or credit card institution immediately to report the scam.

Delete the email.

Remember, never provide any information without checking the source of the request.

Figure 1.46 Phishing Document

3 Previewing and Printing a Document

You created a handout to accompany your oral presentation in the previous exercise. Now you want to print it out so that you can distribute it.

a. If necessary, open the *chap1_pe2_solution* document that you saved in the previous exercise.

b. Click the **Office Button**, point to the arrow after the Print command, and select **Print Preview** to open the Print Preview window with the document displayed.

...continued on Next Page

c. Point the mouse pointer in the document and click to magnify the display. Click the mouse pointer a second time to reduce the display.

d. To change the orientation of the document, click **Orientation** in the Page Setup group and choose **Landscape**.

e. Click **Undo** on the Quick Access Toolbar to undo the last command, which returns the document to portrait orientation. Compare your results to the zoomed document in Figure 1.47.

f. Click **Print** on the Print Preview tab to display the Print dialog box.

g. Click **OK** to print the document.

h. Close the document without saving it.

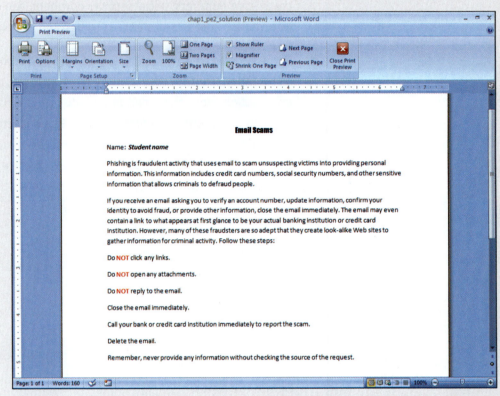

Figure 1.47 Document in Print Preview Window

4 Editing a Promotion Flyer

You work for Business Express, formerly known as Print Express, a regional company specializing in business centers that design and produce documents for local businesses and individuals. Business Express has just undergone a major transition along with a name change. Your job is to edit and refine an existing flyer to inform customers of the new changes. Proceed as follows:

a. Open Word. Click the **Office Button,** and then select **Open**. Use the *Look in* feature to find the *chap1_pe4* document.

b. Click the **Office Button** again and select **Save As**. Type the document name, **chap1_pe4_solution,** be sure that Word document displays in the *Save as type* box, and use the *Look in* option to move to the location where you save your class files.

c. Place the insertion point at the beginning of the document, and then click **Spelling & Grammar** in the Proofing group on the Review tab to open the Spelling and Grammar dialog box.

d. Click the **Change** button three times to correct the spelling errors. Click **OK** to close the completion box.

...continued on Next Page

e. Place the insertion point at the end of the first sentence of the document—just before the period. To insert the following text, press **Spacebar** and type **that offers complete business solutions**.

f. Place the insertion point in *good* in the first sentence of the third paragraph and right-click the mouse.

g. Point to **Synonyms**, and then click **first-rate** to replace the word in the document.

h. Place the insertion point in *bigger* in the last sentence of the third paragraph and click **Thesaurus** in the Proofing group on the Review tab. Point to **superior** and click the drop-down arrow that displays. Click **Insert** from the menu to replace the word in the document, and then click the **Close** button on the Thesaurus.

i. Select the last full paragraph of the document and click **Cut** in the Clipboard group on the Home tab to remove the paragraph from the document.

j. Place the insertion point at the beginning of the new last paragraph and click **Paste** in the Clipboard group on the Home tab to display the text.

k. Click **Undo** on the Quick Access Toolbar twice to undo the paste operation and to undo the cut operation—placing the text back in its original location.

l. Place the insertion point after the colon at the bottom of the document and type **your name**.

m. Compare your results to Figure 1.48, and then save and close the document.

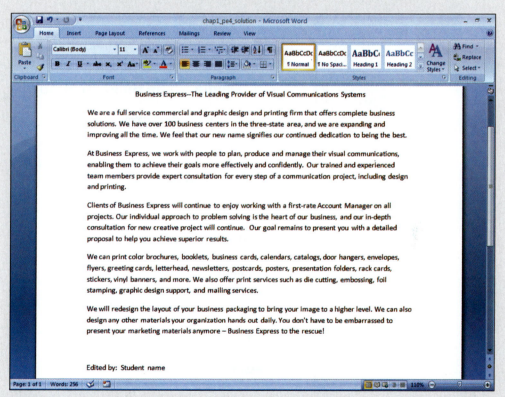

Figure 1.48 Business Flyer

Mid-Level Exercises

1 Updating a Training Document

Your position as trainer for a large building supply company involves training all new employees. It is your job to familiarize new employees with the services provided by Castle Home Building Supply. You distribute a list at the training session and you realize that it needs updating before the next session, so you decide to edit and format it.

a. Start Word. Open the *chap1_mid1* file and save it as **chap1_mid1_solution**.

b. Change the title font to Arial Rounded MT Bold size 16 and change the font color to dark brown.

c. Make the subtitle Arial Unicode MS and italic.

d. Cut the item *Help with permits* and make it the second item on the list.

e. In the first list item, insert **and** after the word *fair*.

f. Change the word *help* in the last list item to **Assistance**.

g. Select the list of items excluding the heading, Services Provided.

h. Bold the list and change the font size to 16.

i. Save the document and compare it to Figure 1.49.

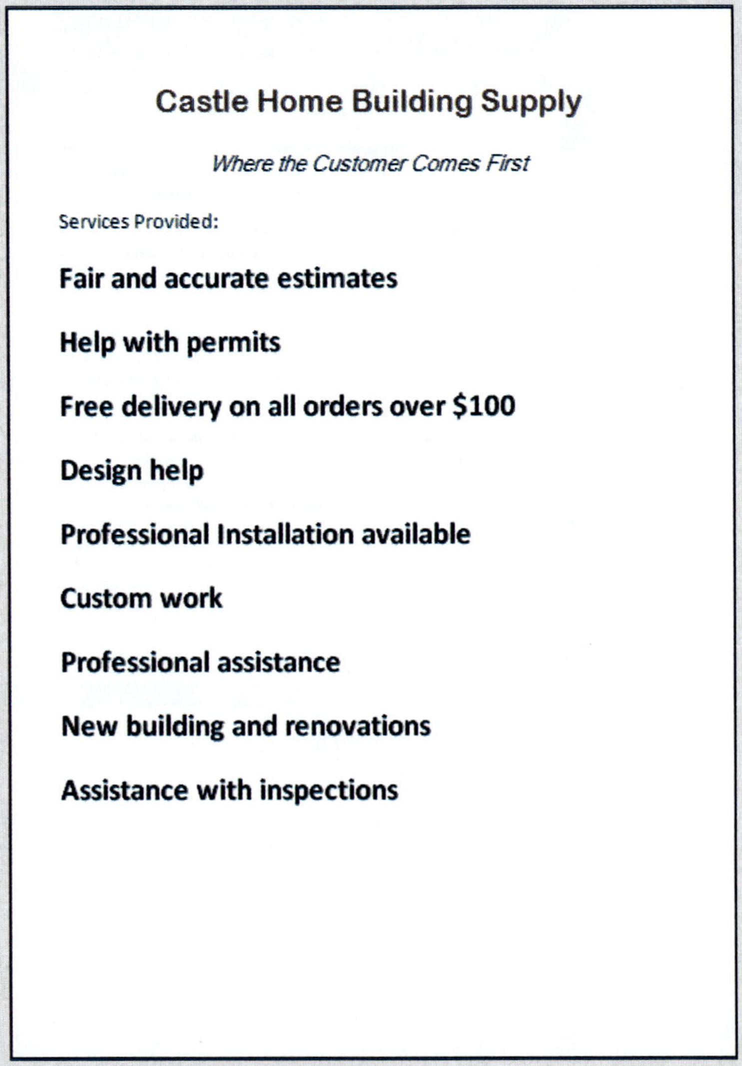
Castle Home Building Supply

Where the Customer Comes First

Services Provided:

Fair and accurate estimates

Help with permits

Free delivery on all orders over $100

Design help

Professional Installation available

Custom work

Professional assistance

New building and renovations

Assistance with inspections

Figure 1.49 Training Document

...continued on Next Page

2 Formatting a Menu

The owner of the Bayside Restaurant wants your help formatting his menu so that it is more pleasing to customers; follow the steps below:

a. Open the *chap1_mid2* document and save it as **chap1_mid2_solution**.

b. Format the menu title as Broadway size 16.

c. Format the three headings: Appetizers, Soups and Salads, and Lunch or Dinner Anytime! as Bodoni MT Black, size 12, and change the font color to Dark Red. Remember to format the first one and use the Format Painter for the second two headings.

d. Format all the dish names, such as Nachos, using the Outline Font Effects.

e. Bold all the prices in the document.

f. Preview the document, compare to Figure 1.50, and then print it.

g. Save and close the document.

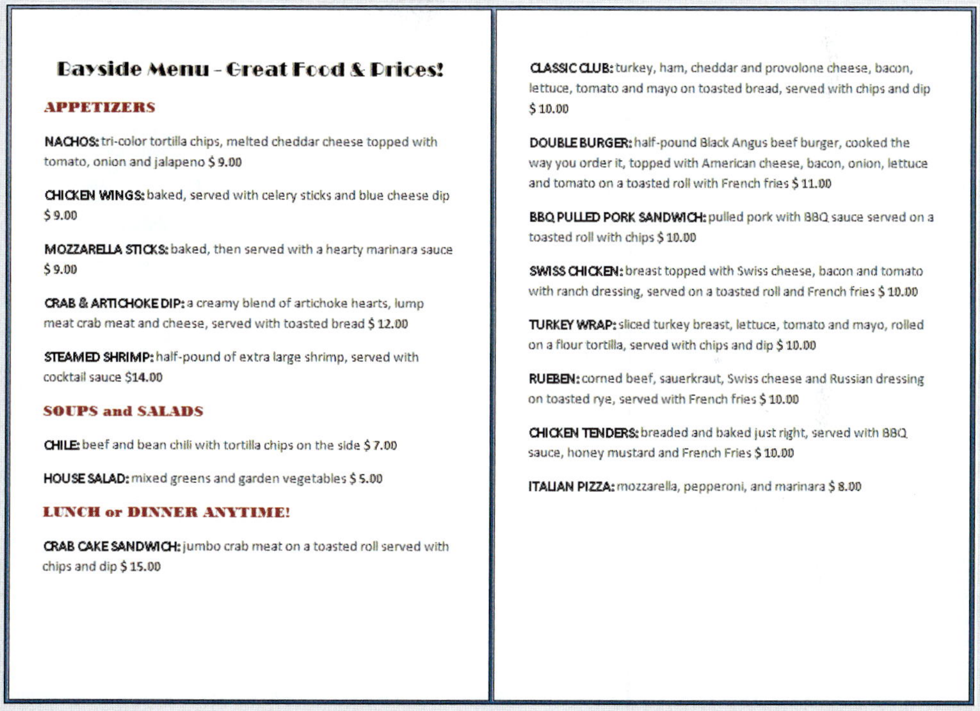

Bayside Menu - Great Food & Prices!

APPETIZERS

NACHOS: tri-color tortilla chips, melted cheddar cheese topped with tomato, onion and jalapeno **$ 9.00**

CHICKEN WINGS: baked, served with celery sticks and blue cheese dip **$ 9.00**

MOZZARELLA STICKS: baked, then served with a hearty marinara sauce **$ 9.00**

CRAB & ARTICHOKE DIP: a creamy blend of artichoke hearts, lump meat crab meat and cheese, served with toasted bread **$ 12.00**

STEAMED SHRIMP: half-pound of extra large shrimp, served with cocktail sauce **$14.00**

SOUPS and SALADS

CHILE: beef and bean chili with tortilla chips on the side **$ 7.00**

HOUSE SALAD: mixed greens and garden vegetables **$ 5.00**

LUNCH or DINNER ANYTIME!

CRAB CAKE SANDWICH: jumbo crab meat on a toasted roll served with chips and dip **$ 15.00**

CLASSIC CLUB: turkey, ham, cheddar and provolone cheese, bacon, lettuce, tomato and mayo on toasted bread, served with chips and dip **$ 10.00**

DOUBLE BURGER: half-pound Black Angus beef burger, cooked the way you order it, topped with American cheese, bacon, onion, lettuce and tomato on a toasted roll with French fries **$ 11.00**

BBQ PULLED PORK SANDWICH: pulled pork with BBQ sauce served on a toasted roll with chips **$ 10.00**

SWISS CHICKEN: breast topped with Swiss cheese, bacon and tomato with ranch dressing, served on a toasted roll and French fries **$ 10.00**

TURKEY WRAP: sliced turkey breast, lettuce, tomato and mayo, rolled on a flour tortilla, served with chips and dip **$ 10.00**

RUEBEN: corned beef, sauerkraut, Swiss cheese and Russian dressing on toasted rye, served with French fries **$ 10.00**

CHICKEN TENDERS: breaded and baked just right, served with BBQ sauce, honey mustard and French Fries **$ 10.00**

ITALIAN PIZZA: mozzarella, pepperoni, and marinara **$ 8.00**

Figure 1.50 The Formatted Menu

...continued on Next Page

Your job duties at Health First Insurance, Inc., involve maintaining the correspondence. You need to update the welcome letter you send to clients to reflect the company's new name, new address, and other important elements, and then address it to a new client. Proceed as follows.

a. Open the *chap1_mid3* document and save it as **chap1_mid3_solution**.

b. Run the Spelling check to eliminate the errors.

c. Use Replace to change **University Insurance, Inc**. to **Health First Insurance, Inc**. throughout the letter.

d. Change the Address from **123 Main St**. to **1717 N. Zapata Way**.

e. Change the inside address that now has **Client name, Client Address, Client City, State and Zip Code** to **your name and complete address**. Also change the salutation to your name.

f. Move the first paragraph so that it becomes the last paragraph in the body of the letter.

g. Preview the letter to be sure that it fits on one page, compare it with Figure 1.51, and then print it.

h. Save and close the document.

Health First Insurance, Inc.

1717 N. Zapata Way

Laredo, TX 78043

Student name

Student Address

Student City, State, and Zip Code

Dear Student name:

Welcome to the Health First Insurance, Inc. We have received and accepted your application and premium for health insurance. Please detach and the ID cards attached to this letter and keep with you at all times for identification, reference and access to emergency phone assistance and Pre Notification numbers in the event of a claim.

Enclosed you will find a Certificate of Coverage detailing the benefits, limits, exclusions and provisions of the Health First Insurance, Inc. Medical Plan. Please review the Certificate of Coverage thoroughly and contact us if you have any questions regarding the terms and provisions.

In order for you and your dependents to receive adequate medical treatment and for your assistance, the Health First Insurance, Inc. Medical Plan requires any insured (or someone on their behalf) to Pre-notify Health First Insurance, Inc., for any hospital admission prior to admittance (or within 36 hours after an emergency admission). Additionally, the Health First Insurance, Inc. Medical Plan requires all insured to utilize the provider network.

We appreciate your confidence in our organization and look forward to serving your insurance needs.

Sincerely,

Maria Fernandez

Agent

Health First Insurance, Inc.

Figure 1.51 The Updated Letter

Capstone Exercise

In this project, you work with a business plan for Far East Trading Company that will be submitted to funding sources in order to secure loans. The document requires editing to polish the final product and formatting to enhance readability and emphasize important information.

Editing the Document

This document is ready for editing, so proceed as follows:

a. Open the *chap1_cap* document. Save the document as **chap1_cap_solution**.

b. Run the Spelling and Grammar check to eliminate all spelling and grammar errors in the document.

c. Use the Thesaurus to find a synonym for the word **unique** in the second paragraph of the document.

d. Use the Go To command to move to page 3 and change the $175,000 to $250,000.

e. Move the entire second section of the document (notice the numbers preceding it) now located at the end of the document to its correct location after the first section.

f. Insert the street **1879 Columbia Ave.** before Portland in the first paragraph.

g. Copy the inserted street address to section 2.3 and place it in front of Portland there also.

h. Replace the initials **FET** with **FETC** for every instance in the document.

i. Type over 1998 in the third paragraph so that it says 2008.

Formatting the Document

Next, you will apply formatting techniques to the document. These format options will further increase the readability and attractiveness of your document.

a. Select the two-line title and change the font to Engravers MT, size 14, and change the color to Dark Red.

b. Select the first heading in the document: 1.0 Executive Summary, then change the font to Gautami, bold, and change the color to Dark Blue.

c. Use the Format Painter to make all the main numbered headings the same formatting, that is 2.0, 3.0, 4.0, and 5.0.

d. The first three numbered sections have subsections such as 1.1, 1.2. Select the heading 1.1 and format it for bold, italic, and change the color to a lighter blue—Aqua, Accents, Darker 25%.

e. Use the Format Painter to make all the numbered subsections the same formatting.

Printing the Document

To finish the job, you need to print the business plan.

a. Preview the document to check your results.

b. Print the document.

c. Save your changes and close the document.

Mini Cases

Use the rubric following the case as a guide to evaluate our work, but keep in mind that your instructor may impose additional grading criteria or use a different standard to judge your work.

A Thank-You Letter

GENERAL CASE

As the new volunteer coordinator for Special Olympics in your area, you need to send out information for prospective volunteers, and the letter you were given needs editing and formatting. Open the *chap1_mc1* document and make necessary changes to improve the appearance. You should use Replace to change the text (insert your state name), use the current date and your name and address information, format to make the letter more appealing, and eliminate all errors. Your finished document should be saved as **chap1_mc1_solution**.

Performance Elements	Exceeds Expectations	Meets Expectations	Below Expectations
Corrected all errors	Document contains no errors.	Document contains minimal errors.	Document contains several errors.
Use of character formatting features such as font, font size, font color, or other attributes	Used character formatting options throughout entire document.	Used character formatting options in most sections of document.	Used character formatting options on a small portion of document.
Inserted text where instructed	The letter is complete with all required information inserted.	The letter is mostly complete.	Letter is incomplete. .

The Information Request Letter

RESEARCH CASE

Search the Internet for opportunities to teach abroad or for internships available in your major. Have fun finding a dream opportunity. Use the address information you find on the Web site that interests you, and compose a letter asking for additional information. For example, you might want to teach English in China, so search for that information. Your finished document should be saved as **chap1_mc2_solution**.

Performance Elements	Exceeds Expectations	Meets Expectations	Below Expectations
Use of character formatting	Three or more character formats applied to text.	One or two character formats applied to text.	Does not apply character formats to text.
Language tools	No spelling or grammar errors.	One spelling or grammar error.	More than one spelling or grammar error.
Presentation	Information is easy to read and understand.	Information is somewhat unclear.	Letter is unclear.

Movie Memorabilia

DISASTER RECOVERY

Use the following rubrics to guide your evaluation of your work, but keep in mind that your instructor may impose additional grading criteria.

Open the *chap1_mc3* document that can be found in the Exploring folder. The advertising document is over-formatted, and it contains several errors and problems. For example, the text has been formatted in many fonts that are difficult to read. The light color of the text also has made the document difficult to read. You should improve the formatting so that it is consistent, helps the audience read the document, and is pleasing to look at. Your finished document should be saved as **chap1_mc3_solution**.

Performance Elements	Exceeds Expectations	Meets Expectations	Below Expectations
Type of font chosen to format document	Number and style of fonts appropriate for short document.	Number or style of fonts appropriate for short document.	Overused number of fonts or chose inappropriate font.
Color of font chosen to format document	Appropriate font colors for document.	Most font colors appropriate.	Overuse of font colors.
Overall document appeal	Document looks appealing.	Document mostly looks appealing.	Did not improve document much.

Microsoft Word

What Will Word Processing Do for Me?

 bjectives

After you read this chapter, you will be able to:

1. Understand Word basics **(page 72)**.

2. Use AutoText **(page 76)**.

3. View a document **(page 78)**.

4. Use the Mini toolbar **(page 80)**.

5. Set margins and specify page orientation **(page 87)**.

6. Insert page breaks **(page 88)**.

7. Add page numbers **(page 90)**.

8. Insert headers and footers **(page 91)**.

9. Create sections **(page 92)**.

10. Insert a cover page **(page 93)**.

11. Use Find and Replace commands **(page 94)**.

12. Check spelling and grammar **(page 103)**.

13. Use save and backup options **(page 104)**.

14. Select printing options **(page 107)**.

15. Customize Word **(page 108)**.

Hands-On Exercises

Exercises	Skills Covered
1. INTRODUCTION TO MICROSOFT WORD (page 81) **Open:** chap1_ho1_credit.docx **Save as:** chap1_ho1_credit_solution.docx	• Open and Save a Word Document • Modify the Document • Insert AutoText • Create an AutoText Entry • Change Document Views and Zoom
2. DOCUMENT ORGANIZATION (page 96) **Open:** chap1_ho1_credit_solution.docx (from Exercise 1) **Save as:** chap1_ho2_credit_solution.docx (additional modifications)	• Set Page Margins and Orientation • Insert a Page Break • Add a Cover Page and Insert a Document Header • Insert a Section Break • Insert a Page Number in the Footer • Use Find, Replace, and Go To
3. THE FINAL TOUCHES (page 110) **Open:** chap1_ho2_credit_solution.docx (from Exercise 2) **Save as:** chap1_ho3_credit_solution.docx (additional modifications), chap1_ho3_credit2_solution.docx, and chap1_ho3_credit_solution.doc	• Perform a Spelling and Grammar Check • Run the Document Inspector and a Compatibility Check • Save in a Compatible Format • Change Word Options • Use Print Preview Features

CASE STUDY
A Question of Ethics

You would never walk into a music store, put a CD under your arm, and walk out without paying for it. What if, however, you could download the same CD from the Web for free? Are you hurting anyone? Or what if you gave a clerk a $5 bill, but received change for a $50? Would you return the extra money? Would you speak up if it was the person ahead of you in line who received change for the $50, when you clearly saw that he or she gave the clerk $5? Ethical conflicts occur all the time and result when one person or group benefits at the expense of another.

Case Study

Your Philosophy 101 instructor assigned a class project whereby students are divided into teams to consider questions of ethics and society. Each team is to submit a single document that represents the collective efforts of all the team members. The completed project is to include a brief discussion of ethical principles followed by five examples of ethical conflicts. Every member of the team will receive the same grade, regardless of his or her level of participation; indeed, this might be an ethical dilemma, in and of itself.

Your Assignment

- Read the chapter, paying special attention to sections that describe how to format a document using page breaks, headers and footers, and page numbers.
- Open the *chap1_case_ethics* document, which contains the results of your team's collaboration, but which requires further formatting before you submit it to your professor.
- Create a cover page for the document. Include the name of the report, the team members, and your course name.
- View the document in draft view and remove any unnecessary page breaks.
- Set the margins on your document to a width and height that allows for binding the document.
- Set page numbers for each page of the document except the cover page. The page numbers should display in the center of the footer. Page numbering should begin on the page that follows the cover page.
- Perform a spelling and grammar check on the document, but proofread it also.
- Save your work in a document named **chap1_case_ethics_solution.docx**.
- Run a compatibility check, and then save it also in Word 97–2003 format, as **chap1_case_ethics_solution.doc**, in case your professor, who does not have Office 2007, requests a digital copy.

Introduction to Word Processing

Word processing software is probably the most commonly used type of software. You can create letters, reports, research papers, newsletters, brochures, and other documents with Word. You can even create and send e-mail, produce Web pages, and update blogs with Word.

Word processing software is probably the most commonly used type of software. People around the world—students, office assistants, managers, and professionals in all areas—use word processing programs such as Microsoft Word for a variety of tasks. You can create letters, reports, research papers, newsletters, brochures, and other documents with Word. You can even create and send e-mail, produce Web pages, and update blogs with Word. Figure 1.1 shows examples of documents created in Word.

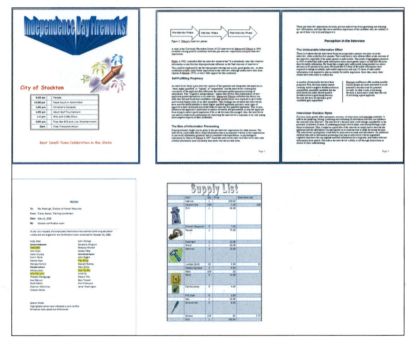

Figure 1.1 The Versatility of Microsoft Word 2007

Microsoft Word provides a multitude of features that enable you to enhance documents with only a few clicks of the mouse. You can change colors, add interesting styles of text, insert graphics, use a table to present data, track changes made to a document, view comments made about document content, combine several documents into one, and quickly create reference pages such as a table of contents, an index, or a bibliography.

This chapter provides a broad-based introduction to word processing in general and Microsoft Word in particular. All word processors adhere to certain basic concepts that must be understood to use the program effectively.

In this section, you learn about the Word interface, word wrap, and toggles. You learn how to use the AutoText feature to insert text automatically in your document, and then you change document views and learn to use the new Mini toolbar.

Understanding Word Basics

The Exploring series authors used Microsoft Word to write this book. You will use Word to complete the exercises in this chapter. When you start Word, your screen might be different. You will not see the same document shown in Figure 1.2, nor is it likely that you will customize Word in exactly the same way. You should, however, be able to recognize the basic elements that are found in the Microsoft Word window that are emphasized in Figure 1.2.

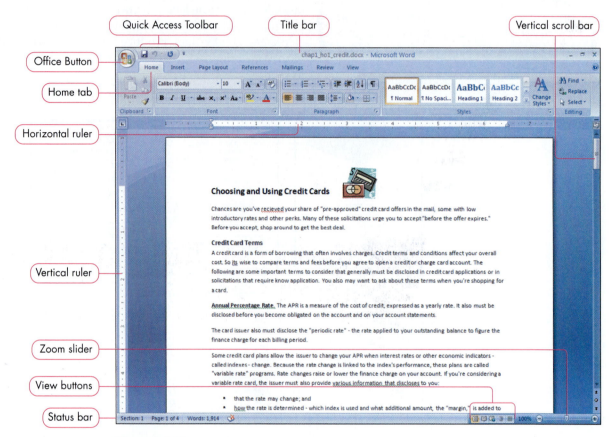

Figure 1.2 The Microsoft Word Window

Figure 1.2 displays two open windows—an application window for Microsoft Word and a document window for the specific document on which you are working. However, only one title bar appears at the top of the application window, and it reflects the application (Microsoft Word) as well as the document name (chap1_ho1_credit.docx). If you want to close the document but not the Word program, click the Office Button and select Close. To close both the document and the application, click Close in the upper-right corner.

The Quick Access Toolbar appears on the left side of the title bar. This toolbar contains commands that are used very frequently, such as Save, Undo, and Repeat. Vertical and horizontal scroll bars appear at the right and bottom of a document window. You use them to view portions of a document that do not display on the screen. Each Microsoft Office application includes the Ribbon, which contains tabs that organize commands into task-oriented groups. The active tab is highlighted, and the commands on that tab display immediately below the title bar. The tabs can change according to the current task, or you can display a different tab by clicking the tab name. The tabs in Word are displayed in the Reference on the next two pages.

The status bar at the bottom of the document window displays information about the document such as the section and page where the insertion point is currently positioned, the total number of pages in the document, and the total number of words in the document. At the right side of the status bar, you find command buttons that enable you to quickly change the View and zoom level of the document.

Word Tabs | Reference

Tab and Group	Description
Home Clipboard Font Paragraph Styles Editing	The basic Word tab. Contains basic editing functions such as cut and paste along with most formatting actions. Some groups contain Dialog Box Launchers that offer more commands and increase functionality.

Insert Pages Tables Illustrations Links Header & Footer Text Symbols	Brings together all insert functions in one area. Includes ability to create graphs and add tables. Contains powerful picture functions. Headers and footers are inserted here.

Page Layout Themes Page Setup Page Background Paragraph Arrange	Contains all functions associated with page appearance, setup, and printing. Provides features that facilitate document customization.

References Table of Contents Footnotes Citations & Bibliography Captions Index Table of Authorities	Provides functions for automating references in a document. Includes assistance using popular writing styles.

Mailings

Create
Start Mail Merge
Write & Insert Fields
Preview Results
Finish

Contains commands used in the process of combining data from multiple sources and providing useful information.

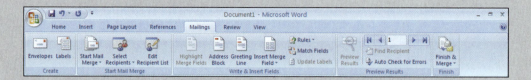

Review

Proofing
Comments
Tracking
Changes
Compare
Protect

Contains all reviewing tools in Word, including spelling and grammatical check, the management of comments, sharing, and protection.

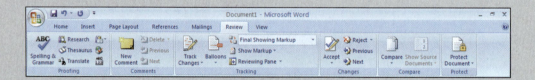

View

Document Views
Show/Hide
Window
Macros

Contains basic and advanced view settings. Some of these options also appear below the horizontal and vertical scroll bars.

Learn About Word Wrap

A word processor is a software tool that enables you to document your thoughts or other information. Whether you are new to using a word processor or have been using one for a period of time, you will notice that certain functions seem to happen automatically. As you type, you probably don't think about how much text can fit on one line or where the sentences must roll from one line to the other. Fortunately, the word processor takes care of that for you. This function is called *word wrap* and enables you to type continually without pressing Enter at the end of a line within a paragraph. The only time you press Enter is at the end of a paragraph or when you want the insertion point to move to the next line.

Word wrap moves words to the next line if they do not fit on the current line.

Word wrap is closely associated with another concept, that of hard and soft returns. A *hard return* is created by the user when he or she presses the Enter key at the end of a line or paragraph; a *soft return* is created by the word processor as it wraps text from one line to the next. The locations of the soft returns change automatically as a document is edited (e.g., as text is inserted or deleted, or as margins or fonts are changed). The locations of hard returns can be changed only by the user, who must intentionally insert or delete each hard return.

A *hard return* is created when you press Enter to move the insertion point to a new line.

A *soft return* is created by the word processor as it wraps text to a new line.

The paragraphs at the top of Figure 1.3 show two hard returns, one at the end of each paragraph. It also includes four soft returns in the first paragraph (one at the end of every line except the last) and three soft returns in the second paragraph. Now suppose the margins in the document are made smaller (that is, the line is made longer), as shown in the bottom paragraphs of Figure 1.3. The number of soft returns drops to three and two (in the first and second paragraphs, respectively) as more text fits on a line and fewer lines are needed. The revised document still contains the two original hard returns, one at the end of each paragraph.

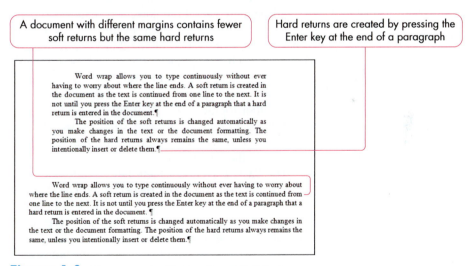

Figure 1.3 Document with Hard and Soft Returns

Use Keyboard Shortcuts to Scroll

The horizontal and vertical scrollbars frequently are used to move around in a document. However, clicking the scroll arrows does not move the insertion point; it merely lets you see different parts of the document in the document window and leaves the insertion point where it was last positioned. You can use the mouse or the keyboard to move the insertion point in a document. Table 1.1 shows useful keyboard shortcuts for moving around in a document and relocating the insertion point.

Table 1.1 Keyboard Scrolling Methods

Key	Moves the Insertion Point . . .	Key	Moves the Insertion Point . . .
Left arrow	one character to the left	Ctrl + Home	to the beginning of the document
Right arrow	one character to the right	Ctrl + End	to the end of the document
Up arrow	up one line	Ctrl + Left arrow	one word to the left
Down arrow	down one line	Ctrl + Right arrow	one word to the right
Home	to the beginning of the line	Ctrl + Up arrow	up one paragraph
End	to the end of the line	Ctrl + Down arrow	down one paragraph
PgUp	up one window or page	Ctrl + Pgup	to the top of the previous page
PgDn	down one window or page	Ctrl + PgDn	to the top of the next page

Discover Toggle Switches

Suppose you sat down at the keyboard and typed an entire sentence without pressing Shift; the sentence would be in all lowercase letters. Then you pressed the Caps Lock key and retyped the sentence, again without pressing the Shift key. This time, the sentence would be in all uppercase letters. Each time you pressed the Caps Lock key, the text you type would switch from lowercase to uppercase and vice versa.

The **toggle switch** is a device that causes the computer to alternate between two states.

The point of this exercise is to introduce the concept of a **toggle switch**, a device that causes the computer to alternate between two states. Caps Lock is an example of a toggle switch. Each time you press it, newly typed text will change from uppercase to lowercase and back again. In the Office Fundamentals chapter, you read about other toggle switches. Some toggle switches are physical keys you press, such as the Insert key (which toggles to Overtype). Some toggle switches are software features such as the Bold, Italic, and Underline commands (which can be clicked to turn on and off).

The **Show/Hide feature** reveals where formatting marks such as spaces, tabs, and returns are used in the document.

Another toggle switch that enables you to reveal formatting applied to a document is the **Show/Hide feature**. Click Show/Hide ¶ in the Paragraph group on the Home tab to reveal where formatting marks such as spaces, tabs, and hard returns are used in the document.

The Backspace and Delete keys delete one character immediately to the left or right of the insertion point, respectively. The choice between them depends on when you need to erase character(s). The Backspace key is easier if you want to delete a character (or characters) immediately after typing. The Delete key is preferable during subsequent editing.

You can delete several characters at one time by selecting (clicking and dragging the mouse over) the characters to be deleted, then pressing the Delete key. You can delete and replace text in one operation by selecting the text to be replaced and then typing the new text in its place. You can also select a block of text by clicking to place the insertion point in front of the first character, holding down Shift and then clicking to the right of the last character. Double-click a word to select it, and triple-click to select a paragraph. These forms of selecting text enable you to quickly format or delete text.

Using AutoText

The **AutoText** feature substitutes a predefined item for specific text but only when the user initiates it.

You learned about the AutoCorrect feature in the Office Fundamentals chapter. The **AutoText** feature is similar in concept to AutoCorrect in that both substitute a predefined item for a specific character string or group of characters. The difference is that the substitution occurs automatically with the AutoCorrect entry, whereas you have to take deliberate action for the AutoText substitution to take place. AutoText entries can also include significantly more text, formatting, and even clip art.

Microsoft Word includes a host of predefined AutoText entries such as days of the week and months of the year. For example, if you start typing today's date, you see a ScreenTip that displays the entire date, as shown in Figure 1.4. Press Enter while the ScreenTip is visible to insert the date automatically.

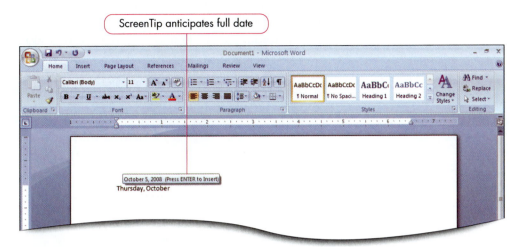

ScreenTip anticipates full date

Figure 1.4 Insert AutoText

As with the AutoCorrect feature, you can define additional entries of your own. (However, you may not be able to do this in a computer lab environment.) This is advisable if you use the same piece of text frequently, such as a disclaimer, a return address, a company logo, or a cover page. You first select the text, click Quick Parts in the Text group on the Insert tab, and select Save Selection to Quick Part Gallery. In the Create New Building Block dialog box, make sure the Gallery option displays Quick Parts, and click OK. After you add entries to the Quick Parts gallery, they are included in the ***Building Blocks*** library, which contains document components you use frequently, such as those mentioned above. After you add the text to the Quick Parts gallery, you can type a portion of the entry, then press F3 to insert the remainder into your document. Figure 1.5 demonstrates the creation of the AutoText entry.

Building Blocks are document components used frequently, such as disclaimers, company addresses, or a cover page.

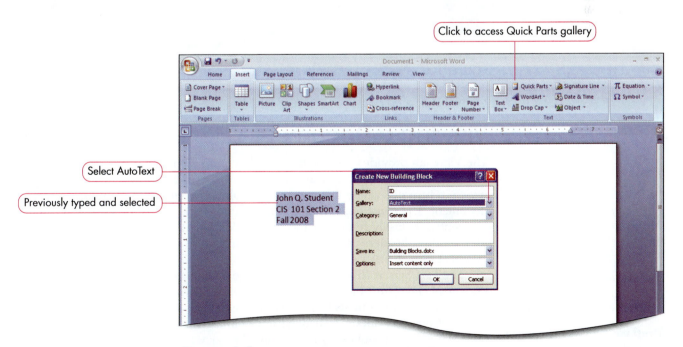

Click to access Quick Parts gallery

Select AutoText

Previously typed and selected

Figure 1.5 Adding an AutoText Building Block

TIP   Insert the Date and Time

Some documents include the date and time they were created. A time and date stamp can help determine the most recent edition of a document, which is important if the document is updated frequently. To create a time and date stamp, click the Insert tab, click Date and Time in the Text group to display the Date and Time dialog box, then choose a format. Click the *Update automatically* check box to update the date automatically if you want your document to reflect the date on which it is opened, or clear the box to retain the date on which the date was inserted (see Figure 1.6).

Click to update the time automatically when the file is saved

Click to display Date and Time dialog box

Select from a variety of date and time formats

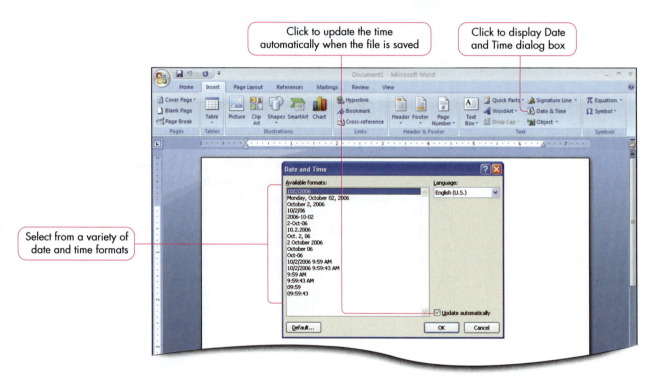

Figure 1.6 The Date and Time Dialog Box

Viewing a Document

The View tab provides options that enable you to display a document in many different ways. Each view can display your document at different magnifications, which in turn determine the amount of scrolling necessary to see remote parts of a document. The *Print Layout view* is the default view and is the view you use most frequently. It closely resembles the printed document and displays the top and bottom margins, headers and footers, page numbers, graphics, and other features that do not appear in other views.

The *Full Screen Reading view* hides the Ribbon, making it easier to read your document. The *Draft view* creates a simple area in which to work; it removes white space and certain elements from the document, such as headers, footers, and graphics, but leaves the Ribbon. It displays information about some elements, such as page and section breaks, not easily noticed in other views. Because view options are used frequently, buttons for each also are located on the status bar, as shown in Figure 1.2.

The Zoom command displays the document on the screen at different magnifications—for example, 75%, 100%, or 200%. But this command does not affect

Print Layout view is the default view and closely resembles the printed document.

Full Screen Reading view eliminates tabs and makes it easier to read your document.

Draft view shows a simplified work area, removing white space and other elements from view.

the size of the text on the printed page. It is helpful to be able to zoom in to view details or to zoom out and see the effects of your work on a full page. When you click Zoom in the Zoom group on the View tab, a dialog box displays with several zoom options (see Figure 1.7).

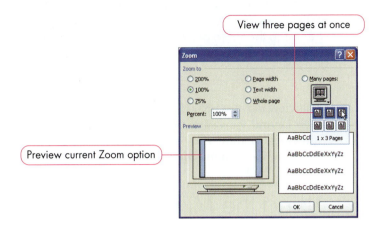

Figure 1.7 The Zoom Dialog Box

Word automatically will determine the magnification if you select one of the Zoom options—Page width, Text width, Whole page, or Many pages (Whole page and Many pages are available only in the Print Layout view). Figure 1.8, for example, displays a four-page document in Print Layout view. The 28% magnification is determined automatically after you specify the number of pages. If you use a wide screen, the magnification size might differ slightly.

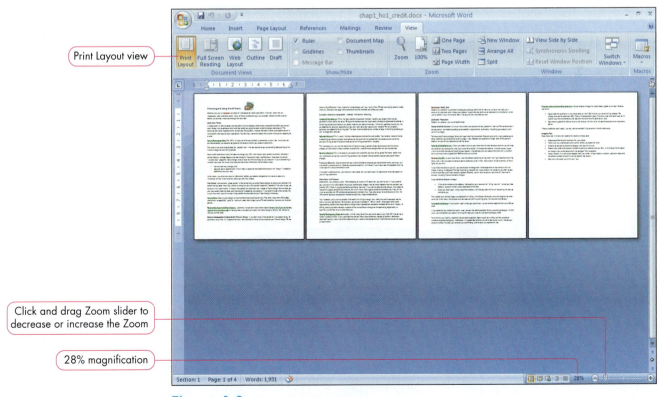

Figure 1.8 View Four Pages of Document

The **Outline view** displays a structural view of the document that can be collapsed or expanded.

The **Web Layout view** is used when creating a Web page.

The View tab also provides access to two additional views—the Outline view and the Web Layout view. The *Outline view* does not display a conventional outline, but rather a structural view of a document that can be collapsed or expanded as necessary. The *Web Layout view* is used when you are creating a Web page.

Using the Mini Toolbar

The **Mini toolbar** contains frequently used formatting commands and displays when you select text.

Several formatting commands, such as Bold, Center, and Italic, are used frequently, and although they can be found on the Home tab, you can also apply them using the Mini toolbar. The *Mini toolbar* contains frequently used formatting commands and displays when you select text or right-click selected text. The Mini toolbar displays faintly at first, then darkens as you move the mouse pointer closer to it, as seen in Figure 1.9. If you move the mouse pointer away from it, it becomes fainter; if you do not want to use the Mini toolbar and prefer it to disappear from view, press Esc when it displays. The Mini toolbar reduces the distance your mouse pointer has to travel around the screen and enables you to quickly and easily apply the most frequently used commands.

The Mini toolbar darkens as the mouse pointer moves closer

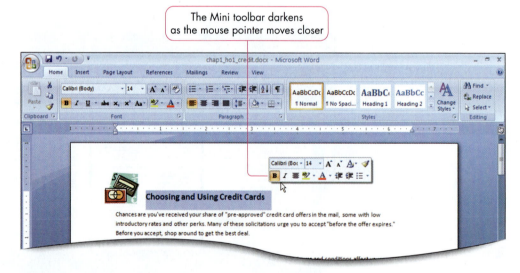

Figure 1.9 The Mini Toolbar

Hands-On Exercises

1 | Introduction to Microsoft Word

Skills covered: 1. Open and Save a Word Document **2.** Modify the Document **3.** Insert AutoText **4.** Create an AutoText Entry **5.** Change Document Views and Zoom

Step 1
Open and Save a Word Document

Refer to Figure 1.10 as you complete Step 1.

a. Click **Start** to display the Start menu. Click (or point to) **All Programs**, click **Microsoft Office**, and then click **Microsoft Office Word 2007** to start the program.

b. Click the **Office Button** and select **Open**. Navigate to the Exploring Word folder and open the *chap1_ho1_credit* document.

You should see the document containing the title *Choosing and Using Credit Cards*.

c. Click the **Office Button**, point to **Save As**, and select **Word Document**.

The Save As dialog box displays so that you can save the document in a different location, with a different name, or as a different file type. The **Exploring Word folder** is the active folder, as shown in Figure 1.10.

TIP — Use Save and Save As

You should practice saving your files often. If you open a document and you do not want to change its name, the easiest way to save it is to click Save on the Quick Access Toolbar. You can also click the Office button and select Save, but many users press the Ctrl+S keyboard command to save quickly and often. The first time you save a document, use the Save As command from the Microsoft Office menu. The command displays the Save As dialog box that enables you to assign a descriptive file name (*job cover letter*, for example) and indicate where the file will be saved. Subsequent saves will be to the same location and will update the file with new changes.

d. Click the **Save in drop-down arrow**. Click the appropriate drive, such as (C:), where you want to store your completed files.

e. In the **File name** box, click once to position the insertion point at the end of the word *credit*. Type **_solution** to rename the document as *chap1_ho1_credit_solution*.

f. Click **Save** or press **Enter**. The title bar changes to reflect the new document name, *chap1_ho1_credit_solution.docx*. Depending on the user's settings, the file extension may not appear in the title bar.

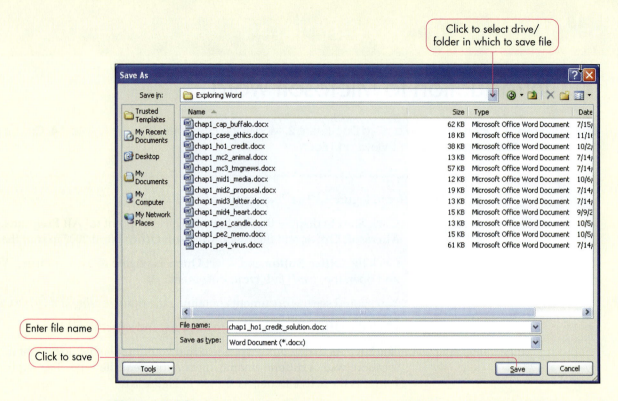

Click to select drive/ folder in which to save file

Enter file name

Click to save

Figure 1.10 Save As Dialog Box

<table>
<tr><td>Step 2
Modify the Document</td><td>Refer to Figure 1.11 as you complete Step 2.</td></tr>
</table>

a. Use the vertical scroll bar to move down to the bottom of the third page in the document. Select the text ***Insert Text Here*** and press **Delete**.

You will add the heading and introduction to this paragraph in the next step.

b. Click **Bold** in the Font group on the Home tab to toggle the format on, if necessary, and then type **Unauthorized Charges.**, including the period.

c. Click **Bold** in the Font group again to toggle the format off. Press **Spacebar** once to insert a space after the period typed in the step above. Then type **If your card is used without your permission, you can be held responsible for up to $50 per card**.

d. Press **Enter** after you complete the sentence. Select the *$50* that you just typed, and then click **Bold** on the Mini toolbar.

You completed the sentence using toggle switches, and you used the Mini toolbar to apply formatting.

e. Click **Show/Hide ¶** in the Paragraph group on the Home tab, if necessary, to display formatting marks in the document.

Notice the formatting marks display to indicate where each space, tab, and soft and hard return occurs.

f. Select the hard return character that follows the sentence typed above, as shown in Figure 1.11. Press **Delete** to delete the unnecessary hard return.

You also can place the insertion point on either side of the formatting mark and press Delete or Backspace to remove it, depending on the location of the insertion point.

g. Click **Save** on the Quick Access Toolbar.

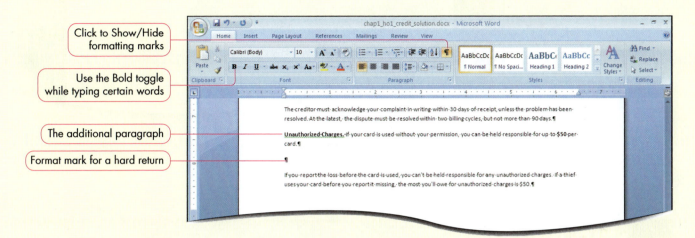

Figure 1.11 The Modified Document

Step 3
Insert AutoText

Refer to Figure 1.12 as you complete Step 3.

a. Press **Ctrl+End** to move to the end of the document and press **Enter** two times.

b. Type the first few letters of the current day of the week, such as **Tues** for *Tuesday*.

Notice that after you type the first few letters, a ScreenTip displays the full name.

c. Press **Enter** to accept the AutoText, and then type a comma.

Now a ScreenTip displays with the complete date—day or week, month, day, and year, as shown in Figure 1.12.

TROUBLESHOOTING: If the complete date does not display, press **Spacebar**, then type the first few letters of the current month, such as **Oct** for October. Press **Enter** to accept the AutoText after a ScreenTip displays with the full name of the month. Then continue until a ScreenTip displays with the complete date—month, day, and year, then press **Enter** to accept and insert the date.

d. Press **Enter** to accept the date. Press **Enter** one more time to insert a hard return.

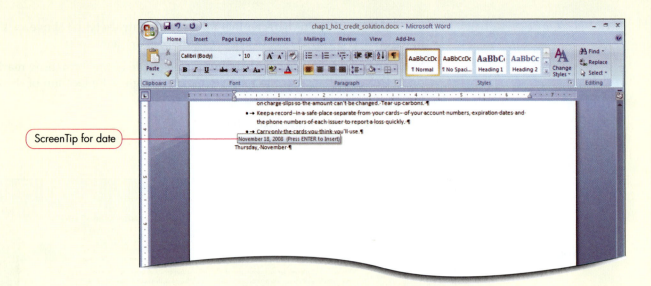

ScreenTip for date

Figure 1.12 Use AutoText to Insert the Date

Step 4
Create an AutoText Entry

Refer to Figure 1.13 as you complete Step 4.

a. Type your name on the line you just added, and then select it.

b. Click the **Insert tab** and click **Quick Parts** in the Text group. Select **Save Selection to Quick Part Gallery**.

The Create New Building Block dialog box displays.

c. In the **Name box**, type your initials.

The text in this box is what you begin to type, then press F3 to insert the actual building block content.

d. Click the **Gallery drop-down arrow**. Select **AutoText**, as shown in Figure 1.13. Click **OK.**

This procedure adds an AutoText entry to the Normal template. If you are in a lab environment, you might not have permission to add this item or save the changes to the Normal template.

e. Select your name in the document, but do not select the hard return mark, and then press **Delete** to remove it. Click **Quick Parts**, and then select **Building Blocks Organizer**.

The Building Blocks Organizer dialog box opens so that you can manage building blocks.

f. Click the **Gallery** heading at the top of the Building Blocks Organizer dialog box to sort the entries.

The AutoText entries display first. You should be able to see your new entry near the top of the list.

g. Select your entry in the Name column. Click **Insert** at the bottom of the dialog box.

Your name displays at the bottom of the page.

h. Click **Undo** in the Quick Access Toolbar to remove your name. Type your initials, and then press **F3**.

Your name, as saved in the Building Block, displays. You now have experience inserting a Building Block using two different methods.

i. Click **Save** on the Quick Access Toolbar.

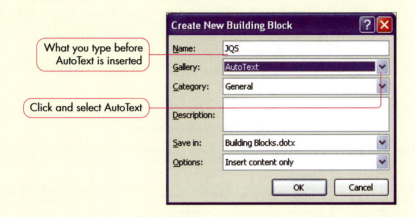

What you type before AutoText is inserted

Click and select AutoText

Figure 1.13 The Create New Building Block Dialog Box

Step 5
Change Document Views and Zoom

Refer to Figure 1.14 as you complete Step 5.

a. Press **Ctrl+Home** to move the insertion point to the beginning of the document. Click the **View tab** and click **Full Screen Reading** in the Document Views group.

The document looks different, pages one and two display, the Ribbon is removed, and only a few buttons display (see Figure 1.14).

TROUBLESHOOTING: If you do not see two pages, click **View Options** in the upper-right corner and select **Show Two Pages**.

b. Hover your mouse pointer over the arrow in the lower-right corner of the screen, and then click the arrow to scroll to the next set of pages. Click the arrow twice to view the last pages.

Once you reach the end of the document, the navigation arrow moves to the lower-left side of the screen.

c. Click the left-pointing arrow twice to display the first two pages again.

Press **Esc** to return to Print Layout view and close the Full Screen Reading view.

d. Click **Close** in the upper-right corner of the screen to return to the default view.

e. Click **Zoom** in the Zoom group on the View tab. Click the icon below **Many pages** and roll your mouse to select 1 × 3 Pages. Click when you see 1 x 3 Pages pop up. Click **OK** to change the view and display three pages on the top of the screen and one page at the bottom.

Notice the Zoom slider in the lower-right corner of the window displays 39%. If you use a wide-screen monitor, the size might differ slightly.

f. Save the *chap1_ho1_credit_solution* document and keep it onscreen if you plan to continue with the next exercise. Close the file and exit Word if you do not want to continue with the next exercise at this time.

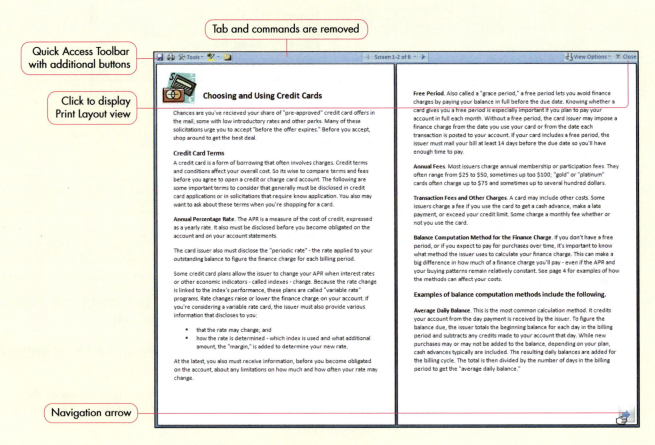

Figure 1.14 Full Screen Reading View

Document Formatting

Throughout your college and professional career, you will create a variety of documents. As you compose and edit large documents, you want to set them up so they have title pages, display a certain way when printed, or include page numbers at the top or bottom of a page. All of these options are available using features in Microsoft Word.

In this section, you make formatting changes to a Word document, such as changing the document margins and orientation. You insert page breaks, page numbers, headers and footers, sections, and cover pages. You also learn how to use the Find and Replace commands.

Setting Margins and Specifying Page Orientation

When you create a document, you consider the content you will insert, but you also should consider how you want the document to look when you print or display it. Many of the settings needed for this purpose are found on the Page Layout tab. The first setting most people change is *margins*. Margins determine the amount of white space from the text to the edges of the page. You should adjust margins to improve the appearance and readability of your document.

Margins are the amount of white space around the top, bottom, left, and right edges of the page.

The default margins, indicated in Figure 1.15, are 1" on the top, bottom, left, and right of the page. You can select different margin settings from the gallery that displays when you click Margins in the Page Setup group on the Page Layout tab, or you can select the Custom Margins option to enter specific settings.

> When you create a document, you consider the content you will insert, but you should also consider how you want the document to look when you print or display it... to have title pages, or include page numbers at the top or bottom of a page. All of these options are available using features in Microsoft Word.

When you create a short business letter, you want to increase the margins to a larger size, such as 1.5" on all sides, so the letter contents are balanced on the printed page. When you print a long document, you might want to reduce the margins to a small amount, such as 0.3" or 0.5", in order to reduce the amount of paper used. If you print a formal or research paper, you want to use a 1.5" left margin and a 1" right margin to allow extra room for binding. The margins you choose will apply to the whole document regardless of the position of the insertion point. You can establish different margin settings for different parts of a document by creating sections. Sections are discussed later in this chapter.

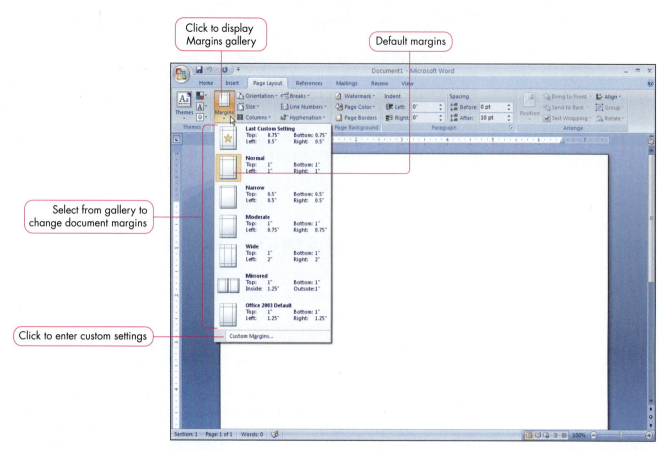

Figure 1.15 Setting Margins

Another setting to consider for a document is orientation. The Page Layout tab contains the Orientation command with two settings—portrait and landscape. *Portrait orientation,* the default setting, positions text parallel with the short side of the page so that the printed page is taller than it is wide. *Landscape orientation* flips the page 90 degrees so that text displays parallel with the longer side of the page, so that the printed page is wider than it is tall. The type of document you create and the manner in which you wish to display the information will dictate which type of orientation you use. Most documents, such as letters and research papers, use portrait orientation, but a brochure, large graphic, chart, or table might display better on a page with landscape orientation.

Portrait orientation positions text parallel with the short side of the page.

Landscape orientation positions text parallel with the long side of the page.

If you need to print a document on special paper, such as legal size ($8\frac{1}{2}'' \times 14''$) or on an envelope, you should select the paper size before you create the document text. The Size command in the Page Setup group on the Page Layout tab contains several different document sizes from which you can choose. If you have special paper requirements, you can select More Paper Sizes to enter your own custom size. If you do not select the special size before you print, you will waste paper and find yourself with a very strange looking printout.

Inserting Page Breaks

When you type more text than can fit on a page, Word continues the text on another page using soft and hard page breaks. The *soft page break* is a hidden marker that automatically continues text on the top of a new page when text no longer fits on the current page. These breaks adjust automatically when you add and delete text. For the most part, you rely on soft page breaks to prepare multiple-page documents. However, at times you need to start a new page before Word inserts a soft page break.

A *soft page break* is inserted when text fills an entire page, then continues on the next page.

A **hard page break** forces the next part of a document to begin on a new page.

You can insert a **hard page break**, a hidden marker, to force text to begin on a new page. A hard page break is inserted into a document using the Breaks command in the Page Setup group on the Page Layout tab, or Page Break in the Pages group on the Insert tab. To view the page break markers in Print Layout view, you must click Show/Hide ¶ on the Home tab, to toggle on the formatting marks, as seen in Figure 1.16. You can view the page break markers without the Show/Hide toggled on when you switch to Draft view (see Figure 1.17).

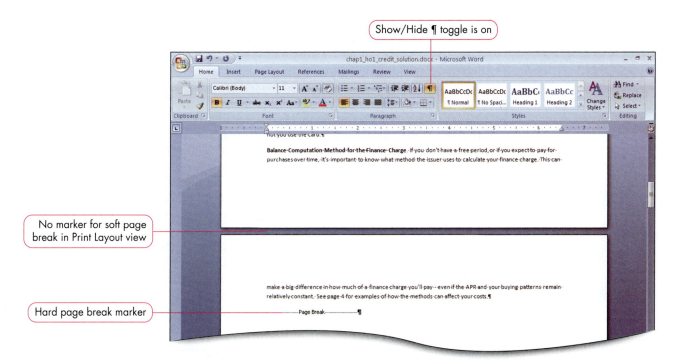

Figure 1.16 View Page Breaks in Print Layout View

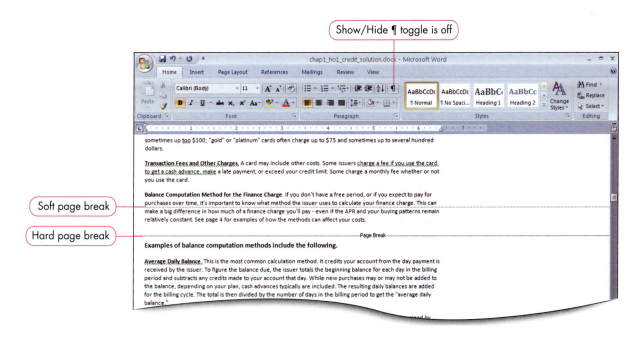

Figure 1.17 View Page Breaks in Draft View

TIP Hard Page Break Shortcut

You can use the keyboard shortcut **Ctrl+Enter** to insert a hard page break.

Adding Page Numbers

Page numbers are essential in long documents. They serve as a convenient reference point for the writer and reader. If you do not include page numbers in a long document, you will have difficulty trying to find text on a particular page or trying to tell someone where to locate a particular passage in the document. Have you ever tried to reassemble a long document that was out of order and did not have page numbers? It can be very frustrating and makes a good case for inserting page numbers in your documents.

The Page Number command in the Header & Footer group on the Insert tab is the easiest way to place page numbers into a document. When you use this feature, Word not only inserts page numbers but also automatically adjusts the page numbering when you add or delete pages. Page numbers can appear at the top or bottom of a page, and can be left-, center-, or right-aligned. Your decision on whether to place page numbers in a header or footer might be based on personal preference, whether the writing guide for your paper dictates a specific location, or if you have other information to include in a header or footer also.

Word 2007 provides several galleries with options for formatting page numbers. New to Office 2007 is the Page Margin option, which enables you to put a page number on the side of a page. This feature adds a nice element of style to a multipage document that will be distributed as a flyer or annual report. Figure 1.18 displays a few gallery options for placing a page number at the bottom of a page.

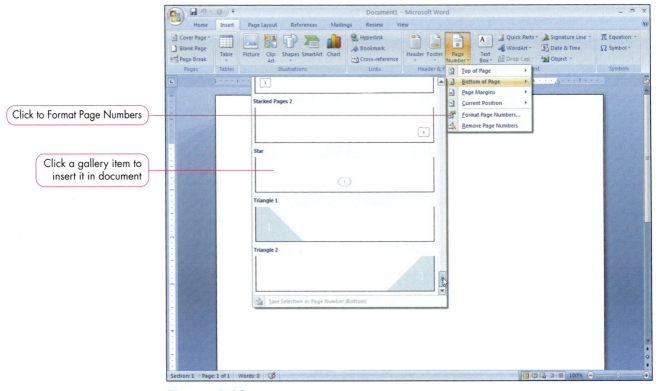

Click to Format Page Numbers

Click a gallery item to insert it in document

Figure 1.18 Insert Page Numbers at Bottom of Page

Word enables you to customize the number format for page numbers to use Roman rather than Arabic numerals, which often are used for preliminary or preface pages at the beginning of a book. You also can adjust the page numbering so that it starts numbering at a page other than the first. This is useful when you have a report with a cover page; you typically do not consider the cover as page one but instead begin numbering with the page that follows it. You use the Format Page Numbers command to display the Page Number Format dialog box (see Figure 1.19) where you can make these changes. If you are not satisfied with the page numbering in a document, use the Remove Page Numbers command to remove them.

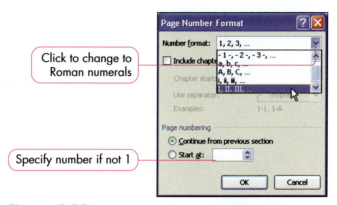

Figure 1.19 Page Number Format Dialog Box

Inserting Headers and Footers

A **header** is information printed at the top of document pages.

A **footer** is information printed at the bottom of document pages.

Headers and footers give a professional appearance to a document. A **header** consists of one or more lines that are printed at the top of a page. A **footer** is printed at the bottom of the page. A document may contain headers but not footers, footers but not headers, both headers and footers, or neither. Footers often contain the page number and a date the document was created. Headers might contain the name of an organization, author, or title of the document. Take a moment to notice the type of information you see in the headers/footers of the books or magazines you are reading.

Headers and footers are added from the Insert tab. You can create a simple header or footer by clicking Page Number, depending on whether the page number is at the top or bottom of a page. Headers and footers are formatted like any other paragraph and can be center, left or right aligned. You can format headers and footers in any typeface or point size and can include special codes to automatically insert the page number, date, and time a document is printed.

The advantage of using a header or footer (over typing the text yourself at the top or bottom of every page) is that you type the text only once, after which it appears automatically according to your specifications. In addition, the placement of the headers and footers is adjusted for changes in page breaks caused by the insertion or deletion of text in the body of the document.

Headers and footers can change continually throughout a document. Once you insert one, the Header & Footer Tools tab displays and contains many options (see Figure 1.20). For instance, you can specify a different header or footer for the first page; this is advisable when you have a cover page and do not want the header (or footer) to display on that page. You also can have different headers and footers for odd and even pages. This feature is useful when you plan to print a document that will be bound as a book. Notice the different information this book prints on the footer of odd versus even pages, and how the page numbers display in the corners of each page. If you want to change the header (or footer) midway through a document, you need to insert a section break at the point where the new header (or footer) is to begin. These breaks are discussed in the next section.

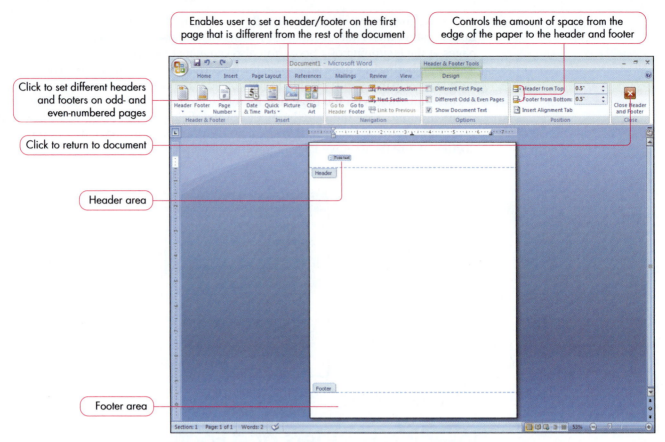

Enables user to set a header/footer on the first page that is different from the rest of the document

Controls the amount of space from the edge of the paper to the header and footer

Click to set different headers and footers on odd- and even-numbered pages

Click to return to document

Header area

Footer area

Figure 1.20 Header and Footer Tools Commands

Creating Sections

Formatting in Word occurs on three levels: character, paragraph, and section. Formatting at the section level controls headers and footers, page numbering, page size and orientation, margins, and columns. All of the documents in the text so far have consisted of a single section, and thus any section formatting applied to the entire document. You can, however, divide a document into sections and format each section independently.

You determine where one section ends and another begins by clicking Breaks in the Page Setup group on the Page Layout tab. A *section break* is a marker that divides a document into sections. It enables you to decide how the section will be formatted on the printed page; that is, you can specify that the new section continues on the same page, that it begins on a new page, or that it begins on the next odd or even page even if a blank page has to be inserted. Formatting at the section level gives you the ability to create more sophisticated documents. You can use section formatting to do the following:

- Change the margins within a multipage letter, where the first page (the letterhead) requires a larger top margin than the other pages in the letter.

- Change the orientation from portrait to landscape to accommodate a wide table at the end of the document.

- Change the page numbering to use Roman numerals at the beginning of the document for a table of contents and Arabic numerals thereafter.

- Change the number of columns in a newsletter, which may contain a single column at the top of a page for the masthead, then two or three columns in the body of the newsletter.

A *section break* is a marker that divides a document into sections, thereby allowing different formatting in each section.

Word stores the formatting characteristics of each section in the section break at the end of a section. Thus, deleting a section break also deletes the section formatting, causing the text above the break to assume the formatting characteristics of the next section.

Figure 1.21 displays a multipage view of a six-page document. The document has been divided into two sections, and the insertion point is currently on the last page of the document, which is also the first page of the second section. Note the corresponding indications on the status bar and the position of the headers and footers throughout the document.

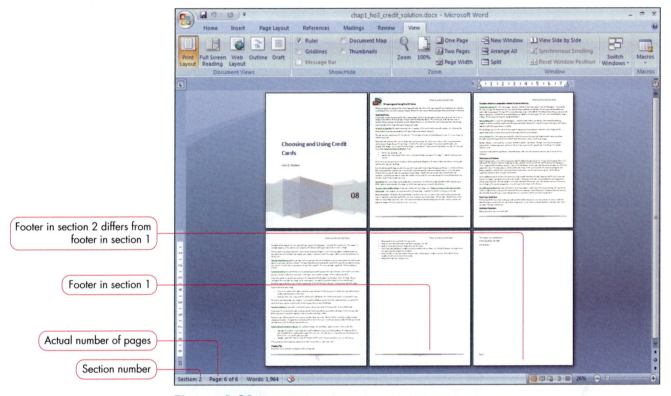

Figure 1.21 A Document with Two Sections

Inserting a Cover Page

You can use commands such as page break and keystrokes such as Ctrl+Enter, mentioned in previous sections, to create a cover page for a document. But Word 2007 offers a feature to quickly insert a preformatted cover page in your document. The Cover Page feature in the Pages group of the Insert tab includes a gallery with several designs, as seen in Figure 1.22. Each design includes building block fields, such as Document Title, Company Name, Date, and Author, which you can personalize. Additionally, the title pages already are formatted with the different first page option in the header and footer, so you don't have to change that setting after you insert the page. After you personalize and make any additional modifications of your choice, your document will include an attractive cover page.

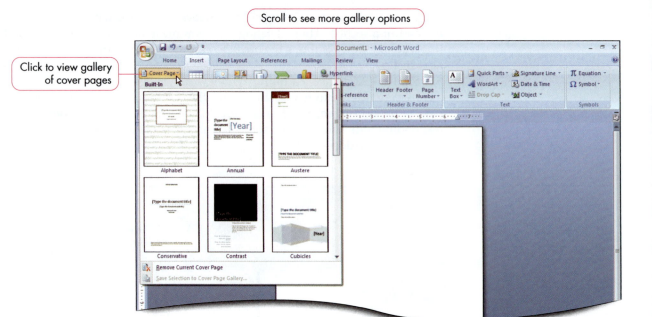

Scroll to see more gallery options

Click to view gallery of cover pages

Figure 1.22 Insert a Cover Page

Using Find and Replace Commands

Even though Find and Replace have individual commands in the Editing group, on the Home tab, they share a common dialog box with different tabs for each command as well as the Go To command. The Find command locates one or more occurrences of specific text (e.g., a word or phrase). The Replace command goes one step further in that it locates the text, and then enables you to optionally replace (one or more occurrences of) that text with different text. The Go To command goes directly to a specific place (e.g., a specific page) in the document. If you use the find function and then decide you want to replace text, you can simply click the Replace tab to initiate the process. These functions are very helpful when working in a long document; you can use them to quickly locate text or jump to a different location in the document.

A ***case-sensitive search*** matches not only the text but also the use of upper- and lowercase letters.

A ***case-insensitive search*** finds a word regardless of any capitalization used.

Selective replacement lets you decide whether to replace text.

Automatic replacement makes a substitution automatically.

The search in both the Find and Replace commands is case sensitive or case insensitive. A ***case-sensitive search***, where the Match Case option is selected, matches not only the text but also the use of upper- and lowercase letters. Thus, *There* is different from *there*, and a search on one will not identify the other. A ***case-insensitive search***, where Match Case is *not* selected, is just the opposite and finds both *There* and *there*. A search also may specify whole words only to identify *there*, but not *therefore* or *thereby*. And finally, the search and replacement text also can specify different numbers of characters; for example, you could replace *flower* with *daisy*.

The Replace command implements either ***selective replacement***, which lets you examine each occurrence of the character string in context and decide whether to replace it, or ***automatic replacement***, where the substitution is made automatically. Selective replacement is implemented by clicking the Find Next command, then clicking (or not clicking) Replace to make the substitution. Automatic replacement (through the entire document) is implemented by clicking Replace All. This feature can save you a great deal of time if you need to make a replacement throughout a document, but it also can produce unintended consequences. For example, if you substitute the word *text* for *book*, the word *textbook* would become *texttext*, which is not what you had in mind.

The Find and Replace commands can include formatting and/or special characters. This command is helpful in situations where you need to make changes to the way text is formatted, but not necessarily to the text itself. You can, for example, change all italicized text to boldface, as shown in Figure 1.23, or you can change five consecutive spaces to a tab character, which makes it easier to align text. You also can use special characters in the character string, such as the "any character" (consisting of ^?). For example, to find all four-letter words that begin with "f" and end with "l" (such as *fall, fill,* or *fail*), search for f^?^?l. (The question mark stands for any character, just like a wildcard in a card game.) You also can search for all forms of a word; for example, if you specify *am,* it will also find *is* and *are.* You can even search for a word based on how it sounds. When searching for *Marion,* for example, check the Sounds like check box, and the search will find both *Marion* and *Marian.*

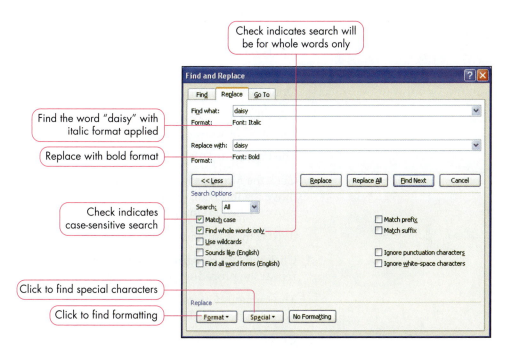

Figure 1.23 The Find and Replace Dialog Box

TIP   The Go To Command

The Go To command moves the insertion point to a designated location in the document. The command is accessed by clicking the Find down arrow in the Editing group on the Home tab, by pressing **Ctrl+G**, or by clicking the page number on the status bar. After you activate the command, the Find and Replace dialog box displays the Go To tab in which you enter a page number, section, line, footnote, or other areas in the Go to what list. You also can specify a relative page number—for example, +2 to move forward two pages or –1 to move back one page.

Hands-On Exercises

2 | Document Organization

Skills covered: 1. Set Page Margins and Orientation **2.** Insert a Page Break **3.** Add a Cover Page and Insert a Document Header **4.** Insert a Section Break **5.** Insert a Page Number in the Footer **6.** Use Find, Replace, and Go To

Step 1 **Set Page Margins and Orientation**	Refer to Figure 1.24 as you complete Step 1. **a.** Open the *chap1_ho1_credit_solution* document if you closed it after the last hands-on exercise and save it as **chap1_ho2_credit_solution**. Be sure you are in the single page view, which you can access by selecting View Options and clicking Show One Page. **b.** Click the **Page Layout tab** and click **Margins** in the Page Setup group. Click **Custom Margins**. The Page Setup dialog box displays. **c.** Click the **Margins tab**, if necessary. Type **.75** in the Top margin box. Press **Tab** to move the insertion point to the Bottom margin box. Type **.75** and press **Tab** to move to the Left margin box. 0.75″ is the equivalent of ¾ of one inch. **d.** Click the **Left margin down arrow** to reduce the left margin to **0.5″**, and then repeat the procedure to set the right margin to **0.5″**. The top and bottom margins are now set at 0.75″ and the left and right margins are set at 0.5″ (see Figure 1.24). **e.** Check that these settings apply to the **Whole document**, located in the lower portion of the dialog box. Click **OK**. You can see the change in layout as a result of changing the margins. More text displays on the first three pages, and there is only one line of text remaining on the fourth page. **f.** Click **Orientation** in the Page Setup group on the Page Layout tab, and then select **Landscape**. The pages now display in landscape orientation. Whereas the document looks fine, we will return to portrait orientation to prepare for the remaining exercises. **g.** Click **Undo** on the Quick Access Toolbar. Save the document.

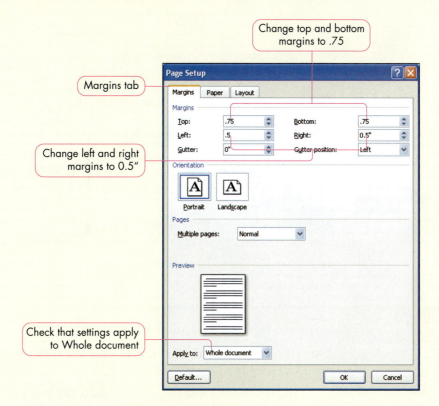

Figure 1.24 Change the Margins

Step 2
Insert a Page Break

Refer to Figure 1.25 as you complete Step 2.

a. Click the **Zoom slider** and increase the zoom to **100%**.

b. Place the insertion point on the left side of the heading *Examples of balance computation methods include the following* on the bottom of the first page.

c. Press **Ctrl+Enter** to insert a page break.

The heading and paragraph that follows move to the top of the second page. It leaves a gap of space at the bottom of the first page, but you will make other adjustments to compensate for that.

d. Place the insertion point on the left side of the paragraph heading *Prompt Credit for Payment* on the bottom of the second page. Press **Enter** one time.

The hard returns force the paragraph to relocate to the top of the next page.

e. Click the **Zoom slider** and decrease the zoom to **50%**, and then display pages one and two. If necessary, click **Show/Hide ¶** in the Paragraph group on the Home tab to view formatting marks.

Notice the marks that indicate the Page Break and hard return at the bottom of the first and second pages, as seen in Figure 1.25.

f. Save the document.

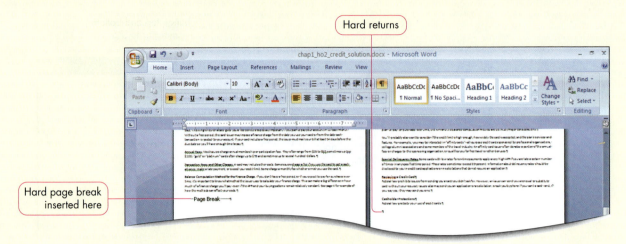

Hard returns

Hard page break inserted here

Figure 1.25 Insert a Hard Page Break

Step 3

Add a Cover Page and Insert a Document Header

Refer to Figure 1.26 as you complete Step 3.

a. Click the **Insert tab**, click **Cover Page** in the Pages group, and then click **Cubicles** from the gallery.

You now have a title page that already displays the report title, and the rest of the document begins at the top of page two. The insertion point does not have to be at the beginning of a document to insert a cover page.

TROUBLESHOOTING: If the document title does not display automatically, click the Title field and replace the text *Type the document title* with **Choosing and Using Credit Cards**.

b. Right-click the Subtitle field and click **Cut**. Right-click the company name field at the top of the page, and then click **Cut**. Click the Year field and type the current year. If necessary, click the Author Name field and type your name.

Due to the preset format of the title page, the date 2008 will change to 08 automatically.

c. Click the **Zoom slider** and increase the zoom to **100%**. Click **Header** on the Insert tab and click **Edit Header** at the bottom of the gallery list.

The Design tab displays and the header area of the page is bordered by a blue line.

d. Look at the status bar on the bottom of the page to determine the page where the insertion point is located. If necessary, place your insertion point in the header of page two. Confirm that the **Different First Page** option is selected in the Design tab's Options group.

The cover page you created does not require a heading, and this setting prevents the heading from displaying on that page.

e. Press **Tab** two times to move the insertion point to the right side of the header.

The title of the document, *Choosing and Using Credit Cards*, displays in the header, as seen in Figure 1.26.

f. Scroll down and notice the header on the remaining pages. Click **Close Header and Footer**.

g. Save the document.

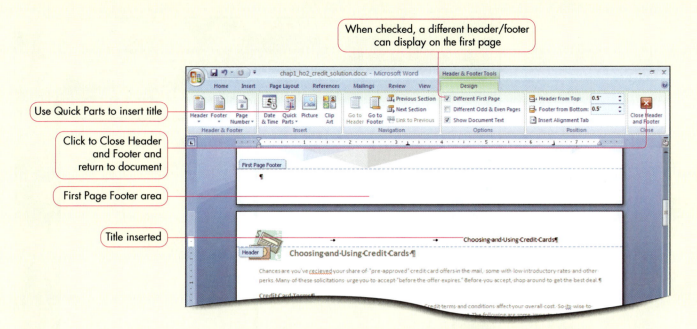

When checked, a different header/footer can display on the first page

Use Quick Parts to insert title

Click to Close Header and Footer and return to document

First Page Footer area

Title inserted

Figure 1.26 Create a Header

Step 4
Insert a Section Break

Refer to Figure 1.27 as you complete Step 4.

a. Press **Ctrl+End** to move to the end of the document, then place the insertion point on the left side of the date. Click the **Page Layout tab**, click **Breaks** in the Page Setup group, and then click **Next Page** under Section Breaks.

By inserting this section break, you are now free to make modifications to the last page without changing the previous pages.

b. Double-click in the header or footer area of the last page to display the Design tab. Click in the header of the last page, and then click **Link to Previous** in the Navigation group to deselect it.

Even though you insert a section break, the header and footer of this page take on the same formatting as the first section. When you remove that link, you can set up an independent header and/or footer.

c. In the header of the last page, type **This project was completed on**, as shown in Figure 1.27.

d. Click **Go To Footer** in the Navigation group. Click **Link to Previous** to toggle it off. In the Position group, click the **Footer from Bottom** up arrow until .8" displays.

This footer is now independent from all other document footers, and the page number at the bottom that you will insert in the next step will print in a different location on the page

e. Click **Close Header and Footer**. Save the document. Zoom two pages in order for your screen to look like Figure 1.27.

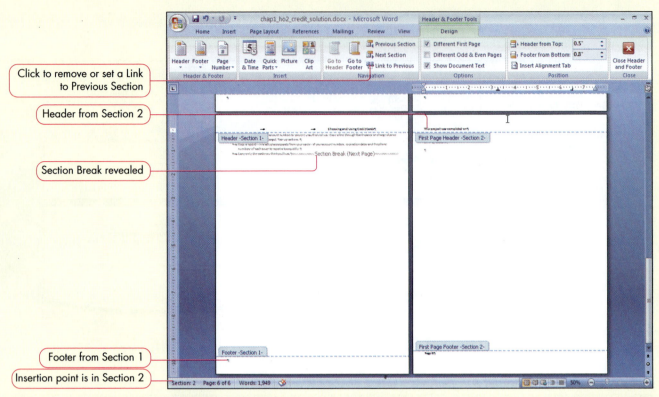

Click to remove or set a Link to Previous Section

Header from Section 2

Section Break revealed

Footer from Section 1

Insertion point is in Section 2

Figure 1.27 Header in Section 2

Step 5
Insert a Page Number in the Footer

Refer to Figure 1.28 as you complete Step 5.

a. Place your insertion point anywhere on the second page. Click the **Insert tab**, if necessary. Click **Page Number** in the Header & Footer group, and then point to **Bottom of Page**.

A dark line and the page number display on the bottom of each page except the first and last because you changed the Different First Page and Link to Previous options.

TROUBLESHOOTING: If your insertion point was on the first page, the footer will display on that page only. Click Undo on the Quick Access Toolbar, place your insertion point on page two, and repeat the step above to add the footer to the remaining pages.

b. Click **Page Number** in the Header & Footer group of the Design tab and click **Format Page Numbers**.

The Page Number Format dialog box displays.

c. Click **Start at**, then click the down arrow until **0** displays. Click **OK**.

If you begin page numbering with zero, the second page, which is the first page of content, displays as page 1.

d. Scroll to the bottom of page 6. Place the insertion point on the left side of the footer area, type **Page**, and then press **Spacebar** one time.

e. Click **Quick Parts** in the Insert group and select **Field**. Click the **Categories drop-down arrow** and select **Numbering**.

You can insert many different items in your document; use the category option to minimize the number of fields to browse through to find the one you want.

f. Select **Page** in the **Field names** list and select the first option displayed in the Format list, as seen in Figure 1.28. Click **OK**.

The end result for this operation will be similar to one that you can reach using the Page Number feature; however, this exercise demonstrates the field feature that allows you to use more customization in headers and footers by combining the field with text of your choice.

g. Click **Close Header and Footer**.

h. Save the document.

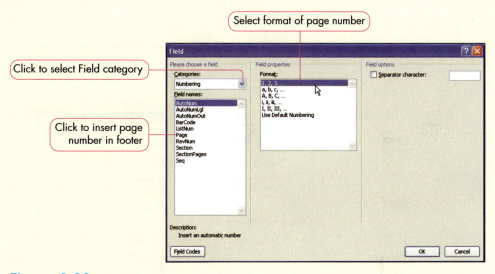

Figure 1.28 Insert a Field in a Footer

<table>
<tr><td>

Step 6

Use Find, Replace, and Go To

</td><td>

Refer to Figure 1.29 as you complete Step 6.

a. Press **Ctrl+Home** to move to the beginning of the document. Click the **Home tab** and click **Find** in the Editing group.

b. Type **APR** in the *Find what* text box, and then click **Find Next**.

The first occurrence of the text appears on the second page.

c. Click the **Replace tab** in the Find and Replace dialog box. Type **annual percentage rate** in the *Replace with* box. Click **Replace All**.

A dialog box displays, indicating seven replacements were made.

d. Click **OK** to remove the dialog box. In the Find what text box, type **$50**. Click **More**, if necessary, then click **Format** and click **Font**. In the Find Font dialog box, click **Bold** in the *Font style* list, and then click **OK**.

e. In the *Replace with* text box, type **$50**. Click **Format** and click **Font**. In the Replace Font dialog box, click **Regular** in the *Font style* list, and then click **OK**. Compare your window to Figure 1.29.

TROUBLESHOOTING: If you applied the Bold format to the text in the *Replace with* box instead of the *Find what* box, click **No Formatting** on the bottom of the window, then start again. Be sure the insertion point is in the desired box before you click **Format**.

</td></tr>
</table>

f. Click **Find Next**.

The bolded occurrence of $50 displays near the bottom of the fourth page.

g. Click **Replace** to remove the formatting from the text, and then click **OK** in the dialog box that informs you Word has finished searching the document.

h. Click the **Go To tab**.

The Go To tab of the Find and Replace dialog box displays, and the insertion point is in the *Enter page number* box.

i. Type **1** in the *Enter page number* box, then click **Go To**.

The top of page 1 displays on your screen, and the Find and Replace dialog box is still onscreen.

j. Click **Section** in the **Go to what** box, type **2** in the *Enter section number* box, and then click **Go To**.

The top of page 6 displays, which is the beginning of the section you added in Step 4.

k. Click **Close**. Save the document.

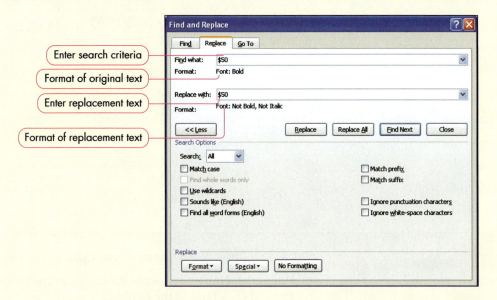

Figure 1.29 Find and Replace Text

The Final Touches

You can create a document that is, for the most part, free of typographical and grammatical errors. Word provides many features that assist in correcting a variety of grammatical mistakes.

As you work on a document, you should save changes frequently. Word even has an option to create backup copies of your work periodically in case of a system failure. When you believe that your document is complete, you should take one last look and run a few diagnostics to check for mistakes in spelling and grammar. If you are sending the document to another person, you also should use the tools that locate compatibility issues your document has with older versions of Word. If you print your document, be sure to use features that avoid wasting paper.

In this section, you check for spelling and grammatical errors. You also revisit the important process of saving files as well as backup options, the Compatibility Checker, and the Document Inspector. You learn different print options, and you learn about the many customization options available in Word 2007.

Checking Spelling and Grammar

You can create a document that is, for the most part, free of typographical and grammatical errors. However, you should always proofread a document at the conclusion of your edits because it is possible the automated spelling and grammar checker did not find every error. Word provides many features that assist in correcting a variety of grammatical mistakes. In the Office Fundamentals chapter, you learned how to use the Spelling and Grammar and the Thesaurus features to assist in writing and proofing. In the following paragraphs, you will learn about other features that help you create error-free documents.

Perform a Spelling and Grammar Check

The **Spelling and Grammar** feature looks for mistakes in spelling, punctuation, writing style, and word usage.

The **Spelling and Grammar** feature attempts to catch mistakes in spelling, punctuation, writing style, and word usage by comparing strings of text within a document to a series of predefined rules. When located, you can accept the suggested correction and make the replacement automatically, or more often, edit the selected text and make your own changes.

You also can ask the grammar check to explain the rule it is attempting to enforce. Unlike the spell check, the grammar check is subjective, and what seems appropriate to you may be objectionable to someone else. Indeed, the grammar check is quite flexible, and can be set to check for different writing styles; that is, you can implement one set of rules to check a business letter and a different set of rules for casual writing. Many times, however, you will find that the English language is just too complex for the grammar check to detect every error, although it will find many. Depending on your reliance on the grammar check, you can set the option for it to run all the time by marking the selection in the Word Options, Proofing category.

TIP Custom Dictionaries

If you work in a field that uses technical terminology, such as nursing or aviation, you need to include those terms with the existing dictionary in the Spelling and Grammar feature. To use the custom dictionary, click the Office Button, click Word Options, click Proofing, click Custom Dictionary, and then navigate to the location where the dictionary is stored.

Check Contextual Spelling

In addition to spelling and grammar checking, Word 2007 has added a contextual spelling feature that attempts to locate a word that is spelled correctly, but used incorrectly. For example, many people confuse the usage of words such as *their* and *there*, *two* and *too*, and *which* and *witch*. The visual indication that a contextual spelling error occurs is a blue wavy line under the word, as shown in Figure 1.30. By default, this feature is not turned on; to invoke the command, click the Office Button, select Word Options at the bottom, select the Proofing category, then click to select the Use contextual spelling check box.

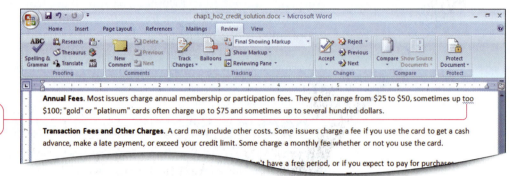

Blue wavy line indicates contextual spelling error

Figure 1.30 Check Contextual Spelling

Using Save and Backup Options

It is not a question of *if* it will happen but *when*. Files are lost, systems crash, and viruses infect a system. That said, we cannot overemphasize the importance of saving your work frequently. Additionally, you should use available resources to provide a backup copy (or two) of your most important documents and back up your files at every opportunity. For example, the Exploring series authors back up all of their manuscript files in case one system crashes. Graduate students periodically back up their lengthy theses and dissertations so that they do not have to recreate these research documents from scratch if one system fails.

Save a Document in Compatible Format

After reading the Office Fundamentals chapter, you know the Save and Save As commands are used to copy your documents to disk and should be used frequently in order to avoid loss of work and data. Because some people may use a different version of Microsoft Word, you should know how to save a document in a format that they can use. People cannot open a Word 2007 document in earlier versions of Word unless they update their earlier version with the Compatibility Pack that contains a converter. If you are not sure if they have installed the Compatibility Pack, it is best to save the document in an older format, such as Word 97–2003.

To save a document so that someone with a different version of Office can open it, click the Office Button and point to the arrow on the right side of the Save As command. The option to save in Word 97–2003 format appears (see Figure 1.31), and after

you click it, you can use the Save As dialog box normally. The saved file will have the .doc extension instead of the Word 2007 extension, .docx. Another way to save in the older format is to double-click Save As, then select the Word 97–2003 format from the *Save as type* list in the Save As dialog box.

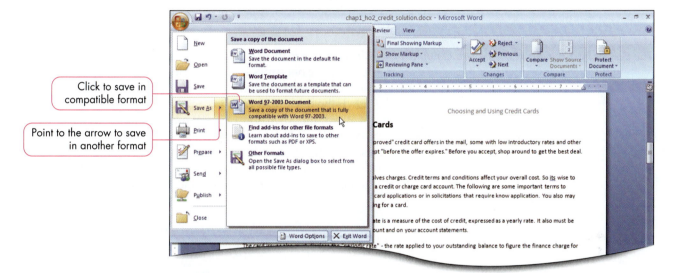

Figure 1.31   Save a File in Compatible Format

If you open a Word document created in an earlier version, such as Word 2003, the title bar will include *(Compatibility Mode)* at the top. You can still work with the document and even save it back in the same format for a Word 97–2003 user. However, some newer features of Word 2007, such as SmartArt and other graphic enhancement options used in the Cover Page and custom headers and footers, are not viewable or available for use in compatibility mode. To remove the file from compatibility mode, click the Office Button and select Convert. It will convert the file and remove the *(Compatibility Mode)* designator, but the .doc extension still displays. The next time you click Save, the extension will change to .docx, indicating that it is converted into a Word 2007 file, and then you can use all of the application features.

Understand Backup Options

Microsoft Word offers several different backup options, the most important of which is to save AutoRecover information periodically. If Microsoft Word crashes, the program will be able to recover a previous version of your document when you restart Word. The only work you will lose is anything you did between the time of the last AutoRecover operation and the time of the crash. The default *Save AutoRecover information every 10 minutes* ensures that you will never lose more than 10 minutes of work.

You also can set Word to create a backup copy in conjunction with every Save. You set these valuable backup and AutoRecover options from the Save and Advanced categories of the Word Options menu. Assume, for example, that you have created the simple document *The fox jumped over the fence* and saved it under the name *Fox*. Assume further that you edit the document to read *The quick brown fox jumped over the fence* and that you saved it a second time. The second Save command changes the name of the original document from *Fox* to *Backup of Fox*, then saves the current contents of memory as *Fox*. In other words, the disk now contains two versions of the document: the current version *Fox* and the most recent previous version *Backup of Fox*.

The cycle goes on indefinitely, with *Fox* always containing the current version and *Backup of Fox* the most recent previous version. So, if you revise and save the document a third time, *Fox* will contain the latest revision while *Backup of Fox* would contain the previous version alluding to the quick brown fox. The original (first) version of the document disappears entirely because only two versions are kept.

The contents of *Fox* and *Backup of Fox* are different, but the existence of the latter enables you to retrieve the previous version if you inadvertently edit beyond repair or accidentally erase the current *Fox* version. Should this situation occur, you can always retrieve its predecessor and at least salvage your work prior to the last save operation. But remember, this process only takes place if you enable the Always create backup copy option in the Advanced category of the Word Options dialog box.

Run the Compatibility Checker

The **Compatibility Checker** looks for features that are not supported by previous versions of Word.

The *Compatibility Checker* is a feature in Word 2007 that enables you to determine if you have used features that are not supported by previous versions. After you complete your document, click the Office Button, point to Prepare, and then select Run Compatibility Checker. If the document contains anything that could not be opened in a different version of Word, the Microsoft Office Word Compatibility Checker dialog box will list it. From this dialog box, you also can indicate that you want to always check compatibility when saving this file (see Figure 1.32). If you are saving the document in a format to be used by someone with an earlier version, you will want to make corrections to the items listed in the dialog box before saving again and sending the file.

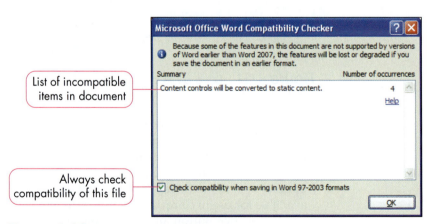

Figure 1.32 The Compatibility Checker

Run the Document Inspector

The **Document Inspector** checks for and removes different kinds of hidden and personal information from a document.

Before you send or give a document to another person, you should run the *Document Inspector* to reveal any hidden or personal data in the file. For privacy or security reasons, you might want to remove certain items contained in the document such as author name, comments made by one or more persons who have access to the document, or document server locations. Some inspectors are specific to individual Office applications, such as Excel and PowerPoint. Word provides inspectors that you can invoke to reveal different types of information, including:

- Comments, Revisions, Versions, and Annotations
- Document Properties and Personal Information
- Custom XML Data
- Headers, Footers, and Watermarks
- Hidden Text

The inspectors also can locate information in documents created in older versions of Word. Because some information that the Document Inspector might remove cannot be recovered with the Undo command, you should save a copy of your original document, using a different name, just before you run any of the inspectors. After you save the copy, click the Office Button, point to Prepare, and then select the Inspect Document option to run the inspector (see Figure 1.33). When it is complete, it will list the results and enable you to choose whether to remove the information from the document. If you forget to save a backup copy of the document, you can use the Save As command to save a copy of the document with a new name after you run the inspector.

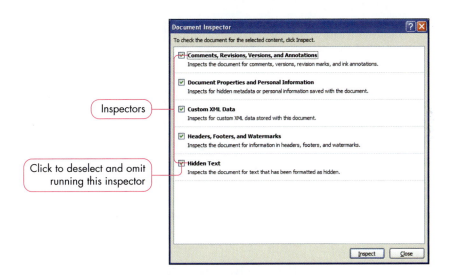

Figure 1.33 The Document Inspector

Selecting Printing Options

People often print an entire document when they want to view only a few pages. All computer users should be mindful of the environment, and limiting printer use is a perfect place to start. Millions of sheets of paper have been wasted because someone did not take a moment to preview his or her work and then had to reprint due to a very minor error that is easily noticed in a preview window.

Click the Office Button and click the Print arrow to see three settings to consider when you are ready to print your work: Print, Quick Print, and Print Preview. You should select the Print Preview option first to see a preview of what the document will look like when you print it. In the Print Preview window, you have several settings that enable you to magnify the page onscreen, display multiple pages, and even make changes to the page layout so you can view the results immediately. If you are satisfied with the document, you can launch the Print dialog box from that window.

The Quick Print option sends a document straight to the printer without prompting you for changes to the printer configuration. If you have only one printer and rarely change printer options, this is an efficient tool.

The final print option is Print, which always displays the Print dialog box and contains many useful options. For example, you can print only the page that contains the insertion point (Current page) or a specific range of pages, such as pages 3–10 (Pages). Furthermore, you can print more than one copy of the document (Number of copies), print miniature copies of pages on a single sheet of paper (Pages per sheet), or adjust the document text size to fit on a particular type of paper (Scale to paper size). If you do not have a duplex printer, you can select the option to print only even numbered pages, flip the paper over and put it back in the printer, then select the option to print only odd pages, as seen in Figure 1.34. This method is used frequently by some of the Exploring authors because they do not own duplex printers and also because they want to conserve paper!

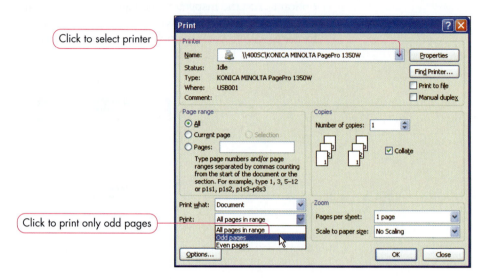

Figure 1.34 Print Options

Customizing Word

As installed, Word is set up to be useful immediately. However, you might find options that you would prefer to customize, add, or remove from the document window. For example, you can add commands to the Quick Access Toolbar (QAT) that do not currently display on any tabs. Or you can add commands that you use so frequently you prefer to access them from the always-visible QAT.

You can customize Word in many ways. To begin the process, or just to view the options available for customization, click the Office button, then select Word Options. Table 1.2 describes the main categories that you can customize and some of the features in each category. You should take some time to glance through each category as you continue to read this chapter. Keep in mind that if you are working in a school lab, you might not have permission to change options on a permanent basis.

Table 1.2 Word Options

Menu Category	Description	Sample of Options to Change
Popular	Change the most popular options in Word.	Show Mini toolbar; show Enhanced ScreenTips; change color scheme; change user name and initials.
Display	Change how documents are displayed on the screen and in print.	Show white space between pages in Print Layout view; always show formatting marks such as spaces on the screen; print document properties.
Proofing	Modify how Word corrects and formats your text.	Ignore words in uppercase (do not flag as incorrect); use Spellchecker; use contextual spelling (checks for words that sound alike but are spelled differently such as two, too, and to); mark grammatical errors.
Save	Customize how documents are saved.	Default locations and format to save files; AutoRecover file location; Web server location.
Advanced	Specify editing options; cut, copy, and paste options; show document content options; display options; print options; and save options.	Allow text to be dragged and dropped; enable click and type; default paragraph style; show paste option buttons; show smart tags; number of recent documents to show in file menu; print pages in reverse order; always create backup copy; embed smart tags; update automatic links at open; compatibility options.
Customize	Customize the Quick Access Toolbar and other keyboard shortcuts.	Add or remove buttons from the QAT; determine location of QAT; customize keyboard shortcuts.
Add-Ins	View the add-ins previously installed, customize settings for add-ins, and install more add-ins.	View settings for active and inactive application add-ins; manage smart tags, templates, and disabled items.
Trust Center	View online documentation about security and privacy and change settings to protect documents from possible infections.	Enable and disable macros; change ActiveX settings; set privacy options; select trusted publishers and locations.
Resources	Provide links to Microsoft sites where you can find online resources and keep your Office application updated.	Download updates for Office; diagnose and repair problems with Office; contact Microsoft; activate your license for Office; register for free online services; view product specifications.

As you can see, you are able to customize dozens of settings in Word. Table 1.2 mentions only a small sample of them; fortunately, most users do not need to change any settings at all.

Hands-On Exercises

3 | The Final Touches

Skills covered: 1. Perform a Spelling and Grammar Check **2.** Run the Document Inspector and a Compatibility Check **3.** Save in a Compatible Format **4.** Change Word Options **5.** Use Print Preview Features

Step 1
Perform a Spelling and Grammar Check

Refer to Figure 1.35 as you complete Step 1.

a. Open the *chap1_ho2_credit_solution* document if you closed it after the last hands-on exercise and save it as **chap1_ho3_credit_solution**.

b. Press **Ctrl+Home** to move to the beginning of the document. Click the **Review tab** and click **Spelling & Grammar** in the Proofing group.

   The Spelling and Grammar dialog box displays with the first error indicated in red text.

c. Click **Change All** to replace all misspellings of the word *recieved* with the correct *received*, then view the next error.

d. Click **Change** to replace *its* with the correct usage, *it's*.

e. Click **Ignore Once** to keep the heading *Annual Percentage Rate*.

   Remember that not all grammar usage flagged may be incorrect. Use your best judgment for those occasions.

f. Remove the check from the **Check grammar** option.

   Most of the headings in the document will be flagged for incorrect grammar, so this will let you bypass all of them and check the spelling only.

g. Click **Change** to replace the contextual spelling error *too* with *to* near the bottom of the first page and fix the next spelling error, Errurs, with Errors, as shown in Figure 1.35. Click **Change** to replace the incorrect spelling of Errors on the third page. Click **OK** in the box that informs you the spelling and grammar check is complete.

h. Save the document.

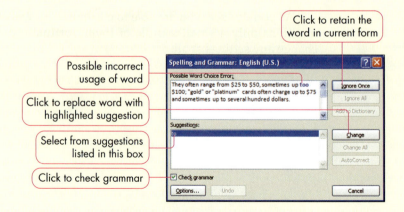

Figure 1.35 Check Spelling and Grammar

Step 2

Run the Document Inspector and a Compatibility Check

Refer to Figure 1.36 as you complete Step 2.

a. Click the **Office Button**, select **Prepare**, and then select **Run Compatibility Checker**.

A list of any non-compatible items in the document will display in the Microsoft Office Word Compatibility Checker dialog box.

b. Click **OK** after you view the incompatible listings.

c. Click the **Office Button** and select **Save As**. Save the document as **chap1_ho3_credit2_solution**.

Before you run the Document Inspector you save the document with a different name in order to have a backup.

d. Click the **Office Button**, point to **Prepare**, and then select **Inspect Document**.

TROUBLESHOOTING: An informational window might display with instructions to save the document before you run the Document Inspector. You should save the document first because the Document Inspector might make changes that you cannot undo.

e. Click to select any inspector check box that is not already checked. Click **Inspect**.

The Document Inspector results display, as shown in Figure 1.36, and Remove All buttons enable you to remove the items found in each category.

f. Click **Close**; do not remove any items at this time.

g. Save the document as **chap1_ho3_credit_solution**. Click **OK** to overwrite the existing file with the same name.

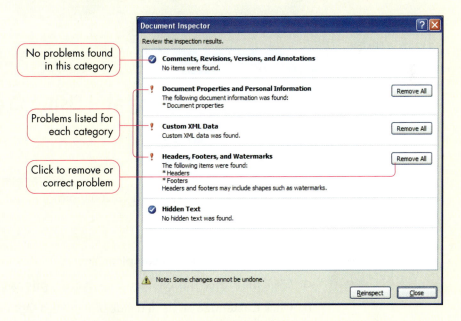

Figure 1.36 Document Inspector Results

Step 3
Save in a Compatible Format

Refer to Figure 1.37 as you complete Step 3.

a. Click the **Office Button**, click the **Save As** arrow, and select **Word 97–2003 Format**.

b. Confirm the *Save as type* box displays **Word 97–2003 Document (*.doc)**, then click **Save**.

The Compatibility Checker dialog box displays to confirm the compatibility issues you have seen already.

c. Click **Continue** to accept the alteration.

The title bar displays *(Compatibility Mode)* following the file name. If you set the option to display file extensions on your computer, the document extension .doc displays in the title bar instead of .docx, as shown in Figure 1.37.

d. Click the **Office Button** and select **Convert**.

The Compatibility Mode designation is removed from the title bar. If a dialog box displays stating the document will be converted to the newest file format, click OK. You can check the option that prevents the dialog box from displaying each time this situation occurs.

e. Click **Save** on the Quick Access Toolbar. Click **Save** in the Save As dialog box and click **OK** if the authorization to overwrite the current file displays.

The document extension has been restored to .docx.

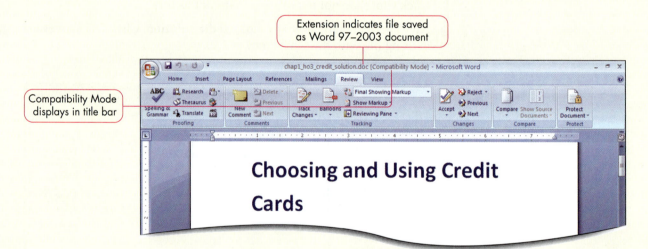

Figure 1.37 File Saved in Word 97–2003 Format

Step 4
Change Word Options

Refer to Figure 1.38 as you complete Step 4.

a. Click the **Office Button**, then click **Word Options** at the bottom of the menu.

b. Click **Customize** on the left side of the Word Options dialog box.

Look at other Word Options also, to view the many different features you can modify.

c. Select **Print Preview** from the *Choose commands from* list and click **Add** in the middle of the dialog box.

Print Preview displays in the Customize Quick Access Toolbar list.

d. Click the *Choose Commands from* drop-down arrow and click **All Commands**. Scroll down the list and click **Inspect Document** from the *Choose commands from* list and click **Add**.

e. Select **Print Preview** from the Customize Quick Access Toolbar list and click **Remove**.

Print Preview no longer displays in the list of icons for the Quick Access Toolbar, as seen in Figure 1.38.

f. Click **OK** at the bottom of the dialog box to return to the document.

The Quick Access Toolbar includes a new icon—the Document Inspector.

TROUBLESHOOTING: If you work in a lab environment, you might not have permission to modify the Word application. Accept any error messages you might see when saving the Word options and proceed to the next step.

g. Click the **Office Button**, click **Word Options** at the bottom of the menu, then click **Customize** on the left side of the Word Options dialog box. Select **Inspect Document** from the Customize Quick Access Toolbar list and click **Remove**. Click **OK** to close the Word Options dialog box.

The Quick Access Toolbar returns to the default setting.

h. Save the document.

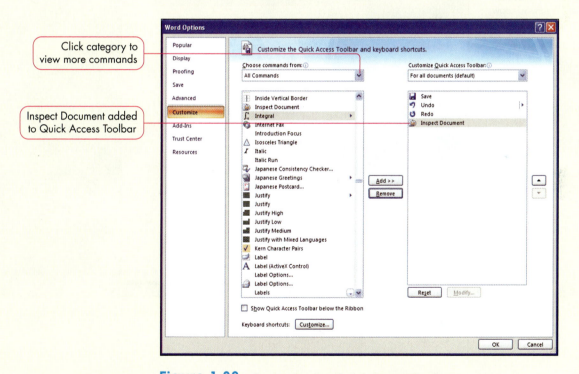

Figure 1.38 Customize the Quick Access Toolbar

Step 5
Use Print Preview Features

Refer to Figure 1.39 as you complete Step 5.

a. Click **Ctrl+Home**, if necessary, to move to the beginning of the document. Click the **Office Button**, click the **Print** arrow, and then select **Print Preview**.

The Print Preview dialog box displays the first page (see Figure 1.39).

b. Click **Two Pages** in the Zoom group to view the first two pages in this document. Click the check box next to **Magnifier** in the Preview group to remove the check mark.

This step removes the magnifying glass displayed on the mouse pointer and displays the insertion point. When you remove the magnifier, you can edit the file in the Print Preview window.

c. Place the insertion point on the left side of your name and type **Presented by:**. Click anywhere on the second page to move the insertion point out of the field.

d. Click **Margins** and select the **Narrow** setting.

Margins in section one of the document change to .5" on each side.

e. Click **Next Page** to view each page in the document. Click **Close Print Preview** to return to the document.

f. Save the document and exit Word.

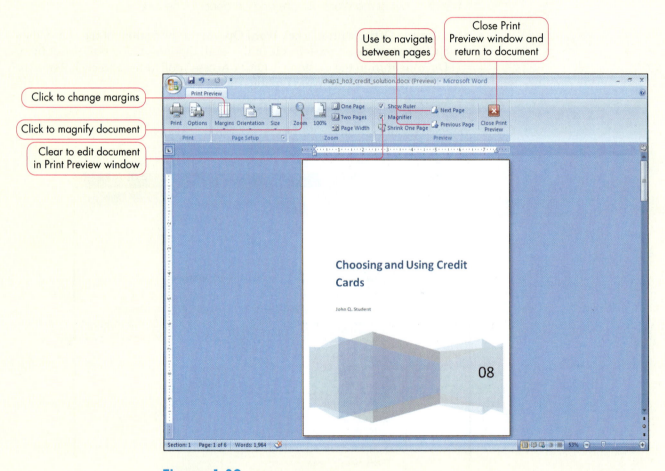

Figure 1.39 Print Preview Options

Summary

1. **Understand Word basics.** A word processing window is made up of several components including the title bar, Quick Access Toolbar, status bar, and the document area. Several tabs contain the commands that you use while working in Word, and the tabs might change according to the current task. As you type in a document, the word wrap feature automatically positions text for you using soft returns; however, you can insert a hard return to force text to the next line. Toggle switches such as the Caps Lock key or Bold feature are often used to alternate between two states while you work. The Show/Hide ¶ feature toggles on to reveal formatting marks in a document. The AutoText feature enables you to quickly insert predefined text or graphics.

2. **Use AutoText.** The AutoText feature substitutes a predefined item for specific text when the user initiates the replacement. Predefined and frequently used items, such as a logo, company name, author name, or return address, are stored as building blocks. You can type a portion of the building block entry, then press F3 to insert the remainder into your document.

3. **View a document.** The View tab provides options that enable you to display a document in many different ways. Views include Print Layout, Full Screen Reading, Web Layout, Outline, and Draft. To quickly change the view, click a button on the status bar in the lower-right corner of the window. You can use the Zoom slider to very quickly change magnification by sliding to a different percentage such as 75%. The Zoom dialog box includes options to change to whole page or multipage view.

4. **Use the Mini toolbar.** The Mini toolbar contains frequently used formatting commands such as Bold, Italic, Underline, Center, and Font Size. It displays faintly when you select text or right-click selected text, but it darkens as you move the mouse pointer closer to it. If you move the mouse pointer away from the Mini toolbar, it becomes fainter; if you do not want to use the Mini toolbar and prefer it disappears from view, press Esc when it displays.

5. **Set margins and specify page orientation.** When you create a document, you should consider how it will look when you print or display it. Margins determine the amount of white space from the text to the edge of the page. Pages can be set to display in portrait or landscape orientation. In portrait orientation, the text runs parallel to the shorter side of the paper. In landscape orientation, the text runs parallel to the longer side of the paper.

6. **Insert page breaks.** Soft page breaks occur when text no longer fits on the current page and automatically wraps to the top of a new page. The break is signified by a hidden marker that you can view using the Show/Hide ¶ feature. Hard page breaks can be used to force text onto a new page. A hard page break is inserted into a document using the Breaks command in the Page Setup group on the Page Layout tab, or Page Break in the Pages group on the Insert tab, but more easily through the Ctrl+Enter keyboard shortcut.

7. **Add page numbers.** Page numbers serve as a convenient reference point and assist in reading through a document. They can appear in the side margins or at the top or bottom of a page and can be left, center, or right aligned. The easiest way to place page numbers into a document is to click Page Number in the Header & Footer group on the Insert tab. When you use this feature, Word not only inserts page numbers but also adjusts automatically the page numbering when you add or delete pages.

8. **Insert headers and footers.** Headers and footers give a professional appearance to a document and are the best location to store page numbers. A header consists of one or more lines that are printed at the top of a page. A footer is printed at the bottom of a page. Footers often contain the page number and the date the document was created. Headers might contain the name of an organization, author, or title of the document. Headers and footers are added from the Insert tab. A simple header or footer also is created automatically by the Insert Page Number command.

9. **Create sections.** A section break is a marker that divides a document into sections, thereby allowing different formatting in each section. You determine where one section ends and another begins by using Breaks in the Page Setup group on the Page Layout tab. By using section breaks, you can change the margins within a multipage letter, where the first page (the letterhead) requires a larger top margin than the other pages in the letter. You also can change the page numbering within a document or even change the number of columns in a newsletter, which may contain a single column at the top of a page for the masthead, then two or three columns in the body of the newsletter.

...continued on Next Page

10. **Insert a cover page.** Word 2007 offers a feature to quickly insert a preformatted cover page in your document. The Cover Page feature includes a gallery with several designs, and each includes building block fields, such as Document Title, Company Name, Date, and Author, which you can personalize.

11. **Use Find and Replace commands.** Find and Replace commands include settings that enable you to look for or replace specific formatting on text. They also include options to conduct a case-sensitive or case-insensitive search. You can also use automatic replacement or selective replacement where you determine on an individual basis whether to replace the text or format. You can search for formatting and special characters. The Go To command moves the insertion point to a designated location in the document. You can go to a page, a section, or specify the number of pages to move forward or backward.

12. **Check spelling and grammar.** The grammar check feature looks for mistakes in punctuation, writing style, and word usage. If it finds an error, it will underline it with a green wavy line. You also can ask the grammar check to explain the rule it is attempting to enforce. When a possible error is found, you can accept the suggested correction, or determine if it is appropriate. The contextual spelling feature attempts to locate a word that is spelled correctly but used incorrectly. For example, it looks for the correct usage of the words *there* and *their*. A contextual spelling error is underlined with a blue wavy line.

13. **Use save and backup options.** To prevent loss of data you should save and back up your work frequently. You also should be familiar with commands that enable you to save your documents in a format compatible with older versions of Microsoft Word. You can use the convert command to alter those files into Word 2007 format, which is more efficient. Several backup options can be set, including an AutoRecover setting you can customize. This feature is useful for recovering a document when the program crashes. You can also require Word to create a backup copy in conjunction with every save operation. Word 2007 includes a compatibility checker to look for features that are not supported by previous versions of Word, and it also offers a Document Inspector that checks for and removes different kinds of hidden or personal information from a document.

14. **Select printing options.** You have three options to consider when you are ready to print your work: Print, Quick Print, and Print Preview. In the Print Preview window, you have several settings that enable you to magnify the page onscreen, display multiple pages, and even make changes to the page layout so you can view the results immediately. The Quick Print option sends a document straight to the printer without prompting you for changes to the printer configuration. The Print dialog box contains many useful options including print only the current page, a specific range of pages, or a specific number of copies.

15. **Customize Word.** After installation, Word is useful immediately. However, many options can be customized. The Word Options dialog box contains nine categories of options you can change including Personalize, Proofing, and Add-Ins. You can add to or remove commands from the Quick Access Toolbar using the Customize section of the Word Options dialog box.

Key Terms

Multiple Choice

1. When entering text within a document, you normally press Enter at the end of every:

   (a) Line
   (b) Sentence
   (c) Paragraph
   (d) Page

2. How do you display the Print dialog box?

   (a) Click the Print button on the Quick Access Toolbar.
   (b) Click the Office button, and then click the Print command.
   (c) Click the Print Preview command.
   (d) Click the Home tab.

3. Which view removes all tabs from the screen?

   (a) Full Screen Reading
   (b) Print Layout
   (c) Draft
   (d) Print Preview

4. You want to add bold and italic to a phrase that is used several times in a document. What is the easiest way to make this update?

   (a) Use the Go To feature and specify the exact page for each occurrence.
   (b) Use the Find feature, then use overtype mode to replace the text.
   (c) Use the Find and Replace feature and specify the format for the replacement.
   (d) No way exists to automatically complete this update.

5. You are the only person in your office to upgrade to Word 2007. Before you share documents with co-workers you should

   (a) Print out a backup copy.
   (b) Run the Compatibility Checker.
   (c) Burn all documents to CD.
   (d) Have no concerns that they can open your documents.

6. A document has been entered into Word using the default margins. What can you say about the number of hard and soft returns if the margins are increased by 0.5" on each side?

   (a) The number of hard returns is the same, but the number and/or position of the soft returns increases.
   (b) The number of hard returns is the same, but the number and/or position of the soft returns decreases.
   (c) The number and position of both hard and soft returns is unchanged.
   (d) The number and position of both hard and soft returns decreases.

7. Which of the following is detected by the contextual spell checker?

   (a) Duplicate words
   (b) Irregular capitalization
   (c) Use of the word *hear* when you should use *here*
   (d) Improper use of commas

8. Which option on the Page Layout tab allows you to specify that you are printing on an envelope?

   (a) Orientation
   (b) Margins
   (c) Breaks
   (d) Size

9. You need to insert a large table into a report, but it is too wide to fit on a standard page. Which of the following is the best option to use in this case?

   (a) Put the table in a separate document and don't worry about page numbering.
   (b) Insert section breaks and change the format of the page containing the table to landscape orientation.
   (c) Change the whole document to use landscape orientation.
   (d) Change margins to 0" on the right and left.

10. What feature adds organization to your documents?

    (a) Print Preview
    (b) Orientation
    (c) Page Numbers
    (d) Find and Replace

11. What might cause you to be unsuccessful in finding a specific block of text in your document?

    (a) You are performing a case-sensitive search.

    (b) You have specified formatting that is not used on the text.

    (c) You are not using wildcard characters even though you are uncertain of the proper spelling of your target.

    (d) All of the above.

12. Which action below is the result of using the AutoText feature?

    (a) When you click the Print button on the Quick Access Toolbar, the document prints.

    (b) When you select text, the Mini toolbar displays.

    (c) When you press Ctrl+F, the Find dialog box displays.

    (d) You start typing the date, a ScreenTip displays the date on the screen, and you press Enter to insert it.

13. If you cannot determine why a block of text starts at the top of the next page, which toggle switch should you invoke to view the formatting marks in use?

    (a) Word wrap

    (b) Show/Hide

    (c) Bold font

    (d) Caps Lock

14. If you use the margins feature frequently, what action should you take to make it more accessible?

    (a) Use the Customization category of Word Options and add Margins to the Quick Access Toolbar.

    (b) Use the Customization category of Word Options and add Margins to the Status bar.

    (c) Use the Personalization category of Word Options and add Margins to the Quick Access Toolbar.

    (d) No way exists to make it more accessible.

15. You are on page 4 of a five-page document. Which of the following is not a way to move the insertion point to the top of the first page?

    (a) Press Ctrl+Home.

    (b) Press Ctrl+G, type 1 in the Enter page number box, and click Go To.

    (c) Press PageUp on the keyboard one time.

    (d) Press Ctrl+F, click the Go To tab, type 1 in the Enter page number box, and click Go To.

16. What visual clue tells you a document is not in Word 2007 format?

    (a) The status bar includes the text (Compatibility Mode).

    (b) The file extension is .docx.

    (c) The title bar is a different color.

    (d) The title bar includes (Compatibility Mode) after the file name.

Practice Exercises

1 Impress a Potential Customer

Chapter 1 introduced you to many of the basic features and abilities of a word processor. In the following steps, you use those tools to make modifications and enhancements to a letter that will be sent to a potential customer. It is important to write in a professional manner, even if the letter is casual. In this case, you use Find and Replace to change a misspelled word. You also insert the date and a page number and observe the AutoCorrect feature as you misspell text while typing.

a. Start Word, if necessary, and open the *chap1_pe1_candle* document. Save the file as **chap1_pe1_candle_solution**.

b. Click **Replace** in the Editing group on the Home tab, and then type **cents** in the *Find what* box and type **Scents** in the *Replace with* box. Click **More**, if necessary, to display additional search options. **Click Find whole words only**, and then click **No Formatting**, if necessary, to remove format settings from the previous Find and Replace operation.

c. Click **Find Next** and click **Replace** when the word is found. Click **OK** to close the dialog box that indicates Word has finished searching the document. Close the Find and Replace dialog box.

   The first sentence of the first paragraph contains the first occurrence of the word. You must select *Find whole words only* to prevent replacing the occurrences of *Scents* that are spelled correctly.

d. Move the insertion point to the left of the phrase that starts with *Take a look*. Press **Insert** to change into Insert mode, if necessary, and type the sentence **We offer teh above scented candles in four sizes, just right for any room.** As you enter the word *the*, type **teh** instead and watch as the spelling is automatically corrected.

e. Click the **Insert tab** and click **Page Number** in the Header and Footer group. Point to **Bottom of Page** and select **Plain Number 2** from the gallery.

f. Press **Ctrl + Home** to move the insertion point to the top of the page. Type the current month, then press **Enter** when the ScreenTip displays the full date.

   TROUBLESHOOTING: If you begin to type the date and the ScreenTip does not display, continue to manually type the current date.

g. Click the **View tab** and select **Full Screen Reading** in the Document Views group. Compare your document to Figure 1.40. Click **Close** to return to Print Layout view.

h. Click **Ctrl+S** to save the document. Click the **Office Button** and select **Close**.

...continued on Next Page

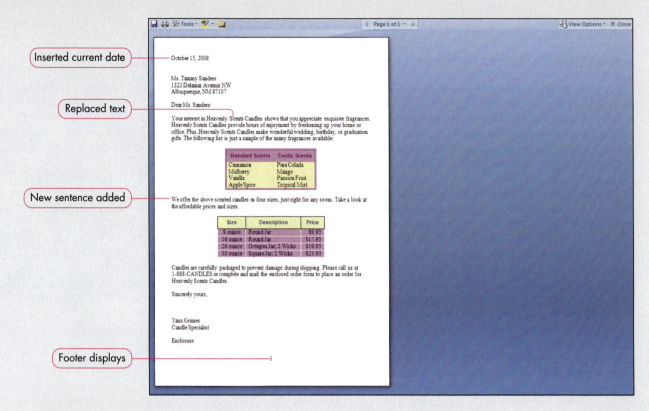

Inserted current date

Replaced text

New sentence added

Footer displays

Figure 1.40 Updated Word Processing Document

2 Use Spelling and Grammar Check on a Memo

Mr. McGary, the Human Resources director of a medium-sized company, sends several memos each week to the employees in his company. It is important to communicate effectively with the employees, so he relies heavily on Word to locate errors in spelling, contextual spelling, and grammar as denoted by the wavy red, blue, and green lines, respectively. Even though Word contains these features, some mistakes may go unnoticed by the program. Mr. McGary, as well as anyone who uses a word processor, should always proofread documents carefully in addition to running the electronic spelling and grammar checkers. Your assignment is to correct the document so that it is error free and Mr. McGary can convey his message to employees without the distraction of poor spelling and grammar.

a. Open the *chap1_pe2_memo* document and save it as **chap1_pe2_memo_solution**.

b. Click the **Office Button** and click **Word Options** to display the Word Options dialog box. Click **Proofing** and click **Use contextual spelling**, if necessary, to enable that feature. Click **OK**.

c. Press **Ctrl+Home** to move to the beginning of the document. Click the **Review tab** and click **Spelling & Grammar** to check the document and correct errors. The first error displays in Figure 1.41. Use the following table to validate your corrections.

Error	Correction
Employeees	Employees
As you probably no	As you probably know
seminars are held inn the Cowboy Hat Hotel	seminars are held in the Cowboy Hat Hotel
managers have been instructed too allow employees in their department too attend	managers have been instructed to allow employees in their department to attend
MEntoring	Mentoring
attend..	attend.

...continued on Next Page

d. Right-click the words *These seminars* in the last sentence of the first paragraph. Click **These seminars** to remove the extra space between the words.

e. Click to the right of the letter b in the word *Subrdinate* in the first seminar listed in the table. Type **o** to correct the misspelling of subordinate.

f. Click the **Insert tab** and click **Footer** in the Header and Footer group. Click **Edit Footer** and type **Updated by**, then press **Spacebar** one time. Type your initials, then press **F3** to insert the AutoText entry that contains your name. Click **Close Header and Footer**.

g. Save the document.

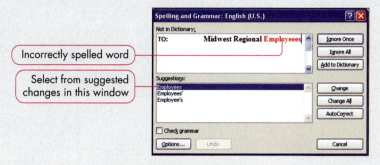

Figure 1.41 The Spell Check Process

3 Keyboard Shortcuts

Keyboard shortcuts are especially useful if you are a good typist because your hands can remain on the keyboard, as opposed to continually moving to and from the mouse. We never set out to memorize the shortcuts; we just learn them along the way as we continue to use Microsoft Office. It is much easier than you think, and the same shortcuts apply to multiple applications, such as Microsoft Excel, PowerPoint, and Access.

a. Open the *chap1_pe3_shortcuts* document. Click the **Office Button** and select **Convert**. Save the document as **chap1_pe3_shortcuts_solution**, paying special attention that it is saved in Word format (*.docx).

b. Click the **Page Layout tab**, click **Margins** in the Page Setup group, and click **Normal**. Click **Orientation**, and then click **Portrait**.

c. Click the **Home tab** and click **Show/Hide ¶** in the Paragraph group, if necessary, to display formatting marks.

It will be helpful to see the formatting marks when you edit the document in the following steps.

d. Move the insertion point to the left side of the hard return mark at the end of the line containing Ctrl+B. Press **Ctrl+B,** then type the word **Bold**.

e. Move the insertion point to the left side of the hard return mark at the end of the line containing Ctrl+I. Press **Ctrl+I,** then type the word **Italic**.

f. Scroll to the bottom of the first page and place the insertion point on the left side of the title *Other Ctrl Keyboard Shortcuts*. Press **Ctrl+Enter** to insert a hard page break and keep the paragraph together on one page.

g. Click the **Insert tab**, click **Page Number** in the Header & Footer group, point to **Bottom of Page**, and select **Brackets 1** from the gallery.

h. Click **Header** in the Header & Footer group and select **Edit Header**. Click **Different First Page** in the Options group of the Design tab to insert a check mark. Place the insertion point in the header area of the second page and type **Keyboard Shortcuts**.

Because you selected the *Different First Page* option, the header does not display on the first page as it is not needed there. However, the footer on the first page has been removed, so you will have to reinsert it.

...continued on Next Page

i. Move the insertion point to the first page footer. With the Design tab selected, click **Page Number** in the Header & Footer group, point to **Bottom of Page**, then select **Brackets 1** from the gallery. Click **Close Header and Footer**.

j. Click the **Zoom button** in the status bar, click **Many pages**, then drag to select **1 x 2 Pages**. Click **OK** to close the Zoom dialog box. Click **Show/Hide ¶** in the Paragraph group on the Home tab to toggle off the formatting marks. Compare your document to Figure 1.42.

k. Save the document.

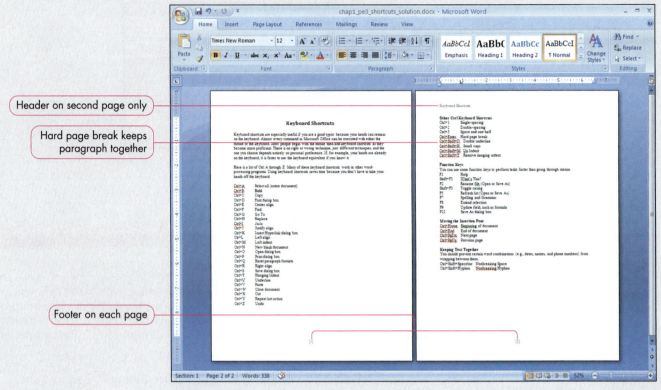

Header on second page only

Hard page break keeps paragraph together

Footer on each page

Figure 1.42 Keyboard Shortcut Document

4 Protecting Your System

The document you use in this exercise discusses computer viruses and backup procedures. It is not a question of *if* it will happen, but *when*—hard drives die, removable disks are lost, or viruses may infect a system. You can prepare for the inevitable by creating an adequate backup before the problem occurs. The advice in this document is very important; you should take it very seriously, and then protect yourself and your data.

a. Open the *chap1_pe4_virus* document and save it as **chap1_pe4_virus_solution**.

b. Click **Ctrl+H** to display the Find and Replace dialog box. In the *Find what* box, type **virus**. In the *Replace with* box, type **virus**. Click **More**, if necessary, then click the **Match case** check box.

c. Confirm that the *Replace with* text is selected or that the insertion point is in that box. Click **Format** at the bottom of the window and select **Font**. Click **Bold Italic** under the *Font Style* section, then click **OK**. Click **Replace All**, then click **OK** to confirm 17 replacements in the document. Click **Close** to remove the Find and Replace dialog box.

d. Scroll to the bottom of the first page and place the insertion point on the left side of the title *The Essence of Backup*. Press **Ctrl+Enter** to insert a hard page break.

This step creates a more appropriate break and keeps the heading and content together on one page.

...continued on Next Page

e. Press **Ctrl+End** to move to the end of the document. Type your name, press **Enter**, type the name of your class, then use the mouse to select both. Click **Quick Parts** in the Text group on the **Insert tab**, then click **Save Selection to Quick Part Gallery**.

The Create New Building Block dialog box displays, and you will add your name as an AutoText entry.

f. Replace your name in the *Name* box with the word **me**. Change the *Gallery* option to **AutoText**, and then click **OK**.

Even though you replaced your name in the dialog box, the text that is high-lighted in the document will be used when you invoke the AutoText feature.

g. Delete your name at the end of the document. Click **Page Number** in the Header & Footer group on the **Insert tab**, click **Bottom of Page**, and then click **Circle** from the gallery.

h. The insertion point is on the left margin of the footer. Type **Created by: me** and press **F3**.

When you click F3, the AutoText entry should replace the text *me* with your name and your class displays on the line below.

i. Click **Close Header and Footer**.

j. Click **Zoom** in the status bar, click **Many pages**, then drag to select **1 × 2 pages**. Click **OK** to close the Zoom dialog box. Click **Show/Hide ¶** in the Paragraph group on the Home tab to toggle off the formatting marks, if necessary. Compare your document to Figure 1.43.

k. Save the document. Click the **Office Button**, click **Prepare**, and then click **Run Compatibility Checker**.

The results indicate that some text box positioning will change if opened in an older version of Word. It was good to check this before you save the document in Word 97–2003 format.

l. Click **OK** to close the Compatibility Checker window. Click the **Office Button**, point to **Save As**, and select **Word 97–2003 Format**. Confirm the *Save as type* box displays Word 97–2003 document (*.doc), then click **Save**. Click **Continue** when the Compatibility Checker box shows the information you viewed previously.

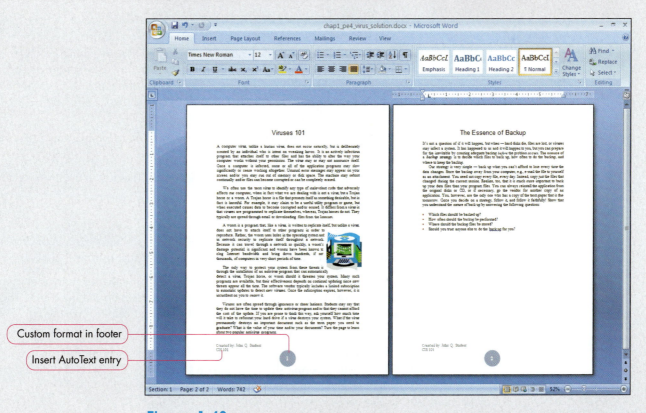

Figure 1.43 Protecting Your System

Mid-Level Exercises

1 Media-Blitz

Media-Blitz is a locally owned store that specializes in both new and used copies of popular music and movies. Its proximity to a local college campus provides a steady flow of customers during the school year. To increase sales during the typically slow summer season, it is offering discounts to students who have already enrolled in classes for the upcoming semester. You are working for the store this summer, and your assistance is needed to put the finishing touches on a flyer it wants to distribute in the area.

a. Open the *chap1_mid1_media* document and save it as **chap1_mid1_media_solution**.

b. Insert hard returns to create a list of discounts using the information below the first paragraph. Use the Mini toolbar to apply Bold and Center formatting to this group of items.

c. Perform a spelling and grammar check on the document to correct errors.

d. Create an AutoText entry for the name and address of the business. Name the entry Blitz. This entry will be useful in other documents you create for the business. Test the entry to make sure it works properly.

e. The school recently changed its name to Greene County Community College. Make appropriate changes in the flyer so each use of the name is updated and bolded.

f. Change to Full Screen Reading view, then change back to Print Layout view.

g. Display the document in the Print Preview window. Change orientation to Landscape.

h. Save and close the document.

2 Training Proposal

All About Training is an established computer training company that actively markets its services to the community. You have the opportunity to preview a document it will be sending to prospective clients and you notice several modifications that would add a professional appearance to the document. Use your skills to make the changes listed in the steps below.

a. Open the *chap1_mid2_proposal* document and save it as **chap1_mid2_proposal_ solution**.

b. Insert a section break at the beginning of the document that forces the proposal to start on the second page.

c. Set 1" margins on all sides of the whole document.

d. At the end of the last page, insert several hard returns, then type a line that says **Last Updated on:** and insert the current date using the AutoText feature.

e. Create a title page, without using the Cover Page feature, that contains a copy of the text *All About Training*. Use a 36 pt bold font and center it on the line. Type **Training Proposal** on the second line; use a 26 pt bold font, and center it on the line. Set 1.5" margins on all sides for this page.

f. Display page numbers on the side margin. The title page should not display a page number, so page numbering should begin on the second page. (Hint: you must change a setting in the Header and Footer Design tab.)

...continued on Next Page

g. Replace each instance of the company name to display in bold, italic, and red font color. Allow the replacement only when it appears in a paragraph, not in the banner that appears at the top of the document.

h. Perform a spelling and grammar check on the document.

i. Save the document in both Word 2007 and Word 97–2003 formats so it will be available for prospective clients regardless of the version of Word they use. Close all documents.

3 Fundraiser

The organizer of a craft fair has contacted your school to request permission to conduct a fundraiser. Your work in the office of College Relations includes returning the responses from administrators on matters such as this. The response letter has been drafted, and you will complete the letter by adding the recipient's name and address; then you create an envelope in which to mail it.

a. Open a blank document and type your name on a blank line. Use your name to create a Building Block AutoText entry.

b. Open the *chap1_mid3_letter* document and save it as **chap1_mid3_letter_solution**.

c. Move the insertion point to the bottom of the letter and replace the text *Your Name Here* with your name using the AutoText entry you created in the first step.

d. Insert a Next Page Section Break at the end of the letter and apply landscape orientation to the second page.

e. Confirm that the headers and footers in the second section are not linked to the first section. Then use the AutoText entry to insert your name in the header.

f. Use copy and paste to insert the recipient's name and address from the letter in the second section. Center the address so it resembles an envelope.

g. Save and close the document.

4 Heart Disease Prevention

Millions of people suffer from heart disease and other cardiac-related illnesses. Of those people, several million will suffer a heart attack each year. Your mother volunteers for the American Heart Association and has brought you a document that explains what causes a heart attack, the signs of an attack, and what you can do to reduce your risk of having one. The information in the document is very valuable, but she needs you to put the finishing touches on this document before she circulates it in the community.

a. Open the *chap1_mid4_heart* document and save it as **chap1_mid4_heart_solution**.

b. Convert the solution file so it does not open in Compatibility Mode.

c. Create a cover page for the report. Use **Tiles** in the cover page gallery. Add text where necessary to display the report title and subtitle (use *What You Should Know* as the subtitle), and your name as author. Delete any unused fields on the cover page.

d. Change the document margins to .75" on all sides.

e. Create a section break between the cover page and the first page of the report. Set appropriate options to prevent a footer from displaying on the cover page. A page number should display at the bottom of the remaining pages, and you should display the number one on the first page of the report that follows the cover page.

...continued on Next Page

f. Create a header that displays the report title. It should not display on the cover or first page of the report (the page that follows the cover page). Confirm that the headers and footers in the second section are not linked to the first section.

g. Toggle the Show/Hide ¶ feature on, then select Draft view. Remove any page breaks that cause the report data to display on separate pages. Do not remove the page break that immediately follows the cover page. View the document in Print Layout view and insert page breaks where necessary to prevent a paragraph or list from breaking across pages.

h. You are investing a lot of time in this project, so confirm that Word is performing back-ups every 5 minutes using the Word Options.

i. Save and close the document.

Capstone Exercise

After a hard week of work, you decide to enjoy the great outdoors by taking a canoe trip with your friends. Your friend researched the Buffalo National River and e-mailed you a document that describes the activities and preparations needed before visiting the area. You want to send the information to others who will accompany you on the trip, but the document needs some formatting modifications.

Spelling and Grammar

The first thing you notice about the report is the number of spelling and grammatical errors detected by Word. You will fix those as well as correct all references to the river that omit its status as a National River.

a. Open the *chap1_cap_buffalo* document, found in the Exploring Word folder. Save the document as **chap1_cap_buffalo_solution**.

b. Display the document in Full Screen Reading view. Use the navigation tool to view each page. Return to Print Layout view.

c. Display the Word Options dialog box and engage the Contextual Spelling feature if it is not already in use.

d. Run the spell checker and correct grammar and contextual spelling errors also.

e. Replace all occurrences of *Buffalo River* with **Buffalo National River**. When you make the replacements, add a bold font.

Revise Page Layout

When you zoom out to view multiple pages of the document, you notice that several lines and paragraphs break at odd places. Use formatting tools and page layout options to improve the readability of this file. Take special consideration of the picture on the last page; it seems to be too wide to display on a standard page.

a. Change the Zoom to 50% and determine where the content makes awkward breaks. Click Show/Hide ¶, if necessary, to display formatting marks that will assist you in determining which format options are in use.

b. Remove any unnecessary hard returns that interfere with word wrapping in the first paragraph.

c. Adjust margins to use the Normal setting (1" on each side). Insert hard page breaks where necessary to keep paragraphs together.

d. Create a footer that displays page numbers. Select the **Annual** format for the page numbers.

e. Insert a Next Page Section break before the picture of the river. Change the orientation of the last page so the whole picture displays on the page.

Save in Multiple Formats

After improving the readability of the document, you remember that it has not yet been saved. Saving work is very important, and you will save it immediately. Since you will be sharing the document with friends, you also decide to save it in a format compatible with older versions.

a. Save the document again as **chap1_cap_buffalo2_solution**, then run the Compatibility Checker and Document Inspector, but do not take any suggested actions at this time.

b. Save the document in Word 97–2003 format.

c. Use the Print Preview feature to view the document before printing. Do not print unless instructed to by your teacher.

Mini Cases

Use the rubric following the case as a guide to evaluate your work, but keep in mind that your instructor may impose additional grading criteria or use a different standard to judge your work.

Letter of Appreciation

GENERAL CASE

Have you taken time to think about the people who have helped you get to where you are? For some, parents have provided encouragement and financial assistance so their children can enjoy the privileges of a higher education. Many other students receive the moral support of family but are financing their education personally. Regardless of how your education is funded, there are people who deserve your appreciation. Take this opportunity to write a letter that you can send to those people. In the letter, you can give an update on your classes, tell them about your future plans, and don't forget to express your appreciation for their support. Create an attractive document using skills learned in this chapter, then save your letter as **chap1_mc1_appreciate_solution**.

Performance Elements	Exceeds Expectations	Meets Expectations	Below Expectations
Completeness	Document contains all required elements.	Document contains most required elements.	Document contains elements not specified in instructions.
Page setup	Modified or added at least three Page Layout elements.	Modified or added at least two Page Layout elements.	Did not modify or add any Page Layout elements.
Accuracy	No errors in spelling, grammar, or punctuation were found.	Fewer than two errors in spelling, grammar, or punctuation were found.	More than two errors in spelling, grammar, or punctuation were found.

Animal Concerns

RESEARCH CASE

As the population of family pets continues to grow, it is imperative that we learn how to be responsible pet owners. Very few people take the time to perform thorough research on the fundamental care of and responsibility for animal populations. Open the *chap1_mc2_animal* document and proceed to search the Internet for information that will contribute to this report on animal care and concerns. Compare information from at least three sources. Give consideration to information that is copyrighted and do not reprint it. Any information used should be cited in the document. As you enter the information and sources into the document, you will be reminded of concepts learned in Chapter 1, such as word wrap and soft returns. Use your knowledge of other formatting techniques, such as hard returns, page numbers, and margin settings, to create an attractive document. Create a cover page for the document, perform a spell check, and view the print preview before submitting this assinment to your instructor. Create headers and/or footers to improve readability. Name your completed document **chap1_mc2_animal_solution**.

Performance Elements	Exceeds Expectations	Meets Expectations	Below Expectations
Research	All sections were completed with comprehensive information and citations.	All sections were updated but with minimal information and no citations.	Sections were not updated, no citations were given.
Page setup	Modified or added at least three Page Layout elements.	Modified or added at least two Page Layout elements.	Did not modify or add any Page Layout elements.
Accuracy	No errors in spelling, grammar, or punctuation were found.	Fewer than two errors in spelling, grammar, or punctuation were found.	More than two errors in spelling, grammar, or punctuation were found.

The *chap1_mc3_tmgnews* document was started by an office assistant, but she quickly gave up on it after she moved paragraphs around until it became unreadable. The document contains significant errors, which cause the newsletter to display in a very disjointed way. Use your knowledge of Page Layout options and other Word features to revise this newsletter in time for the monthly mailing. Save your work as **chap1_mc3_tmgnews_solution**.

Performance Elements	Exceeds Expectations	Meets Expectations	Below Expectations
Page setup	Modified Page Layout options in such a way that newsletter displays on one page.	Few Page Layout modifications applied; newsletter displays on more than one page.	No Page Layout modifications applied; newsletter displays on more than one page.
Accuracy	No errors in spelling, grammar, or punctuation were found.	Fewer than two errors in spelling, grammar, or punctuation were found.	More than two errors in spelling, grammar, or punctuation were found.

Gaining Proficiency

Editing and Formatting

Objectives

After you read this chapter, you will be able to:

1. Apply font attributes through the Font dialog box **(page 133)**.

2. Highlight text **(page 136)**.

3. Control word wrapping with nonbreaking hyphens and nonbreaking spaces **(page 137)**.

4. Copy formats with the Format Painter **(page 139)**.

5. Set off paragraphs with tabs, borders, lists, and columns **(page 143)**.

6. Apply paragraph formats **(page 148)**.

7. Create and modify styles **(page 159)**.

8. Create a table of contents **(page 171)**.

9. Create an index **(page 171)**.

Hands-On Exercises

Exercises ○	Skills Covered
1. **CHARACTER FORMATTING (page 140)** **Open:** chap2_ho1_description.docx **Save as:** chap2_ho1_description_solution.docx	• Change Text Appearance • Insert Nonbreaking Spaces and Nonbreaking Hyphens • Highlight Text and Use Format Painter
2. **PARAGRAPH FORMATTING (page 152)** **Open:** chap2_ho1_description_solution.docx (from Exercise 1) **Save as:** chap2_ho2_description_solution.docx (additional modifications)	• Set Tabs in a Footer • Select Text to Format • Specify Line Spacing, Justification, and Pagination • Indent Text • Apply Borders and Shading • Change Column Structure • Insert a Section Break and Create Columns
3. **STYLES (page 164)** **Open:** chap2_ho3_gd.docx **Save as:** chap2_ho3_gd_solution.docx	• Apply Style Properties • Modify the Body Text Style • Modify the Heading 3 Style • Select the Outline View • Create a Paragraph Style • Create a Character Style • View the Completed Document
4. **REFERENCE PAGES (page 173)** **Open:** chap2_ho3_gd_solution.docx (from Exercise 3) **Save as:** chap2_ho4_gd_solution.docx (additional modifications)	• Apply a Style • Insert a Table of Contents • Define an Index Entry • Create the Index • Complete the Index • View the Completed Document

CASE STUDY

Treyserv-Pitkin Enterprises

Treyserv, a consumer products manufacturing company, has recently acquired a competitor, paving the way for a larger, stronger company poised to meet the demands of the market. Each year Treyserv generates a corporate annual report and distributes it to all employees and stockholders. You are the executive assistant to the president of Treyserv and your responsibilities include preparing and distributing the corporate annual report. This year the report emphasizes the importance of acquiring Pitkin Industries to form Treyserv-Pitkin Enterprises.

As with most mergers or acquisitions, the newly created Treyserv-Pitkin organization will enable management to make significant changes to establish a more strategic and profitable company. Management will focus on reorganizing both companies to eliminate duplication of efforts and reduce expenses; it will reduce long-term debt when possible and combine research and development activities. The annual report always provides a synopsis of recent changes to upper management, and this year it will introduce a new Chair and Chief Executive Officer, Mr. Dewey A. Larson. The company also hired Ms. Amanda Wray as chief financial officer; both positions are very high profile and contribute to the stockholders' impression of the company's continued success. Information about these newly appointed executives and other financial data have been gathered, but the report needs to be formatted attractively before it can be distributed to employees and stockholders.

Case Study

Your Assignment

- Read the chapter, paying special attention to sections that describe how to apply styles, create a table of contents, and create an index.
- Open the document, *chap2_case_treyserv*, which contains the unformatted report that was provided to you by the president of the company.
- Add format features such as borders and shading, line spacing, justification, paragraph indention, and bullet and number lists to enhance the appearance of information in the report.
- Use tabs or columns, when appropriate, to align information in the report.
- Use predefined styles, such as Heading 1 and Heading 2, to format paragraph headings throughout the document.
- Apply paragraph formats such as widow/orphan control to prevent text from wrapping awkwardly when it spans from one page to the next.
- Add a table of contents and page numbering to assist readers in locating information.
- Save your work in a document named **chap2_case_treyserv_solution**.

Text Formatting

> The ultimate success of any document depends greatly on its appearance. Typeface should reinforce the message without calling attention to itself and should be consistent with the information you want to convey.

The arrangement and appearance of printed matter is called *typography*. You also may define it as the process of selecting typefaces, type styles, and type sizes. The importance of these decisions is obvious, for the ultimate success of any document depends greatly on its appearance. Typeface should reinforce the message without calling attention to itself and should be consistent with the information you want to convey. For example, a paper prepared for a professional purpose, such as a résumé, should use a standard typeface and abstain from using one that looks funny or cute. Additionally, you want to minimize the variety of typefaces in a document to maintain a professional look.

A *typeface* or *font* is a complete set of characters—upper- and lowercase letters, numbers, punctuation marks, and special symbols. A definitive characteristic of any typeface is the presence or absence of thin lines that end the main strokes of each letter. A *serif typeface* contains a thin line or extension at the top and bottom of the primary strokes on characters. A *sans serif typeface* (sans from the French for without) does not contain the thin lines on characters. Times New Roman is an example of a serif typeface. Arial is a sans serif typeface.

Serifs help the eye to connect one letter with the next and generally are used with large amounts of text. This book, for example, is set in a serif typeface. A sans serif typeface is more effective with smaller amounts of text such as titles, headlines, corporate logos, and Web pages.

A second characteristic of a typeface is whether it is monospaced or proportional. A *monospaced* typeface (such as Courier New) uses the same amount of horizontal space for every character regardless of its width. A *proportional* typeface (such as Times New Roman or Arial) allocates space according to the width of the character. For example, the lowercase *m* is wider than the lowercase *i*. Monospaced fonts are used in tables and financial projections where text must be precisely lined up, one character underneath the other. Proportional typefaces create a more professional appearance and are appropriate for most documents, such as research papers, status reports, and letters. You can set any typeface in different *type styles* such as regular, **bold**, *italic*, or ***bold italic***.

In this section, you apply font attributes through the Font dialog box, change casing, and highlight text so that it stands out. You also control word wrapping by inserting nonbreaking hyphens and nonbreaking spaces between words. Finally, you copy formats using the Format Painter.

Typography is the appearance of printed matter.

A **typeface** or **font** is a complete set of characters.

A **serif typeface** contains a thin line at the top and bottom of characters.

A **sans serif typeface** does not contain thin lines on characters.

A **monospaced typeface** uses the same amount of horizontal space for every character.

A **proportional typeface** allocates horizontal space to the character.

Type style is the characteristic applied to a font, such as bold.

Applying Font Attributes Through the Font Dialog Box

In the Office Fundamentals chapter, you learned how to use the Font group on the Home tab to apply font attributes. The Font group contains commands to change the font, font size, and font color; and apply bold, italic, and underline. In addition to applying commands from the Font group, you can display the Font dialog box if you click the Font Launcher, the small icon in the right corner in the Font group, to give you complete control over the typeface, size, and style of the text in a document. Making selections in the Font dialog box before entering text sets the format of the text as you type. You also can change the font of existing text by selecting the text and then applying the desired attributes from the Font dialog box, as shown in Figure 2.1.

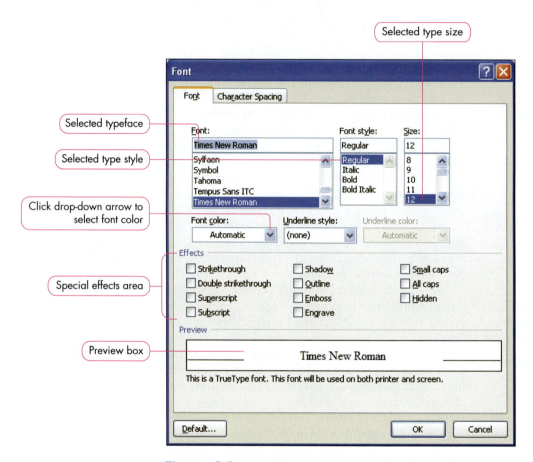

Figure 2.1 Font Dialog Box

Change Text Case (Capitalization)

Use **Change Case** to change capitalization of text.

To quickly change the capitalization of text in a document use **Change Case** in the Font group on the Home tab. When you click Change Case, the following list of options display:

- **Sentence case.** (capitalizes only the first word of the sentence or phrase)
- **lowercase** (changes the text to lowercase)
- **UPPERCASE** (changes the text to all capital letters)
- **Capitalize Each Word** (capitalizes the first letter of each word; effective for formatting titles, but remember to lowercase first letters of short prepositions, such as *of*)
- **tOGGLE cASE** (changes lowercase to uppercase and uppercase to lowercase)

    This feature is useful when generating a list and you want to use the same case formatting for each item. If you do not select text first, the casing format will take effect on the text where the insertion point is located. You can toggle among upper-case, lowercase, and sentence case formats by pressing Shift+F3.

Select Font Options

In addition to changing the font, font style, and size, you can apply other font attributes to text. Although the Font group on the Home tab contains special effects commands such as strikethrough, subscript, and superscript, the *Effects* section in the Font tab in the Font dialog box contains a comprehensive set of options for applying color and special effects, such as SMALL CAPS, superscripts, or subscripts. Table 2.1 lists and defines more of these special effects. You also can change the underline options and indicate if spaces are to be underlined or just words. You can even change the color of the text and underline.

Table 2.1 Font Effects

Effect	Description	Example
Strikethrough	Displays a horizontal line through the middle of the text	~~strikethrough~~
Superscript	Displays text in a smaller size and raised above the baseline	Super^{script}
Subscript	Displays text in a smaller size and lowered below the baseline	Sub$_{script}$
Shadow	Displays text with a 3D shadow effect	Shadow
Emboss	Displays text as if it has been raised from the page	Emboss
Engrave	Displays text as if it has been pressed down into the page	Engrave
Small caps	Displays letters as uppercase but smaller than regular-sized uppercase letters	SMALL CAPS

> **TIP   Hidden Text**
>
> ***Hidden text*** is document text that does not appear on screen, unless you click Show/Hide ¶ in the Paragraph group on the Home tab. You can use this special effect format to hide confidential information before printing documents for other people. For example, an employer can hide employees' Social Security numbers before printing a company roster.

Set Character Spacing

Hidden text does not appear onscreen.

Character spacing refers to the amount of horizontal space between characters. Although most character spacing is acceptable, some character combinations appear too far apart or too close together in large-sized text when printed. If so, you might want to adjust for this spacing discrepancy. The Character Spacing tab in the Font dialog box contains options in which you manually control the spacing between characters. The Character Spacing tab shown in Figure 2.2 displays four options for adjusting character spacing: Scale, Spacing, Position, and Kerning.

Character spacing is the horizontal space between characters.

   Scale increases or decreases the text horizontally as a percentage of its size; it does not change the vertical height of text. You may use the scale feature on justified text, which does not produce the best-looking results—adjust the scale by a low percentage (90%–95%) to improve text flow without a noticeable difference to the reader.

Scale increases or decreases text as a percentage of its size.

You may select the *Expanded* option to stretch a word or sentence so it fills more space; for example, use it on a title you want to span across the top of a page. The *Condensed* option is useful to squeeze text closer together, such as when you want to prevent one word from wrapping to another line.

> **Position** raises or lowers text from the baseline.

Position raises or lowers text from the baseline without creating superscript or subscript size. Use this feature when you want text to stand out from other text on the same line; or use it to create a fun title by raising and/or lowering every few letters. *Kerning* automatically adjusts spacing between characters to achieve a more evenly spaced appearance. Kerning primarily allows letters to fit closer together, especially when a capital letter can use space unoccupied by a lowercase letter beside it. For example, you can kern the letters *Va* so the top of the *V* extends into the empty space above the *a* instead of leaving an awkward gap between them.

> **Kerning** allows more even spacing between characters.

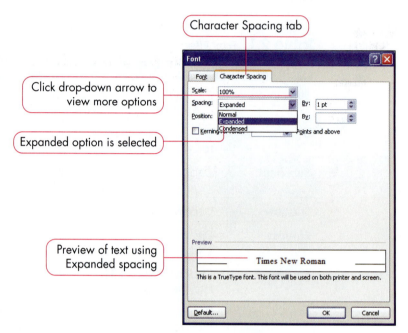

Figure 2.2 Character Spacing Tab in the Font Dialog Box

Highlighting Text

> Use the **Highlighter** to mark text that you want to locate easily.

People often use a highlighting marker to highlight important parts of textbooks, magazine articles, and other documents. In Word, you use the *Highlighter* to mark text that you want to stand out or locate easily. Highlighted text draws the reader's attention to important information within the documents you create, as illustrated in Figure 2.3. The Text Highlight Color command is located in the Font group on the Home tab and also on the Mini toolbar. You can click Text Highlight Color before or after selecting text. When you click Text Highlight Color before selecting text, the mouse pointer resembles a pen that you can click and drag across text to highlight it. The feature stays on so you can highlight additional text. When you finish highlighting text, press Esc to turn it off. If you select text first, click Text Highlight Color to apply the color. To remove highlights, select the highlighted text, click the Text Highlight Color arrow, and choose No Color.

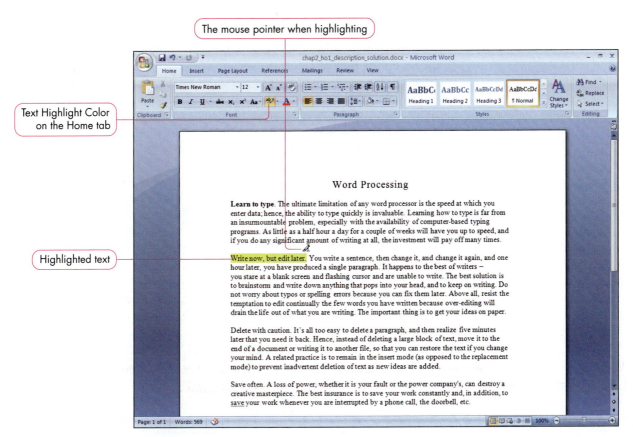

The mouse pointer when highlighting

Text Highlight Color on the Home tab

Highlighted text

Figure 2.3 The Highlight Tool

If you use a color printer, you see the highlight colors on your printout. If you use a monochrome printer, the highlight appears in shades of gray. Be sure that you can easily read the text with the gray highlight. If not, select a lighter highlight color, and print your document again. You can create a unique highlighting effect by choosing a dark highlight color, such as Dark Blue, and applying a light font color, such as White.

TIP   Impose a Time Limit

Word 2007 is supposed to save time and make you more productive. It will do exactly that, provided you use Word for its primary purpose—writing and editing. It is all too easy, however, to lose sight of that objective and spend too much time formatting the document. Concentrate on the content of your document rather than its appearance and remember that the success of a document ultimately depends on its content. Impose a limit on the amount of time you will spend on formatting.

Controlling Word Wrapping with Nonbreaking Hyphens and Nonbreaking Spaces

In Word, text wraps to the next line when the current line of text is full. Most of the time, the way words wrap is acceptable. Occasionally, however, text may wrap in an undesirable location. To improve the readability of text, you need to proofread word-wrapping locations and insert special characters. Two general areas of concern are hyphenated words and spacing within proper nouns.

Insert Nonbreaking Hyphens

A ***nonbreaking hyphen*** prevents a word from becoming separated at the hyphen.

If a hyphenated word falls at the end of a line, the first word and the hyphen may appear on the first line, and the second word may wrap to the next line. However, certain hyphenated text, such as phone numbers, should stay together to improve the readability of the text. To keep hyphenated words together, replace the regular hyphen with a nonbreaking hyphen. A ***nonbreaking hyphen*** keeps text on both sides of the hyphen together, thus preventing the hyphenated word from becoming separated at the hyphen, as shown in Figure 2.4. To insert a nonbreaking hyphen, press Ctrl+Shift+Hyphen. When you click Show/Hide ¶ in the Paragraph group on the Home tab to display formatting symbols, a regular hyphen looks like a hyphen, and a nonbreaking hyphen appears as a wider hyphen. However, the nonbreaking hyphen looks like a regular hyphen when printed.

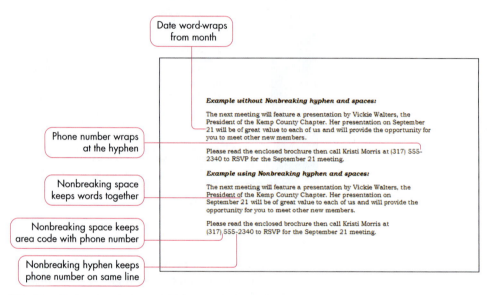

Figure 2.4 Nonbreaking Hyphens and Spaces

Insert Nonbreaking Spaces

A ***nonbreaking space*** keeps two or more words together on a line.

Because text will wrap to the next line if a word does not fit at the end of the current line, occasionally word-wrapping between certain types of words is undesirable; that is, some words should be kept together for improved readability. For example, the date *March 31* should stay together instead of word-wrapping after March. Other items that should stay together include names, such as *Ms. Stevenson*, and page references, such as *page 15*. To prevent words from separating due to the word-wrap feature, you can insert a ***nonbreaking space***—a special character that keeps two or more words together. To insert a nonbreaking space, press Ctrl+Shift+Spacebar between the two words that you want to keep together. If a space already exists, the result of pressing the Spacebar, you should delete it before you insert the nonbreaking space.

Copying Formats with the Format Painter

You should format similar headings and text within a document with the same formatting. However, it is time-consuming to select every heading individually and apply the desired format (such as bold, underline, and font color). You can use the *Format Painter* to copy existing text formats to other text to ensure consistency. Using the Format Painter helps you improve your efficiency because you spend less time copying multiple formats rather than applying individual formats to each heading or block of text one at a time. When you single-click Format Painter in the Clipboard group on the Home tab, you can copy the formats only one time, then Word turns off Format Painter. When you double-click Format Painter, it stays activated so you can format an unlimited amount of text. To turn off Format Painter, click Format Painter once or press Esc.

Use the **Format Painter** to copy existing text formats to other text.

> You can use Format Painter to . . . ensure consistency . . . and improve your efficiency by spending less time copying multiple formats rather than applying individual formats to each heading or block of text one at a time.

Display Nonprinting Formatting Marks

As you type text, Word inserts nonprinting marks or symbols. While these symbols do not display on printouts, they do affect the appearance. For example, Word inserts a "code" every time you press Spacebar, Tab, and Enter. The paragraph mark ¶ at the end of a paragraph does more than just indicate the presence of a hard return. It also stores all of the formatting in effect for the paragraph. To preserve the formatting when you move or copy a paragraph, you must include the paragraph mark in the selected text. Click Show/Hide ¶ in the Paragraph group on the Home tab to display the paragraph mark and make sure it has been selected. Table 2.2 lists several common formatting marks. Both the hyphen and nonbreaking hyphen look like a regular hyphen when printed.

Table 2.2   Nonprinting Symbols

Symbol	Description	Create by
•	Regular space	Pressing Spacebar
°	Nonbreaking space	Pressing Ctrl+Shift+Spacebar
–	Regular hyphen	Pressing Hyphen
—	Nonbreaking hyphen	Pressing Ctrl+Shift+Hyphen
→	Tab	Pressing Tab
¶	End of paragraph	Pressing Enter
. . .	Hidden text	Selecting Hidden check box in Font dialog box
↵	Line break	Pressing Shift+Enter

Hands-On Exercises

1 | Character Formatting

Skills covered: 1. Change Text Appearance **2.** Insert Nonbreaking Spaces and Nonbreaking Hyphens
3. Highlight Text and Use Format Painter

Step 1
Change Text Appearance

Refer to Figure 2.5 as you complete Step 1.

a. Start Word. Open the *chap2_ho1_description* document in the **Exploring Word folder** and save it as **chap2_ho1_description_solution**.

You must select the text for which you want to adjust the character spacing.

b. Select the heading *Word Processing*, then click the **Font Dialog Box Launcher** in the Font group on the Home tab.

The Font dialog box displays with the Font tab options.

c. Click the **Character Spacing tab** and click the **Spacing drop-down arrow**. Select **Expanded** and notice how the text changes in the preview box. Click **OK**.

Word expands the spacing between letters in the heading *Word Processing*, as shown in Figure 2.5.

d. Save the document.

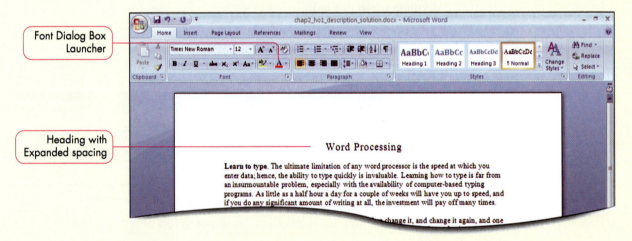

Figure 2.5 Text Formatting

Step 2
Insert Nonbreaking Spaces and Nonbreaking Hyphens

Refer to Figure 2.6 as you complete Step 2.

a. Place the insertion point between the words *you stare* in the third sentence of the second paragraph.

Before inserting a nonbreaking space, you must position the insertion point between the two words you want to keep together.

b. Delete the existing space, and then press **Ctrl+Shift+Spacebar** to insert a nonbreaking space.

The nonbreaking space keeps the words *you stare* together, preventing word wrapping between the two words.

c. Select the hyphen between the text *five-minute* in the third sentence of the sixth paragraph. Delete the hyphen, and then press **Ctrl+Shift+Hyphen** to insert a nonbreaking hyphen, as shown in Figure 2.6.

TROUBLESHOOTING: If text continues word-wrapping between two words after you insert a nonbreaking space or nonbreaking hyphen, click Show/Hide ¶ in the Paragraph group on the Home tab to display symbols and then identify and delete regular spaces or hyphens that still exist between words.

d. Save the document.

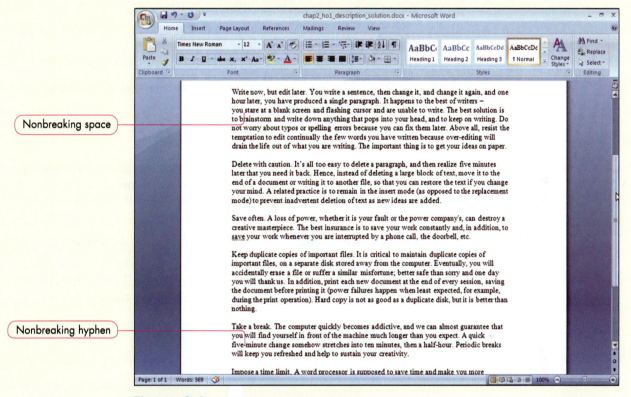

Figure 2.6 Nonbreaking Characters

TIP Another Way to Insert Nonbreaking Spaces and Hyphens

An alternative to using keyboard shortcuts to insert nonbreaking spaces and hyphens is to use the Symbols gallery on the Insert tab. Click **More Symbols** to display the Symbol dialog box, click the Special Characters tab, select the Nonbreaking Hyphen or the Nonbreaking Space character option, and click **Insert** to insert a nonbreaking hyphen or a nonbreaking space, respectively. Close the Symbol dialog box after inserting the nonbreaking hyphen or nonbreaking space.

Step 3
Highlight Text and Use Format Painter

Refer to Figure 2.7 as you complete Step 3.

a. Select the text *Learn to type.* in the first paragraph.

b. Click **Text Highlight Color** in the Font group on the Home tab.

Word highlighted the selected text in the default highlight color, yellow.

TROUBLESHOOTING: If Word applies a different color to the selected text, that means another highlight color was selected after starting Word. If this happens, select the text again, click the Text Highlight Color arrow, and select Yellow.

c. Click anywhere within the sentence *Learn to type.* Double-click **Format Painter** in the Clipboard group on the Home tab. (Remember that clicking the Format Painter button once, rather than double-clicking it, enables you to copy the format only one time.)

The mouse pointer changes to a paintbrush, as shown in Figure 2.7.

d. Drag the mouse pointer over the first sentence in the second paragraph, *Write now, but edit later.*, and release the mouse.

The formatting from the original sentence (bold font and yellow highlight) is applied to this sentence as well.

e. Drag the mouse pointer (in the shape of a paintbrush) over the remaining titles (the first sentence in each paragraph) to copy the formatting. You can click the scroll down arrow on the vertical scroll bar to display the other headings in the document.

f. Press **Esc** to turn off Format Painter after you copy the formatting to the last tip.

g. Save the *chap2_ho1_description_solution* document and keep it onscreen if you plan to continue with the next hands-on exercise. Close the file and exit Word if you will not continue with the next exercise at this time.

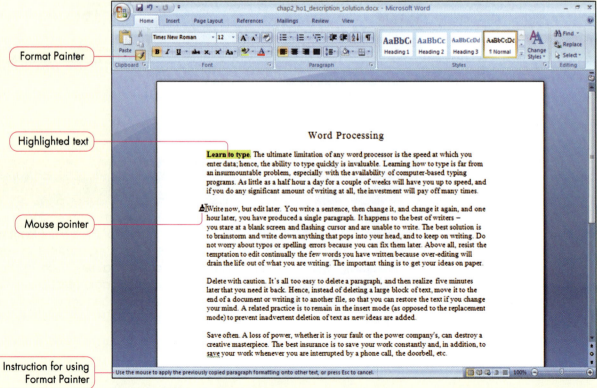

Figure 2.7 The Format Painter

Paragraph Formats

A change in typography is only one way to alter the appearance of a document. You also can change the alignment, indentation, tab stops, or line spacing for any paragraph(s) within the document. You can control the pagination and prevent the occurrence of awkward page breaks by specifying that an entire paragraph must appear on the same page, or that a one-line paragraph (e.g., a heading) should appear on the same page as the next paragraph. You can include borders or shading for added emphasis around selected paragraphs.

Word implements all of these paragraph formats for all selected paragraphs. If no paragraphs are selected, Word applies the formats to the current paragraph (the paragraph containing the insertion point), regardless of the position of the insertion point within the paragraph when you apply the paragraph formats.

(Word implements all of these paragraph formats for all selected paragraphs. If no paragraphs are selected, Word applies the feature to the current paragraph.)

In this section, you set tabs, apply borders, create lists, and format text into columns to help offset text for better readability. You also change text alignment, indent paragraphs, set line and paragraph spacing, and control pagination breaks.

Setting Off Paragraphs with Tabs, Borders, Lists, and Columns

Many people agree that their eyes tire and minds wander when they read page after page of plain black text on white paper. To break up long blocks of text or draw attention to an area of a page, you can format text with tabs, borders, lists, or columns. These formatting features enable you to modify positioning, frame a section, itemize for easy reading, order steps in a sequence, or create pillars of text for visual appeal and easy reading. For example, look through the pages of this book and notice the use of bulleted lists, tables for reference points, and borders around TIP boxes to draw your attention and enhance the pages.

Set Tabs

Tabs are markers for aligning text in a document.

Tabs are markers that specify the position for aligning text and add organization to a document. They often are used to create columns of text within a document. When you start a new document, the default tab stops are set every one-half inch across the page and are left aligned. Every time you press Tab, the insertion point moves over ½". You typically press Tab to indent the first line of paragraphs in double-spaced reports or the first line of paragraphs in a modified block style letter.

You access the Tabs feature by first clicking the Paragraph Dialog Box Launcher in the Paragraph group on the Home tab, then click the Tabs button. The Tabs dialog box displays so that you can set left, center, right, decimal, and bar tabs.

A **left tab** marks the position to align text on the left.

A **center tab** marks where text centers as you type.

A **right tab** marks the position to align text on the right.

A **decimal tab** marks where numbers align on a decimal point as you type.

A **bar tab** marks the location of a vertical line between columns.

- A **left tab** sets the start position on the left so as you type, text moves to the right of the tab setting.

- A **center tab** sets the middle point of the text you type; whatever you type will be centered on that tab setting.

- A **right tab** sets the start position on the right so as you type, text moves to the left of that tab setting and aligns on the right.

- A **decimal tab** aligns numbers on a decimal point. Regardless of how long the number, each number lines up with the decimal in the same position.

- A **bar tab** does not position text or decimals, but inserts a vertical bar at the tab setting. This bar is useful as a separator for text printed on the same line.

Instead of setting tabs in the Tabs dialog box, you can set tabs on the ruler. First, click the Tabs button to the left of the ruler (refer to Figure 2.8) until you see the tab alignment you want. Then click on the ruler in the location where you want to set the type of tab you selected. To delete a tab, click the tab marker on the ruler, then drag it down and off the ruler.

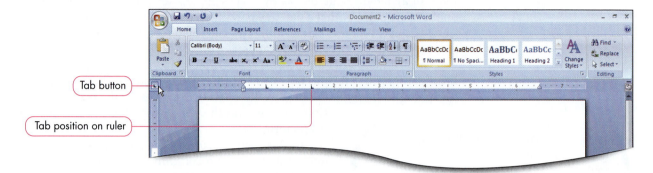

Tab button

Tab position on ruler

Figure 2.8 Tab Button and Ruler

TIP Deleting Default Tabs

When you set a tab on the ruler, Word deletes all of the default tab settings to the *left* of the tab you set. If you need to delete a single tab setting, click the tab marker on the ruler and drag it down. When you release the mouse, you delete the tab setting.

A *leader character* is dots or hyphens that connect two items.

In the Tabs dialog box, you also can specify a *leader character*, typically dots or hyphens, to draw the reader's eye across the page. For example, in a table of contents you can easily read a topic and the associated page where it is found when tab leaders connect the two, as shown in Figure 2.9. Notice also in Figure 2.9 that the default tab settings have been cleared, and a right tab is set at 5".

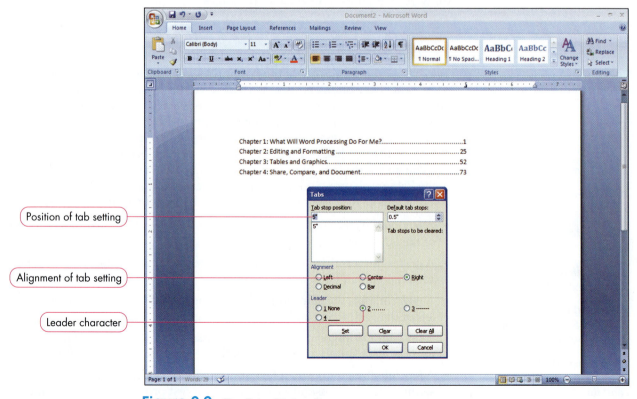

Position of tab setting

Alignment of tab setting

Leader character

Figure 2.9 The Tabs Dialog Box

Apply Borders and Shading

You can draw attention to a document or an area of a document by using the Borders and Shading command. A **border** is a line that surrounds a paragraph, a page, a table, or an image, similar to how a picture frame surrounds a photograph or piece of art. **Shading** is a background color that appears behind text in a paragraph, a page, or a table. You can apply specific borders, such as top, bottom, or outside, from the Border command in the Paragraph group on the Home tab. To allow more customization of borders, open the Borders and Shading dialog box when you click the Borders arrow in the Paragraph group on the Home tab, as shown in Figure 2.10. Borders or shading is applied to selected text within a paragraph, to the entire paragraph if no text is selected, to the entire page if the Page Border tab is selected, and also can be used on tables and images. You can create boxed and/or shaded text as well as place horizontal or vertical lines around different quantities of text. A good example of this practice is used in the *Exploring* series: The TIP boxes are surrounded by a border with dark shading and a white font color for the headings to attract your attention.

You can choose from several different line styles in any color, but remember you must use a color printer to display the line colors on the printed page. Colored lines appear in gray on a monochrome printer. You can place a uniform border around a paragraph (choose Box), or you can choose a shadow effect with thicker lines at the right and bottom. You also can apply lines to selected sides of a paragraph(s) by selecting a line style, then clicking the desired sides as appropriate.

The horizontal line button at the bottom of the Borders and Shading dialog box provides access to a variety of attractive horizontal line designs.

(Use page borders on . . . fliers, newsletters, and invitations, but not on formal documents such as research papers and professional reports.)

The Page Border tab enables you to place a decorative border around one or more selected pages. As with a paragraph border, you can place the border around the entire page, or you can select one or more sides. The page border also provides an additional option to use preselected clip art instead of ordinary lines. Note that it is appropriate to use page borders on documents such as fliers, newsletters, and invitations, but not on formal documents such as research papers and professional reports.

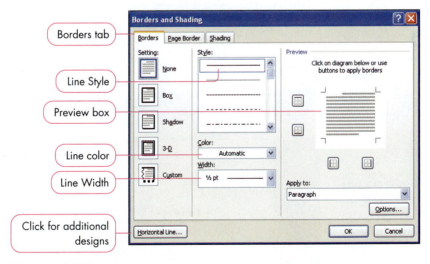

Figure 2.10 Apply a Border Around Text, Paragraphs, or Pages

Shading is applied independently of the border and is accessed from the Borders and Shading dialog box or from Shading in the Paragraph group on the Home tab. Clear (no shading) is the default. Solid (100%) shading creates a solid box where the text is turned white so you can read it. Shading of 10% or 20% generally is most effective to add emphasis to the selected paragraph (see Figure 2.11). The Borders and Shading command is implemented on the paragraph level and affects the entire paragraph unless text has been selected within the paragraph.

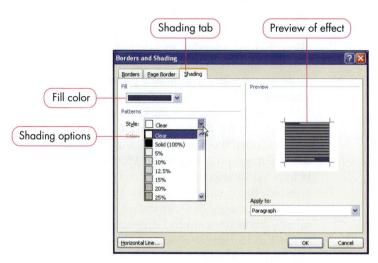

Figure 2.11 Apply Shading to Text or a Paragraph

Create Bulleted and Numbered Lists

A **bulleted list** itemizes and separates paragraph text to increase readability.

A **numbered list** sequences and prioritizes items.

A **multilevel list** extends a numbered list to several levels.

A list helps you organize information by highlighting important topics. A **bulleted list** itemizes and separates paragraphs to increase readability. A **numbered list** sequences and prioritizes the items and is automatically updated to accommodate additions or deletions. A **multilevel list** extends a numbered list to several levels, and it too is updated automatically when topics are added or deleted. You create each of these lists from the Paragraph group on the Home tab.

To apply bullet formatting to a list, click the Bullets arrow and choose one of several predefined symbols in the Bullet library (see Figure 2.12). Position your mouse over one of the bullet styles in the Bullet Library and a preview of that bullet style will display in your document. To use that style, simply click the bullet. If you want to use a different bullet symbol, click the Define New Bullet option below the Bullet Library to choose a different symbol or picture for the bullet.

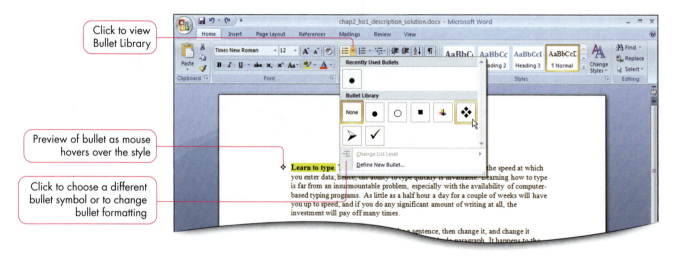

Figure 2.12 Bulleted List Options

Click the Numbering arrow in the Paragraph group to apply Arabic or Roman numerals, or upper- or lowercase letters, for a numbered list. When you position the mouse pointer over a style in the Numbering Library, you see a preview of that numbering style in your document. As with a bulleted list, you can define a new style by selecting the Define New Number Format option below the Numbering Library. Note, too, the options to restart or continue numbering found by selecting the Set Numbering Value option. These become important if a list appears in multiple places within a document. In other words, each occurrence of a list can start numbering anew, or it can continue from where the previous list left off.

The Mulitlevel List command enables you to create an outline to organize your thoughts in a hierarchical structure. As with the other types of lists, you can choose one of several default styles, and/or modify a style through the Define New Multilevel List option below the My Lists gallery. You also can specify whether each outline within a document is to restart its numbering, or whether it is to continue numbering from the previous outline.

Format Text into Columns

Columns format a section of a document into side-by-side vertical blocks.

Columns format a section of a document into side-by-side vertical blocks in which the text flows down the first column and then continues at the top of the next column. The length of a line of columnar text is shorter, enabling people to read through each article faster. To format text into columns, click the Page Layout tab and click Columns in the Page Setup group. From the Columns gallery, you can specify the number of columns or select More Columns to display the Columns dialog box. The Columns dialog box provides options for setting the number of columns and spacing between columns. Microsoft Word calculates the width of each column according to the left and right document margins on the page and the specified (default) space between columns.

The dialog box in Figure 2.13 implements a design of three equal columns. The 2" width of each column is computed based on current 1" left and right document margins and the ¼" spacing between columns. The width of each column is determined by subtracting the sum of the margins and the space between the columns (a total of 2½" in this example) from the page width of 8½". The result of the subtraction is 6", which is divided by 3 columns, resulting in a column width of 2".

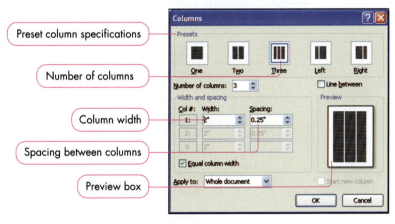

Figure 2.13 The Columns Dialog Box

One subtlety associated with column formatting is the use of sections, which control elements such as the orientation of a page (landscape or portrait), margins, page numbers, and the number of columns. All of the documents you have worked with so far have consisted of a single section, so section formatting was not an issue. It becomes important only when you want to vary an element that is formatted at the section level. You could, for example, use section formatting to create a document that has one column on its title page and two columns on the remaining pages. Creating this type of formatting requires you to divide the document into two sections by inserting a section break. You then format each section independently and specify the number of columns in each section. Table 2.3 guides you in formatting text into columns.

Table 2.3 Formatting with Columns

If your document contains . . .	And you want to apply column formatting to . . .	Do this:
only one section	the entire document	apply column formatting from anywhere within the document
two or more sections	only one section	position the insertion point in that section, and apply column formatting
one or more sections	only part of the document within a section	select the text you want to format, and then apply column formatting

Applying Paragraph Formats

The Paragraph group on the Home tab contains commands to set and control several format options for a paragraph. The options include alignment, indentation, line spacing, and pagination. These features also are found in the Paragraph dialog box. All of these formatting features are implemented at the paragraph level and affect all selected paragraphs. If no paragraphs are selected, Word applies the formatting to the current paragraph—the paragraph containing the insertion point.

Change Text Alignment

Horizontal alignment refers to the placement of text between the left and right margins.

Horizontal alignment refers to the placement of text between the left and right margins. Text is aligned in four different ways as shown in Figure 2.14. Alignment options are justified (flush left/flush right), left aligned (flush left with a ragged right margin), right aligned (flush right with a ragged left margin), or centered within the margins (ragged left and right). The default alignment is left.

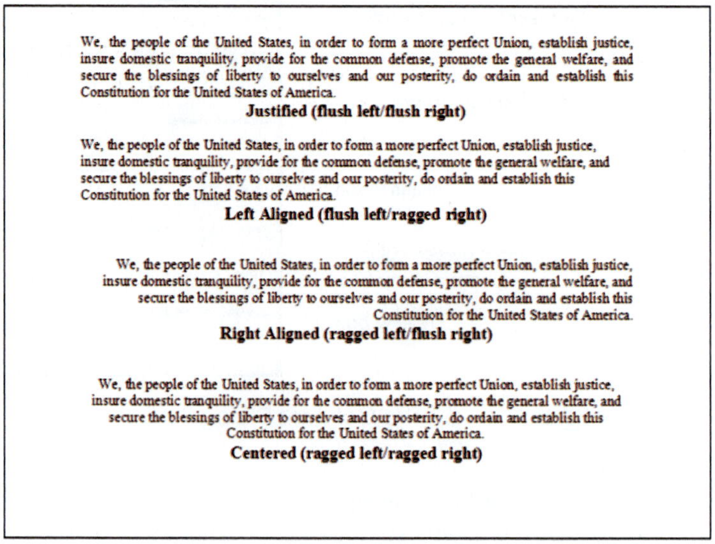

We, the people of the United States, in order to form a more perfect Union, establish justice, insure domestic tranquility, provide for the common defense, promote the general welfare, and secure the blessings of liberty to ourselves and our posterity, do ordain and establish this Constitution for the United States of America.
Justified (flush left/flush right)

We, the people of the United States, in order to form a more perfect Union, establish justice, insure domestic tranquility, provide for the common defense, promote the general welfare, and secure the blessings of liberty to ourselves and our posterity, do ordain and establish this Constitution for the United States of America.
Left Aligned (flush left/ragged right)

We, the people of the United States, in order to form a more perfect Union, establish justice, insure domestic tranquility, provide for the common defense, promote the general welfare, and secure the blessings of liberty to ourselves and our posterity, do ordain and establish this Constitution for the United States of America.
Right Aligned (ragged left/flush right)

We, the people of the United States, in order to form a more perfect Union, establish justice, insure domestic tranquility, provide for the common defense, promote the general welfare, and secure the blessings of liberty to ourselves and our posterity, do ordain and establish this Constitution for the United States of America.
Centered (ragged left/ragged right)

Figure 2.14 Horizontal Alignment

Left-aligned text is perhaps the easiest to read. The first letters of each line align with each other, helping the eye to find the beginning of each line. The lines themselves are of irregular length. Uniform spacing exists between words, and the ragged margin on the right adds white space to the text, giving it a lighter and more informal look.

Justified text, sometimes called fully justified, produces lines of equal length, with the spacing between words adjusted to align at the margins. Look closely and you will see many books, magazines, and newspapers fully justify text to add formality and "neatness" to the text. Some find this style more difficult to read because of the uneven (sometimes excessive) word spacing and/or the greater number of hyphenated words needed to justify the lines. But it also can enable you to pack more information onto a page when space is constrained.

Text that is centered or right aligned is usually restricted to limited amounts of text where the effect is more important than the ease of reading. Centered text, for example, appears frequently on wedding invitations, poems, or formal announcements. In research papers, first-level titles often are centered as well. Right-aligned text is used with figure captions and short headlines.

The Paragraph group on the Home tab contains the four alignment options: Align Text Left, Center, Align Text Right, and Justify. To apply the alignment, select text, then click the alignment option on the Home tab. You can also set alignment from the Paragraph dialog box; the Indents and Spacing tab contains an Alignment drop-down box in the General section.

Indent Paragraphs

You can indent individual paragraphs so they appear to have different margins from the rest of a document. Indentation is established at the paragraph level; thus, it is possible to apply different indentation properties to different paragraphs. You can indent one paragraph from the left margin only, another from the right margin only, and a third from both the left and right margins. For example, the fifth edition of the *Publication Manual of the American Psychological Association* specifies that quotations consisting of 40 or more words should be contained in a separate paragraph that is indented ½" from the left margin. Additionally, you can indent the first line of any paragraph differently from the rest of the paragraph. And finally, a paragraph may have no indentation at all, so that it aligns on the left and right margins.

Three settings determine the indentation of a paragraph: the left indent, the right indent, and a special indent, if any (see Figure 2.15). The left and right indents are set to 0 by default, as is the special indent, and produce a paragraph with no indentation at all. Positive values for the left and right indents offset the paragraph from both margins.

A **first line indent** marks the location to indent only the first line in a paragraph.

A **hanging indent** marks how far to indent each line of a paragraph except the first.

The two types of special indentation are first line and hanging. The **first line indent** affects only the first line in the paragraph, and you apply it by pressing the Tab key at the beginning of the paragraph or by setting a specific measurement in the Paragraph dialog box. Remaining lines in the paragraph align at the left margin. A **hanging indent** aligns the first line of a paragraph at the left margin and indents the remaining lines. Hanging indents often are used with bulleted or numbered lists and to format citations on a bibliography page.

Set Line and Paragraph Spacing

Line spacing is the space between the lines in a paragraph.

Line spacing determines the space between the lines in a paragraph and between paragraphs. Word provides complete flexibility and enables you to select any multiple of line spacing (single, double, line and a half, and so on). You also can specify line spacing in terms of points (1" vertical contains 72 points). Click the Line spacing command in the Paragraph group on the Home tab to establish line spacing for the current paragraph. You can also set line spacing in the *Spacing* section on the Indents and Spacing tab in the Paragraph dialog box.

Paragraph spacing is the amount of space before or after a paragraph.

Paragraph spacing is the amount of space before or after a paragraph, as indicated by the paragraph mark when you press Enter between paragraphs. Unlike line spacing that controls *all* spacing within and between paragraphs, paragraph spacing controls only the spacing between paragraphs.

Sometimes you need to single-space text within a paragraph but want to have a blank line between paragraphs. Instead of pressing Enter twice between paragraphs, you can set the paragraph spacing to control the amount of space before or after the paragraph. You can set paragraph spacing in the *Spacing* section on the Indents and Spacing tab in the Paragraph dialog box. Setting a 12-point *After* spacing creates the appearance of a double-space after the paragraph even though the user presses Enter only once between paragraphs.

The Paragraph dialog box is illustrated in Figure 2.15. The Indents and Spacing tab specifies a hanging indent, 1.5 line spacing, and justified alignment. The Preview area within the Paragraph dialog box enables you to see how the paragraph will appear within the document.

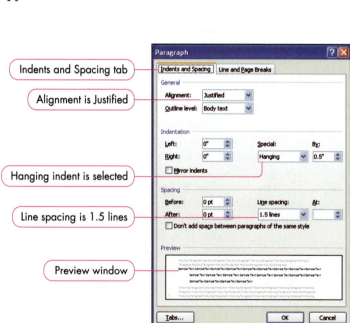

Figure 2.15 Indents and Spacing

Control Widows and Orphans

A **widow** is the last line of a paragraph appearing by itself at the top of a page.

An **orphan** is the first line of a paragraph appearing by itself at the bottom of a page.

Some lines become isolated from the remainder of a paragraph and seem out of place at the beginning or end of a multipage document. A **widow** refers to the last line of a paragraph appearing by itself at the top of a page. An **orphan** is the first line of a paragraph appearing by itself at the bottom of a page. You can prevent these from occurring by clicking the *Widow/Orphan control* check box in the *Pagination* section of the Line and Page Breaks tab of the Paragraph dialog box.

To prevent a page break from occurring within a paragraph and ensure that the entire paragraph appears on the same page use the *Keep lines together* option in the *Pagination* section of the Line and Page Breaks tab of the Paragraph dialog box. The paragraph is moved to the top of the next page if it does not fit on the bottom of the current page. Use the *Keep with next* option in the *Pagination* section to prevent a soft page break between the two paragraphs. This option is typically used to keep a heading (a one-line paragraph) with its associated text in the next paragraph. The check boxes in Figure 2.16 enable you to prevent the occurrence of awkward soft page breaks that detract from the appearance of a document.

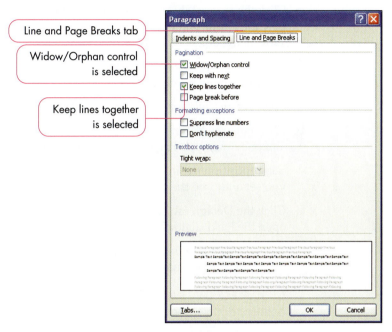

Figure 2.16 Line and Page Breaks

TIP   The Section Versus the Paragraph

Line spacing, alignment, tabs, and indents are implemented at the paragraph level. Change any of these parameters anywhere within the current (or selected) paragraph(s) and you change *only* those paragraph(s). Margins, page numbering, orientation, and columns are implemented at the section level. Change these parameters anywhere within a section and you change the characteristics of every page within that section.

Hands-On Exercises

2 | Paragraph Formatting

Skills covered: **1.** Set Tabs in a Footer **2.** Select Text to Format **3.** Specify Line Spacing, Justification, and Pagination **4.** Indent Text **5.** Apply Borders and Shading **6.** Change Column Structure **7.** Insert a Section Break and Create Columns

Step 1
Set Tabs in a Footer

Refer to Figure 2.17 as you complete Step 1.

a. Open the *chap2_ho1_description_solution* document if you closed it after the last hands-on exercise and save it as **chap2_ho2_description_solution**.

b. Click the **Insert tab**, and then click **Footer** in the Header & Footer group. Click **Edit Footer** and notice the document text is dimmed except for the footer area.

c. Click the **Home tab**, and then click the **Paragraph Dialog Box Launcher** to display the Paragraph dialog box. Click **Tabs** in the lower-left corner to display the Tabs dialog box.

This footer contains no tab settings. You will add a 3" center tab that will be used for a page number.

d. Type **3** in the *Tab stop position* box. Click **Center**, and then click **OK**.

e. Click near the bottom of your page to display the footer area, if necessary. Press **Tab** one time, type **Page**, and press **Spacebar** one time.

You reposition the insertion point to the middle of the footer area using the tab you set and type the text you want to precede the page number.

f. Click the **Design tab** and click **Quick Parts** in the Insert group, then click **Field** to open the Field dialog box. Click **Page** in the *Field names* box, then click **OK**.

The actual page number displays in the footer, as shown in Figure 2.17, and will automatically paginate for any additional pages added to your document.

TROUBLESHOOTING: If the page number is not horizontally centered at the 3" position, double-check the tab settings on the ruler. If tab settings appear to the left of the 3" tab setting, drag the tab markers off the ruler to delete them.

g. Click **Close Header and Footer** in the Close group of the Header and Footer Tools tab.

h. Save the document.

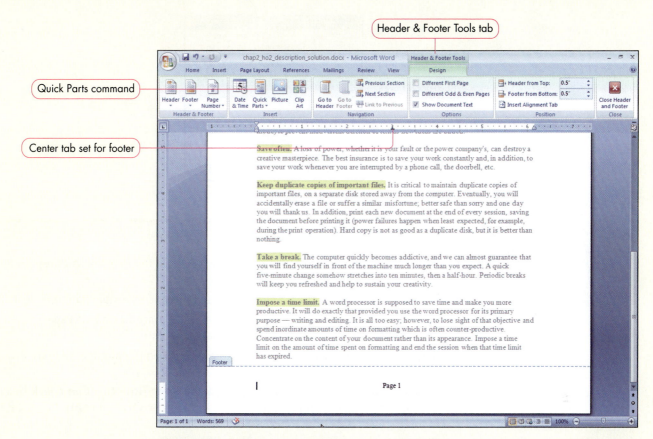

Header & Footer Tools tab

Quick Parts command

Center tab set for footer

Figure 2.17 Insert Tab in Footer

Step 2
Select Text to Format

Refer to Figure 2.18 as you complete Step 2.

a. Position your insertion point at the end of the title, *Word Processing*, then press **Ctrl+Enter**.

You inserted a manual page break between the title and the list of tips.

b. Click **Zoom** in the status bar to display the Zoom dialog box. Click **Many pages** and drag to select the first two icons that represent two pages, as shown in Figure 2.18. Click **OK**.

You can see the entire document as you select text to format.

c. Select the entire second page.

d. Save the document.

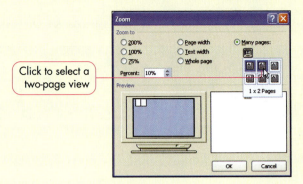

Click to select a two-page view

Figure 2.18 Zoom Dialog Box

Refer to Figure 2.19 as you complete Step 3.

a. Select page 2, if necessary, and then click **Justify** in the Paragraph group on the Home tab.

b. Click **Line Spacing** in the Paragraph group on the Home tab, and then select **1.5**.

These settings align the text on the right and left margins and add spacing before and after lines of text, making it easier to read.

c. Right-click the selected text and select **Paragraph** on the menu to display the Paragraph dialog box.

d. Click the **Line and Page Breaks tab**. Click the **Keep lines together check box** in the *Pagination* section, if necessary. Click the **Widow/Orphan control check box** in the *Pagination* section, if necessary.

e. Click **OK** to accept the settings and close the dialog box.

These settings prevent paragraphs from being split at a page break.

f. Click anywhere in the document to deselect the text and see the effects of the formatting changes that were just specified.

Three paragraphs now display on a third page, and none are split at the page break, as shown in Figure 2.19.

g. Save the document.

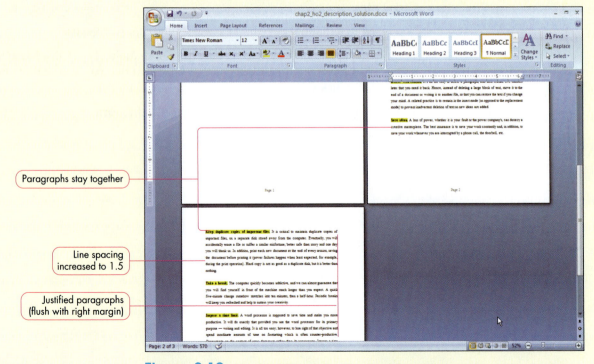

Paragraphs stay together

Line spacing increased to 1.5

Justified paragraphs (flush with right margin)

Figure 2.19 Result of Changing Line Spacing, Alignment, and Pagination

Step 4
Indent Text

Refer to Figure 2.20 as you complete Step 4.

a. Click the **Zoom slider** in the status bar and select **100%**. Select the second paragraph, as shown in Figure 2.20.

The second paragraph will not be indented yet.

b. Right-click the selected text and select **Paragraph** from the shortcut menu.

c. If necessary, click the **Indents and Spacing tab** in the Paragraph dialog box.

d. Click the **Left indentation** up arrow to display 0.5". Set the **Right indention** to 0.5" also. Click **OK**.

Your document should match Figure 2.20.

e. Save the document.

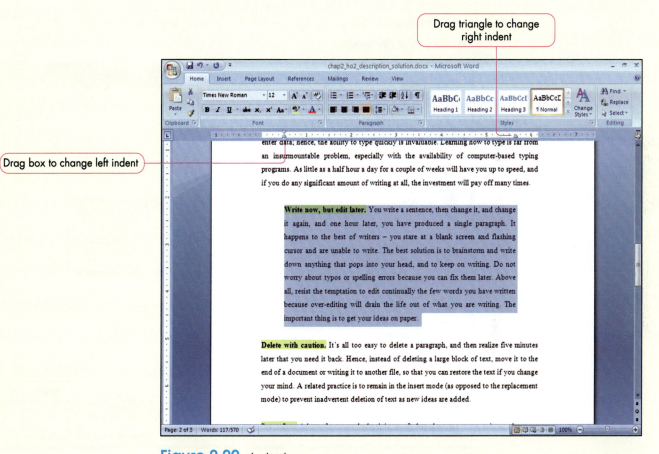

Figure 2.20 Indent

TIP | **Indents and the Ruler**

You can use the ruler to change the special, left, and/or right indents. Select the paragraph (or paragraphs) in which you want to change indents, and then drag the appropriate indent markers to the new location(s) on the ruler. If you get a hanging indent when you wanted to change the left indent, it means you dragged the bottom triangle instead of the box. Click Undo on the Quick Access Toolbar and try again. You can always use the Paragraph dialog box rather than the ruler if you continue to have difficulty.

Step 5
Apply Borders and Shading

Refer to Figure 2.21 as you complete Step 5.

a. Click the **Home tab**, click the **Borders arrow**, and then click **Borders and Shading** to display the Borders and Shading dialog box shown in Figure 2.21.

b. Click the **Borders tab**, if necessary, then click the double line style in the *Style* list. Click ¾ **pt** in the *Width* list, then click **Box** in the *Setting* section.

A preview of these settings will display on the right side of the window in the Preview area.

c. Click the **Shading tab**, then click the **Fill drop-down arrow** and select **Dark Blue, Text 2, Lighter 80%** from the palette. It is located in the fourth column from the left and in the second row from the top. Click **OK** to accept the settings for both Borders and Shading.

The paragraph is surrounded by a ¾ point double-line border, and a light blue shading appears behind the text.

d. Click outside the paragraph to deselect it and view your formatting changes.

e. Save the document.

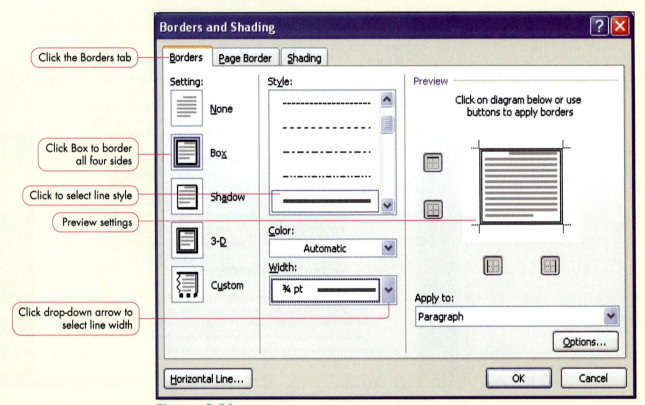

Figure 2.21 Borders and Shading Dialog Box

Step 6
Change Column Structure

Refer to Figure 2.22 as you complete Step 6.

a. Click the **Page Layout tab** and click **Margins** in the Page Setup group. Click **Custom Margins** and select the **Margins tab** if necessary.

b. Click the spin arrows to set **1"** left and right margins. Click **OK**.

The document is now formatted by 1" left, right, top, and bottom margins.

c. Click the **Zoom button** in the status bar, select **Page width,** and then click **OK**. Press **PgUp** or **PgDn** on the keyboard to scroll until the second page comes into view.

d. Click anywhere in the paragraph, *Write now, but edit later*. Right-click and select **Paragraph**, click the **Indents and Spacing tab** if necessary, then change left and right to **0"** in the *Indentation* section. Click **OK**.

These settings prepare your document for the changes you make in the next steps.

e. Click the **Page Layout tab** and click **Columns** in the Page Setup group. Click **More Columns** to display the Columns dialog box.

Because you will change several settings related to columns, you clicked the More Columns option instead of clicking the gallery option to create three columns.

f. Click **Three** in the *Presets* section of the dialog box. The default spacing between columns is 0.5", which leads to a column width of 1.83". Change the spacing to **.25"** in the **Spacing** list, which automatically changes the column width to 2".

g. Click the **Line between** check box, as shown in Figure 2.22. Click **OK**.

The document is now formatted in three columns with 0.25" space between columns. Vertical lines appear between columns.

h. Save the document.

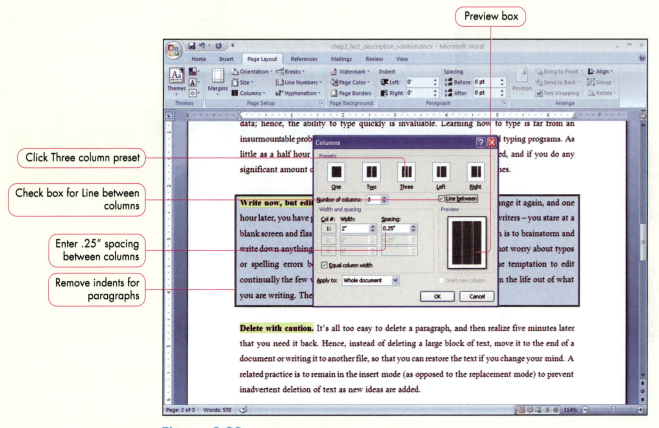

Figure 2.22 Change Column Structure

Refer to Figure 2.23 as you complete Step 7.

Step 7
Insert a Section Break and Create Columns

a. Click **Zoom** on the status bar to display the Zoom dialog box. Click **Many pages**, drag to select **1x3** Pages, and then click **OK**.

The document displays the column formatting.

b. Place the insertion point immediately to the left of the first paragraph on the second page. Click the **Page Layout tab** and click **Breaks** to display the list shown in Figure 2.23. Click **Continuous** under *Section Breaks*.

c. Click anywhere on the title page, above the section break you just inserted. Click **Columns**, then click **One** to display the content in one column.

The formatting for the first section of the document (the title page) should change to one column; the title of the document is centered across the entire page.

d. Save and close the *chap2_ho2_description_solution* document. Exit Word if you will not continue with the next exercise at this time.

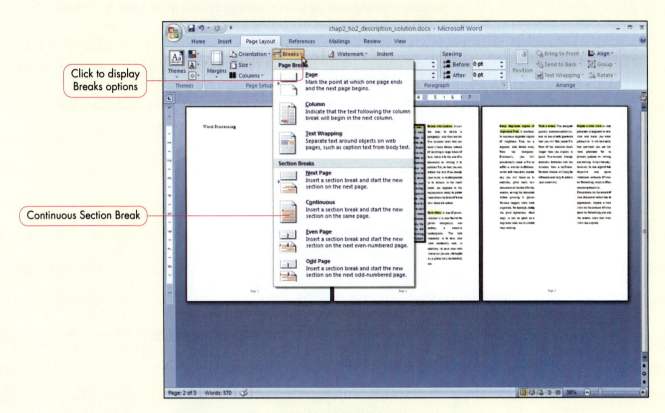

Figure 2.23   Insert a Continuous Section Break

Styles and Document References

As you complete reports, assignments, and projects for other classes or in your job, you probably apply the same text, paragraph, table, and list formatting for similar documents. Instead of formatting each document individually, you can create your own custom style to save time in setting particular formats for titles, headings, and paragraphs. Styles and other features in Word then can be used to automatically generate reference pages such as a table of contents and indexes.

In this section, you create and modify styles. You also display a document in the Outline view. Finally, you learn how to use the AutoFormat feature.

Creating and Modifying Styles

One way to achieve uniformity throughout a document is to store the formatting information as a style. Change the style and you automatically change all text defined by that style.

One characteristic of a professional document is the uniform formatting that is applied to similar elements throughout the document. Different elements have different formatting. For headings you can use one font, color, style, and size, and then use a completely different format design on text below those headings. The headings may be left aligned, while the text is fully justified. You can format lists and footnotes in entirely different styles.

One way to achieve uniformity throughout the document is to use the Format Painter to copy the formatting from one occurrence of each element to the next, but this step is tedious and inefficient. And if you were to change your mind after copying the formatting throughout a document, you would have to repeat the entire process all over again. A much easier way to achieve uniformity is to store all the formatting information together, which is what we refer to as a *style*. Styles automate the formatting process and provide a consistent appearance to a document. It is possible to store any type of character or paragraph formatting within a style, and once a style is defined, you can apply it to any element within a document to produce identical formatting. Change the style and you automatically change all text defined by that style.

A *style* is a set of formatting options you apply to characters or paragraphs.

Styles are created on the character or paragraph level. A *character style* stores character formatting (font, size, and style) and affects only the selected text. A *paragraph style* stores paragraph formatting such as alignment, line spacing, indents, tabs, text flow, and borders and shading, as well as the font, size, and style of the text in the paragraph. A paragraph style affects the current paragraph or, if selected, multiple paragraphs. You create and apply styles from the Styles group on the Home tab, as shown in Figure 2.24.

A *character style* stores character formatting and affects only selected text.

A *paragraph style* stores paragraph formatting of text.

The Normal template contains more than 100 styles. Unless you specify a style, Word uses the Normal style. The Normal style contains these settings: 11-point Calibri, 1.15 line spacing, 10-point spacing after, left horizontal alignment, and Widow/Orphan control. You can create your own styles to use in a document, modify or delete an existing style, and even add your new style to the Normal template for use in other documents.

The document in Figure 2.25 is a report about the Great Depression. Each paragraph begins with a one-line heading, followed by the supporting text. The task pane in the figure displays all of the styles used in the document. The Normal style contains the default paragraph settings (left aligned, 1.15 line spacing, 10 pt. spacing after, and a default font) and is assigned automatically to every paragraph unless a different style is specified. The Clear All style removes all formatting from selected text. It is the Heading 3 and Body Text styles, however, that are of interest to us, as these styles have been applied throughout the document to the associated elements.

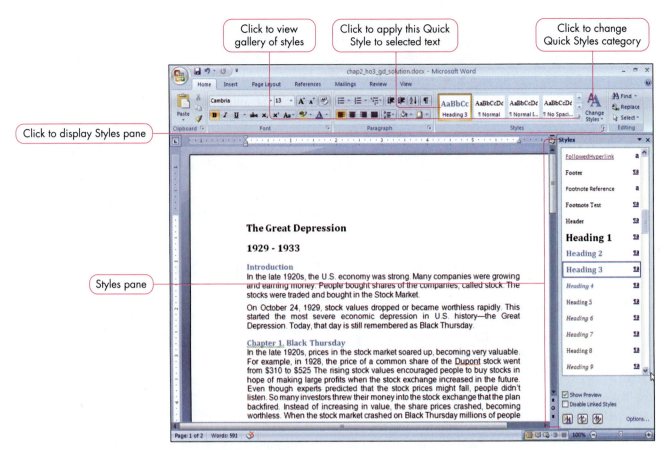

Click to view gallery of styles

Click to apply this Quick Style to selected text

Click to change Quick Styles category

Click to display Styles pane

Styles pane

Figure 2.24 The Styles Group

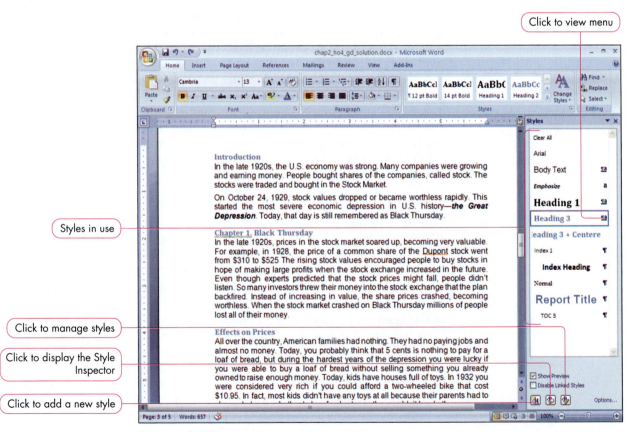

Click to view menu

Styles in use

Click to manage styles

Click to display the Style Inspector

Click to add a new style

Figure 2.25 Styles Task Pane

You can change the specifications of a style by clicking the down arrow for the particular style, then selecting Modify. The specifications for the Heading 3 style are shown in Figure 2.26. The current settings within the Heading 3 style call for 13-point Cambria bold type using a custom color. There is a 12-point space before the text, and the heading appears on the same page as the next paragraph. The preview frame in the dialog box shows how paragraphs formatted in this style display. Click the Format button in the Modify Style dialog box to select and open other dialog boxes where you modify settings that are used in the style. And, as indicated earlier, any changes to the style are reflected automatically in any text or element defined by that style.

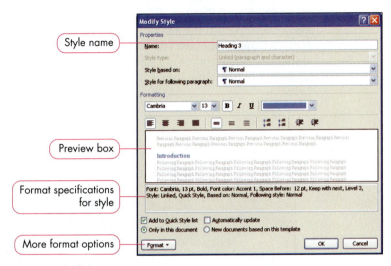

Figure 2.26 Modify a Style

TIP Styles and Paragraphs

A paragraph style affects the entire paragraph; that is, you cannot apply a paragraph style to only part of a paragraph. To apply a style to an existing paragraph, place the insertion point anywhere within the paragraph, click the Styles Dialog Box Launcher on the Home tab to display the Styles pane, then click the name of the style you want to use. The Styles pane can display in several locations. Initially, it might display as a floating window, but you can drag the title bar to move it. Drag to the far left or right side, and it will dock on that side of the window.

Use the Styles Pane Options

When you display the Styles pane in your document, it might contain only the styles used in the document, as in Figure 2.25, or it might list every style in the Word document template. If the Styles pane only displays styles used in the document, you are unable to view or apply other styles. You can change the styles that display in the Styles pane by using the Styles Gallery Options dialog box, which displays when you click *Options* in the lower-right corner of the Styles pane. In the *Select styles to show* box, you select from several options including Recommended, In use, In current document, and All styles. Select *In use* to view only styles used in this document; select *All styles* to view all styles created for the document template as well as any custom styles you create. Other options are available in this dialog box, including how to sort the styles when displayed and whether to show Paragraph or Font or both types of styles. To view the style names with their styles applied, click the *Show Preview* check box near the bottom of the Styles pane.

Reveal Formatting

To display complete format properties for selected text in the document, use the Reveal Formatting task pane, as shown in Figure 2.27. The properties are displayed by Font, Paragraph, and Section, enabling you to click the plus or minus sign next to each item to view or hide the underlying details. The properties in each area are links to the associated dialog boxes. Click Alignment or Justification, for example, within the Paragraph area to open the Paragraph dialog box, where you can change the indicated property. This panel is often helpful for troubleshooting a format problem in a document. To view this pane, click the Styles Dialog Box Launcher on the Home tab, click Style Inspector at the bottom of the Styles pane, then click Reveal Formatting in the Style Inspector pane. If you use this feature often, you can add it to the Quick Access Toolbar. To add it, click the Office Button, then click Word Options; select *Customize* on the left side of the Word Options dialog box, then click the drop-down arrow for *Choose commands from* and select *All Commands*. Scroll down the alphabetical list and select *Reveal Formatting*, then click the Add button displayed between the two large lists. Click OK to save the addition.

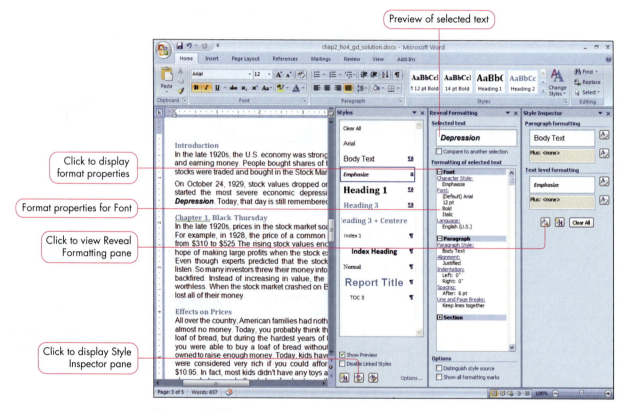

Figure 2.27 Reveal Formatting

Use the Outline View

Outline view is a structural view that displays varying amounts of detail.

One additional advantage of styles is that they enable you to view a document in the Outline view. The *Outline view* does not display a conventional outline, but rather a structural view of a document that can be collapsed or expanded as necessary. Consider, for example, Figure 2.28, which displays the Outline view of a report about the Great Depression. The heading for each tip is formatted according to the Heading 3 style. The text of each tip is formatted according to the Body Text style.

The advantage of Outline view is that you can collapse or expand portions of a document to provide varying amounts of detail. We have, for example, collapsed almost the entire document in Figure 2.28, displaying the headings while suppressing the body text. We also expanded the text for two sections (*Introduction* and *The New Deal*) for purposes of illustration.

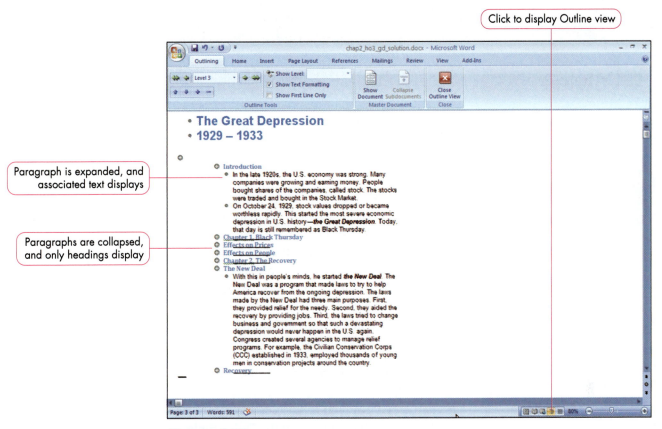

Paragraph is expanded, and associated text displays

Paragraphs are collapsed, and only headings display

Figure 2.28   The Outline View

Now assume that you want to move one paragraph from its present position to a different position in the document. Without the Outline view, the text might stretch over several pages, making it difficult to see the text of both areas at the same time. Using the Outline view, however, you can collapse what you do not need to see, then simply click and drag headings to rearrange the text within the document. The Outline view is very useful with long documents, but it requires the use of styles throughout the document.

TIP   The Outline Versus the Outline View

A conventional outline is created as a multilevel list using the Multilevel List command in the Paragraph group on the Home tab. Text for the outline is entered in the Print Layout view, *not* the Outline view. The latter provides a condensed view of a document that is used in conjunction with styles.

Use the AutoFormat Feature

Styles are extremely powerful. They enable you to impose uniform formatting within a document, and they let you take advantage of the Outline view. What if, however, you have an existing or lengthy document that does not contain any styles (other than the default Normal style, which is applied to every paragraph)? Do you have to manually go through every paragraph in order to apply the appropriate style? Fortunately, the answer is no, because the AutoFormat feature provides a quick solution. The **AutoFormat** feature analyzes a document and formats it for you; it evaluates an entire document and determines how each paragraph is used, then it applies an appropriate style to each paragraph. To use the AutoFormat feature, you must add it to the Quick Access Toolbar using the same procedure explained previously in the Reveal Formatting section.

The **AutoFormat** feature analyzes a document and formats it for you.

Hands-On Exercises

3 | Styles

Skills covered: 1. Apply Style Properties **2.** Modify the Body Text Style **3.** Modify the Heading 3 Style **4.** Select the Outline View **5.** Create a Paragraph Style **6.** Create a Character Style **7.** View the Completed Document

---

Step 1
Apply Style Properties

Refer to Figure 2.29 as you complete Step 1.

a. Open the document *chap2_ho3_gd* in the **Exploring Word folder** and save it as **chap2_ho3_gd_solution**.

b. Press **Ctrl+Home** to move to the beginning of the document.

Notice the headings have been formatted with 12-point bold font.

c. Select the first two lines, *The Great Depression* and *1929–1933*, then click **Heading 1** from the Quick Style gallery in the Styles group on the Home tab.

d. Click anywhere in the word *Introduction*. Click the **Styles Dialog Box Launcher** on the Home tab. Double-click the title bar of the task pane to dock it, if necessary, so it does not float on the screen. Click the down arrow that displays when you hover over the *12 pt Bold* style listed in the Styles pane, then click **Select All 7 Instance(s)**.

All paragraph headings in this document are selected, as shown in Figure 2.29.

e. Click **More** on the right side of the **Quick Style** gallery in the Styles group on the Home tab to display more styles, then click the **Heading 3** style.

When you hover your mouse over the different styles in the gallery, the Live Preview feature displays the style on your selected text but will not apply it until you click on the style.

f. Save the document.

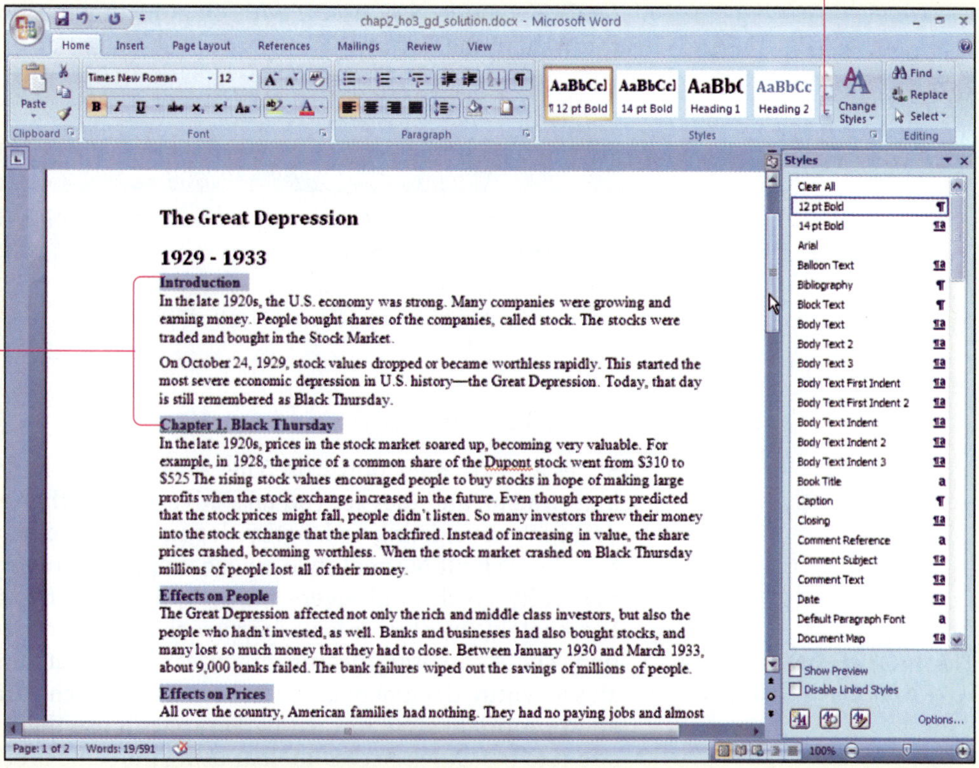

Click to view more formats

Style applied to text

Figure 2.29 View Style Properties

Refer to Figure 2.30 as you complete Step 2.

a. Press **Ctrl+Home** to move to the beginning of the document. Place the insertion point in the first paragraph, then notice the Body Text style is selected in the Styles pane. Click the down arrow next to the style and click **Modify** to display the Modify Style dialog box.

> **TROUBLESHOOTING:** If you click the style name instead of the down arrow, you will apply the style to the selected text instead of modifying it. Click Undo on the Quick Access Toolbar to cancel the command. Click the down arrow next to the style name to display the associated menu and click the Modify command to display the Modify Style dialog box.

b. Change the font to **Arial**. Click **Justify** to change the alignment of every paragraph in the document formatted with the *Body Text* style.

c. Click **Format** in the lower-left corner of the window, as shown in Figure 2.30, then click **Paragraph** to display the Paragraph dialog box. If necessary, click the **Line and Page Breaks tab**.

The box for Widow/Orphan control is checked by default. This option ensures that any paragraph defined by the Body Text style will not be split, leaving a single line of text at the bottom or top of a page.

d. Click the **Keep lines together check box** in the *Pagination* section.

This option is a more stringent requirement and ensures that the entire paragraph is not split.

e. Click **OK** to close the Paragraph dialog box. Click **OK** to close the Modify Style dialog box.

All of the multiline paragraphs in the document change automatically to reflect the new definition of the Body Text style, which includes full justification, a new font, and ensuring that a paragraph is not split across pages.

f. Save the document.

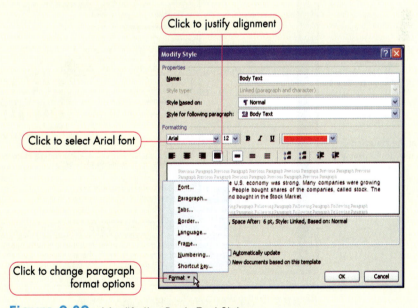

Figure 2.30 Modify the Body Text Style

Refer to Figure 2.31 as you complete Step 3.

a. Place the insertion point in one of the headings that has been formatted with the *Heading 3* style. Scroll, if necessary, to view *Heading 3* in the Styles pane. Hover your mouse over Heading 3, click the down arrow, then click **Modify** to display the Modify Style dialog box.

b. Click the **Font Color drop-down arrow** to display the palette in Figure 2.31. Click **Blue, Accent 1**, the blue color swatch on the first row, to change the color of all of the headings in the document.

c. Click **Format** at the bottom of the dialog box, then click **Paragraph** to display the Paragraph dialog box. Click the **Indents and Spacing tab**, then change the **Spacing After** to 0. Click **OK** to accept the settings and close the Paragraph dialog box.

You modified the style by changing the spacing after the heading to 0, which forces the paragraph text to display closer to the heading.

d. Click **OK** to close the Modify Style dialog box.

The formatting in your document has changed to reflect the changes in the Heading 3 style.

e. Save the document.

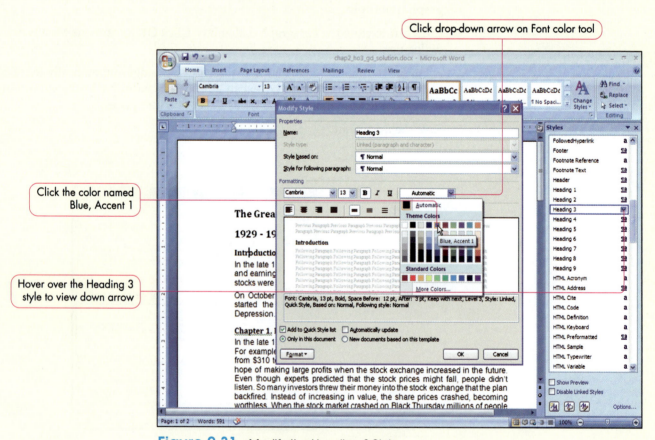

Figure 2.31 Modify the Heading 3 Style

Step 4
Select the Outline View

Refer to Figure 2.32 as you complete Step 4.

a. Close the Styles pane. Click the **View tab**, then click **Outline** to display the document in Outline view.

b. Place the insertion point to the left of the first paragraph heading, *Introduction*, and select the rest of the document. Click the **Outlining tab**, if necessary, then click **Collapse** in the Outline Tools group.

The entire document collapses so that only the headings display.

c. Click in the heading titled *The New Deal*, as shown in Figure 2.32. Click **Expand** in the Outline Tools group to see the subordinate items under this heading.

d. Select the paragraph heading *Effects on Prices*, then click **Move Up** on the Outline Tools group.

You moved the paragraph above the paragraph that precedes it in the outline. Note that you also can drag and drop a selected paragraph.

e. Save the document.

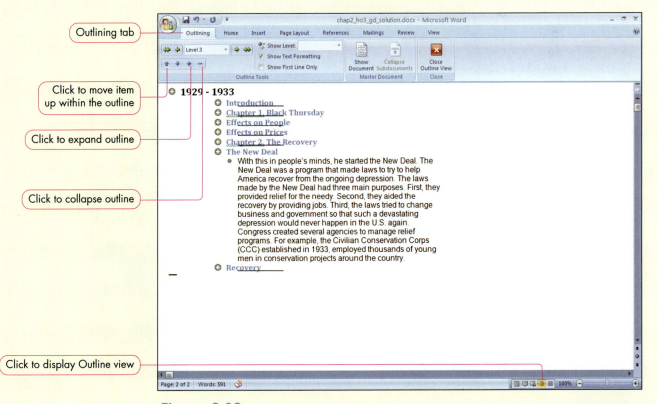

Figure 2.32 The Outline View

Refer to Figure 2.33 as you complete Step 5.

a. Click Close Outline View to change to return to Print Layout view. Click the **Home tab**, if necessary, and then click the **Styles Dialog Box Launcher** to open the Styles pane.

b. Press **Ctrl+Home** to move the insertion point to the beginning of the document, then place the insertion point to the right of *1933* and press **Ctrl+Enter**.

Inserting a page break creates space where you can add a title page.

c. Press **Ctrl+Home** to move the insertion point to the beginning of the new page, then select both lines on the title page. Scroll up if necessary and click **Clear All** in the Styles pane. Click the **Font arrow** on the Home tab and select **Arial**, then click the **Font Size arrow**, select **24**, and click **Bold** and **Center** in the Paragraph group on the Home tab. Click the **Font Color arrow** and select **Blue, Accent 1** on the color palette (the blue color swatch on the first row) to change the color of the text to blue.

The Styles task pane displays the specifications for the text you just entered. You have created a new style, but the style is not yet named.

d. Point to the description for the title on the Styles pane (you may only be able to see the first or last few format effects such as Bold, Accent 1), hover your mouse over the description to view the down arrow, click the down arrow, as shown in Figure 2.33, and then select **Modify Style** to display the Modify Style dialog box.

e. Click in the **Name text box** in the Properties area and type **Report Title** as the name of the new style. Click **OK**.

f. Save the document.

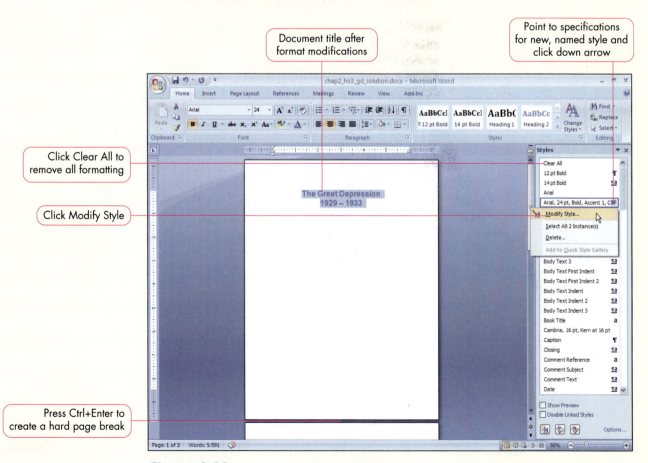

Figure 2.33 Create a Paragraph Style

Refer to Figure 2.34 as you complete Step 6.

a. Select the words *the Great Depression* (that appear within the second paragraph of the Introduction). Click **Bold** and **Italic** in the Font group on the Home tab.

b. Click **New Style** on the bottom of the Styles pane, and then type **Emphasize** as the name of the style.

c. Click the **Style type drop-down arrow** and select **Character** (see Figure 2.34). Click **OK**.

The style named Emphasize is listed in the Style pane and can be used throughout your document.

d. Select the words *the New Deal* in the first sentence of the *New Deal* section. Click **More** in the Quick Style gallery on the Home tab and apply the newly created *Emphasize* character style to the selected text. Close the Styles task pane.

e. Save the document.

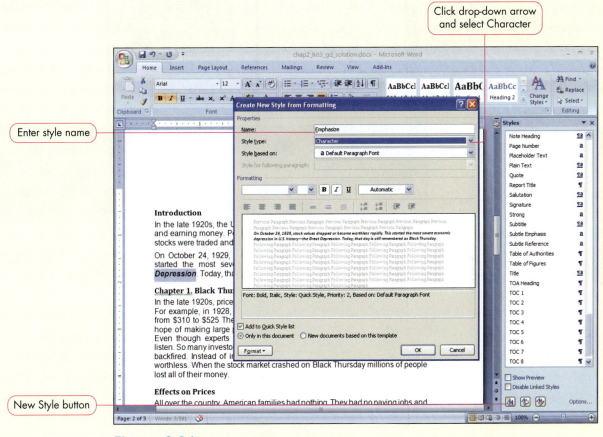

Figure 2.34 Create a Character Style

Refer to Figure 2.35 as you complete Step 7.

a. Click **Zoom** on the status bar, click **Many pages**, then click and drag to select 1 x 3 pages. Click **OK**.

You should see a multipage display similar to Figure 2.35. The text on the individual pages is too small to read, but you can see the page breaks and overall document flow. According to the specifications in the Body Text style, the paragraphs should all be justified and each should fit completely on one page without spilling over to the next page.

b. Click to the left of the title on the first page and press **Enter** three times to position the title further down the page.

c. Save the *chap2_ho3_gd_solution* document and keep it onscreen if you plan to continue with the next hands-on exercise. Close the file and exit Word if you will not continue with the next exercise at this time.

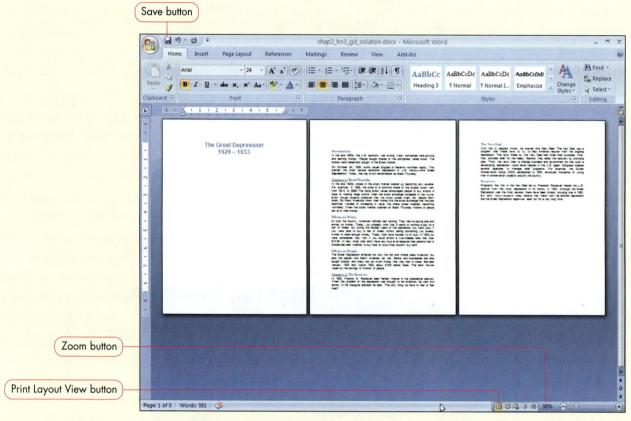

Figure 2.35 The Completed Document

Table of Contents and Indexes

Well-prepared long documents include special features to help readers locate information easily. You can use Word to help you create these supplemental document components with minimal effort.

Well-prepared long documents include special features to help readers locate information easily. For example, people often refer to the table of contents or the index in a long document—such as a book, reference manual, or company policy—to locate particular topics within that document. You can use Word to help you create these supplemental document components with minimal effort.

In this section, you generate a table of contents at the beginning of a document. You then learn how to designate text to include in an index and then generate the index at the end of a document.

Creating a Table of Contents

A **table of contents** lists headings and the page numbers where they appear in a document.

A **table of contents** lists headings in the order they appear in a document and the page numbers where the entries begin. Word can create the table of contents automatically, if you apply a style to each heading in the document. You can use built-in styles, Heading 1 through Heading 9, or identify your own custom styles to use when generating the table of contents. Word also will update the table to accommodate the addition or deletion of headings and/or changes in page numbers brought about through changes in the document.

The table of contents is located on the References tab. You can select from several predefined formats such as Classic and Formal, as well as determine how many levels to display in the table; the latter correspond to the heading styles used within the document. You can determine whether or not to right-align the page numbers; and you also can choose to include a leader character to draw the reader's eyes across the page from a heading to a page number.

Creating an Index

An **index** is a listing of topics and the page numbers where the topic is discussed.

An index puts the finishing touch on a long document. The **index** provides an alphabetical listing of topics covered in a document, along with the page numbers where the topic is discussed. Typically, the index appears at the end of a book or document. Word will create an index automatically, provided that the entries for the index have been previously marked. This result, in turn, requires you to go through a document, select the terms to be included in the index, and mark them accordingly. It is not as tedious as it sounds. You can, for example, select a single occurrence of an entry and tell Word to mark all occurrences of that entry for the index. You also can create cross-references, such as "see also Internet."

After you specify the entries, create the index by choosing the Insert Index command on the References tab. You can choose a variety of styles for the index, just as you can for the table of contents. Word arranges the index entries in alphabetical order and enters the appropriate page references. You also can create additional index entries and/or move text within a document, then update the index with the click of a mouse.

Table of Contents and Index Styles | Reference

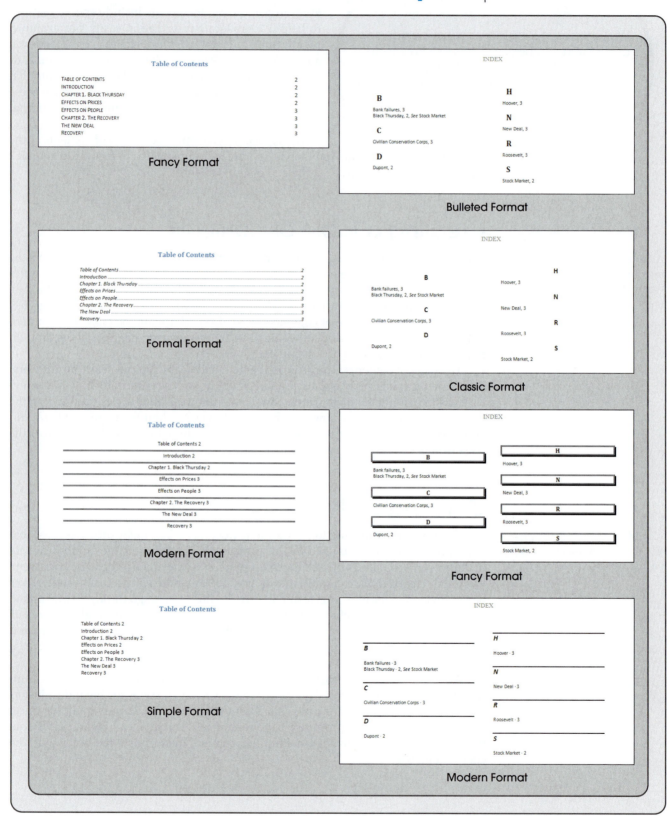

Fancy Format

Formal Format

Modern Format

Simple Format

Bulleted Format

Classic Format

Fancy Format

Modern Format

Hands-On Exercises

4 | Reference Pages

Skills covered: 1. Apply a Style **2.** Insert a Table of Contents **3.** Define an Index Entry **4.** Create the Index
5. Complete the Index **6.** View the Completed Document

<table>
<tr><td>

Step 1

Apply a Style

</td><td>

Refer to Figure 2.36 as you complete Step 1.

a. Open the *chap2_ho3_gd_solution* document if you closed it after the last hands-on exercise and save it as **chap2_ho4_gd_solution**.

b. Click **Zoom** in the status bar, click **Page width**, then click **OK**. Scroll to the top of the second page.

c. Click to the left of the *Introduction* title. Type **Table of Contents**, and then press **Enter** two times. Press **Ctrl+Enter** to insert a page break.

The table of contents displays on a page between the title page and the body of the document using the Heading 3 style you modified in the previous exercise.

d. Click anywhere in the *Table of Contents* heading.

TROUBLESHOOTING: If the Heading 3 style does not display, click Heading 3 from the Quick Style gallery on the Home tab.

e. Click **Center** in the Paragraph group on the Home tab and compare your document to Figure 2.36.

f. Save the document.

</td></tr>
</table>

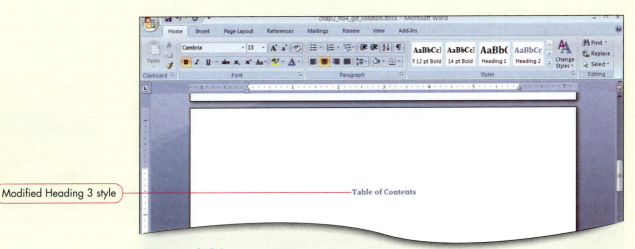

Modified Heading 3 style

Table of Contents

Figure 2.36 Apply a Style to a Heading

Refer to Figure 2.37 as you complete Step 2.

a. Place the insertion point immediately under the *Table of Contents* title, then click **Zoom** on the status bar. Click **Many pages**, then click and drag to select 1 x 4 pages. Click **OK**.

The display changes to show all four pages in the document.

b. Click the **References tab**, and then click **Table of Contents** in the Table of Contents group. Select **Insert Table of Contents**.

The Table of Contents dialog box displays (see Figure 2.37).

c. If necessary, click the **Show page numbers check box** and the **Right align page numbers check box**.

d. Click the **Formats drop-down arrow** in the *General* section and select **Distinctive**. Click the **Tab leader drop-down arrow** in the *Print Preview* section and choose a **dot leader**. Click **OK**.

Word takes a moment to create the table of contents, and then displays it in the location of your insertion point.

e. Save the document.

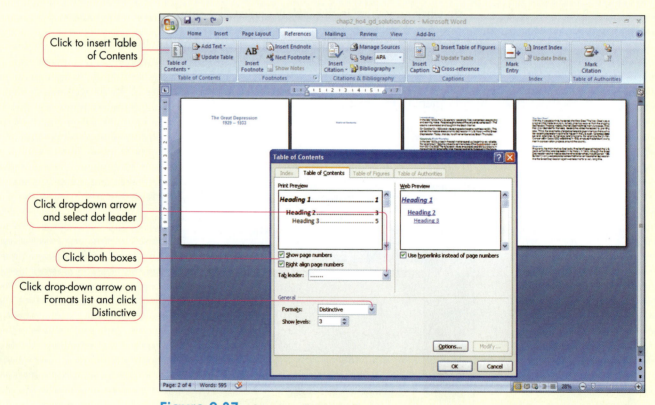

Click to insert Table of Contents

Click drop-down arrow and select dot leader

Click both boxes

Click drop-down arrow on Formats list and click Distinctive

Figure 2.37 Create a Table of Contents

TIP Updating the Table of Contents

You can use a shortcut menu to update the table of contents. Point to any entry in the table of contents, then press the right mouse button to display the menu. Click **Update Field**, click **Update Entire Table**, and then click **OK**. The table of contents is adjusted automatically to reflect page number changes as well as the addition or deletion of any text defined by a style.

Step 3
Define an Index Entry

Refer to Figure 2.38 as you complete Step 3.

a. Press **Ctrl+Home** to move to the beginning of the document. Drag the Zoom Slider on the task bar to 100%. Click the **Home tab**, then click **Find** in the Editing group. Type **Black Thursday** in the *Find what* box, and then click **Find Next** two times.

You click Find Next two times because the first occurrence of *Black Thursday* is in the table of contents, but that is not the occurrence you want to mark for the index.

b. Click **Cancel** to close the Find and Replace dialog box. Click **Show/Hide ¶** in the Paragraph group on the Home tab so you can see the nonprinting characters in the document, if necessary.

The index entries that were created by the authors appear in curly brackets and begin with the letters XE.

c. Check that the text *Black Thursday* is selected within the document, then press **Alt+Shift+X** to display the Mark Index Entry dialog box, as shown in Figure 2.38.

TROUBLESHOOTING: If you forget the shortcut, click Mark Entry on the References tab.

d. Click **Mark** to create the index entry.

After you create the index entry, you see the field code, {XE "Black Thursday"}, to indicate that the index entry is created. The Mark Index Entry dialog box stays open so that you can create additional entries by selecting additional text.

e. Click the **Cross-reference check box** in the *Options* section. Type **Stock Market** in the Cross-reference text box following the word *See*, then click **Mark**.

f. Click in the document, scroll down to the next paragraph, select the text *Dupont*, then click in the Mark Index Entry dialog box and notice Main entry automatically changes to Dupont. Click **Mark** to create the index entry, then close the Mark Index Entry dialog box.

g. Save the document.

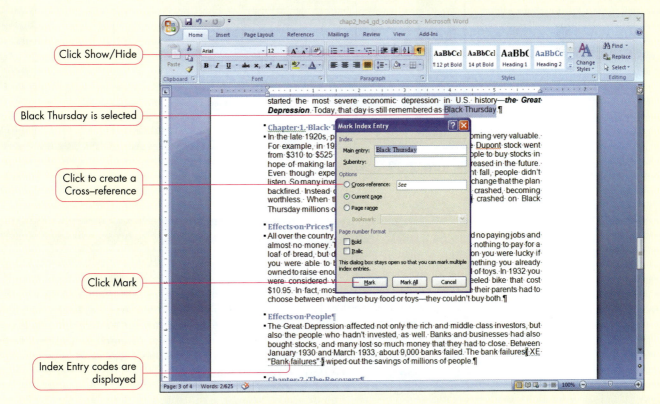

Figure 2.38 Create an Index Entry

Refer to Figure 2.39 as you complete Step 4.

a. Press **Ctrl+End** to move to the end of the document, then press **Enter** to begin a new line.

This spot is where you will insert the index.

b. Click the **References tab**, and then click **Insert Index** in the Index group.

The Index dialog box displays, as shown in Figure 2.39.

c. Click the **Formats drop-down arrow** and select **Classic**. If necessary, click the **Columns spin box arrows** until **2** displays. Click **OK** to create the index.

TROUBLESHOOTING: Click Undo on the Quick Access Toolbar if you are not satisfied with the appearance of the index or if it does not display at the end of the document, then repeat the process.

d. Save the document.

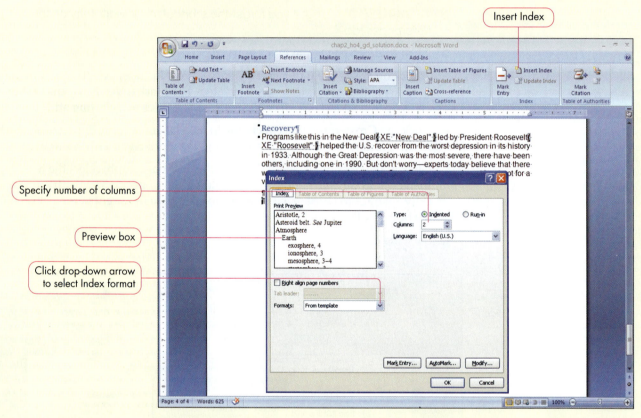

Figure 2.39 Create the Index

AutoMark Index Entries

The AutoMark command will, as the name implies, automatically mark all occurrences of all entries for inclusion in an index. To use the feature, you have to create a separate document that lists the terms you want to reference, then you execute the AutoMark command from the Index dialog box. The advantage is that it is fast. The disadvantage is that every occurrence of an entry is marked in the index so that a commonly used term may have too many page references. You can, however, delete superfluous entries by manually deleting the field codes. Click **Show/Hide ¶** in the Paragraph group of the Home tab if you do not see the entries in the document.

Step 5
Complete the Index

Refer to Figure 2.40 as you complete Step 5.

a. At the beginning of the index click to position the insertion point on the left of the letter "B".

b. Click the **Page Layout tab**, then click **Breaks** and select **Next Page**.

The index moves to the top of a new page.

c. Click the **Insert tab**, click **Page Number** in the Header & Footer group, and then select **Format Page Numbers** to display the Page Number Format dialog box. Click **Continue from previous section**, if necessary, then click **OK**.

d. Click **Header** in the Header & Footer group, and then click **Edit Header** to display the Design tab as shown in Figure 2.40. Click **Link to Previous**.

When you toggle the Link to Previous indicator off, you create a new header for this section that is independent of and different from the header in the previous section. Notice other Header and Footer options that display in the tab.

e. Type **INDEX** in the header. Select *INDEX* then on the Mini toolbar click **Center**. Click **Close Header and Footer** in the Close group to return to the document. Click **Show/Hide ¶** in the Paragraph group on the Home tab to turn off display of field codes.

f. Save the document.

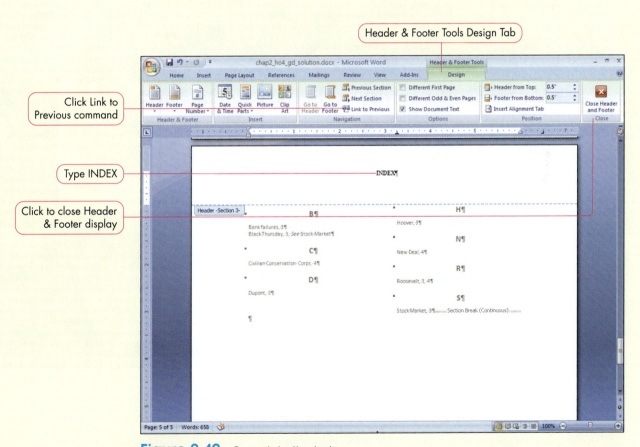

Figure 2.40 Complete the Index

TIP Check the Index Entries

Every entry in the index should begin with an uppercase letter. If this is not the case, it is because the origin entry within the body of the document was marked improperly. Click **Show/Hide ¶** in the Paragraph group on the Home tab to display the indexed entries within the document, which appear within brackets; e.g., {XE "Practice Files"}. Change each entry to begin with an uppercase letter as necessary.

Step 6
View the Completed Document

Refer to Figure 2.41 as you complete Step 6.

a. Click **Zoom** on the status bar. Click **Many pages** and drag to display 2 x 3. Click **OK**.

The completed document is shown in Figure 2.41. The index appears by itself on the last page of the document.

b. Save and close the *chap2_ho4_gd_solution* document.

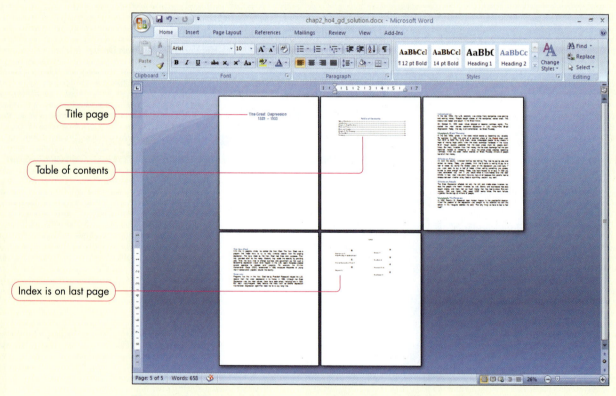

Figure 2.41 The Completed Document

Summary

1. **Apply font attributes through the Font dialog box.** Formatting occurs at the character, paragraph, or section level. The Font dialog box allows you to change spacing of the characters and also provides special formatting options for text that only appears on the screen. Through this dialog box, you can change the font and character spacing attributes including font, font size, font color, underline color, and effects. Use the character spacing options to control horizontal spacing between letters. You also can adjust the scale, position, and kerning of characters.

2. **Highlight text.** The Text Highlight Color command provides the ability to color text on screen so it stands out or resembles highlighting marks you often make in books. The Text Highlight Color command is located on the Home tab and also on the Mini toolbar that appears when you select text.

3. **Control word-wrapping with nonbreaking hyphens and nonbreaking spaces.** Occasionally, text wraps in an undesirable location in your document, or you just want to keep words together for better readability. To keep hyphenated words together on one line, use a nonbreaking hyphen to replace the regular hyphen. You insert a nonbreaking hyphen by pressing Ctrl+Shift+Hyphen in place of a hypen. You also can keep words together on one line by inserting a nonbreaking space instead of using the spacebar. To insert a nonbreaking space, click Ctrl+Shift+Spacebar.

4. **Copy formats with the Format Painter.** Use the Format Painter to copy existing format features to other text for consistency in appearance. The Format Painter uses fewer clicks than formatting from scratch. You can use it one time by single-clicking Format Painter in the Clipboard group on the Home tab, then selecting the text to format. If you double-click Format Painter, it toggles on and you can select many items to format the text. To toggle off the Format Painter, press Esc or click Format Painter again.

5. **Set off paragraphs with tabs, borders, lists, and columns.** You can change the appearance and add interest to documents by using paragraph formatting options. Tabs allow you to set markers in the document to use for aligning text. Borders and shading are set at the character or paragraph level and enable you to use boxes and/or shading to highlight an area of your document. A bulleted or numbered list helps to organize information by emphasizing and/or ordering important topics. Columns add interest to a document by formatting text into side-by-side vertical blocks of text and are implemented at the section level.

6. **Apply paragraph formats.** You can use additional formatting options in the Paragraph dialog box. Paragraph alignment refers to the placement of text between the left and right margins; text can be aligned left, right, centered between, or justified, which allows it to touch both margins. Another option that incorporates the distance from margins is indention. You can specify indention from the left margin, right margin, or both, or use special indents such as hanging or first-line. Line spacing determines the space between lines in a document and can be customized as single, double, or 1.5, for example. You also can specify an amount of space to insert before or after a paragraph, which is more efficient than pressing Enter. Widow/Orphan control prevents a single line from displaying at the top or bottom of a page, separate from the rest of a paragraph.

7. **Create and modify styles.** A style is a set of formatting instructions that has been saved under a distinct name. Styles are created at the character or paragraph level and provide a consistent appearance to similar elements throughout a document. You can modify any existing style to change the formatting of all text defined by that style. You can even create a new style for use in the current or any other document. Styles provide the foundation to use other tools such as outlines and the table of contents. The Outline view displays a condensed view of a document based on styles within the document. Text may be collapsed or expanded as necessary to facilitate moving text within long documents. The Outline view does not display a conventional outline, which is created in Print Layout view using the Multilevel List command on the Home tab.

8. **Create a table of contents.** A table of contents lists headings in the order they appear in a document with their respective page numbers. Word can create it automatically, provided the built-in heading styles were applied previously to the items for inclusion.

9. **Create an index.** Word also will create an index automatically, provided that the entries for the index have been marked previously. This result, in turn, requires you to go through a document, select the appropriate text, and mark the entries accordingly.

Key Terms

Multiple Choice

1. Which of the following can be stored within a paragraph style?
   - (a) Tabs and indents
   - (b) Line spacing and alignment
   - (c) Shading and borders
   - (d) All of the above

2. What is the easiest way to change the alignment of five paragraphs scattered throughout a document, each of which is formatted with the same style?
   - (a) Select the paragraphs individually, then click the appropriate alignment button.
   - (b) Select the paragraphs at the same time, then click the appropriate alignment button on the Home tab.
   - (c) Change the format of the existing style, which changes the paragraphs.
   - (d) Retype the paragraphs according to the new specifications.

3. Which feature analyzes a document and formats it for you?
   - (a) Character styles
   - (b) AutoFormat
   - (c) Multilevel list
   - (d) Table of contents

4. Which of the following is used to create a conventional outline?
   - (a) A Numbered list
   - (b) The Outline view
   - (c) A table of contents
   - (d) An index

5. A(n) _____ occurs when the first line of a paragraph is isolated at the bottom of a page and the rest of the paragraph continues on the next page.
   - (a) widow
   - (b) section break
   - (c) footer
   - (d) orphan

6. What is the keyboard shortcut to mark an index entry?
   - (a) Index entries cannot be marked manually.
   - (b) Press Ctrl+Enter
   - (c) Ctrl+I
   - (d) Alt+Shift+X

7. Which of the following is true regarding the formatting within a document?
   - (a) Line spacing and alignment are implemented at the section level.
   - (b) Margins, headers, and footers are implemented at the paragraph level.
   - (c) Nonbreaking hyphens are implemented at the paragraph level.
   - (d) Columns are implemented at the section level.

8. Which tab contains the Table of Contents and Index features?
   - (a) Home
   - (b) Insert
   - (c) View
   - (d) References

9. After you create and insert a table of contents into a document,
   - (a) any subsequent page changes arising from the insertion or deletion of text to existing paragraphs must be entered manually.
   - (b) any additions to the entries in the table arising due to the insertion of new paragraphs defined by a heading style must be entered manually.
   - (c) an index can not be added to the document.
   - (d) you can right-click, then select Update Field to update the table of contents.

10. Which of the following is a false statement about the Outline view?
    - (a) It can be collapsed to display only headings.
    - (b) It can be expanded to show the entire document.
    - (c) It requires the application of styles.
    - (d) It is used to create a conventional outline.

11. What is the best way to create a conventional outline in a Word document?
    - (a) Use the Outline view.
    - (b) Use the Mulitlevel List command in the Paragraph group in Print Layout view.
    - (c) Use the Outlining toolbar.
    - (d) All of the above are equally acceptable.

12. Which of the following is not a predefined Word style that is available in every document?

  (a) Normal

  (b) Heading 1

  (c) Body Text

  (d) Special 1

13. What happens if you modify the Body Text style in a Word document?

  (a) Only the paragraph where the insertion point is located is changed.

  (b) All paragraphs in the document will be changed.

  (c) Only those paragraphs formatted with the Body Text style will be changed.

  (d) It is not possible to change a Word default style such as Body Text.

14. Which of the following are not set at the paragraph level?

  (a) Alignment

  (b) Tabs and indents

  (c) Line spacing

  (d) Columns

15. Which of the following is a true statement regarding indents?

  (a) Indents are measured from the edge of the page.

  (b) The left, right, and first line indents must be set to the same value.

  (c) The insertion point can be anywhere in the paragraph when indents are set.

  (d) Indents must be set within the Paragraph dialog box.

16. The default tab stops are set to:

  (a) Left indents every ½".

  (b) Left indents every ¼".

  (c) Right indents every ½".

  (d) Right indents every ¼".

17. The spacing in an existing multipage document is changed from single spacing to double spacing throughout the document. What can you say about the number of hard and soft page breaks before and after the formatting change?

  (a) The number of soft page breaks is the same, but the number and/or position of the hard page breaks is different.

  (b) The number of hard page breaks is the same, but the number and/or position of the soft page breaks is different.

  (c) The number and position of both hard and soft page breaks is the same.

  (d) The number and position of both hard and soft page breaks is different.

18. Which of the following is not a valid use of the Format Painter?

  (a) View formatting codes assigned to a paragraph.

  (b) Copy the font style of a paragraph heading to other paragraph headings.

  (c) Restore character style to a paragraph (whose style was deleted accidentally) using the style from a properly formatted paragraph.

  (d) Copy the format of a paragraph that includes a hanging indent to a paragraph formatted in the Normal style.

19. If you want to be sure the phone number 555-1234 does not word-wrap what should you do?

  (a) Use a nonbreaking hyphen in place of the hyphen.

  (b) Use expanded spacing on the whole number.

  (c) Use a nonbreaking space in place of the hyphen.

  (d) Press Ctrl+Enter before you type the phone number.

Practice Exercises

1 The Purchase of a PC

You can purchase a PC from any number of vendors, each of which offers multiple models and typically enables you to upgrade individual components. You want to remember a few important tips as you shop for your next system. We have provided a few of those tips for you, but the document is difficult to read in its current state. Follow instructions to change the formatting of this document and improve readability. Refer to Figure 2.42 as you complete this exercise.

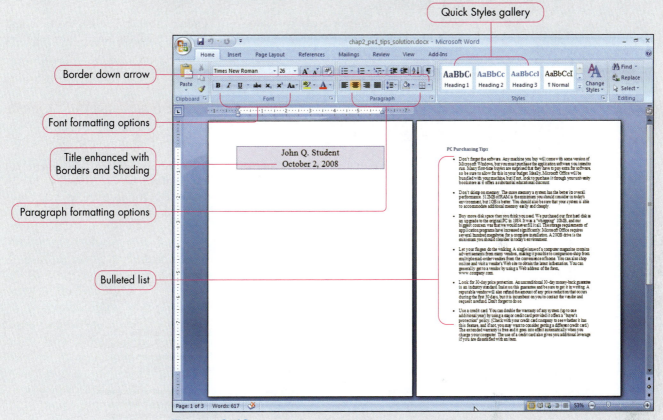

Figure 2.42 PC Purchasing Tips

a. Open the *chap2_pe1_tips* document in the Exploring Word folder and save the document as **chap2_pe1_tips_solution**.

b. Press **Ctrl+Home** to go to the beginning of the document, and then press **Ctrl+Enter** to insert a page break. Press **Ctrl+Home** to move to the beginning of the document and type your name. Press **Enter**, then type today's date. This is your title page.

c. Click the **Home tab**, select your name and date, and then click the **Borders arrow** in the Paragraph group on the Home tab. Select **Borders and Shading** to open the dialog box.

d. In the Borders tab, select **Box** in the *Setting* section. Click the **Color drop-down arrow** and select **Purple, Accent 4**. Click the **Width drop-down arrow** and select 2¼.

e. Click the **Shading tab**. Click the **Fill drop-down arrow**, then select **Purple, Accent 4, Lighter 60%**. Click **OK** to close the Borders and Shading dialog box.

f. Select your name again, if necessary, click the **Font size arrow** in the Font group on the Home tab, and select **26**. Click **Center** in the Paragraph group on the Home tab. Click the **Styles Dialog Box Launcher** to display the Styles Pane, then scroll to find the format applied to your name. Move your mouse over the style, then click the down arrow and select **Modify** to display the Modify Style dialog box. Type **PCTitle** in the Name box, then click **OK**.

g. Select the date, then click **PCTitle** in the Styles pane to apply the style to the second line of your title page. Close the Styles pane.

...continued on Next Page

h. The second page of the document contains various tips that we provide, but it is up to you to complete the formatting. Select the title *PC Purchasing Tips* at the top of this page. Click **Heading 1** in the Quick Styles gallery on the Home tab to format this title.

i. To create a bulleted list for the tips on this page, select all remaining text that has not been formatted, then click the **Bullets arrow** in the Paragraph group on the Home tab. Select a round black circle from the bullet Style gallery.

j. The bullets help differentiate each point, but they are still spaced pretty close together. To make the document easier to read, click the **Paragraph Dialog Box Launcher**, and then click the **After spin box up arrow** until **12 pt** displays. Click the **Don't add space between paragraphs of the same style** check box (this will remove the check mark from the check box).

k. One paragraph splits between two pages. To eliminate that split, click the **Line and Page Breaks tab** in the Paragraph dialog box, and then click the **Keep lines together check box**. Click **OK**.

l. Compare your document to Figure 2.42. Save and close the document.

2 Creating a List of Job Descriptions

You work for a major book publisher, and your supervisor asked you to prepare a document that lists key personnel and their job descriptions. This information sheet will be sent to each author on the Microsoft Office 2007 team, so they will know who is responsible for different aspects of the publication process. Refer to Figure 2.43 as you complete this exercise.

Office 2007 Series

Publisher Contact	Job Description
Rachel Starkey	**Executive Editor**: Coordinate all books in the Office 2007 series. Contact potential authors and issue contracts to final authors. Work with all publishing personnel. Determine budgets, sales forecasts, etc.
Marilyn Kay	**Developmental Editor**: Work with author to organize topics for a final TOC. Review incoming chapters and provide suggestions for organization, content, and structure. Ensure that author correctly formats the manuscript according to series specifications.
Scott Umpir	**Project Manager**: Coordinate the publishing process with the authors, developmental editors, technical editors, copy editors, and production team members.
Brittany Shaymonu	**Technical Editor**: Review first-draft of manuscript to ensure technical accuracy of the step-by-step lessons. Make notes of any missing or extra steps. Point out inconsistencies with menu names, options, etc., including capitalization. Make other notes from a student's perspective.
Darleen Terry	**Copy Editor**: Proofread manuscript and correct errors in spelling, grammar, punctuation, wording, etc. Use the tracking feature in Word to make the online edits.

Figure 2.43 Publisher Job Descriptions

a. Click the **Office Button**, click **New**, and then double-click **Blank document** to open a new document. Save as **chap2_pe2_personnel_solution**.

b. Click the **Page Layout tab**, click **Margins** in the Page Setup group, and then click **Custom Margins** to display the Page Setup dialog box. Click the **Top margin spin box up arrow** until **2** displays, and then click **OK**.

...continued on Next Page

c. Type the title shown in Figure 2.43. Press **Enter** three times to triple-space after the title. Select the title, and then on the Mini Toolbar click **Center**, click the **Font arrow** and select **Arial,** click the **Font size arrow** and select **16,** and click **Bold**.

d. Click the **Font Dialog Box Launcher** on the Home tab and select the **Character Spacing tab**. Click the **Spacing drop-down arrow** and select **Expanded**. Click **OK**. Click on one of the blank lines below the title to deselect it.

e. Click the **View tab** and click the **Ruler check box**, if necessary. The ruler should display at the top of your page.

f. Click on the **2"** mark on the ruler to insert a Left tab. The Left tab mark displays on the ruler.

g. Click the **Home tab**. Click the **Paragraph Dialog Box Launcher**. Click the **Special drop-down arrow** in the *Indention* section and select **Hanging**. Click in the **After text box** in the Spacing section and type **12**. Click **OK**.

h. Type the column heading **Publisher Contact**. Press **Tab** and type the column heading **Job Description**. Press **Enter** to move your cursor to the next line. Select the column headings and on the Mini toolbar, click **Bold**. Finish typing the rest of the columnar text, as shown in Figure 2.43; notice the 12-point After paragraph spacing creates the equivalent of one blank line between rows.

i. Select the first job description, *Executive Editor,* and click **Underline** in the Font group on the Home tab. Double-click **Format Painter** in the Clipboard group on the Home tab, then select the remaining job descriptions to apply the Underline format to each job. After you format the last job description, press **Esc** to turn off the Format Painter.

j. Select the name of each person and apply bold formatting. Save and close the *chap2_pe2_personnel_solution* document.

3 Creating and Updating a Table of Contents and an Index

You have received an ISO 9000 document that lists standards for quality management and assurance and is used by international manufacturing and service organizations. You need to distribute the standards to your employees. It is a multipage document that does not contain a table of contents or index for easy reference. You decide to add each before making copies. After creating the table of contents, you decide only two levels of headings are necessary, so you update it to reflect your changes. After adding the index, you decide to make it more detailed, so you edit and update it as well. Refer to Figure 2.44 as you complete this exercise.

a. Open the *chap2_pe3_iso* document and save it as **chap2_pe3_iso_solution**.

b. Place the insertion point at the end of *ISO 9000* at the top of the first page and press **Ctrl+Enter** to create a hard page break. The page break creates a page for the table of contents.

c. Click the **References tab**, click **Table of Contents** in the Table of Contents group, and then select **Table of Contents** from the gallery. Select **Update Entire Table** if the Update Table of Contents dialog box appears.

d. Click to place the insertion point on the left of the heading *I. Introduction* and press **Ctrl+Enter** to create a hard page break.

e. Click one time anywhere in the table of contents to select it, click **Table of Contents** on the References tab, and then click **Insert Table of Contents**. Click the **Show levels spin box down arrow** until **2** displays. Click **OK**, and then click **OK** again at the prompt asking to replace the selected table of contents.

f. Before you insert the index, you must mark several words as entries. Locate, then select the word *quality* in the *Quality Policy* paragraph, and then press **Alt+Shift+X** to display the Mark Index Entry dialog box. Click **Mark** to create the index entry.

g. Locate and select the following words, and then click **Mark** for each one, just as you did in the previous step:

authority	In heading *Responsibility and authority*
procedures	In heading *Quality System Procedures*
supplier	First sentence under heading *Quality System Procedures*
testing	In heading *Inspection and Testing*

...continued on Next Page

h. Press **Ctrl+End** to go to the end of the document. Press **Ctrl+Enter** to insert a new page where you will display the index. Click **Insert Index** from the Index group on the References tab, and then click **OK** to create the Index.

i. You decide your index is incomplete and should include more words. Locate and select the words below. Remember to press **Alt+Shift+X** to display the Mark Index Entry dialog box and click **Mark** to create the index entry.

data control	In heading *Document and Data Control*
training	In heading *Training*
records	In heading *Control of Quality Records*

j. Close the Mark Index Entry dialog box. Position the insertion point anywhere in the index and click **Update Index** in the Index group on the References tab. Your additional entries will display in the updated index.

k. Select all entries, then click **Change Case** in the Font group on the Home tab. Select **lowercase** to change the case of all entries.

l. Position the insertion point left of the section break that precedes the first index entry heading and press **Enter** two times. Move the insertion point up to the first empty line and type **INDEX**, and then select it and click **Heading 1** in the Quick Styles gallery on the Home tab.

m. Save the document and compare your results to Figure 2.44.

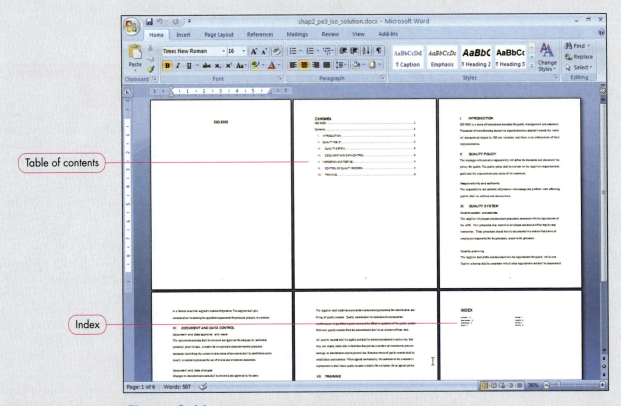

Figure 2.44 Report Including Table of Contents and Index

4 Editing a Memo to the HR Director

Tracey Spears is the training coordinator for a local company, and her responsibilities include tracking employees' continuing education efforts. The company urges employees to pursue educational opportunities that add experience and knowledge to their positions, including taking any certification exams that enhance their credentials. The human resources director has asked Ms. Spears to provide him with a list of employees who have met minimum qualifications to take an upcoming certification exam. In its present state, the memo prints on two pages; you will

...continued on Next Page

format the memo using columns in order to save paper and display the entire list on one page. Refer to Figure 2.45 as you complete this exercise.

a. Open the *chap2_pe4_training* document and save it as **chap2_pe4_training_solution**.

b. Select the word *MEMO*, click **Heading 1** in the Quick Styles gallery on the Home tab, and then click **Center** in the Paragraph group on the Home tab.

c. Several employees have a work conflict and will be unable to sit for the certification exam in October. To specify the people who fall into that category scroll over *Alana Bell* to select her name, and then on the Mini toolbar click **Text Highlight Color** or click **Text Highlight Color** in the Font group on the Home tab. Repeat this process for *Amy Kay Lynn*, *Piau Shing*, and *Ryan Stubbs*.

d. Employees can opt out of the exam for personal reasons, and we need to specify those as well. Hold down **Ctrl** and select the following employees: *Simon Anderson, Randall Larsen*, and *Winnifred Roark*. Click the **Font Dialog Box Launcher**, and then click the **Strikethrough check box** in the *Effects* section on the Font tab; click **OK** to return to the memo.

e. Now you list the employees in two columns so you can print the memo on one sheet of paper instead of two. Drag your mouse over the list of employees to select all names. Click the **Page Layout tab**, click **Columns**, and then select **Two**. The names now display in two columns, and the entire memo fits on one page, as shown in Figure 2.45.

f. Save your work and close the document.

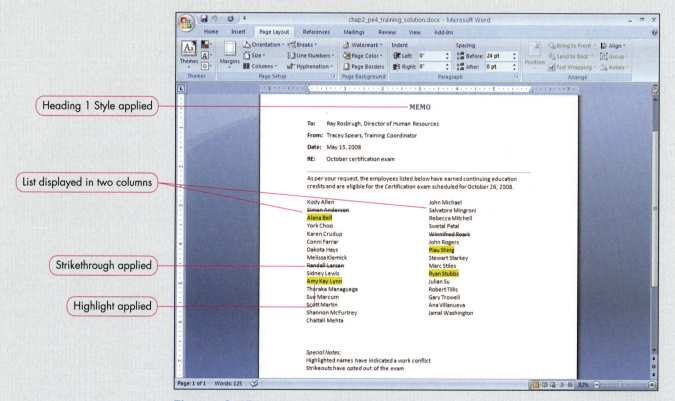

Figure 2.45 The Formatted Memo

Mid-Level Exercises

1 Creating and Applying Styles

You created a status report to inform committee members about an upcoming conference of which you are in charge. You want it to look attractive and professional, and you decide to create and apply your own styles rather than use those already available in Word. You create a paragraph style named Side Heading to format the headings, and then you create a character style named Session to format the names of the conference sessions and apply these formats to document text. You then copy these two styles to the Normal template. Eventually, you delete these two styles from the Normal template. Refer to Figure 2.46 as you complete this exercise.

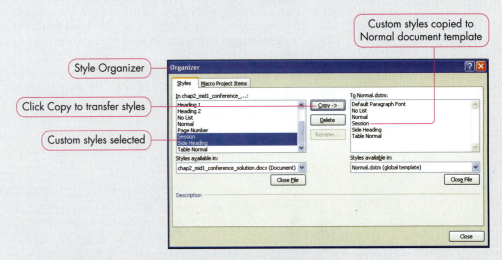

Figure 2.46 Transfer Custom Styles to the Global Template

a. Open the *chap2_mid1_conference* document and save it as **chap2_mid1_conference_solution**.

b. Create a new paragraph style named **Side Heading** using the following properties: Style based on is Normal, Style for following paragraph is Normal. Font properties are Arial, 14-pt, Bold, Red, Accent 2, Darker 50% font color.

c. Set the following paragraph formats: 12-point Before paragraph spacing, 6-point After paragraph spacing.

d. Apply the Side Heading style to the three headings *The Committee*, *Training Sessions*, and *Training Goal*.

e. Create a new character style named **Session** using the following specifications: Bold and Red, Accent 2, Darker 50% font color.

f. In the bulleted list, apply the Session style to the following: *Word*, *Web Page Development*, *Multimedia*, and *Presentations Graphics*.

g. Open the **Manage Styles** dialog box, then click **Import/Export**. In the Organizer dialog box, copy the **Side Heading** and **Session** styles from the **chap2_mid1_conference_solution.docx** list to the **Normal.dotm** list, as shown in Figure 2.46. Close the Organizer dialog box.

h. Save and close *chap2_mid1_conference_solution*.

i. Open a new document. Display the Styles pane, if necessary, then verify that the Session and Side Heading styles are listed. This step proves that you copied the two styles to the Normal template so that they are available for all new documents.

j. Open the **Manage Styles** dialog box, then click the **Import/Export button**. In the Organizer dialog box, delete the two styles from the **In Normal.dotm** list. Click **Yes to All** when prompted. Close the Organizer dialog box.

k. Close the blank document without saving it.

...continued on Next Page

As a student in the Physician Assistant program at a local university you create a document containing tips for healthier living. The facts have been typed into a Word 2007 document but are thus far unformatted. You will modify it to incorporate styles and add readability as you follow the steps below. Refer to Figure 2.47 as you complete this exercise.

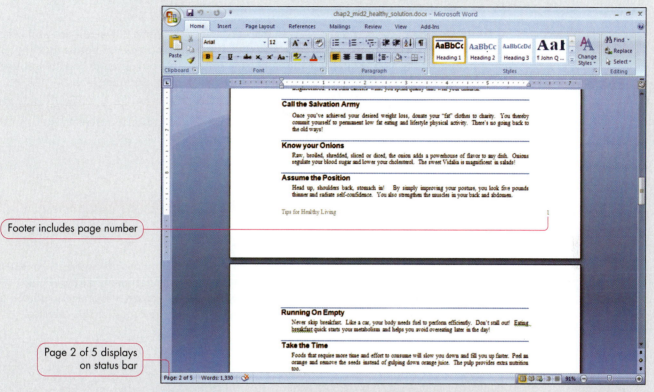

Footer includes page number

Page 2 of 5 displays on status bar

Figure 2.47 Tips for Healthy Living

a. Open the *chap2_mid2_healthy* document and save it as **chap2_mid2_healthy_solution**.

b. Apply the **Heading 1** and **Body Text** styles throughout the document. The Format Painter is a useful tool to copy formats.

c. Change the specifications for the *Body Text* and *Heading 1* styles so that your document matches the document in Figure 2.47. The Heading 1 style is 12-point Arial bold with a blue top border. The Body Text style is 10-point Times New Roman, justified, ¼" left indent, and 12-point spacing After.

d. Create a title page for the document consisting of the title, *Tips for Healthy Living*, and an additional line of text that indicates the document was prepared by you. Format the title page content using a custom style named after yourself. The custom style should contain 28-point Times New Roman font that is bold, centered, and colored in Dark Blue, Text 2 (a blue color).

e. Create a footer for the document consisting of the title, **Tips for Healthy Living**, and a page number. (You can see the footer in Figure 2.47.) The footer should not appear on the title page; that is, page 1 is actually the second page of the document. Look closely at the status bar in Figure 2.47 and you will see that you are on page 1, but that this is the second page of a five-page document.

f. Click Outline View, collapse the text, and view the headings only.

g. Save and close the document.

...continued on Next Page

3 Enhance the Healthy Living Document

Your modifications to the Healthy Living document in the last exercise set it up nicely for the next step in creating a comprehensive document that includes a table of contents and index.

a. Open the *chap2_mid2_healthy_solution* document you created in the last exercise and save it as **chap2_mid3_healthy_solution**. Change the document view to Print Layout so the whole document displays.

b. Create a page specifically for the table of contents, then give the page a title and generate a table of contents using the Healthy Living tip headings. Do not include the custom styles you created for the Title page in the table of contents. You should use a dashed leader to connect the headings to the page numbers in the table.

c. Mark the following text for inclusion in the index: *diet, exercise, metabolism, vegetables, fat.* At the end of your document, create the index and take necessary steps so the index heading displays in the table of contents.

d. Save and close the document.

4 Editing a Welcome Letter

You composed a letter to welcome new members to an organization of which you are president. Now, you need to apply various paragraph formatting, such as alignment, paragraph spacing, and a paragraph border and shading. In addition, you want to create a customized bulleted list that describes plans for the organization. Refer to Figure 2.48 as you complete this exercise.

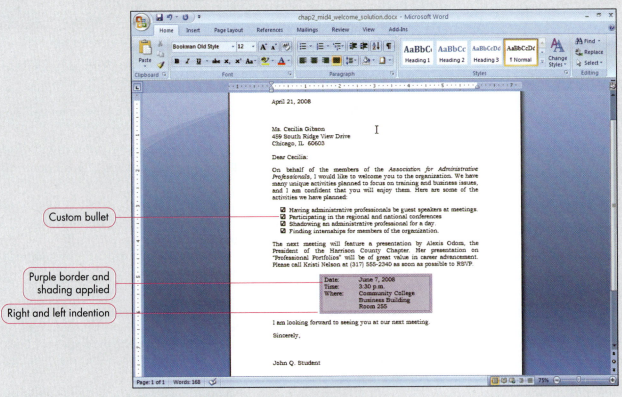

Figure 2.48 Formatted Welcome Letter

...continued on Next Page

a. Open the *chap2_mid4_welcome* document and save it as **chap2_mid4_welcome_solution**. Change Ken's name to your name in the signature block.

b. Apply Justified alignment to the entire document. Delete the asterisk (*) and create a customized bulleted list, selecting a picture bullet of your choice. Type the following items in the bulleted list:

Having administrative professionals be guest speakers at meetings.
Participating in the regional and national conferences.
Shadowing an administrative professional for a day.
Finding internships for members of the organization.

c. Select text from the salutation, *Dear Cecilia*, through the last paragraph that ends with *next meeting*. Set 12-point spacing After paragraph.

d. Select the italicized lines of text and remove the italics. For these lines of text, set 1.5" left and right indents and 0-point spacing After paragraph. Apply a triple-line border, Purple, Accent 4 border color, ¾ pt border width, and Purple, Accent 4, Lighter 60% shading color.

e. Click on the line containing the text *Room 255* and set 12-point spacing After paragraph.

f. Select the entire document, and then change the Font to 12-point Bookman Old Style.

g. If needed, delete an extra tab formatting mark to the left of *Community College* to prevent it from word-wrapping. Compare your work to Figure 2.48.

h. Save and close the document.

Capstone Exercise

In this project, you work with a document prepared for managers involved in the hiring process. This report analyzes the validity of the interview process and suggests that selection doesn't depend only on quality information, but on the quality of the interpretation of information. The document requires formatting to enhance readability and important information; you will use skills from this chapter to format multiple levels of headings and figures. To make it easy for readers to locate topics in your document, create and use various supplemental document components such as a table of contents and index.

Adding Style

This document is ready for enhancements, and the styles feature is a good tool that allows you to add them quickly and easily.

a. Open the file *chap2_cap_interview* document and save it as **chap2_cap_interview_solution**.

b. Create a paragraph style named **Title_Page_1** with these formats: 22-point size, Shadow font effect, character spacing expanded by 1 point, horizontally centered, and no Widow/Orphan control. Apply this style to the first line of the title on the title page.

c. Create a paragraph style named **Title_Page_2** based on the first style you created, with these additional formats: 20-point size, custom color 66, 4, 66. Apply this style to the subtitle on the title page.

d. Replace the * in the middle of the first page with your name. Apply the Heading 3 style to your name and the line that precedes it.

e. Apply the Body Text style to all regular paragraphs.

f. Apply the Heading 2 style to the side headings and the Heading 1 style to the main headings throughout the document.

Formatting the Paragraphs

Next, you will apply paragraph formatting to the document. These format options will further increase the readability and attractiveness of your document.

a. Select the second paragraph in the *Introduction* section and apply these formats: 0.7" left and right indent, 6-point spacing after the paragraph, boxed 1½-point border with a custom color (31, 73, 125 RGB), and custom shading color (210, 218, 229 RGB).

b. Select the second and third paragraphs in *The Unfavorable Information Effect* section and create a two-column format with a line between the columns.

c. Use Keep Lines Together controls to prevent paragraphs from being separated across pages.

d. Insert nonbreaking spaces and nonbreaking hyphens where appropriate.

e. Apply the arrow bulleted-list format for the five-item list in the *Introduction*.

f. Apply the (1) numbered-list format for the three phases in the *Pre-Interview Impressions* section.

Inserting References

To put the finishing touches on your document, you will add a table of contents and index. These additions enable the reader to quickly locate topics in your document and add a level of professionalism to your work.

a. Create a table of contents based on the styles you applied to paragraph headings; do not include the style you used for the title page.

b. Mark these words as index entries: behavior, favorable, impression, interview, interviewer, perceptions, personal interview, reference, unqualified. Add an index to the end of the document. Use the Classic index format.

c. A page number should display in the footer of the document. Use the **Accent Bar 4** format, but prevent it from displaying on the title page and start numbering on the page that contains the table of contents.

d. Save your changes and close the document.

Mini Cases

Use the rubric following the case as a guide to evaluate your work, but keep in mind that your instructor may impose additional grading criteria or use a different standard to judge your work.

A Fundraising Letter

GENERAL CASE

Each year, you update a letter to several community partners soliciting support for an auction. The auction raises funds for your organization, and your letter should impress your supporters by using several formatting styles and options that give it a very professional look. Open the *chap2_mc1_auction* document and make necessary changes to improve the appearance. Consider the use of columns for auction items, bullets to draw attention to the list of forms, and page borders—and that is just for starters! Your finished document should be saved as **chap2_mc1_auction_solution**.

Performance Elements	Exceeds Expectations	Meets Expectations	Below Expectations
Enhanced document using the following paragraph formatting features: columns, bullets/numbering, borders/shading	Document contains at least three of the paragraph formatting features.	Document contains at least two of the paragraph formatting features.	Document contains one or none of the paragraph formatting features.
Use of character formatting features such as Font, Font Size, Font color, or other attributes from Font dialog box	Used character formatting options throughout entire document.	Used character formatting options in most sections of document.	Used character formatting options on a small portion of document.
Overall appearance of document	Used formatting tools to create a very attractive document that is easy to read.	Some formatting has been applied, but more updates are required for an attractive and readable document.	Minimal formatting has been applied, resulting in a plain and somewhat unattractive document.

The Invitation

RESEARCH CASE

Search the Internet for an upcoming local event at your school or in your community and produce the perfect invitation. You can invite people to a charity ball, a fun run, or to a fraternity party. Your laser printer and abundance of fancy fonts enable you to do anything a professional printer can do. Your finished document should be saved as **chap2_mc2_invitation_solution**.

Performance Elements	Exceeds Expectations	Meets Expectations	Below Expectations
Use of character formatting	Three or more character formats applied to text.	One or two character formats applied to text.	Does not apply character formats to text.
Use of styles	Created custom paragraph or character style.	Used at least two predefined styles.	Used one or no predefined style.
Use of paragraph formatting	Two or more paragraph format options used.	Used one paragraph format option.	Does not use paragraph format options.
Presentation	Invitation is formatted attractively; information is easy to read and understand.	Special formatting has been applied, but information is somewhat cluttered.	Invitation lists basic information with no special formatting for attractiveness.

Open the *chap2_mc3_wintips* document. The document is formatted, but it contains several errors and problems. For example, the paragraph titles are not all formatted with the same style, so they do not all display in the table of contents. You will notice most of the problems easily and you must fix them before the document can be useful. Your finished document should be saved as **chap2_mc3_wintips_solution**.

Performance Elements	Exceeds Expectations	Meets Expectations	Below Expectations
Paragraph and text formatting	Standardized style used on all paragraph text and headings.	Standardized style used on either text or headings, but not both.	Did not standardize styles on text or headings.
Table of contents	All appropriate paragraph titles are listed in the TOC.	Most paragraph titles are listed; no inappropriate titles are listed.	Some paragraph titles are not listed, and TOC contains some inappropriate titles.
Updated footer	Made all necessary updates to footer.	Made some updates to footer.	Did not update footer.

Enhancing a Document

Tables and Graphics

Objectives

After you read this chapter, you will be able to:

1. Insert a table (**page 197**).

2. Format a table (**page 205**).

3. Sort and apply formulas to table data (**page 207**).

4. Convert text to a table (**page 210**).

5. Insert clip art and images into a document (**page 219**).

6. Format a graphic element (**page 220**).

7. Insert WordArt into a document (**page 225**).

8. Insert symbols into a document (**page 226**).

Hands-On Exercises

Exercises	Skills Covered
1. **INSERT A TABLE (page 201)** **Open:** Blank document **Save as:** chap3_ho1_vacation_solution.docx	• Create a Table • Insert Rows and Columns • Change Row Height and Column Width • Merge Cells to Create Header Row
2. **ADVANCED TABLE FEATURES (page 212)** **Open:** chap3_ho1_vacation_solution.docx (from Exercise 1) **Save as:** chap3_ho2_vacation_solution.docx (additional modifications) **Open:** chap3_ho2_expenses.docx (Step 7) **Save as:** chap3_ho2_expenses_solution.docx	• Apply a Table Style • Add Table Borders and Shading • Enter Formulas to Calculate Totals • Add a Row and Enter a Formula • Sort Data in a Table • Align Table and Data • Convert Text to a Table
3. **CLIP ART, WORDART, AND SYMBOLS (page 227)** **Open:** chap3_ho3_ergonomics.docx **Save as:** chap3_ho3_ergonomics_solution.docx	• Insert a Clip Art Object • Move and Resize the Clip Art Object • Create a WordArt Object • Modify the WordArt Object • Insert a Symbol

CASE STUDY

The Ozarks Science and Engineering Fair

Each spring Luanne Norgren is responsible for coordinating the Science and Engineering Fair at Southwest State University. The premier science event for the Ozarks region attracts middle school and high school students from 28 counties. You have been hired to serve as the assistant coordinator for the event and are responsible for communications with school administrators and faculty. You prepared an informational letter that will be sent to each school explaining the event registration procedures and project criteria. At your suggestion, Luanne agreed to let you

Case Study

develop a one-page flyer that can be mailed independently or with the informational letter. The flyer will be an attractive source of information that will encourage participation by faculty and students at the schools.

The event takes place April 4–6, 2008, on the university campus. The students who participate will be entered into either the Junior or Senior division, depending on their grade (7–9 in Junior, 10–12 in Senior). In both divisions students can enter a science project in any of the following categories: Biochemistry, Botany, Chemistry, Computer Science, Earth and Space Sciences, Engineering, Environmental Sciences, Physics, or Zoology.

Your Assignment

- Read the chapter, paying special attention to sections that describe how to insert and format tables and graphics.
- As assistant coordinator in charge of communications, you develop a flyer in Word that can be used as a quick source of information about the event. The flyer must include the date, divisions, and categories listed above, and contact information.
- You consider the use of a table, primarily as a placeholder for other information that you will add. Merge and split cells as necessary to create the effect you want to portray using the flyer. Use table styles to enhance color and readability of data in the table. Use borders and shading where appropriate or to supplement any table style you use.
- Insert clip art or other science-oriented graphics to add emphasis and excitement to the flyer. Use graphic formatting tools as needed to enhance colors, change styles, and compress the graphics.
- Use WordArt to create an exciting heading and in any other place it can be used to enhance the flyer.
- Add a "For more information" section to the flyer and list your contact information, Phone: (555) 111-2222 and e-mail: yourname@swsu.edu.
- Save the document as **chap3_case_science_solution**.

Tables

A ***table*** is a series of columns and rows that organize data.

A ***cell*** is the intersection of a column and row in a table.

A *table* is a series of columns and rows that organize data effectively. The columns and rows in a table intersect to form *cells*. The table feature is one of the most powerful in Word and is an easy way to organize a series of data in a columnar list format such as employee names, inventory lists, and e-mail addresses. The Vacation Planner in Figure 3.1, for example, is actually a 4x9 table (4 columns and 9 rows). The completed table looks impressive, and it is very easy to create once you understand how a table works. In addition to the organizational benefits, tables make an excellent alignment tool. For example, you can create tables to organize data such as employee lists with phone numbers and e-mail addresses. The Exploring series uses tables to provide descriptions for various software commands. Although you can align text with tabs, you have more format control when you create a table. (See the Practice Exercises at the end of the chapter for other examples.)

(The table feature is one of the most powerful in Word and is the basis for an almost limitless variety of documents. It is very easy to create once you understand how a table works.)

Vacation Planner			
Item	Number of Days	Amount per Day (est)	Total Amount
Airline Ticket			449.00
Amusement Park Tickets	4	50.00	200.00
Hotel	5	120.00	600.00
Meals	6	50.00	300.00
Rental Car	5	30.00	150.00
Souvenirs	5	20.00	100.00
TOTAL EXPECTED EXPENSES			$1799.00

Figure 3.1 The Vacation Planner

In this section, you insert a table in a document. After inserting the table, you can insert or delete columns and rows if you need to change the structure. Furthermore, you learn how to merge and split cells within the table. Finally, you change the row height and column width to accommodate data in the table.

Inserting a Table

You can create a table from the Insert tab. Click Table in the Tables group on the Insert tab to see a gallery of cells from which you select the number of columns and rows you require in the table, or you can choose the Insert Table command below the gallery to display the Insert Table dialog box and enter the table composition you prefer. When you select the table dimension from the gallery or from the Insert Table dialog box, Word creates a table structure with the number of columns and rows you specify. After you define a table, you can enter text, numbers, or graphics in individual cells. The text wraps itself as it is entered within a cell so that you can add or delete text without affecting the entries in other cells.

You format the contents of an individual cell the same way you format an ordinary paragraph; that is, you change the font, apply boldface or italic, change the text alignment, or apply any other formatting command. You can select multiple cells and apply the formatting to all selected cells at once, or you can format a cell independently of every other cell.

After you insert a table in your document, use commands in the Table Tools Design and Layout tabs to modify and enhance it. Place the insertion point anywhere in the table, then click either the Design or Layout tab to view the commands. In either tab, just point to a command and a ScreenTip describes its function.

TIP   Tabs and Tables

The Tab key functions differently in a table than in a regular document. Press Tab to move to the next cell in the current row or to the first cell in the next row if you are at the end of a row. Press Tab when you are in the last cell of a table to add a new blank row to the bottom of the table. Press Shift+Tab to move to the previous cell in the current row (or to the last cell in the previous row). You must press Ctrl+Tab to insert a regular tab character within a cell.

Insert and Delete Rows and Columns

You can change the structure of a table after it has been created. If you need more rows or columns to accommodate additional data in your table, it is easy to add or insert them using the Rows & Columns group on the Table Tools Layout tab. The Insert and Delete commands enable you to add new or delete existing rows or columns. When you add a column, you can specify if you want to insert it to the right or left of the current column. Likewise, you can specify where to place a new row—either above or below the currently selected row—based on where you need to add the new row.

You can delete complete rows and columns using the commands mentioned above, or you can delete only the data in those rows and columns using the Delete key on your keyboard. Keep in mind that when you insert or delete a complete row or a column, the remaining rows and columns will adjust to the positioning. For example, if you delete the third row of a 5x5 table, the data in the fourth and fifth rows move up and become the third and fourth rows. If you delete only the data in the third row, the cells would be blank and the fourth and fifth rows would not change at all.

Merge and Split Cells

You can use the Merge Cells command in the Merge group on the Table Tools Layout tab to join individual cells together (merge) to form a larger cell, as was done in the first and last rows of Figure 3.1. People often merge cells to enter a main title at the top of a table. Conversely, you can use the Split Cells command in the Merge group to split a single cell into multiple cells if you require more cells to hold data.

Change Row Height and Column Width

Row height is the vertical space from the top to the bottom of a row.

Column width is the horizontal space or length of a column.

When you create a table, Word builds evenly spaced columns. Frequently you need to change the row height or column width to fit your data. *Row height* is the vertical distance from the top to the bottom of a row. *Column width* is the horizontal space or width of a column. You might increase the column width to display a wide string of text, such as first and last name, to prevent it from wrapping in the cell. You might increase row height to better fit a header that has been enlarged for emphasis.

The table command is easy to master, and as you might have guessed, you will benefit from reviewing the available commands listed in the Design and Layout tabs as shown in the reference pages. You will use many of these commands as you create a table in the hands-on exercises.

Table Tools Layout Ribbon | Reference

Group	Commands	Enables You to
Table	Select ▾ View Gridlines Properties **Table**	• Select particular parts of a table (entire table, column, row, or cell). • Show or hide the gridlines around the table. • Display the Table Properties dialog box to format the table.
Rows & Columns	Delete ▾ Insert Above Insert Below Insert Left Insert Right **Rows & Columns**	• Delete cells, columns, rows, or the entire table. • Insert rows and columns. • Display the Insert Cells dialog box.
Merge	Merge Cells Split Cells Split Table **Merge**	• Merge (join) selected cells together. • Split cells into additional cells. • Split the table into two tables.
Cell Size	0.22" 6.15" AutoFit ▾ **Cell Size**	• Adjust the row height and column width. • Adjust the column width automatically based on the data in the column. • Display the Table Properties dialog box.
Alignment	Text Direction Cell Margins **Alignment**	• Specify the combined horizontal and vertical alignment of text within a cell. • Change the text direction. • Set margins within a cell.
Data	Sort Repeat Heading Rows Convert to Text Formula **Data**	• Sort data within a table. • Repeat heading rows when tables span multiple pages. • Convert tabulated text to table format. • Insert a formula in a table.

Hands-On Exercises

1 | Insert a Table

Skills covered: 1. Create a Table **2.** Insert Rows and Columns **3.** Change Row Height and Column Width **4.** Merge Cells to Create Header Row

Step 1
Create a Table

Refer to Figure 3.2 as you complete Step 1.

a. Start Word and press **Enter** two times in the blank document, then click the **Insert tab**.

The Insert tab contains the Table command.

b. Click **Table** in the Tables group, and then drag your mouse over the cells until you select 3 columns and 7 rows; you will see the table size, 3x7, displayed above the cells, as shown in Figure 3.2. Click the lower-right cell (where the 3rd column and the 7th row intersect) to insert the table into your document.

Word creates an empty table that contains three columns and seven rows. The default columns have identical widths, and the table spans from the left to the right margin.

c. Practice selecting various elements from the table, something that you will have to do in subsequent steps:

- To select a single cell, click inside the left grid line (the pointer changes to a black slanted arrow when you are in the proper position).
- To select a row, click outside the table to the left of the first cell in that row.
- To select a column, click just above the top of the column (the pointer changes to a small black downward pointing arrow).
- To select adjacent cells, drag the mouse over the cells.
- To select the entire table, drag the mouse over the table or click the table selection box that appears at the upper-left corner of the table.

d. Save the document as **chap3_ho1_vacation_solution**.

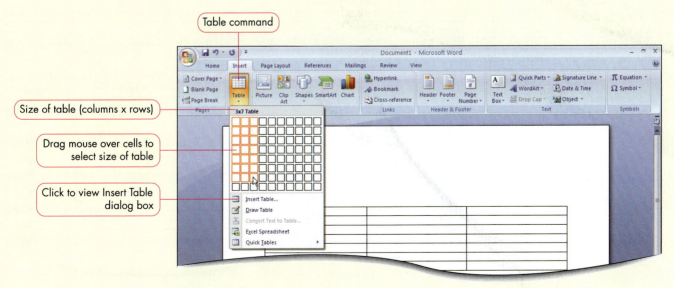

Figure 3.2 Inserting a Table

Refer to Figure 3.3 as you complete Step 2.

a. Click in the first cell of the first row and type **Vacation Planner**.

b. Click the first cell in the second row and type **Item**. Press **Tab** (or **right arrow**) to move to the next cell. Type **Number of Days**. Press **Tab** to move to the next cell, and then type **Amount per Day (est)**.

Notice you do not have enough columns to add the last heading, *Total Amount*.

c. Click anywhere in the last column of your table, then click the **Layout tab**. Click **Insert Right** in the Rows & Columns group to add a new column to your table. Click in the second row of the new column and type **Total Amount**.

You added a new column on the right side of the table. Notice that the column widths decrease to make room for the new column you just added.

TROUBLESHOOTING: If the column you insert is not in the correct location within the table, click Undo on the Quick Access Toolbar, confirm your insertion point is in the last column, and then click the appropriate Insert command.

d. Select the text *Vacation Planner* in the first row. On the Mini toolbar, click the **Font Size arrow** and click **18**, click **Bold**, and click **Center** to center the heading within the cell.

The table title stands out with the larger font size, bold, and center horizontal alignment.

e. Click outside and left of the second row to select the entire row. On the Mini toolbar, click the **Font Size arrow** and select **16**, and then click **Bold** and **Center**.

f. Enter the remaining data, as shown in Figure 3.3. When you get to the last row and find the table is too small to hold all the data, place the insertion point in the last cell (in the Total Amount column) and press **Tab** to add a row to the end of your table. Then enter the last item and amounts.

g. Save the document.

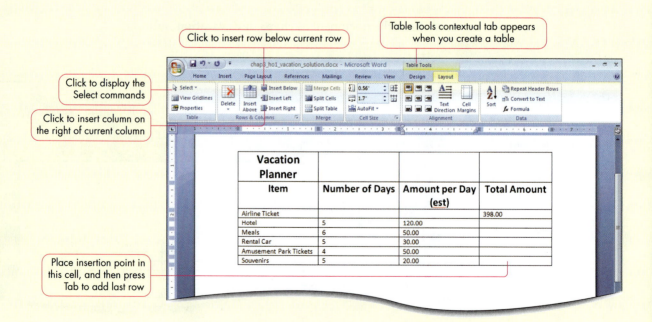

Figure 3.3 Enter the Vacation Planner Data

Step 3
Change Row Height and Column Width

Refer to Figure 3.4 as you complete Step 3.

a. Hold your mouse over the second column of data until the small black arrow appears, then hold down your mouse and drag to the right to select the last three columns of the table.

b. Click the **Layout tab**, then type **1.2** in the **Width** box in the Cell Size group, as shown in Figure 3.4. Click anywhere in the table or document to view the change.

You changed the width of the last three columns so that they are each 1.2" wide. They are now narrower, and the headings wrap even more in the cells.

c. Place the insertion point anywhere in the cell containing the text *Airline Ticket*, then click **Select** in the Table group on the Layout tab. Click **Select Row**, then hold down **Shift** and press the **down arrow** on your keyboard five times to select the remaining rows in the table. Click the **Height spin arrow** in the Cell Size group on the Layout tab to display 0.3".

You changed the height of the last five rows in the table to 0.3" tall.

d. Save the document.

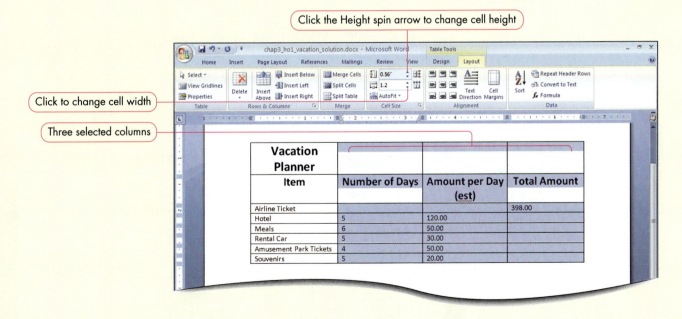

Figure 3.4 Adjust Cell Height and Width

TIP Adjusting Column Width and Row Height

If you are not certain of the exact measurements needed for row height or column width, you can use the mouse to increase or decrease the size. Position the mouse pointer on the gridline that separates the rows (or columns) until the pointer changes to a two-headed arrow. The two-headed arrow indicates you can adjust the height (or width) by clicking and dragging the gridline up or down (right or left) to resize the cell.

Step 4

Merge Cells to Create Header Row

Refer to Figure 3.5 as you complete Step 4.

a. Click outside the table to the left of the first cell in the first row to select the entire first row.

b. Click **Merge Cells** in the Merge group on the Layout tab, as shown in Figure 3.5.

You merged or joined the selected cells. The first row now contains a single cell.

c. Place the insertion point anywhere in the first row, click **Select** in the Table group on the Layout tab, then choose **Select Row**. Click the **Home tab**, click the **Font Size arrow,** and select **24**. Click **Center** in the Paragraph group.

d. Click the **Layout tab**, then click the **Height spin arrow** in the Cell Size group to display **0.5"**.

After increasing the size of the cell contents, you increased the height of the cell so the text is easier to read.

e. Save the *chap3_ho1_vacation_solution* document and keep it onscreen if you plan to continue to the next hands-on exercise. Close the file and exit Word if you do not want to continue with the next exercise at this time.

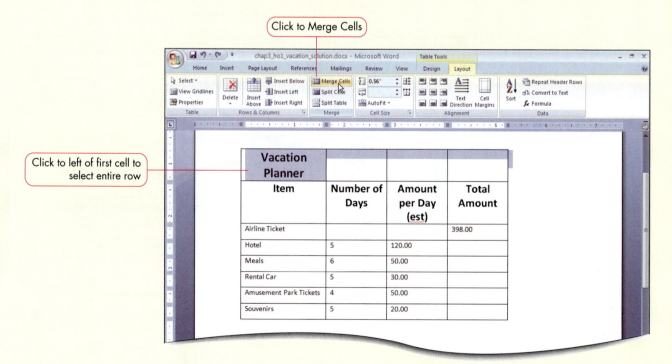

Figure 3.5 Merge First Row Cells

Advanced Table Features

After you create a basic table, you will want to enhance the appearance to create interest for the reader and improve readability. Microsoft Word 2007 provides many predefined styles, which contain borders, shading, font sizes, and other attributes that enhance a table.

You now have a good understanding of the table features and realize there are many uses for them in your Word documents. After you create the basic table, you want to enhance the appearance to create interest for the reader and improve readability. Microsoft Word 2007 includes many tools to assist with these efforts, and you will use several of them to complete the Vacation Planner table.

In this section, you learn how to format a table. Specifically, you apply borders and shading to table cells, apply table styles to the entire table, and select table alignment and position. In addition, you sort data within a table and insert formulas to perform calculations. Finally, you convert text to a table format.

Formatting a Table

You can use basic formatting options to enhance the appearance of your table. The Borders and Shading commands, for example, offer a wide variety of choices for formatting the table structure. *Shading* affects the background color within a cell or group of cells. Table shading is similar to the Highlight feature that places a color behind text. You often apply shading to the header row of a table to make it stand out from the data. *Border* refers to the line style around each cell in the table. The default is a single line, but you can choose from many styles to outline a table such as a double, triple, or a wavy line. You can even choose invisible borders if you want only data to display in your document without the outline of a table. Borders and Shading commands are located on the Design tab so you do not have to return to the Home tab to use them.

Shading affects the background color within a cell.

Border refers to the line style around each cell.

Apply Table Styles

When you do not have time to apply custom borders and shading, you will find the Table Styles feature very helpful. Microsoft Word 2007 provides many predefined *table styles* that contain borders, shading, font sizes, and other attributes that enhance readability of a table. The custom styles are available in the Table Styles group on the Design tab. To use a predefined table style, click anywhere in your table, and then click a style from the Table Styles gallery. A few styles from the gallery display, but you can select from many others by clicking the down arrow on the right side of the gallery, as shown in Figure 3.6. The Live preview of a style displays on your table when you hover your mouse over it in the gallery. To apply a style, click it one time.

A **table style** contains borders, shading, and other attributes to enhance a table.

You can modify a predefined style if you wish to make changes to features such as color or alignment. You also can create your own table style and save it for use in the current document or add it to a document template for use in other Word documents. Click the More arrow in the Table Styles group to access the Modify Table Style and New Table Style commands.

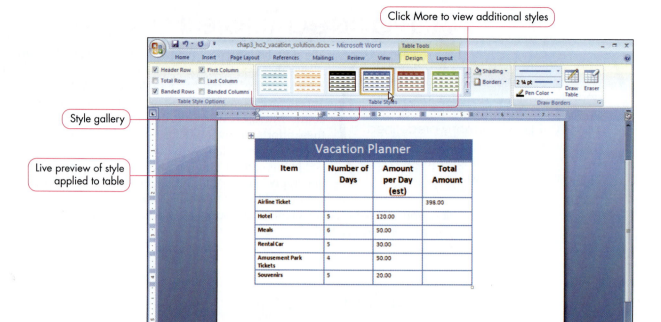

Figure 3.6 Table Styles Command

Select the Table Position and Alignment

Table alignment is the position of a table between the left and right margins.

When you insert a table, Word aligns it at the left margin by default. However, you can click Properties in the Table group on the Layout tab to change the *table alignment*, the position of a table between the left and right document margins. For example, you might want to center the table between the margins or align it at the right margin.

You also can change alignment of the data in a table separately from the table itself using the Properties dialog box. The Layout tab includes the Alignment group that contains many options to quickly format table data.

Table data can be formatted to align in many different horizontal and vertical combinations. We often apply horizontal settings, such as center, to our data, but using vertical settings also increases readability. For example, when you want your data to be centered both horizontally and vertically within a cell so it is easy to read and does not appear to be elevated on the top or too close to the bottom, click Align Center in the Alignment group to apply that setting.

Text direction refers to the degree of rotation in which text displays.

The default *text direction* places text in an upright position. However, you can rotate text so it displays sideways. To change text direction, click Text Direction in the Alignment group on the Layout tab. Each time you click Text Direction, the text rotates. This is a useful tool for aligning text that is in the header row of a narrow column.

Cell margins are the amount of space between data and the cell border in a table.

The *Cell margins* command in the Alignment group on the Layout tab enables you to adjust the amount of white space inside a cell as well as spacing between cells. Use this setting to improve readability of cell contents by adjusting white space around your data or between cells if they contain large amounts of text or data. If you increase cell margins, it prevents data from looking squeezed together.

Sorting and Applying Formulas to Table Data

Sorting is the process of rearranging data.

Because tables provide an easy way to arrange numbers within a document, it is important to know how to use table calculations. This feature gives a Word document the power of a simple spreadsheet. Additional organization of table data is possible by the use of *sorting*, or rearranging data based on a certain criteria. Figure 3.7 displays the vacation expenses you created previously, but this table illustrates two additional capabilities of the table feature—sorting and calculating.

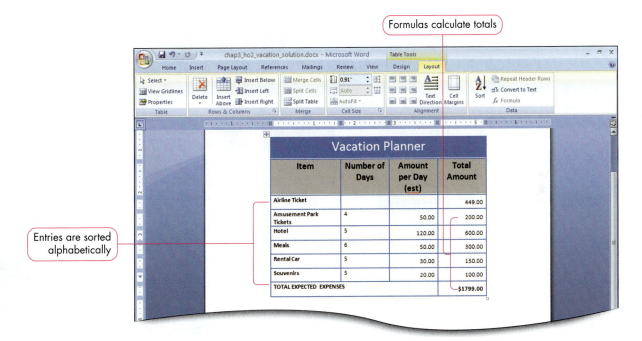

Figure 3.7 The Vacation Planner Table with Enhancements

Calculate Using Table Formulas

In this table, the entries in the Total Amount column consist of formulas that were entered into the table to perform a calculation. The entries are similar to those in a spreadsheet. Thus, the rows in the table are numbered from one to nine while the columns are labeled from A to D. The row and column labels do not appear in the table, but are used in the formulas.

You know that the intersection of a row and column forms a cell. Word uses the column letter and row number of that intersection to identify the cell and to give it an address. Cell D5, for example, contains the entry to compute the total hotel expense by multiplying the number of days (in cell B5) by the amount charged per day (in cell C5). In similar fashion, the entry in cell D6 computes the total expense for meals by multiplying the values in cells B6 and C6, respectively. The formula is not entered (typed) into the cell explicitly, but is created using the Formula command in the Data group on the Layout tab.

Figure 3.8 is a slight variation of Figure 3.7 in which the field codes have been toggled on to display the formulas, as opposed to the calculated values. The cells are shaded to emphasize that these cells contain formulas (fields), as opposed to numerical values. The field codes are toggled on and off by selecting the formula and pressing Shift+F9 or by right-clicking the entry and selecting the Toggle Field Codes command.

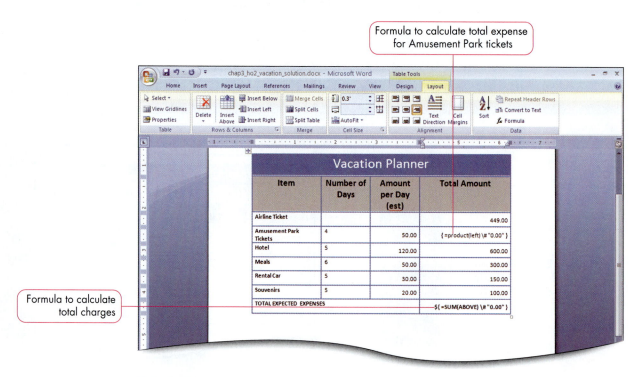

Figure 3.8 The Vacation Planner Table Displaying Formulas

The formula in cell D9 has a different syntax and adds the value of all cells directly above it. You do not need to know the syntax because Word provides a dialog box that supplies the entry for you, but once you use it to create the formula, you will find it easy to understand. It is better to use the Formula command to calculate totals than to type a number because if you add data to the table, you can use formula tools to recalculate for you.

Sort Data in a Table

Ascending order arranges data from lowest to highest.

Descending order arranges data from highest to lowest.

At times, you might need to sort data in a table to enhance order or understand the data. For example, when a list of employees is reviewed, a manager would prefer to view the names in alphabetical order by last name or department. You can sort data according to the entries in a specific column or row of the table. Sort orders include *ascending order*, which arranges text in alphabetical or sequential order starting with the lowest letter or number and continuing to the highest (A–Z or 0–9). Or you can sort in *descending order*, where data is arranged from highest to lowest (Z–A or 9–0).

You can sort the rows in a table to display data in different sequences as shown in Figure 3.9, where the vacation items are sorted from lowest to highest expense. You also could sort the data in descending (high to low) sequence according to the Total Amount. In descending order, the hotel (largest expense) displays at the top of the list, and the souvenirs (smallest expense) appear last. The second row of the table contains the field names for each column and is not included in the sort. The next six rows contain the sorted data, while the last row displays the total for all expenses and is not included in the sort.

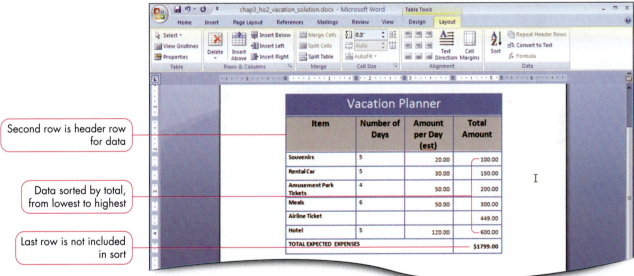

Figure 3.9 Sort the Table Data

Sorting is accomplished according to the select-then-do methodology that is used for many operations in Microsoft Word. You select the rows that are to be sorted, rows three through nine in this example, and then you click Sort in the Data group on the Layout tab. The Sort dialog box displays, as shown in Figure 3.10, which enables you to select the direction and sort criteria.

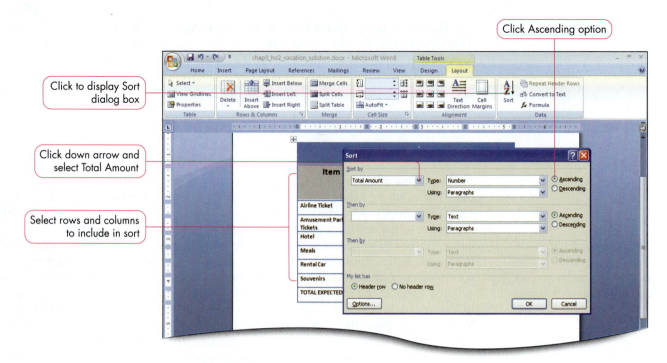

Figure 3.10 The Sort Command

Converting Text to a Table

The tables feature is outstanding. But what if you are given a lengthy list of items—for example, two items per line separated by a tab that should have been formatted as a table? The Table command on the Insert tab includes the Convert Text to Table command, and it can aid you in this transformation. After you select the text and choose this command, the Convert Text to Table dialog box displays and offers several options to assist in a quick conversion of text into a table. The command also works in reverse; you can convert a table to text. You will perform a table conversion in the next set of hands-on exercises.

Table Tools Design Ribbon | Reference

Group	Commands	Enables you to
Table Style Options	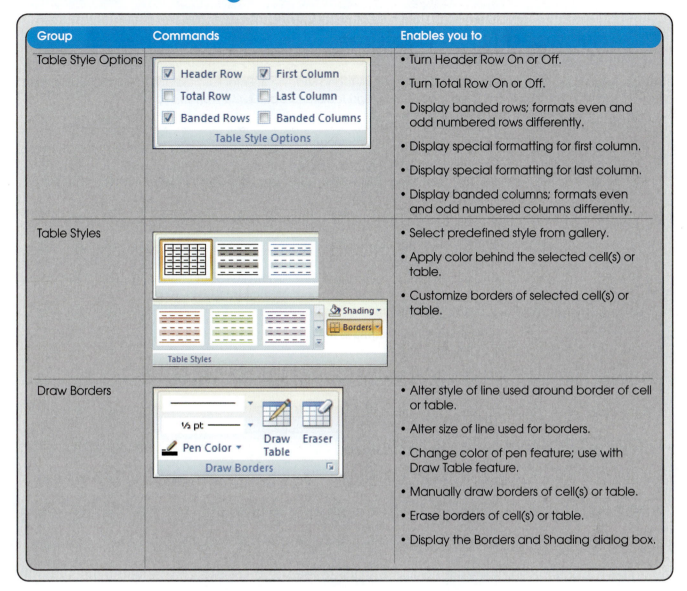	• Turn Header Row On or Off. • Turn Total Row On or Off. • Display banded rows; formats even and odd numbered rows differently. • Display special formatting for first column. • Display special formatting for last column. • Display banded columns; formats even and odd numbered columns differently.
Table Styles		• Select predefined style from gallery. • Apply color behind the selected cell(s) or table. • Customize borders of selected cell(s) or table.
Draw Borders		• Alter style of line used around border of cell or table. • Alter size of line used for borders. • Change color of pen feature; use with Draw Table feature. • Manually draw borders of cell(s) or table. • Erase borders of cell(s) or table. • Display the Borders and Shading dialog box.

Hands-On Exercises

2 | Advanced Table Features

Skills covered: 1. Apply a Table Style **2.** Add Table Borders and Shading **3.** Enter Formulas to Calculate Totals **4.** Add a Row and Enter a Formula **5.** Sort Data in a Table **6.** Align Table and Data **7.** Convert Text to a Table

---

Step 1
Apply a Table Style

Refer to Figure 3.11 as you complete Step 1.

a. Open the *chap3_ho1_vacation_solution* document if you closed it at the end of the first exercise and save it as **chap3_ho2_vacation_solution**. Then click anywhere in the table.

The insertion point must be somewhere within the table before the Table Tools tabs display.

b. Click the **Design tab**, and then click **More** on the right side of the Table Styles gallery. Hover your mouse over several styles and notice how the table changes to preview that style. Click once on the **Light List – Accent 1** style to apply it to your table, as shown in Figure 3.11.

Previous cell shading is replaced by the formatting attributes for the **Light List – Accent 1** style.

c. Save the document.

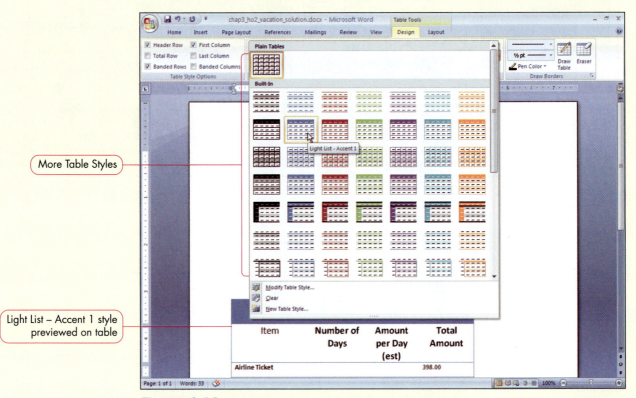

Figure 3.11 Style Applied to Vacation Planner Table

Step 2
Add Table Borders and Shading

Refer to Figure 3.12 as you complete Step 2.

a. Click anywhere in the Vacation Planner table. Click the **Borders arrow** in the Table Styles group and select **Borders and Shading**.

b. Click **All** in the *Setting* section on the left side of the Borders tab. Then click the **Width drop-down arrow** and select 2¼ pt. Click **OK** to close the Borders and Shading dialog box.

Your table has a darker blue border surrounding each cell.

c. Drag your mouse across the cells in the second row of the table to select them, then click **Shading** in the Table Styles group. Click the swatch in the fourth row of the first column named **White, Background 1, Darker 25%**, as shown in Figure 3.12.

The table now displays a large, blue title row, a gray colored header row, and blue borders around the remaining data.

d. Save the document.

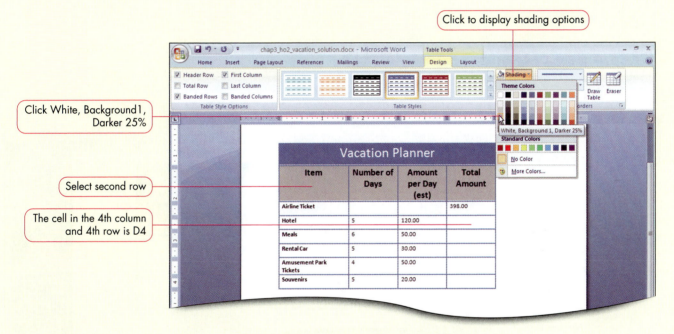

Figure 3.12 Borders and Shading Applied to Table

Step 3
Enter Formulas to Calculate Totals

Refer to Figure 3.13 as you complete Step 3.

a. Click in **cell D4**, the cell in the fourth column and fourth row. Click the **Layout tab** and click **Formula** in the Data group to display the formula box.

b. Click and drag to select the =SUM(ABOVE) function, which is entered by default. Type **=b4*c4**, as shown in Figure 3.13, to replace the existing formula and compute the total hotel expense. Click the **Number format drop-down arrow** and select **0.00**, and then click **OK**.

The formula is not case sensitive; you can type formula references in lowercase or capital letters. The total is computed by multiplying the number of days (in cell B4) by the amount per day (in cell C4). The result, 600, displays in a number format with two decimal places because these numbers represent a monetary value in dollars and cents.

c. Click in **cell D5**, directly below the cell you edited in the last step, then click **Formula**. In the Formula box, click and drag to select SUM(ABOVE) but do not select the equal sign, then press **Delete** to remove the formula. Click the **Paste function drop-down arrow**, and then scroll and select **PRODUCT**. Type **left** between the parentheses where the insertion point is blinking in the Formula box. Click the **Number format drop-down arrow**, select **0.00**, and then click **OK**.

This formula performs the same function as the one you used in Step B, but it references cells to the left of the current cell instead of using actual cell addresses.

d. Calculate the total expenses for cells D6, D7, and D8 using either formula used in the previous steps.

e. Save the document.

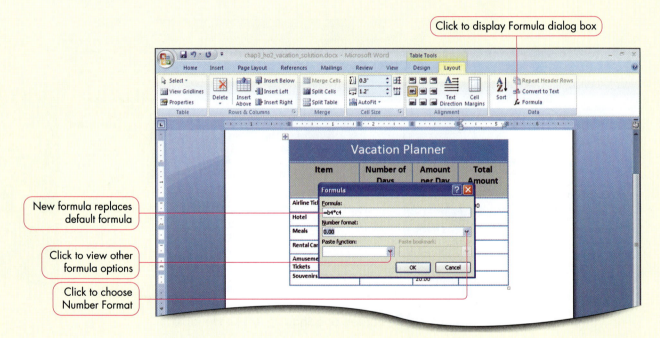

Figure 3.13 Compute a Formula in a Table

Step 4
Add a Row and Enter a Formula

Refer to Figure 3.14 as you complete Step 4.

a. Click the last cell in the table and press **Tab** to add another row to the table. Drag your mouse across all four cells in this row to select them, and then click **Merge Cells** in the Merge group on the Layout tab. Type the words **TOTAL EXPECTED EXPENSES** in the newly merged cell.

b. Click **Split Cells** in the Merge group to display the Split Cells dialog box. If necessary, click the **Number of columns spin box** to display **2**, then click **OK**.

The last row displays two cells of equal size. You will display the total vacation expense amount in the last cell, but you need to resize it to the same size as cells in the last column so the numbers will align correctly.

c. Hold your mouse over the border between the cells in the last row until a two-headed arrow displays. Then click and drag to the right until the border aligns with the border of the last column in the rows above, as shown in Figure 3.14.

d. Click in the last cell of the table, click **Formula**, click the **Number format drop-down arrow**, select **0.00**, and then click **OK** to accept the default formula, =SUM(ABOVE).

You should see 1748.00 (the sum of the cells in the last column) displayed in the selected cell.

e. Click the number, 1748.00, one time so that it is shaded in grey, then press **Shift+F9** to display the code {=SUM(ABOVE)\#"0.00"}. Press **Shift+F9** a second time to display the actual value.

f. Click in **cell D3** (the cell containing the airfare). Replace 398.00 with **449.00** and press **Tab** to move out of the cell.

The total expenses are not yet updated in cell D9.

g. Right-click on the number that displays in **cell D9** to display a shortcut menu, then select **Update Field**.

Cell D9 displays 1799.00, the updated total for all expenses.

h. Save the document.

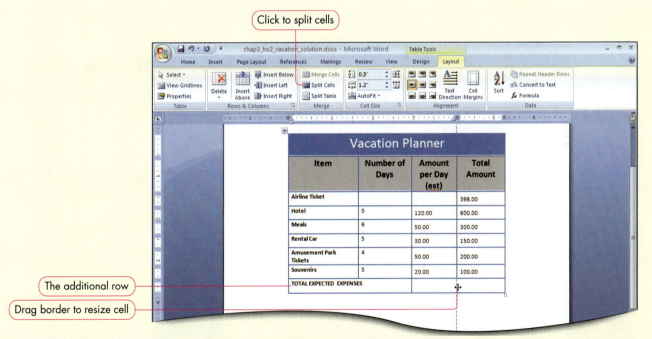

Figure 3.14 Drag to Resize Cell Width

<table>
<tr><td>

Step 5
Sort Data in a Table
</td><td>

Refer to Figure 3.15 as you complete Step 5.

a. Click and drag to select rows two through eight in the table. Click **Sort** in the Data group on the Layout tab.

b. Click **Header row** in the *My list has* section, at the bottom of the dialog box.

c. If necessary, click the **Sort by drop-down arrow** and select **Item** (the column heading for the first column). The Ascending option is selected by default, as shown in Figure 3.15. Click **OK**.

The entries in the table are rearranged alphabetically according to the entry in the Item column. The Total row remains at the bottom of the table since it was not included in the sort.

TROUBLESHOOTING: If you do not first click Header row, the headings for each column will not display in the Sort by drop-down list; instead, you will see the Column numbers listed. You can sort by Column number (1, 2, 3, or 4), but it is important to click the Header row option before you leave this dialog box so the header row is not included in the sort.

d. Select rows four through six, some of which have lost formatting along the left and right borders. Click the **Design tab**, click the **Borders arrow** in the Table Styles group, and then select **All Borders**.

The dark blue borders fill the left and right borders of the selected cells, matching the remainder of the table.

e. Save the document.
</td></tr>
</table>

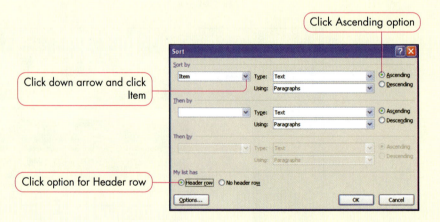

Figure 3.15 Sort Data in a Table

<table>
<tr><td>

Step 6
Align Table and Data
</td><td>

Refer to Figure 3.16 as you complete Step 6.

a. Click the table selector to select the entire table. Click the **Layout tab**, then click **Properties** in the Table group.

b. Click the **Table tab**, if necessary, and then click **Center** in the *Alignment* section, as shown in Figure 3.16. Click **OK**.

Your table is now centered between the left and right margins.

c. Click anywhere to deselect the whole table, then drag your mouse to select the last two columns of rows three through eight. Select entries listed under Amount Per Day (est) and Total Amount, but do not select data in the header
</td></tr>
</table>

row. Click **Align Center Right** from the Alignment group. Select the last cell in the table and click **Align Center Right** to align it with other data.

Because these columns contain numerical data, you right align them to give the effect of decimal alignment. However, the numbers are not decimal aligned, so if you display an additional digit in a value, it will result in misaligned numbers.

d. Click in the last cell and insert a dollar sign ($) in front of the amount of expected expenses.

e. Save and close the *chap3_ho2_vacation_solution* document.

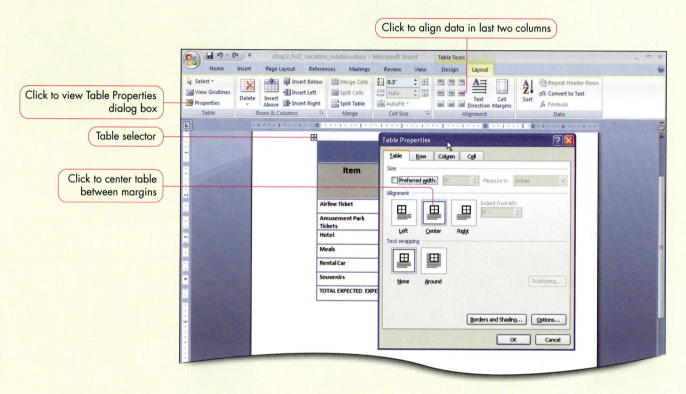

Figure 3.16 Apply Alignment to Vacation Planner Table

Step 7	
Convert Text to a Table	Refer to Figure 3.17 as you complete Step 7.

a. Open the *chap3_ho2_expenses* document and save it as **chap3_ho2_expenses_ solution**.

b. Press **Ctrl+A** to select all text in this document and then click the **Insert tab**.

c. Click **Table**, and then select **Convert Text to Table**. View the options in the Convert Text to Table dialog box, as shown in Figure 3.17, but do not make any changes at this time. Click **OK**.

The list of items display in a table that can now be sorted and formatted.

d. Save and close the *chap3_ho2_expenses_solution* document.

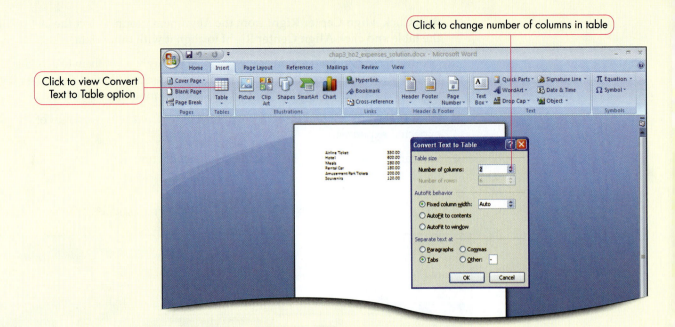

Click to change number of columns in table

Click to view Convert Text to Table option

Figure 3.17 Convert Text to Table Dialog Box

Graphic Tools

Clip art is a graphical image, illustration, drawing, or sketch.

One of the most exciting features of Word is its graphic capabilities. You can use clip art, images, drawings, and scanned photographs to visually enhance brochures, newsletters, announcements, and reports. **Clip art** is a graphical image, illustration, drawing, or sketch. In addition to inserting clip art in a document, you can insert photographs from a digital camera or scanner, graphically shaped text, and special boxes to hold text. After inserting a graphical image or text, you can adjust size, choose placement, and perform other graphical formatting options.

> One of the most exciting features of Word is its graphic capabilities. You can use clip art, images, drawings, and scanned photographs to visually enhance brochures, newsletters, announcements, and reports.

In this section, you will learn to insert a clip art and an image in a document. Then you format the image by changing the height and width, applying a text-wrapping style, applying a quick style, and adjusting graphic properties. Finally, you will insert WordArt and symbols in a document.

Inserting Clip Art and Images into a Document

Clip art and other graphical images or objects may be stored locally, purchased on a CD at a computer supply store, or downloaded from the Internet for inclusion into a document. Whether you use Microsoft's online clip gallery or purchase clip art, you should read the license agreements to know how you may legally use the images. A **copyright** provides legal protection to a written or artistic work, giving the author exclusive rights to its use and reproduction, except as governed under the fair use exclusion. Anything on the Internet should be considered copyrighted unless the document specifically says it is in the public domain. The Fair Use doctrine allows you to use a portion of the work for educational, nonprofit purposes, or for the purpose of critical review or commentary. All such material should be cited through an appropriate footnote or endnote. Using clip art for a purpose not allowed by the license agreement is illegal.

A **copyright** provides legal protection to a written or artistic work.

Manage Clips with the Microsoft Clip Organizer

The Clip Art command displays a task pane through which you can search, select, and insert clip art, photographs, sounds, and movies (collectively called clips). The clips can come from a variety of sources. They may be installed locally in the My Collections folder, in conjunction with Microsoft Office in the Office Collections folder, and/or they may have been downloaded from the Web and stored in the Web Collections folder. You can insert a specific clip into a document if you know its location. You also can search for a clip that will enhance the document on which you are working.

The **Microsoft Clip Organizer** catalogs pictures, sounds, and movies stored on your hard drive.

The **Microsoft Clip Organizer** brings you out of potential chaos by cataloging the clips, photos, sounds, and movies that are available. You enter a keyword that describes the clip you are looking for, specify the collections that are to be searched, and indicate the type of clip(s) you are looking for. The results are returned in the task pane, as shown in Figure 3.18, which displays the clips that are described by the keyword *computer*. You can restrict the search to selected collections but request that all media types be displayed. If you also specify to search for items stored locally, the search is faster than one that searches online as well. When you see a clip that you want to use, click the clip to insert it into your document. For more options, point to the clip, click the down arrow that appears, and then select from the menu.

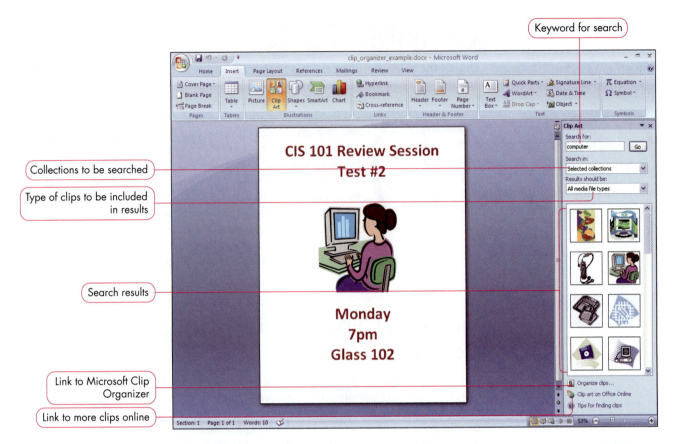

Keyword for search

Collections to be searched

Type of clips to be included in results

Search results

Link to Microsoft Clip Organizer

Link to more clips online

Figure 3.18 The Clip Art Task Pane

You can access the Microsoft Clip Organizer (to view the various collections) by clicking Organize clips at the bottom of the Clip Art task pane. You also can access the Clip Organizer when you are not using Word; click the Start button on the taskbar, click All Programs, Microsoft Office, Microsoft Office Tools, and Microsoft Clip Organizer. Once in the Organizer, you can search through the clips in the various collections, reorganize the existing collections, add new collections, and even add new clips (with their associated keywords) to the collections. The other links at the bottom of the task pane in Figure 3.18 provide access to additional clip art online and tips for finding more relevant clips.

Insert a Picture

In addition to the collection of clip art and pictures that you can access from Word, you also can insert your own pictures into a document. If you have a scanner or digital camera attached to your computer, you can scan or download a picture for use in Word. After you save the picture to your disk, click Picture in the Illustrations group on the Insert tab to locate and insert it in the document. The Insert Picture dialog box opens so that you can navigate to the location where the picture is saved. After you insert the picture, there are many commands you can use to format it. Those commands are discussed in the next section.

Formatting a Graphic Element

Remember that graphical elements should enhance a document, not overpower it.

When you insert an image in a document, it comes in a predefined size. For example, the clip art image in Figure 3.18 was very large and took up much space on the page before it was resized. Most times, you need to adjust an image's size so it fits within the document and does not greatly increase the document file size. Remember that graphical elements should enhance a document, not overpower it.

Adjust the Height and Width of a Graphic

Sizing handles are the small circles and squares that appear around a selected object and enable you to adjust the height and width of an object.

Word provides different tools you can use to adjust the height or width of an image, depending on how exact you want the measurements. The Picture Tools Format tab contains Height and Width commands that enable you to specify exact measurements. You can use *sizing handles*, the small circles and squares that appear around a selected object, to size an object by clicking and dragging any one of the handles. When you use the circular sizing handles in the corner of a graphic to adjust the height (or width), Word also adjusts the width (or height) simultaneously. If needed, hold down Shift while dragging the corner sizing handle to maintain the correct proportion of the image. If you use square sizing handles on the right, left, top, or bottom, you adjust that measurement without regard to any other sides.

Adjust Text Wrapping

Text wrapping style refers to the way text wraps around an image.

When you first insert an image, Word treats it as a character in the line of text, which leaves a lot of empty space on the left or right side of the image. You may want it to align differently, perhaps allowing text to display very tightly around the object or even behind the text. *Text wrapping style* refers to the way text wraps around an image. Table 3.1 describes the different wrapping options.

Table 3.1 Text Wrapping Styles

Text Wrapping Style	Description
Square	Allows text to wrap around the graphic frame that surrounds the image.
Tight	Allows text to wrap tightly around the outer edges of the image itself instead of the frame.
Through	Select this option to wrap text around the perimeter and inside any open portions of the object.
Top and Bottom	Text wraps to the top and bottom of the image frame, but no text appears on the sides.
Behind Text	Allows the image to display behind the text in such a way that the image appears to float directly behind the text and does not move if text is inserted or deleted.
In Front of Text	Allows the image to display on top of the text in such a way that the image appears to float directly on top of the text and does not move if text is inserted or deleted.
In Line with Text	Graphic displays on the line where inserted so that as you add or delete text, causing the line of text to move, the image moves with it.

Apply Picture Quick Styles

The **Picture Styles** gallery contains preformatted options that can be applied to a graphical object.

Word 2007 introduces the *Picture Styles* gallery that contains many preformatted picture formats. The gallery of styles you can apply to a picture or clip art is extensive, and you also can modify the style after you apply it. The quick styles provide a valuable resource if you want to improve the appearance of a graphic but are not familiar with graphic design and format tools. For example, after you insert a graphic, with one click you can choose a style from the Quick Styles gallery that adds a border and displays a reflection of the picture. You might want to select a style that changes the shape of your graphic to an octagon, or select a style that applies a 3-D effect to the image. To apply a quick style, select the graphical object, then choose a quick style from the Picture Styles group on the Picture Tools Format tab. Other style formatting options, such as Soft Edges or 3-D Rotation, are listed in Picture Effects on the Picture Styles group, as shown in Figure 3.19.

Adjust Graphic Properties

Crop or Cropping is the process of trimming the edges of an image or other graphical object.

Scale or scaling is the adjustment of height or width by a percentage of the image's original size.

Contrast is the difference between light and dark areas of an image.

Brightness is the ratio between lightness and darkness of an image.

After you insert a graphic or an image, you might find that you need to edit it before using a picture style. One of the most common changes includes *crop or cropping*, which is the process of trimming edges or other portions of an image or other graphical object that you do not wish to display. Cropping enables you to call attention to a specific area of a graphical element while omitting any unnecessary detail. When you add images to enhance a document, you may find clip art that has more objects than you desire or you may find an image that has damaged edges that you do not wish to appear in your document. You can solve the problems with these graphics by cropping. The cropping tool is located in the Size group on the Format tab.

Instead of cropping unused portions of a graphic, you may need to enlarge or reduce its size to fit in the desired area. The easiest method for sizing is selecting the image and dragging the selection handles. For more exact measurements, however, you can use the *scale or scaling*, which adjusts the height or width of an image by a percentage of its original size. The scale adjustment is located in the Size dialog box, which you display by clicking the Size Dialog Box Launcher on the Format tab.

Other common adjustments to a graphical object includes contrast and/or brightness. Adjusting the *contrast* increases or decreases the difference in dark and light areas of the image. Adjusting the *brightness* lightens or darkens the overall image.

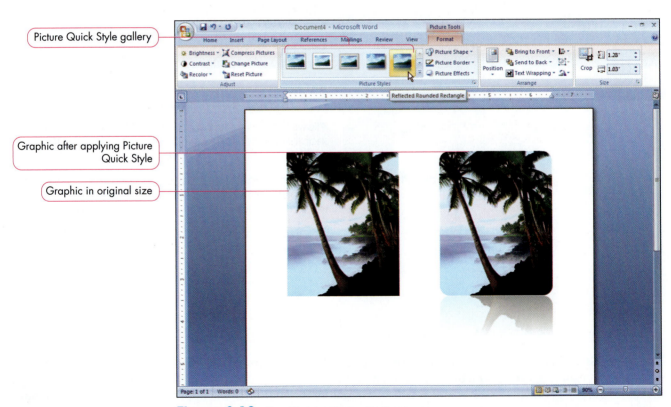

Figure 3.19 The Picture Styles Gallery

These adjustments often are made on a picture taken with a digital camera in poor lighting or if a clip art image is too bright or dull to match other objects in your document. Adjusting contrast or brightness can improve the visibility of subjects in a picture. You may want to increase contrast for a dramatic effect or lower contrast to soften an image. The Brightness and Contrast adjustments are in the Picture Tools group on the Format tab.

Even though graphical objects add a great deal of visual enhancement to a document, they also can increase the file size of the document. If you add several graphics to a document, you should view the file size before you copy or save it to a portable storage device, and then confirm the device has enough empty space to hold the large file. Additional consideration should be given to files you send as e-mail attachments. Many people have space limitations in their mailboxes, and a document that contains several graphics can fill their space or take a long time to download. To decrease the size a graphic occupies, you can use the *Compress* feature, which reduces the size of an object. When you select a graphical object, you can click the Compress Pictures command on the Picture Tools group in the Format tab, to display the Compression Settings dialog box. Here you can select from options that allow you to reduce the size of the graphical elements, thus reducing the size of the file when you save.

The Picture Tools tab offers many additional graphic editing features, which are described on the following reference page.

Compress reduces the file size of an object.

Graphic Editing Features | Reference

Feature	Button	Description
Height		Height of an object in inches.
Width		Width of an object in inches.
Crop		Remove unwanted portions of the object from top, bottom, left, or right to adjust size.
Align		Adjust edges of object to line up on right or left margin or center between margins.
Group		Process of selecting multiple objects so you can move and format them together.
Rotate		Ability to change the position of an object by rotating it around its own center.
Text Wrapping		Refers to the way text wraps around an object.
Position		Specify location on page where object will reside.
Border		The outline surrounding an object; it can be formatted using color, shapes, or width, or can be set as invisible.
Shadow Effects		Ability to add a shadow to an object.
Compress		Reduce the file size of an object.
Brightness		Increase or decrease brightness of an object.
Contrast		Increase or decrease difference between black and white colors of an object.
Recolor		Change object to give it an effect such as washed-out or grayscale.

Inserting WordArt into a Document

Microsoft WordArt creates decorative text for a document.

Microsoft WordArt is a Microsoft Office application that creates decorative text that can be used to add interest to a document. You can use WordArt in addition to clip art, or in place of clip art if the right image is not available. You can rotate text in any direction, add three-dimensional effects, display the text vertically, slant it, arch it, or even print it upside down.

WordArt is intuitively easy to use. In essence, you choose a style from the gallery (see Figure 3.20). Then you enter the specific text in the Edit WordArt Text dialog box, after which the results display (see Figure 3.21). The WordArt object can be moved and sized, just like any object. A WordArt Tools tab provides many formatting features that enable you to change alignment, add special effects, and change styles quickly. It is fun and easy, and you can create some truly unique documents.

Click to select style

Figure 3.20   The WordArt Gallery

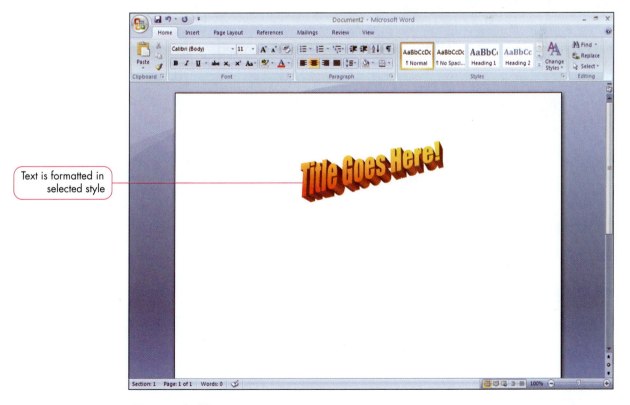

Text is formatted in selected style

Figure 3.21   The Completed WordArt Object

Inserting Symbols into a Document

The Symbol command enables you to enter typographic symbols and/or foreign language characters into a document in place of ordinary typing—for example, ® rather than (R), © rather than (c), ½, and ¼, rather than 1/2 and 1/4, or é rather than e (as used in the word résumé). These special characters give a document a very professional look.

You may have already discovered that some of this formatting can be done automatically through the AutoCorrect feature that is built in to Word. If, for example, you type the letter "c" enclosed in parentheses, it will automatically be converted to the copyright symbol. You can use the Symbol command to insert other symbols, such as accented letters like the é in résumé or those in a foreign language (e.g., ¿Cómo está usted?).

The installation of Microsoft Office adds a variety of fonts onto your computer, each of which contains various symbols that can be inserted into a document. Selecting "normal text," however, as was done in Figure 3.22, provides access to the accented characters as well as other common symbols. Other fonts—especially the Wingdings, Webdings, and Symbol fonts—contain special symbols, including the Windows logo. The Wingdings, Webdings, and Symbol fonts are among the best-kept secrets in Microsoft Office. Each font contains a variety of symbols that are actually pictures. You can insert any of these symbols into a document as text, select the character and enlarge the point size, change the color, then copy the modified character to create a truly original document.

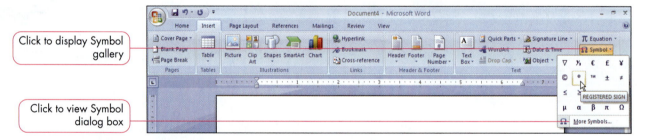

Click to display Symbol gallery

Click to view Symbol dialog box

Figure 3.22 Insert Symbol Command

Hands-On Exercises

3 | Clip Art, WordArt, and Symbols

Skills covered: 1. Insert a Clip Art Object **2.** Move and Resize the Clip Art Object **3.** Create a WordArt Object
4. Modify the WordArt Object **5.** Insert a Symbol

Step 1
Insert a Clip Art Object

Refer to Figure 3.23 as you complete Step 1.

a. Open the *chap3_ho3_ergonomics* document and save it as **chap3_ho3_ergonomics _solution**.

b. Click to move the insertion point to the beginning of the document, if necessary. Click the **Insert tab** and click **Clip Art** in the Illustrations group.

The Clip Art task pane opens, as shown in Figure 3.23.

c. Type **computer** in the **Search for box** to search for any clip art image that is indexed with this keyword. Click the **Search in drop-down arrow** and click **Office Collections**, then click to deselect My Collections and Web Collections, if necessary. Click **Go**.

The images display in the task pane. If the the Microsoft Clip Organizer displays and asks "Do you want to include thousands of additional clip art images and photos from Microsoft Office Online when you search?" click No.

d. Point to the first image to display a down arrow, and then click the arrow to display a menu.

e. Click **Insert** to insert the image into the document. Do not be concerned about its size or position at this time. Close the task pane.

f. Save the document.

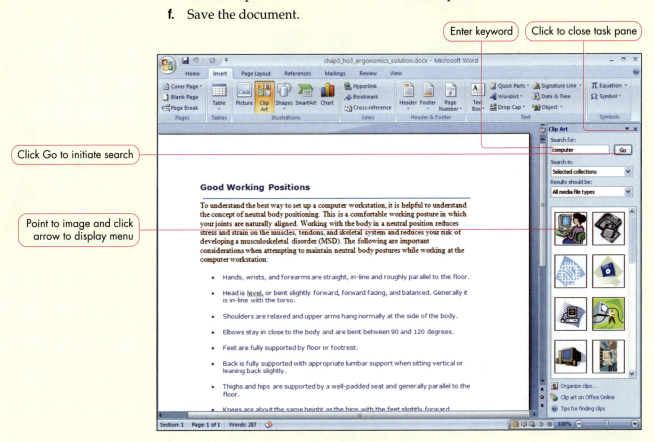

Figure 3.23 Clip Art Task Pane

Step 2
Move and Resize the Clip Art Object

Refer to Figure 3.24 as you complete Step 2.

a. Click once on the clip art object to select it. Click **Text Wrapping** in the Arrange group on the Picture Tools Format tab to display the text wrapping options, and then select **Square**, as shown in Figure 3.24.

You must change the layout in order to move and size the object.

b. Click **Position** in the Arrange group, and then click **More Layout Options.** Click the **Picture Position tab** in the Advanced Layout dialog box, if necessary, then click **Alignment** in the *Horizontal* section. Click the **Alignment drop-down arrow** and select **Right**. Deselect the **Allow overlap check box** in the *Options* section. Click **OK**.

c. Click **Crop** in the Size group, then hold your mouse over the sizing handles and notice how the pointer changes to angular shapes. Click the **bottom center handle** and drag it up. Drag the side handles inward to remove excess space surrounding the graphical object.

d. Click the Shape **Height box** in the Size group and type **2.77**. Click anywhere in the document to view the changes.

Notice the width is changed automatically to retain the proportion.

e. Save the document.

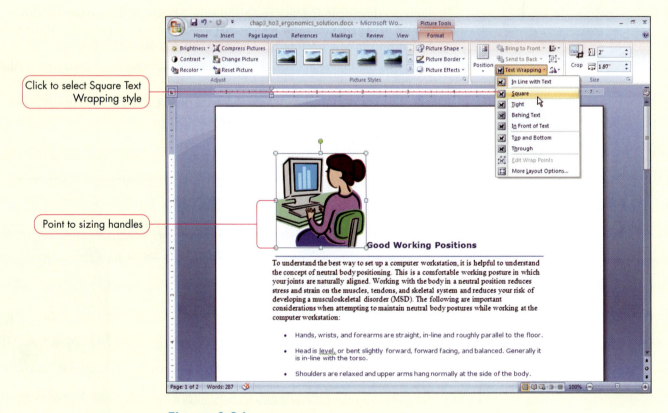

Figure 3.24 Formatting Clip Art

Click to select Square Text Wrapping style

Point to sizing handles

Step 3
Create a WordArt Object

Refer to Figure 3.25 as you complete Step 3.

a. Press **Ctrl+End** to move to the end of the document. Click the **Insert tab**, and then click **WordArt** in the Text group to display the WordArt gallery.

b. Click **WordArt style 28** on the bottom row of the gallery.

The Edit WordArt Text dialog box displays, as shown in Figure 3.25.

c. Type **WWW.OSHA.GOV,** and then click OK.

The WordArt object appears in your document in the style you selected.

TROUBLESHOOTING: If the WordArt object displays on another page, you can correct it in the next steps.

d. Point to the WordArt object and right-click to display a shortcut menu. Select **Format WordArt** to display the Format WordArt dialog box.

e. Click the **Layout tab** and click **Square** in the *Wrapping style* section. Click **OK**.

It is important to select this wrapping option to facilitate placing the WordArt at the bottom of the first page.

f. Save the document.

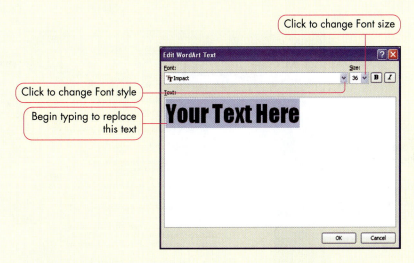

Figure 3.25 Edit WordArt Text Dialog Box

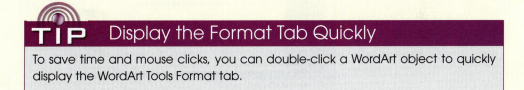

TIP Display the Format Tab Quickly

To save time and mouse clicks, you can double-click a WordArt object to quickly display the WordArt Tools Format tab.

Step 4
Modify the WordArt Object

Refer to Figure 3.26 as you complete Step 4.

a. Click and drag the WordArt object to move it to the bottom-right corner of the document, below the text.

The Format WordArt dialog box is not yet visible.

b. Point to the WordArt object, right-click to display a menu, and then click **Format WordArt** to display the Format WordArt dialog box.

Remember that many of the options in this dialog box also are displayed in the WordArt Tools Format tab.

c. Click the **Colors and Lines tab** and click the **Color drop-down arrow** in the *Fill* section to display the color palette. Click **Orange, Accent 6, Lighter 40%**, which is in the last column. Click **OK**.

This action enables you to customize the colors used in the WordArt graphic. In this case, you minimize much of the bright orange tint in the WordArt.

d. Click **3-D Effects** on the Format tab, then click **3-D Effects** to display the 3-D Effects gallery, as shown in Figure 3.26. Click **3-D Style 1** from the Parallel group.

TROUBLESHOOTING: If your monitor uses a high resolution, or if you have a wide monitor, the 3-D Effects gallery might display immediately after you click 3-D Effects the first time. In that case, you will not click 3-D Effects twice, as instructed in Step D.

e. Save the document.

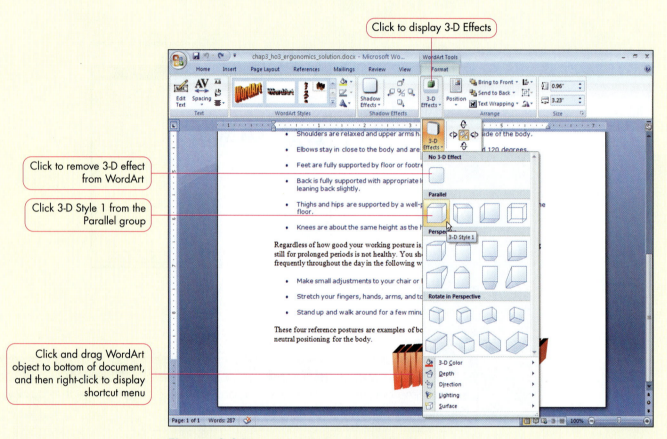

Click to display 3-D Effects

Click to remove 3-D effect from WordArt

Click 3-D Style 1 from the Parallel group

Click and drag WordArt object to bottom of document, and then right-click to display shortcut menu

Figure 3.26 3-D Style Gallery for WordArt

Step 5
Insert a Symbol

Refer to Figure 3.27 as you complete Step 5.

a. Select the word *degrees* that displays at the end of the fourth bullet item in the document. Press **Backspace** to remove the word and the space that follows 120.

b. Click the **Insert tab**, click **Symbol** in the Symbols group, and click **More Symbols** to display the Symbol dialog box. Click the **Font** drop-down box, and then select **Verdana** as shown in Figure 3.27. If necessary, click the *Subset* drop-down box and select **Basic Latin**.

c. Click the **Degree symbol** (the last character in the seventh line), click **Insert**, and close the Symbol dialog box.

d. Save the *chap3_ho3_ergonomics_solution* document and close Word if you do not want to continue with the end-of-chapter exercise at this time.

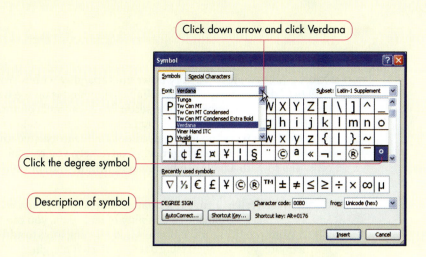

Figure 3.27 The Insert Symbol Command Symbol Dialog Box

Summary

1. **Insert a table.** Tables represent a very powerful capability within Word and are used to organize a variety of data in documents. The Table command is on the Insert tab, and tables are made up of rows and columns; the intersection of a row and column is called a cell. You can insert additional rows and columns if you need to add more data to a table, or you can delete a row or column if you no longer need data in the respective row or column. Individual cells can be merged to create a larger cell. Conversely, you can split a single cell into multiple cells. The rows in a table can be different heights and/or each column can be a different width.

2. **Format a table.** Each cell in a table is formatted independently and may contain text, numbers, and/or graphics. To enhance readability of table data, you can apply a predefined style, which Word provides, or use Borders and Shading tools to add color and enhance it. Furthermore, you can align table data—at the left margin, at the right margin, or centered between the margins. You also can change the text direction within a cell.

3. **Sort and apply formulas to table data.** You can sort the rows in a table to display the data in ascending or descending sequence, according to the values in one or more columns in the table. Sorting is accomplished by selecting the rows within the table that are to be sorted, then executing the Sort command on the Layout tab. Calculations can be performed within a table using the Formula command in the same tab.

4. **Convert text to a table.** If you have a list of tabulated items that would be easier to manipulate in a table, you can use the Convert Text to Table command. The command also works in reverse, enabling you to remove data from a table and format it as tabulated text.

5. **Insert clip art and images into a document.** You often add graphics to enhance a document. When you click the Clip Art command, Office displays a task pane where you enter a keyword to describe the clip you are looking for. The search is made possible by the Microsoft Clip Organizer, which organizes the media files available to you into collections, then enables you to limit the search to specific media types and/or specific collections. Resources (such as clip art or photographs) can be downloaded from the Web for inclusion in a Word document. Although clip art is often acceptable for educational or nonprofit use, it may not be permitted in some advertising situations. You should always assume a graphic is copyrighted unless noted otherwise.

6. **Format a graphic element.** After you insert the clip art object, you can use a variety of tools to refine the object to fit in your document, such as changing height and width, cropping, rotating, or aligning.

7. **Insert WordArt into a document.** Microsoft WordArt is an application within Microsoft Office that creates decorative text that can be used to add interest to a document. WordArt can be used in addition to clip art or in place of clip art if the right image is not available. You can rotate text in any direction, add three-dimensional effects, display the text vertically down the page, or print it upside down.

8. **Insert symbols into a document.** The Insert Symbol command provides access to special characters, making it easy to place typographic characters into a document. The symbols can be taken from any font and can be displayed in any point size.

Key Terms

Multiple Choice

1. You have created a table containing numerical values and have entered the SUM(ABOVE) function at the bottom of a column. You then delete one of the rows included in the sum. Which of the following is true?

   (a) The row cannot be deleted because it contains a cell that is included in the sum function.

   (b) The sum is updated automatically.

   (c) The sum cannot be updated.

   (d) The sum will be updated provided you right-click the cell and click the Update Field command.

2. Which process below is the best option to change the size of a selected object so that the height and width change in proportion to one another?

   (a) Enter the Height and allow Word to establish the Width.

   (b) Click and drag the sizing handle on the top border, then click and drag the sizing handle on the left side.

   (c) Click and drag the sizing handle on the bottom border, then click and drag the sizing handle on the right side.

   (d) Click only the sizing handle in the middle of the left side.

3. How do you search for clip art using the Clip Organizer?

   (a) By entering a keyword that describes the image you want.

   (b) By selecting the photo album option.

   (c) By clicking the Clip Organizer command on the Insert tab.

   (d) There is no such thing as a Clip Organizer.

4. What guideline should you remember when inserting graphics into a document?

   (a) It is distasteful to insert more than two graphics into a document.

   (b) It is not necessary to consider copyright notices if the document is for personal use.

   (c) WordArt should always be center aligned on a page.

   (d) Graphic elements should enhance a document, not overpower it.

5. Which of the following commands in the Picture Tools Format tab would you use to remove portions of a graphic that you do not wish to see in your document?

   (a) Height

   (b) Position

   (c) Crop

   (d) Reset Picture

6. Which of the following is not an example of how to use the Symbols feature in a document?

   (a) You can type (c) to insert the copyright symbol.

   (b) You can insert WordArt from the Symbol dialog box.

   (c) You can insert the Windows logo from the Symbol dialog box.

   (d) You can insert special characters from the Symbol dialog box.

7. Which of the following is true regarding objects and their associated tabs?

   (a) Clicking a WordArt object displays the WordArt Tools tab.

   (b) Right-clicking on a Picture displays the Picture Tools tab.

   (c) You can only display a tab by clicking the tab across the top of the screen.

   (d) Neither (a) nor (b).

8. Which wrap style allows text to wrap around the graphic frame that surrounds the image?

   (a) Top and Bottom

   (b) Tight

   (c) Behind Text

   (d) Square

9. What provides legal protection to the author for a written or artistic work?

   (a) Copyright

   (b) Public domain

   (c) Fair use

   (d) Footnote

10. Microsoft WordArt cannot be used to:

(a) Arch text, or print it upside down

(b) Rotate text, or add three-dimensional effects

(c) Display text vertically down a page

(d) Insert a copyright symbol

11. What happens when you press Tab from within the last cell of a table?

(a) A Tab character is inserted just as it would be for ordinary text.

(b) Word inserts a new row below the current row.

(c) Word inserts a new column to the right of the current column.

(d) The insertion point appears in the paragraph below the table.

12. What happens when you type more than one line of text into a cell?

(a) The cell gets wider to accommodate the extra text.

(b) The row gets taller as word wrapping occurs to display the additional text.

(c) The other lines are hidden by default.

(d) A new column is inserted automatically.

13. Assume you created a table with the names of the months in the first column. Each row lists data for that particular month. The insertion point is in the first cell on the third row—this row lists goals for April. You realize that you left out the goals for March. What should you do?

(a) Display the Insert tab and click the Table command.

(b) Display the Table Tools Design tab and click the Insert Cell command.

(c) Display the Table Tools Layout tab and click the Insert Left command.

(d) Display the Table Tools Layout tab and click the Insert Above command.

14. You have a list of people who were sent an invitation to a wedding. You are responsible for monitoring their responses to the invitation, whether they will attend or not, and to determine the grand total of those attending. Using skills learned in this Chapter what would be a good way to track this information?

(a) Use pen and paper to mark through names of those who decline the invitation and put stars by those who accept.

(b) Convert the list of names to a table; add columns that allow you to mark their response, including the number who will attend, and use a formula to add up the numbers when all responses are received.

(c) Insert wedding clip art in the document so you will know the purpose of the document.

(d) Insert a two-column table beside the names and mark the responses as declined or attending.

15. If cell A1 contains the value 2 and A2 contains the value 4, what value will be displayed if cell A3 contains the formula =PRODUCT(ABOVE)?

(a) 8

(b) 2

(c) 6

(d) This is not a valid formula.

16. What option would you use if you were given a lengthy list of items that are separated by tabs and that would be easier to format in a table?

(a) Insert Table

(b) Convert Table to Text

(c) Convert Text to Table

(d) Insert Text Box

17. Which option should you use to add color to improve the attractiveness and readability of a table?

(a) Text wrapping

(b) Sort

(c) Add column to right

(d) Borders and shading

While working as a volunteer at the local library, you are asked to create a flyer to advertise the upcoming annual book sale, as shown in Figure 3.28. You are required to use a combination of tables, clip art, WordArt, and symbols to create an informative and attractive flyer. If you are unable to find the exact same graphics, find something as similar as possible; you need not match our flyer exactly.

a. Open a new document and save it as **chap3_pe1_flyer_solution**.

b. Click the **Page Layout tab** and click **Margins** in the Page Setup group. Click **Normal**, if necessary, to set all four margins to 1˝.

c. Click the **Insert tab** and click **Table** in the Tables group to insert a table. Click only one cell to insert a **1x1** table.

d. Click the **Home tab**, and then click the **Font Dialog Box Launcher**. Select **Comic Sans MS** in the **Font list**, select **Bold** in the **Font style list**, and select **36** in the **Size list**. Click the **Font color drop-down arrow**, select **Red, Accent 2, Darker 25%** (a shade of red). Click **OK** to close the Font dialog box.

e. Type **Annual Book Sale** in the table. Click **Center** in the Paragraph group to center the text within the table cell.

f. Click the **Design tab**, click the **Borders arrow**, and click **Borders and Shading**. Select **None** in the *Setting* section to remove all current borders around the table. Click the **Color drop-down arrow** and select **Red, Accent 2, Darker 50%** (at the bottom of the red column). Then click the **Width drop-down arrow** and select **3 pt**.

g. Click once on the top of the diagram in the *Preview* section to insert a top border, and then click once on the bottom of the diagram to insert a bottom border. If necessary, click the **Apply to drop-down arrow**, select **Table**, and click **OK**.

h. Click below the table to move the insertion point. Click the **Home tab**, and then click the **Font Size arrow** and select **28**. Type the date of the sale, **March 1**, and click **Align Text Right** in the Paragraph group to move the date to the right side of the flyer.

i. Press **Enter** two times to move the insertion point down the page, click the **Insert tab,** and click **WordArt** in the Text group. Click **WordArt style 28** on the bottom row. In the Edit WordArt Text dialog box, type **The Library Station** and click **OK**.

j. The WordArt object needs to be resized and relocated to have a bigger impact on our flyer. Click **Position** in the Arrange group of the Format tab and click **Position in Middle Center with Tight Text Wrapping**.

k. Click the **Height box** and type **2** to increase the height of the object. Click the **Width box** and type **6** to elongate the object. Click the uppermost handle on the top of the object and notice the insertion point changes to a curved arrow. Click this handle and hold down while rotating the object to the left so that it appears similar to Figure 3.28.

l. Click anywhere to deselect the WordArt object. Click the **Insert** tab, and then click **Clip Art**. When the Clip Art task pane displays, type **book** in the **Search for** box, click the **Search in drop-down arrow**, and click **Office Collections**. Deselect My Collections and Web Collections, if necessary, and click **Go**. Click one time on the first object to insert it in your document, then close the Clip Art task pane.

m. Click the clip art object to display the Format tab, if necessary. Click **Text Wrapping** in the Arrange group, and then select **Square**. Now you can move the object anywhere in your document. Move it to the left side above the WordArt object, as it appears in Figure 3.28.

n. Double-click anywhere in the bottom of your document to reposition the insertion point. Click the **Insert tab**, and then click **Table**. Drag your mouse over the cells until **2x3 Table** displays (a 2 column, 3 row table), and click to insert it in the document.

o. Click the table selector in the upper-left corner to select the whole table and click the **Layout** tab. Click **Properties** in the Table group to display the Table Properties dialog box. Click the **Table tab**, and then click the **Preferred width check box**. Type **8** in the **Preferred width box** and click **OK**.

p. Drag your mouse across the two cells in the first row to select it, then right-click and select **Merge Cells**. Type **Hourly Drawings for FREE Books!** in the first row.

q. Click the **Design tab**, and then click **More** in the Table Styles group. Scroll to view the **B2 Dark List Accent 2** style. Click once to apply the style to your table.

...continued on Next Page

r. Right-click the table, click **Table Properties**, click **Center** alignment, and click **OK**.

s. Select the two empty cells in the first (left) column of the table, right-click, and click **Merge Cells**. In this column enter the phrase **Discounts of 50% or More**. Select the two empty cells in the right column of the table, right-click, and select **Merge Cells** in the Alignment group. In this column, type the phrase **Only at our North Glenstone Location**.

t. Click anywhere in the table, if necessary, and click the **Layout tab**. Click **Cell Margins**, click the **Allow spacing between cells check box**, then type **.1** as the spacing amount. Click **OK** and notice the improvement.

u. Select only the text in the table, but do not click the table selector; on the Mini toolbar, click **Center**.

v. Make minor adjustments to each element as necessary so your flyer looks attractive and spacing is retained. Save and close the document.

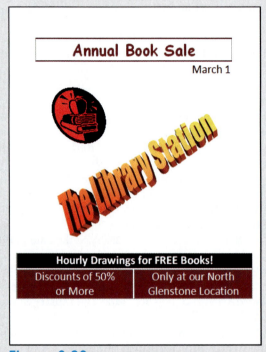

Figure 3.28 The Book Sale Flyer

2 Lost Pet

In an unfortunate mishap, your 3-year-old dog escaped from your fenced yard and is now missing. After calling local shelters and pet stores, you decide to create a flyer to post around the neighborhood and shops so that people will know whom to contact if they see her. Figure 3.29 displays a flyer that is intended to give information about your dog, Dakota, and also provide a tag with contact information that someone can pull from the flyer and take with him or her. The tag displays your name and phone number. Use a table as the basis of this document; you can use the picture of our pet or any other picture you like.

a. Open a new document and save it as **chap3_pe2_lostpet_solution**.

b. Click the **Insert tab** and click **Table** in the Tables group. Drag to select cells to create a table with 10 columns and 4 rows (**10x4 Table**), then click on the last cell to insert the table.

c. Click left of the first cell in the first row to select the entire row. Right-click the selected row and select **Merge Cells** to merge all the cells in the first row. Repeat the step to merge the cells in rows 2, and then the cells in row 3.

d. Click in the first row and enter the text **Lost Pet**. Select the text, and then on the Mini toolbar click the **Font size arrow** and select **26**. The row height will increase automatically to accommodate the larger text. On the Mini toolbar, click **Center** to center the text in the cell.

e. Select the cell in the second row. Click the **Design tab** and click **Shading** in the Table Styles group. Click **Black, Text 1** (the black swatch in the first row), which will place a black background in the cell.

...continued on Next Page

f. Click **Insert tab** and click **Picture** in the Illustrations group. Locate pictures of your pet or pets; we have provided a picture of Dakota, dakota.jpg, in the Exploring Word folder. When you locate the file, double-click to insert the picture. The row height will expand automatically to accommodate the picture. Click once to select the picture, if necessary, and then press **Ctrl+E** to center the picture.

g. Click in the third row and enter text to describe your pet or pets. Feel free to duplicate the information we have provided in Figure 3.29. Select the text, then on the Mini tool-bar, click the **Font size arrow**, select **14**, and click **Center**.

h. Type your name and phone number . . . on two lines . . . in the first cell of the fourth row. Display the **Layout tab**, and then click **Text Direction** one time to rotate the text (see Figure 3.29). Click **Align Top Center** to align the text vertically on the top of the cell. Right-click the cell and click **Copy**. Select the empty cells on that row, right-click, and click **Paste Cells** to populate the remaining cells with the owner information.

i. Select the entire row, right-click, and select **Borders and Shading**. Click the **Borders** tab, if necessary, and click a dashed line in the **Style list**. Click **OK**.

j. Click the **Height** box in the Cell Size group and increase the size to at least **1.5"**. The contact information now displays correctly.

k. Click **Zoom** in the task bar, click **Whole page**, and click **OK**.

l. Save and close the document.

Figure 3.29 The Lost Pet Flyer

3 The Study Schedule

Your midterm grades reveal the need to set up a solid study schedule. The best way to plan your study time is to create a daily schedule, mark the times you are in class or at work, then find the needed study time. Your work in this chapter provided information you can use to create a document that lists days and times and allows you to establish your new study schedule. You can even add colorful borders and shading, as well as graphics, to create a document you can proudly display.

a. Open a new blank document and save it as **chap3_pe3_schedule_solution**.

b. Click the **Page Layout tab**. Click **Margins** in the Page Setup group, and then click **Custom Margins** to display the Page Layout dialog box. Type **.75** in the **Top** and **Bottom** boxes, then type **.5** in the **Left** and **Right** boxes. Click **Landscape** in the *Orientation* section and click **OK**.

...continued on Next Page

c. Click the **Insert tab** and click **Table**. Click **Insert Table** to display the Insert Table dialog box. Type **8** in the **Number of columns** box and type **12** in the **Number of rows** box. Click **OK**.

d. Click left of the first cell in the first row to select the entire first row, then **right-click** and select **Merge Cells**. Click in the merged cell, then type **Weekly Class and Study Schedule**. Select the text you typed. On the Mini toolbar, click the **Font arrow** and select **Arial**, click the **Font size arrow** and select **24**, and click **Bold** and **Center**.

e. Click left of the first cell in the last row to select the entire row, then right-click and select **Merge Cells**. Click in the merged cell, type **Notes:**, then press **Enter** five times. The height of the cell increases to accommodate the blank lines.

f. Select the text you typed. On the Mini toolbar, click the **Font arrow** and select **Arial**, click the **Font size arrow** and select **12**, and click **Bold**.

g. Click the second cell in the second row. Type **Monday**. Press **Tab** (or right arrow key) to move to the next cell. Type **Tuesday**. Continue until the days of the week have been entered. Select the entire row. On the Mini toolbar, click the **Font arrow** and select **Arial**, click the **Font size arrow** and select **10**, and then click **Bold** and **Center**.

h. Click the first cell in the third row. Type **8:00 a.m.** Press the **down arrow key** to move to the first cell in the fourth row. Type **9:00 a.m.** Continue to enter the hourly periods up to **4:00 p.m.**

i. Select the cells containing the hours of the day, and then right-click and select **Table Properties**. Click the **Row tab**, then click the **Specify height check box**. Click the spin button until the height is **0.5"**. Click the **Row height is drop-down arrow** and select **Exactly**.

j. Click the **Cell tab** in the Table Properties dialog box and click **Center** in the *Vertical alignment* section. Click **OK** to accept the settings and close the dialog box.

k. Select the first row, containing the title of your table. Click the **Design tab** and click **Shading**. Click **Orange, Accent 6**, the orange color at the end of the first row.

l. Click and drag to select the first four cells under Sunday, then right-click and select **Merge Cells**. Type **Reserved for services** in the new large cell. Select this text, then click the **Layout tab**. Click **Text Direction** one time to rotate the text, and then click **Align Center** to display the text, as shown in Figure 3.30.

m. Click anywhere in the cell in the last row of the table. Click the **Insert tab** and click **Clip Art** to display the task pane. Type **books** in the **Search for** box, and then click **Go** or press **Enter**. Click the first clip art object to insert it in your table.

n. Click the newly inserted clip art to display the Format tab, if necessary, and click **Text Wrapping** and select **Square**. Click the sizing handle on the upper-right corner, hold down **Shift**, and drag the sizing handle to reduce the size of the object and maintain proportions. Move the object to the lower-right corner of the last row and close the Clip Art task pane.

o. Save and close the document.

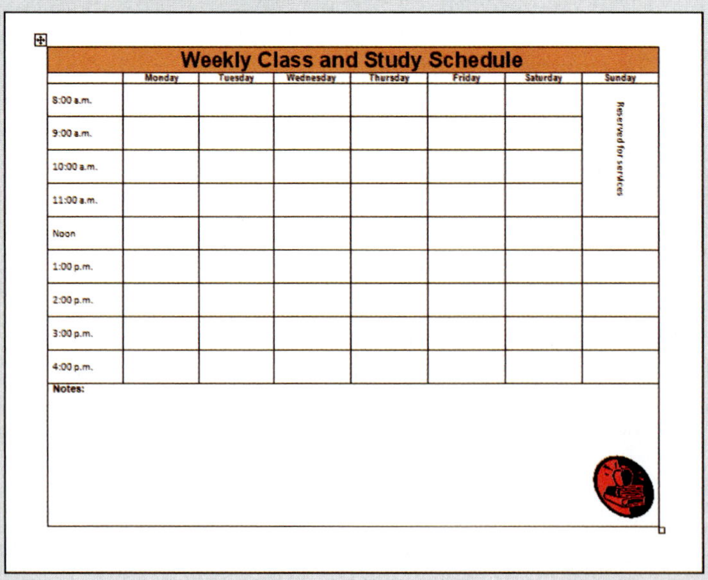

Figure 3.30 The Completed Study Schedule

...continued on Next Page

You work as a bank consultant for a software firm and must bill for services each month. Traditionally, you type the amount of your invoice in the document, but after a discussion with a coworker you discover how to use table formulas and begin to use them to calculate your total fees on the invoice. In this exercise, you develop a professional-looking invoice and use formulas to calculate totals within the table.

a. Open a blank document and save it as **chap3_pe4_invoice_solution**.

b. Click the **Page Layout tab**, click **Margins**, and click **Office 2003 Default**, which sets 1.25" left and right margins. Click the **Insert tab** and click **Table**. Drag to select eight rows and two columns (**2x8 Table**).

c. Click left of the first cell in the first row to select the entire first row, right-click, and select **Merge Cells**. Click in the merged cell, and then type **Invoice**. Select the text you typed, click the **Home tab**, and click **Heading 1** from the Styles gallery. Click **Center** in the Paragraph group to complete the first row of the table.

d. Select the second and third cells in the first column, and then click the **Layout tab**. Click **Merge Cells**, click the **Height box** in the Cell Size group, and type **1** to increase the size of the cell. In this cell, enter the following text:

TO:
Jack Hendrix Technologies
4999 Garland Street
Fayetteville, AR 72703

e. Select the second and third cells in the right column and click **Merge Cells**. They inherit the size from the cell on their left. Click **Align Top Right** in the Alignment group and type the following text in the cell:

FROM:
John Q. Student
9444 Elton Lane
Tulsa, OK 74129

f. Select the last five cells in the first column, then click the **Width box** in the Cell Size group and type **5**. The cells on the right might extend beyond the borders of the page, but you will fix that next. Select the five cells in the second column, then click the **Width box** and type **1.15**. Now the cells should align with the cells in the first two rows.

g. Type the following text in the third through sixth cells of the two columns, as shown in Figure 3.31:

Description	Amount
Consulting Fee for June	$5640.00
Travel Expenses	500.00
Supplies	200.00

h. In the first column of the last row, type **TOTAL**. Click in the second column in the last row and click **Formula** on the Layout tab. Click **OK** to accept the formula, =SUM(ABOVE), which is correct for our calculation. The total is $6340.00.

i. Your invoice is correct, but formatting changes are needed to give it a more professional appearance. Select the third row, which contains the Description and Amount titles, and hold down **Ctrl**, and select the last row of the table. Click the **Design tab**

...continued on Next Page

and click **Shading**. Click **White, Background 1, Darker 15%** from the first column. Do not deselect the rows.

j. While the rows are selected, click the **Home tab** and click **Heading 3** from the Styles gallery. You may need to click the **More button** in the Styles group, select **Apply Styles** from the gallery, type **Heading 3** in the Apply Styles dialog box, and click **Apply**. Click anywhere to deselect the rows and view the format changes.

k. Select the last four cells in the second column, click the **Layout tab**, and click **Align Center Right** on the tab. The result gives the effect of decimal alignment. However, the numbers are not decimal aligned, so if you display an additional decimal place, it will result in misaligned numbers.

l. Select the fourth, fifth, and sixth rows, which contain the items you bill for, then click **Sort** in the Data group. Click **OK**. Deselect the rows to view the newly sorted list.

m. You determine the travel expenses were incorrect; change the amount to **550.00**. Right-click the cell that contains the formula and select **Update Field** to recalculate the total. The new total $6390.00 displays.

n. Save and close the document.

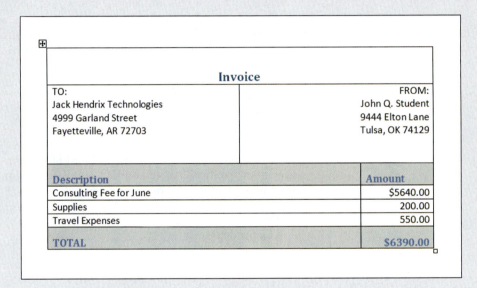

Figure 3.31 The Completed Invoice

Microsoft Word 2007 includes a Résumé template, but you can achieve an equally good result through the tables feature. In this exercise you create a resume for yourself using the tools learned in this chapter 3. Follow the instructions below to create a résumé similar to the document in Figure 3.32. Remember that a resume often serves as the first impression between you and a potential employer, so you must include all the information expected by an employer and display it in a manner that is easy to read and follow.

a. Open a new blank document and save it as **chap3_mid1_resume_solution**. Set margins at 1" on the top and bottom, and 1.25" on the left and right. Insert a 2-column, 10-row table into your document. Additional rows can be added as needed. Conversely, rows can be deleted at a later time if they are not needed.

b. Merge the two cells in the first row. Type your name in the cell, and then center it. Change the font to Times New Roman, 24 pt, and bold, as shown in Figure 3.32.

c. Enter your addresses in the second row. Type your campus address, telephone number, and e-mail address in the cell on the left and your permanent address and telephone number in the cell on the right. Format the text in Times New Roman, 12 pt. Left align the text in the cell on the left and right align the text in the cell on the right.

d. Enter the categories in the left cell of each row, being sure to include the following categories: **Objective**, **Professional Accomplishments**, **Education**, **Honors**, and **References**. Format the text in Times New Roman, 12 pt, boldface and right align the text in these cells. (Not all of these categories are visible in Figure 3.32.)

e. Enter the associated information in the right cell of each row. Be sure to include all information that would interest a prospective employer. Format the text in Times New Roman, 12 pt. Left align the text in these cells, using boldface and italics where appropriate.

f. Select rows three through ten in the first column, then change the width of the cells to 1.5". Select the same rows in the second column and increase the width of the cells until they align with the first two rows.

g. Select the entire table and remove the borders surrounding the individual cells. (Figure 3.32 displays gridlines, which—unlike borders—do not appear in the printed document.) For the first row only, set a bottom line border.

h. Save and close the document.

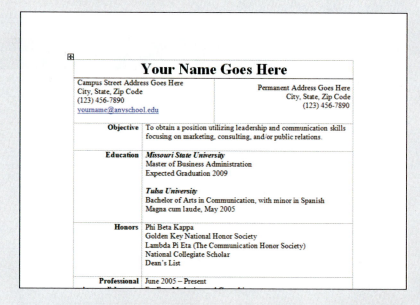

Figure 3.32   The Completed Résumé

...continued on Next Page

You work as an intern for the Human Resources department of a company that offers home health consulting services. Your manager mentions the need for a new employment application form and asks you to create an application form similar to the document in Figure 3.33. Use the skills you recently acquired about the tables feature in Word to follow our design and create the application form. Remember that the Tables and Borders toolbar can be used in place of the Table menu to execute various commands during the exercise. Proceed as follows:

a. Open a blank document and save it as **chap3_mid2_application_solution**.

b. Create a 3 × 8 (three columns and eight rows) table to match our design. Select the entire table after it is created initially. Change the before paragraph spacing to 6 pt. The result will drop the text in each cell half a line from the top border of the cell, and also determine the spacing between paragraphs within a cell.

c. Merge the cells in the first row to create the title for the application. Enter the text for the first line, press **Shift+Enter** to create a line break instead of a paragraph break (to minimize the spacing between lines), then enter the text on the second line. Center the text. Select the first cell, and then shade the cell with the color **Black, Text 1** to create white letters on a dark background. Increase the font size of the title to 22 pt.

d. Enter the text in the next several cells, as shown in Figure 3.33. Select cells individually and adjust the width to create the offsetting form fields.

e. Move down in the table until you can select the cell for the highest degree attained. Enter the indicated text, click and drag to select all four degrees, and create a custom bulleted list using the check box character in the Wingdings font.

f. Merge the cells in row 7, then enter the text that asks the applicant to describe the skills that qualify him or her for the position. Merge the cells in row 8 (these cells are not visible in Figure 3.33) to create a single cell for employment references.

g. Reduce the zoom setting to view the entire document. Change the row heights as necessary so that the completed application fills the entire page.

h. Complete the finished application as though you were applying for a job. Replace the check box next to the highest degree earned (remove the bullet) with the letter X.

i. Save and close the document.

Figure 3.33 The Employment Application

...continued on Next Page

You are the marketing manager for a private pilot flight school. Periodically, you perform a review of marketing tools used in the company, then make a list of items that must be changed. In your last review, you noticed the company letterhead is quite dated and should be changed. Since the change is being made, all company stationery will be replaced with the new logo. Figure 3.34 displays an envelope and matching letterhead designed by an intern. Replicate that design as closely as possible, creating both the letterhead and matching envelope.

a. Begin with the stationery. Open a blank document and save it as **chap3_mid3_ stationery_solution**.

b. Click the **Narrow** margin setting, which sets 1/2" margins all around. Enter the company name, address, telephone, and e-mail information at the top of the page. Use a larger font and distinguishing color for your name, then center all of the text at the top of the page.

c. After you type your information, convert the text into a table. Split the table into three columns so you can add a logo to each side of your information.

d. Use the Clip Organizer to locate the clip art image shown in Figure 3.34. (If you cannot find the same clip art image, use one with the same theme.) Use that image as a logo by inserting it in the first column of the table. Click the Square text wrap style. Change the image height to **1"**. Crop the image to decrease width to approximately **1.1"**. Select the clip art, click Copy, then Paste the image in the third column of the table on the right side of the page.

e. Center align the information in each cell both horizontally and vertically. Use the Borders command to add a 3-pt wide horizontal line below the text that contains your address information. Do not extend the border below the clip art images.

f. Insert a new page section break at the beginning of the document. (The result creates a new page as well as a new section. The latter enables you to change the page orientation within a document.)

g. Click on the newly inserted page and select landscape orientation. Change the **Size** to **Envelope #10** (the standard business envelope).

h. Copy the clip art and address information from the letterhead to the envelope. Make adjustments as necessary to align your address beside the logo.

i. Save and close the document.

Figure 3.34 Custom Stationery

...continued on Next Page

You work as an intern for the mayor's office in City Hall. The office sponsors a yearly fireworks display near the local airport and posts informational flyers in local businesses prior to the event. The community relations director has asked for your help to create the flyers they will distribute because of your experience using Microsoft Word 2007. You are responsible for creating an exciting and attractive flyer for this year's event using the guidelines below.

a. Open a new blank document and save it as **chap3_mid4_fireworks_solution**.

b. Set the following margins: 0.6" top, 0.3" bottom, 0.5" left, and 0.5" right. If a warning appears mentioning that the margins are outside the boundary, choose the option to fix the problem.

c. Create a WordArt object with these settings: Click WordArt style 11 in the WordArt gallery. Type **Independence Day Fireworks!** in the WordArt box. Add the **3-D Style 11** effect. Change the Shape Fill, located in the WordArt Styles group of the Format tab, to use the **Linear Down** gradient color scheme. Change the height to **1.5"** and the width to **7"**, then Format the object to use **Square Text Wrapping**, and center it horizontally on the page.

d. Use the Clip Art task pane and search for **fireworks** in the Web Collections. Find and insert the image, as shown in Figure 3.35. Adjust the height to **3"**, then crop the image to trim white space from the top and bottom of the picture. Adjust the brightness to **+20%**. Apply square text wrapping, and then move the object to the right side of the flyer, as shown in Figure 3.35.

e. Place the insertion point on the left side of the document and type **City of Stockton** on the left side of the clip art object. Format the text in Comic Sans MS, 26-pt size, and change the font color to red.

f. Insert a table to list the events shown in Figure 3.35. Align text on the left and right as displayed. In addition to increasing Cell Margins, insert an extra column to create the gap between columns. Apply a Dark Red Double-line outside border, then left-align the table.

g. Below the table insert the text **Best Small-Town Celebration in the State**, as shown in Figure 3.35. Format the text using Comic Sans MS 18-pt, change the font color to red, and center the text on the page.

h. Save and close the document.

Figure 3.35 Fireworks Announcement Flyer

Capstone Exercise

You are the executive assistant to a general contractor, and your duties include listing the materials that will be used on a home remodeling project. Due to the large number of people who work on the project, from plumbers to electricians to carpenters, it is necessary to keep detailed records of the materials and supplies to use during the remodel. After the first job, you decide to provide the crew with a table of materials that includes pictures. This also might be helpful for any crewmember who does not speak English.

Create the Table

Fortunately, a list of materials has been provided, which will eliminate the need for you to type a list of supplies. However, the preexisting list is weak. You decide to modify the document to increase organization and clarity by putting the list in table format, creating a header row and labels, and also adding visual enhancements with WordArt.

a. Open the *chap3_cap_construction* document and save it as **chap3_cap_construction_solution**. You wisely decide to convert this list to a three-column table so you can organize the list of materials and add more data.

b. Insert two rows at the top to use for a heading and item descriptions.
   - Create a title row on the table by merging cells in the first row.
   - Use WordArt to create a title using the phrase **Supply List**.
   - Use the second row as a header for the columns.
   - Enter an appropriate label for each column.

Format the Table

Your table is functional now, but it would look even better with additional improvements. Enhance the table of materials by aligning the data in columns, sorting the data, and using formulas to calculate costs. Since the table spans more than one page, you also should change the table properties so that the header row repeats on every page.

a. Use the Table Properties dialog box to indicate the first row should repeat as a header row at the top of each page if your table spans more than one page.

b. Align the prices of each item in the third column. The prices should appear to align on the decimal point.

c. Center the data in the second column, which displays the quantity of each item you will use in the project.

d. Sort the data in ascending order by Item.

e. Use the Split cell option to add a column to calculate the total cost of materials.

f. Use a formula to calculate the total cost of any item that has a quantity of 10 or more.

Add Visual Enhancements

Your table is very factual, but to assist members of the crew who need more visual information, you will enhance the table with pictures. Insert pictures from the Clip Organizer and then use formatting tools, when appropriate, to modify the graphics so they will fit into the table cells.

a. Insert a column to the left of the first column.

b. Insert a picture of each item in the first column.
   - Use symbols, clip art, or pictures to visually describe the following materials in your table: Drill, Faucet, Hammer, Paint, Paintbrushes, Screwdriver, Toilet, and Towel holder.
   - You might not be able to locate a graphic for each item, but you should be able to find at least five to use in the table.
   - Crop or resize the graphics as necessary so they do not exceed 2" in height or width.
   - All graphics should align in the center of the cell.

TROUBLESHOOTING: If your Clip Organizer query does not return any results, click Clip art on Office Online. The Online organizer will display in a new Internet Explorer window, but you can return to Word and continue your clip art search. Your search should now return more results.

c. Apply the **Light Grid Accent 1** style to the table. Add a double-line outside border to the table, then center it horizontally on the page. If necessary, click Table Properties and verify that the setting for the first row will repeat as a header row on the top of each page.

d. Save and close the document.

Mini Cases

Holiday Greetings

GENERAL CASE

After learning how to use the creative tools in Microsoft Word 2007, you decide to create your own holiday greeting card. Your greeting card should include a picture of a family (feel free to use your own or one from the Clip Organizer) and decorative text. Use several editing features on the graphics so the greeting card reflects your personality or sentiment during the holidays. Due to printing constraints for special paper used for cards, design only the cover of your Greeting card. Save the document as **chap3_mc1_greeting_solution**.

Performance Elements	Exceeds Expectations	Meets Expectations	Below Expectations
Use of tables and table formatting	Inserted table; applied two or more table format options.	Inserted table; applied one table format option.	Inserted table; did not apply additional formatting.
Use of graphics	Inserted at least two graphical objects and used at least three formatting options.	Inserted at least one graphical object and applied formatting.	Inserted zero or one graphical object.
Presentation	Greeting card is formatted attractively; information is easy to read and understand.	Special formatting has been applied, but information is somewhat cluttered.	Greeting card lists basic information with no special formatting for attractiveness.

Travel World

RESEARCH CASE

You have been hired at *Let's Go!* Travel Agency and asked to create a flyer to distribute on campus. Search the Internet to find a company that offers cruises to Alaska and sails through the Inside Passage. Then create a flyer that provides information about one of the cruises through the Alaska Inside Passage. You should include your name and e-mail address as the travel agent. Use a combination of clip art, photographs, and/or WordArt to make the flyer as attractive as possible. Use a table to list the Ports of Call in Alaska. Save your work as **chap3_mc2_alaska_solution**.

Performance Elements	Exceeds Expectations	Meets Expectations	Below Expectations
Use of tables and table formatting	Inserted table; applied three or more table formats.	Inserted table; applied one or two table format options.	Inserted table; did not apply additional formatting.
Use of graphics	Inserted at least two graphical objects and applied formatting to objects.	Inserted at least two graphical objects and resized them.	Inserted zero or one graphical object.
Use of research	Two or more pieces of information are included in flyer, reflecting adequate research was performed.	Includes one piece of information reflecting research of topic.	Does not include data that indicate research was performed.
Presentation	Flyer is formatted attractively; information is easy to read and understand.	Special formatting has been applied, but information is somewhat cluttered.	Flyer lists basic information with no special formatting for attractiveness.

Payroll Report

You are assigned the job of proofreading a payroll report before it goes to the department head who issues checks. After looking at the data you find several errors that must be corrected before the report can be submitted. Open the *chap3_mc3_payroll_report* document and correct the errors. Remember to use the keyboard shortcut that reveals formulas in a table. Make further adjustments that enhance your ability to view the information easily and to make the report look more professional. Save your work as **chap3_mc3_payroll_solution**.

Performance Elements	Exceeds Expectations	Meets Expectations	Below Expectations
Use of table formulas	Table formulas applied correctly to all entries.	Table formulas applied correctly to two entries.	Table formulas applied incorrectly to at least one item.
Use of other table formatting options	Used at least three table format options.	Used two table format options.	Does not use table format options.
Presentation	Report is formatted attractively; information is easy to read and understand.	Some report formatting corrections have been applied, but information is somewhat cluttered.	Report contains errors in formatting and presentation is poor.

Share, Compare, and Document

Workgroups, Collaboration, and References

Objectives

After you read this chapter, you will be able to:

1. Insert comments in a document **(page 251)**.
2. Track changes in a document **(page 254)**.
3. View documents side by side **(page 263)**.
4. Compare and combine documents **(page 264)**.
5. Create master documents and subdocuments **(page 265)**.
6. Use navigation tools **(page 267)**.
7. Acknowledge a source **(page 277)**.
8. Create a bibliography **(page 279)**.
9. Select the writing style **(page 280)**.
10. Create and modify footnotes and endnotes **(page 281)**.
11. Add figure references **(page 287)**.
12. Insert a table of figures **(page 288)**.
13. Add legal references **(page 289)**.
14. Create cross-references **(page 289)**.
15. Modify document properties **(page 290)**.

Hands-On Exercises

Exercises	Skills Covered
1. DOCUMENT COLLABORATION (page 258) **Open:** chap4_ho1_proposal.docx **Save as:** chap4_ho1_proposal_solution.docx	• Set User Name and Customize the Track Changes Options • Track Document Changes • View, Add, and Delete Comments • Accept and Reject Changes
2. DOCUMENT COMPARISON, MERGERS, AND NAVIGATION (page 270) **Open:** chap4_ho1_proposal_solution.docx (from Exercise 1) chap4_ho2_proposal2.docx **Save as:** chap4_ho2_compare_solution.docx and chap4_ho2_combine_solution.docx **Open:** chap4_ho2_master.docx chap4_ho2_background.docx **Save as:** chap4_ho2_master_solution.docx, Overview.docx, Ideology.docx, Time Frame.docx, Budget.docx, and Conclusion.docx **Open:** chap4_ho1_proposal_solution.docx (from Exercise 1) **Save as:** chap4_ho2_map_solution	• Compare and Combine Documents • View Documents Side by Side • Create Master Documents and Subdocuments • Modify Master Documents and Subdocuments • Use Document Map and Create Bookmarks
3. REFERENCE RESOURCES (page 283) **Open:** chap4_ho3_plagiarism.docx and chap4_ho3_plmasterlist.xml **Save as:** chap4_ho3_plagiarism_solution.docx	• Create and Search for a Source • Select a Writing Style and Insert a Bibliography • Create and Modify Footnotes • Convert Footnotes to Endnotes and Modify Endnotes
4. ADDITIONAL REFERENCE RESOURCES (page 292) **Open:** chap4_ho4_tables.docx **Save as:** chap4_ho4_tables_solution.docx	• Add Captions and Create a Table of Figures • Create a Table of Authorities • Create a Cross-Reference • Modify Document Properties

CASE STUDY

Compiling an Employee Handbook

After years of planning and saving, Alex Caselman has recently started his own company. He will be hiring 20 employees initially and anticipates hiring 40 more by the end of the first fiscal year. He understands the importance of establishing goals and procedures that the employees can use to guide their efforts, so he has been working with the Small Business Development Center in his community to create these documents. The SBDC suggested Alex partner with a local business college and recruit students to assist him in writing a Staff Handbook for his

Case Study

employees. There are many laws which must be considered for employee hiring and management, and Alex wants to be sure his company stays in compliance with all regulations.

The two students who have volunteered to help Alex, Tanner and Elexis, have spent a number of hours researching employee handbooks and the laws that regulate hiring and employee leave in their state. They decide to assign a section to each person; after each section is written and reviewed, they will combine them. Knowing they would be viewing and editing all pages for each section, each person tracked the changes in their respective documents so the person in charge of combining them can easily view the modifications. Their work has been hard and they have only completed the first five sections of the handbook, but so far everyone is pleased with their progress.

Your Assignment

- Read the chapter, paying special attention to sections that describe how to use the Track Changes and Master Document features in Word.
- Open the *chap4_case_handbook* document, which contains the opening section of the employee handbook, and save the file as **chap4_case_handbook_ solution**. This will become the master document for the handbook.
- Insert the following files, in this order, as subdocuments into the master document: *chap4_case_eligibility, chap4_case_employment, chap4_case_leave, chap4_case_ conduct*.
- Display the document in Print Layout view, then turn on track changes. Accept all changes to the eligibility, employment, and leave sections of the document. Reject changes to the conduct section of the document.
- Renumber the conduct section so that all paragraph numbers begin with 5 instead of 7.
- Save and close the *chap4_case_handbook_solution* document.

Workgroups and Collaboration

This chapter introduces several features that go beyond the needs of the typical student and extend to capabilities that you will appreciate in the workplace, especially as you work with others on a collaborative project. This chapter opens with a discussion of workgroup editing, where suggested revisions from one or more individuals can be stored electronically within a document. This feature enables the original author to review each suggestion individually before it is incorporated into the final version of the document, and further, enables multiple people to work on the same document in collaboration with one another.

In this section, you insert comments to provide feedback or to pose questions to the document author. Then you track editing changes you make so that others can see your suggested edits.

Inserting Comments in a Document

In today's organizational environment, teams of people with diverse backgrounds, skills, and knowledge prepare documentation. Team members work together while planning, developing, writing, and editing important documents. If you have not participated in a team project yet, most likely you will. When you work with a team, you can use collaboration tools in Word such as the Comments feature. A *comment* is a note or annotation to ask a question or provide a suggestion to another person about the content of a document.

> In today's organizational environment, teams of people with diverse backgrounds, skills, and knowledge prepare documentation. When you work with a team, you can use collaboration tools in Word such as the Comment feature.

Before you use the comment and other collaboration features, you should click the Office Button, click Word Options, and then view the Personalize section and confirm that your name is displayed as the user. Word uses this information to indicate the name of the person who uses collaboration tools, such as Comments. If you are in a lab environment, you might not have permission to modify settings or change the User name; however, you should be able to change these settings on a home computer.

A *comment* is a note or annotation about the content of a document.

Add a Comment

Add comments to a document to remind yourself (or a reviewer) of action that needs to be taken. Click in the document where you want the comment to appear, display the Review tab, and click New Comment in the Comments group to open the markup balloon (see Figure 4.1), and enter the text of the comment and click outside the comment area. *Markup balloons* are colored circles that contain comments, insertions, and deletions in the margin with a line drawn to where the insertion point was in the document prior to inserting the comment or editing the document. After you complete the comment, the word containing the insertion point is highlighted in the color assigned to the reviewer. If you do not select anything prior to clicking New Comment, Word selects the word or object to the left of the insertion point for the comment reference.

Markup balloons are colored circles that contain comments and display in the margins.

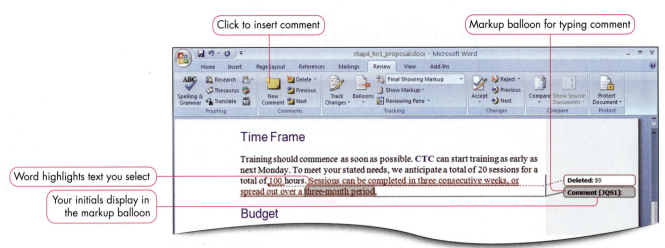

Figure 4.1 Insert a Comment

TIP   Record Voice Comments

You can record voice comments if your computer contains a sound card and a microphone. The Insert Voice command is not found in a tab; therefore, you must add it to the Quick Access Toolbar using the Customize section of the Word Options command. To create the sound comment, position the insertion point where you want to insert the sound comment, click Insert Voice on the Quick Access Toolbar, click the Record button in the Sound Object dialog box, record your voice, and then click the Stop button. Click the Rewind button to rewind the sound clip, and click the Play button to hear your recording. People can listen to the voice comment by double-clicking the sound icon within the document.

View, Modify, and Delete Comments

The ***Reviewing Pane*** displays comments and changes made to a document.

Comments appear in markup balloons in Print Layout, Web Layout, and Full Screen Reading views. In Draft view, comments appear as tags embedded in the document; when you hover the mouse over the tag, it displays the comment. In any view, you can display the *Reviewing Pane*, a pane that displays all comments and editorial changes made to the main document. To display or hide the Reviewing Pane, click Reviewing Pane on the Review tab. You can display the pane vertically on the left side of the document window, as shown in Figure 4.2, or horizontally at the bottom. The Reviewing Pane is useful when the comments are too long to display completely in a markup balloon.

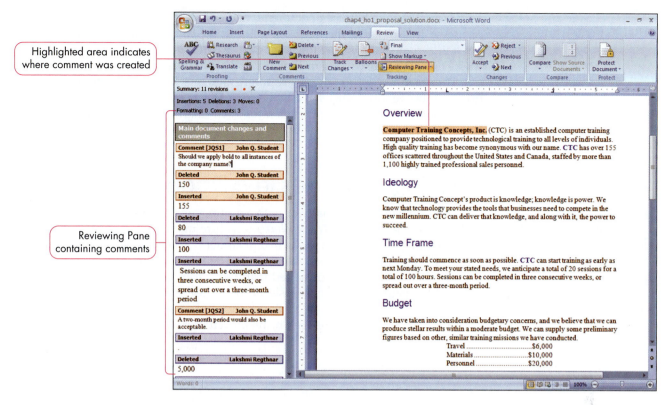

Figure 4.2 The Reviewing Pane

Show Markup enables you to view document revisions by reviewer.

If you do not see comments initially, click Show Markup on the Review tab and confirm that Comment is toggled on. The *Show Markup* feature enables you to view document revisions by reviewers. It also enables you to choose which type of revisions you want to view, such as Comments, Ink annotations (made on a tablet PC), insertions and deletions, or formatting changes. Each can be toggled on or off and you can view one or all at the same time. Show Markup also color codes each revision or comment with a different color for each reviewer. If you want to view changes by a particular reviewer, you simply toggle off all others in the Show Markup reviewers list, as shown in Figure 4.3.

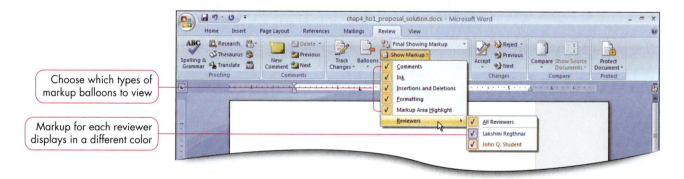

Figure 4.3 Show Markup Features

You can modify comments easily. When you click inside a markup balloon, the insertion point will relocate and you can use word processing formatting features, such as bold, italic, underline, and color, in the comment. If a document contains many comments, or the document is lengthy, you can click Previous and Next in the Comments group of the Review tab to navigate from comment to comment. This is a quick way to move between comments without scrolling through the entire document and it also places the insertion point in the comment automatically. You also can edit comments from the Reviewing Pane. After you edit a comment, click anywhere outside of the balloon or Reviewing Pane to save the changes.

After reading, acting on, or printing comments, you can delete the comments from within the Reviewing Pane by clicking Delete in the Comments group on the Review tab. You also can right-click a comment markup balloon and choose Delete Comment from the shortcut menu.

Tracking Changes in a Document

Use **Track Changes** to insert revision marks and markup balloons for additions, deletions, and formatting changes.

Revision Marks indicate where text is added, deleted, or formatted while the Track Changes feature is active.

Whether you work individually or with a group, you can monitor any revisions you make to a document. The **Track Changes** feature monitors all additions, deletions, and formatting changes you make in a document. When Track Changes is active, it applies **Revision Marks**, which are onscreen elements that indicate locations where a person added, deleted, or formatted text. Word uses colors for different reviewers who edit a document. You can position the mouse pointer over revision marks or markup balloons to see who made the change and on what date and time, as shown in Figure 4.4. The vertical line may be on the left or right side of the screen.

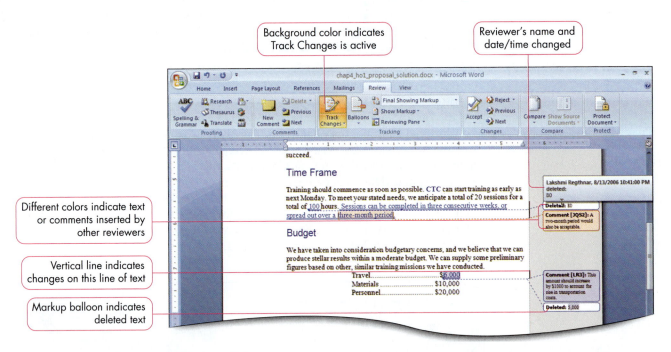

Figure 4.4 An Example of Track Changes

Word also includes markup tools, some of which enable you to accept or reject changes indicated by revision marks. The Changes group on the Review tab includes Accept, to accept a suggested change, and Reject, which removes a suggested change. When you accept or reject a change, the revision marks and markup balloon disappear.

The Track Changes feature is useful in situations where a document must be reviewed by several people, each of whom can offer suggestions or changes, and then returned to one person who must finalize the document. The last person can view all suggestions at the same time, and then accept or reject the suggested changes with the click of a mouse. If the process takes place using paper copies of a document, it is difficult to visualize all the suggested changes at one time, and then the last person must manually change the original document. While writing the Exploring series, the authors, editors, and reviewers each inserted comments and tracked changes to the manuscript for each chapter. Each person's comments or changes displayed in different colored balloons, and because all edits were performed in one document, the last person could accept and reject changes before sending it to the next step of the publishing process.

TIP | Accepting or Rejecting All Changes

To accept all changes in a document at once, click the Accept arrow on the Review tab and select Accept All Changes in Document. To delete all changes in a document at once, click the Reject arrow on the Review tab and select Reject All Changes in Document.

Select Markup Views

Original Showing Markup view shows a line through deleted text and puts inserted text in a markup balloon.

Final Showing Markup view shows inserted text in the body and puts deleted text in a markup balloon.

The suggested revisions from the various reviewers display in one of two ways, as the Original Showing Markup or as the Final Showing Markup. The *Original Showing Markup* view shows the deleted text within the body of the document (with a line through the deleted text) and displays the inserted text in a balloon to the right of the actual document, as shown in Figure 4.5. The *Final Showing Markup* view is the opposite; that is, it displays the inserted text in the body of the document and shows the deleted text in a balloon. The difference is subtle and depends on personal preference with respect to displaying the insertions and deletions in a document. (All revisions fall into one of these two categories: insertions or deletions. Even if you substitute one word for another, you are deleting the original word and then inserting its replacement.) Both views display revision marks on the edge of any line that has been changed. Comments are optional and enclosed in balloons in the side margin of a document.

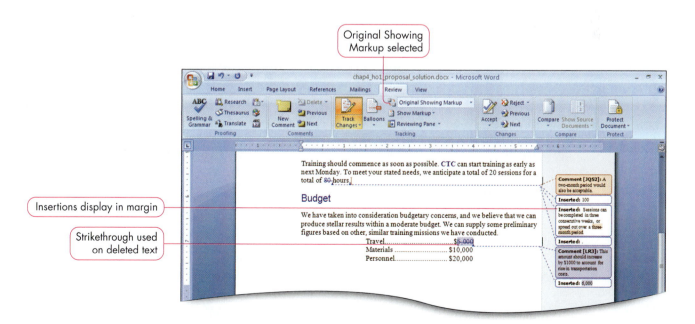

Figure 4.5 Original Showing Markup View

When you click the Display for Review arrow in the Review tab, two additional view options are listed—Final and Original. Final shows how the document looks if you accept and incorporate all tracked changes. Original shows the document prior to using the Track Changes feature.

The review process is straightforward. The initial document is sent for review to one or more individuals, who record their changes by executing the Track Changes command on the Review tab to start (or stop) the recording process. The author of the original document receives the altered document and then uses Accept and Reject in the Changes group on the Review tab to review the document and implement the suggested changes.

Customize Track Changes Options

Although the feature seems to have many options for viewing and displaying changes, you can further customize the Track Changes feature. The following reference page describes the sections and settings you can change in the Track Changes dialog box.

The beginning of this chapter mentioned that you should check the Word Options, making changes if necessary, so your name is associated with any tracked changes you make in the document. You also can access those settings from the Review tab when you click the Track Changes arrow and click Change User Name, as shown in Figure 4.6. This step takes you to the Popular category of the Word Options dialog box, where you have the opportunity to enter your name and initials in the Personalize your copy of Microsoft Office section.

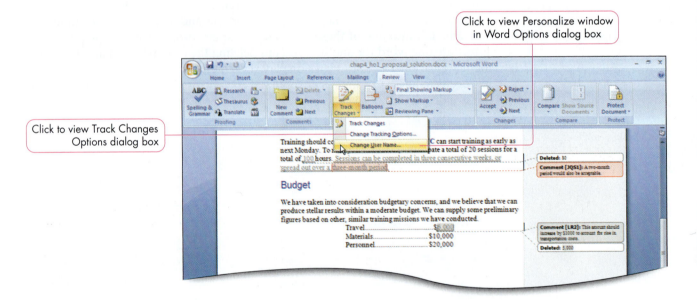

Figure 4.6 Track Changes Customization Options

Track Changes Options Dialog Box | Reference

Markup

Specify format property (color, bold, italic, underline, strikethrough) used for insertions and deletions.

Specify location (left border, right border, outside border, none) of marks that indicate a change has been made to text on a line.

Specify color to use for comments, insertions, deletions, and changed lines. Select a standard color for each or assign color by author/reviewer.

Moves

Specify format property (double strikethrough, double underline) used on text that is moved within the document.

Specify color to use for text that is moved within the document.

Select a standard color for each or assign color by author/reviewer.

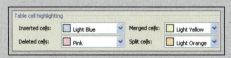

Table cell highlighting

Specify highlight color used to indicate a change in the layout of a table (insert cells, delete cells, merge or split cells).

Select a standard color for each type of modification or assign color by author/reviewer.

Formatting

Turn on Track formatting. Tracks any change made to the format of text or an object.

Specify format property (color, bold, italic, underline, strikethrough) used to indicate a format change.

Specify color of balloon used to indicate a format change.

Balloons

Specify when to use balloons in Print and Web Layout views (always, never, only for comments/formatting).

Specify width of balloon.

Specify width measurement (inches or percentage of page width).

Specify in which margin (right or left) to display balloons.

Specify if lines will connect balloons to text.

Hands-On Exercises

1 | Document Collaboration

Skills covered: 1. Set User Name and Customize the Track Changes Options **2.** Track Document Changes **3.** View, Add, and Delete Comments **4.** Accept and Reject Changes

---

Step 1
Set User Name and Customize the Track Changes Options

Refer to Figure 4.7 as you complete Step 1.

a. Start Word. Open the *chap4_ho1_proposal* document and save it as **chap4_ho1_ proposal_solution**.

b. Click the **Review tab** and click the upper portion of **Track Changes** in the Tracking group.

The command should display with an orange background color indicating the feature is turned on. When you click the upper portion of Track Changes, you toggle the feature on or off. When you click the lower portion of Track Changes, a menu of options displays, which you use in the next step.

c. Click the **Track Changes down arrow**, and then select **Change User Name**. In the *Personalize your copy of Microsoft Office* section, type your name in the **User name** box and type your initials in the **Initials** box, if necessary. Click **OK** to close the Word Options dialog box.

You want to be sure your name and initials are correct before you add any comments or initiate any changes in the document. After you update the User information, your initials display with any comments or changes you make.

d. Click the **Track Changes** arrow and click **Change Tracking Options**. In the *Markup* section, click the **Insertions drop-down arrow**, and then click **Double underline**. In the *Formatting* section, click the **Track formatting check box**.

e. In the *Balloons* section, click the **Use Balloons (Print and Web Layout) drop-down arrow** and select **Always**, if necessary. Click the **Preferred width spin arrow** until **1.8"** displays. Click the **Margin drop-down arrow** and select **Left**, as shown in Figure 4.7. Click **OK** to close the Track Changes Options dialog box.

Your revisions to the Track Changes options enable you to quickly view any additions to the document because they will be identified in balloons and insertions will display with a double underline. Additionally, you altered the location of all comment and editing balloons to display on the left side of your document instead of on the right, which is the default. You also decreased the width of the markup balloons so they will take up less space in the margins.

f. Save the document.

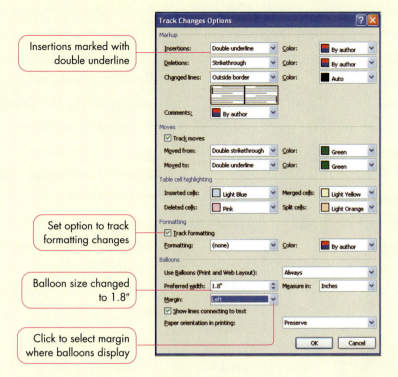

Insertions marked with double underline

Set option to track formatting changes

Balloon size changed to 1.8"

Click to select margin where balloons display

Figure 4.7 Track Changes Options Dialog Box

Step 2
Track Document Changes

Refer to Figure 4.8 as you complete Step 2.

a. Click the **Display for Review arrow** in the Tracking group on the Review tab and select **Final Showing Markup**, if necessary. Scroll down to view the bottom of the first page.

One comment and two previous changes display in balloons. Because of the changes you made in Steps 1a and 1b, any future changes you make in the document also display in balloons in the margin of the document.

b. Scroll to the top of the page, select the number 150 in the first paragraph, and replace it with **155**.

TROUBLESHOOTING: If a balloon does not display, indicating the number 150 was deleted, make sure the Track Changes is on. When on, Track Changes is highlighted in an orange color. If necessary, click Track Changes again to turn it on, then repeat Step 2b.

c. Select *Computer Training Concepts, Inc.* in the first sentence of the first paragraph and apply **Bold** from the Mini toolbar.

The changed line appears on the right side of the line you formatted, a markup balloon indicates the formatting change, and the text you inserted in Step 2b is colored with a double underline, as shown in Figure 4.8.

d. Click the **Display for Review arrow** in the Tracking group and select **Final**.

The formatting change indicators do not display, and the text in the first sentence displays in bold.

e. Save the document.

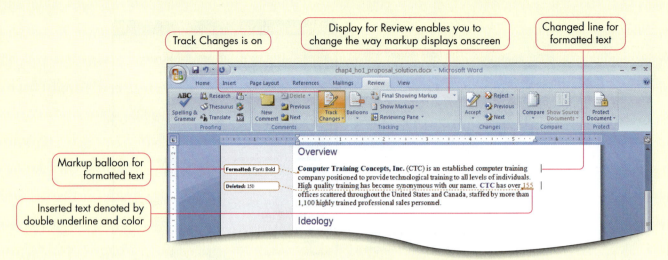

Figure 4.8 View Changes in a Document

<table>
<tr>
<td>

Step 3
View, Add, and Delete Comments

</td>
<td>

Refer to Figure 4.9 as you complete Step 3.

a. Click the **Display for Review arrow** in the Tracking group and select **Final Showing Markup**.

b. Select *three-month period* at the end of the *Time Frame* paragraph. Click **New Comment** in the Comments group, and then type **A four-month period would also be acceptable.**

If you do not select anything prior to clicking New Comment, Word selects the word or object to the left of the insertion point for the comment reference.

c. Select *Computer Training Concepts, Inc.* in the first sentence of the first paragraph. Click **New Comment**, and then type **Should we apply bold to all instances of the company name?** in the markup balloon.

d. Click inside the first markup balloon you created. Edit the comment by replacing *four-month* with **two-month**. Click outside of the balloon to deselect it.

e. Position the mouse pointer over the comment balloon in the Budget paragraph.

When you position the mouse pointer over a markup balloon, Word displays a ScreenTip that tells you who created the comment and when.

f. Click the comment by Lakshmi Regthnar one time to select it, and then click **Delete** in the Comments group of the Review tab (see Figure 4.9).

You removed the selected comment and the markup balloon. If you click the arrow on the right side of Delete, you can select from several options, including Delete all Comments in Document.

g. Save the document.

</td>
</tr>
</table>

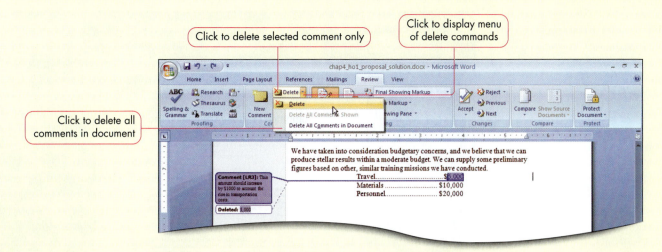

Figure 4.9 Deleting Comments

<table>
<tr>
<td>

Step 4
Accept and Reject Changes

</td>
<td>

Refer to Figure 4.10 as you complete Step 4.

a. Press **Ctrl+Home** to place the insertion point at the beginning of the document.

b. Click **Next** in the Changes group to highlight the first change, and then position the mouse pointer over the tracked change.

When you position the mouse pointer on the revision mark, a ScreenTip appears that tells you who made the change and the date and time the change was made.

TROUBLESHOOTING: If you click Next in the Comments group instead of Next in the Changes group, click Previous in the Comments group, and then click Next in the Changes group.

c. Click **Accept** in the Changes group.

The formatting change is accepted. When the suggested change is accepted, the markup balloons and other Track Changes markups disappear. Additionally, the markup balloon for the next change or comment is highlighted. As with other commands, you can click the upper portion of the Accept command to accept this change only or you can click the lower portion of the command to view a menu of options for accepting changes.

d. Click **Next** in the Changes group to pass the comment and view the next markup balloon. Click **Accept** two times to accept the change to 155 offices.

e. Click **Next** in the Changes group to view the next markup balloon. Click **Reject** two times to retain the session time frame of *80 hours*.

f. Click the **Accept arrow** and click **Accept All Changes in Document**. Click the **Display for Review** arrow and select **Final**.

Figure 4.10 shows the first page after accepting and rejecting changes.

g. Save and close *chap4_ho1_proposal_solution*. Exit Word if you will not continue with the next exercise at this time.

</td>
</tr>
</table>

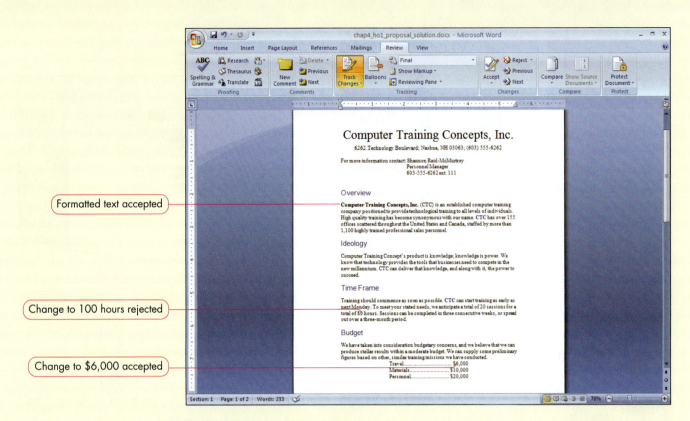

Formatted text accepted

Change to 100 hours rejected

Change to $6,000 accepted

Figure 4.10 The Revised Document

Multiple Documents

Features in Word enable you to work with multiple documents simultaneously—you can view multiple documents at one time, as well as combine them into one.

The collaboration features in Word facilitate an easy exchange of ideas and revisions to a document. But some users do not use the collaboration features, which causes the process of combining information into one document to be less efficient. Fortunately, other features in Word enable you to work with multiple documents simultaneously—you can view multiple documents at one time, as well as combine them into one.

In this section, you display multiple documents side by side as well as compare and combine documents into a new file. You create a document that contains subdocuments and then use tools to navigate within lengthy documents. Finally, you create an electronic marker for a location in a document and use the Go To feature.

Viewing Documents Side by Side

View Side by Side enables you to display two documents on the same screen.

The *View Side by Side* feature enables you to display two documents on the same screen. This is a useful tool when you want to compare an original to a revised document or when you want to cut or copy a portion from one document to another. To view two documents side by side, you must open both documents. The View Side by Side command is grayed out if only one document is open. When the documents are open, click View Side by Side in the Window group on the View tab, and the Word window will split to display each document, as shown in Figure 4.11. If you have more than two documents open, the Compare Side by Side dialog box displays and you select which document you want to display beside the active document.

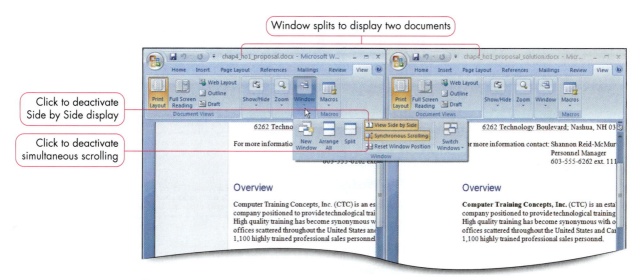

Figure 4.11 View Documents Side by Side

Synchronous scrolling enables you to simultaneously scroll through documents in Side by Side view.

When the documents display side by side, synchronous scrolling is active by default. *Synchronous scrolling* enables you to scroll through both documents at the same time. If you want to scroll through each document independently, click Synchronous Scrolling on the View tab to toggle it off. If you are viewing two versions of the same document, synchronous scrolling enables you to view both documents using only one scroll bar. If you scroll through each document asynchronously, you must use the respective scroll bars to navigate through each document.

While in Side by Side view, you can resize and reposition the two document windows. If you want to reset them to the original side-by-side viewing size, click Reset Window Position on the View tab. To close Side by Side view, click View Side by Side to toggle it off. The document that contains the insertion point when you close Side by Side view will display as the active document.

Comparing and Combining Documents

The **Compare** feature evaluates the contents of two or more documents and displays markup balloons showing the differences.

Ideally, when you have a document to submit to others for feedback, you want everyone to use the Track Changes feature in Word. However, sometimes it is necessary to have several people editing their own copy of the document simultaneously before they return it to you. When this occurs, you have several similar documents but with individual changes. Instead of compiling results from printed copies or viewing each one in Side by Side view to determine the differences, you can use a Compare feature. *Compare* automatically evaluates the contents of two or more documents and displays markup balloons that show the differences between the documents. You can display the differences in the original document, the revised document, or in a new document. You also can display query on the screen with the new document, as shown in Figure 4.12. The Compare command is in the Compare group of the Review tab.

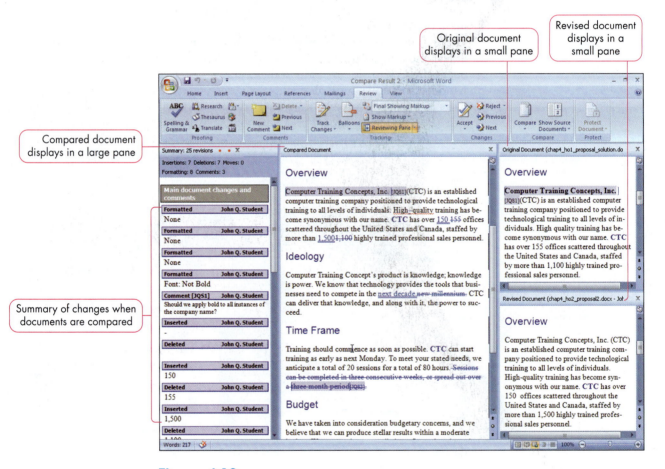

Figure 4.12 Results of Comparing Two Documents

The **Combine** feature incorporates all changes from multiple documents into a new document.

If you want to go a step further than just viewing the differences, you can use the *Combine* feature to integrate all changes from multiple documents into one document. To use the Combine feature, click the Compare arrow in the Review tab and select Combine. The Combine Documents dialog box opens displaying a variety of options you can invoke, as shown in Figure 4.13. The option you are most likely to change is in the Show Changes section, where you determine where the Combined documents will display—in the original document, the revised document, or in a new document. If you want to be certain not to modify the original documents, you should combine the changes into a new document.

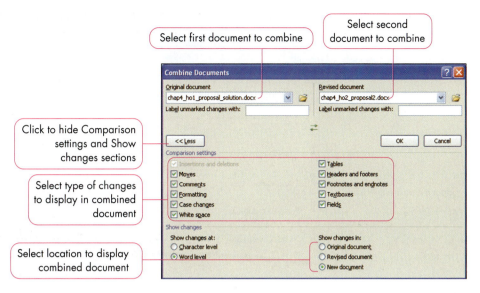

Figure 4.13 The Combine Documents Dialog Box

Creating Master Documents and Subdocuments

Working with long documents can be cumbersome. You may notice your computer slows down when you are working in a lengthy document. Scrolling, finding and replacing, editing, and formatting typically take longer. To improve this situation, you can create a *master document*, a document that acts like a binder for managing smaller documents. A smaller document that is a part of a master document is called a *subdocument*. The advantage of the master document is that you can work with several smaller documents, as opposed to a single large document. Thus, you edit the subdocuments individually and more efficiently than if they were all part of the same document. You can create a master document to hold the chapters of a book, where each chapter is stored as a subdocument. You also can use a master document to hold multiple documents created by others, such as a group project, where each member of the group is responsible for a section of the document.

The Outlining tab contains the Collapse and Expand Subdocuments buttons, as well as other tools associated with master documents. Figure 4.14 displays a master document with five subdocuments. The subdocuments are collapsed in Figure 4.14 and expanded in Figure 4.15. The collapsed structure enables you to see at a glance the subdocuments that comprise the master document. You can insert additional subdocuments or remove existing subdocuments from the master document. Deleting a subdocument from within a master document does not delete the actual subdocument file.

A *master document* is a document that acts like a binder for managing smaller documents.

A *subdocument* is a smaller document that is a part of a master document.

Figure 4.14 Master Document Showing Collapsed Subdocuments

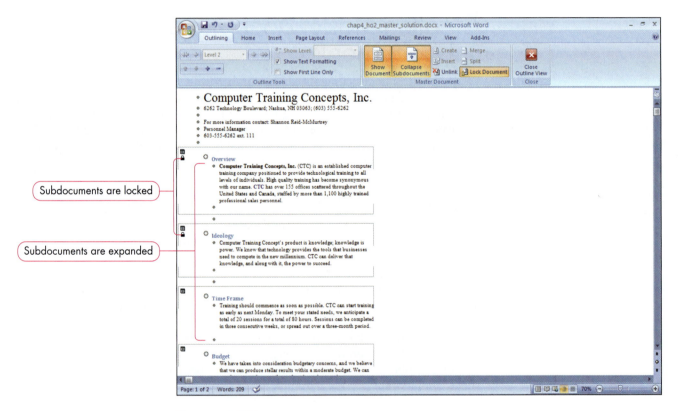

Figure 4.15 Master Document Showing Expanded Subdocuments

The expanded structure enables you to view and/or edit the contents of the subdocuments. Look carefully, however, at the subdocuments in Figure 4.15. A padlock appears to the left of the first line in the first and second subdocuments, whereas it is absent from the third and fourth subdocuments. These subdocuments are locked and unlocked, respectively. (All subdocuments are locked when collapsed, as in Figure 4.14.)

You can make changes to the master document at any time. However, you can make changes to the subdocuments only when the subdocument is unlocked. Note, too, that you can make changes to a subdocument in one of two ways, either when the subdocument is expanded (and unlocked) within a master document, as in Figure 4.15, or by opening the subdocument as an independent document within

Microsoft Word. Both techniques work equally well, and you will find yourself alternating between the two. You lock the subdocuments to prevent making changes to their content but also to prevent the subdocument from being deleted from the master document.

Regardless of how you edit the subdocuments, the attraction of a master document is the ability to work with multiple subdocuments simultaneously. The subdocuments are created independently of one another, with each subdocument stored in its own file. Then, when all of the subdocuments are finished, the master document is created, and the subdocuments are inserted into the master document, from where they are easily accessed. Inserting page numbers into the master document, for example, causes the numbers to run consecutively from one subdocument to the next. You also can create a table of contents or index for the master document that will reflect the entries in all of the subdocuments. And finally, you can print all of the subdocuments from within the master document with a single command.

Alternatively, you can reverse the process by starting with an empty master document and using it as the basis to create the subdocuments. This process is ideal for organizing a group project in school or at work, the chapters in a book, or the sections in a report. Start with a new document, and then enter the topics assigned to each group member. Format each topic in a heading style within the master document, and then use the Create Subdocument command to create subdocuments based on those headings. Saving the master document will automatically save each subdocument in its own file. This is the approach that you will follow in the next hands-on exercise.

TIP Printing a Master Document

If you click Print when a master document is displayed and the subdocuments are collapsed, the message Do you want to open the subdocuments before continuing with this command? appears. Click Yes to open the subdocuments so that they will print as one long document. Click No to print the master document that lists the subdocument filenames as they display onscreen.

Using Navigation Tools

Without a reference source, such as a table of contents, it can be difficult to locate information in a long document. Even scrolling through a long document can be inefficient if you are uncertain of the exact location that you want to view. Fortunately, Word provides navigation tools that assist the author and reader in locating content quickly and easily.

Display a Document Map and Thumbnails

The **Document Map** is a pane that lists the structure of headings in your document.

You can use the Find and Go To features in Word to move through a document. Another helpful navigation feature is the **Document Map**, a pane that lists the structure of headings in your document. The headings in a document are displayed in the left pane, and the text of the document is visible in the right pane. You can click a heading in the Document Map to move the insertion point to that heading in the document. When working in long documents, the Document Map provides a way to navigate quickly to a particular topic, as shown in Figure 4.16.

Click to toggle Document Map on and off

Document Map task pane

Figure 4.16 The Document Map

To display the Document Map pane, click Document Map in the Show/Hide group on the View tab. If you want to display the Document Map for a master document, be sure the master document is expanded to display the text of the subdocuments. This feature is a toggle; to close the Document Map, remove the check mark from the Document Map check box. The Document Map can be used on any document that uses the styles feature to format headings. The best way to format headings is to apply the built-in Title or Heading styles from the Styles group on the Home tab.

Thumbnails are small pictures of each page in your document that display in a separate window pane.

In lieu of the Document Map, you can display ***Thumbnails***—small pictures of each page in your document that display in a pane on the left side of the screen. As with the Document Map, you can click a thumbnail to move the insertion point to the top of that page. This is another method of navigating quickly through a document.

Even though you cannot read the text on a thumbnail, you can see the layout of a page well enough to determine if that is a location you want to display. And if you display markup, the revision marks and comments also display in the thumbnails, as shown in Figure 4.17. The Thumbnails view is a toggle; click the Thumbnails check box on the Show/Hide group of the View tab to display the pane, and remove the check to turn it off.

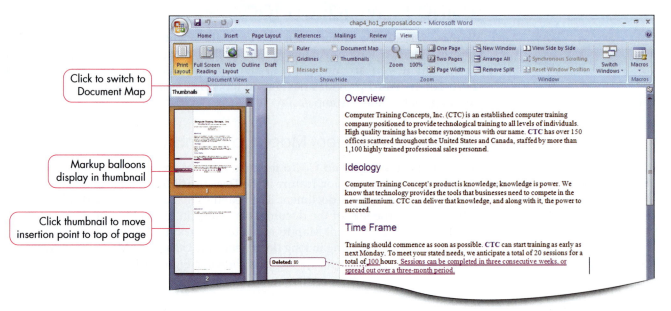

Click to switch to Document Map

Markup balloons display in thumbnail

Click thumbnail to move insertion point to top of page

Figure 4.17 Show Markup Features

Insert Bookmarks

The **bookmark** feature is an electronic marker for a specific location in a document

When you read a book you use a bookmark to help you return to that location quickly. Word provides the **bookmark** feature as an electronic marker for a specific location in a document, enabling the user to go to that location quickly. Bookmarks are helpful to mark a location where you are working. You can scroll to other parts of a document and then quickly go back to the bookmarked location. The Bookmark command is in the Links group on the Insert tab. After you click the command, the Bookmark dialog box displays, and you can designate the name of the bookmark, as shown in Figure 4.18. Bookmarks are inserted at the location of the insertion point. Bookmark names cannot contain spaces or hyphens; however, they may contain the underscore character to improve readability.

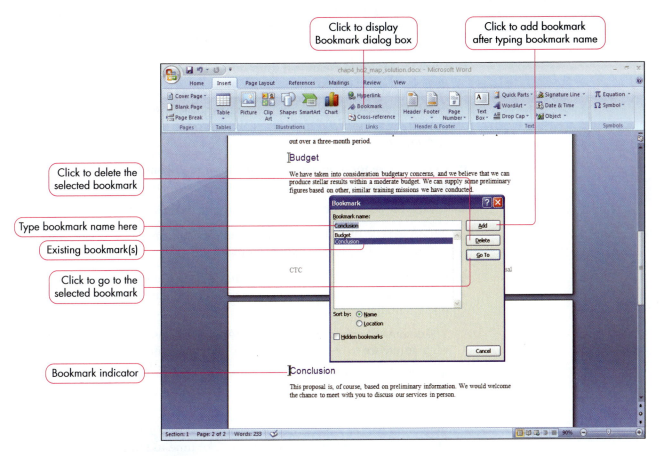

Figure 4.18 Bookmark a Location in the Document

After you insert a bookmark, you can click Bookmark on the Insert tab to see a list, of bookmarks in the current document. Click a bookmark in the Bookmark name list and then click Go To to move the insertion point to that bookmarked location. You can also press Ctrl+G to open the Go To tab of the Find and Replace dialog box. When you click Bookmark in the *Go to what* section, a drop-down list of bookmarks is available to choose from.

TIP   Using Numbers in Bookmark Names

You can use numbers within bookmark names, such as Quarter1. However, you cannot start a bookmark name with a number.

Hands-On Exercises

2 | Document Comparison, Mergers, and Navigation

Skills covered: 1. Compare and Combine Documents **2.** View Documents Side by Side **3.** Create Master Documents and Subdocuments **4.** Modify Master Documents and Subdocuments **5.** Use Document Map and Create Bookmarks

Step 1
Compare and Combine Documents

Refer to Figure 4.19 as you complete Step 1.

a. Click the **Office Button**, select **New**, and double-click **Blank document**. Click the **Review tab**. Click **Compare**, and then click **Compare** to display the Compare Documents dialog box.

b. Click the **Original document drop-down arrow** and select the *chap4_ho1_proposal_solution* document.

> **TROUBLESHOOTING:** If the chap4_ho1_proposal_solution document does not display in the drop-down list, click the Browse for Original button to locate the document.

c. Click **Browse for Revised** beside the **Revised document** text box, and then browse to locate and open the *chap4_ho2_proposal2* document.

d. Click **New document** under *Show changes in*, if necessary.

> **TROUBLESHOOTING:** If the Comparison settings and Show changes sections do not display, click More to display them.

e. Click **OK**, and then click **Yes** in the Microsoft Office Word dialog box that explains how the tracked changes in each document will be accepted before the document displays.

The document opens in a new window and contains markup balloons to indicate each difference in the two documents. The Reviewing Pane might also display.

f. Save the document as **chap4_ho2_compare_solution**. If the Reviewing Pane displays, click **Reviewing Pane** in the Tracking group on the Review tab to remove it.

In the first part of this exercise, you compared two documents. In the next series of steps, you combine the documents. Take time to notice how Word tracks the differences in compared versus combined documents.

g. In the Compare group, click **Compare**, and then click **Combine** to display the Combine Documents dialog box.

h. Click the **Original document drop-down arrow** and select the *chap4_ho1_proposal_solution* document. Click **Browse for Revised** and browse to locate the *chap4_ho2_proposal2* document.

i. Click **New document** under *Show changes in*, if necessary. Click **OK**, and then click **Continue with Merge**.

> **TROUBLESHOOTING:** If the two documents you just merged display in small windows on the screen, click **Show Source Documents** in the Compare group on the Review tab, and then click **Hide Source Documents** to close them.

The document opens in a new window and contains markup balloons to indicate each difference in the two documents, as shown in Figure 4.19. Depending on your Track Changes settings, the balloons might display on either the left or right side of your document.

j. Save the document as **chap4_ho2_combine_solution**.

k. Leave both documents open for Step 2. If the two documents you just merged display in small windows on the screen, click **Show Source Documents** in the Compare group on the Review tab, and then click **Hide Source Documents** to close them.

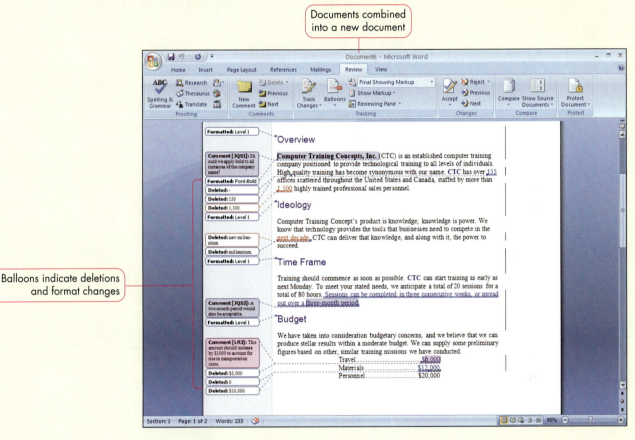

Figure 4.19 Combining Documents

Step 2
View Documents Side by Side

Refer to Figure 4.20 as you complete Step 2.

a. If *chap4_ho2_combine_solution* is not the active document, click the **View tab**, click **Switch Windows**, and then click *chap4_ho2_combine_solution* from the list. Click **View Side by Side** in the Window group.

Two windows display containing the files you created using the compare and combine features. Notice in the Window group on the View tab that Synchronous Scrolling is highlighted in an orange color to indicate the setting is on. As you scroll in one document, the other will scroll also.

TROUBLESHOOTING: If your view of one or both of the documents is insufficient, you can use the mouse to resize the window. Click and drag the border of the window until you reach an acceptable size to view the document information.

b. Scroll down to view the Time Frame paragraph and compare the differences.

In the *chap4_ho2_compare_solution* document, the last sentence in this section is deleted and displays in a markup balloon. In the *chap4_ho2_combine_solution* document, the last sentence displays in the paragraph.

c. Click **Synchronous Scrolling** on the View tab, as shown in Figure 4.20, to turn the toggle off. Scroll down in the *chap4_ho2_combine_solution* document until the Conclusion paragraph displays.

Since the Synchronous Scrolling toggle is off, the *chap4_ho2_compare_solution* document does not scroll, and the Time Frame paragraph remains in view.

d. Scroll to the top of the page. Click the **Review tab**, click the **Tracking arrow**, click the **Display for Review arrow**, and then click **Final**. Do this for both documents.

Notice the bold formatting is only applied to the company name in the *chap4_ho2_combine_solution* document.

e. Close *chap4_ho2_compare_solution* without saving.

f. In the *chap4_ho2_combine_solution* document, click the **Accept arrow** in the Changes group of the Review tab, and then click **Accept All Changes in Document**.

g. Save and close the *chap4_ho2_combine_solution* document.

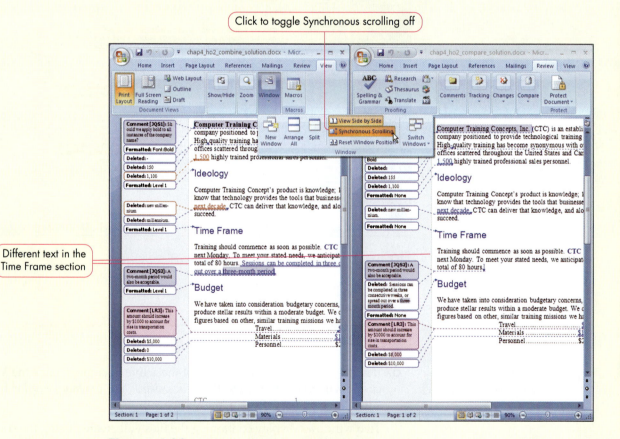

Figure 4.20 View Documents Side by Side

Refer to Figure 4.21 as you complete Step 3.

a. Open the *chap4_ho2_master* document and save it as **chap4_ho2_master_solution**.

b. Press **Ctrl+End** to move to the end of the document. Type the following headings for the subdocuments: **Overview**, **Ideology**, **Time Frame**, **Budget**, and **Conclusion**. Each word should have its own line.

c. Select the topics you just typed, and then click **Heading 2** from the Quick Styles gallery on the Home tab. Click the **Outline** button on the status bar.

The Outlining tab displays and the document text displays in Outline view. Be sure all five headings are still selected before you perform the next step.

d. Click **Show Document** in the Master Document group to display more master document commands. Click **Create**.

Individual subdocuments are created for the selected headings. A box surrounds each subdocument, and you see a subdocument icon in the top-left corner of each subdocument box, as shown in Figure 4.21. You also will see section breaks and other formatting marks if your Show/Hide ¶ feature is turned on.

e. Click **Collapse Subdocuments** in the Master Document group to collapse the subdocuments in the document and display the name and path where each subdocument is saved. Click **OK** if prompted to save changes to the master document.

f. Click **Expand Subdocuments** in the Master Document group to reopen and display the subdocuments.

g. Save the document.

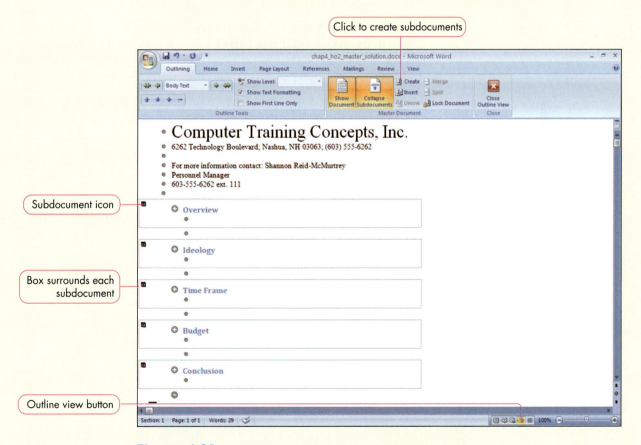

Figure 4.21 View Subdocuments in a Master Document

Refer to Figure 4.22 as you complete Step 4.

a. Press **Ctrl+End** to move to the end of the master document.

b. Click **Insert** in the Master Document group to display the Insert Subdocument dialog box. If necessary, click the **Look in drop-down arrow** to change to the **Exploring Word folder** and select *chap4_ho2_background*. Then click **Open** to insert this document into the master document. If prompted to rename the style in the subdocument, click **Yes**.

The Background Information and Financial Statement paragraphs display as a subdocument at the bottom of the page.

c. Click within the third subdocument, Time Frame, which will eventually summarize the amount of time the company requires for training.

d. Click **Lock Document** in the Master Document group of the Outlining tab. Press the letter **a** on the keyboard.

The padlock icon displays below the subdocument icon and the Lock Document command is highlighted in an orange color to indicate the toggle is on. Attempts to type or edit text are not successful because the document is locked.

e. Click **Lock Document** a second time to unlock the document. Click below the Time Frame heading and type the text, as shown in Figure 4.22. Then click **Save** to save changes to the Master document.

TROUBLESHOOTING: Be sure the subdocument is unlocked so the changes you make will be reflected in the subdocument file as well.

f. Click **Close Outline View** to return to Print Layout view.

The document now displays on two pages.

g. Click **Show/Hide ¶** in the Paragraph group on the Home tab to display section breaks in the document. Press **Ctrl+End** to view the end of the document. Place the insertion point on the *Section Break (Continuous)* mark that displays below the *Financial Statement* paragraph, and then press **Delete**.

The *Background Information* and *Financial Statement* paragraphs display on page one with the other subdocument headings.

TROUBLESHOOTING: If the last two paragraphs still display on page two, position the insertion point on the left of the last paragraph mark in the document and press **Delete** to remove the empty second page.

h. Click **Show/Hide ¶** to toggle off paragraph marks.

i. Save and close the document. Exit Word if you will not continue with the next step at this time.

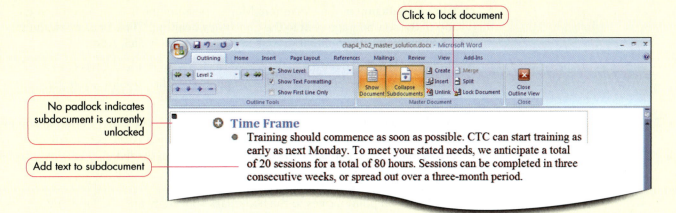

Figure 4.22 Modify a Subdocument

Refer to Figure 4.23 as you complete Step 5.

a. Open the *chap4_ho1_proposal_solution* document you completed in Step 1 and save it as **chap4_ho2_map_solution**. Click the **View tab** and click **Thumbnails** in the Show/Hide group to display the Thumbnails pane on the left side of the screen.

The Thumbnails appear as a separate pane on the left side of your screen. An orange border appears around the thumbnail of the currently viewed page.

b. Click the thumbnail for the second page.

Word positions the insertion point at the beginning of the second page.

c. Click **Thumbnails** to hide the thumbnails pane. Click **Document Map**.

The Document Map contains a list of text formatted with built-in heading styles. Like Thumbnails, it is a toggle. Clicking it again hides the Document Map pane.

d. Click **Overview** in the Document Map. Click **Computer Training Concepts, Inc.** in the Document Map.

Because of your actions, Word moves the insertion point to the left side of the *Overview* heading near the top of the first page, and then moves it to the left of *Computer Training Concepts*. Because *Overview* and other headings are formatted with the Heading 2 style, they display in the Document Map.

e. Click **Budget** in the Document Map.

You moved the insertion point and now you will insert a bookmark in this location.

f. Click the **Insert tab** and click **Bookmark** in the Links group. Type **Budget** in the Bookmark name text box, then click **Add**.

Word inserts a bookmark with the name you entered. A large, gray-colored I-beam indicates the location of the bookmark.

TROUBLESHOOTING: If you do not see the bookmark indicator, you can change a setting that enables it. Click the Office Button, then click Word Options. Click Advanced, and then scroll down and click the Show bookmarks check box in the Show document content section. Click OK to save the settings and return to the document.

g. Click **Conclusion** in the Document Map to position the insertion point on the top of the second page next to the *Conclusion* heading. Click **Bookmark**, type **Conclusion** in the Bookmark name text box, and then click **Add**.

h. Press **Ctrl+Home** to return to the top of the document. Press **Ctrl+G** to display the *Go To* tab of the Find and Replace dialog box. Click **Bookmark** in the *Go to what* list.

Word displays the first bookmark name, Budget, in the Enter bookmark name text box, as shown in Figure 4.23. If you click the *Enter bookmark name* drop-down arrow, the Conclusion bookmark also will display in the list.

i. Click **Go To**.

The insertion point moves to the bookmark's location, and the Find and Replace dialog box remains onscreen in case you want to go to another bookmark.

j. Click **Close** to remove the Find and Replace dialog box. Click **Close** in the upper-right corner of the Document Map pane.

k. Save and close the file. Exit Word if you will not continue with the next exercise at this time.

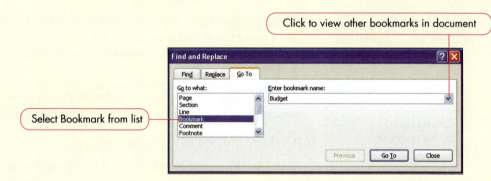

Figure 4.23 Go to a Bookmark

Reference Resources

Well-prepared documents often include notes that provide supplemental information or citations for sources quoted in the document. Some documents also contain other valuable supplemental components, such as a list of figures or legal references. Word 2007 includes many features that can help you create these supplemental references, as well as many others described in the following paragraphs.

In this section, you use Word to create citations used for reference pages, create a bibliography page that displays works cited in the document, and select from a list of writing styles that are commonly used to dictate the format of reference pages. You also create and modify footnote and endnote citations, which display at the bottom or end of the document.

Acknowledging a Source

Failure to acknowledge the source of information you use in a document is a form of plagiarism. Word includes a robust feature for tracking sources and producing the supplemental resources to display them.

It is common practice to use a variety of sources to supplement your own thoughts when writing a paper, report, legal brief, or many other types of document. Failure to acknowledge the source of information you use in a document is a form of plagiarism. *Webster's New Collegiate Dictionary* defines *plagiarism* as the act of using and documenting the ideas or writings of another as one's own. Plagiarism has serious moral and ethical implications and is taken very seriously in the academic community, and is often classified as academic dishonesty. It is also a violation of U.S. Copyright law, so it should be avoided in any professional and personal setting also.

Plagiarism is the act of using and documenting the ideas or writings of another as one's own.

To assist in your efforts to avoid plagiarism, which is frequently a thoughtless oversight rather than a malicious act, Word includes a robust feature for tracking sources and producing the supplemental resources to display them.

Create a Source

Word provides the citation feature to track, compile, and display your research sources for inclusion in several types of supplemental references. To use this feature you use the Insert Citation command in the Citations & Bibliography group on the References tab to add data about each source, as shown in Figure 4.24. A *citation* is a note recognizing the source of information or a quoted passage. The Create Source dialog box includes fields to catalog information, such as author, date, publication name, page number, or Web site address, from the following types of sources:

A *citation* is a note recognizing a source of information or a quoted passage.

- Book
- Book Section
- Journal Article
- Article in a Periodical
- Conference Proceedings
- Report
- Web Site
- Document from Web Site
- Electronic Source

- Art
- Sound Recording
- Performance
- Film
- Interview
- Patent
- Case
- Miscellaneous

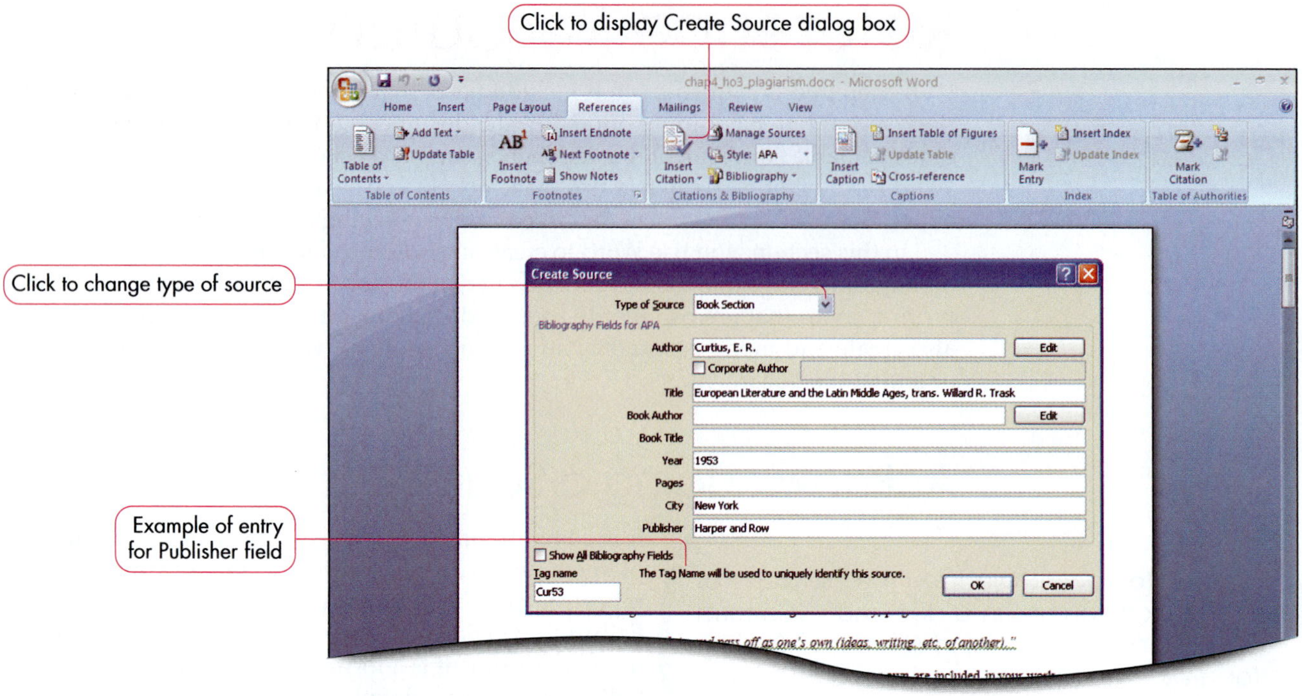

Figure 4.24 Add a Source Citation

After you create the citation sources, you can insert them into a document using the Insert Citation command. When you click the command, a list of your sources displays; click a source from the list, and the proper citation format is inserted in your document.

Share and Search for a Source

The **Master List** is a database of all citation sources created in Word.

The **Current List** includes all citation sources you use in the current document.

After you add sources, they are saved in a Master List. The **Master List** is a database of all citation sources created in Word on a particular computer. The source also is stored in the **Current List**, which contains all sources you use in the current document. Sources saved in the Master List can be used in any Word document. This feature is very helpful to those who use the same sources on multiple occasions. Master Lists are stored in XML format, so you can share the Master List file with coworkers or other authors, eliminating the need to retype the information and to ensure accuracy. The Master List file is stored in \Application Data\Microsoft\Bibliography, which is a subfolder of the user account folder stored under C:\Documents and Settings. For example, a path to the Master File might be C:\Documents and Settings\John Q. Student\Application Data\Microsoft\Bibliography\Sources.xml.

The Source Manager dialog box (see Figure 4.25) displays the Master List you created, and you also can browse to find others. If you do not have access to a Master List on a local or network drive, you can e-mail the Master List file. After you open the Master List, you can copy sources to your Current List. You also can use the Research and Reference Pane to search external libraries for Master Lists of sources. If a library or host service makes its sources available in a format compatible with Office 2007, you can import its files, open the Master File, and insert a citation, avoiding the need to fill out a new Source form in Word.

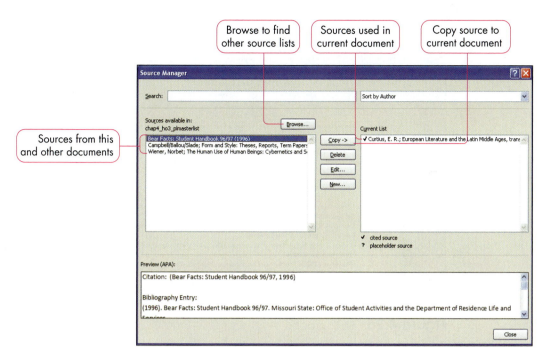

Figure 4.25 Source Manager Dialog Box

Creating a Bibliography

A *bibliography* is a list of works cited or consulted by an author in a document.

A *bibliography* is a list of works cited or consulted by an author and should be included with the document when published. Some reference manuals use the terms Works Cited or References instead of Bibliography. A bibliography is just one form of reference that gives credit to the sources you consulted or quoted in the preparation of your paper. The addition of a bibliography to your completed work demonstrates respect for the material consulted and proves that you are not plagiarizing. It also gives the reader an opportunity to validate your references for accuracy.

Word includes a bibliography feature that makes the addition of this reference page very easy. After you add the sources using the Insert Citation feature, you click Bibliography in the Citations & Bibliography group of the References tab, and then click Insert Bibliography. Any sources used in the current document will display in the appropriate format as a Bibliography, as shown in Figure 4.26.

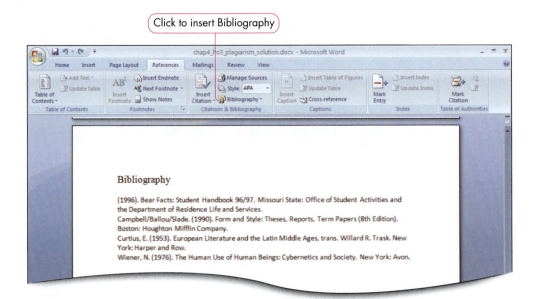

Click to insert Bibliography

Figure 4.26 Bibliography

Selecting the Writing Style

When research papers are prepared the author often must conform to a particular writing style. The writing style, also called an editorial style, consists of rules and guidelines set forth by a publisher of a research journal to ensure consistency in presentation of research documents. Some of the presentation consistencies that a style enforces are use of punctuation and abbreviations, format of headings and tables, presentation of statistics, and citation of references. The style guidelines differ depending on the discipline the research topic comes from. For example, the APA style originates with the American Psychological Association, but many other disciplines use this style as well. Another common style is MLA, which is sanctioned by the Modern Language Association. The topic of your paper and the audience you write to will determine which style you should use while writing.

Word 2007 incorporates several writing style guidelines, which makes it easier for you to generate supplemental references in the required format. The Style list in the Citations & Bibliography group on the References tab includes the most commonly used international styles, as shown in Figure 4.27. When you select the style before creating the bibliography, the citations that appear in the bibliography will be formatted exactly as required by that style.

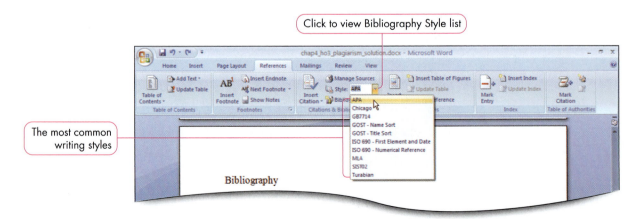

Click to view Bibliography Style list

The most common writing styles

Figure 4.27 Style Options

Creating and Modifying Footnotes and Endnotes

A *footnote* is a citation that appears at the bottom of a page, and an *endnote* is a citation that appears at the end of a document. You use footnotes or endnotes to credit the sources you quote or cite in your document. You also can use footnotes or endnotes to provide supplemental information about a topic that is too distracting to include in the body of the document. Footnotes, endnotes, and bibliographies often contain the same information. Your use of one of the three options is determined by the style of paper (MLA for example) or by the person who oversees your research. When you use a bibliography, the information about a source is displayed only one time at the end of the paper, and the exact location in the document that uses information from the source may not be obvious. When you use a footnote, the information about a source displays on the specific page where a quote or information appears. When you use endnotes, the information about a source displays only at the end of the document; however, the number that identifies the endnote displays on each page, and you can use several references to the same source throughout the document.

The References tab includes the Insert Footnote and Insert Endnote commands. If you click the Footnote and Endnote Dialog Box Launcher, the Footnote and Endnote dialog box opens, and you can modify the location of the notes and the format of the numbers. By default, Word sequentially numbers footnotes with Arabic numerals (1, 2, and 3), as shown in Figure 4.28. Endnotes are numbered with lowercase Roman numerals (i, ii, and iii) based on the location of the note within the document. If you add or delete notes, Word renumbers the remaining notes automatically.

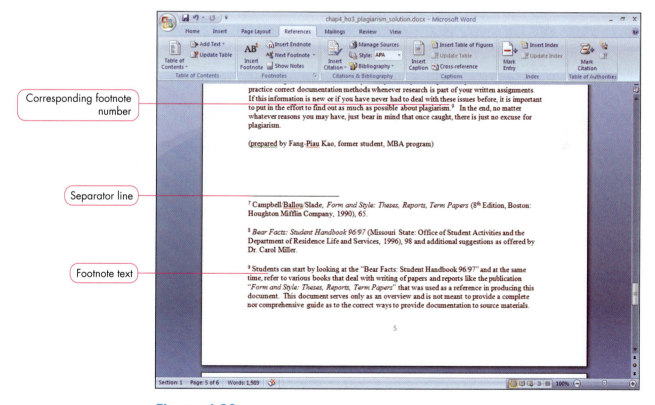

Figure 4.28   Document Containing Footnotes

You can easily make modifications to footnotes and endnotes. In Print Layout view, scroll to the bottom of the page (or for endnotes, to the end of the document or section), click inside the note, and then edit it. In Draft view, double-click the footnote or endnote reference mark to see the Footnotes or Endnotes pane, then edit the note.

TIP   Relocating a Footnote or Endnote

If you created a note in the wrong location, select the note reference mark, cut it from its current location, and then paste it in the correct location within the document text. You also can use the drag-and-drop method to move a selected note reference mark to a different location.

Hands-On Exercises

3 | Reference Resources

Skills covered: 1. Create and Search for a Source **2.** Select a Writing Style and Insert a Bibliography **3.** Create and Modify Footnotes **4.** Convert Footnotes to Endnotes and Modify Endnotes

---

<table>
<tr>
<td>

Step 1
Create and Search for a Source

</td>
<td>

Refer to Figure 4.29 as you complete Step 1.

a. Open the *chap4_ho3_plagiarism* document and save it as **chap4_ho3_ plagiarism_ solution**.

b. Click the **References tab**, click **Manage Sources** in the Citations & Bibliography group, and then click **New** in the middle of the dialog box.

Because you want to create a citation source without inserting it into the document, you use the Source Manager instead of Create Citation. After you click New in the Source Manager, the Create Source dialog box displays.

c. Click the **Type of Source drop-down arrow** and select **Book Section**. Type the source information in the Bibliography fields, as shown in Figure 4.29, and then click **OK** to add the source to your document and return to the Source Manager dialog box.

d. Click **Browse** in the Source Manager dialog box to display the Open Source List dialog box. Click the **Look in drop-down arrow** and navigate to the Exploring Word folder. Select *chap4_ho3_plmasterlist*, and then click **OK**.

You return to the Source Manager dialog box, and three sources display in the *Sources available in* box.

e. Click the first source entry, if necessary, to select it. Then press and hold **Shift** and select the last entry. Click **Copy** to insert the sources into the current document.

The three sources you copied and the one source you created display in the Current List box.

f. Click **Close** to return to the document. Save the document.

</td>
</tr>
</table>

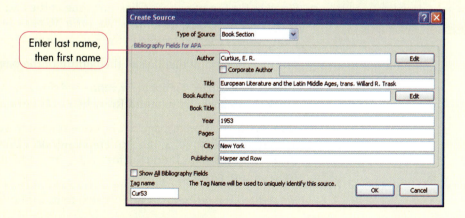

Figure 4.29 Add a New Source

Refer to Figure 4.30 as you complete Step 2.

a. Click the **Style arrow** in the Citations and Bibliography group and select **MLA**.

b. Press **Ctrl+End** to position the insertion point at the end of the document, press **Ctrl+Enter** to add a blank page, type **Bibliography** at the top of the new page, and then press **Enter** two times.

c. Click **Bibliography**, and then click **Insert Bibliography**.

The sources cited in the document display in the MLA format for bibliographies, as shown in Figure 4.30.

d. Click the **Style arrow** again and select **APA**.

The format of the bibliography changes to reflect the standards of the APA style.

e. Save the document.

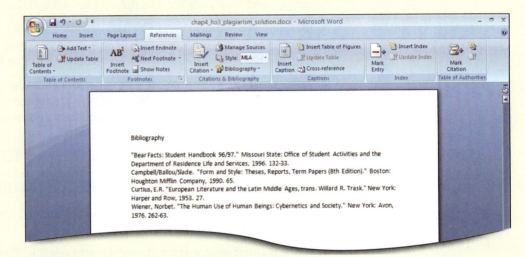

Figure 4.30 Bibliography in MLA Style

Refer to Figure 4.31 as you complete Step 3.

a. Scroll to the top of page 3. Click one time at the end of the paragraph that begins with *Ernst Robert Curtius's term "the Latin Middle Ages"* to move the insertion point. Click **Insert Footnote** in the Footnotes group on the References tab.

The insertion point displays at the bottom of the page, below the horizontal line.

b. Type **E. R. Curtius,** *European Literature and the Latin Middle Ages,* **trans. Willard R. Trask (New York: Harper and Row, 1953), 27**. Format the endnote as displayed.

c. Scroll to the bottom of page 5. Click one time at the end of the seventh footnote, a reference to *Bear Facts*, the Student Handbook. Remove the period that follows the page number and type the following: **and additional suggestions as offered by Dr. Carol Miller.**

You edited the footnote by adding text to it, as shown in Figure 4.31.

d. Save the document.

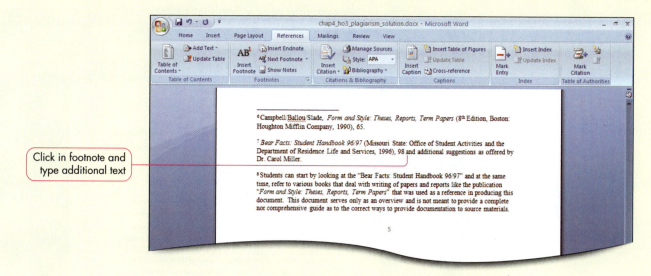

Click in footnote and type additional text

Figure 4.31 Modify a Footnote

Refer to Figure 4.32 as you complete Step 4.

Step 4

Convert Footnotes to Endnotes and Modify Endnotes

a. Click the **Footnote and Endnote Dialog Box Launcher**. Click **Convert**, click **Convert all footnotes to endnotes**, and then click **OK**. Click **Close** to close the Footnote and Endnote dialog box.

All footnotes relocate to the last page, below the Bibliography, and the number format is changed to Roman numerals.

b. Scroll to the bottom of page 3. Move the insertion point to the end of the first example paragraph, which ends with *subject to law*. Click **Insert Endnote** and type **Norbet Wiener,** *The Human Use of Human Beings: Cybernetics and Society* **(New York: Avon, 1976), 262–63**. Format the endnote as displayed.

The endnote displays at the end of the document and the endnote numbers adjust for the addition, as shown in Figure 4.32.

c. Save and close the document. Exit Word if you will not continue with the next exercise at this time.

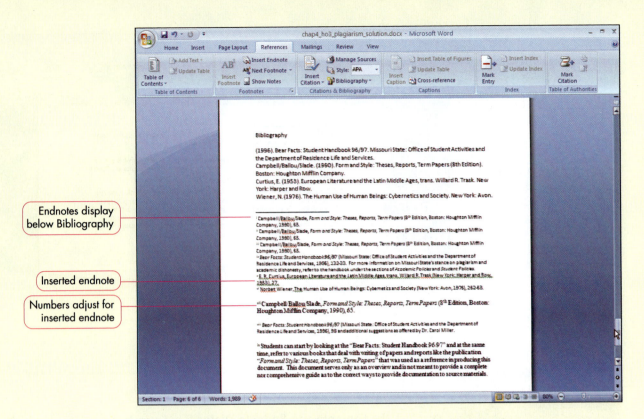

Endnotes display below Bibliography

Inserted endnote

Numbers adjust for inserted endnote

Figure 4.32 Modify an Endnote

Additional Reference Resources

The previous section mentioned several types of reference features that should be used when a document refers to outside information or sources. Some reference features are used less frequently, yet are valuable for creating professional quality documents. These supplements include a list of captions used on figures, a list of figures presented in a document, references to other locations in a document, and a list of legal sources referenced. You also can attach information that refers to the contents and origin of a document.

In this section, you add descriptions to visual elements and create a list of the visuals used in a document. You create a cross-reference, or note that refers the reader to another location in the document, and you create a list of references from a legal document. Finally, you modify the properties associated with a document.

> Some reference features are used less frequently, yet are valuable for creating professional quality documents. You also can attach information that refers to the contents and origin of a document.

Adding Figure References

Documents and books often contain several images, charts, or tables. For example, this textbook contains several screenshots in each project. To help readers refer to the correct image or table, you can insert a caption. A *caption* is a descriptive title for an image, a figure, or a table. To add a caption, click Insert Caption in the Captions group on the References tab. By default, Word assigns a number to the equation, figure, or table at the beginning of the caption. When you click Insert Caption, the Caption dialog box appears, as shown in Figure 4.33, and you can edit the default caption by adding descriptive text.

A *caption* is a descriptive title for an equation, a figure, or a table.

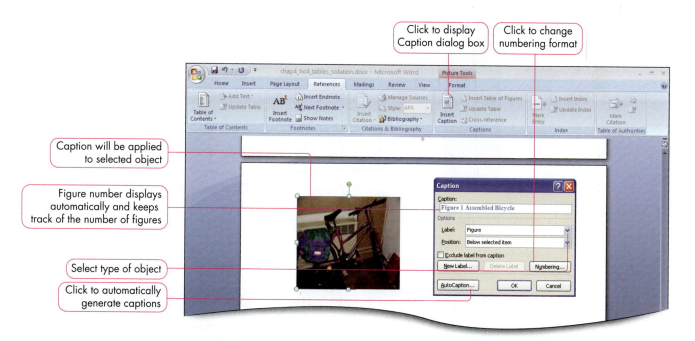

Click to display Caption dialog box

Click to change numbering format

Caption will be applied to selected object

Figure number displays automatically and keeps track of the number of figures

Select type of object

Click to automatically generate captions

Figure 4.33 Insert Caption Dialog Box

To automatically generate captions, click AutoCaption in the Caption dialog box. In the *Add caption when inserting* list, in the AutoCaption dialog box, click the check box next to the element type for which you want to create AutoCaptions. Specify the default caption text in the *Use label* text box, and specify the location of the caption by clicking the Position drop-down arrow. If your document will contain several captions, this feature helps you to ensure each caption is named and numbered sequentially.

Inserting a Table of Figures

A **table of figures** is a list of the captions in a document.

If your document includes pictures, charts and graphs, slides, or other illustrations along with a caption, you can include a **table of figures**, or list of the captions, as a reference. To build a table of figures, Word searches a document for captions, sorts the captions by number, and displays the table of figures in the document. A table of figures is placed after the table of contents for a document. The Insert Table of Figures command is in the Captions group on the References tab. The Table of Figures dialog box, shown in Figure 4.34, enables you to select page number, format, and caption label options.

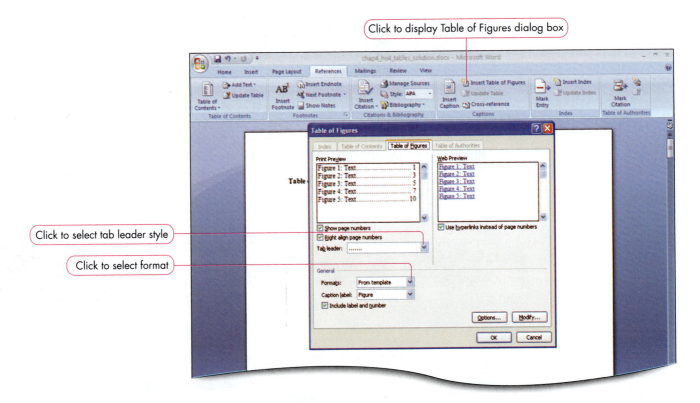

Click to display Table of Figures dialog box

Click to select tab leader style

Click to select format

Figure 4.34 The Table of Figures Dialog Box

TIP   Update a Table of Figures

If the figures or figure captions in a document change or are removed, you should update the table of figures. To update the table, right-click on any table entry to select the entire table and display a menu. Click Update Field, and then choose between the options Update Page Numbers only or Update entire table. If significant changes have been made, you should update the entire table.

Adding Legal References

A **table of authorities** is used in legal documents to reference cases, rules, treaties, and other documents referred to in a legal brief. You typically compile the table of authorities on a separate page at the beginning of a legal document, as shown in Figure 4.35. Word's table of authorities feature enables you to track, compile, and display citations, or references to specific legal cases and other legal documents, to be included in the table of authorities. Before you generate the table of authorities, you must indicate which citations you want to include using the Mark Citation command in the Table of Authorities group on the References tab. To mark citations, select text and then click Mark Citation. After you mark the citations, click Insert Table of Authorities in the Table of Authorities group on the References tab to generate the table at the location of your insertion point.

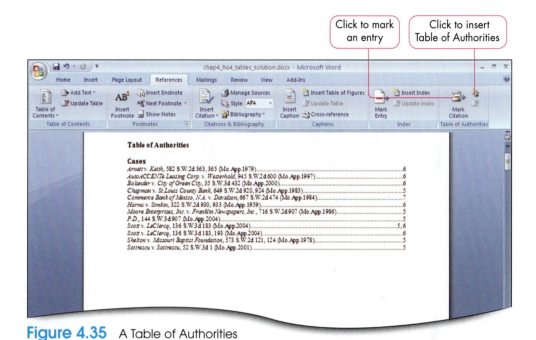

Figure 4.35 A Table of Authorities

To modify a table of authorities entry, you must display the table of authorities fields by clicking Show/Hide ¶ in the Paragraph group on the Home tab. Locate the entry that you wish to modify and edit the text inside the quotation marks. Do not change the entry in the finished table of authorities or the next time you update the table of authorities, your changes will be lost.

To delete a table of authorities entry, select the entire entry field, including the braces {}, and press Delete. After you modify or delete a marked entry, click Update Table in the Table of Authorities group on the References tab to display the changes in the table.

Creating Cross-References

A **cross-reference** is a note that refers the reader to another location for more information about a topic. You can create cross-references to headings, bookmarks, footnotes, endnotes, captions, and tables. A typical cross-reference looks like this: *See page 4 for more information about local recreation facilities.* For files you make available via e-mail or on an intranet, you can create an electronic cross-reference. However, if you are distributing printed copies of your document, you need printed references so the readers can find the location themselves.

To create a cross-reference, position the insertion point in the location where the reference occurs. Display the References tab and click Cross-reference in the Captions group. When the Cross-reference dialog box displays, as shown in Figure 4.36, you choose the type of reference (such as Heading, Bookmark, Figure, or Footnote), and then the reference element to display (such as page number or paragraph text). You can specify whether it displays as a hyperlink in the document, causing a ScreenTip to appear when the mouse pointer is over the cross-reference.

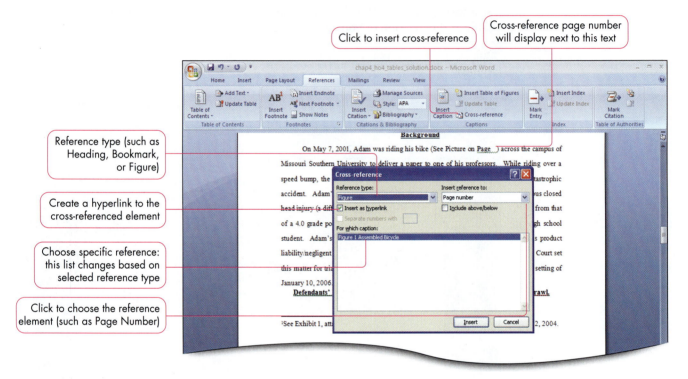

Figure 4.36 Insert a Cross-Reference

Modifying Document Properties

The **Document Information panel** allows you to enter descriptive information about a document.

Sometimes, you want to record information about a document but do not want to include the information directly in the document window. For example, you might want to record some notes to yourself about a document, such as the document's author, purpose, or intended audience. To help maintain documents, you can use the **Document Information panel** to store descriptive information about a document, such as a title, subject, author, keywords, and comments. When you create a document summary and save the document, Word saves the document summary with the document. You can update the document summary at any time by opening the Document Information panel for the respective document. To display the Document Information panel, as shown in Figure 4.37, click the Office Button, point to Prepare, and then select Properties.

> Sometimes, you want to record information about a document but do not want to include the information directly in the document window . . . you can use the Document Information panel to store descriptive information about a document, such as a title, subject, author, keywords, and comments.

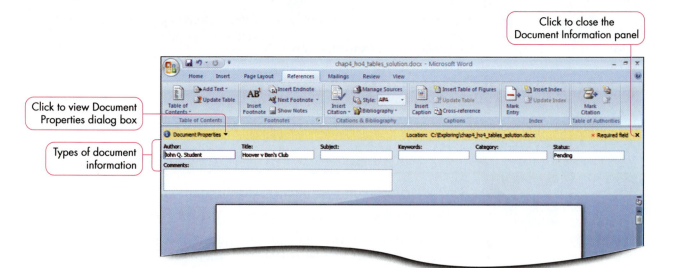

Click to close the Document Information panel

Click to view Document Properties dialog box

Types of document information

Figure 4.37 Document Information Panel

TIP Search for a Document Using Document Properties

After you insert information into the Document Information panel, you can use it as search criteria when using the Windows search tool. The information entered as document title, comments, author, or any other field will be searched in the same manner as text that displays in the document.

Customize Document Properties

In addition to creating, modifying, and viewing a document summary, you might want to customize the document properties in the Document Information panel. When you click the arrow next to Document Properties and then click Advanced Properties, the Properties dialog box displays. The Custom tab of the Properties dialog box enables you to add other properties and assign values to those properties. For example, you might want to add the *Date completed* property and specify an exact date for reference. This date would reflect the completion date, not the date the file was last saved—in case someone opens a file and saves it without making changes. You also might create a field to track company information such as warehouse location or product numbers.

You can create and modify document summaries directly from the Open dialog box, through Windows Explorer, or in other file management windows. You do not have to create the document summary when the document is open within Microsoft Word.

Print Document Properties

You can print document properties to have hard copies to store in a filing cabinet for easy reference. To do this, display the Print dialog box, click the Print what drop-down arrow, choose Document properties, and click OK.

Hands-On Exercises

4 | Additional Reference Resources

Skills covered: 1. Add Captions and Create a Table of Figures **2.** Create a Table of Authorities **3.** Create a Cross-Reference **4.** Modify Document Properties

<table>
<tr>
<td>

Step 1

Add Captions and Create a Table of Figures

</td>
<td>

Refer to Figure 4.38 as you complete Step 1.

a. Open the *chap4_ho4_tables* document and save it as **chap4_ho4_ tables_solution**.

b. Press **Ctrl+End** to view the end of the document. Click once on the picture to select it. Click the **References tab** and click **Insert Caption** in the Captions group.

The Caption dialog box displays, and the insertion point is positioned at the end of the caption text that displays automatically.

c. Press **Spacebar** to insert a space and then type **Assembled Bicycle** after the existing text in the Caption box, as shown in Figure 4.38. Click **OK**.

The caption *Figure 1 Assembled Bicycle* displays below the picture in a text box.

d. Press **Ctrl+Home** to view page 1. Press **Ctrl+Enter** to insert a page, move your insertion point to the top of the new page, and then type **Table of Figures**. Press **Enter** two times.

e. Click **Insert Table of Figures** in the Captions group to display the Table of Figures dialog box. Click **OK**.

The table displays, showing only one entry at this time.

f. Save the document.

</td>
</tr>
</table>

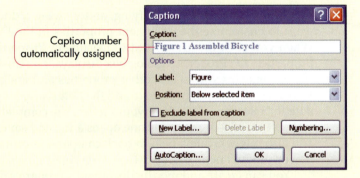

Caption number automatically assigned

Figure 4.38 Add a Caption to a Picture

Refer to Figure 4.39 as you complete Step 2.

a. Go to page 4 in the document. Locate the *Shelton v. Missouri Baptist Foundation* case and select the case information from *Shelton* up to and including the date *(1978)*. Click **Mark Citation** in the Table of Authorities group on the References tab. Click **Mark All**, as shown in Figure 4.39, and then click **Close**.

b. Search through the remainder of the document and mark all case references. Click the **Home tab**, and then click **Show/Hide ¶** to turn off display of formatting marks.

c. Press **Ctrl+Home** to position the insertion point at the beginning of the document, press **Ctrl+Enter** to add a blank page, type **Table of Authorities** at the top of the new page, and then press **Enter** one time. Click the **References tab**, and then click **Insert Table of Authorities** in the Table of Authorities group. Click **OK**.

The Table of Authorities, which lists information about the cases mentioned in the brief, is shown in Figure 4.35.

d. Save the document.

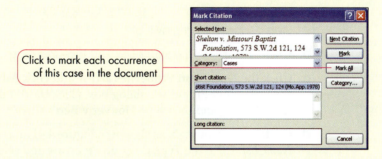

Click to mark each occurrence of this case in the document

Figure 4.39 Mark Citation Dialog Box

Refer to Figure 4.40 as you complete Step 3.

a. Scroll to page 3 and place the insertion point on the right side of the word *bike* in the first sentence of the *Background* section.

b. Press **Spacebar** and type **(See picture on page**. Click the **References tab**, if necessary, and click **Cross-Reference** in the Captions group. Click the **Reference type drop-down arrow** and click **Figure**, click **Figure 1** in the **For which caption** list, click the **Insert reference to drop-down arrow** and select **Page number**, as shown in Figure 4.40, and then click **Insert**.

The cross-reference displays 8, the page where the picture displays.

c. Click **Close** to close the Cross-reference dialog box. Type **)** to end the cross-reference.

Hold your mouse over the cross-reference page number and view the ScreenTip that instructs you to press **Ctrl** while you click on the number *8* to move the insertion point to the location of the picture.

d. Save the document.

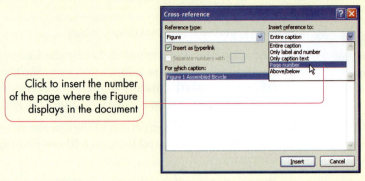

Click to insert the number of the page where the Figure displays in the document

Figure 4.40 Insert Cross-Reference

Refer to Figure 4.41 as you complete Step 4.

a. Click the **Office Button**, select **Prepare**, and then select **Properties**.

The Document Information panel displays above your document.

TROUBLESHOOTING: If the Document Information panel disappears, repeat Step a. above to display it again.

b. Click one time in the *Status* box and type **Pending**.

c. Click the **Document Properties arrow** and click **Advanced Properties** to display the Document Properties dialog box. Click the Summary tab, click one time in the *Title* box, and then type **Hoover v Ben's Club**.

d. Click the **Custom tab,** as shown in Figure 4.41, and select **Date completed** in the *Name list*. Click the **Type drop-down arrow** and select **Date**. Type today's date in the *Value box* using MM/DD/YY format, and then click **Add**. Click **OK** to close the dialog box.

e. Save and close the document.

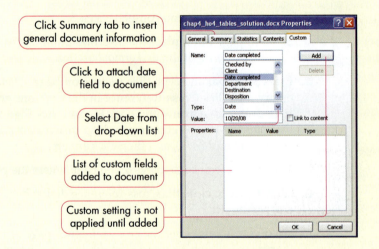

Click Summary tab to insert general document information

Click to attach date field to document

Select Date from drop-down list

List of custom fields added to document

Custom setting is not applied until added

Figure 4.41 Change Document Properties

Summary

1. **Insert comments in a document.** When you work as part of a team you can use the Comment feature to collaborate. Comments enable you to ask a question or provide a suggestion to another person in a document, without modifying the content of the document. Comments are inserted using colored Markup balloons, and a different color is assigned to each reviewer. Comments appear in the Print Layout, Web Layout, and Full Screen Reading views. You can display comments in the margins of a document or in a reading pane.

2. **Track changes in a document.** This feature monitors all additions, deletions, and formatting changes you make to a document. When active, the Track Changes feature applies revision marks to indicate where a change occurs. When you move your mouse over a revision mark, it will display the name of the person who made the change as well as the date and time of change. You can use markup tools to accept or reject changes that have been tracked. These tools are especially helpful when several people make changes to the same document. If comments and tracked changes do not display initially, you can turn on the Show Markup feature to view them. You also can view the document as a final copy if all tracked changes are accepted or as the original before any changes were made and tracked. You can modify the Track Changes options to change settings such as fonts, colors, location, and size of markup balloons.

3. **View documents side by side.** This feature enables you to view two documents on the same screen. It is useful when you want to compare the contents of two documents or if you want to cut or copy and paste text from one document to another. To view two documents side by side, they must both be open in Word. While you display the two documents, you can use synchronous scrolling to move through both using only one scroll bar.

4. **Compare and combine documents.** When you have several copies of the same document submitted from different people, you can use the compare and combine features. The compare feature evaluates the contents of two or more documents and displays markup balloons that show the differences between the documents. You can determine if the differences display in the original document, a revised document, or a new document. The combine feature goes a step further and integrates all changes from multiple documents into one.

5. **Create master documents and subdocuments.** Working with long documents can be cumbersome, and a document that is very long can even slow down your computer. As an alternative to creating long documents, you can create a master document that acts like a binder for managing smaller documents. The smaller document is called a subdocument and can be edited individually at any time. It can be modified when displayed as part of the master document if it is not locked for editing. The Outlining tab contains the Collapse and Expand buttons, as well as other tools used to work on master documents. The great benefit of master and subdocuments is the ability to work with multiple subdocuments simultaneously. For example, you can create page numbers in a master document, and it will cause the numbers to run consecutively from one subdocument to the next.

6. **Use navigation tools.** When you use the Document Map feature, the headings in a document are displayed in a pane on the left, and the text of the document is visible on the right. You can click a heading in the Document Map to move the insertion point to that heading in the document. The feature is only available when headings are formatted using the styles feature. You also can use Thumbnails to navigate quickly through a document. Thumbnails are small pictures of each page that display on the left in a pane when the feature is toggled on. When you click a thumbnail, the insertion point moves to the top of that page. The bookmark feature is an electronic marker for a specific location in a document. You can designate a bookmark in a particular location in a document, then use the Go To feature to return to that bookmark.

7. **Acknowledge a source.** It is common practice to use a variety of sources to supplement your own thoughts when authoring a paper, report, legal brief, or many other types of document. Failure to acknowledge the source of information you use in a document is a form of plagiarism. Word provides the citation feature to track, compile, and display your research sources for inclusion in several types of supplemental references. After you add sources, they are saved in a Master List, a database of all citation sources created in Word on a particular computer. The source also is stored in the Current List, which contains all sources you use in the current document. These lists are stored in XML format and can be used in any Word document.

...continued on Next Page

8. **Create a bibliography.** A bibliography is a list of works cited or consulted by an author and should be included with the document when published. The addition of a bibliography to your completed work demonstrates respect for the material consulted and proves that you are not plagiarizing. It also gives the reader an opportunity to validate your references for accuracy. Any sources added with the citation feature and used in the current document will display in the appropriate format as a bibliography.

9. **Select the writing style.** When research papers are prepared, the author often must conform to a particular writing style. The writing style, also called an editorial style, consists of rules and guidelines set forth by a publisher to ensure consistency in presentation of research documents. The Style list in the Citations & Bibliography group of the References tab includes the most commonly used international styles. When you select the style before creating the bibliography, the citations that appear in the bibliography will be formatted exactly as required by that style.

10. **Create and modify footnotes and endnotes.** A footnote is a citation that appears at the bottom of a page, and an endnote is a citation that appears at the end of a document. You use footnotes or endnotes to credit the sources you quote or cite in your document. If you click the Footnotes Dialog Box Launcher, the Footnotes and Endnotes dialog box opens, and you can modify the location of the notes and the format of the numbers.

11. **Add figure references.** Documents and books often contain several images, charts, or tables. To help readers refer to the correct image or table, you can insert a caption that is a descriptive title. To add a caption, click Insert Caption in the Captions group of the References tab. To automatically generate captions, click AutoCaption in the Caption dialog box.

12. **Insert a table of figures.** If your document includes pictures, charts and graphs, slides, or other illustrations along with a caption, you can include a table of figures, or list of the captions, as a reference. To build a table of figures, Word searches a document for captions, sorts the captions by number, and displays the table of figures in the document. A table of figures is commonly placed after the table of contents for a document.

13. **Add legal references.** A table of authorities is used in legal documents to reference cases, rules, treaties, and other documents referred to in a legal brief. Word's Table of Authorities feature enables you to track, compile, and display citations, or references to specific legal cases and other legal documents, to be included in the table of authorities. Before you generate the table of authorities, you must indicate which citations you want to include using the Mark Citation command. To modify a table of authorities entry, locate the entry that you wish to modify and edit the text inside the quotation marks. To delete a table of authorities entry, select the entire entry field, including the braces {}, and then press Delete. If you do not wish to use the existing categories of citations in your table of authorities, you can add or change the categories.

14. **Create cross-references.** A cross-reference is a note that refers the reader to another location for more information about a topic. You can create cross-references to headings, bookmarks, footnotes, endnotes, captions, and tables.

15. **Modify document properties.** You can create a document summary that provides descriptive information about a document, such as a title, subject, author, keywords, and comments. When you create a document summary, Word saves the document summary with the saved document. You can update the document summary at any time by opening the Document Information panel for the respective document. The Custom tab of the Document Properties dialog box enables you to add other properties and assign values to those properties. You also can print document properties from the Print dialog box.

Key Terms

Multiple Choice

1. Which of the following statements about Comments is false?

   (a) Comment balloons appear on the right side in Print Layout view by default.

   (b) A ScreenTip showing the reviewer's name and date/time of comment creation appears when the mouse pointer is over a markup balloon.

   (c) You cannot print comments with the rest of the document.

   (d) You can use the Show Markup feature on the Review tab to filter markup balloons so only comments display on the page.

2. Which dialog box gives you the ability to enter the name of the person using the computer so that person's name appears in ScreenTips for tracked changes and markup balloons?

   (a) View

   (b) File Properties

   (c) Paragraph

   (d) Word Options (located in Office menu)

3. What option enables you to see the document appearance if you accept all tracked changes?

   (a) Final Showing Markup

   (b) Final

   (c) Original Showing Markup

   (d) Original

4. Which of the document elements listed below can you find using the Go To command?

   (a) Bookmark

   (b) Hyperlink

   (c) Table of Contents

   (d) Cross-reference notation

5. Which procedure is a method used to view and edit footnote text?

   (a) By positioning the mouse pointer over the footnote reference mark and clicking inside the ScreenTip that appears

   (b) Through the Footnote and Endnote dialog box

   (c) By double-clicking the footnote reference mark and typing from within the Footnotes pane in Print Layout view

   (d) By clicking Citation on the References tab

6. When you use the styles feature to format headings, you can use this feature to view an outline of your document and click on a heading in the outline to relocate the insertion point in your document.

   (a) Bookmarks

   (b) Document Map

   (c) Thumbnails

   (d) Navigation

7. What navigation tool do you use to display images of document pages that you can click to move the insertion point to the top of a particular page?

   (a) Task pane

   (b) Document Map

   (c) Thumbnails

   (d) Zoom

8. Which option is not true about plagiarism?

   (a) It is the act of using another person's work and claiming it as your own.

   (b) It is an illegal violation of U.S. Copyright law.

   (c) It only applies to written works; ideas, spoken words, or graphics are not included.

   (d) It has serious moral and ethical implications and is taken very seriously in academic communities.

9. What document item directs a reader to another location in a document by mentioning its location?

   (a) Cross-reference

   (b) Bookmark

   (c) Endnote

   (d) Thumbnail

10. A table of figures is generated from what type of entries?

    (a) Bullets

    (b) Bookmarks

    (c) Comments

    (d) Captions

11. What does a table of authorities display?

    (a) A list of pictures, tables, and figures in a document

    (b) A list of cases, rules, treaties, and other documents cited in a legal document

    (c) A list of key words and phrases in the document

    (d) A sequential list of section headings and their page numbers

12. What comprises a master document?

   (a) Subdocuments

   (b) Bibliographies

   (c) Completed document

   (d) Legal citations

13. Which feature enables you to attach information to a document such as author name, subject, title, keywords, and comments?

   (a) Track changes

   (b) Bibliography

   (c) Master document

   (d) Document Information panel

14. Select the sequence of events you undertake to include a bibliography in your document.

   (a) Insert a citation, select writing style, insert bibliography.

   (b) Type citations into document, insert bibliography, select writing style.

   (c) Select writing style, mark legal references, insert bibliography.

   (d) Select writing style, insert bibliography, insert citations.

15. Which feature enables you to display the differences in two documents in a separate document?

   (a) Side by side view

   (b) Compare documents

   (c) Combo documents

   (d) Subdocuments

Periodically, it is helpful to step back and review the basics. In this case, you have the opportunity to read and work in a document that describes the reviewing features in Word. These features are extremely helpful when working on a group project, and you should take time to evaluate and practice using these features.

a. Open the *chap4_pe1_review* and *chap4_pe1_review2* document. Click the **View tab** and click **View Side by Side**. After you view the differences in the two documents, click **Window** on the View tab for the *chap4_pe1_review2* document and click **View Side by Side** to close the Side by Side view and display only one file.

b. Click the **Review tab**, click **Compare**, and then click **Combine**. Click **Browse for Original**, navigate to the *chap4_pe1_review* document, and then click **Open**. Click **Browse for Revised**, navigate to the *chap4_pe1_review2* document, and then click **Open**. Click **OK** and then click **Continue with Merge**.

c. Save the new document as **chap4_pe1_review_solution**.

d. Click **Show Source Documents** in the Compare group on the Review tab, and then click **Hide Source Documents**, if necessary. Click **Reviewing Pane** in the Tracking group to hide the reviewing pane that displays on the left side of the screen, if necessary.

e. Click the **Track Changes arrow** and click **Change Tracking Options**. Take a moment to review the variety of options you can set in this dialog box. In the *Formatting* section, click the **Formatting drop-down arrow** and select **Double underline**, if necessary. Click the **Color drop-down arrow** in the *Formatting* section and select **Violet**. In the *Balloons* section, click the **Margin drop-down arrow** and select **Right**, if necessary. In the Balloons section click the **Preferred width spin arrow** until **1.8** displays, if necessary. Click **OK** to close the dialog box.

f. Click **Show Markup** in the Tracking group, and then point to **Reviewers** to display the names of the reviewers, each of whom is displayed in a different color. Click **All Reviewers** to remove the check mark. Click **Show Markup**, click **Reviewers**, and then click **John Doe**. Only revisions by John Doe display, as shown in Figure 4.42. Click **Show Markup**, point to **Reviewers**, and then click **All Reviewers** to display all markup balloons again. Note that reviewer colors may be different on your screen.

g. Click the **Display for Review down arrow** on the Review tab and select **Original Showing Markup**. Click the **Display for Review down arrow** again and select **Final Showing Markup**.

h. Press **Ctrl+Home** to move the insertion point to the beginning of the document, if necessary. Click **Next** in the Changes group to move to the first revision. Click **Accept** in the Changes group to accept this change. Click the **Accept arrow** and select **Accept and Move to Next**.

i. Click to place the insertion point after the letter *A* at the beginning of the second sentence. Press **Spacebar** to insert a space between *A* and *line*. Click the **Accept arrow** and select **Accept All Changes in Document**.

j. Press **Ctrl+End** to move to the end of the document. Click **New Comment** and type **Review completed by *your name* on *current date***. Substitute your name and the current date in the sentence, where appropriate.

k. Save and close the document. Close the *chap4_pe1_review* and *chap4_pe1_review2* documents without saving.

...continued on Next Page

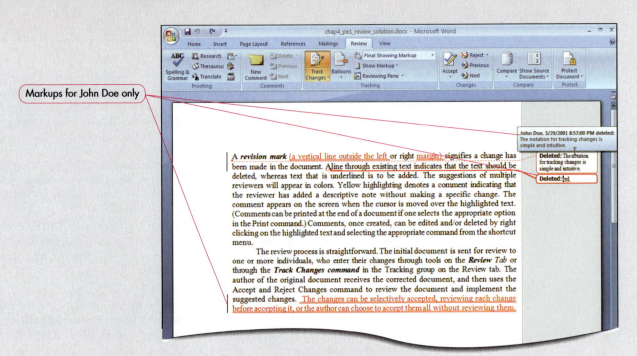

Figure 4.42 Review a Document

2 Create a Master Document

You volunteer in a middle school library and have the opportunity to observe the computer skill level of many students. You decide to create a document that contains tips for using Windows XP for the students to use as a reference. You found three sources of information and want to combine them into one document. Fortunately, you are familiar with the Master and Subdocument features in Word, so you can easily combine the documents into one.

a. Create a new document. Click the **Outline button** on the status bar. The Outlining tab should display automatically. Save the document as **chap4_pe2_tips_solution**.

b. Type the title of the document, **Tips for Windows XP**, and then apply **24-point Arial** and **Center** it using the Mini toolbar. Click to move the insertion point to the right side of the heading and press **Enter** two times.

c. Click **Show Document** in the Master Document group on the Outlining tab to display other features. Click **Insert**, and then open the file *chap4_pe2_tips1*. Insert two additional documents, *chap4_pe2_tips2* and *chap4_pe2_tips3*, that are stored in the same folder. When you get a Microsoft Office Word dialog box that asks if you want to rename the style in the subdocument, click **Yes to All**.

d. Click **Close Outline View**, and then click the **View tab**. Click **Document Map** in the Show/Hide group to display the Document Map pane; click **Select Multiple Files** from the list in the pane, as shown in Figure 4.43.

e. After the *Select Multiple Files* heading and paragraph display, click the **Insert tab**, and then in the Links group, click **Bookmark**. Type **multiple** in the Bookmark name box, and then click **Add**.

f. Click the **Switch Navigation Window** arrow in the Document Map pane and click **Thumbnails**. Click the **page 6 thumbnail** and view the *Customize Windows Explorer* paragraph at the top of the page. Click **Bookmark**, type **customize** in the Bookmark name box, and then click **Add**.

g. Click **Close** in the Thumbnails pane. Press **Ctrl+G**, select **Bookmark** in the *Go to what* list, and then select **multiple**, if necessary, in the **Enter bookmark name** list. Click **Go To** and view the *Select Multiple Files* paragraph. Click **Close** to remove the Find and Replace dialog box.

h. Save and close the document.

...continued on Next Page

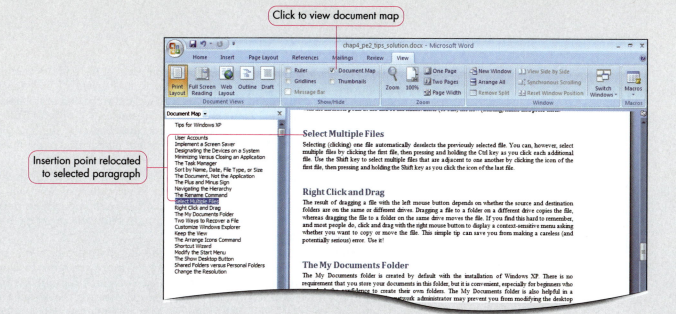

Figure 4.43 Use the Document Map

3 Planting Tulips

You are a member of the Izzard County Horticulture Society and have been asked to assist in the development of information packets about a variety of flowers and plants. You are responsible for developing an informational report about tulips that will be distributed at the fall meeting. After viewing sources of information on the Internet, in books, and in journals, you have created a short paper that includes information and pictures. In the following steps, you create additional resources to accompany your report, such as a table of figures and a bibliography.

a. Open the *chap4_pe3_tulip* document and save it as **chap4_pe3_tulip_solution**.

b. Press **Ctrl+End** to view the sources at the bottom of the document. Click the **References tab**, click **Manage Sources**, and then click **New**. Click the **Type of Source drop-down arrow** and click **Article in a Periodical**. In the Author box, type **Lauren Bonar Swezey**. In the Title box, type **A Westerner's Guide to Tulips**. In the Year box, type **1999**. In the Month box, type **October**. Click **OK** to close the dialog box.

c. Select the first Web site listed in the Sources list and press **Ctrl+C** to copy it to the Clipboard. Click **Insert Citation**, and then click **Add New Source**. Click the **Type of Source drop-down arrow** and click **Web site**. Click once in the URL box to move the insertion point, and then press **Ctrl+V** to paste the Web site address. Type **http://americanmeadows.com** in the Name of Web Site box, as shown in Figure 4.44. Click **OK**. Repeat this procedure for the remaining Web site sources in the list.

d. Scroll up to view the page that contains pictures of different varieties of tulips. Click one time on the first image. Click **Insert Caption** in the Captions group on the References tab. The caption number is already entered; press **Spacebar** one time, and then type **Angelique** to add more detail to the caption information. Click **OK** to close the Caption dialog box. Add the following tulip classifications to the captions for the remaining images on the first row: **Beauty of Apeldoorn**, **Black Parrot**. Add the following classifications to the captions for the images on the second row: **Candela**, **Plaisir**. Remember to insert a space between the caption number and tulip classification.

e. Scroll down to the top of the page 4. Click one time on the *Planting Guide at a Glance* graphic. Click **Insert Caption**. Press **Spacebar** one time in the Caption box, which already displays *Figure 6*, and type **Planting Depth Guide**, and then click **OK**. Scroll down to the bottom of the page. Click one time on the cross-section graphic of a bulb. Click **Insert Caption**. Press **Spacebar** one time in the Caption box, which already displays *Figure 7*, type **Dissecting a Bulb**, and then click **OK**.

...continued on Next Page

f. Scroll up to page 3. Click one time to place the insertion point at the end of the third paragraph in the *Planting* section, which ends with *made by the planter*. Click **Insert Endnote** and notice the insertion point blinking on a blank line at the end of the document. Type the following: **Swezey, Lauren Bonar, A Westerner's Guide to Tulips (Sunset, October 1999)**. Click the **Footnotes Dialog Box Launcher**, click the **Number format drop-down arrow**, click **1, 2, 3** to change the format of marks used in the document to denote endnotes, and then click **Apply**.

g. Scroll to the third page and find the sentence *See the depth chart in Figure 6*, which displays in the third paragraph in the *Planting* section. Click to place the insertion point at the end of the sentence, and then add the following text before the period: **on page**. Be sure to include a space before and after the text you type. Now you insert a cross-reference to complete the sentence.

h. Click **Cross-reference** in the Captions group on the References tab. Click the **Reference type drop-down arrow** and click **Figure**. Click the **Insert reference to drop-down arrow** and click **Page Number**. Click **Figure 6** in the **For which caption** list, and then click **Insert**. The number four completes the sentence, informing the reader that the graphic is found on page 4. Click **Close** to remove the Cross-reference dialog box.

i. Place the insertion point at the end of the table of contents. Press **Ctrl+Enter** to insert a page. Type **Table of Figures.** Click at the end of the heading, and then press **Enter** two times. Click **Insert Table of Figures**, and then click **OK**. Select the Table of Figures heading, and then click **Heading 3** from the Styles Quick gallery in the Home tab.

j. Place the insertion point at the end of the last paragraph in the report, *Forcing Tulips*. Press **Ctrl+Enter** to insert a page. Type **Bibliography** and press **Enter** two times. Click the **References tab**. In the Citations & Bibliography group, click the **Style arrow** and click **APA**, if necessary. Click **Bibliography**, and then click **Insert Bibliography**. Select the bibliography heading, and then click **Heading 3** from the Styles Quick gallery in the Home tab.

k. Select the list of sources that were in the document before you inserted the bibliography and press **Delete** to remove them from the document.

l. Scroll to the second page that contains the table of contents. Click one time anywhere in the table of contents and press **F9**. Click **Update Entire Table**, and then click **OK**.

m. Save and close the document.

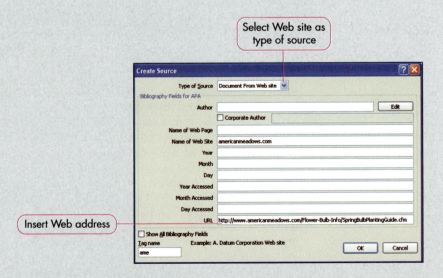

Figure 4.44 Insert Citation from Web Site

...continued on Next Page

You work as a clerk in a law firm and are responsible for preparing documentation used in all phases of the judicial process. A senior partner in the firm asks you to complete a document by inserting a table of authorities based on the cases cited in the document. You will mark the references to other cases in the document, then prepare a table of authorities based on those cases.

a. Open *chap4_pe4_legal* and save it as **chap4_pe4_legal_solution**.

b. Press **Ctrl+Home** to move the insertion point to the beginning of the document. Display the **Page Layout tab**, click **Breaks** in the Page Setup group, and then click the **Next Page section break**.

c. Press **Ctrl+End** to move the insertion point to the end of the document. Display the **Insert tab**, click **Page Number** in the Header & Footer group, and click **Format Page Numbers**. In the Page Number Format dialog box, click the **Start at** option button to display the number **1**. Click **OK** to close the dialog box.

d. Double-click the footer area on the second page. Click **Link to Previous** in the Navigation group of the Design tab to toggle the setting off. Click **Page Number** in the Header and Footer group, point to **Bottom of Page**, and then select **Plain Number 2** from the gallery. Click **Close Header and Footer**.

e. Press **Ctrl+Home** to move the insertion point to the beginning of the document. Type the title **TABLE OF AUTHORITIES** at the top of the page. Press **Enter** twice, and then click **Align Text Left** in the Paragraph group on the Home tab. Select the *Table of Authorities* title, and then click **Center** and **Underline** on the Home tab.

f. Select the citation *Utah Code Ann.' 33-8-34 (1994)* in the *Statutes Involved* section on the second page. Click the **References tab** and click **Mark Citation** in the Table of Authorities group. Click **Mark All**, and then click **Close**. Click the **Home tab** and click **Show/Hide ¶** on the Paragraph group to turn off the display of formatting marks.

g. Scroll to the top of the document and position the insertion point on the second line following the *Table of Authorities* heading. Click **Insert Table of Authorities** in the Table of Authorities group on the References tab. In the Table of Authorities dialog box, click **Cases** in the Category list, and then click **OK** to display the table in your document, as shown in Figure 4.45.

h. Select the heading **Cases** and the five citations, click the **Home tab**, click **Line spacing** in the Paragraph group, and select **2.0** to double-space the entries in the table.

i. Click the **Office Button** and select **Prepare**. Click **Properties** to display the Document Information Panel above the document. Click one time in the **Author** box, delete the current name if necessary, and type your name. Click once in the Title box and type **Motion for Appeal**. Click once in the Comment box and type **Utah District Court**.

j. Save and close the document.

...continued on Next Page

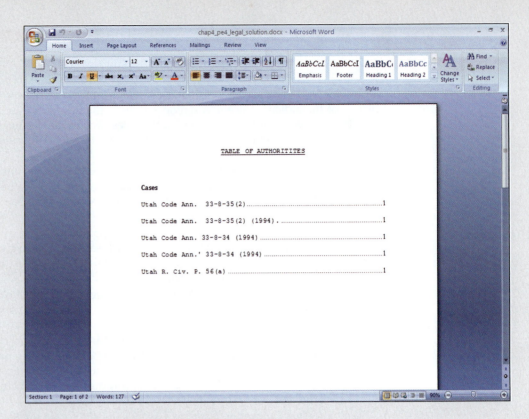

Figure 4.45 Table of Authorities

1 Recipe Book

You work as a volunteer at the local humane society. The board of directors asked you to coordinate a fund-raising effort in which animal recipe books will be sold. You have been receiving recipes from several supporters via e-mail and decide to create a master document that contains all of the recipe documents. After you combine the recipes, you can print the document in preparation for the big sale.

a. Create a new master document. Save the file as **chap4_mid1_recipes_solution**.

b. At the top of the page add the title **Recipes for the Animals in Your Life** and format it using the Heading 1 style, then insert two blank lines.

c. Below the heading type the following categories on different lines: **Dogs**, **Cats**, **Birds**, and **Horses**. These category headings classify the type of recipes that follow. Format the category headings using the Heading 2 style.

d. Insert the following subdocuments into the master document below the appropriate category heading: *chap4_mid1_dogs*, *chap4_mid1_cats*, *chap4_mid1_birds*, *chap4_mid1_horses*.

e. Change the document properties and specify the following:

Title	Humane Society Animal Recipe Book
Author	Friends of the Humane Society
Comments	Distributed Fall 2008

f. Take appropriate actions so the recipes for each type of animal start on the top of a page. Remove any section breaks that create large gaps of white space within the group of recipes for a particular animal. If removal of breaks changes formatting of category headings, reapply the Heading 2 style.

g. Save and close the master document. If a window asks you to overwrite the original subdocuments, click No.

2 Sidewalk Café

Your friend Sue McCrory just purchased the Sidewalk Cafe restaurant. She prepared an information sheet to distribute to several office buildings within the neighborhood. As you review the information sheet, you annotate the document with comments. After you review your comments, you edit one comment and delete another comment. Later, you receive a revision of the document from Sue. With two different documents, you use the Compare and Combine features to consolidate the documents into one final copy that Sue will distribute.

a. Open the *chap4_mid2_cafe* document and save it as **chap4_mid2_cafe_solution**.

b. Position the insertion point at the end of the subtitle and type the comment **Placing the italicized slogan below the restaurant name is a good idea.** Position the insertion point after *Turkey Club* and type the comment **Adding some photos of lunch items will enhance the information sheet.** In the fourth paragraph below the list, select *Sunday brunch* and insert the comment **What's on this menu?**

c. Change the Track Changes options to view markup balloons on the left side of the screen and resize the markup balloons to 1.5" wide. Select the Track formatting check box, if necessary. Change the Formatting option to display double underline and, if necessary, change the formatting color to show **By Author**.

...continued on Next Page

d. Position the mouse pointer over the first comment markup balloon to see the comment with your name as the reviewer. Edit your second comment by adding **full-color** between *some* and *photos*. Delete the third comment.

e. Confirm the Track Changes option is toggled on. Delete the words *diverse and eclectic* on the second line of the first main paragraph and replace them with the word **wide**. In the second paragraph, delete *on a daily basis*, including the space before *on*, but do not delete the colon at the end of that line. Italicize all instances of *Sue McCrory* and *Ken McCrory*, or any variation of their names.

f. Change the Display for Review option to Final Showing Markup, if necessary. Make appropriate adjustments so that only your changes display onscreen. Accept all of your changes.

g. Display comments and changes by all reviewers. Accept the change to delete the words *restaurant, bar, and grill*, but reject the change to delete the words *is homey and*.

h. Open the original file, **chap4_mid2_cafe**, and view it side by side with the revised file you have edited. Close the *chap4_mid2_cafe* document when your review is complete.

i. Sue made revisions to another copy of the original, named *chap4_mid2_caferevision*, and sent a copy to you. Combine that document with the *chap4_mid2_cafe_solution* document and display the results in a new document named **chap4_mid2_caferevision_solution**.

j. View Sue's markups only and accept all of her changes. View all remaining markups; reject only the deletion of the phrase "is homey and" and accept all remaining changes.

k. Delete all comments.

l. Save and close all documents.

3 Web Design

You work as a Web designer at a local advertising agency and have been asked to provide some basic information to be used in a senior citizens workshop. You want to provide the basic elements of good Web design and format the document professionally. Use the basic information you have already, in a Word document, and revise it to include elements appropriate for a research-oriented paper.

a. Open the *chap4_mid3_web* document and save it as **chap4_mid3_web_solution**.

b. On the cover page, insert your name at the bottom.

c. Place the insertion point at the end of the *Proximity* paragraph on the page numbered 2. Insert the following text into an endnote: **Max Rebaza, Effective Web Sites, Chicago: Windy City Publishing, Inc. (2004): 44.**

d. Change all endnotes into footnotes.

e. In preparation for adding a Bibliography to your document, create a citation using the book source from Step c. If a selection from the citation displays in the document, delete it.

f. Select the Chicago style of writing and add a bibliography at the end of the document. Use the default format and settings for the bibliography. Type a heading on the page and format it using the Heading 2 style.

g. Add captions to each graphic that displays in the paper. Allow Word to number the captions sequentially and display the caption below the graphic. Add a caption to the table on page six and display the caption below the table.

h. Create a Table of Figures at the beginning of the document, on a separate page after the table of contents. If the Table 1 entry displays instead of figures, click the Caption label

...continued on Next Page

drop down list in the Table of Figures dialog box and select Figure. Give the page an appropriate heading and format the heading using the Heading 2 style.

i. Create bookmarks for the three major headings, *Proximity and Balance*, *Contrast and Focus*, and *Consistency*. The bookmarks should be named **proximity, contrast,** and **consistency**.

j. Insert a cross-reference at the end of the *Font Size and Attributes* paragraph on the seventh page. Type **See also**, then insert a **Heading** *reference type* for the **Contrast and Focus** heading. End the sentence with a period.

k. Display the Document Map and click on **Table of Contents**. Update the table and select the option to update the entire table. Close the Document Map.

l. Save and close the document.

4 Table of Authorities

As the junior partner in a growing law firm, you must proofread and update all legal briefs before they are submitted to the courts. You are in the final stage of completing a medical malpractice case, but the brief cannot be filed without a Table of Authorities.

a. Open the file *chap4_mid4_authorities* and save the file as **chap4_mid4_authorities_ solution**.

b. Mark all references to legal cases throughout the document.

c. Insert a Table of Authorities at the beginning of the document. Insert an appropriate header at the top of the page and format it using Heading 1 style.

d. Change document properties, insert your name as Author, title the document **Bradford v Hillcrest**, and use **Medical malpractice** as the subject.

e. Save and close the document.

Capstone Exercise

You work in a medical office where many patients have been examined or screened for cancer. The disease is a huge threat to society and a major focus of the health care system. Because of the potential risk and consequences of this disease, you decide to perform research to learn more about it, and the preventive measures you should undertake to avoid it. Your coworkers have similar concerns, and you discover they also have been researching the topic. After a few conversations, the staff of nurses and administrative assistants decide to create an informational document that can be distributed to patients. They offer to e-mail you the documents that contain information they found.

Combine Documents

You receive two documents from coworkers who searched for information about cancer on the Internet. The information is interesting and could be valuable to other people you know, so you decide to create a well-formatted document that you can distribute to anyone who expresses an interest in basic information about cancer.

a. Open the two files *chap4_cap_cancer1* and *chap4_cap_cancer2*, then view them side by side.

b. Combine the two documents into a new document. Show the source documents after you combine them into a new document.

c. The new document should contain all information from both files. Accept all insertions and reject any deletions.

d. Save the new file as **chap4_cap_cancer_solution**.

Credit Sources

You notice several places in the document where the source of the information is listed. Remembering the documentation features in Word 2007, you decide to create citations and add a bibliography to your document.

a. Insert a citation for each source posted in the document.

b. Create a footnote that displays at the end of the paragraph preceding the source listing. Cut each source listing and paste it into the footnote area. Make adjustments as necessary so the source information displays next to the number in the footnote.

c. You decide to include a bibliography as well. Use a page break to add a page to the end of the document and insert a bibliography there. Use the APA writing style for the bibliography, and provide a title formatted in the Heading 2 style. Remove any comments after creating the reference page.

Figure References

The graphics in the document are quite informative, and you want to add descriptive captions to them, and also list them on a reference page.

a. Select the first table and type the following caption: **Table 1. Cancer-related deaths from 1990–1998**. Display the captions above the graphics.

b. Select the second graphic and display the following caption above it: **Figure 1. Rate* of prostate cancer deaths, 1990–1998**.

c. Select the final graphic and display the following caption above it: **Figure 2. Rate* of female breast cancer deaths, 1990–1998**.

d. At the beginning of the document, insert a cover page using the Mod theme. Type **Cancer Information** as the document title and remove all other fields except the author name. If necessary, replace the existing author name with your own.

e. Create a blank page following the cover page and type **Table of Figures** at the top. Format the text with the Heading 2 style.

f. Below the heading insert a table of figures, using the Distinctive format. Change table of figure options so that it builds the table from captions (found in the Table of Figures Options dialog box).

Add Navigation

The document is becoming complex, and you decide to add a few bookmarks to help the reader find information quickly.

a. Display the Document Map. Click *Other primary causes of cancer include:* Place the insertion point at the left side of the heading, and then insert a bookmark named **causes**.

b. Use the Document Map to place the insertion point at the left side of the heading *What are the symptoms of cancer?* and insert a bookmark named **symptoms**.

c. Place the insertion point at the left side of the heading *Cancer treatment can take the following forms:* and insert a bookmark named **treatment**.

d. Click Go To and use the bookmarks to move the insertion point to the section about *causes*. Close the Document Map.

e. Place the insertion point to the left side of the line directly below the heading Cancer: Choosing a Treatment Program and insert a cross-reference to another paragraph heading in the document. The text for the cross-reference should begin **See also the section titled**. Allow the cross-reference to complete the statement by inserting the heading text *What are the treatments for cancer?*

f. Modify document properties and type your name in the Author field. In the Title text box, type **Cancer Information**.

g. Save and close all documents.

Mini Cases

Use the rubric following the case as a guide to evaluate your work, but keep in mind that your instructor may impose additional grading criteria or use a different standard to judge your work.

Group Collaboration

GENERAL CASE

This case requires collaboration between members of a group. Two people in the group will open the *chap4_mc1_collaborate* document. Each member will turn on track changes and proceed to make corrections and add suggestions to the document. Each group member should save the modified file, adding their group number to the file name. Upon completion, the first two people will send the document to two additional group members who also will turn on Track Changes and make additional corrections and suggestions. It is acceptable to correct the previous member's corrections, but do not accept or reject changes at this time. After each member corrects the document, the group should meet together and combine the two documents using the Compare and Combine feature in Word. Combine the documents into a new document, accept and reject changes to the document, and save the final version as **chap4_mc1_collaborate_solution**. View the final version side by side with the original document.

Performance Elements	Exceeds Expectations	Meets Expectations	Below Expectations
Collaboration	Each member of the group participated by using the Track Changes feature while making modifications.	At least half of the members of the group participated.	Fewer than half of the members of the group participated.
Use of tools	Each member of the group used Changes feature at all times while making modifications.	The group used Track Changes at least half of the time while making modifications.	The group did not use the Track Changes feature while making modifications to the document.
Final product	The final version of the document contained proper spelling, punctuation, grammar, and well-written and complete thoughts.	The final version of the document requires additional edits to achieve proper spelling, punctuation, grammar, and well-written and complete thoughts.	The final version of the document requires vast improvements to achieve proper spelling, punctuation, grammar, and well-written and complete thoughts.

Learn to Use Writing Styles

Do you know someone who has been the victim of identity theft? It occurs every day. But what exactly is involved in this growing crime? Use your research skills to locate information about identity theft. You should find at least one source from the Internet, at least one source from a book, and at least one source from a journal. Use your school's library or online library resources to help locate the information sources. After you find your sources, write a two-page report, double spaced, describing identity theft. Include information about the crime, statistics, government policies, and laws that have been passed because of this crime, and the effects on victims. Cite the sources in your paper, use footnotes where appropriate, and develop a bibliography for your paper based on the APA writing style. Save the report as **chap4_mc2_idtheft_solution**.

Performance Elements	Exceeds Expectations	Meets Expectations	Below Expectations
Research	Report cites more than one source each from a book, a journal, and an Internet site.	Report cites one source each from a book, a journal, and an Internet site.	Report cites fewer than three total sources.
Content	Report contains at least four categories of information about identity theft.	Report contains two or three topics of information about identity theft.	Report contains a minimum amount of information about identity theft.
Citations	Report includes citations, footnotes, and bibliography in APA style.	Report includes bibliography, but not in APA style. Some sources are included in footnotes, but not in bibliography.	Sources are not cited. Bibliography is missing.

Repairing Bookmarks

You work in the city's Planning and Zoning department as an analyst. You begin to prepare the Guide to Planned Developments document for posting on the city's intranet. The administrative clerk who typed the document attempted to use bookmarks for navigation purposes, but he did not test the bookmarks after inserting them. You must review the document and repair the bookmarks. Additionally, several cross-reference statements are embedded in the document, but appear to be erroneous. The cross-references are highlighted in the document so you can locate them; the highlights should be removed when you have corrected the references. Open *chap4_mc3_bookmarks* and save your revised document as **chap4_mc3_bookmarks_solution**.

Performance Elements	Exceeds Expectations	Meets Expectations	Below Expectations
Bookmarks	All erroneous bookmarks were repaired, and links work properly.	At least half of the erroneous bookmarks were repaired, and links work properly.	Fewer than half of the erroneous bookmarks were repaired.
Cross-references	All erroneous cross-references were repaired, and links work properly.	At least half of the erroneous cross-references were repaired, and links work properly.	Fewer than half of the erroneous cross-references were repaired.

Productivity Tools

Templates, Themes, and Mail Merge

Objectives

After you read this chapter, you will be able to:

1. Select a template from the New Document window **(page 313)**.
2. Use a resume template **(page 314)**.
3. Create a Word template **(page 316)**.
4. Customize theme colors **(page 321)**.
5. Customize theme fonts and effects **(page 322)**.
6. Select a main document **(page 329)**.
7. Select or create recipients **(page 330)**.
8. Sort records in a data source **(page 331)**.
9. Insert merge fields **(page 332)**.
10. Merge a main document and a data source **(page 333)**.
11. Use Excel worksheets as a data source **(page 342)**.
12. Use Access databases as a data source **(page 343)**.

Hands-On Exercises

Exercises	Skills Covered
1. DESIGN A DOCUMENT USING TEMPLATES (page 318) **Open:** Blank document **Save as:** chap5_ho1_resume1_solution.docx **Open:** Blank document **Save as:** chap5_ho1_resume2_solution.docx and chap5_ho1_resume2_solution.dotx	• Select an Installed Resume Template • Download a Resume Template • Save a Document as a Template
2. USE OFFICE 2007 THEMES (page 324) **Open:** chap5_ho1_resume1_solution. docx (from Exercise 1) **Save as:** chap5_ho2_theme1_solution. docx, chap5_ho2_theme2_solution. dotx, and Resume_Theme.thmx	• Apply a Theme to a Document • Revise Theme Color • Revise Theme Fonts • Save a Custom Theme
3. USE MAIL MERGE (page 336) **Open:** chap5_ho3_cover.docx **Save as:** chap5_ho3_cover_solution.docx, chap5_ho3_recipients.mdb, and chap5_ho3_coverletters_solution.docx **Open:** New document **Save as:** chap5_ho3_mergelabels_solution.docx and chap5_ho3_labels_solution.docx	• Start the Mail Merge Process and Create a Recipient List • Complete the Main Document • Complete the Mail Merge and View Results • Use Mail Merge Wizard to Create Mailing Labels
4. USE EXCEL AND ACCESS DATA SOURCES (page 344) **Open:** chap5_ho4_cover.docx and chap5_ho4_source.xlsx **Save as:** chap5_ho4_excover_solution.docx and chap5_ho4_exletters_solution.docx **Open:** chap5_ho4_cover.docx and chap5_ho4_source.accdb **Save as:** chap5_ho4_accover_solution.docx and chap5_ho4_acletter_solution.docx	• Perform a Mail Merge Using an Excel Data Source • Perform a Mail Merge Using an Access Data Source

CASE STUDY

Community Disaster Relief Center

Micah Ward is the Director of Fundraising at the local Community Disaster Relief Center (CDRC). He spends many hours giving speeches to local companies, organizations, and civic groups so they will be familiar with the efforts and activities of the Relief Center. Because the CDRC is a nonprofit organization, Micah as well as other CDRC staffers must demonstrate the need, the benefit, and the success of the service they provide. They understand that promotional appearances are a marketing tool they must use wisely and often to generate the income necessary to sustain the CDRC. But their marketing efforts also include print media, such as flyers and correspondence.

Case Study

Micah always sends a letter of appreciation to the people who donate and support the CDRC, but his latest marketing efforts have increased the response of the community. Typically he sends one or two per week, but now he is in a position where he needs to send several dozen letters. His coworker maintains a list of the donors, their addresses, and their contribution amounts in an Excel worksheet. She also created a document template of the standard donation response letter and advised Micah to set up a mail merge so that he can complete the letters quickly and efficiently. After all, his time is better spent giving speeches than typing letters.

Your Assignment

- Read the chapter, paying special attention to sections that describe how to use templates, themes, and mail merge.
- Put yourself in Micah's place and open the document template, *chap5_case_thanks.dotx*, which contains the standard letter of appreciation he sends to donors.
- The executive assistant used a document theme that is not appropriate for the organization, so you should select a theme with more subtle coloring.
- Revise theme colors and fonts as needed.
- Use the mail merge feature to create individual letters that thank the donors for their contributions. The letter should include the donor name and contribution amount.
- If the donor does not have an address on file, do not send a letter at this time.
- Donor information is stored in the Excel worksheet *chap5_case_donors.xlsx*. Save your work as **chap5_case_thanks_solution**.

Document Templates

Word 2007 is useful for creating very interesting and complex documents, and usually you format the document entirely on your own. You can jump-start the formatting process by using professional designs provided in the form of templates. A *template* is a partially completed document that contains formatting, text, and/or graphics. Microsoft Word provides a variety of templates for common documents, and additional templates can be downloaded from Microsoft Office Online. You can use Word templates to create letters, memos, reports, resumes, agendas, calendars, and brochures, as well as other documents. Each template contains the framework of formats and text to decrease the time it takes you to create a document. You can even develop your own templates to use when you create certain types of documents, such as specialized reports.

> A *template* is a partially completed document containing preformatted text or graphics.

In this lesson, you use a resume template to start a document. You save time doing so because you do not have to set fonts, bullets, or create a style for the resume. You also download and use a template from Microsoft Office Online.

(Word provides a variety of templates for common documents, and additional templates can be downloaded from Microsoft Office Online. You can use Word templates to create letters, memos, reports, resumes, agendas, calendars, and brochures, as well as other documents.)

Selecting a Template from the New Document Window

> **Normal template** is the framework that defines the default page settings.

Each time you create a new blank document, you use the **Normal template**, the framework that defines the 1″ left, right, top, and bottom margins, left horizontal alignment, 11-point Calibri font, and other settings. When you click the Office Button and then click New, the New Document window displays with a variety of template options you can select and use, as shown in Figure 5.1.

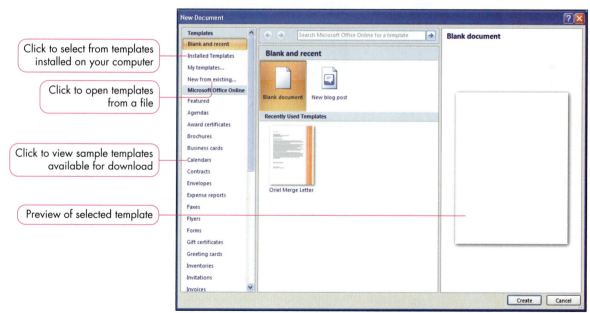

Click to select from templates installed on your computer

Click to open templates from a file

Click to view sample templates available for download

Preview of selected template

Figure 5.1   Selecting a Document Template

When you use a template, it will display under Blank and recent, but you can also view other templates installed on your PC or templates you have created. If you cannot find a template that meets your immediate needs, you can view templates available for download from the Microsoft Web site.

Using a Resume Template

A *placeholder* is a field or block of text used to determine the position of objects in a document.

Building Blocks are document components used frequently such as disclaimers, company addresses, or names.

By default, five resume templates are installed in Word: Equity, Median, Oriel, Origin, and Urban, which display on the following reference page. To preview the templates, click Installed Templates in the New Document dialog box, as shown in Figure 5.2. Each template provides a different style and when opened contains placeholders for information you provide to complete the resume. A *placeholder* is a field or block of text used to determine the position of objects in a document. If you insert text beside a placeholder instead of replacing it, you should be sure to delete the placeholder before you save the document. You can also replace the placeholders with Building Blocks. ***Building Blocks*** are document components you use frequently such as disclaimers, company addresses or logos, or your name and address.

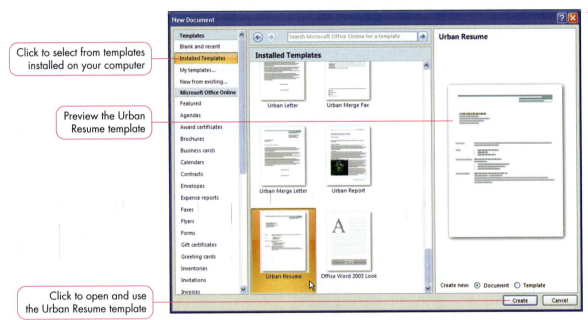

Click to select from templates installed on your computer

Preview the Urban Resume template

Click to open and use the Urban Resume template

Figure 5.2 Select a Resume Template

If the default resume templates do not meet your needs, you can select from others on the Microsoft Web site. When you click Resumes and CVs in the New Document window, listed below Microsoft Office Online, you then select from three categories of resume templates: Basic, Job specific, and Situation specific.

After you select a template category, you then choose a style from the long list of choices before you transfer it to your own computer (see Figure 5.3). Some templates are set up for resumes and some are set up for a vitae. A *curriculum vitae*, or *CV*, is similar to a resume; it displays your skills, accomplishments, job history, or other employment information, and is often used by academics.

A ***curriculum vitae (CV)***, like a resume, displays your skills, accomplishments, and job history.

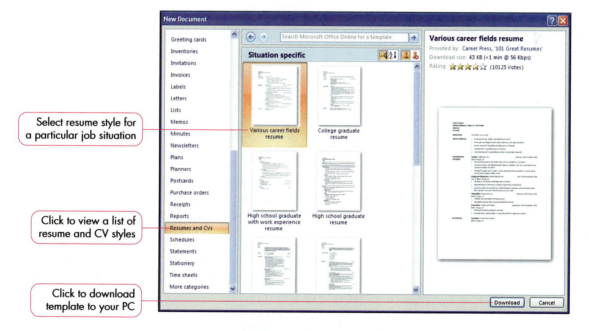

Figure 5.3 Select a Situation Specific Resume Template

To transfer the template to your own PC, click Download after you select a template from the gallery. After the template downloads, it opens in a new document window to display placeholders and sample text as shown in Figure 5.4. You can then begin the process of replacing placeholders with your personal information. When you save the resume, it will save as a Word document, not a document template, unless you change the file type to template.

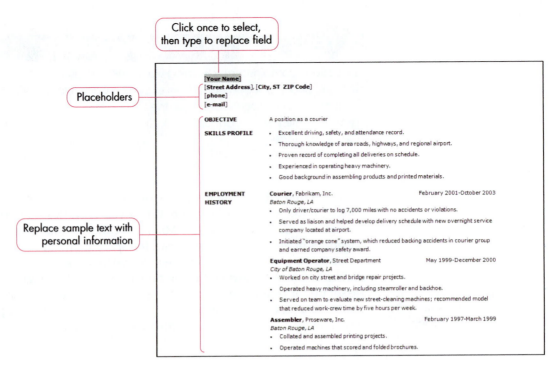

Figure 5.4 The Various Career Fields Resume Template

Creating a Word Template

If you create or use a particular document frequently, with only minor modifications each time, you should save the document as a template. When you create the template, you can insert placeholders for the information you change frequently. You can create a document template that contains a company letterhead, greeting, body, and salutation, thereby requiring you to replace only the information for the recipient. Or if you have a report that you update on a regular basis, which is contained in a very structured and detailed table, you might consider making it a template as well.

To save a document as a template, simply click the Office Button, click the Save As arrow, and then click Word Template. The file extension is then set for you and all you have to do is click Save. You should, however, note the location where the template saves. You can specify a location on your own hard drive or portable storage device, or you can specify Trusted Templates, which displays in the My Places bar in the Save As dialog box, and it will save to your hard drive. When you create and save a Word template, it displays when you click My templates in the New Document dialog box.

Resume Templates | Reference

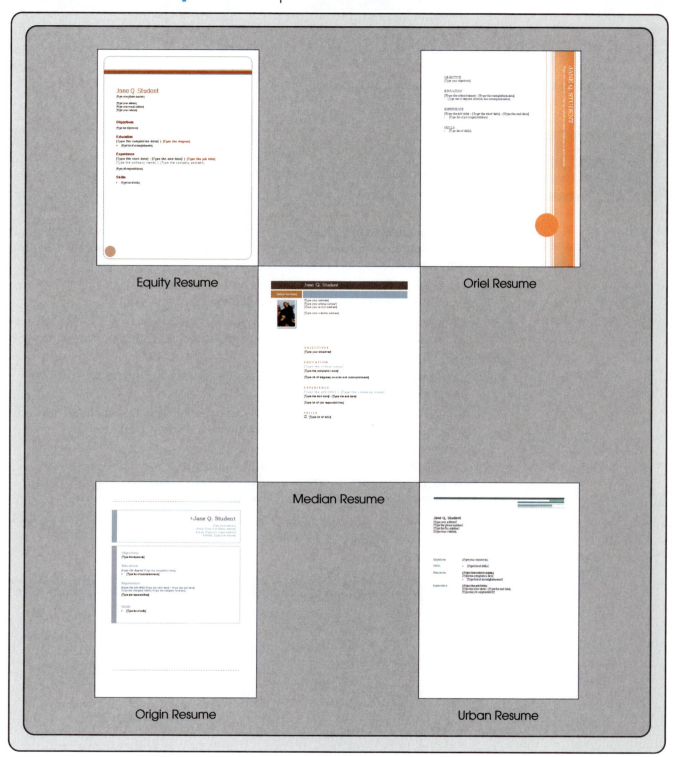

Equity Resume

Oriel Resume

Median Resume

Origin Resume

Urban Resume

Hands-On Exercises

1 | Design a Document Using Templates

Skills covered: 1. Select an Installed Resume Template **2.** Download a Resume Template **3.** Save a Document as a Template

<table>
<tr>
<td>

Step 1

Select an Installed Resume Template

</td>
<td>

Refer to Figure 5.5 as you complete Step 1.

a. Start Word. Click the **Office Button**, and then click **New**.

The New Document window displays and the Templates pane displays on the left.

b. Click **Installed Templates** in the Templates pane. Scroll down, and then click the **Median Resume** template, as shown in Figure 5.5. Click **Create** to open the template.

The Median Resume template opens as a new document and the User Name specified in Word Options displays at the top.

TROUBLESHOOTING: If your name does not display at the top of the resume, you can click any or all parts of the name placeholder, and then type to replace it with your name.

c. Click **Select the Date** in the template to view a down arrow control. Click the **down arrow**, and then click **Today**.

d. Replace the address, phone number, e-mail, and Web site information with your personal information. Use fictional information if you prefer; delete any fields you may not want to include, such as Web site.

e. Click the **Office Button** and click **Save As**. In the File name box, type **chap5_ho1_resume1_solution**. Confirm the Save as type box displays *Word Document (*.docx)*, and then click **Save**.

TROUBLESHOOTING: If the Save as type box displays *Word Template (*.dotx)*, click the down arrow and click **Word Document (*.docx)** before you save.

f. Close the document.

</td>
</tr>
</table>

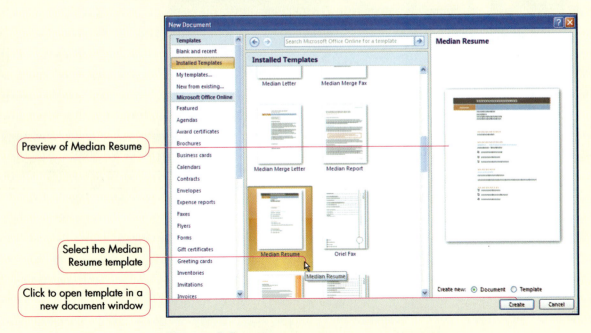

Preview of Median Resume

Select the Median Resume template

Click to open template in a new document window

Figure 5.5 Select the Median Resume Template

Step 2
Download a Resume Template

Refer to Figure 5.6 as you complete Step 2.

a. Click the **Office Button**, and then click **New**. In the Templates pane, scroll down in the Microsoft Office Online section and click **Resumes and CVs**. Click **Job Specific** in the center pane, click **Chef resume**, and then click **Download**.

TROUBLESHOOTING: If a Microsoft Office Genuine Advantage dialog box displays, click **Do not show this message again**, and then click **Continue**. If you work in a lab environment, you may not have permission to download document templates from Microsoft Office online. If that is the case, read Steps 2 and 3, and then continue to the next section.

A download window appears briefly, then the Chef resume template displays with placeholders and sample text.

b. Save the document as **chap5_ho1_resume2_solution.docx**.

Be sure to save the file as a document (.docx) and not a template (.dotx).

TROUBLESHOOTING: If a Microsoft Office Word dialog box displays, click **Do not ask me again**, and then click **OK**.

c. Click one time to select the placeholder that displays the sample text *Your Name* on the first line of the template. Type your name to replace that placeholder.

d. Place your insertion point on the left side of the second line of the resume, which includes placeholders for Street Address, City, ST, and ZIP code, and then click once to select the entire row, as shown in Figure 5.6. Type your local address.

e. Replace the placeholders for the phone and e-mail address with your own information. Save the document.

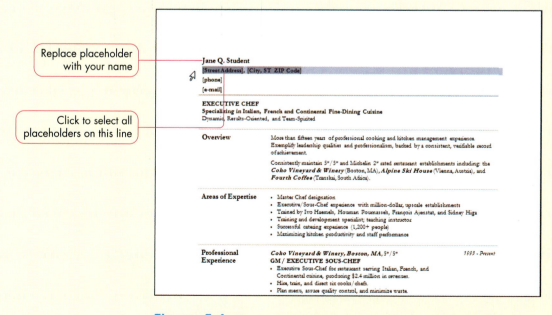

Figure 5.6 Revise the Resume Template for the Chef Position

Step 3
Save a Document as a Template

Refer to Figure 5.7 as you complete Step 3.

a. Click the **Office Button**, and then click the **Save As arrow**. Click **Word Template**.

The Save As dialog box opens and the Save as type box displays *Word Template (*.dotx)*, as shown in Figure 5.7. When you save this document as a template, you can open it later and make modifications without changing the original.

TROUBLESHOOTING: If the Save as type box displays *Word Document (*.docx)*, click the Save as type down arrow, and then scroll down and click **Word Template (*.dotx)**.

b. Click **Save**.

c. Close all documents and exit Word.

This folder on the hard drive is provided specifically to hold your templates

Specify Word Template

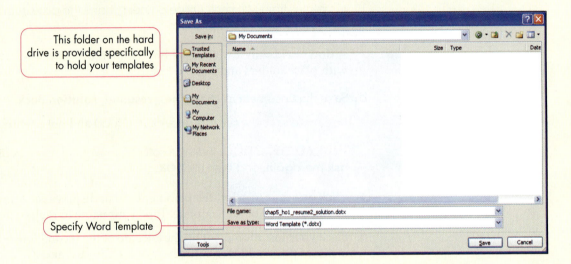

Figure 5.7   Save Chef Resume as a Template

Document Themes

To create a professional-looking document, you want to select features and styles that coordinate, but creating and managing document design is very time-consuming. Word 2007 contains several document themes that enable you to focus on the content of your document instead of spending time creating a design for it. A *document theme* is a set of coordinating fonts, colors, and special effects, such as shadowing or glows, that work together to provide a stylish appearance. Document themes are available in other Office applications also. This means you can use the same theme on different types of files that are used in a project, such as a report created in Word and a worksheet and chart created in Excel.

A *document theme* is a set of coordinating fonts, colors, and special effects that give a stylish and professional look.

In this lesson, you apply themes to a document. You also customize the theme elements and create a new theme.

> Creating and managing document design is very time-consuming. Word 2007 contains several document themes that enable you to focus on the content of your document instead of spending time creating a design for it.

Customizing Theme Colors

You can select a document theme from the Themes group on the Page Layout tab. When you select a document theme, formatting occurs immediately. If you wish to make changes to the design, you can modify the theme elements individually.

Theme colors represent the current text and background, accent, and hyperlinks.

Theme colors include four text and background colors, six accent colors, and two hyperlink colors. When you click Theme Colors in the Themes group on the Page Layout tab, the accent and hyperlink colors display, as shown in Figure 5.8. To create a custom color theme you can modify the colors in the current theme and then save the set with a new name. The new color theme will then display at the top of the theme color gallery.

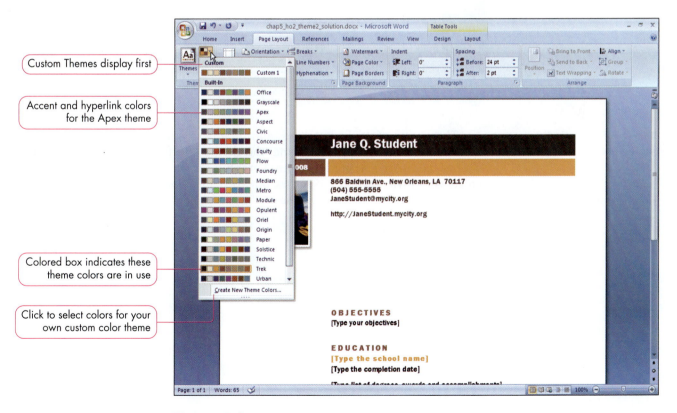

Custom Themes display first

Accent and hyperlink colors for the Apex theme

Colored box indicates these theme colors are in use

Click to select colors for your own custom color theme

Figure 5.8 View Theme Colors

Customizing Theme Fonts and Effects

Theme fonts contain a heading and body text font.

The *Theme fonts* contain a coordinating heading and body text font for each different theme. You can view the fonts used in the theme when you click Theme Fonts in the Themes group on the Page Layout tab, as shown in Figure 5.9. Theme fonts display at the top of the font list when you click the Font down arrow on the Home tab or in the Mini toolbar. As with theme colors, you can change the fonts used in a theme, and you can create a new theme font set.

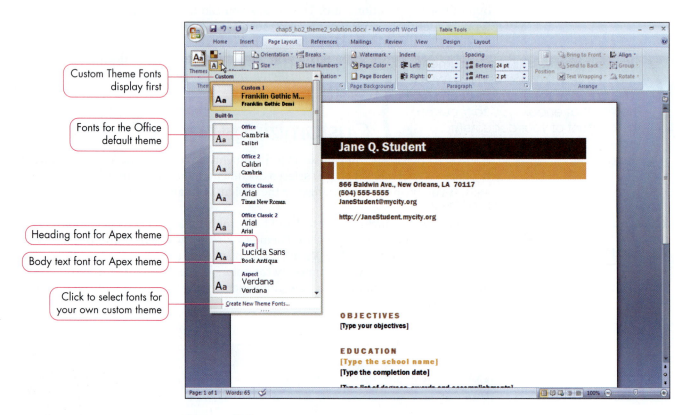

Figure 5.9 View Theme Fonts

Theme effects include lines and fill effects.

The *Theme effects* include lines and fill effects, such as shadowing, glows, and borders. When you apply a theme, the theme effects will affect objects such as shapes, SmartArt, and borders around graphics, as shown in Figure 5.10. You cannot create your own set of theme effects, but you can choose from the built-in sets when compiling your own document theme.

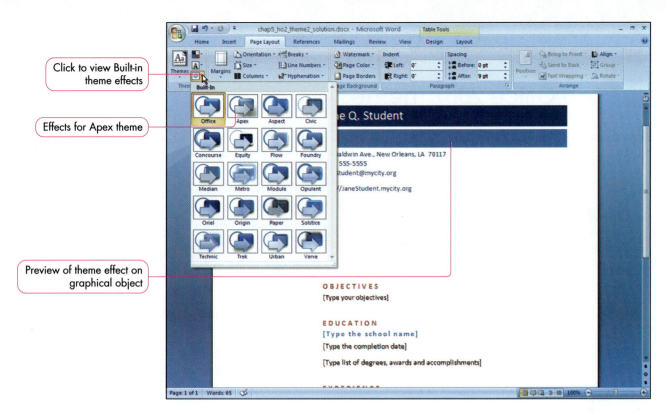

Click to view Built-in theme effects

Effects for Apex theme

Preview of theme effect on graphical object

Figure 5.10 View Theme Effects

TIP Delete Custom Theme Colors and Fonts

You can easily delete a custom theme, a custom theme color set, or custom theme fonts. To remove these custom sets, click Themes (or Theme Colors or Theme Fonts) on the Page Layout tab, right-click the custom set that displays in the top of the gallery, and then click Delete. You will see a confirmation dialog box before the set is removed permanently. You cannot delete the themes, color themes, or font themes that are installed.

Hands-On Exercises

2 | Use Office 2007 Themes

Skills covered: 1. Apply a Theme to a Document **2.** Revise Theme Color **3.** Revise Theme Fonts **4.** Save a Custom Theme

---

Step 1

Apply a Theme to a Document

Refer to Figure 5.11 as you complete Step 1.

a. Open *chap5_ho1_resume1_solution.docx*, which you created in Step 1. Save it as **chap5_ho2_theme_solution.docx**.

The partially completed resume displays using the Median theme.

b. Click the **Page Layout tab**, and then click **Themes**.

The gallery of themes displays and a shaded box surrounds the Median theme to indicate it is in use.

c. Hold your mouse over the Verve theme, but do not click it, and notice how the resume features change to reflect that theme, as shown in Figure 5.11. Click **Trek** to apply the Trek theme to your resume.

d. Save the document.

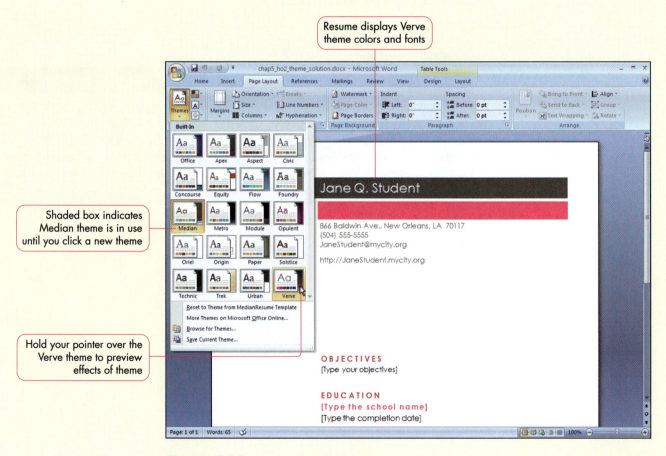

Figure 5.11 Select a New Theme

TIP Using Themes in Compatibility Mode

If you click the Page Layout Tab and notice Theme is grayed out, and thus unavailable, your current document is probably open in Compatibility Mode. To use Themes, you must save your document in Word 2007 format (.docx). If you save a Word 2007 document in a compatible format, such as Word 97–2003, any Theme previously applied to the document will be removed.

Step 2
Revise Theme Color

Refer to Figure 5.12 as you complete Step 2.

a. Click the **Page Layout tab**, if necessary, and click **Theme Colors**.

A colored box displays around the color swatch for Trek to indicate it is in use. You can select the colors for other built-in themes from this gallery.

b. Click **Create New Theme Colors** at the bottom of the gallery.

The Create New Theme Color dialog box displays, as shown in Figure 5.12. Now you can customize the colors used in the theme that is currently applied to your document.

c. Click the **Text/Background – Dark 2 drop-down arrow** and click **Orange, Accent 6** from the top row of the color palette.

d. Click the **Accent 1 drop-down arrow** and click **Orange, Accent 1, Lighter 60%** from the fifth column.

e. Type **Custom 1** in the Name box, if necessary, then click **Save** to save this color scheme.

The Custom 1 color theme is automatically applied to your document. When you click Theme Colors, Custom 1 displays at the top of the gallery with a box around it.

f. Save the document as **chap5_ho2_theme2_solution**.

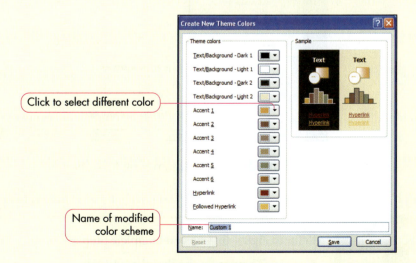

Figure 5.12 Revise Theme Colors

Refer to Figure 5.13 as you complete Step 3.

a. Click **Theme Fonts** in the Themes group of the Page Layout tab.

The fonts for each theme display. The fonts in use for the Trek theme are Franklin Gothic Medium and Franklin Gothic Book.

b. Click **Create New Theme Fonts** at the bottom of the gallery.

c. Click the **Body font drop-down arrow** and select **Franklin Gothic Demi**.

d. Type **Custom 1** in the Name box, if necessary, then click **Save** to save this font scheme.

The text used for specific information in your resume changes to reflect the new font.

e. Click **Theme Fonts** and notice *Custom 1* displays at the top of the list with orange shading to indicate it is in use, as shown in Figure 5.13. Click **Esc** to return to the document.

f. Save the document.

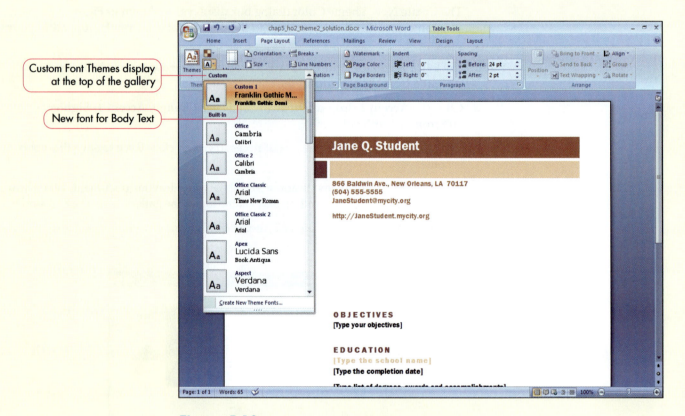

Figure 5.13 Select Custom Fonts for a Theme

Refer to Figure 5.14 as you complete Step 4.

a. Click **Themes** on the Page Layout tab.

b. Click **Save Current Theme** at the bottom of the gallery.

The Save Current Theme dialog box displays, as shown in Figure 5.14. By default, the new themes are saved in the Document Themes folder for the current user. They are not stored in a folder with the themes that install with Word 2007.

c. Type **Resume_Theme** in the File name box.

d. Click **Save**.

> **TROUBLESHOOTING:** If your lab environment does not allow you to save the template to the default folder, or if instructed by your teacher, save the theme file to your own storage media.

e. Close *Resume_Theme.thmx* and exit Word.

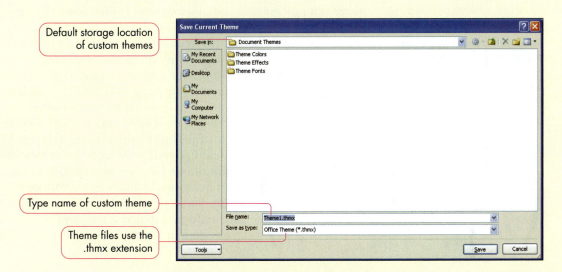

Default storage location of custom themes

Type name of custom theme

Theme files use the .thmx extension

Figure 5.14 Save Custom Theme

Mail Merge

At some point in your personal or professional life, you will need to send the same message to a number of different people. For example, you will send a graduation announcement to all your family and friends, you might send a resume to several organizations, or you might need to send a letter to a group of customers informing them of an upcoming sale. In each case, you will need to personalize either the letter or the recipient's address on the letter or an envelope. You can use Microsoft Word's mail merge feature to generate these types of documents easily and efficiently. *Mail merge* is a process that combines content from a main document and a data source, with the option of creating a new document.

Mail merge is a process that combines content from a main document and a data source.

Form letters are letters you will print or e-mail many times, personalizing each one for the recipient.

Mail merge is used most frequently to create a set of *form letters*, which are letters you might print or e-mail many times, personalizing or modifying each one for the recipient. When you apply for a job after graduation, you might send the same cover letter to many different companies. You could spend hours personalizing and resaving individual letters, but when you use mail merge, you can update several letters simultaneously and quickly. An example of a mail merge is illustrated in Figures 5.15, 5.16, and 5.17, in which Jane Q. Student has written a cover letter describing her professional qualifications for a job as a chef, then merges that letter with a set of names and addresses to produce individualized letters.

> . . . you might send the same cover letter to many different companies. You could spend hours personalizing and resaving individual letters, but when you use mail merge, you can update several letters simultaneously and quickly.

In this section, you learn the mail merge process by creating a main document and a recipient list. You then create form letters by combining the information from both sources.

Figure 5.15 The Main Document

Title	First Name	Last Name	Company Name	Address Line 1	City	State	ZIP Code
Mr.	Michael	Scroggins	Charlamain's	1151 South Cannon Parkway	New Orleans	LA	70128
Mr.	Edward	Matthews	Casper's	6969 Fugate Road	New Orleans	LA	70121
Mr.	Harry	Shea	Harbor House Seafood	10 Front Street	New Orleans	LA	70119

Figure 5.16 A List of Recipients

Figure 5.17 The Merged Form Letters

Selecting a Main Document

The mail merge process uses two files as input, a main document and a data source; and by merging these two files you can create a set of individualized letters, envelopes, e-mails, or other documents. The *main document*, also known as a source or starting document, contains the information that stays the same for all recipients. The main document also includes one or more *merge fields* that serve as placeholders for the variable data that will be inserted into the individual letters, as shown in Figure 5.15.

You can use an existing document as a main document, or you can create one from a blank document. When you click Start Mail Merge in the Start Mail Merge group of the Mailings tab, you can choose from several types to use as your main document. Table 5.1 describes the document types and how they are typically used in a mail merge.

The last option displayed when you click Start Mail Merge is the Step-by-Step Mail Merge Wizard. A *wizard* makes a process easier by asking a series of questions, then creating a customized document structure based on your answers. In this case, the wizard simplifies the process of creating form letters and other types of merge documents through step-by-step directions that appear automatically on the task pane.

The ***main document*** contains the information that stays the same for all recipients.

Merge fields serve as placeholders for the variable data that will be inserted into the main document during the mail merge.

A ***wizard*** makes a process easier by asking a series of questions, then creating a document structure based on your answers.

Table 5.1 Main Document Types

Document Type	How It's Typically Used
Letters	To send letters to a group after personalizing each letter.
E-mail messages	To send e-mail messages to a group of people after personalizing each message.
Envelopes	To print an address on an envelope for each person in the group.
Labels	To print address labels for each person in the group, which can then be attached to an envelope for mailing.
Directory	To create a single document that contains a list of addresses.

The options for the current step appear in the top portion of the task pane and are self-explanatory. Click the link to the next step at the bottom of the pane to move forward in the process, or click the link to the previous step to correct any mistakes you might have made. This is a very easy-to-follow process and helps you work through the mail merge process without knowing exactly what you need to click in the Mailings tab.

> **TIP   Printing Mailing Labels or Envelopes**
>
> If you want to create mailing labels or envelopes, the Create group on the Mailings tab includes commands that you use to select the correct settings. You can use these options to print items that would not necessarily be included in a mail merge, such as a single envelope or a sheet of return address labels.

Selecting or Creating Recipients

The next step in setting up a mail merge is to create or select a list of recipients. Typically, this is the information you need to insert in an address block, or personal information, such as a company name. A recipient list, sometimes called a *data source*, contains individual pieces of data known as *fields*. Common fields in a data source include first name, last name, address, city, state, ZIP code, phone number, and e-mail address. A group of fields for a particular person or thing is called a *record*. Figure 5.16 demonstrates a sample data source. Your data source might come from

- a Microsoft Word document that contains information stored in a table
- a Microsoft Access database
- a Microsoft Excel worksheet
- your Outlook Contacts

The first row in the data source is called the *header row* and identifies the fields in the remaining rows. Each additional row contains a record, and every record contains the same fields in the same order—for example, Title, FirstName, LastName, and so on.

A *data source* is a listing of information.

A *field* is a single piece of data used in a source document, such as last name.

A *record* is a group of related fields.

The *header row* is the first row in a data source.

> **TIP   Using a Word Table as a Data Source**
>
> When your source data are stored in a table in Microsoft Word, you can ensure the mail merge will work correctly if you save the table by itself in a separate file with no blank lines above the table. The first row of the table must contain field names. To use your table as a recipient list, click *Use Existing List* after you click Select Recipients in the Start Mail Merge group on the Mailings tab. Navigate to the location where the document is saved, select the file, and click Open.

If you do not have a preexisting list to use as a data source, you can create one in Word. Click Select Recipients in the Start Mail Merge group of the Mailings tab, and then click Type New List. A New Address List dialog box displays with the most commonly used fields for a mail merge, as shown in Figure 5.18. You can enter data immediately or click Customize Columns to add, delete, or rename the fields to meet your particular needs.

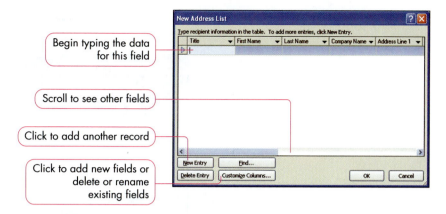

Begin typing the data for this field

Scroll to see other fields

Click to add another record

Click to add new fields or delete or rename existing fields

Figure 5.18   Create a New Data Source

If you want to add new records to a source file you created in Word, you can click Edit Recipient List in the Start Mail Merge group of the Mailings tab. When the Mail Merge Recipients dialog box displays, click the name of the data source, and then click Edit. The Edit Data Source dialog box displays. Click New Entry and a blank entry displays as the last record and you can immediately populate the fields with your data (see Figure 5.19).

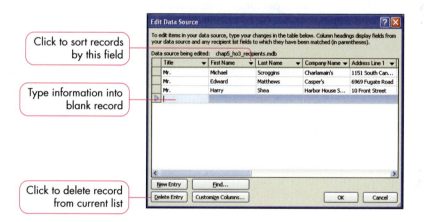

Click to sort records by this field

Type information into blank record

Click to delete record from current list

Figure 5.19   Edit a Data Source in Word

Sorting Records in a Data Source

Before merging the data source with the main document, you might want to rearrange the records in the data source. For example, you might want to sort the data source in alphabetical order by last name, or in descending order by sales, if included. If you have a large number of form letters to send, you can receive a discount at the post office if you follow certain procedures. One procedure is to sort the letters by ZIP code. You can save a lot of work hours if you sort the data source before merging instead of after merging and printing. When you click Edit Recipient List on the Mailings tab to display the Mail Merge Recipients dialog box, several options offer a variety of methods to sort the source data, as shown in Figure 5.20.

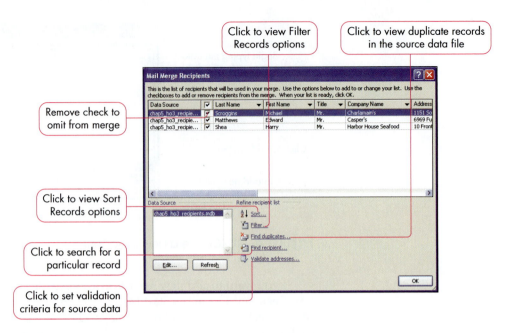

Figure 5.20 Refining the Data Source Records

A *filter* specifies criteria for including records that meet certain conditions.

When you click Sort or Filter, the Filter and Sort dialog box displays and enables you to perform more complex sorts. The Filter Records tab enables you to *filter*, or specify criteria for including records that meet certain conditions during the merge process. For example, you may want to filter the source data by state so only companies in the state of California will be used in the mail merge.

The Sort Records tab enables you to specify up to three levels for sorting records. For example, you can first sort by state, further sort by city within state, and finally sort by last name within city (see Figure 5.21).

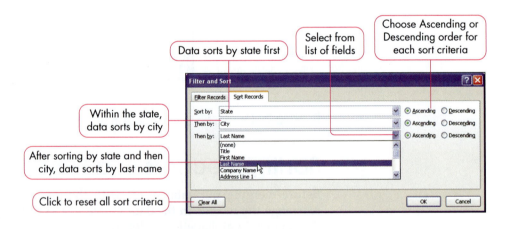

Figure 5.21 Sort Source Data

Inserting Merge Fields

When you write your letter or set up your e-mail in preparation for a mail merge, you insert a merge field in the main document. The merge field is a placeholder that specifies where information from the data source will display in the main document. Because it corresponds with a field in the data source, matching the two fields guarantees that the right data will be inserted into the main document when you complete the merge. View Figure 5.16 again to view the merge fields that correspond to the fields in the source document in Figure 5.15.

The merge fields display in the main document within angle brackets, for example <<Title>> <<FirstName>> <<LastName>>. These entries are not typed explicitly but are entered automatically when you select one of the source data fields that display when you click Insert Merge Field from the Write & Insert Fields group of the Mailings tab. (See Figure 5.22.)

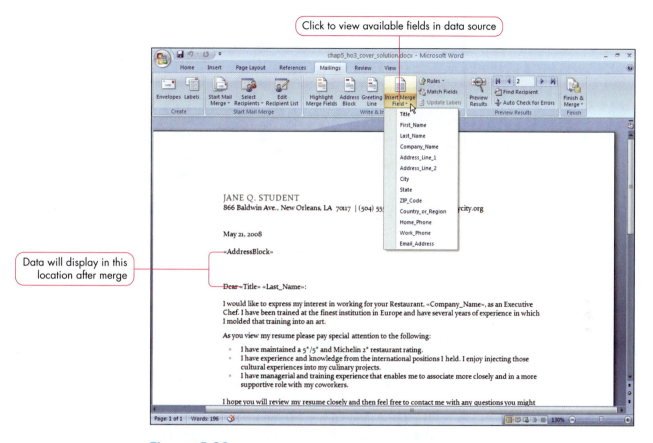

Figure 5.22 Insert Merge Fields into the Main Document

Merging a Main Document and a Data Source

After you create the main document and identify the source data, you are ready to merge them. The merge process examines each record in the data source, and when a match is found, it replaces the merge field in the main document with the information from the data source. A copy of the main document is created for each record in the data source, thus creating individual form letters. Figure 5.17 displays the mail merge results—three personalized cover letters.

To complete the merge, click Finish & Merge in the Finish group on the Mailings tab. Three options display when you click Finish & Merge: Edit Individual Documents, Print Documents, and Send E-mail Messages. To create a new document that contains the results of the merge, you should select Edit Individual Documents. This enables you to preview each page of the merged documents prior to printing. If you select Print Documents, you will have the opportunity to specify which pages to print; however, you cannot preview the document prior to printing. To conserve paper, you should choose Edit Individual Documents and use Print Preview before you print. The last option, Send E-mail Messages, enables you to make selections and complete the e-mail information prior to sending, as shown in Figure 5.23.

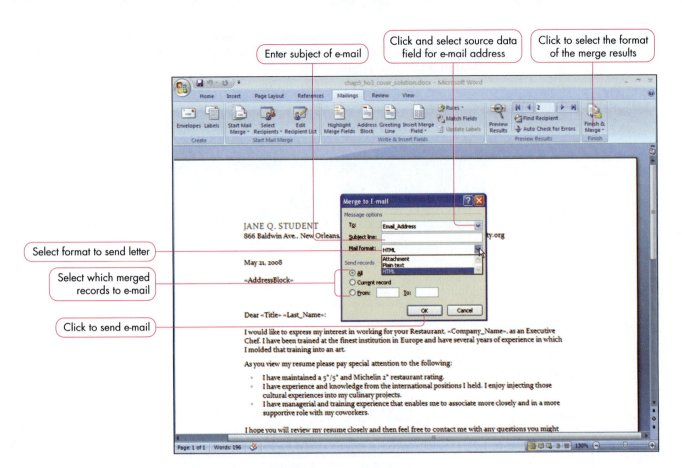

Figure 5.23 Merge to E-Mail Dialog Box

The same data source can be used to create multiple sets of form letters. You could, for example, create a marketing campaign in which you send an initial letter to the entire list, and then send follow-up letters at periodic intervals to the same mailing list. Alternatively, you could filter the original mailing list to include only a subset of names, such as the individuals who responded to the initial letter. You could also create a different set of documents, such as envelopes and/or e-mail messages.

If you want to generate a list from the source data, you can use a Directory mail merge. Select Directory as your source document type and Word will merge all the source data onto the same page instead of merging each record onto a separate page.

The mail merge feature is exciting, yet a bit complex. Use the following reference page to acquaint yourself with the commands on the Mailings tab. Once you successfully complete a mail merge, you'll enjoy finding ways to use it over and over!

Mail Merge Commands | Reference

Icon	Command Name	Description
	Envelopes	Opens the Envelopes and Labels dialog box. Lets you insert recipient and return address information.
	Labels	Opens the Envelopes and Labels dialog box. Lets you insert address for labels and select to print a full page of the same label or a single label.
	Start Mail Merge	Enables you to choose the type of main document, such as letters or envelopes, to create. Enables you to use Mail Merge Wizard.
	Select Recipients	Enables you to select the data source file that you want to open and use with the main document or opens a New Address List dialog box to create a data source.
	Edit Recipient List	Opens the Mail Merge Recipients dialog box. Lets you sort or select records to include in a merge. Also lets you add, edit, and delete the data source records.
	Highlight Merge Fields	Shades the fields in the main document so you can quickly see where the merged information will display.
	Address Block	Opens the Insert Address Block dialog box. Lets you choose the formats for the inside address.
	Greeting Line	Opens the Greeting Line dialog box. Lets you choose the level of formality for the salutation.
	Insert Merge Field	Opens the Insert Merge Field dialog box. Lets you select and insert fields in the main document.
	Rules	Displays decision-making criteria to increase your options for filtering records.
	Match Fields	Opens the Match Fields dialog box. Lets you select fields from another data source, such as an Access database table, to match with required fields in Word.
	Update Labels	Copies the merge fields from the first label to the other labels.
	Preview Results	Displays the data from the data source in the respective fields in the main document so that you can verify correct placement.
	First Record	Displays the first merged record. Works with the View Merged Data button.
	Previous Record	Displays the previous merged record. Works with the View Merged Data button.
1	Go to Record	Lets you enter the number of a specific record to go to.
	Next Record	Displays the next merged record. Works with the View Merged Data button.
	Last Record	Displays the last merged record. Works with the View Merged Data button.
	Find Recipient	Opens the Find Entry dialog box. Lets you find data in a particular field or in all fields.
	Auto Check for Errors	Helps you check for errors and report those errors during the merge process.
	Finish & Merge	Enables you to choose how to display or process the results of the mail merge.

Hands-On Exercises

3 | Use Mail Merge

Skills covered: 1. Start the Mail Merge Process and Create a Recipient List **2.** Complete the Main Document **3.** Complete the Mail Merge and View Results **4.** Use Mail Merge Wizard to Create Mailing Labels

Step 1

Start the Mail Merge Process and Create a Recipient List

Refer to Figure 5.24 as you complete Step 1.

a. Open *chap5_ho3_cover.docx* and save it as **chap5_ho3_cover_solution**.

The document contains a cover letter that you will mail with your resume.

b. Click the **Mailings tab**, click **Start Mail Merge** in the Start Mail Merge group, and then click **Letters**.

c. Click **Select Recipients** in the Start Mail Merge group on the **Mailings tab**, and then click **Type New List**.

The New Address List dialog box displays and you can now type in the information you'll use to complete the mail merge. Press **Tab** to move to the next field after you fill in information.

d. Type the following information in the first record:

Field Name	Value
Title	Mr.
First Name	Michael
Last Name	Scroggins
Company Name	Charlamain's
Address Line 1	1151 South Cannon Parkway
Address Line 2	
City	New Orleans
State	LA
ZIP Code	70128

e. Click **New Entry** and type the following information in the second record:

Field Name	Value
Title	Mr.
First Name	Edward
Last Name	Matthews
Company Name	Casper's
Address Line 1	6969 Fugate Road
Address Line 2	
City	New Orleans
State	LA
ZIP Code	70121

f. Click **New Entry** and type the following information in the third record:

Field Name	Value
Title	Mr.
First Name	Harry
Last Name	Shea
Company Name	Harbor House Seafood
Address Line 1	10 Front Street
Address Line 2	
City	New Orleans
State	LA
ZIP Code	70119

g. Click the **ZIP Code down arrow**, and then click **Sort Ascending**.

The recipient list is sorted by ZIP code, as shown in Figure 5.24.

h. Click **OK**.

The Save Address List dialog box appears, where you can enter a name for your list and save it.

i. Navigate to the location where you save your work. Type **chap5_ho3_recipients** in the File name box, and then click **Save**.

The recipient list is now a Microsoft Access database file.

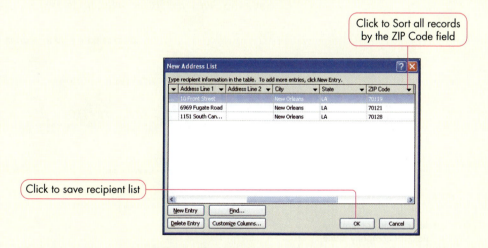

Figure 5.24 Sort the Recipient List by ZIP Code

Step 2
Complete the Main Document

Refer to Figure 5.25 as you complete Step 2.

a. Select the line that displays the text *Insert Date Here*, and then type the current date. Press the **right arrow key** two times to move the insertion point two lines below the date.

b. Click **Address Block** in the Write & Insert Fields group on the **Mailings tab**.

The Insert Address Block dialog box displays. In the Preview window, the first address in the recipient list displays.

c. Click **Next** in the Preview section of the Insert Address Block dialog box.

The entry for Mr. Edward Matthews displays in the Preview section of the dialog box.

d. Click **OK** to close the Insert Address Block dialog box.

The AddressBlock field displays in the document.

e. Click one time on the left side of the colon in the salutation line *Dear :*, and then click **Insert Merge Field** (do not click the icon above the words) in the Write & Insert group on the Mailings tab. Click **Title**, press the **Spacebar**, click **Insert Merge Field** again, and click **Last_Name**.

The merge fields display the recipient's title and last name in the salutation line.

TROUBLESHOOTING: You can click the Insert Merge Field icon to display the Insert Merge Field dialog box and insert the merge fields. If you insert the merge fields from this dialog box, you must insert the space between title and last name after you close this dialog box.

f. Click to place the insertion point on the immediate right side of the word *Restaurant* in the first line of the first paragraph. Type a **comma** after the word, and then press the **spacebar** one time to insert a space.

g. Click **Insert Merge Field** on the Write & Insert Fields group of the Mailings tab, and then click **Company_Name**.

The placeholder for the company name displays on the right side of the word *Restaurant* in the first sentence.

h. Type a **comma** after the Company_Name field as shown in Figure 5.25. Press the **spacebar** one time to insert a space.

i. Save the *chap5_ho3_cover_solution* document.

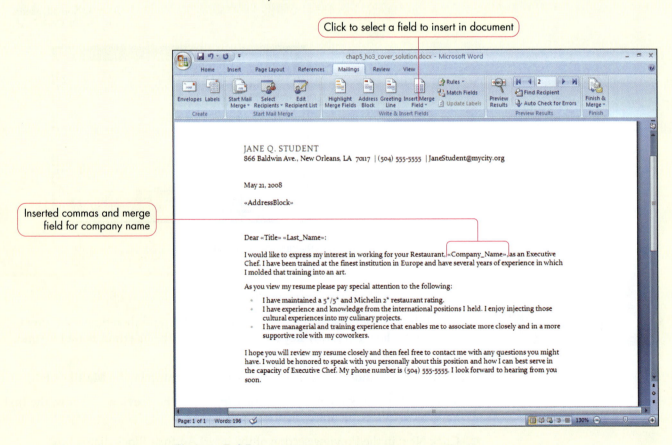

Figure 5.25 Insert Merge Field into Body of Letter

Refer to Figure 5.26 as you complete Step 3.

a. Click **Preview Results** in the Preview Results group on the Mailings tab. Click **Next Record** to preview the letter addressed to Mr. Edward Matthews.

You can navigate from record to record or specify a record to preview using the *First Record*, *Previous Record*, *Go To Record*, *Next Record*, and *Last Record* navigational commands in the Preview Results group on the Mailings tab.

b. Click **Preview Results** to return to the letter and view the mail merge fields.

The Preview Results command is a toggle switch that alternates between the source and a preview of the merged documents.

c. Click **Finish & Merge** in the Finish group on the Mailings tab, and then click **Edit Individual Documents**. Click **OK** to merge all records with the letter.

The letter merges with the recipients and displays in a completely new document, as shown in Figure 5.26. The new document contains three pages, one for each letter.

d. Press **CTRL+S** to display the Save As dialog box, then type **chap5_ho3_coverletters_solution** in the File name box. Click **Save**.

e. Save and close all documents.

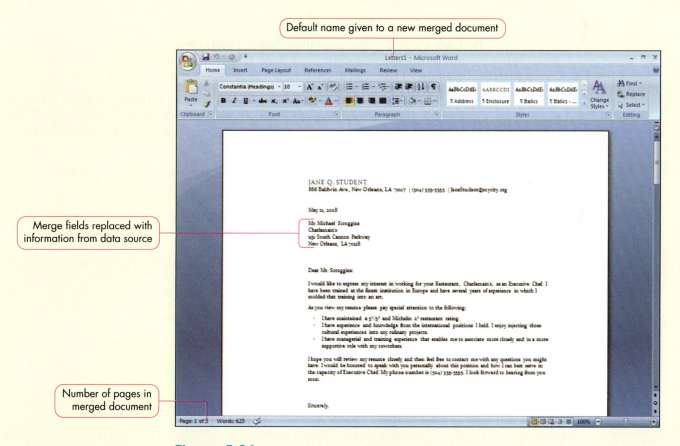

Default name given to a new merged document

Merge fields replaced with information from data source

Number of pages in merged document

Figure 5.26 View the Merged Documents

Refer to Figure 5.27 as you complete Step 4.

a. Press **CTRL+N** to display a new document. Save the document as **chap5_ho3_mergelabels_solution.docx**. Click the **Mailings tab**, click **Start Mail Merge**, and then click **Step by Step Mail Merge Wizard**.

The Mail Merge task pane displays.

b. Click **Labels** in the Select document type section of the Mail Merge task pane, and then click **Next: Starting document** at the bottom of the task pane.

c. Click **Label options** in the Change document layout section of the task pane.

The Label Options dialog box displays.

d. Click the **Label vendors drop-down arrow** and click **Avery A4/A5**. Click **C2651** from the Product number list. Click **OK**. Click **Next: Select recipients** at the bottom of the task pane.

e. Click **Use an existing list**, if necessary, in Step 3 of 6 of the Mail Merge Wizard. Click **Browse** in the Use an existing list section of the task pane, and then navigate to the location where you saved the recipient list, *chap5_ho3_recipients.mdb*, in Step 1. Click the file, and then click **Open**.

The Mail Merge Recipients dialog box displays with three records.

f. Click the **Last Name drop down arrow**. Click **Sort Ascending**. Click **OK** to select all recipients and close the dialog box.

The document displays the *Next Record* code throughout the document to indicate the labels are ready.

g. Click **Next: Arrange your labels** in the bottom of the Mail Merge task pane. Click **Address block** in the Arrange your labels section of the task pane.

The Insert Address Block dialog box displays.

h. Click to remove the check mark beside **Insert company name** in the Specify address elements section of the Insert Address Block dialog box. Click **OK**. Click **Update all labels** in the Replicate labels section of the task pane.

The Address Block field displays on each label, as shown in Figure 5.27. The default font size for the document is so large the addresses will not display correctly on the labels. You will reduce the size of the font to allow the address information to fit.

i. Press **CTRL+A** to select all the label fields. Click the **Home tab**, and then click the **Font Size down arrow** and select **10**.

TROUBLESHOOTING: If the address block is too large to fit on the label, select a smaller font, such as 9 or 8.

j. In Step 4 of 6, click **Next: Preview your labels** in the Mail Merge task pane. In Step 5 of 6, click **Next: Complete the merge**.

k. In Step 6 of 6, click **Edit individual labels** in the Merge section of the task pane. Click **OK** in the Merge to New Document dialog box.

A new document displays with three labels at the top of the page.

l. Press **CTRL+S** to display the Save As dialog box. Save the document as **chap5_ho3_labels_solution**. Close the file.

m. Save and close *chap5_ho3_mergelabels_solution*.

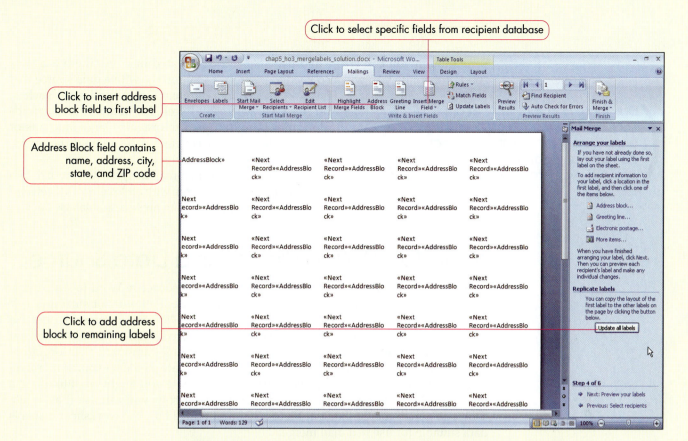

Figure 5.27 Arranging Labels Before Merge

External Data Sources

Even though you can create and use data sources created in Word, there is a very good probability you will also need to perform a mail merge with a data source that was created and saved in a different Office application such as Microsoft Access or Microsoft Excel. The database and spreadsheet applications are designed to organize large amounts of information, so they are perfect candidates to hold the source data you want to use in a mail merge.

> Database and spreadsheet applications are designed to organize large amounts of information, so they are perfect candidates to hold the source data you want to use in a mail merge.

In this section, you perform a mail merge with external data sources. You complete a mail merge with an Excel worksheet, and then you complete a mail merge with an Access database query.

Using Excel Worksheets as a Data Source

In the previous hands-on exercise, you created a data source in Word to store information that you use in a mail merge. That is an adequate way of storing a few records, but you might also save the information in a Microsoft Excel worksheet. An Excel worksheet is comparable to a giant table in Word; it can contain hundreds of rows and columns of data. Many companies have large amounts of information stored in a worksheet, which makes it a good candidate as a data source in a mail merge and prevents you from having to retype any data you might want to use in a merge. As long as the worksheet data has a header row, you can use it as a data source in a mail merge. Look at Figure 5.28 and notice how the worksheet displays data suitable for use in a mail merge.

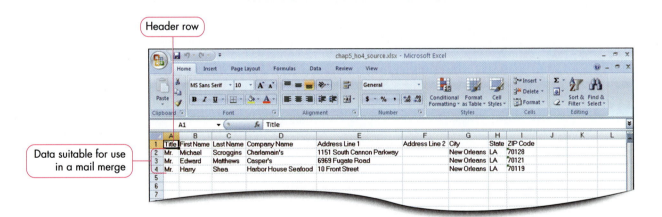

Figure 5.28   Use an Excel Worksheet as a Data Source

To merge a Word document with data stored in Excel, click Select Recipients in the Start Mail Merge group on the Mailings tab, and then click Use Existing List. When the Select Data Source dialog box opens, browse to the location where the Excel worksheet is stored, click the file name, and then click Open. Excel worksheets have the extension .xlsx (or .xls if an older version), so you might need to change the type of file in the Files of type box at the bottom of the window.

Using Access Databases as a Data Source

A ***database table*** is a collection of related records that contain fields to organize data.

Microsoft Access is a database program, and databases are designed to store large amounts of data. Information in a database is stored in tables. A ***database table*** is a collection of related records that contain fields to organize data. Access also includes features that enable you to query the database tables so you can extract and view only data that meet your search criteria. Figure 5.29 provides a look at a database file. Because database files can contain so much data, it is advisable to use the query feature to narrow down the data to only that which will be needed in the mail merge. Filtering the data from the database is much more efficient and easier than sorting and deleting unwanted pages in a Word document after a mail merge.

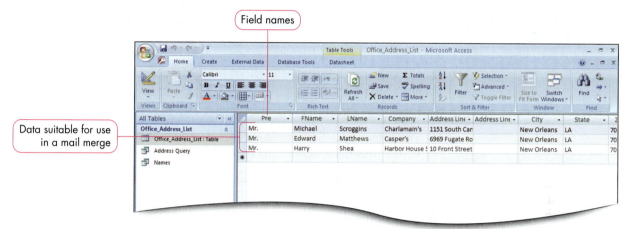

Figure 5.29 Use an Access Database as a Data Source

The process of selecting recipients from a database for use in a mail merge is the same as in Excel. However, when you merge a Word document with an Access database, you can select to use a table or a query as the source of your data. If a database includes queries, the query names will display in the Select Table dialog box along with any tables it contains, as shown in Figure 5.30. When you select to use the query as a data source, only records that meet the query criteria will be available for your mail merge. This can be beneficial if you are certain all the data you need is extracted by that query, but it can limit your data and omit necessary records if the query is too restrictive.

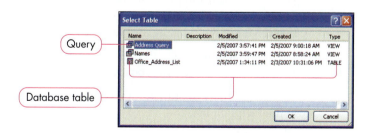

Figure 5.30 Select from Table and Queries in the Select Table Dialog Box

Access database files have the extension .accdb (or .mdb if an older version). A database uses field names to classify the data it contains, which makes it very compatible for a mail merge. However, the Access file you use as a data source might not use the same field names as Word expects; for example, a database may use LNAME as a field name instead of Last_Name. In this situation, you can use the Match Fields command to create a link between the Word document fields and the Access database fields. After you select the recipient list for your mail merge, click Match Fields to display a list of fields that Word often uses and drop-down lists of the fields found in the data source. You can then click the lists and select a database field that matches the required fields in Word.

Hands-On Exercises

4 | Use Excel and Access Data Sources

Skills covered: 1. Perform a Mail Merge Using an Excel Data Source **2.** Perform a Mail Merge Using an Access Data Source

Step 1 **Perform a Mail Merge Using an Excel Data Source**	Refer to Figure 5.31 as you complete Step 1. **a.** Open *chap5_ho4_cover.docx* and save it as **chap5_ho4_excover_solution**. The document contains a cover letter that you will mail with your resume. **b.** Click the **Mailings tab**, click **Start Mail Merge** in the Start Mail Merge group, and then click **Letters**. **c.** Click **Select Recipients**, and then click **Use Existing List**. The Select Data Source dialog box displays. You will navigate to the location where your data files are stored, as shown in Figure 5.31. **d.** Click **chap5_ho4_source.xlsx**, and then click **Open**. When the Select Table dialog box displays, click **OK**. **e.** Replace the text *Insert Date Here* with today's date. Then press the down arrow two times to move the insertion point down two lines. **f.** Click **Insert Merge Field** to display the gallery of fields. Click **First_Name**, press the **spacebar**, then click **Insert Merge Field** again and click **Last_Name**. Press **Enter** to move the insertion point to the next line. **g.** On the next line, use the method used in the previous step to insert **Address_Line_1**. On the following line, insert the **City**, **State**, and **ZIP_Code** fields. After completing steps F and G, you will have a complete address for the recipient of the letter at the top of the document. Be sure to insert spaces or commas in appropriate places between the merge fields you insert. **h.** Place your insertion point on the left side of the colon, following the salutation *Dear*, and then click **Insert Merge Field**. Click **Title**, press the **spacebar**, click **Insert Merge Field** again, and then select **Last_Name**. **i.** Click **Finish & Merge**, and then click **Edit Individual Documents**. Click **From**, and then type **1** in the first box and **2** in the second box. Click **OK**. You create a new document that contains letters for only the first two individuals in the recipient list. **j.** Save the file as **chap5_ho4_exletters_solution.docx**. Close the document. Save and close *chap5_ho4_excover_solution*.

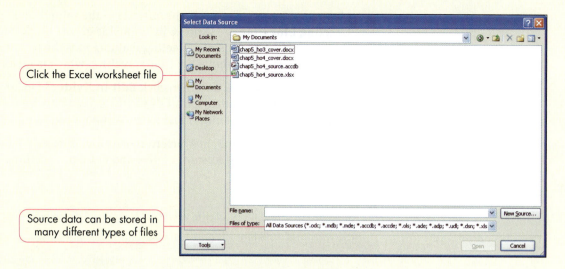

Click the Excel worksheet file

Source data can be stored in many different types of files

Figure 5.31 Use a Worksheet as a Data Source

Step 2

Perform a Mail Merge Using an Access Data Source

Refer to Figure 5.32 as you complete Step 2.

a. Open *chap5_ho4_cover.docx* and save it as **chap5_ho4_accover_solution**.

b. Click the **Mailings tab**, click **Start Mail Merge** in the Start Mail Merge group, and then click **Letters**.

c. Click **Select Recipients**, and then click **Use Existing List**.

The Select Data Source dialog box displays. You will navigate to the location where your data files are stored.

d. Click **chap5_ho4_source.accdb**, and then click **Open**. When the Select Table dialog box displays, click **Address Query**, and then click **OK**.

The Access database file contains a table of data, but it also includes queries that are created to extract specific information from the tables. You can use either the tables or the queries as your data source. In previous exercises, you used the tables, but in this exercise, you use a query.

TROUBLESHOOTING: If you click the Names query or Office_Address_List table in the Select Table dialog box by mistake, you can repeat steps C and D to select the Address Query. You can use the Office_Address_List table for the merge, but you will have more fields to select from than you have in the Address Query.

e. Click **Match Fields** in the Write & Insert Fields group.

The Match Fields dialog box displays, as shown in Figure 5.32.

f. Click the **Courtesy Title drop-down arrow** and select **Pre**. Click **OK**.

The Greeting Line and Address Block fields use the courtesy title, but it will not display unless you match the field from the Access database to your Word fields.

g. Replace the text *Insert Date Here* with today's date. Then press the down arrow two times to move the insertion point down two lines.

h. Click **Address Block** on the Mailings to display the Insert Address Block dialog box, and then click **OK** to insert the merge fields for the address into the letter.

Using the Address Block is faster than inserting each field individually.

i. Move your insertion point to the left side of the salutation *Dear :*, and then click **Greeting Line** from the Write & Insert Fields group. Click **OK** to keep the default settings and insert a greeting that includes the recipient name. Press **Delete** six times to remove the *Dear :* greeting, which is no longer needed.

j. Click **Finish & Merge**, and then click **Edit Individual Documents**. Click **Current Record**, and then click **OK** to create a new document that contains a letter for only the first individual in the recipient list.

k. Save the letter as **chap5_ho4_acletter_solution.docx**, and then close the document. Save *chap5_ho4_accover_solution* and close the document.

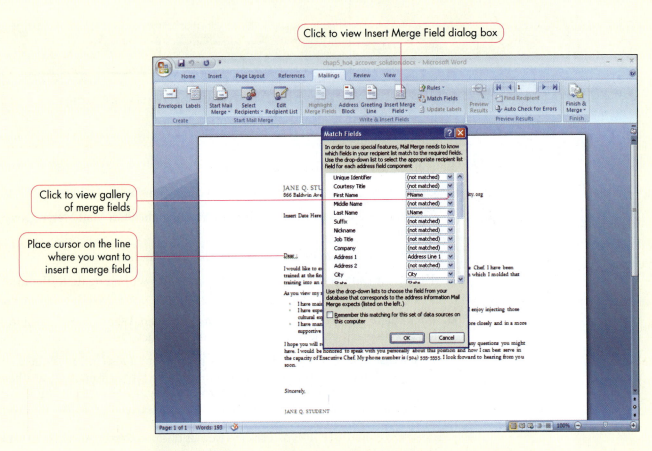

Click to view Insert Merge Field dialog box

Click to view gallery of merge fields

Place cursor on the line where you want to insert a merge field

Figure 5.32 Insert Merge Fields from an Access Database Query

Summary

1. **Select a template from the New Document window**. Each time you create a new blank document, you use the Normal template, the framework that defines the 1" left, right, top, and bottom margins, left horizontal alignment, 11-point Calibri font, and other settings. When you use a template, it will display under Blank and recent, but you can also view other templates installed on your PC or templates you have created.

2. **Use a resume template.** By default, five resume templates are installed in Word: Equity, Median, Oriel, Origin, and Urban. A placeholder is a field or block of text used to determine the position of objects in a document. If you insert text beside a placeholder instead of replacing it, you should be sure to delete the placeholder before you save the document. You can also replace the placeholders with Building Blocks. Building Blocks are document components you use frequently such as disclaimers, company addresses or logos, or your name and address. A curriculum vita, or CV, is similar to a resume; it displays your skills, accomplishments, job history, or other employment information, and is often used by academics.

3. **Create a Word template.** If you create or use a particular document frequently, with only minor modifications each time, you should save the document as a template. When you create the template, you can insert placeholders for the information you change frequently. To save a Word document as a template, simply click the Office Button, click the Save As arrow, and then click Word Template.

4. **Customize theme colors.** You can select a document theme from the Themes group on the Page Layout tab. When you select a document theme, formatting occurs immediately. Theme colors represent the current text and background, accent, and hyperlinks. To create a custom color theme, you can modify the colors in the current theme, and then save the set with a new name.

5. **Customize theme fonts and effects.** The Theme Fonts contain a coordinating heading and body text font for each different theme. Theme fonts display at the top of the font list when you click the Font down arrow on the Home tab or in the Mini toolbar. The Theme Effects include lines and fill effects, such as shadowing, glows, and borders. You cannot create your own set of theme effects, but you can choose from the built-in sets when compiling your own document theme.

6. **Select a main document.** The mail merge process uses two files as input, a main document and a data source; by merging these two files, you can create a set of individualized letters, envelopes, e-mails, or other documents. The main document, also known as a source or starting document, contains the information that stays the same for all recipients. When you click Start Mail Merge in the Start Mail Merge group of the Mailings tab, you can choose from several types, such as Letters, Envelopes, or Labels, to use as your main document. A wizard makes a process easier by asking a series of questions, and then creating a template based on your answers. If you want to create individual envelopes or a sheet of mailing labels, which are not part of a mail merge process, the Create group on the Mailings tab includes commands that you use to select the correct settings.

7. **Select or create recipients.** A recipient list, sometimes called a data source, contains individual pieces of data known as fields. Common fields in a data source include first name, last name, address, city, state, ZIP code, phone number, and e-mail address. A group of fields for a particular person or thing is called a record. If you want to add new records to a source file you created in Word, you can click Edit Recipient List in the Start Mail Merge group of the Mailings tab.

8. **Sort records in a data source.** Before merging the data source with the main document, you might want to rearrange the records in the data source. When you click Edit Recipient List on the Mailings tab, several options display that offer a variety of methods to sort the source data. When you click Sort or Filter, the Filter and Sort dialog box displays and enables you to perform more complex sorts. The Filter Records tab enables you to filter, or specify criteria for including records that meet certain conditions during the merge process. The Sort Records tab enables you to specify up to three levels for sorting records.

9. **Insert merge fields.** When you write your letter or set up your e-mail in preparation for a mail merge, you insert a merge field in the main document. The merge field is a placeholder that specifies where information from the data source will display in the main document. The merge fields display in the main document within angle brackets. Because it corresponds with a field in the data source, matching the two fields guarantees that the right data will be inserted into the main document when you complete the merge.

...continued on Next Page

10. **Merge a main document and a data source.** The merge process examines each record in the data source, and when a match is found, it replaces the merge field in the main document with the information from the data source. A copy of the main document is created for each record in the data source, thus creating individual form letters. To complete the merge, click Finish & Merge in the Finish group on the Mailings tab. Three options display when you click Finish & Merge: Edit Individual Documents, Print Documents, and Send E-mail Messages.

11. **Use Excel worksheets as a data source.** An Excel worksheet is comparable to a giant table in Word; it can contain hundreds of rows and columns of data. Many companies have large amounts of information stored in a worksheet, which makes it a good candidate as a data source in a mail merge and prevents you from having to retype any data you might want to use in a merge. As long as the worksheet has a header row, you can use it as a data source in a mail merge.

12. **Use Access databases as a data source.** Microsoft Access is a database program, and databases are designed to store large amounts of data. Information in a database is stored in tables and that makes them good data sources for a mail merge. Access also includes features that enable you to query the database tables so you can extract and view only data that meet your search criteria. Filtering the data from the database is much more efficient and easier than sorting and deleting unwanted pages in a Word document after a mail merge.

Key Terms

Multiple Choice

1. When you generate a new data source during the mail merge process, what type of file do you create when it saves?

   (a) Document (.docx)

   (b) Worksheet (.xlsx)

   (c) Database (.mdb)

   (d) Rich text (.rtf)

2. What term refers to a group of data for one person?

   (a) Field

   (b) Record

   (c) Main document

   (d) Data source

3. During a mail merge process, what operation can you perform on a data source so only data that meet specific criteria, such as a particular city, are included in the merge?

   (a) Sort

   (b) Propagate

   (c) Delete

   (d) Filter

4. When you click **Edit Individual Documents** on the Mail Merge task pane, and then click **OK**, the merged document _____.

   (a) Overwrites the main document

   (b) Is automatically printed

   (c) Is saved to a new document file

   (d) Appears in a new document window

5. When you use mail merge to create address labels, what option do you click to copy the address field from the first label to the rest of the labels before performing the merge?

   (a) Copy and paste

   (b) Update all labels

   (c) Edit recipient list

   (d) Sort and filter

6. Which of the following best describes the documents that are associated with a mail merge?

   (a) The main document is typically saved, but not necessarily printed.

   (b) The names and addresses are typically saved, but not necessarily printed.

   (c) The individual form letters are printed, but not necessarily saved.

   (d) The main document is not saved and always printed.

7. Which of the following is not an example of why mail merge is a good tool?

   (a) You can print mailing labels for Christmas cards.

   (b) Your business sends personalized letters to all clients.

   (c) You use the same basic document every day.

   (d) Each month you e-mail a meeting announcement to every member of your professional organization.

8. If you use a document every day that contains your company letterhead, which productivity tool would best fit your need?

   (a) Mail merge

   (b) Building blocks

   (c) Document themes

   (d) Document templates

9. Which of the following is not a way you can obtain a document template?

   (a) Select it from the Styles gallery

   (b) Download from Microsoft Office Online

   (c) Installed on your computer

   (d) Create a document yourself and save it as a template

10. What file extension is given to a template?

    (a) .dotx

    (b) .docx

    (c) .xlsx

    (d) .accdb

11. What is another name for the text or fields that display in a document template so you will know where to insert your own information?

    (a) Flag

    (b) Extension

    (c) CV

    (d) Placeholder

12. If you open a curriculum vitae template, what type of document are you creating?

   (a) A calendar

   (b) A job history or resume

   (c) A cover letter

   (d) A lesson plan

13. Why would you use a document theme?

   (a) So you can restrict the use of color in the document

   (b) To merge information from a data source into a document

   (c) To add a stylish and professional appearance

   (d) So you can preserve the format of a document

14. Which theme element are you unable to customize and save?

   (a) Theme Effect

   (b) Theme Font

   (c) Theme Color

   (d) Document Theme

15. What feature makes a process easier by asking a series of questions, then creating a document based on your answers?

   (a) Themes

   (b) Wizard

   (c) Template

   (d) Merge

Practice Exercises

1 Prepare a Form Letter for Theatre Patrons

You are the manager of the Jacksonville City Theatre and each month you mail tickets to patrons who have placed orders over the phone or online. You know that it is too time-consuming to copy and paste the patrons' names and addresses from your Excel worksheet into the cover letter you send with the tickets, so you decide to create a mail merge document that you can quickly update and send each month. You also decide to take advantage of the new Themes in Word 2007 and apply one to your letter.

a. Open *chap5_pe1_theatre* and save it as **chap5_pe1_theatre_solution**.

b. Click the **Page Layout tab**, click **Themes**, and then click **Opulent**.

c. Click **Theme Colors**, and then click **Create New Theme Colors**. Click the **Accent 1 drop-down arrow** and click **Purple, Accent 2, Lighter 60%** in the sixth column. Type **Theatre Colors** in the Name box, replacing any text that currently displays. Click **Save**.

d. Click **Themes** in the Page Layout tab, and then click **Save Current Theme**. Type **Theatre_Theme** in the File name box, and then click **Save**.

e. Click the **Mailings** tab, click **Start Mail Merge** in the Start Mail Merge group, and then click **Letters**.

f. Click **Select Recipients**, and then click **Use Existing List**. Navigate to the location where data files are stored, select **chap5_pe1_patrons.xlsx**, and then click **Open**. Click **OK** when the Select Table dialog box displays.

g. Click to move the insertion point two lines below the date. Click **Address Block**, and then click **OK** to insert the patron's address at the top of the letter. Move the insertion point to the left side of the comma in the salutation line *Dear*, and then click **Insert Merge Field**. Click **Fname**, press **Spacebar**, click **Insert Merge Field**, and then click **Lname**.

h. Click to place the insertion point between the two spaces on the right side of the word *of* in the last sentence of the second paragraph. Click **Insert Merge Field**, and then click **Show**.

TROUBLESHOOTING: If you find it difficult to determine where to place the cursor, click Show/Hide ¶ on the Home tab to display formatting marks such as spaces.

i. Move the insertion point to the end of the last sentence of the second paragraph, just before the ending period. Click **Insert Merge Field**, and then click **Date**. Compare your letter to Figure 5.33.

j. Click **Finish & Merge** in the Finish group on the Mailings tab. Click **Edit Individual Documents**, click **From**, type **1** in the first box, type **34** in the second box, and then click **OK**. There were four records at the end of the list that did not contain addresses. You do not want to print those letters.

k. Save the new document as **chap5_pe1_ticketletter_solution**. Save *chap5_pe1_theatre_solution*, and then close all documents.

...continued on Next Page

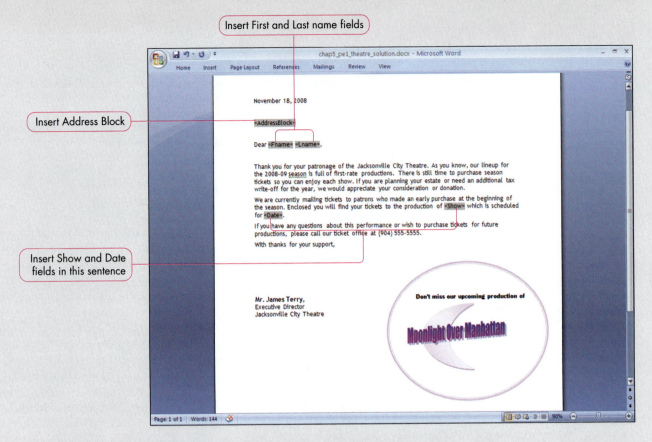

Figure 5.33 Prepare a Form Letter for Mail Merge

2 Sort the Data Source for a Theatre Patron Form Letter

After you create the form letters you want to mail patrons of the Jacksonville City Theatre, you realize you did not want to send letters to all the patrons, only those who purchased tickets for the production that is held in January. You remember that you can take steps to restrict the source data so that you merge only selected records with your source document and proceed to make those changes to the documents you created in Practice Exercise 1.

a. Open *chap5_pe1_theatre_solution*. If a Microsoft Office Word dialog box displays a message and asks if you want to continue, click **Yes**. Save the document as **chap5_pe2_theatre_solution**.

b. Click the **Mailings tab**, and then click **Edit Recipient List** to display the Mail Merge Recipients dialog box.

c. Click **Filter** to display the Filter and Sort dialog box. Click the **Filter Records** tab, if necessary. Click the **Field drop-down arrow** and click **Show**. Click the **Comparison drop-down arrow** and click **Contains**. In the **Compare to box**, type **Moon**, as shown in Figure 5.34, and then click **OK**. Click **OK** again to close the Mail Merge Recipients dialog box.

d. Click **Preview Results** on the Mailings tab, and then click **Last Record** to determine how many pages your merge will create. If the filter is set correctly, your merge will create 12 letters.

e. Click **Finish & Merge**, click **Edit Individual Documents**, and then click **OK**.

f. Save the new document as **chap5_pe2_moonletter_solution**. Close the document.

g. Save changes to *chap5_pe2_theatre_solution*, and then close the document.

...continued on Next Page

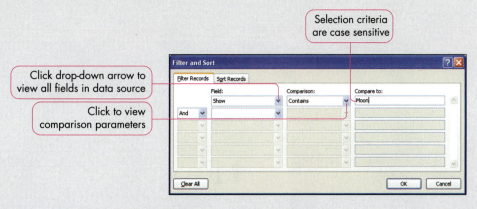

Figure 5.34 Filter a Data Source

3 Create a Fax from a Template

As a mortgage broker, you need to send a fax and other documents to a customer who will complete closing on her new home this week. Instead of formatting a new blank document as a fax, you decide to choose a fax template to save time. After starting the document with the fax template, you quickly replace placeholders with text and type a short paragraph.

a. Click the **Office Button**, click **New**, click **Installed Templates**, click **Origin Fax**, and then click **Create**.

b. If necessary, replace the name of the sender with your name. To make that change, select the sender name, and then type your name to replace it.

c. Use the following table as a guide to replace the placeholders with information about the sender.

Field Name	Value
Phone:	(479) 555-5555
Fax:	(479) 555-5556
Company Name:	Bronson Abstract

d. Click the **Office Button**, click the **Save As arrow**, and then click **Word Template**. Type **chap5_pe3_faxtemplate_solution** in the File name box, and then click **Save**. Notice the file name in the Title Bar reflects the template extension (see Figure 5.35). You can now use the template for any faxes you send in the future.

e. Use the following table as a guide to replace the placeholders with information about the recipient of the fax.

Field Name	Value
To:	Alana Bell
Phone:	(479) 555-1234
Fax:	(479) 555-9876
Company Name:	Reed Educational Supplies

f. Click the **Pick a date drop-down arrow**, and then click **Today**.

g. Select the *Type Comments* placeholder, press **Delete**, and then type the following paragraph: **Alana, the following pages contain the preliminary closing papers for your loan. Please bring a cashier's check in the amount of $50,000 with you when you come to the closing next week. Please call me if you have any questions**.

h. Click the **Office Button**, click the **Save As arrow**, click **Word Document**, and then name the document **chap5_pe3_fax_solution**. Close the document.

...continued on Next Page

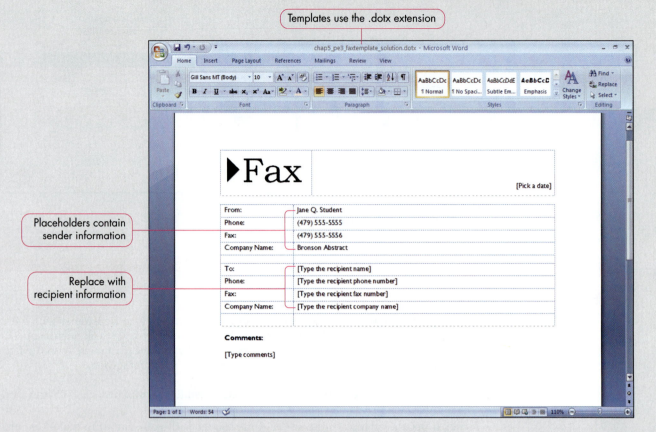

Figure 5.35 Create a Document Template for a Fax

4 Create a Home Inspection Checklist for Home Buyers

You are a real estate agent who develops close relationships with your customers and works diligently to insure a positive home-buying experience for each family. Providing lists of homes for sale is only the first of many value-added services you offer. You also arm your clients with a Home Inspection Checklist that contains the addresses of houses they plan to view so they will be able to take notes during their walk-through of the home. You download the checklist from Microsoft Office Online, and then update the template so it is ready for a mail merge with a list of addresses.

a. Click the **Office Button**, click **New**, click **Lists** from the Microsoft Office Online section of the New Document window, click **Buyer's home inspection checklist**, and then click **Download**. If the Microsoft Office Genuine Advantage dialog box displays, click **Do not show this message again**, and then click **Continue**.

b. Click the **Mailings tab**, click **Select Recipients**, click **Use Existing List**, navigate to the location where you store data files, click *chap5_pe4_homes.accdb*, and then click **Open**.

c. Position the insertion point in the cell that intersects the first row and second column, click **Address Block**, and then click **OK**. Click the **Layout tab**, and then click the **Table Row Height spin arrow** until .6" displays. The additional space enables the whole address to display in the cell.

d. Position the insertion point in the cell opposite the Listing agent's name and type **Lisa Prince**. In the third row, type **Lisa@homes4you.com** in the cell for e-mail address.

e. Click the **Insert tab**, click **Header**, and then click **Edit Header**. Click **Next Section**, click to select the *Address of the house* field that displays on the right side, and then press **Delete** to remove the field. Click the **Mailings tab**, click **Address Block**, and then click **OK**. Double-click anywhere outside of the header to close the header.

f. Click the **Office Button**, click the **Save As arrow**, click **Word Template**, and then save the file as **chap5_pe4_checklist**. If necessary, click **OK** to the Microsoft Office Word

...continued on Next Page

dialog box that alerts you to the fact you are saving it with the newer version of Word. You have created a document template that can be used each time you want to provide a customer with a list of homes to view.

g. Click **Edit Recipient List**, and then click the **Data Source checkbox** to remove all recipients from the merge, as shown in Figure 5.36. Click **Find recipient**, type **GA** in the *Find* box, click the drop-down arrow for *This Field* and click **State**, and then click **Find Next**. Click **Cancel** to close the Find Entry dialog box. The home with the address 3288 Piper Gln is highlighted because it is the first item to meet the criteria. Click the **data source check box** beside that entry, and then click **OK**.

h. Click **Finish & Merge** in the Mailings tab, click **Edit Individual Documents**, and then click **OK**. The new document contains a nine-page checklist for the house on 3288 Piper Gln. The header of pages two through nine displays the address in the upper right corner.

i. Save the file as **chap5_pe4_inspection_solution.docx**. Save and close all documents.

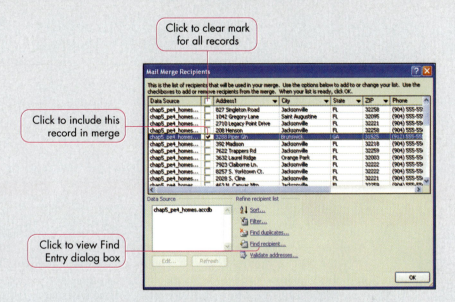

Figure 5.36 Create a Document Template for a Fax

Mid-Level Exercises

1 Science Fair Volunteers

The Regional Science Fair will occur on the campus of Missouri State University in the spring, and students from schools across the southwest portion of the state compete in areas such as physics, chemistry, environment, meteorology, and astronomy. As the Volunteer Coordinator, you must maintain a list of people who will donate their time to the event. You decide to send a reminder to each volunteer so they will be sure to arrive at their designated time.

a. Open the *chap5_mid1_reminder* document and save it as **chap5_mid1_reminder_solution**.

b. Use the reminder as the main document in a mail merge.

c. Use *chap5_mid1_times.xlsx* as your data source. Insert fields for name, start time, and end time in the appropriate locations in the reminder document.

d. Preview the merge results, then edit the recipient list. Sort the source data so that it sorts the *Time In* field in ascending order.

e. Filter the source data so that any record that contains a Time Out later than 9:00 PM will not be included in the merge.

f. Merge the documents and display the results in a new file. Save the merged reminders as **chap5_mid1_mergedreminder_solution.docx**.

g. Save and close all documents.

2 Family Newsletter

At the end of every year, your family compiles a newsletter that summarizes the important events from the past 12 months. This year, you found the variety of templates that Office 2007 provides and offers as downloads from Microsoft Office Online. You decide to make your correspondence very efficient this year by using a template for the newsletter and using mail merge to insert the addresses of your family and friends.

a. Open a new document, and then browse the newsletter templates available from Microsoft Office Online. Select the Family Christmas newsletter.

b. Scroll to the bottom of the newsletter and replace the return address with your own. Save the newsletter as a Word template named **chap5_mid2_newsletter_solution.dotx**.

c. Run the Step-by-Step Mail Merge Wizard and use the template as a starting document.

d. Type a new list to use as a source. Enter the information from the table below into your address list:

Field Name	Value	Value	Value
First Name	Randy	Brian	Scott
Last Name	Smith	Turner	Lewis
Address Line 1	901 S. National	109 Lombard St.	558 Justice Blvd
City	Las Cruces	San Francisco	Norman
State	NM	CA	OK
ZIP Code	88001	94122	73070

...continued on Next Page

e. Save the source data file as **chap5_mid2_addresses**.

f. Go to the bottom of the newsletter and replace the friend's name and address with the source data fields.

g. Complete the Mail Merge Wizard steps, and then display the results in a new file. Save the new document containing the newsletters as **chap5_mid2_letters_solution.docx**.

h. Save and close all documents.

3 Creating Themes

Because you learned about the themes that Word 2007 provides, you decide that you need to use them more often and also create your very own custom theme. You download a letter that incorporates a theme already, and then you make modifications and save the custom theme for use in future documents.

a. Open a new document, and then browse the installed templates. Find the Median Letter template, and then use it to create a new document. The template has a few fields defined and might display information you store in the Windows options, such as your name and organization. Save the file as **chap5_mid3_theme_solution**.

b. If necessary, type your name at the top of the document. Insert today's date.

c. Display the **Theme** gallery and select the **Module** theme. Display the Theme Colors gallery. Create a new Color Theme. Change the *Text/Background – Dark 2* color to **Rose, Accent 3**, which is located on the top of the seventh column. Change the *Accent 1* color to **Gold, Accent 1, Lighter 60%** and change *Accent 2* to **Green, Accent 4**. Save the new color theme as **chap5_mid3_color**.

d. Create a new Font Theme. Change the Heading font to Times New Roman and change the Body font to Microsoft San Serif. Save the Font theme as **chap5_mid3_font**.

e. Because you are making many changes, save the Current Document Theme as **chap5_mid3_theme**.

f. Save and close the document.

Capstone Exercise

You work as the Business Manager for the local Sports Medicine Clinic. Each week your office mails a letter of reminder to patients who are scheduled for treatment or consultation the following week. In the past, the letters were very plain and simple. However, because you now use Word 2007, you decide to improve the look of the letters and implement a mail merge with the patient database so you can produce the letters quickly and accurately.

Create a Word Template

You will create a new letter and add the appropriate information that reminds patients of their appointments. You will select your document style by using one of the installed templates. Once you create the file, you personalize the document and save it as a document template so that you can use it for other types of correspondence.

a. Create a new document using the Urban Merge Letter template.

b. Save the file as a Word template named **chap5_cap_ appt_merge.dotx**.

c. Modify the Sender Company information and address in the upper-right corner of the document. Change the name of the organization to **Sports Medicine Clinic**, and change the address to **997 Foster Lane, Pittsburgh, PA 15697**.

d. Replace the body of the template with the following paragraph: **Please remember that you have an appointment at the Sports Medicine Clinic on at. If you have paperwork to fill out, please arrive at our office 15 minutes prior to your appointment time stated above. Thank you!**

e. Remove any building blocks that you do not use in the letter. Do not remove the Address Block or Greeting Line.

f. Save the template.

Apply a Theme to the Letter

After you set up the template, you decide to change the color scheme that the template uses. You will use the Themes feature and modify the themes when necessary to achieve a professional look for the letter.

a. Change the theme to Foundry so the colors do not overpower the document.

b. Create a new Theme color and name it **chap5_cap_ color**. This color scheme should use *Light Green, Accent 2* as the Accent 1 color. It should also modify Accent 2 to use *Green, Accent 1*.

c. Modify the Theme Fonts so that the Heading font is **Arial Black**. The Body font should be **Arial Rounded MT**. Save the Font Theme as **chap5_cap_font**.

d. Save the Theme as **chap5_cap_theme**.

Set Up a Mail Merge

Once your document has the basic elements in place, such as themes and text, you can begin the mail merge process.

a. Start the mail merge process by using this template as your main source document.

b. Select your source data from *chap5_cap_patients.accdb*. When you select the file, click the Patients table.

c. Insert the fields for day, date, and time in the first sentence.

d. Pick the date, and preview the results of a merge to make sure all fields display properly.

e. Edit the recipient list and add your name, address, and a date for an appointment. If file or network security does not enable you to modify the source data file, copy the file to your own disk and redirect the mail merge to use the file from the new location. If you cannot copy the file, omit this step.

f. Sort the recipient list by appointment date, and then appointment time. Do not print letters for people who do not have a scheduled appointment.

g. Merge the documents into a new document, and then save it as **chap5_cap_appt_solution.docx**. If a Mail Merge dialog box displays indicating Word found locked fields during the update, click OK to clear the dialog box.

h. Save and close all documents.

Mini Cases

Use the rubric following the case as a guide to evaluate your work, but keep in mind that your instructor may impose additional grading criteria or use a different standard to judge your work.

Create an Employee Directory

GENERAL CASE

The management of your company requires you to keep a current list of employee contact information in case you need to contact someone for an emergency situation. You have a worksheet that contains the contact information, but you do not yet know how to use Microsoft Excel and you need to create and format a list very quickly. You are mastering the mail merge feature of Word 2007 and remember you have the option of creating a directory, which lists the source data on one page instead of printing each one on a separate page. This would be a good tool to use in generating the master list. Open a new document and prepare the contact information list using a mail merge operation. Use the file *chap5_mc1_personnel.xlsx* as your data source. Save the main document as **chap5_mc1_directory_solution.docx**, and save the result of your mail merge as **chap5_mc1_directorylist_solution.docx**. Use the Microsoft Help feature, if necessary. It might be helpful to format your data in a table so it is easier to read.

Performance Elements	Exceeds Expectations	Meets Expectations	Below Expectations
Directory mail merge	Successfully created a listing of all employee information, using mail merge, and displayed the information on a single page.	Created a listing of all employee information using mail merge, but information displays on a new page for each employee.	Did not use mail merge to create a listing of employee information.
Directory format	Formatted the employee information to display evenly by using layout tools such as tabs or tables.	Employee information displays in a general sense of alignment, but could improve upon the layout.	Employee information displays in uneven rows and wraps awkwardly.

Use the Calendar Wizard

RESEARCH CASE

You want to create a monthly calendar for the current year. However, you do not want to manually create and populate 12 tables, one for each month, typing in dates within cells. You know there are many calendar templates on the Microsoft Office Online site and decide to find one there. Find and download the Calendar Wizard, and after you complete the steps you can type in important dates such as birthdays and anniversaries. Save the calendar as **chap5_mc2_calendar_solution.docx**.

Performance Elements	Exceeds Expectations	Meets Expectations	Below Expectations
Search abilities	Successfully downloaded and completed the calendar wizard.	Downloaded a calendar template, but not the calendar wizard.	Did not download a calendar template or wizard. Created a calendar from scratch.
Visual aspects	Objects such as clip art or pictures are used generously. They enhance and add understanding of information on the calendar.	Some clip art or pictures seem to be unrelated to the presentation purpose and content and do not enhance the overall concepts. Images are too large/small in size. Colors are distracting.	No background or theme is applied, or the document is distracting to the topic. Images do not enhance understanding of the content or are unrelated.
Layout	The layout is visually pleasing and contributes to the overall message purpose of a calendar.	The layout shows some structure, but placement of dates, images, and/or white space is distracting.	The layout is cluttered and confusing. Placement of dates, images, and/or white space detracts from readability.

Your friend is experiencing high levels of anxiety because she cannot complete a mail merge operation to create labels for her wedding invitations. She has used the mail merge feature previously; however, when you open the labels, a dialog box appears and indicates there is no link from that main document to the data source (address list). You decide to troubleshoot the operation by first opening the file **chap5_mc3_invlabels**, to see how it was set up to use the addresses in **chap5_mc3_addr.accdb**, and then determine if you can find the reason why it does not work. If you can solve the problem, rename and save the original file to **chap5_mc3_invlabels_solution**.

Performance Elements	Exceeds Expectations	Meets Expectations	Below Expectations
Problem-solving	Successfully determined source of error message, resolved database field inconsistencies, and performed mail merge.	Solved the problem that prevented the merge from completing, but did not complete the merge.	Did not determine source of problem and did not complete a mail merge.
Layout	The labels are formatted so they display properly and will look neat when printed.	The labels display all address information, but are not formatted to print correctly.	The address is formatted in such a way that information cannot fit completely on the label.

Desktop Publishing

Creating a Newsletter, Using Graphic Design, and Linking Objects

bjectives

After you read this chapter, you will be able to:

1. Construct a newsletter **(page 363)**.
2. Develop a document design **(page 367)**.
3. Insert drawing shapes **(page 377)**.
4. Insert SmartArt **(page 378)**.
5. Insert a text box **(page 380)**.
6. Format graphical objects **(page 382)**.
7. Group and layer objects **(page 385)**.
8. Flip and rotate objects **(page 387)**.
9. Use OLE to insert an object **(page 393)**.
10. Update a linked object **(page 396)**.

Hands-On Exercises

Exercises	Skills Covered
1. DESIGN A NEWSLETTER (page 370) **Open:** chap6_ho1_newsletter.docx **Save as:** chap6_ho1_newsletter_solution.docx	• Change Page Setup Options and Implement Column Formatting • Change Column Layout • Create a Masthead and a Reverse • Modify Heading Styles and Apply Numbering • Create a Pull Quote and Create a Drop Cap • Apply Borders and Shading and Insert Clip Art
2. WORK WITH OBJECTS (page 388) **Open:** chap6_ho1_newsletter_solution.docx (from Exercise 1) **Save as:** chap6_ho2_newsletter_solution.docx **Open:** Blank document **Save as:** chap6_ho2_acme_solution.docx	• Create the Autoshape and Apply Formatting • Create a Text Box • Layer and Group Drawing Objects • Insert SmartArt
3. OBJECT LINKING AND EMBEDDING (page 398) **Open:** chap6_ho2_acme_solution.docx (from Exercise 2) **Save as:** chap6_ho3_acme_solution.docx	• Copy and Link a Worksheet • Change the Source Data and Update the Document • Embed and Modify an Excel Chart

CASE STUDY

Astronomy Is Fun!

Amateur astronomy is a favorite pastime, and many people who enjoy it as a serious or casual hobby join astronomy groups. Many individuals and organizations share ideas, pictures, and information through newsletters, Web sites, and group meetings. The local astronomical society you attend distributes a monthly newsletter, but because of the number of requests for information from schools and families who home-school their children, they decide to create a newsletter just for young people. They ask for a volunteer to create the newsletter, which will be printed and mailed to several schools and families, but will also be posted on the society's Web site.

Case Study

You fondly recall how many children in your neighborhood come running when they see you outside looking through a telescope, and you realize that you would be proud to help them, and others like them, learn even more about astronomy. You gladly volunteer to create the youth newsletter because you are familiar with desktop publishing and you have the tools at hand to make it happen.

The president of the organization provided you with a Word document that contains a few brief articles and information that would be appropriate for your first edition. You decide it is now time to reorganize that information and form it into an eye-catching and fun newsletter that children of all ages will enjoy reading.

Your Assignment

- Read the chapter, which describes how to create and format a newsletter.
- Open the president's file, *chap6_case_astronomy*, which contains the information for the first edition of your newsletter, and save it as **chap6_case_astronomy_solution**.
- Create a grid to plan the layout of your newsletter. Then use the column formatting that best displays the articles.
- Determine how the information will align in the columns. Move the articles around, as necessary, to try to prevent an article from spanning across columns.
- Insert a masthead for the newsletter and place a border around the page.
- Insert clip art or shapes, pull quotes, and borders and shading to add visual stimulation and emphasis to the page.
- Change typography as needed to make the document easy to read in a printed format.

Desktop Publishing

Desktop publishing is the merger of text with graphics to produce a professional-looking document.

Desktop publishing evolved through a combination of technologies, including faster computers, laser printers, and sophisticated page composition software to manipulate text and graphics to produce a professional-looking document. Before computers made it so easy, desktop publishing was accomplished by using services of professionals such as art directors, paste-up artists, typographers, plate makers, and printers. The level of acceptable quality has declined, but you can produce acceptable quality entirely on your own with your computer. Desktop publishing was initially considered a separate application, but today's generation of word processors has matured to such a degree that it is difficult to tell where word processing ends and desktop publishing begins. Microsoft Word is, for all practical purposes, a desktop publishing program that can be used to create all types of documents.

Desktop publishing will save you time and money because you are doing the work yourself rather than sending it out as you did in traditional publishing. You can enjoy the challenge of creating a document that contains many graphical design techniques, but it can be time-consuming and require an eye for detail, which is why documents such as brochures, newsletters, and flyers are often prepared by skilled professionals. Nevertheless, with a little practice and a basic knowledge of graphic design, you will be able to create effective and attractive documents.

In this section, you develop a simple newsletter that includes a multicolumn layout, clip art, and other objects, and position those objects within a document.

Reverse is the technique that uses light text on a dark background.

A **masthead** is the identifying information at the top of a newsletter or other periodical.

> When you use desktop publishing to create a document such as a newsletter, you can use several techniques to enhance readability and attractiveness. Your objective should be to create a document that is easy to read and visually appealing.

Constructing a Newsletter

When you use desktop publishing to create a document, such as the newsletter you see in Figure 6.1, you should use several techniques to enhance readability and attractiveness. One favorite technique of desktop publishers to emphasize a specific element is *reverse*, using light text on a dark background. It is often used in the *masthead*, which is the identifying information at the top of the newsletter or other periodical. It provides a distinctive look to the publication and often has the characteristics of a banner. The number of the newsletter and the date of publication also appear in the masthead in smaller letters.

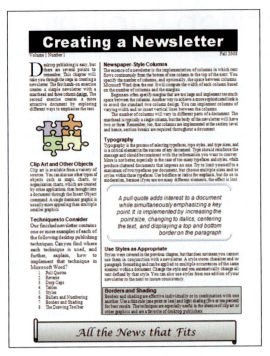

Figure 6.1 The Newsletter

A *pull quote* is a phrase or sentence taken from an article to emphasize a key point.

A *sidebar* is supplementary text that appears on the side of the featured information.

A *drop cap* is a large capital letter at the beginning of a paragraph.

A *pull quote* is a phrase or sentence taken from an article to emphasize a key point. It is typically set in larger type, often in a different typeface and/or italics, and may be offset with borders at the top, bottom, or on the sides. Pull quotes display throughout this book to draw attention to important topics in each chapter. *Sidebars* also enable you to call attention to information in a document by displaying it in a space along the side of the featured information. Sidebars might display supplementary information, or they can simply display information of interest to the reader.

A *drop cap*, or dropped-capital letter, is a large capital letter at the beginning of a paragraph. It, too, catches the reader's eye and calls attention to the associated text. The Drop Cap command enables you to determine if the dropped cap will align with the text or display off to the side. The choice you make will largely depend on the style of the newsletter and how you design it. You can determine the size of a drop cap initial from the Drop Cap dialog box. Options for a drop cap include how many lines to drop, or how far from the text the drop cap displays. You can display a drop cap in the margin and turn it off from this dialog box. Click Drop Cap on the Insert tab, and then click Drop Cap Options to display the dialog box, as shown in Figure 6.2.

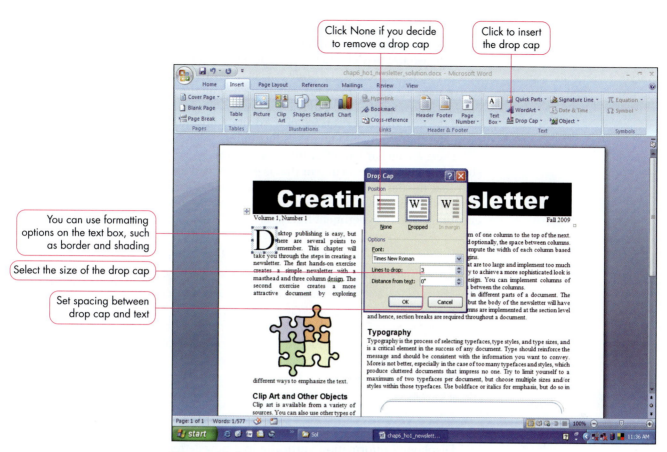

Click None if you decide to remove a drop cap

Click to insert the drop cap

You can use formatting options on the text box, such as border and shading

Select the size of the drop cap

Set spacing between drop cap and text

Figure 6.2 The Drop Cap Dialog Box

Microsoft Office 2007 enables you to quickly insert a pull quote, sidebar, or drop cap using commands on the Insert tab. The Text Box command (which you learn more about later in this chapter) includes a gallery of pull quotes and sidebars.

Clip art is a graphical image, illustration, drawing, or sketch. When used in moderation, clip art will catch the reader's eye and enhance almost any newsletter. It is also used to prevent using so much text on a page that the document bores the reader. Clip art is available from a variety of sources including CDs you purchase and the Microsoft Online Clip Gallery, which is included in Office 2007. Clip art can also be downloaded from the Web, but be sure you are allowed to reprint the image. The banner at the bottom of the newsletter is not a clip art image per se, but was created using various tools on the Drawing toolbar. These tools will be discussed later in this chapter.

Borders and shading are effective individually, or in combination with one another, to emphasize important stories within the newsletter. ***Border*** refers to whatever displays around an element. A line border might surround a paragraph, or a page border might consist of a series of small graphics. ***Shading*** affects the background color of an element, such as a text box. Simple vertical and/or horizontal lines are also effective. These techniques are especially useful in the absence of clip art or other graphics and are a favorite of desktop publishers to draw the reader's eye to a location on the document.

Lists, whether bulleted or numbered, help to organize information by emphasizing important topics. A ***bulleted list*** emphasizes and separates information. A ***numbered list*** sequences and prioritizes information, and is automatically updated to accommodate additions or deletions.

The use of typography is essential in adding personality to your newsletter. ***Typography*** is the arrangement and appearance of printed matter. It involves selecting fonts, font styles, and font sizes that enhance the appearance of a document. It is a critical, often subtle, element in the success of a document, and its importance cannot be overstated. You should not, for example, use the same design to announce

Clip art is a graphical image, illustration, drawing, or sketch.

Border refers to the line style around the element.

Shading affects the background color of an element.

A ***bulleted list*** emphasizes and separates information.

A ***numbered list*** sequences and prioritizes information, and is automatically updated to accommodate additions or deletions.

Typography is the arrangement and appearance of printed matter.

A **style** is a set of formatting options you apply to characters or paragraphs.

a year-end bonus and a plant closing. Indeed, good typography goes almost unnoticed, whereas poor typography draws attention to and detracts from a document. You can also use predefined styles in desktop publishing to add personality to your newsletter. Remember that a **style** is a set of formatting options you apply to characters or paragraphs. It can store formats such as alignment, line spacing, indents, tabs, borders, and shading. You can use the same styles from one edition of your newsletter to the next to ensure consistency. Additionally, the use of styles in any document promotes uniformity and increases flexibility.

There are no hard and fast rules for the selection of type and style. Your objective should be to create a document that is easy to read and visually appealing. You will find that the design that worked so well in one document may not work at all in a different document. Good typography is often the result of trial and error, and we encourage you to experiment freely.

TIP   Limit Use of Typography

More is not better, especially in the case of too many typefaces and styles, which produce cluttered documents that impress no one. Try to limit yourself to a maximum of two fonts per document, but choose multiple sizes and/or styles within those fonts. Use boldface or italic for emphasis, but do so in moderation, because if you emphasize too many elements, the effect is lost. A simple design is often the best design.

Displaying information vertically in a newsletter is implemented through the Columns command, as shown in Figure 6.3. Start by selecting one of the column preset designs, and Microsoft Word takes care of everything else. It calculates the width of each column based on the number of columns, the left and right margins on the page, and the specified (default) space between columns. The newsletter in Figure 6.1, for example, uses a two-column layout with wide and narrow columns. We prefer this design to columns of uniform width, as we think it adds interest to our document. Note, too, that once columns have been defined, text will flow continuously from the bottom of one column to the top of the next. Notice also that in Figure 6.1, the number of columns varies from one part of the newsletter to another. The masthead is displayed over a single column at the top of the page, whereas the remainder of the newsletter is formatted in two columns of different widths. The number of columns is specified at the section level, and thus, a section break is required whenever the column specification changes. A section break is also required at the end of the last column to balance the text within the columns.

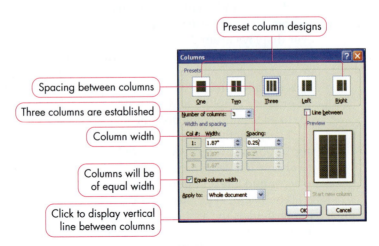

Figure 6.3 The Columns Command

Developing a Document Design

The most difficult aspect of creating a newsletter is to develop the design in the first place; the mere availability of a desktop publishing program does not guarantee an effective document any more than a word processor will turn its author into another Shakespeare. Other skills are necessary, and so we continue with a brief introduction to graphic design.

Much of what we say is subjective, and what works in one situation will not necessarily work in another. Your eye is the best judge of all, and you should follow your own instincts. Experiment freely and realize that successful design is the result of trial and error. Seek inspiration from others by collecting samples of real documents that capture your attention, and then use those documents as the basis for your own designs.

A ***grid*** is an underlying, but invisible, set of horizontal and vertical lines that determine the placement of major elements.

The design of a document is developed on a ***grid***, an underlying, but invisible, set of horizontal and vertical lines that determine the placement of major elements. A grid establishes the overall structure of a document by indicating the number of columns, the space between columns, the size of the margins, and the placement of headlines, art, sidebars, and so on. The grid does not appear in the printed document—you draw or sketch it on a piece of paper to solidify the layout prior to creating the newsletter in Word.

Figures 6.4, 6.5, and 6.6 show the same document in three different designs. The left half of each design displays the underlying grid, whereas the right half displays the completed document.

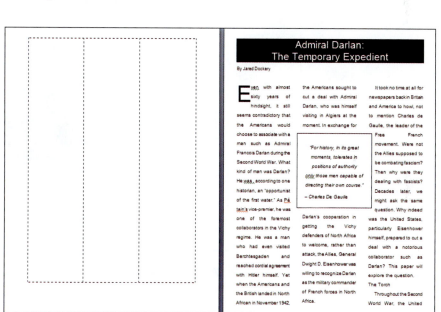

Figure 6.4 A Three-Column Grid

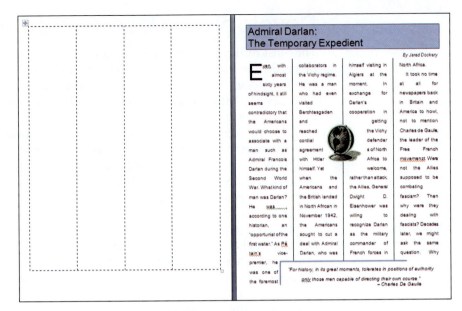

Figure 6.5 A Four-Column Grid

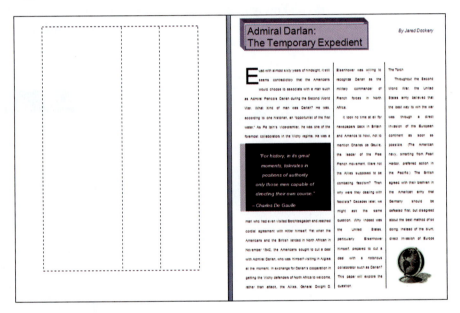

Figure 6.6 A Three-Column Grid with Unequal Column Widths

A grid may be simple or complex, but it is always distinguished by the number of columns it contains. The three-column grid of Figure 6.4 is one of the most common and utilitarian designs. Figure 6.5 shows a four-column design for the same document. Figure 6.6 illustrates a three-column grid with unequal column widths to provide interest. Many other designs are possible as well. A one-column grid is used for term papers and letters. A two-column, wide-and-narrow format is appropriate for some textbooks and manuals. Two- and three-column formats are used for newsletters and magazines.

The simple concept of a grid should make the underlying design of any document obvious, and it also helps you determine the page composition. Moreover, the conscious use of a grid will help you organize your material and will result in a more polished and professional-looking publication. It will also help you to achieve consistency from page to page within a document (or from issue to issue of a newsletter). Indeed, much of what goes wrong in desktop publishing stems from failing to follow or use the underlying grid.

Good design makes it easy for the reader to determine what is important. As indicated earlier, emphasis can be achieved in several ways, the easiest being variations in type size and/or type style. Headings should be set in type sizes at least two points larger than body copy. The use of boldface is effective, as are italics, but both should be done in moderation. UPPERCASE LETTERS and underlining are alternative techniques that we believe are less effective. Uppercase letters are often associated with screaming, because that is how we portray a raised voice in e-mail. They can also be harder to read because of the close spacing. Underlining is often associated with hyperlinks on a Web page, so it should be used on a limited basis, unless you are actually displaying a Web link.

Boxes and/or shading call attention to selected articles. Horizontal lines are effective to separate one topic from another or to call attention to a pull quote. A reverse can be striking for a small amount of text. Clip art, used in moderation, will catch the reader's eye and enhance almost any newsletter. Color is also effective, but it is more costly if you print a document.

All of the techniques and definitions we have discussed can be implemented with commands you already know, as you will see in the following hands-on exercise.

Hands-On Exercises

1 | Design a Newsletter

Skills covered: 1. Change Page Setup Options and Implement Column Formatting **2.** Change Column Layout **3.** Create a Masthead and a Reverse **4.** Modify Heading Styles and Apply Numbering **5.** Create a Pull Quote and Create a Drop Cap **6.** Apply Borders and Shading and Insert Clip Art

Step 1
Change Page Setup Options and Implement Column Formatting

Refer to Figure 6.7 as you complete Step 1.

a. Start Word. Open *chap6_ho1_newsletter* and save it as **chap6_ho1_newsletter_ solution**.

b. Click the **Page Layout tab**, click **Margins**, and then click **Custom Margins**.

   Because the newsletter contains many items, you need smaller margins that allow more usable space on the document.

c. Type **.75** in the Top margin box. Press **Tab** to move the insertion point to the Bottom margin box. Type **.75** and press **Tab** to move to the Left margin box. Type **.75** and press **Tab** to move to the Right margin box. Type **.75**, and then click **OK**.

d. Click **Columns** in the Page Setup group on the Page Layout tab, and then click **Two**.

   The text of the newsletter displays in two columns. The column width for each column and the spacing between columns is determined automatically from the existing margins.

e. Click the **Zoom slider** and decrease the zoom to **50%**.

   You can see the entire newsletter, as shown in Figure 6.7.

f. Save the document.

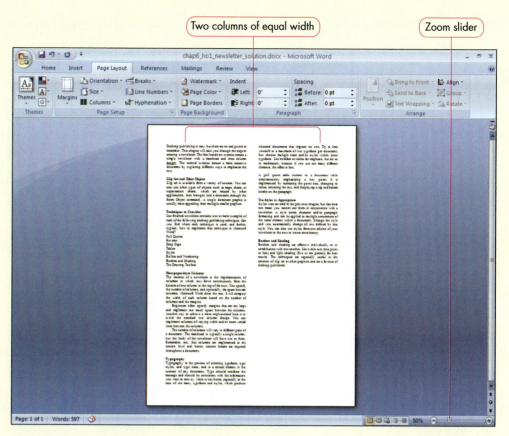

Figure 6.7 A Two-Column Newsletter

Step 2
Change Column Layout

Refer to Figure 6.8 as you complete Step 2.

a. Click **Columns** in the Page Setup group on the Page Layout tab, and then click **More Columns** to display the Columns dialog box.

b. Click **Left** in the *Presets* section, and then click the **Line between check box** to insert a line between the columns.

c. Press **Tab** to select the **Width** list for the first column, then type **2.25**. Press **Tab**, and then type **.25** in the **Spacing** list for the first column. Press **Tab** and notice that the width of the second column automatically changes to 4.5", as shown in Figure 6.8. Click **OK**.

The columns are no longer the same width, and the vertical line displays as a separator.

d. Press **Ctrl+End** to move the insertion point to the end of the document. Click **Breaks** in the Page Setup group on the Page Layout tab. Click **Continuous** under Section Breaks.

The columns are now balanced.

e. Save the document.

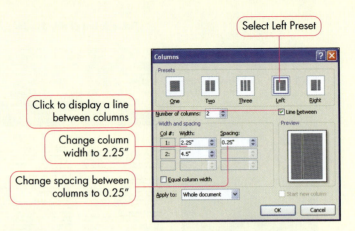

Select Left Preset

Click to display a line between columns

Change column width to 2.25"

Change spacing between columns to 0.25"

Figure 6.8 Modify Column Settings

Refer to Figure 6.9 as you complete Step 3.

a. Click the **Zoom slider** and increase the zoom to **110%**.

b. Click the **Home tab**, and then click **Show/Hide ¶**, if necessary, to display formatting marks in the document.

c. Press **Ctrl+Home** to move the insertion point to the beginning of the document. Click the **Page Layout tab**, click **Breaks** in the Page Setup group, and then click **Continuous** under Section Breaks.

You should see a double dotted line indicating a section break at the top of the document.

d. Click on the left side of the dotted line to move the insertion point, click **Columns**, and then click **One**.

The section break extends across the top of the document.

e. Type **Creating a Newsletter**, and then press **Enter** twice. Select the text you just typed, and then click **Center** on the Mini toolbar. Click the Font down arrow on the Mini toolbar, click **Arial Black**, and then click the Font size down arrow and click **36**.

This large heading is the masthead for the newsletter.

f. Click on the left side of the section break, just below the masthead, to move the insertion point. Click the **Insert tab**, click **Table**, and drag your mouse over the cells until you select two columns and one row (2x1 Table). Click the right cell to insert the table.

A table displays below the masthead and above the section break.

g. Click in the left cell of the table, if necessary, and type **Volume 1, Number 1**. Click in the right cell (or press Tab) and type **Fall 2009**. Click the **Home tab**, then click **Align Text Right** in the Paragraph group.

h. Press **Ctrl+Home** to move the insertion point to the beginning of the masthead. Click the **Border** down arrow in the Paragraph group, and then click **Borders and Shading**.

The Borders and Shading dialog box displays. The Borders tab is active.

i. Click the **Shading tab**, click the **Style drop-down arrow**, click **Solid (100%)**, and then click **OK**. Click in the table to deselect the masthead.

The masthead displays white text on a black background.

j. Click the table selector to select the entire table. Click the **Borders and Shading** down arrow in the Paragraph group on the Home tab, and then click **No Border.** Compare your work to Figure 6.9.

k. Save the document.

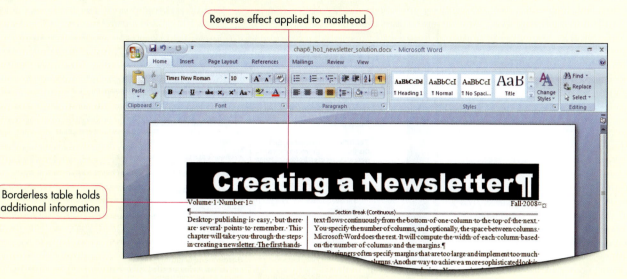

Figure 6.9 Create a Newsletter Masthead

Step 4
Modify Heading Styles and Apply Numbering

Refer to Figure 6.10 as you complete Step 4.

a. Click the **Home tab**, if necessary, and then click the **Styles Dialog Box Launcher** to display the Styles task pane.

Two styles have been set for you in the newsletter. Click in any paragraph and you see that the Body Text style displays with a box around it in the Styles task pane. The Heading 1 style displays on all paragraph headings.

b. Click to place the insertion point anywhere in the heading *Clip Art and Other Objects*, then scroll, if necessary, to display Heading 1 in the Styles task pane. Click the down arrow that displays when you move the mouse over the Heading 1 style in the Styles task pane, and then click **Modify**. Click the **Font list** down arrow and click **Arial**. Click the **Font size** down arrow and click **12**. Click **OK**. Close the Styles task pane.

All of the paragraph headings in the document change automatically to reflect the changes in the Heading 1 style.

c. Scroll down the document until the heading *Techniques to Consider* displays. Select the entire list of techniques that display below this paragraph (starting with *Pull Quotes* and ending with *The Drawing Toolbar*), and then click **Numbering** on the Paragraph group of the Home tab.

Your list should look like the list in Figure 6.10.

TROUBLESHOOTING: If the Arabic Numbers (followed by periods) do not apply to the list, as shown in Figure 6.10, click the **Numbering down arrow** and select the appropriate style from the Numbering Library gallery.

d. Click anywhere in the newsletter to deselect the numbered list. Save the document.

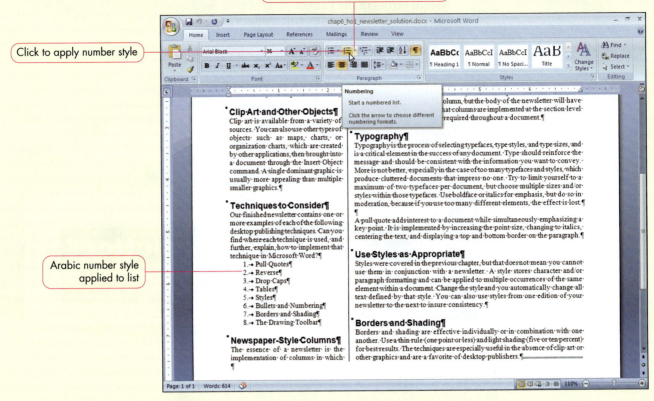

Figure 6.10 Numbered List in a Newsletter

Step 5

Create a Pull Quote and Create a Drop Cap

Refer to Figure 6.11 as you complete Step 5.

a. Select the paragraph that is located on the right side of the numbered list you just created; it starts with the text *A pull quote adds interest* and describes a pull quote. Click the **Font size** down arrow on the Mini toolbar and click **14**. Click the **Font** down arrow and select **Arial**. Click **Italic**. Click **Ctrl+X** to cut the text from the document.

b. Click the **Insert tab**, click **Text Box** in the Text group, and then scroll down and click **Motion Quote** from the gallery.

The Text Box gallery includes building blocks that are preformatted for a variety of pull quote styles.

c. Click once on the blue text in the middle to select the text portion of the box, if necessary. Click **Ctrl+V** to insert the text you copied earlier.

d. Click on the blue dotted border of the box; when the mouse pointer changes to a four-headed arrow, click and drag the box and drop it close to the left side of the column, below the *Typography* paragraph and above the *Use Styles as Appropriate* paragraph.

The box does not fill the whole column and some of the text might wrap on the right or left side of it, but you will fix that next.

e. Click the lower-right sizing handle and drag it to the right until the box spans the width of the column and text no longer wraps on the side. Click on the sizing handles to adjust size as necessary, and use Ctrl+arrow to nudge the box into the exact position. Delete any extra line returns, if necessary, to prevent a large gap of white space between the pull quote and the surrounding paragraphs.

f. Click to move the insertion point to the left of the first letter in the first paragraph on the top left of the page, which starts *Desktop publishing is easy.* Click the **Insert tab**, click **Drop Cap** in the Text group, and then click **Dropped**.

g. Click anywhere outside the Drop Cap frame, and then compare your document to Figure 6.11.

h. Save the document.

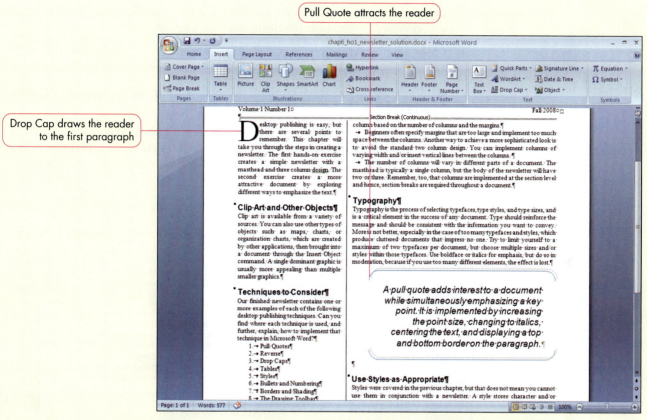

Figure 6.11   Insert a Pull Quote and a Drop Cap

Step 6

Apply Borders and Shading and Insert Clip Art

Refer to Figure 6.12 as you complete Step 6.

a. Press **Ctrl+End** to move the insertion point to the end of the document. Select the heading *Borders and Shading* and the paragraph, but do not select the ending paragraph mark that displays at the end of the last line in the paragraph.

TROUBLESHOOTING: If you find it difficult to select the text without the ending paragraph mark, hold down **Shift** and use the arrow keys to select the paragraph text.

b. Click the **Home tab,** click the **Border down arrow,** click **Borders and Shading,** and click the Borders tab, if necessary.

c. Click **Box** in the *Setting* section. Click the **Width down arrow** and click **1 pt**.

d. Click the **Shading** tab, click the **Style list drop-down arrow**, click **15%**, and then click **OK**. Click anywhere to deselect the paragraph.

A black border and gray shading display around and behind the Borders and Shading paragraph, as shown in Figure 6.12.

e. Click the **Insert tab**, click **Clip Art**, and type **puzzle** in the Search for box. Click the **Four Interlocking Puzzle Pieces** clip art to insert it into the document. Click one time on the clip art object to select it, then click the **Format tab**. Click **Text Wrapping**, and then click **Square**. In the **Format tab**, type **1.5** in the **Shape Height** box and type **1.5** in the **Shape Width** box. Drag the clip art to the top of the document and display it below the introductory paragraph and above the *Clip Art* paragraph.

Use Ctrl+arrow to nudge the clip art into place, if needed, so the paragraphs do not wrap around it. If you do not have the Four Interlocking Puzzle Pieces clip art on your PC, you can substitute different clip art.

f. Close the Clip Art task pane. Click **Show/Hide ¶** on the Home tab to turn off the formatting marks. Click the **Zoom Slider** to decrease the view to **50%**.

As you view the whole document, notice how your changes greatly improve the look of the newsletter.

g. Save the *chap6_ho1_newsletter_solution* document and keep it onscreen if you plan to continue with the next hands-on exercise. Close *chap_ho1_newsletter_solution* and exit Word if you will not continue with the next exercise at this time.

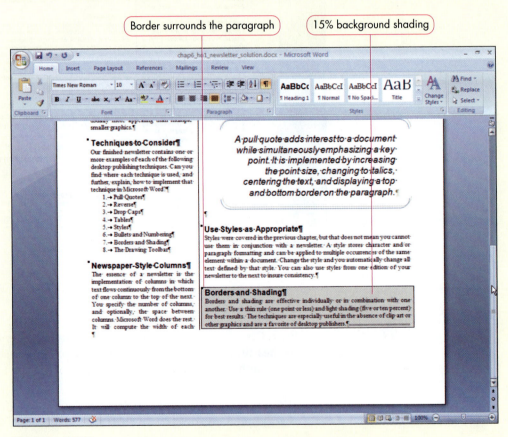

Figure 6.12 Borders and Shading Enhance a Paragraph

Drawing Tools and Special Effects

You can use shape and text tools on the Insert tab to modify an existing image or create simple shapes of your own that can enhance a document.

Did you ever stop to think how the images in the Clip Organizer were developed? Undoubtedly, they were drawn by someone with artistic ability using basic shapes, such as lines and curves in various combinations, to create the images. We don't expect you to create clip art comparable to the images in the Clip Organizer. You can, however, use shape and text tools on the Insert tab to modify an existing image or create simple shapes of your own that can enhance a document.

Graphical elements—such as lines, arrows, stars, and other shapes—help enhance your documents by adding visual interest. Microsoft Word enables you to combine graphical elements to produce one-of-a-kind drawings. For example, you can create shapes that represent balloons on strings and format the shapes by applying different fill colors. You can position, size, and overlap shapes to achieve the visual effect you desire.

Inserting Drawing Shapes

A **shape** is a geometric or non-geometric object, such as a circle or an arrow.

One tool that is especially useful is the Shapes command. A **shape** is a geometric or nongeometric object, such as a circle or an arrow, that you can use as a visual enhancement.

You can use one shape or combine multiple shapes to create a more complex image. When you click Shapes in the Illustrations group on the Insert tab, the Shapes gallery displays the following categories of shapes:

- Lines
- Basic Shapes
- Block Arrows
- Flowchart
- Callouts
- Stars and Banners

To insert a shape, select the shape from the gallery, and then position the mouse pointer in your document where you want to place the shape. The mouse pointer changes to a cross-hair, which enables you to see the beginning and ending points of your shape. Click and drag the cross-hair pointer until the shape is the size you desire. If you need to insert several instances of the same shape, click Shapes on the Insert tab, then right-click the shape object in the gallery and click Lock Drawing Mode (see Figure 6.13).

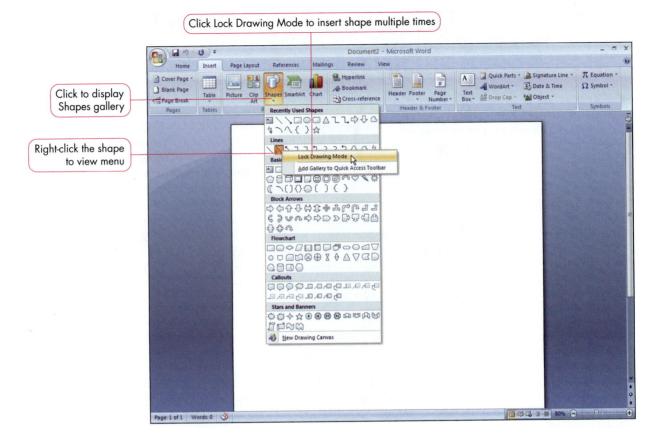

Click Lock Drawing Mode to insert shape multiple times

Click to display
Shapes gallery

Right-click the shape
to view menu

Figure 6.13 Lock Drawing Mode

TIP   Inserting Additional Shapes

The Format tab includes the Insert Shapes group, which displays a small gallery of shapes you can insert. If the small gallery does not display the shape you want, you can click More to view the complete gallery of shapes. This enables you to insert shapes without returning to the Insert tab.

Inserting SmartArt

SmartArt is a diagram that presents information visually to effectively communicate a message.

Using shapes and text allows you to draw attention to your document; however, it is very time-consuming to use these tools to create a complex and designer-quality illustration. Word includes **SmartArt**, which enables you to create a diagram and enter the text of your message in one of many existing layouts in order visually and effectively to communicate your message. For example, you might insert a SmartArt diagram of an organizational chart or food pyramid into your document to illustrate an important concept that is difficult to explain with simple text but easy to understand when viewed in an illustration. When you insert a SmartArt diagram in your document, you can select from several existing layouts and it will conform to any theme you select for your document (see Figure 6.14).

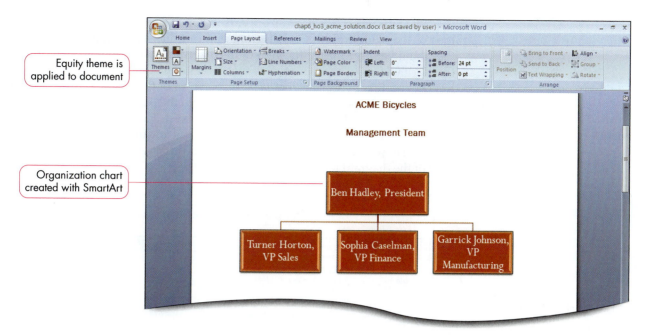

Equity theme is applied to document

Organization chart created with SmartArt

Figure 6.14 A SmartArt diagram

To insert SmartArt into your document, click the Insert tab, click SmartArt, and then click on one of the diagrams that display in the gallery. A short description displays at the side of the gallery pane when you click one of the diagrams, as shown in Figure 6.15. When you select the type and subtype of diagram you want to create, click OK.

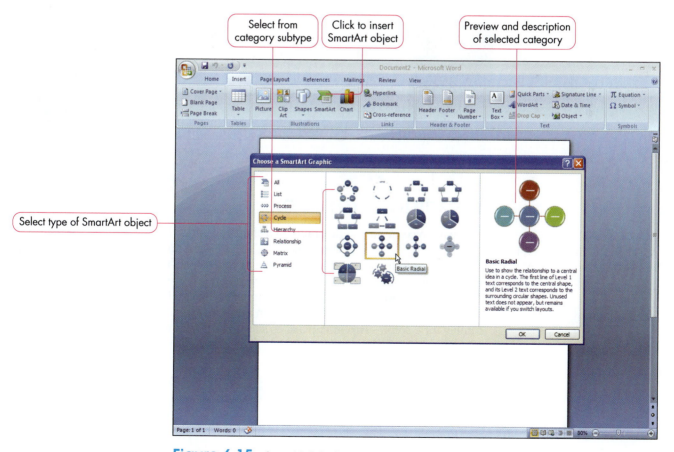

Select from category subtype

Click to insert SmartArt object

Preview and description of selected category

Select type of SmartArt object

Figure 6.15 SmartArt Gallery

When the SmartArt diagram appears in your document, placeholders display for the text that will display in the diagram. You can click a placeholder and type the text that should appear in that location in the diagram. If you do not prefer to type over the placeholders, you can also click the arrows on the left side of the diagram frame to view the Text pane. The **Text pane** displays an outline view of the text items and enables you to type or insert additional text into the outline. The Design and Format tabs also display when you select a SmartArt object. The Design tab provides tools to change the appearance of the diagram, such as adding shapes and changing the style, as shown in Figure 6.16. The Format tab provides tools to modify the appearance of the diagram text.

The **Text pane** is a special pane that opens up for entering text when a SmartArt diagram is selected.

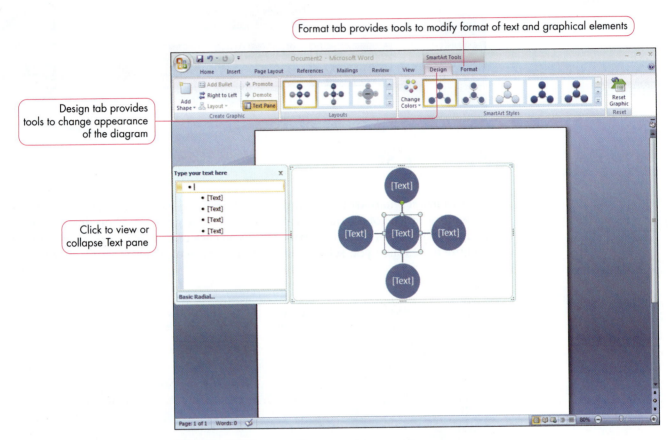

Figure 6.16 Format Options for SmartArt

Inserting a Text Box

A **text box** is simply a graphical object that contains text.

One way to combine the flexibility of a shape object with simple text is to create a text box. A **text box** is simply a graphical object that contains text. Magazine and newspaper articles often use text boxes as a visual tool to entice readers to focus on the contents of the text box, which then encourages them to read the accompanying article. Besides the obvious benefit of displaying text, you can layer it with other shapes. For example, you can position a text box on a callout shape object, and use it as a dialog bubble for a comic strip or clip art, as shown in Figure 6.17.

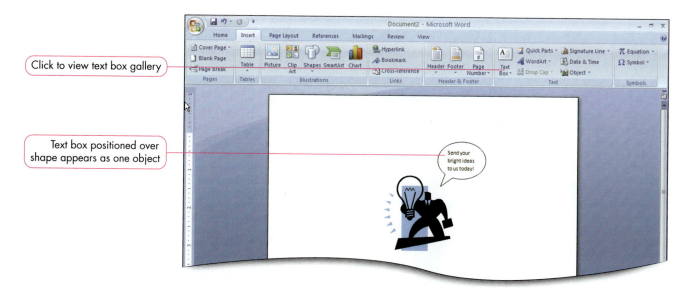

Click to view text box gallery

Text box positioned over shape appears as one object

Figure 6.17 Insert a Text Box

To insert a text box, click the Insert Tab, and then click Text Box. A gallery of pre-formatted text boxes, ready for use as Pull Quotes, displays and you can click one of those or click Draw Text Box to create a plain box with your own dimensions. Because it is a graphical object, you can apply graphical formatting options such as wrapping style, horizontal alignment, and outside borders. When you click a text box, the Format tab displays, enabling you to customize the border of the text box (you can give it a colored border, or no border at all), shadow and 3-D effects, and positional attributes such as how the text box displays on the page and how text wraps around the text box. You can format the text using font properties you are already familiar with, such as size, type, and color, and you also can change the direction text displays within the text box.

You can link one text box to another so that when text runs out of space in one box it automatically continues into another, as shown in Figure 6.18. The best use for linking text boxes is creating a booklet. Each page contains two text boxes that contain the booklet text. Because booklets print on both sides of the paper, the text boxes will link in such a way that the text will flow from the back of one page to the front of another. When you view the pages in Word, they appear out of order, but when assembled for the booklet, they display correctly.

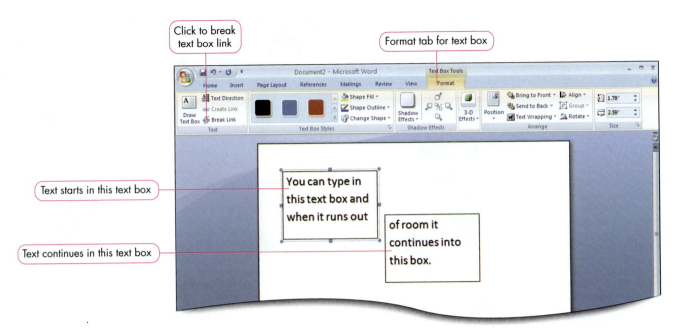

Figure 6.18   Linking Text Boxes

Formatting Graphical Objects

After you insert a shape, SmartArt, or text box, you can enhance its appearance by using one of the commands available on the Format tab for the object. Shapes and text boxes display initially with a simple black border and white fill. Seldom will you want to use such a plain-looking graphic, so you can add color or fill effects, as well as change the border style.

Use Quick Styles

A **Quick Style** is a combination of different formatting options available in the Quick Styles gallery.

The fastest way to change the look of a graphical object is to use a **Quick Style**—a combination of different formatting options—which is available in the Quick Style gallery. When you click a graphical object, and then click the Format tab, the Quick Styles display on the tab. You can display the gallery, and then hold your mouse pointer over a style to preview it on the object, as shown in Figure 6.19. When you find a style you prefer, click to apply the style.

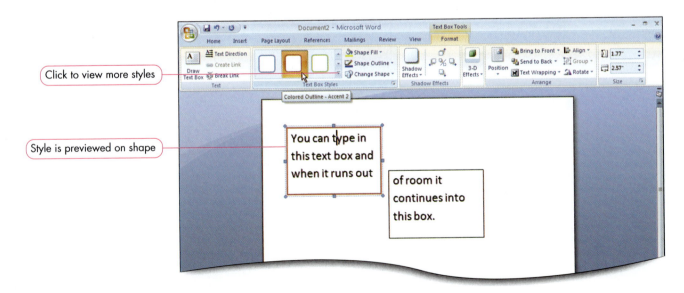

Figure 6.19   Preview Quick Styles on a Shape

Change Shape Fills and Borders

The ***fill*** is the interior space of an object.

Drawing shapes and text boxes have two main components that can contain color: the line or border and the *fill*, or interior space of the object. You might prefer to choose the line and fill colors for your objects instead of using the Quick Styles. You have so many options to use for line and fill that it can be overwhelming. The following reference charts demonstrate several border and fill options. Shapes such as a straight line obviously do not contain an interior area for applying a fill color, but you can change the color, width, and style of the line itself.

Border and Line Options | Reference

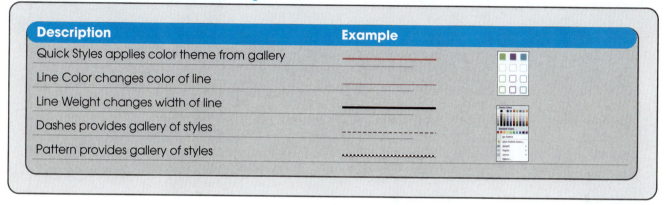

Description	Example	
Quick Styles applies color theme from gallery		
Line Color changes color of line		
Line Weight changes width of line		
Dashes provides gallery of styles		
Pattern provides gallery of styles		

Fill Options for a Shape | Reference

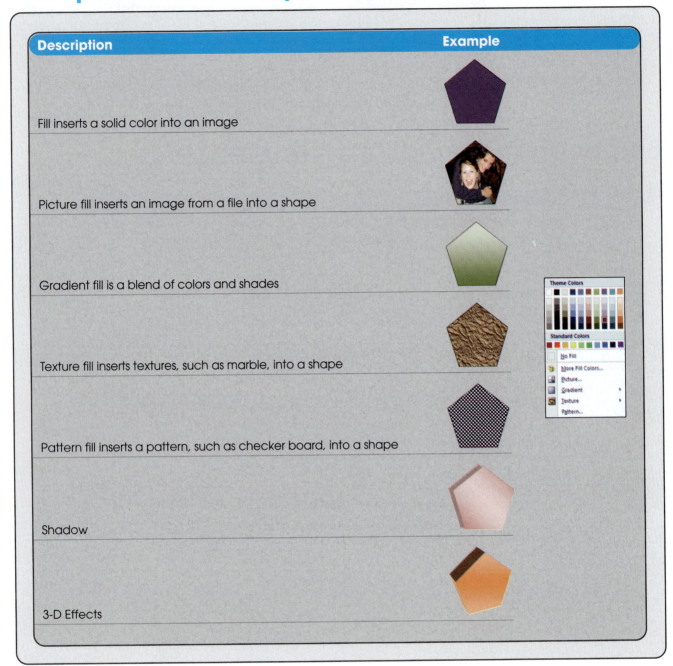

Description	Example
Fill inserts a solid color into an image	
Picture fill inserts an image from a file into a shape	
Gradient fill is a blend of colors and shades	
Texture fill inserts textures, such as marble, into a shape	
Pattern fill inserts a pattern, such as checker board, into a shape	
Shadow	
3-D Effects	

The **Drawing Canvas** is a frame-like area that helps you keep parts of your drawing together.

Grouping and Layering Objects

One reason it is fun to work with shapes is because you can manipulate them in so many different ways. You have already seen how to manipulate their appearance. Not only can you format and manipulate a single shape or object, but you can manipulate several objects together.

When you work with several graphical objects, you might find that you need to arrange them so that one covers a portion of another. This process is appropriately called *layering* because objects are basically stacked on each other. However, the reason for layering is to enable you to separate a complex grouping of objects so you can format and revise each object individually. It is similar to working on a project on a desk: You pick up a piece of paper and place it on top of another piece. At any time, you can rearrange the order of the papers, write on one, or add to the stack of papers on your desk. Figure 6.20 shows two objects that are layered.

Layering is the process of placing one shape on top of another.

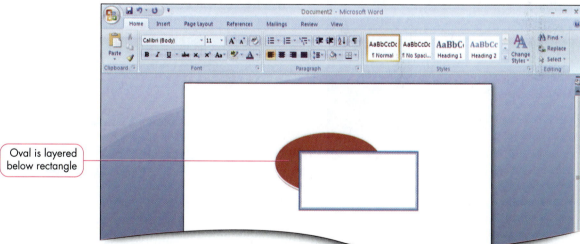

Oval is layered below rectangle

Figure 6.20 Layering Objects

As you work with shapes in Word, you can bring a shape to the front by one layer, push a shape back by one layer, move a shape to the front of all layers, or push a shape to the back of all layers. The commands in Table 6.1 are very valuable when you layer objects and are found in the Arrange group on the Format tab.

Table 6.1 Layering Options

Bring to Front	Moves an object to the top of all other objects
Bring Forward	Places an object on top of the object directly in front of it
Bring in Front of Text	Enables an object to display in front of text
Send to Back	Moves an object to the back of all other objects
Send Backward	Places an object behind the object directly in front of it
Send Behind Text	Enables an object to display behind text

Grouping is the process of combining objects so they appear as a single object.

After you layer objects, you might need to group them so you can manipulate them more easily. *Grouping* is the process of combining selected objects so that they appear as a single object. When objects are grouped, you can move them together or apply a quick style to all the objects at one time. To select multiple objects for grouping, click one object, hold down Shift, and then click the remaining objects. After you select all the objects, click Group on the Format tab, as shown in Figure 6.21.

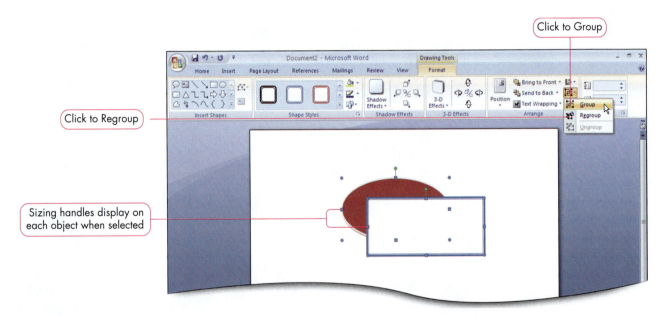

Figure 6.21 Grouping Objects

Ungrouping breaks a combined single object into individual objects.

You can separate grouped objects by ungrouping them. *Ungrouping* breaks a combined single object into individual objects. You might ungroup objects because you need to make modifications to an individual object, such as size or position. Or you might want to delete or add another object to the group. After you ungroup, Word remembers how you grouped the objects originally and enables you to regroup them. *Regrouping* is the process of grouping objects together again. Regrouping only works with the objects you group initially. If you want to add another object to the group, use the Group command instead of Regroup.

Regrouping is the process of grouping objects together again.

You can quickly change the grouping or layering of an object by right-clicking on the object. When the menu displays, click Grouping to view the Group commands, or click Order to view the layering commands.

Flipping and Rotating Objects

If you insert a shape and then decide that it should be turned a different direction, you can quickly make that modification. Word makes it easy to flip or rotate an object using tools on the Format tab. When you click the Rotate command, you select from several commands that enable you to rotate the object in a particular direction, or to flip it in such a way that you get a mirror image. If you click the last command in the list, More Rotate Options, a dialog box displays and you can use precise measurements to modify the object. Figure 6.22 demonstrates the different Rotate commands.

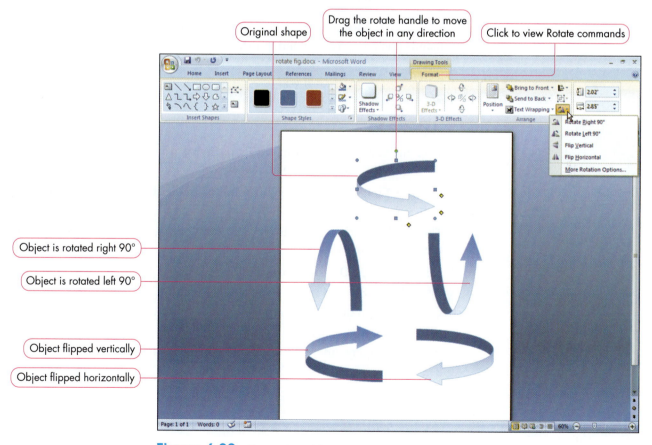

Figure 6.22   Examples of Rotating an Object

Hands-On Exercises

2 | Work with Objects

Skills covered: 1. Create the Autoshape and Apply Formatting **2.** Create a Text Box **3.** Layer and Group Drawing Objects **4.** Insert SmartArt

<table>
<tr>
<td>

Step 1

Create the Autoshape and Apply Formatting

</td>
<td>

Refer to Figure 6.23 as you complete Step 1.

a. Open the *chap6_ho1_newsletter_solution* document, if you closed it after the last hands-on exercise, and save it as **chap6_ho2_newsletter_solution**.

b. Drag the **Zoom slider** to **100%**. Click the **Insert tab**, click **Shapes**, and click **Horizontal Scroll** in the Stars and Banners set.

This shape is on the very bottom row, second from the left. After you click the shape, the mouse cursor takes the form of a cross-hair.

c. Click and drag the mouse at the bottom of the newsletter to create a scroll that extends across the width of the page. If necessary, click the **Height** box and type **.7**, and click the **Width** box and type **6.8**.

The scroll remains selected after you release the mouse, as indicated by the sizing handles. You can click and drag the yellow diamond to change the appearance of the scroll. Additionally, the Format tab displays a variety of formatting commands, including Height and Width.

TROUBLESHOOTING: If you release the mouse before the scroll is the desired size, click the sizing handles to stretch it to the desired size or just type in the Height and Width.

d. Click the **Shape Fill arrow** in the Shape Styles group on the Format tab. Click the color **White, Background 1, Darker 25%** in the first column.

e. Click the **Shape Fill arrow** again, point to **Gradient**, and then click **Linear Up** from the Light Variations section.

The scroll color changes to display a gray color that gradually lightens as it nears the top of the object.

f. Click the **Shape Outline arrow** in the Shape Styles group, point to **Weight**, and then click **2¼ pt**.

g. Click **Rotate** in the Arrange group and click **Flip Vertical**.

The last two steps enhance the outline of the object and flip it so that the edges of the scroll display differently. Compare your object to Figure 6.23.

h. Save the document.

</td>
</tr>
</table>

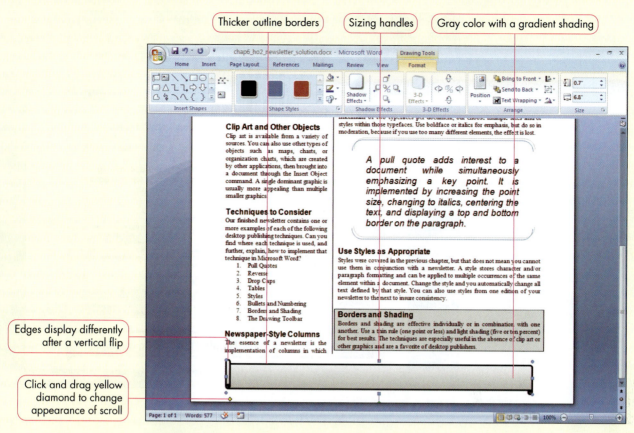

Figure 6.23 Create and Format a Shape Object

Step 2	Refer to Figure 6.24 as you complete Step 2.
Create a Text Box	

a. Click the **Insert tab**, click **Text Box** in the Text group, and then click **Draw Text Box**.

The mouse pointer changes to a cross-hair.

b. Click and drag within the banner object so the text box displays directly in front of it. The text box should be slightly smaller.

c. Type **All the News that Fits** in the text box. Press **Ctrl+E** to center the text in the box.

d. Select the text, click the **Font Size down arrow** on the Mini toolbar, and then click **20**. Click the **Font list box arrow** and click **Lucida Calligraphy**.

TROUBLESHOOTING: If you do not have the Lucida Calligraphy font installed on your computer, feel free to substitute a different font.

e. Click the **Format tab**, click **Shape Fill** in the Text Box Styles group, and click **No Fill**. Click **Shape Outline**, then click **No Outline**, as shown in Figure 6.24.

Removing the fill and outline gives the impression that the text is a part of the banner, instead of a separate object.

f. Click the **sizing handles** and drag to the right and left so the width of the text box is approximately the same width as the banner object. Click anywhere to deselect the text box.

g. Save the document.

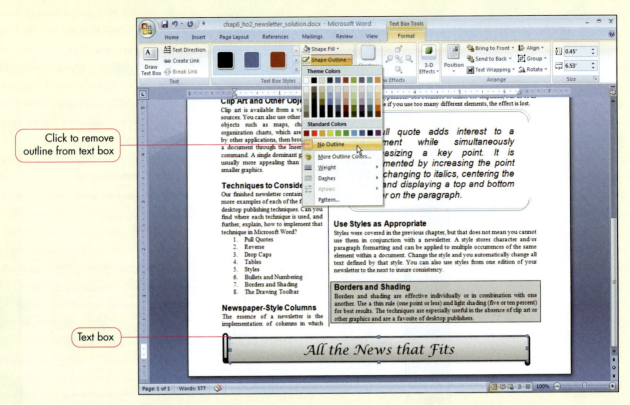

Figure 6.24 Create and Format a Text Box

Step 3

Layer and Group Drawing Objects

Refer to Figure 6.25 as you complete Step 3.

a. Click the text box so that the sizing handles display. Move your mouse over the blue dashed text box border until the mouse pointer displays as a four-headed arrow. Click the border and drag the text box down so that it appears over only half of the banner.

b. Click **Send to Back** in the Arrange group on the Format tab.

The banner displays on top of the text. The text box is now behind the banner object.

c. Click **Bring to Front** to return the text to the front of the banner.

d. Hold down **Ctrl** and press **up arrow** to nudge the text box back into the middle of the banner. Use the right and left arrow keys as needed to center the text box horizontally in the banner.

Using the Ctrl+arrow combination provides much-needed assistance in positioning an object very precisely.

e. Press **Shift**, and then select the banner.

Both objects, the banner and the text box, should be selected and sizing handles for both objects display, as shown in Figure 6.25.

f. Click **Group** in the Arrange group on the Format tab, and then click **Group**.

Only one set of sizing handles displays because the two objects appear as one.

g. Save and close the document.

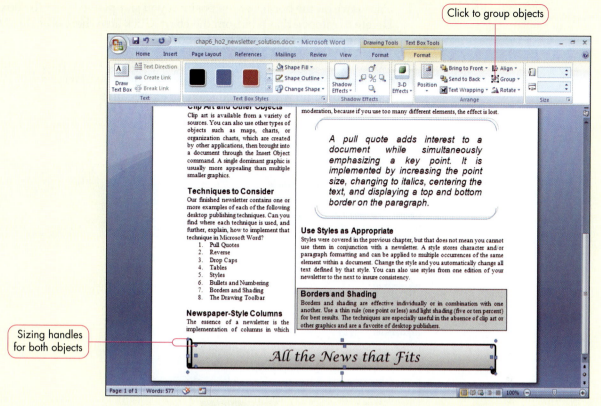

Figure 6.25 Grouping Objects

Step 4
Insert SmartArt

Refer to Figure 6.26 as you complete Step 4.

a. Press **Ctrl+N** to open a new document and save it as **chap6_ho2_acme_ solution**.

b. Type **ACME Bicycles** on the first line of the document. Press **Enter** two times, type **Management Team**, and then press **Enter** two times. Select both lines and click the **Heading 1 Quick Style** on the Home tab. Click **Center** on the Paragraph group of the Home tab.

c. Press **Ctrl+End** to move the insertion point to the end of the document. Click the **Insert tab**, and then in the Illustrations group, click **SmartArt**.

The Choose a SmartArt Graphic dialog box displays with a list of categories on the left side of the box. Your document will include an organizational chart, so you will select a style accordingly.

d. Click **Hierarchy**, click **Organization Chart**, and then click **OK**.

A representation of the organizational chart displays in your document. If the Text pane does not display, click the Text pane arrows to expand the text pane.

e. Click in the first bullet in the Text pane and type **Ben Hadley, President**. Skip the next entry, which is the position that displays on the left side of the chart. In the last three bullets, type the following names:

Turner Horton, VP Sales

Sophia Caselman, VP Finance

Garrick Johnson, VP Manufacturing

Your chart should look like the chart in Figure 6.26.

f. Click once on the border of the position you skipped to select the box. Press **Delete** to remove that box from the chart. Click anywhere outside of the chart to hide the sizing handles and the Text pane.

g. Save *chap6_ho2_acme_solution* and keep it onscreen if you plan to continue with the next hands-on exercise. Close *chap6_ho2_acme_solution* and exit Word if you will not continue with the next exercise at this time.

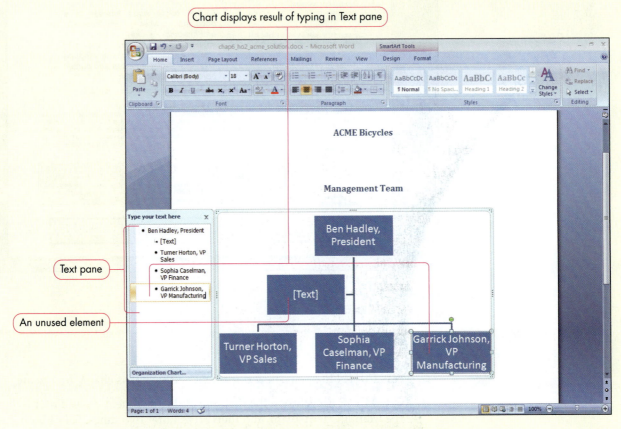

Figure 6.26 Insert a SmartArt Object

Object Linking and Embedding

Microsoft Office enables you to create documents that contain objects from other applications. For example, you might create a report in Word that explains the results of a survey. The data from the survey are saved in an Excel spreadsheet that also includes a chart to summarize the data. You can insert the chart into your Word document, thus combining the object that displays the data with the explanation. The document in Figure 6.27 is a Microsoft Word document that contains objects (a worksheet and a chart) developed in Microsoft Excel. The technology that enables you to insert objects or information into different applications is called *Object Linking and Embedding* (abbreviated OLE, it is pronounced "oh-lay").

> Microsoft Office enables you to create documents that contain objects from other applications. The technology that enables you to insert objects is called Object Linking and Embedding.

Object Linking and Embedding (OLE) is a technology that enables you to insert objects into different applications.

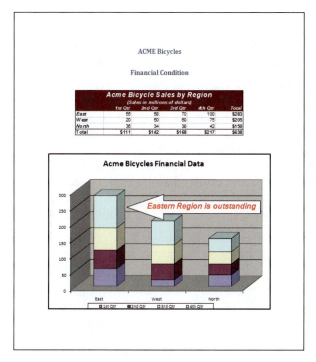

Figure 6.27   Document Containing Linked and Embedded Objects

In this section, you explore the many ways to embed and link an object, and then you learn to update a linked object.

Using OLE to Insert an Object

Embedding pulls an object into a document where you can edit it without changing the source.

When you insert objects into your document, you really have two options on how the object will work within your document. The first option is *embedding*, which enables you to insert and then edit the object within Word. Embedding pulls an object into a document from its original source and enables you to edit it without changing the source. For example, if you copy and paste text from another location, you embed it in your document, but it does not change the source. Additionally, if you embed a portion of an Excel worksheet, it becomes part of your document; you can make modifications to it at any time, and those changes do not affect the original worksheet. Likewise, any changes to the original Excel file will not display in your document.

Linking inserts an object from another program, but retains a connection to the original data.

The second option for inserting an object into your document involves linking. *Linking* is the process of inserting an object from another program, but the object retains a connection to the original data and file. If you change the data in the original source application, you can also quickly update the data in the destination program to reflect the changes. A linked object is stored in its own file and may be tied to many documents. The same Excel chart, for example, can be linked to a Word document and a PowerPoint presentation. Any changes to the Excel chart are automatically reflected in the document and the presentation to which it is linked.

The advantage of linking over embedding is that a linked object will reflect the most current information. This might be important, for example, when you insert the most current stock prices for your company into your weekly newsletter. An embedded object is a snapshot of the information at the time you embedded it; if that is sufficient for your document, it is a good option to use because you don't have to worry about having access to the source file at a later date. If you want to display the previous year-ending sales figures in your January newsletter, you would embed the data because those numbers won't change.

You have several methods to link and embed data into a document including:

- Copy and Paste
- Drag and Drop
- Display the Insert tab and click Object

If you use the Copy and Paste method, you first copy a selection from the source, such as an Excel spreadsheet or a PowerPoint slide, and then you use Paste to insert it into the destination document. If you use a simple paste command, the object will be embedded. When you paste Excel data into Word, the data are pasted into table cells and do not retain Excel spreadsheet capabilities and formatting. For example, all formulas and functions convert to actual values, and if you change one value it will not change any results that use that value. Additionally, the numbers will not align on the decimal points. If you click Paste Special, you can invoke the Paste link option, as shown in Figure 6.28, which creates the connection to the original file.

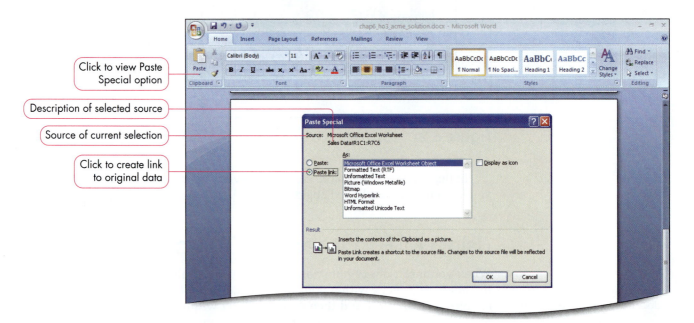

Figure 6.28 The Paste Special Dialog Box

If you use the drag-and-drop method, you display both source and destination documents simultaneously, click the object in the source, and then drag and drop it in the destination. It is important to note that when you want to copy the object from the source to the destination, then you must hold down Ctrl while dragging. If you do not hold down Ctrl during the entire drag-and-drop process, you will move the object instead of copying it.

You can insert an object, such as an Excel workbook, as an object within a Word document without opening the file in Excel. The contents of the entire Excel workbook, which may contain several worksheets, appear as an object in Word. To use this method, click the Insert tab, and then click Object. The Object dialog box displays, as shown in Figure 6.29, with two tabs across the top. Click the Create from File tab to browse to the location of the file you want to insert.

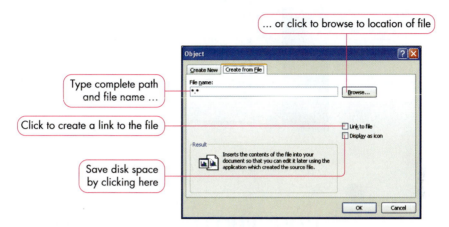

Figure 6.29   The Create from File tab in the Object Dialog Box

TIP   Displaying a Link as an Icon

You can save disk space by inserting the link as an icon instead of displaying the actual linked data. When you are selecting options in the Paste Special dialog box or the Object dialog box, click the Display as icon check box.

The Create New tab, in the Object dialog box, is helpful when you do not have an existing file to insert as an object. The Object type list box displays many types of objects you can create; however, you can only create the object if the respective application, such as Microsoft Excel, is installed on your computer. When you click the Object type, a small window displays (see Figure 6.30), and you can create the content for the object that will display in your document. After it displays in your document, you can edit it by double-clicking the object.

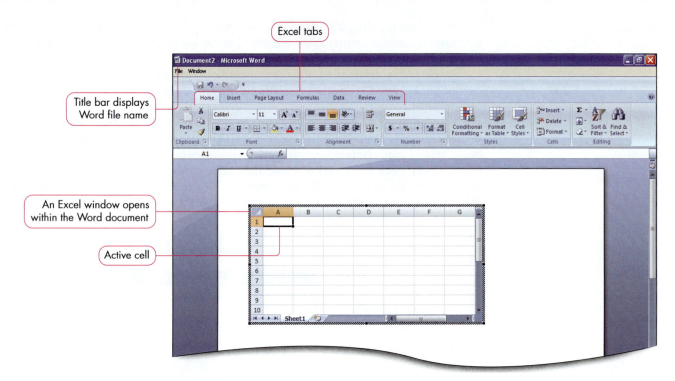

Figure 6.30   Create a New Object

Updating a Linked Object

After you link an object into your document, you can still make modifications to the source file. At any time, you can open a source file in its native application—Microsoft Excel, for example—to make modifications. But you can also open the application by clicking the linked object in a Word document. To use this method, right-click on the linked object in your document, point to Linked Worksheet Object, and then select Edit Link or Open Link, as shown in Figure 6.31. When you click Edit Link, the editing tools display and you can make modifications to the object from within Word. If you click Open Link, the application starts and displays the complete interface and Ribbon.

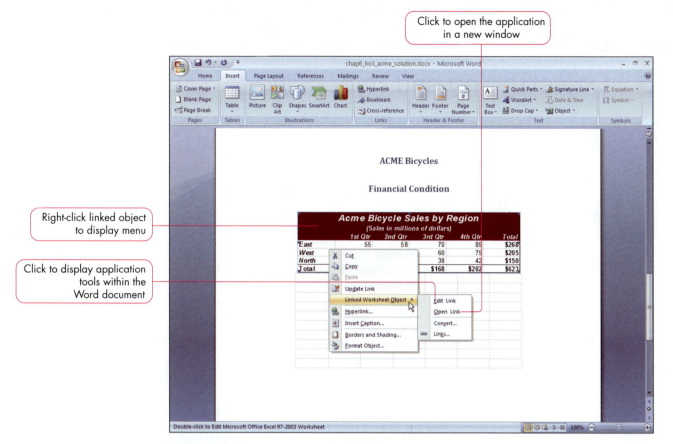

Figure 6.31 Updating a Linked Object

If you linked an object into the document, there is also an Update Link command in the menu, as shown in Figure 6.31. When you click Update Link, Word retrieves the most updated form of the object from the source; any changes in the source file will display in the Word document. Some updates to the source do not display automatically, so this provides you the ability to check and update.

Hands-On Exercises

3 | Object Linking and Embedding

Skills covered: 1. Copy and Link a Worksheet **2.** Change the Source Data and Update the Document **3.** Embed and Modify an Excel Chart

---

Step 1
Copy and Link a Worksheet

Refer to Figure 6.32 as you complete Step 1.

a. Open the *chap6_ho2_acme_solution* document if you closed it after the last hands-on exercise and save it as **chap6_ho3_acme_solution**.

b. Click **Ctrl+End** to move the insertion point to the bottom of the page. Click **Ctrl+Enter** to insert a new page. Type **ACME Bicycles**, press **Enter**, type **Financial Condition**, and then press **Enter** two times. Select the two lines of text, click **Heading 1** in the Quick Styles gallery, and then click **Center**.

   In the next step, you open an Excel workbook. You might find it easier to work with the Excel spreadsheet if you minimize your Word document. Don't forget to save your document.

c. Click the **Start button**, click **All Programs**, click **Microsoft Office**, and then click **Microsoft Office Excel 2007**. Open the *chap6_ho3_acme* workbook in the Exploring Word folder and save it as **chap6_ho3_acme_solution**.

   The file displays in an Excel window. The taskbar now contains buttons for both Word and Excel; click either button to move back and forth between the applications.

d. Click the **Sales Data worksheet tab**. Click and drag to select cells **A1–F7**.

e. Click **Copy** in the Clipboard group on the Home tab (or click **Ctrl+C**).

   A moving border displays around the selection, indicating it has been copied to the Clipboard, as shown in Figure 6.32.

f. Click the Word button on the taskbar to return to the Word document. Press **Ctrl+End** to place the insertion point at the end of the document, where you will insert the Excel worksheet.

g. Click the **Paste down arrow** in the Clipboard group on the Home tab. Click **Paste Special** to display the Paste Special dialog box. In the As list, click **Microsoft Office Excel Worksheet Object**.

h. Click **Paste Link** on the left side of the dialog box, and then click **OK**.

   TROUBLESHOOTING: If you do not see the Update Link option when you right-click an object, it is not linked to the source. Click Undo on the Quick Access Toolbar, and then repeat Steps G and H, making sure you click Paste Special and Paste Link.

i. Press **Enter** two times to create blank lines between the worksheet and the chart you will insert next.

j. Save the document.

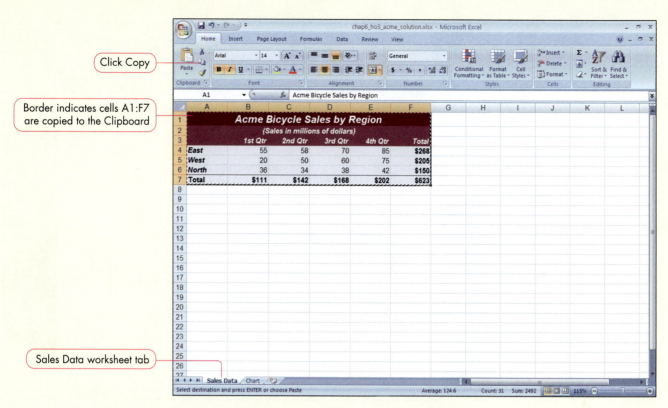

Click Copy

Border indicates cells A1:F7
are copied to the Clipboard

Sales Data worksheet tab

Figure 6.32 Copy Data from an Excel Worksheet

Step 2

Change the Source Data and Update the Document

Refer to Figure 6.33 as you complete Step 2.

a. Click the **Excel button** on the taskbar to return to the worksheet. Press **Esc** to deselect the cells.

b. Click cell E4, type **100**, and press **Enter**.

c. Save the workbook.

d. Click the Word button on the taskbar to return to the Word document. If necessary, right-click the chart and click **Update Link**, as shown in Figure 6.33.

The linked object reflects the changes you made in the Excel workbook.

e. Click the object to select it and click **Center** in the Paragraph group on the Home tab.

f. Save the document.

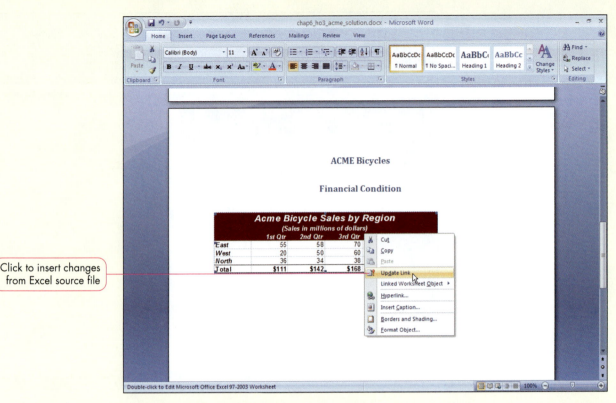

Figure 6.33 Update Linked Data

Step 3

Embed and Modify an Excel Chart

Refer to Figure 6.34 as you complete Step 3.

a. Click the **Excel button** on the taskbar to return to the worksheet. Click the **Chart tab** to select the chart sheet.

b. Point just inside the white border of the chart, then click the left mouse button to select the chart. Be sure the selection border displays around the entire chart. Click **Copy**.

> **TROUBLESHOOTING:** If you have trouble selecting the entire chart, click very near one of the four corners.

c. Click the **Word button** on the taskbar to return to the document. Press **Ctrl+End** to move to the end of the document, where you will insert the chart.

d. Click **Paste** (or **Ctrl+V**) to insert the chart into the document.

e. Click the upper-left corner of the chart area to select the chart, and then click the **Format tab**. Click the **Text Wrapping down arrow**, and then click **Square**.

f. Click **Colored Outline – Dark 1** in the **Quick Style gallery** on the **Shape Styles group** to place a black border around the object.

g. Click the white arrow object in the middle of the chart to display sizing handles for that shape only.

The arrow is layered with the text *Eastern Region is*, but the word *outstanding* does not display after you copy it into the document. You will resize the shape object to allow room to display all of the text.

h. Click the middle sizing handle on the right side of the shape and drag to the right until it nears the edge of the gray chart background, as shown in Figure 6.34.

Click the middle sizing handle on the bottom side of the shape and drag down slightly, so there is white space between the bottom of the shape and the text. Continue to resize as needed until the text *Eastern Region is outstanding* displays completely on one line across the arrow.

i. Click the legend at the bottom of the chart so the sizing handles display. Click the middle sizing handle on the right side and drag to the right until all four legend elements display. Drag the box that contains the legend to the left until it appears centered in the bottom of the chart.

j. Save and close the *chap6_ho3_acme_solution* document and exit Word.

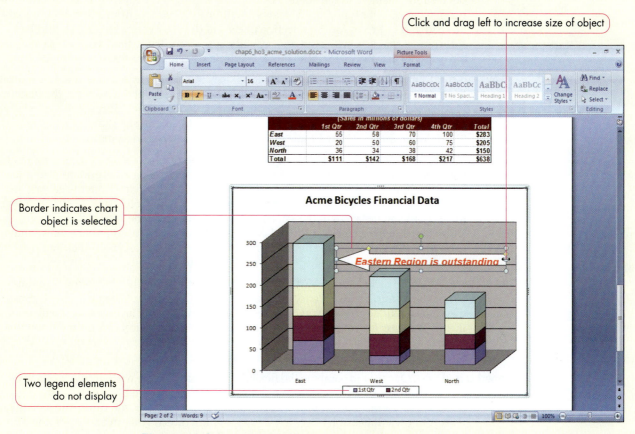

Figure 6.34 Modify an Excel Chart in Word

Summary

1. **Construct a newsletter.** When you use desktop publishing to create a document such as a newsletter, you should use several techniques to enhance readability and attractiveness. You can create a masthead to display at the top of the page to introduce the document and use a reverse to enhance the appearance. When used in moderation, clip art, pull quotes, sidebars, and drop caps will catch the reader's eye and enhance almost any newsletter. Borders and shading are effective individually, or in combination with one another, to emphasize important stories within the newsletter. Lists, whether bulleted or numbered, help to organize information by emphasizing important topics. Typography is a critical, often subtle, element in the success of a document; good typography goes almost unnoticed, whereas poor typography draws attention and detracts from a document. There are no hard and fast rules for the selection of type and style—your objective should be to create a document that is easy to read and visually appealing. Try to limit yourself to a maximum of two fonts per document, but choose multiple sizes and/or styles.

2. **Develop a document design.** A grid establishes the overall structure of a document by indicating the number of columns, the space between columns, the size of the margins, the placement of headlines, art, and so on. The grid does not appear in the printed document—you draw or sketch it on a piece of paper to solidify the layout prior to creating the newsletter in Word. Good design makes it easy for the reader to determine what is important.

3. **Insert drawing shapes.** A shape is a geometric or nongeometric object, such as a circle or an arrow, that you can use as a visual enhancement. You can use one shape or combine multiple shapes to create a more complex image. To insert a shape, select the shape from the gallery, and then position the mouse pointer in your document where you want to place the shape. If you need to insert several instances of the same shape, click Shapes on the Insert tab, right-click the shape object in the gallery, and click Lock Drawing Mode. To insert a shape, select the shape from the gallery, position the mouse pointer in the document, and then click and drag the cross-hair pointer until the shape is the size you desire.

4. **Insert SmartArt.** Word includes SmartArt to assist you in creating visually stimulating diagrams to represent your information and effectively communicate a message. When you insert a SmartArt diagram in your document, you can select from several existing layouts, and it will follow any theme you select for your document. The Text pane displays placeholders for the text that displays in a SmartArt diagram. The Design and Format tabs display when you select a SmartArt object, and they offer many options for modifying the appearance of the diagram and text.

5. **Insert a text box.** One way to combine the flexibility of a shape object with simple text is to create a text box. Besides the obvious benefit of displaying text, you can layer it with other shapes. A gallery of preformatted text boxes displays on the Insert tab, or you can create a plain text box with your own dimensions. Because it is a graphical object, you can apply graphical formatting options such as wrapping style, horizontal alignment, and outside borders to a text box.

6. **Format graphical objects.** After you insert a shape, SmartArt, or text box, you can enhance the appearance by using one of the commands available on the Format tab for the object. Shapes and text boxes display initially with a simple black border and white fill. A Quick Style is a combination of different formatting options available in the Quick Styles gallery on the Format tab. Drawing shapes and text boxes have two main components that can contain color: the border and the fill. You might prefer to choose the line and fill colors for your objects instead of using the Quick Styles. If you plan on combining multiple shapes in one area, you should consider using the Drawing Canvas.

7. **Group and layer objects.** Layering is the process of placing one shape on top of another to simplify editing and formatting. When you work with several graphical objects, you might find that you need to arrange them so that one covers a portion of another. After you layer objects, you might need to group them so you can manipulate them more easily. Grouping is the process of combining selected objects so that they appear as a single object. When objects are grouped you can move them simultaneously or apply a Quick Style to all the objects at one time. Ungrouping breaks a combined single object into individual objects. Regrouping is the process of grouping objects together again.

8. **Flip and rotate objects.** If you insert a shape and then decide it should be turned a different direction, you can quickly make that modification. Word makes it easy to flip or rotate an object

...continued on Next Page

using tools on the Format tab. When you click the Rotate command, you can select from several commands that enable you to rotate the object in a particular direction or to flip it in such a way that you get a mirror image.

9. **Use OLE to insert an object.** When you insert objects into your document, you have two options on how the object will work within your document. The first option, embedding, pulls information from its original source into your document, but does not change or maintain a link to that source file. The second option for inserting an object into your document is linking. Linking is the process of inserting an object from another program, but the object retains a connection to the original data and file. If you change the data in the original source program, you can quickly update the data in the destination program to reflect the changes. The advantage of linking over embedding is that a linked object will reflect the most current information. You have several methods to link and embed data into a document, including: Copy and Paste, Drag and Drop, or click the Insert tab and then click Object.

10. **Update a linked object.** After you link an object into your document, you can still make modifications to the source file. At any time, you can open a source file in its native application, Microsoft Excel, for example, to make modifications. But you can also open the application by double-clicking the linked object in a Word document. When you right-click a linked object, the Linked Worksheet Object command provides the Edit Link and Open Link commands. When you click Update Link, Word retrieves the most updated form of the object from the source; any changes in the source file will display in the Word document.

Key Terms

Multiple Choice

1. What format do you see when you use a reverse effect on a masthead?

   (a) Light text on a clear background

   (b) Dark text on a clear background

   (c) Dark text on a light background

   (d) Light text on a dark background

2. What is the minimum number of sections in a three-column newsletter whose masthead extends across all three columns, with text balanced in all three columns?

   (a) One

   (b) Two

   (c) Three

   (d) Four

3. How do you balance the columns in a newsletter so that each column contains the same amount of text?

   (a) Check the Balance Columns box in the Columns dialog box.

   (b) Insert a page break at the end of the last column.

   (c) Manually set the column widths in the Columns dialog box.

   (d) Press Enter until the text lines up at the bottom of each column.

4. Which feature would not be used to add emphasis to a document?

   (a) Pull Quote

   (b) Borders and Shading

   (c) Paste Link

   (d) Bulleted and Numbered List

5. If you need to quickly add a pull quote to your document, which method gives the fastest results?

   (a) Insert a shape object and a text box, then layer and group them.

   (b) Insert a text box, then change the border and shading.

   (c) Select a built-in style from the Text Box gallery.

   (d) Type text, and then use the Highlighter to shade it yellow.

6. Which feature enables you to quickly insert an organizational chart, which you can modify and enhance as needed?

   (a) Word Art

   (b) SmartArt

   (c) Shapes

   (d) Clip Art

7. You insert an arrow shape in your document that points left, but you need it to point right; which command will you use?

   (a) Flip Horizontal

   (b) Rotate Right 90°

   (c) Flip Vertical

   (d) Rotate Left 90°

8. To move several shapes as one object, you should

   (a) Layer the shapes.

   (b) Anchor the shapes.

   (c) Position the shapes.

   (d) Group the shapes.

9. Which graphic object does not use Shape Fill formatting properties?

   (a) Circle

   (b) Square

   (c) Star

   (d) Line

10. Which of the following inserts Excel data in a way that enables you to edit the values in Word, but does not change the source?

    (a) Embedding

    (b) Copying and pasting

    (c) Linking

    (d) E-mailing

11. When you copy an Excel worksheet and paste it into Word, which of the following is not true?

    (a) Values with decimal points might not align in Word.

    (b) You can use the drawing tools on the Format tab to edit the worksheet object.

    (c) The imported data can be formatted as a table.

    (d) Formulas are converted to values.

12. Which process should you use to insert Excel data into Word so that any changes you make to the original Excel worksheet are automatically made in Word?

    (a) Copying and Pasting

    (b) Linking

    (c) Embedding

    (d) E-mailing

13. To quickly determine if a spreadsheet that displays in a Word document is linked to the source file, what can you do?

(a) Click the Insert tab, and then click Object.

(b) Single-click the object.

(c) Click Paste Special.

(d) Right-click the object and look for the Update Link option.

14. If you want to create a link to an object from your Word document, but you want to keep the size of the file as small as possible, which option should you use in the Paste Special dialog box?

(a) Paste link

(b) Display as icon

(c) Paste

(d) HTML Format

15. You just inserted two shape objects into your document; the second object is larger and was inserted on top of the first. What can you do to display the first object on top of the second one?

(a) Click the second (top) object, and then click Bring to Front.

(b) Click the first (bottom) object, and then click Bring to Front.

(c) Click the second (top) object, and then click Send to Back.

(d) Click the second (top) object, and then click Bring in Front of Text.

Practice Exercises

1 Shopping for a Personal Computer

You are a local computer expert who is often called upon to give advice on purchasing a personal computer. Because the basic considerations are the same for everyone, you decide to create a simple newsletter to explain those steps. You want it to look professional, so you use several commands in Word to develop an attractive document that is easy to read and that will make a good handout for anyone who asks how to buy a PC.

a. Open *chap6_pe1_pc* and save it as **chap6_pe1_pc_solution**.

b. Click the **Page Layout tab**, click **Columns** in the Page Setup group, and then click **More Columns**. Click **Two** in the Presets section, click the **Line Between check box**, and then click **OK**.

c. Press **Ctrl+Home** to move the insertion point to the beginning of the document. Click **Breaks** in the Page Setup group, and then click **Continuous**.

d. Click the **Home tab** and click **Show/Hide ¶** to display formatting marks. Move the insertion point to the left side of the section break. Click the **Page Layout tab**, click **Columns**, and then click **One**.

e. Type the text **Shopping for a Personal Computer**, and then click **Enter** two times. Select the text, then click **Center** on the Mini toolbar. Click the **Font arrow** and click **Arial Black**, then click the **Font size** arrow and click **22**.

f. Click the **Home tab**, and then click **Border.** Click **Borders and Shading**, click the **Shading tab**, click the **Style drop-down arrow**, click **Solid (100%)**, and then click **OK**.

g. Press **Ctrl+End** to move the insertion point to the end of the document. Click the **Page Layout tab**, click **Breaks**, and then click **Continuous**. The columns are now balanced, as shown in Figure 6.35.

h. Save and close the document.

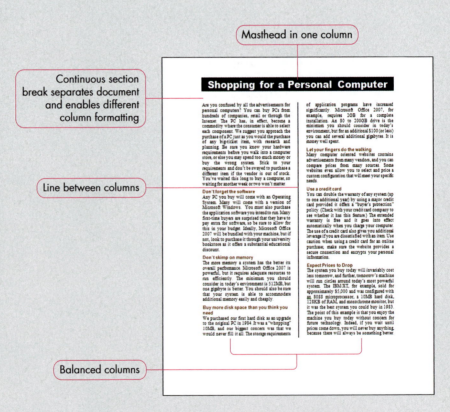

Figure 6.35 Create a Two-Column Newsletter

...continued on Next Page

You enjoyed a very favorable reception from friends who received a copy of the newsletter you created to offer advice for personal computer shopping. However, you realized you are capable of enhancing the document to add even more variety and appeal. In this exercise, you add enhancements to the newsletter you created in Practice Exercise 1.

a. Open *chap6_pe1_pc_solution* and save it as **chap6_pe2_pc_solution**.

b. Click the **Page Layout tab**, click **Margins**, and then click **Custom Margins**. Type **.7** in the Top margin box. Press **Tab** to move the insertion point to the Bottom margin box. Type **.7** and press **Tab** to move to the Left margin box. Type **.7** and press **Tab** to move to the Right margin box. Type **.7**. In the **Apply to** drop-down list, select **Whole document**, and then click **OK**.

c. Select the heading and text for the paragraph titled *Let your fingers do the walking*. Press **Ctrl+X** to cut the paragraph. Click the **Insert tab**, click **Text Box** in the Text group, and then click **Mod Quote**. Click **Ctrl+V** to insert the paragraph you cut in this step.

d. Click the **Format tab**, if necessary. In the Arrange group, click the **Bring to Front down arrow** and click **Bring in Front of Text**.

e. Click the **Shape Height box** and type **2.85**. Click the paragraph heading and text in the pull quote, and then press **Ctrl+E** to center it. If necessary, delete any extra line returns in the pull quote. Select the whole paragraph in the pull quote, click **Font** on the Mini toolbar and select **Arial**. Click the **Font Color arrow** and select **White, Background 1**. Click outside the pull quote to deselect it.

f. Click the **Insert tab**, click **Clip Art**, and then type **computer** in the Search for text box in the Clip Art task pane. Click **Go**. Click the clip of a computer with a blue screen, or substitute as needed. Click the Close button on the task pane. Click the graphic one time, click the Format tab, if necessary, click **Text Wrapping**, and then click **Square**. Click and drag the object to the lower-right side of the left column.

g. Click the **Insert tab**, click **Shapes**, and click the **Explosion1** shape in the Stars and Banners section. Click and drag to create a shape that is approximately the same size as the clip art. Click **More** in the Shape Styles group to display the Quick Styles gallery. Click **Compound Outline – Accent 5**.

h. Click the **Insert tab**, click **Text Box**, and click **Draw Text box**. Click and drag a text box that is almost as large as the explosion. Type **Shop Online** in the text box. Select the text, click the Font Color down arrow on the Mini toolbar, and then click **Dark Blue, Text 2, Lighter 40%**. Click the font size arrow and click **16**. Click the blue dotted line that surrounds the text. Click the border and drag until the text is centered in the explosion shape. Click the **Format tab**, click **Shape Fill**, and then click **No Fill**. Click Shape **Outline**, and then click **No Outline**.

i. Click the text box and drag it to better position the text within the explosion shape, if necessary. Click the text box, press and hold **Shift**, and click the explosion shape. Right-click the mouse, point to **Grouping**, and click **Group**. Click anywhere outside the explosion shape to deselect it.

j. Click the **Home tab**, click **Borders**, then click **Borders and Shading**. Click the **Page Border tab**, click a double line style, click the **Width drop-down arrow,** and then click **2¼ pt**. Click **Box** in the Setting section, and then click **OK**. Click the **Home tab**, then click **Show/Hide ¶** to remove formatting marks, if necessary. Compare your work to Figure 6.36.

k. Save and close the document.

...continued on Next Page

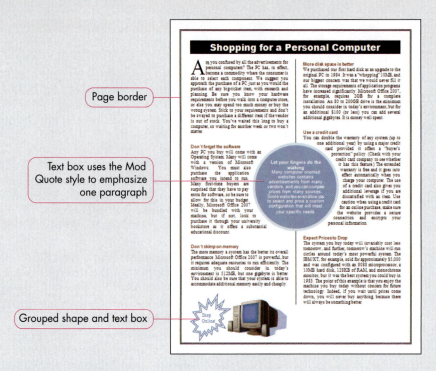

Page border

Text box uses the Mod Quote style to emphasize one paragraph

Grouped shape and text box

Figure 6.36 Enhanced Two-Column Newsletter

3 Enhancing a Financial Report

You are the lead financial analyst for a technology manufacturing organization, and each year you are responsible for preparing a summary of the annual report. After you summarize the main points, you decide the report should include a chart and graph to emphasize certain points as well as give a visual summary of the information. You begin this exercise by opening the general summary, and then you add data from an Excel spreadsheet that contains the information you want to summarize.

a. Open *chap6_pe3_report* and save it as **chap6_pe3_report_solution**.

b. Click once to place the insertion point on the line just above the heading *Capital Expenditures*. Click the **Insert tab**, click **Object**, and then click **Create from File**. Click **Browse**, and then browse your storage devices to find and select *chap6_pe3_dividends.xlsx*. Click **Insert** in the Browse dialog box. Click **OK** in the Object dialog box and scroll down to the next page to view the object, if necessary.

c. Double-click the worksheet object, and then click cell **F5**. Type **10.00**, and then press **Enter**. Click anywhere outside the object to save the change. Click the object one time to display sizing handles, and then click **Center** on the Home tab (or press **Ctrl+E**).

d. Minimize Word and start Microsoft Excel. Open *chap6_pe3_dividends.xlsx*. Click the *Expenses* worksheet tab at the bottom of the Excel window.

e. Position the mouse pointer over cell A4. When the mouse pointer resembles a big plus sign, click and drag down and over to cell C8, which contains the total $265. Click **Copy** in the Clipboard group on the Home tab (or press **Ctrl+C**).

f. Click the Word button on the Windows taskbar to toggle back to the *chap6_pe3_report_solution* document. Click once on the line following the Capital Expenditures paragraph.

g. Click the **Home tab**, if necessary, and then click the **Paste down arrow** in the Clipboard group. Click **Paste Special** to display the Paste Special dialog box. In the As list, click **Microsoft Office Excel Worksheet Object**. Click **Paste Link** on the left side of the window, and then click **OK**.

...continued on Next Page

h. Click the linked object to display sizing handles. Right-click the object, and then click **Format Object**. Click the **Layout tab**, and then click **Square wrapping style**. Under **Horizontal alignment**, click **Center**, and then click **OK.**

i. Click once on the blank line above the *Dividends* heading. Click the Excel button on the Windows taskbar to toggle to the *chap6_pe3_dividends.xlsx* workbook. Save the workbook as **chap6_pe3_dividends_solution.xlsx**.

j. If the moving border remains on the range you copied earlier, press **Esc**. Click the *Earnings* worksheet tab at the bottom of the Excel window. Position the mouse pointer in the white space on the right side of the chart title *Earnings from Continuing Operations*, and then click one time to select the entire chart. Click **Copy** on the Home tab.

k. Click the Word button on the Windows taskbar to toggle back to the *chap6_pe3_report_solution* document. Click the **Home tab**, if necessary, and then click the **Paste down arrow** in the Clipboard group. Click **Paste Special** to display the Paste Special dialog box. In the As list, click **Microsoft Office Excel Chart Object**. Click **Paste Link** on the left side of the window, and then click **OK.**

l. Right-click the white space near the top of the chart, point to **Linked Worksheet Object**, and then click **Open Link**. In the Earnings tab of the Excel worksheet, click cell **F5**, type **270**, and then press **Enter**.

m. Click the Word button on the Windows taskbar to toggle back to the *chap6_pe3_report_solution* document. Right-click the white space near the top of the chart, click **Update Link**, and notice that the column for 2012 increases in height. Drag the Zoom slider in the Status bar to **55%**. Compare your document to Figure 6.37.

n. Save and close all documents.

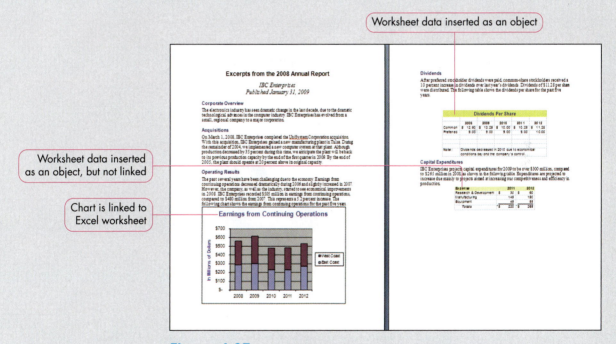

Figure 6.37   Insert Excel Data and Graphs into a Financial Summary

4 Design a Radial Diagram

As an advisor for Business Information Systems (BIS) students, you want to create a simple diagram that shows some of the careers available for BIS majors. You decide to use SmartArt to quickly create a radial diagram. The process is quick and easy, so you can add, remove, or change the diagram, when necessary, to reflect any changes in the program.

...continued on Next Page

a. Open a new document. Save it as **chap6_pe4_careers_solution**.

b. At the top of the document, type **Business Information Systems Careers**. Select the text and on the Mini toolbar, click the **Font size** arrow and click **26**. Click **Bold**, and then click **Center** on the Mini toolbar. Move your insertion point to the end of the text and press **Enter** two times.

c. Click the **Insert tab**, click **SmartArt**, click **Relationship** on the left side of the Choose a SmartArt Graphic dialog box, and then double-click **Diverging Radial** in the third column of the sixth row.

d. Click one time in the middle circle and type **BIS Majors**. In the circle on the top, click one time, and then type **Web Designers**. Click one time on the circle on the right side and type **Network Managers**. Click one time on the circle on the bottom and type **Database Managers**. Click one time on the circle on the left and type **College Instructors**.

e. Click **Add Shape** in the Create Graphic group on the Design tab, and then click **Add Shape After** to insert an additional circle into the diagram.

f. Click once in the new shape and type **Systems Analysts**.

g. Click **More** on the SmartArt Styles group to display a gallery of styles for the object. Click **Polished**, the first design in the 3-D gallery.

h. Click **Change Colors** in the SmartArt Styles group. Click **Colorful Range – Accent Colors 3 to 4**, which is the third item in the Colorful row.

i. Hold your mouse over the lower-right corner of the box that surrounds the object. Click on the box, hold your mouse down, and drag to enlarge the object. Release the mouse when the object enlarges enough to fill most of the page. Compare your chart to Figure 6.38.

j. Save and close the document.

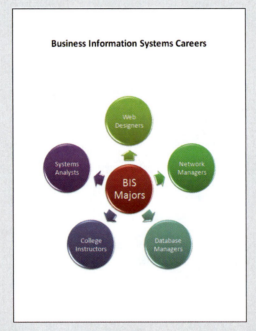

Figure 6.38 Designing a Radial Diagram

1 Link a Chart into a Memo

You are preparing a report that announces the implementation of new technology for your company. You need to include a chart that was created in Excel. Because you want the chart in Word to reflect changes in the original Excel workbook, you need to link the chart.

   a. Open the *chap6_mid1_CTA* document and save it as **chap6_mid1_CTA_solution**.

   b. Open the *chap6_mid1_chart.xlsx* worksheet and save it as **chap6_mid1_chart_solution.xlsx**.

   c. Select the chart in Excel, and then copy it to the Clipboard.

   d. Link the chart to the bottom of the *chap6_mid1_CTA_solution* document.

   e. In the *chap6_mid1_chart_solution* worksheet, make the following changes:

      Phase 1 Hardware value: 1.4

      Phase 2 Software value: .75

      Phase 3 Software value: .80

      Phase 4 Software value: 1.2

      Phase 3 Training value: .5

      Phase 4 Training value: 1.0

   f. Update the linked chart object in the Word document.

   g. Save and close all documents.

2 Bark in the Park Newsletter

You are a member of the Bixby County Citizens Dog Park Committee, which is raising funds to develop an off-leash dog park. You have many events to advertise and volunteers to recruit, so you decide to put some information into a newsletter that can be printed and mailed, or simply e-mailed. A draft of the completed newsletter is provided for you, and the text is included in a file. In this exercise, you re-create the newsletter as you see it in Figure 6.39.

   a. Open the *chap6_mid2_petnews* document and save it as **chap6_mid2_petnews_solution**.

   b. Create a masthead for the newsletter by using the Titles Sidebar. Type **Volume 1 Number 1** on the left side of the masthead, and then type **Editor:** on the right side. Type your name as editor.

   c. Create a two-column newsletter that uses a left preset and displays a line between columns. Use a section break to enable a one-column masthead.

   d. Create a text box using the **Braces Quote** style to emphasize the paragraph that begins *While Raising the funds necessary*. Resize the box as necessary to extend across the column.

   e. Insert a clip art image of a dog to enhance the document with graphics. Insert the picture **dakota.jpg** into the newsletter next to the *Pet of the Month* description. Resize the graphic objects and apply text wrapping or other alignment settings as needed.

   f. Use borders and shading to draw attention to the *Dog Park meeting dates* and the *Committee hotline number*.

   g. Save and close the document.

...continued on Next Page

Figure 6.39 Bark in the Park Newsletter

3 Create a Family Tree

You have decided to begin charting your genealogy. You have a number of different methods for displaying the family tree, but you decide to use SmartArt graphics to show your immediate family. If instructed, substitute your own personal information for that given in the instructions below.

a. Open a new document and save it as **chap6_mid3_family_solution**.

b. Insert the Horizontal Hierarchy SmartArt graphic from the Hierarchy gallery.

c. Click in the first element on the left, and then display the Text pane. Type **Michelle** in the first box.

d. Type **Gary** and **Sandra** in the second-level boxes to represent Michelle's parents.

e. Type **Lester** and **Verdene** in the boxes that represent Gary's parents.

f. Type **Sidney** and **Effie** in the boxes that represent Sandra's parents.

g. Add boxes to represent Lester's parents, Ralph and Emma. Then add boxes to represent Verdene's parents, George and Mary. Add boxes for Sidney's parents, Miles and Minnie, and finally, add boxes for Effie's parents, Jasper and Lou.

h. Modify the chart colors to use **Colorful Range – Accent Colors 3 to 4.**

i. Modify the chart to use the Subtle Effect Style.

j. Change the Position to Middle Center with Square Text Wrapping.

k. At the top of the document, type the heading **My Family Tree**. Format the text using Heading 1 Style and center it.

l. Save and close the document.

Capstone Exercise

You are hired as a marketing manager for a small airline service that provides transportation from Denver to frequently requested locations and vacation cities such as Las Vegas, Orlando, and New York. Your first big assignment is to develop marketing material that can be printed and mailed to potential customers in the Denver area and also in the cities serviced by the airline. From your previous marketing experience, you know that it is important to emphasize the most positive attributes of the airline as well as provide information that will generate interest in, and eventually revenue for, the company.

Create the Masthead

You have a document with several important pieces of information that should be used in the marketing material. You must format the page so it can accommodate the amount of information you display, as well as any graphics you might add later.

a. Open the file named *chap6_cap_airline* and save it as **chap6_cap_airline_solution**.

b. Change the margins to .7" on all sides.

c. Set a Continuous Section Break at the beginning of the document. Use a single-column format for the masthead.

d. Create a masthead with the main heading **Sunset Airlines** and a subheading **As Nice as Riding into the Sunset**. Use a Reverse on both headings. Change the font color of the main heading to **Orange, Accent 6**, and change the color of the subheading to **Orange, Accent 6, Lighter 80%**. Left align the heading and right align the subheading.

Create Columns and Format Text

You now need to adjust the text to display in two columns below the masthead. You will also make several modifications to that text so that it is visually appealing and also conveys all the important information the airline wants the potential customers to be excited about.

a. Set a dropped cap letter on the first letter of the word *Welcome* in the first paragraph.

b. Set a two-column format to arrange the text below the masthead. Display a line between the columns and set equal column width. Set another Continuous Section Break at the end of the text and set the area below to display in one column.

c. Cut the paragraph that starts with the phrase *Because we want to be the airline* and insert it as a text box. Use the **Stars Quote** design from the Text Box gallery, set it to wrap **In Line with Text**, and center the text.

d. Select the paragraph that starts with the phrase *We are always adding* and move it to the bottom of the second column. Apply a border that uses the wavy line style, is colored **Orange, Accent 6**, and is **1½-point width**. Set shading for the paragraph using the color **Orange, Accent 6, Lighter 60%**.

e. Set a Page Border that uses the style found fourth from the bottom of the style list. Use the **Orange, Accent 6** color and a **3-point width**.

f. Use a bullet list to organize the regulations listed in the paragraph that starts *For a more enjoyable flight*. Customize the bullets to use the airplane symbol, **Webdings: 241**.

g. Change the font of the paragraph and bullet list to **Verdana** and set the size as **11 points**.

Add Graphics for Visual Effects

You have several ways to visually stimulate the flyer, but you know that it is easy to add too much and thus defeat the purpose of attracting customers. You decide to use SmartArt, clip art, and a few shapes to complete the look.

a. Position your insertion point in the first paragraph. Insert a clip art picture of an airplane or a sunset. You might have to search the Microsoft Online Clip Gallery to find an appropriate picture. Format the clip art using Behind Text Wrapping style. Resize the graphic as necessary to fit behind the first paragraph only.

b. Position the insertion point at the bottom of the document. Insert a SmartArt object; use the **Diverging Radial** from the Cycle section. Display the Text pane and type **Denver** on the first line to represent the circle in the middle. Click and type the following cities to fill the outer circles: **Las Vegas**, **Orlando**, **New York**, **Chicago**. Press **Enter** after you type Chicago, and then type **Minneapolis (Coming Soon!)**. Click **Enter** once again and type **Salt Lake City (Coming Soon!)**.

c. Format the SmartArt object with **Square Text Wrapping**, and then drag the sizing handles to enlarge the object, if necessary, to fill the width of the column. Drag the object to the bottom of the second column.

d. Place the insertion point on the left side of the paragraph that begins *For a more enjoyable flight*. Open the Excel workbook *chap6_cap_flights.xlsx* and save it as **chap6_cap_flights_solution.xlsx**. Copy the chart from the spreadsheet, and then paste it into the Word document. It should display below the pull quote.

e. Edit the data in the chart so the Los Angeles on-time percentage increases to 93%. Because this operation does not reflect immediately in the newsletter, take steps to create a link between the chart in the document and the spreadsheet. After you update the chart, position it at the bottom of the page, in the one-column section. If necessary, deselect the option to move the object with text.

f. Insert two shape objects, a banner and a text box that displays Let's Go!, at the bottom of the first column. Fill the banner with **Horizontal Gradient – Accent 6** from the Shape Styles gallery. Increase the size of the text to at least 18 pt. Group and layer the objects so they can be moved as one object.

g. Make adjustments to spacing and line returns as necessary to display all text and objects without overlapping. Save and close all files.

Mini Cases

Use the rubric following the case as a guide to evaluate your work, but keep in mind that your instructor may impose additional grading criteria or use a different standard to judge your work.

Evaluating Political Issues

GENERAL CASE

At any given time, there is often a political race or issue that will eventually be voted on by your community. As an informed citizen, you should be aware of any amendments, issues, or candidates running for office; you should also be able to give reasons why you would vote for or against them. Create a SmartArt object that describes a group of candidates or amendments and list the issues they support or oppose. Remember that a few SmartArt objects enable you to include pictures or graphics in the diagram as well as insert bullet points to support the main subject. Save your file as **chap6_mc1_politics_solution**.

Performance Elements	Exceeds Expectations	Meets Expectations	Below Expectations
Organization	SmartArt object contains at least three forms of current information about candidates, amendments, or issues.	SmartArt object contains at least two forms of current information about candidates, amendments, or issues.	SmartArt object omits current information about candidates, amendments, or issues.
Visual aspects	SmartArt object selected is an appropriate and adequate style for displaying information about candidates and/or issues.	SmartArt object selected is an adequate style for displaying information about candidates and/or issues, but is not the most appropriate representation of the information.	SmartArt object selected is neither an appropriate nor an adequate style for displaying information about candidates and/or issues.

Dihydrogen Monoxide: Good or Bad?

RESEARCH CASE

You are a member of the local chemistry club. You have been asked to give a presentation at the next meeting about dihydrogen monoxide. Perform an Internet search to gather information about this substance, and then create a flyer to hand out at the meeting. The flyer should contain a few general facts about the chemical as well as the hazards of exposure (if any). Use the techniques from this chapter to organize your facts and present a professional-looking flyer. Save the document as **chap6_mc2_chemical_solution**.

Performance Elements	Exceeds Expectations	Meets Expectations	Below Expectations
Organization	Document indicates accurate research and significant facts. Evidence exists that information has been evaluated and synthesized showing an understanding of the topic.	Document indicates some research has taken place and that information was included in the content.	Document demonstrates a lack of research or understanding of the topic.
Layout	The layout is visually pleasing and contributes to the overall message with appropriate use of masthead, columns, bullet points, pull quotes, and white space.	The layout shows some structure, but placement of pull quotes, masthead, bullet points, images, and/or white space is distracting.	The layout is cluttered and confusing. Placement of masthead, pull quotes, bullet points, and/or white space detracts from readability.
Mechanics	Presentation has no errors in spelling, grammar, word usage, or punctuation.	Presentation has no more than two errors in spelling, grammar, word usage, or punctuation.	Presentation readability is impaired due to repeated errors in spelling, grammar, word usage, or punctuation.

You work for a local automotive dealer and your supervisor requests your help to fix a document he was unable to complete. He attempted to create a document that describes a vehicle, including a spreadsheet calculation for pricing that can be updated automatically. He thinks this will be a great resource for all sales associates, but his first attempt to create the document was not successful. He did not properly link the document with the source file, nor did his graphical enhancements provide the effect he desires. You have been assigned the task of repairing the document so the pricing information from the *chap6_mc3_payment.xlsx* spreadsheet can be updated easily and automatically. You must also modify the document to display the graphical elements correctly and make any other enhancements that create a professional-looking document. Open the Word document your supervisor created, *chap6_mc3_car.docx*, and save your changes to **chap6_mc3_car_solution.docx**.

Performance Elements	Exceeds Expectations	Meets Expectations	Below Expectations
Organization	Placement of graphical elements enables easy viewing of all text in document.	Placement of graphical elements enables easy viewing of some text in document.	Placement of graphical elements does not enable easy viewing of all text in document.
Linking/embedding	Adjustment to worksheet object provides ability to update information in the spreadsheet and subsequently in the document.	Adjustment to worksheet object provides ability to view but not update information from the spreadsheet.	Did not make adjustment to worksheet object.

The Advanced User

Forms, Document Security, and Macros

Objectives

After you read this chapter, you will be able to:

1. Create an electronic form **(page 419)**.

2. Insert form controls **(page 420)**.

3. Protect a form **(page 422)**.

4. Mark a document as final **(page 432)**.

5. Set formatting restrictions **(page 433)**.

6. Set editing restrictions **(page 434)**.

7. Set passwords to open a document **(page 435)**.

8. Use Digital signatures to authenticate documents **(page 437)**.

9. Record a macro **(page 447)**.

10. Run a macro **(page 450)**.

Hands-On Exercises

Exercises	Skills Covered
1. CREATING A FORM (page 424) **Open:** chap7_ho1_invoice.doc **Save as:** chap7_ho1_invoice_solution.dotx **Open:** chap7_ho1_invoice_solution.dotx **Save as:** chap7_ho1_invoice1_solution.docx	• Create a Document Template • Insert Form Controls in a Document • Insert Form Controls in a Table • Perform Calculations with Form Control Data • Add Check Box Controls and Protect the Form • Use an Electronic Form
2. PROTECTING DOCUMENTS (page 440) **Open:** chap7_ho2_case.docx **Save as:** chap7_ho2_case1_solution.docx, chap7_ho2_case2_solution.docx, chap7_ho2_case3_solution.docx, chap7_ho2_case4_solution.docx, chap7_ho2_case5_solution.docx, and chap7_ho2_case6_solution.docx	• Set a Password to Open a Document and Mark as Final • Set Formatting Restrictions • Set Editing Restrictions • Set Exceptions for Restricted Documents • Attach a Digital Signature to a Document • Insert a Signature Line in a Document
3. USING MACROS (page 451) **Open:** chap7_ho3_cover.docx **Save as:** chap7_ho3_cover_solution.docm	• Record a Macro • Play a Macro • Modify a Macro • Run an Edited Macro

CASE STUDY

Angela Marti Real Estate Appraisals

Angela Marti is a real estate appraiser in Greene County. Each day Angela's assistant provides her with a list of residential houses that she must visit to determine the worth of the structure and surrounding property. At the conclusion of her visit she uses her evaluation to determine the property value and then reports it to the client. This information is valuable when selling the property or for use by an insurance company. At the end of each week, Angela is responsible for preparing a report of all the inspections she completed, and then she must send it to the county assessor. She carries a laptop computer and typically types the addresses in a Word document while she is on location.

Angela's assistant suggested she create a form that she can use while on location. By using the form she has a document she can quickly print or e-mail to the county assessor. Angela is thrilled with this idea and decides the form should include a table that contains the address information, the appraised value, and the date she visited the property. She will include a signature line where she can insert her name prior to submitting the report, and lastly she will authenticate the report with a digital signature. She can also make the form available to coworkers who perform similar work. Her assessment of this project is that it will be very valuable to her for a long time!

Your Assignment

- Read the chapter, paying special attention to the sections that describe how to create forms, protect documents, and use macros.

- You will put yourself in Angela's place and open the document template *chap7_case_appraisal.dotx*, which contains the table where Angela will enter each address, the appraised value, and the date of her visit, and save it as **chap7_case_appraisal_solution**.

- You will insert text controls in the document where Angela enters her name at the beginning of the report, and also in the address column of the table.

- You will add a Combo box control for City and Zip Code because Angela primarily makes assessments in only four cities. Use Ava, Salem, Ozark, and Nixa in the combo box for City and use codes from 65800 to 65810 in the zip code combo box. Type **MO** in each cell in the State column.

- Use a Date Picker control for all areas of the report that require dates.

- Use a text box form field in the cell where she enters the appraised value. Format the field as a number type using a monetary number format. At the bottom of the table enter a text box form field that calculates the total of all appraisals in the table.

- Protect the table so that only the form controls can be modified. Password protect the document using the password **Chap7_case**.

- Enter fictional information into the table, apply a digital signature, and then save the report as a Word document named **chap7_case_appraisalinfo_solution.docx**.

Forms

A **_form_** is a document designed for collecting data for a specific situation.

Forms are quite common in our society. A **_form_** is a document designed for collecting data for a specific situation. For example, you complete a medical history form when you visit a doctor's office, you complete forms when you open a bank account, other forms help you register software and hardware, and you fill out a form when you apply for a job. Forms are also used for class registrations, purchase orders, and invoices. The form may be electronic and completed online, or it may exist as a printed document. Figure 7.1 displays a completed form that is an invoice for goods or services.

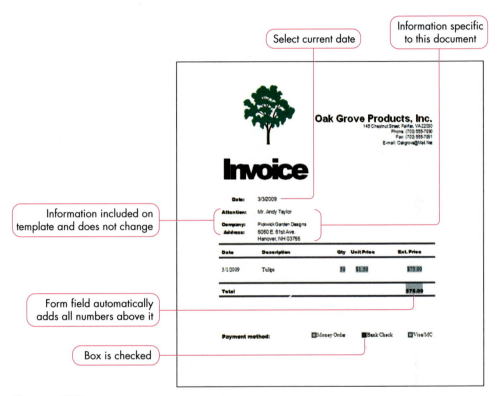

Select current date

Information specific to this document

Information included on template and does not change

Form field automatically adds all numbers above it

Box is checked

Oak Grove Products, Inc.
145 Chestnut Street, Fairfax, VA 22030
Phone: (703) 555-7890
Fax: (703) 555-7891
E-mail: Oakgrove@Mail.Net

Invoice

Date:	3/3/2009			
Attention:	Mr. Andy Taylor			
Company:	Pickwick Garden Designs			
Address:	5050 E. 61st Ave. Hanover, NH 03755			

Date	Description	Qty	Unit Price	Ext. Price
3/1/2009	Tulips	50	$1.50	$75.00
Total				**$75.00**

Payment method: ☐ Money Order   ☒ Bank Check   ☐ Visa/MC

Figure 7.1   A Completed Form Becomes an Invoice

In this section, you create and use a simple form that can be printed and filled in or completed onscreen. You learn how to create and customize form controls, you perform calculations in a table form, and then you protect the document so you can use the form.

Creating an Electronic Form

A **_form template_** is a document that defines the standard layout, structure, and the formatting of a form.

In Microsoft Word, you can create a **_form template_**, a document that defines the standard layout, structure, and formatting of a form. You save the document as a Word template, and then establish settings to enable the user to enter data in specific places, but prevent editing it in any other way. The process requires you to create the form and save it to disk, where it serves as an original template for future documents. Then, when you need to enter data for a specific situation, you open the template form, enter the data, and save the completed form as a new document. This process is more efficient than removing old information from a standard document so you can replace it with current data for the new situation. It also minimizes errors that sometimes occur when you intend to replace old information with updated data

> In Microsoft Word, you can create a **form template**, a document that defines the standard layout, structure, and formatting of a form. You . . . then establish settings to enable the user to enter data in specific places, but prevent editing it in any other way.

but overlook some portion of the older data. Using a form allows you to maintain the integrity of an original document or template while also allowing you to customize it.

Figure 7.2 displays a blank form. The shaded entries indicate where a user enters information into a form. To complete the form, the user presses Tab to go from one field to the next and enters data as appropriate. Then, when all fields have been entered, the form is printed to produce the finished document (an invoice). The data that were entered into the various fields appear as regular text when printed.

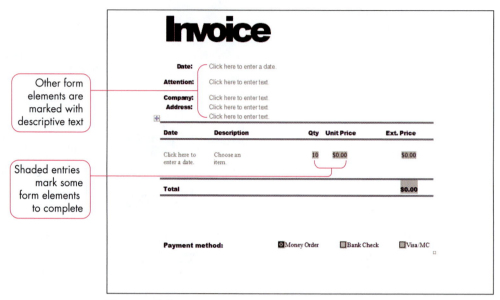

Figure 7.2 A Blank Form

Inserting Form Controls

You must display the Developer tab to use the form development tools in Word. This tab does not display automatically but is easy to activate. Click the Office Button, click Word Options, click Popular, click Show Developer tab in the Ribbon, and then click OK.

After you display the Developer tab, you see the form controls as well as other commands you use while creating the form. Before you insert the controls in your document, you enter Design Mode. *Design Mode* enables you to view and select the control fields so you can make any necessary modifications to their layout or options. Design Mode is a toggle; click it once to activate Design Mode, and then click it again to deactivate it.

Design Mode enables you to view and modify control fields.

Using a table in a form template helps you align information and makes the form easier for users to fill out. In addition, you can use the Table feature to format and manipulate the fields and data in the table to improve the form. For example, you can right-align labels, such as Name and Address, in one table cell and then you can left-align the form field the user completes. This alignment clarifies the instructional information that accompanies the field.

You can design forms that will be printed and also forms that will be completed electronically. If you want users to fill out a form electronically, you must insert *form controls*, also called form fields, into the form template. Form controls help the user complete a form by displaying prompts such as drop-down lists and text boxes. Word 2007 added several new types of form controls to those available in previous versions. Table 7.1 describes several of the most common types of controls.

Form controls help a user complete a form by displaying prompts such as text boxes and drop-down lists.

Table 7.1 Form Controls

Control Type	Description
Rich Text	User can enter text or numbers, and users can modify the format of the text they enter.
Text	User can enter text or numbers, but cannot modify the format of the text.
Picture Content Control	User can insert a drawing, shape, chart, table, clip art, or SmartArt object in a field.
Combo Box	User selects from a list of choices that displays in a drop-down box, but the user can modify the choices in the list.
Drop-Down List	User selects from a predefined list of choices that displays in a drop-down box.
Date Picker	User selects a date from the calendar that displays.
Building Block Gallery	User selects a building block item to insert in the document, such as cover pages, headers, footers, or predefined text such as a disclaimer.
Check Box	User selects or deselects an item by clicking the check box that displays beside the item.
Option Button	User selects from a predefined list by clicking the option button that displays beside the item.

A ***text content control*** is used to enter any type of text into a form.

The controls you use most often are text, check boxes, and drop-down lists. A ***text content control*** is the most common and is used to enter any type of text into a form. It usually displays in the form of a box, and it collects information such as name and address, and even numerical data such as a phone number. The length of a text box can be set exactly or can be left unspecified, in which case the field will expand to the exact number of positions that are required as the data are entered.

A ***check box form field*** consists of a box that is checked or not.

A ***check box form field***, as the name implies, consists of a box that is checked or not. A check box might include the responses Yes or No, or Male or Female, for example. You can customize check box form fields so they display checked by default, or not checked. You can also specify the size of the check box.

A ***drop-down list*** enables the user to choose from one of several existing entries.

A ***drop-down list*** enables the user to choose from one of several existing entries. This type of control should only be used on electronic forms, because the list of options will not display on a printed form. A drop-down list enables users to click a down arrow and then click one option from the list; the option they click will then display on the form. A list of cities or states is appropriate to display in a drop-down list.

The ***Date Picker*** displays a calendar that the user can click rather than typing in a date.

Many forms require a date. The ***Date Picker*** displays a calendar that the user can navigate and click rather than typing in a date. If the user wants to select the current date, the Date Picker calendar has a Today button. The Properties dialog box for the Date Picker enables you to select from several date formats, such as 3/2/2008 or 2-Mar-08.

Legacy form fields are form elements that can be used in Word 2007 and also in previous versions of Word.

ActiveX controls are form elements that work in a Word 2007 document or template.

Some controls are designated as ***Legacy form fields*** because they were used in previous versions of Word. These controls can be used in Word 2007 and also in documents or templates you open in Compatibility Mode, meaning they were created with a previous version of Word. Controls that are new in Word 2007 are called ***ActiveX controls***. These controls are easy to insert in a Word 2007 document or template. You can insert them in a document saved in Compatibility Mode; however, the Properties dialog box is confusing to those not familiar with programming. If you create forms that might be used by people who are not yet using Word 2007, you should remember to use only legacy controls and save the document or template in Compatibility Mode. Figure 7.3 shows the Developer tab and available controls.

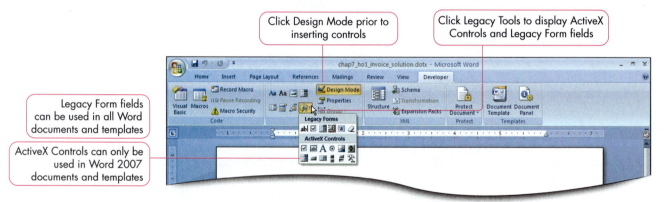

Figure 7.3 Controls on the Developer Tab

Protecting a Form

After the form is created, it is protected to prevent modification other than data entry. To protect the form, deactivate Design Mode, if necessary, and then click Protect Document in the Protect group of the Developer tab. The Restrict Formatting and Editing task pane displays as shown in Figure 7.4. Click Allow only this type of editing in the document in the Editing restrictions section, then click the drop-down arrow and click Filling in forms to enable the user to type in, click, or select only the form fields in the form.

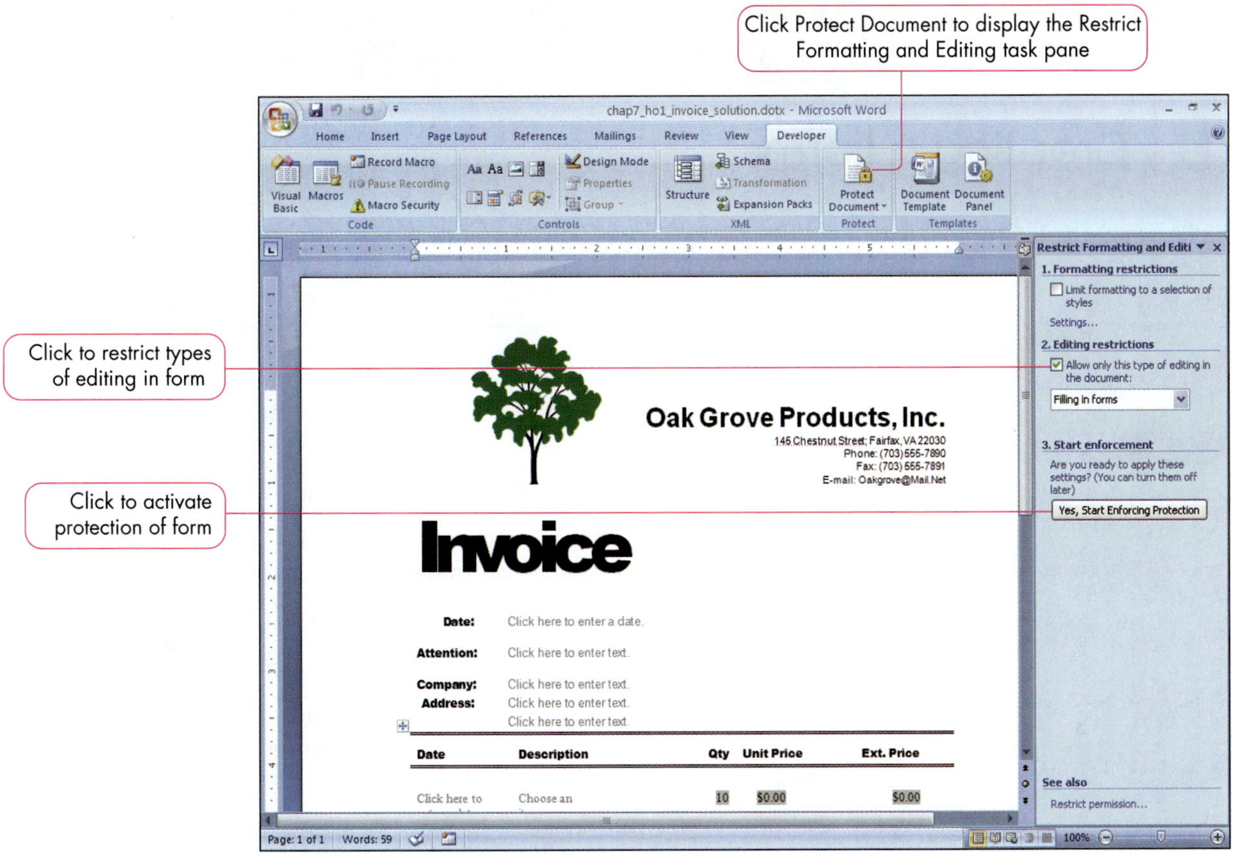

Click Protect Document to display the Restrict Formatting and Editing task pane

Click to restrict types of editing in form

Click to activate protection of form

Figure 7.4 Restrict Formatting and Editing of a Form

A **password** is a security feature required to gain access to a restricted document.

After you enforce the protection of a form, you are prompted for a password. A **password** is a security mechanism consisting of case-sensitive characters entered to gain access to a restricted document. You can create a password for the form that serves as another layer of protection and prevents other users from deactivating the protection unless they know the password. Without a password, anyone can deactivate the protection. However, if you forget the password, it cannot be recovered. You can skip the password protection by omitting a password in the Enter new password box and clicking OK. If you want to revise the form, click Stop Protection in the Restrict Formatting and Editing task pane.

You can protect specific controls on a form without restricting access to the entire document by using the Group command on the Developer tab. When you select a range and apply the Group command, the range is protected from editing. This feature is useful when you want to be able to make modifications to a document that contains form controls, but you do not want to allow any changes to the form controls within that document. After you apply the Group command to the range, click Properties and set one of the two locking options. The first option—Content control cannot be deleted—enables you to edit the content of a control but does not enable you to remove the control. The second option—Contents cannot be edited—enables you to delete the control, but you cannot edit the content in the control.

Hands-On Exercises

1 | Creating a Form

Skills covered: 1. Create a Document Template **2.** Insert Form Controls in a Document **3.** Insert Form Controls in a Table **4.** Perform Calculations with Form Control Data **5.** Add Check Box Controls and Protect the Form **6.** Use an Electronic Form

Step 1 **Create a Document Template**	Refer to Figure 7.5 as you complete Step 1. **a.** Start Word. Click the **Office Button**, then open the document *chap7_ho1_invoice.doc*. This file is saved as a Word 97–2003 document and will open in Compatibility Mode. **b.** Click the **Office Button**, click **Word Options**, click **Popular**, if necessary, and then click **Show Developer tab in the Ribbon**, as shown in Figure 7.5. Click **OK**. This step is necessary to display the Developer tab, which contains all form controls. **c.** Click the **Developer tab** and locate the Controls group. Notice that most of the Controls in the Controls group are grayed out. These ActiveX controls cannot be used in a document that opens in Compatibility Mode. Next you save the document as a Word 2007 template. **d.** Click the **Office Button**, click the **Save As arrow**, and click **Word Template**. Type **chap7_ho1_invoice_solution** in the File name box, and then click **Save**. If a Microsoft Office Word dialog box displays with a warning that you are about to save your document in one of the new formats, click **OK**. If a Microsoft Office Word dialog box asks if you want to continue to save as a macro-free document, click **Yes**.

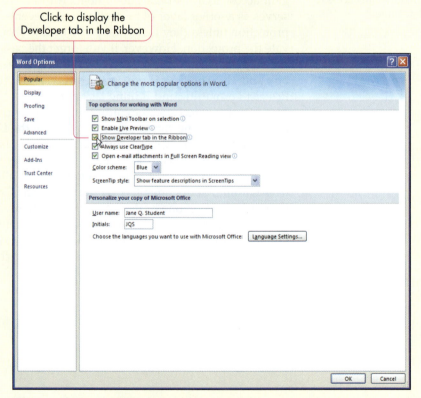

Figure 7.5 Activate the Developer Tab

Refer to Figure 7.6 as you complete Step 2.

a. Click the **Home tab**, and then click **Show/Hide ¶** in the Paragraph group to display formatting marks.

b. Click on the left side of the paragraph mark that displays at the end of the line for *Date*, which is just below the text *Invoice*.

You are positioning the insertion point here prior to inserting a date control.

c. Click the **Developer tab**, click **Design Mode** in the Controls group, and then click **Date Picker**.

The control for choosing a date displays with a light blue border and the text *Click here to enter a date.*

d. Press the **down arrow** one time to move the insertion point to the end of the line for *Attention:* and click **Text** in the Controls group on the Developer tab.

The control for entering text displays with a light blue border and the text *Click here to enter text.*

e. Repeat the process from Step d to insert a Text control at the ends of the *Company:* and *Address:* lines.

f. Click on the left side of the paragraph mark that displays at the end of the line just below the *Address:* line. Click **Text** in the Controls group.

You must insert a second text control here for the City, State, and Zip code portions of the address. The text controls do not align text properly when you press Enter when typing within them, so a second box is necessary to align all the address information.

g. Compare your document to Figure 7.6, and then save the document.

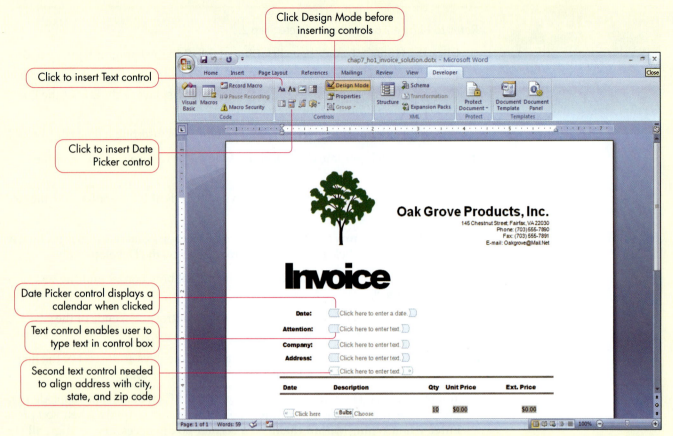

Figure 7.6 Insert Form Controls in the Invoice

Callouts in figure:
- Click Design Mode before inserting controls
- Click to insert Text control
- Click to insert Date Picker control
- Date Picker control displays a calendar when clicked
- Text control enables user to type text in control box
- Second text control needed to align address with city, state, and zip code

Step 3
Insert Form Controls in a Table

Refer to Figure 7.7 as you complete Step 3.

a. Click on the left side of the second row in the table, just below the text *Date*. Click **Date Picker** from the Controls group. Click to move the insertion point to the next cell below the text *Description*.

b. Click **Drop-Down List** in the Controls group. Click **Properties** to display the Content Control Properties dialog box.

Users will select from a predefined list of products when they click this control in the form. In the next step, you populate the list with the available products.

c. Type **Spring Bulbs** in the Title box. Type **Bulbs** in the Tag box.

d. Click **Add** to display the Add Choice dialog box. Type **Tulips** in the Display Name box and click **OK**. Repeat the process in this step to add two more types of bulbs: **Hyacinth** and **Crocus**.

Compare your work to Figure 7.7.

e. Click **OK** to close the dialog box. Save the document.

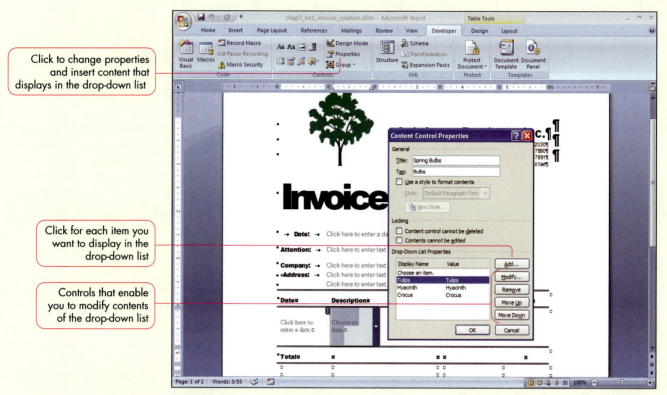

Annotations on figure:

Click to change properties and insert content that displays in the drop-down list

Click for each item you want to display in the drop-down list

Controls that enable you to modify contents of the drop-down list

Figure 7.7 Insert Form Controls to Display Transaction Details

---

Step 4
Perform Calculations with Form Control Data

Refer to Figure 7.8 as you complete Step 4.

a. Click in the cell below *Qty*. Click **Legacy Tools** in the Controls group, and then click **Text Form Field** below the heading *Legacy Forms*.

A series of small circles displays with a gray background.

> **TROUBLESHOOTING:** If the gray background does not display behind the circles, click **Legacy Tools**, and then click **Form Field Shading** below the Legacy Forms heading.

b. Click **Properties** to display the Text Form Field Options dialog box. Click the **Type drop-down arrow** and select **Number**. In the Default number box, type **10**. Click the **Number format drop-down arrow** and click **#,##0**. Press **Tab** three times, and then replace the contents of the Bookmark box with **Qty1**. Click the **Calculate on exit box**, and then click **OK**.

By naming the bookmark *Qty1*, you will be able to add more product items in the invoice. The next row can contain a bookmark named Qty2, and eventually, you can use the bookmark names to create formulas to perform calculations within the form. Checking Calculate on exit ensures that calculations are updated after users enter numbers.

c. Click in the cell below *Unit Price*. Click **Legacy Tools** in the Controls group, and then click **Text Form Field** below the heading *Legacy Forms*. Display the Form Field Properties and use the following information in the Text Form Field Options dialog box to customize this control.

Type:	**Number**
Default number:	**0**
Number format:	**$#,##0.00;($#,##0.00)**
Bookmark:	**UnitPrice1**

d. Click **OK** to close the Text Form Field Options dialog box, and then click in the cell below *Ext. Price*. Click **Legacy Tools** in the Controls group, and then click **Text Form Field**. Click **Properties**. Click the **Type drop-down arrow** and select **Calculation**. In the *Expression* box, type **Qty1*UnitPrice1** after the equal sign.

The equal sign in the Expression box specifies that you are creating a mathematical formula. This formula multiplies the value in the Qty field by the value of the UnitPrice field. Because you assigned bookmark names to the fields, you can use the bookmark names in the formula.

e. Click the **Number format down arrow**, click **$#,##0.00;($#,##0.00)**, as shown in Figure 7.8, and then click **OK**.

The Ext. Price field immediately displays *$0.00*, which is the result of multiplying the default value of 10 in the Qty field by the default entry 0 in the Unit Price field.

f. Click the cell at the end of the Total row, below the Ext. Price. Click **Legacy Tools**, and then click **Text Form Field**. Right-click the shaded field and click **Properties**. Click the **Type down arrow** and select **Calculation**. Click in the *Expression* box and type **SUM(ABOVE)** after the equal sign. Click the **Number format down arrow** and select **$#,##0.00;($#,##0.00)**, and then click **OK**.

You want to add all the values in as many fields as appear in the Ext. Price column. You use the SUM function to add values in all fields in this column. The results display as a dollar value.

g. Save the document.

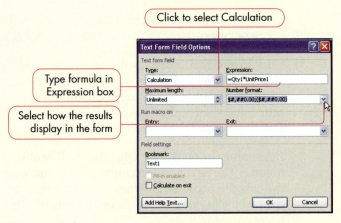

Figure 7.8 Create a Calculation in the Text Form Field Options Dialog Box

Refer to Figure 7.9 as you complete Step 5.

a. Click on the left side of the cell containing *Money Order*, click **Legacy Tools**, and click **Check Box Form Field** below Legacy Forms.

You insert a check box form field in the cell to the left of the Money Order Payment Method option. Users can mark the check box next to the payment method they prefer.

b. Right-click the *Money Order* check box and click **Properties**. Click **Checked** in the *Default value* section, as shown in Figure 7.9. Click **OK**.

The check box for Money Order will be checked automatically when the user opens the form.

c. Click on the left side of the cell containing *Bank Check*, click **Legacy Tools**, and click **Check Box Form Field**. Click at the left side of the cell containing *Visa/MC*, click **Legacy Tools**, and click **Check Box Form Field**.

You now display check boxes next to all the payment methods. The user will check only one.

d. Click **Design Mode** to turn off Design Mode, if necessary. Save the document. Click **Protect Document** in the Protect group on the Developer tab. Click **Restrict Formatting and Editing**, if necessary, to display the task pane.

The Restrict Formatting and Editing task pane displays.

e. If necessary, click **Allow only this type of editing in the document**, which displays in the *2. Editing restrictions* section. If necessary, click the down arrow in the box below this option and click **Filling in forms**. Click **Yes, Start Enforcing Protection**.

TROUBLESHOOTING: If Yes, Start Enforcing Protection is grayed out, make sure you are not in Design Mode.

f. Click **OK** when the Start Enforcing Protection dialog box displays.

If you want to password protect a document, you can insert and confirm the password in this dialog box. Remember that if you forget the password, there is no way to recover it and your document cannot be opened.

g. Click **Close** in the upper-right corner of the Restrict Formatting and Editing task pane. Click the **Home tab** and click **Show/Hide ¶** to turn off formatting marks.

h. Save and close the document.

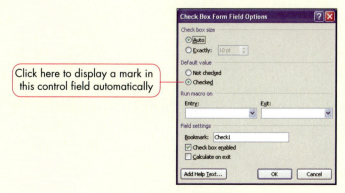

Figure 7.9 Change Check Box Properties

Step 6

Use an Electronic Form

Refer to Figure 7.10 as you complete Step 6.

a. Open the template *chap7_ho1_invoice_solution* and save it as a Word 2007 document named **chap7_ho1_invoice1_solution**.

Word creates the new file based on the template. By default, the first form control is selected. Notice the Ribbon is grayed out, preventing you from using the formatting commands, because the document is protected from editing. You will only be able to click and use the form controls.

b. Click the **Date Picker arrow** in the first control, which is already selected. Click **Today**.

c. Click the control box next to *Attention:* and type **Mr. Andy Taylor**. Press **Tab**.

Word enters the name in the field and moves to the next field when you press Tab.

d. Type **Pickwick Garden Designs**, press **Tab**, type **5050 E. 51st Ave.**, press **Tab**, type **Hanover, NH 03755**, and press **Tab**.

e. Click the **Date Picker arrow** for the date of the first purchase and click **June 7**. Press **Tab**

f. Click the down arrow for the Description drop-down list. Click **Crocus** from the list.

g. Double-click the Qty control field and type **50**, then press **Tab**. Type **1.50** and press **Tab**.

As soon as you click Tab to move out of the Unit Price control field, the insertion point moves forward in the form to the Money Order check box. As you continue completing the form, the calculations will take place.

h. Press the **Spacebar** to deselect Money Order. Press **Tab**, then press **Spacebar** to select Bank Check. Press **Tab** three times to cycle through the text fields and update the calculations.

You have completed the form, as shown in Figure 7.10.

i. Save and close the *chap7_ho1_invoice1_solution* document and exit Word.

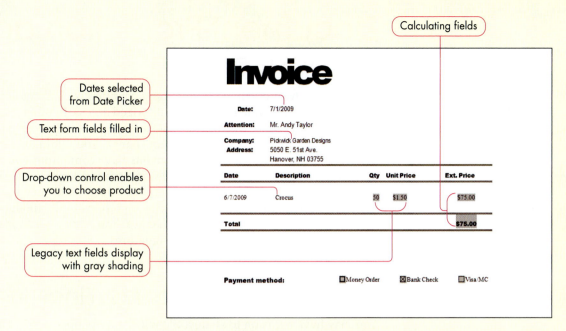

Calculating fields

Dates selected
from Date Picker

Text form fields filled in

Drop-down control enables
you to choose product

Legacy text fields display
with gray shading

Invoice

Date:	7/1/2009
Attention:	Mr. Andy Taylor
Company:	Pickwick Garden Designs
Address:	5050 E. 51st Ave. Hanover, NH 03755

Date	Description	Qty	Unit Price	Ext. Price
6/7/2009	Crocus	50	$1.50	$75.00
Total				**$75.00**

Payment method: ☐ Money Order ☒ Bank Check ☐ Visa/MC

Figure 7.10 The Completed Form

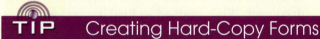

TIP   Creating Hard-Copy Forms

Many offices still use hard-copy forms instead of electronic forms. For example, some job application forms are printed, and the job applicants must write or type on the hard-copy form. These types of forms contain labels, text boxes, and check boxes. Drop-down fields are not applicable to a hard-copy form. To use a hard-copy form, open a document from the form template and print as many copies as you need.

Document Protection and Authentication

As you work with documents containing confidential information, you might want to protect those documents from unauthorized access. In other situations, you might need to store reference documents, such as policies and procedures, on an organization's network for others to read but not change. You might also want to assure document recipients that particular documents have come from you and have not been tampered with during transit. To assist in situations such as these, Microsoft Word provides tools that enable you to protect your documents on many levels.

In this section, you learn to restrict permissions to documents against unauthorized access, formatting, or content changes. You learn how to mark a document as final, set passwords, and add digital signatures.

Marking a Document as Final

Mark as Final creates a read-only file and also sets the property to Final on the status bar.

You may have occasion to share a file with other people, but before you send it you want to make it a read-only file, which prevents others from changing the document. The *Mark as Final* command enables you to create a read-only file and sets the property to Final on the status bar. To alert the reader to this status, it displays an icon in the status bar to indicate the file is in its final form, as shown in Figure 7.11. This is a helpful command for communicating with other people that the document is not a draft but a completed and final version. It also prevents unintentional changes to the document. When marked as final, typing, editing, and proofing marks do not display; all commands in the Ribbon are grayed out; and the document cannot be modified. To use this command, click the Office Button, point to Prepare, and then click Mark as Final.

Even though this feature provides a way to communicate the status of the document and enables you to set it as read-only, it does not completely secure the document. Mark as Final is a toggle setting and anyone can remove the status from the document as easily as it is set. Additionally, if you use the Mark as Final command on a Word 2007 document, it will not retain the read-only status if opened in an earlier version of Word.

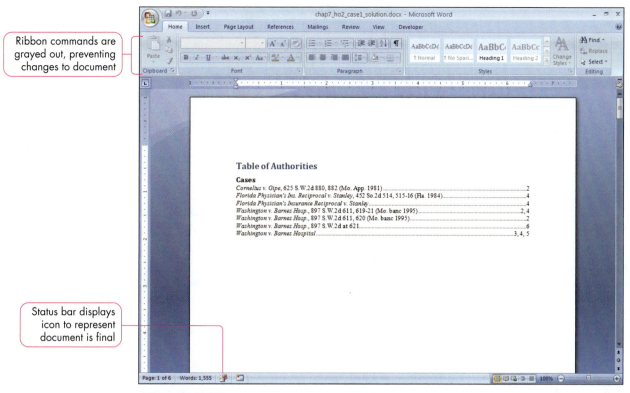

Ribbon commands are grayed out, preventing changes to document

Status bar displays icon to represent document is final

Figure 7.11 Mark as Final Command

Setting Formatting Restrictions

> To ensure that others do not modify formatting or styles, you can set **formatting restrictions** on documents. When you set formatting restrictions, character formatting tools, such as bold and font size, are unavailable.

Organizations often use specific styles and formatting to ensure consistency among documents. The person who oversees document formatting might create or modify styles that should not be changed by other users. To ensure that others do not modify formatting or styles, you can set *formatting restrictions* on documents. When you set formatting restrictions, character formatting tools, such as bold and font size, are unavailable, as shown in Figure 7.12. Users cannot click Bold or press Ctrl+B to bold text.

Formatting restrictions guarantee that others do not modify formatting or styles in a document.

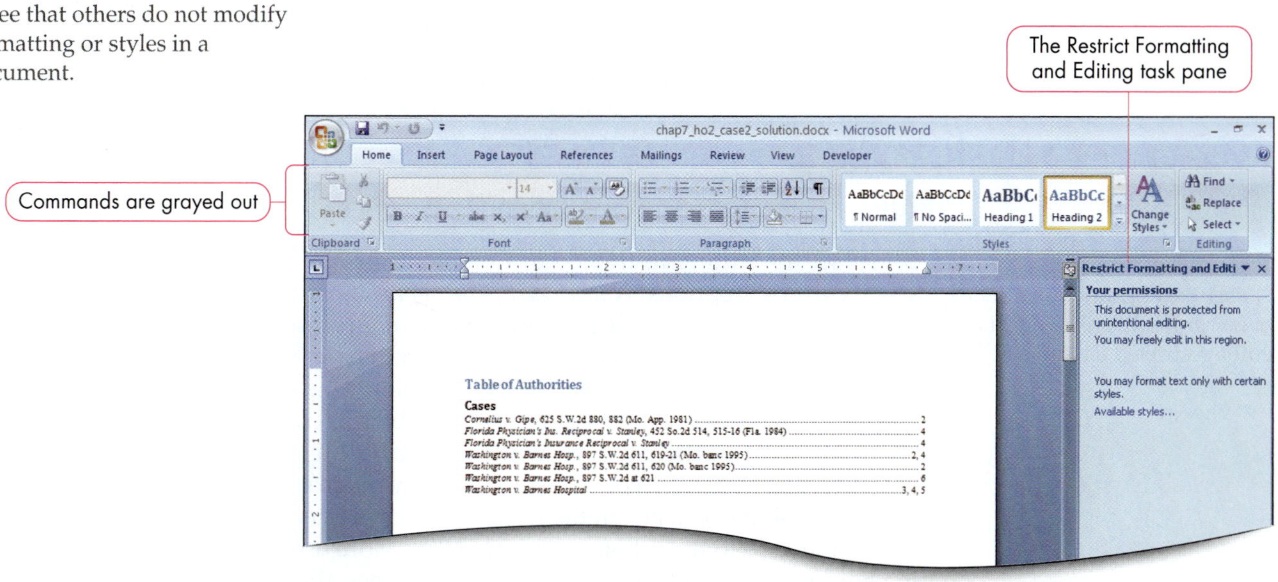

The Restrict Formatting and Editing task pane

Commands are grayed out

Figure 7.12 Formatting Restrictions Disable Commands on the Home Tab

In addition to restricting character format tools, Word also prevents users from changing the formats for font, paragraph, column, drop caps, bullets and numbering, and tabs. You may apply approved styles, such as Heading 1, to text. However, you cannot apply styles that you have restricted. For example, if you restrict the Heading 3 style, you cannot apply that style to text. Furthermore, you cannot modify the format settings for any styles, even those the user is authorized to apply.

To set formatting restrictions on a document, click Protect Document on the Review tab, click Restrict Formatting and Editing, if necessary, and then click Limit formatting to a selection of styles. Click Settings to display the Formatting Restrictions dialog box where you specify exactly which formatting options to disable.

Setting Editing Restrictions

When you set formatting restrictions, Word does not prevent you from changing content in a document. You might also want to set editing restrictions on particular documents. *Editing restrictions* specify limits for users to modify a document. For example, you might want to make sure that the Track Changes feature is active when users make any changes to the document. Doing so lets you know what edits are made to collaborative documents, even if the users forget to activate Track Changes themselves. Other types of editing restrictions include limiting users to inserting comments without changing document content, restricting data entry to fields or unprotected areas within a form, and preventing users from making any changes to a letterhead template.

Editing restrictions specify limits for users to modify a document.

To set editing restrictions on a document, click Protect Document on the Review tab, click Restrict Formatting and Editing, if necessary, and then click Allow only this type of editing in the document. After you click this setting, you can select from four editing restrictions, as outlined in Table 7.2. After the restriction is selected, click Yes, Start Enforcing Protection to activate it.

Table 7.2 Editing Restrictions

Restriction Type	Description
Tracked Changes	Enables the track changes feature automatically and marks document with any changes made.
Comments	Users can add comments to document, but cannot make any other changes.
Filling in forms	Users can insert information into form controls or fields, but cannot modify other content.
No changes (Read only)	Users cannot make any changes to the document; they can only view it.

Allow User Exceptions from Restrictions

If you set the editing restriction to Comments or No changes (Read only), you can specify user exceptions. A *user exception* is an individual or group of individuals who are allowed to edit all or specific parts of a restricted document. For example, you might allow all team members to edit a particular section of a collaborative document. You can create an exception by enabling users to edit that section only. You can create various user exceptions throughout a document by enabling some individuals to edit particular text, while enforcing the editing restrictions for other individuals. Word color-codes text for which you create different user exceptions.

A *user exception* is an individual or group that is allowed to edit a restricted document.

The default check box in the Exceptions list is Everyone. You can add individual users or groups to the list of exceptions. Click More users to open the Add Users dialog box, as shown in Figure 7.13. Type user names, domains, or e-mail addresses for individuals you want to add, separated by semicolons, and click OK. After you add users, you can continue selecting text and clicking the appropriate user name to create a user exception for editing text.

Type name or ID in this area

Figure 7.13 Add Users Who Are Exceptions to Editing Restrictions

Information Rights Management (IRM) services are designed to help control who can access documents.

You must install a special service to add users in the Add Users dialog box. *Information Rights Management (IRM)* services are designed to help you control who can access documents containing sensitive or confidential information. By using an IRM, you can specify different users and the types of permissions you grant to them. If the IRM Services Client is not installed on your computer, a prompt to download it will display when you try to open files that have been rights-managed. Follow the prompts to download and install the software. If you work in a network lab, you might not be able to install it. Use Help to learn more about permissions, IRM, and adding users as exceptions.

Remove Editing Restrictions

To remove editing restrictions, click Stop Protection on the Restrict Formatting and Editing task pane. You can also click the Review tab, click Protect Document, and then click Restrict Formatting and Editing, if necessary. If the formatting restrictions are password-protected, you must enter the correct password and click OK. If you did not assign a password, the restrictions are automatically removed. If you applied both formatting and editing restrictions, clicking the Stop Protection button removes both types of restrictions. If you want to remove only one type of restriction, you must reset the restriction you want to continue to enforce in the Restrict Formatting and Editing task pane.

Setting Passwords to Open a Document

When creating the form in Hands-On Exercise 1, you had the opportunity to set a password for the document. Setting passwords is one way to secure a document. For example, you might want to password-protect highly confidential documents from being opened by unauthorized users. This is helpful when you need to store a document on a network drive but do not want everyone to be able to open the document. When you assign a password to the document, only those who know the password can open the document. You can set a password with up to 15 characters. Passwords are case-sensitive, meaning they must match upper- and lowercase letters perfectly. They may consist of letters, numbers, and symbols; a good password will use a combination of all three. You may even use a combination of upper- and lowercase characters, such as *EW3_proj_2*.

To set a password that must be entered before a document will open, click the Office Button, click Save As, click Tools, and then click General Options, as shown in Figure 7.14. Type your password in the Password to open box, and then click OK. The Confirm Password dialog box will prompt you to reenter the password. After you retype the password, click OK to close the dialog box, and then save the document.

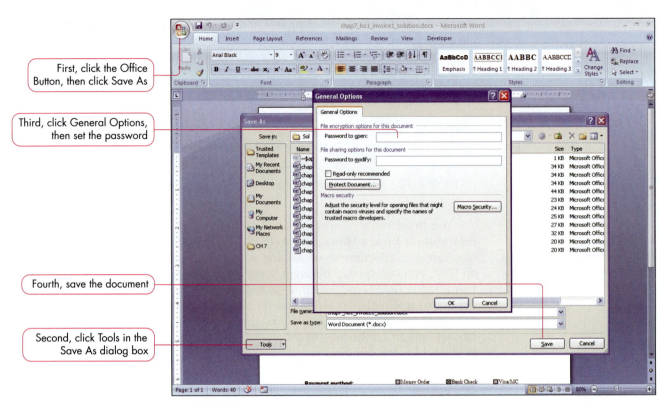

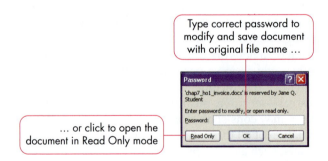

Figure 7.14 Open the General Options Dialog Box to Set a Password

Set a Password to Modify a Document

You may want to allow others to open a document but not be able to modify the content. To restrict users from modifying a document, click the Office Button, Save As, click Tools, and then click General Options. Type your password in the Password to modify box, and then click OK. The Confirm Password dialog box will prompt you to reenter the password, and then you click OK. You return to the Save As dialog box, where you can proceed to save the document. People can now open the document, but they must know the password to modify the document. When users attempt to open a document protected against unauthorized modifications, the Password dialog box opens (see Figure 7.15).

Figure 7.15 The Password Dialog Box

Authorized users can type the password in the Password box and click OK. They are able to make changes and save the document with those changes. Users who do not know the password can click the Read Only button to open the document in Read Only mode. In this mode, users can make changes; however, they cannot save those changes to the original file name. They must choose a different folder or specify a different file name for saving the document through the Save As dialog box.

Modify a Password to Open or Modify a Document

If you want to change a password, you must know the current password to open or modify the document. With the document open, click the Office Button, click Save As, click Tools, and then click General Options. Type the replacement password in the Password to open or the Password to modify box, and then click OK. The Confirm Password dialog box will prompt you to reenter the password. Click OK to close the dialog box and then save the document again.

Delete a Password to Open or Modify a Document

You can remove a password for opening or modifying a document if you decide you no longer want to protect the document with a password. To remove the password, open the document by using the current password for opening or modifying the document. With the document open, click the Office Button, click Save As, click Tools, and then click General Options. Select the password in the Password to open or the Password to modify box, and then press Delete to remove it. Click OK to close the dialog box, and then save the document.

Using Digital Signatures to Authenticate Documents

> A ***digital certificate*** is an attachment to a file that guarantees the authenticity of the file, provides a verifiable signature, or enables encryption.

Word uses Microsoft Authenticode technology to enable you to digitally sign a file by using a ***digital certificate***—an attachment to a file or e-mail that guarantees the authenticity of the file, provides a verifiable signature, or enables encryption. This authentication is important because as you share files with others, you increase your risk of having files tampered with or infected with a virus. By adding a digital signature to your documents, you confirm through electronic encryption that the information comes from you, is valid, and has not been changed after you signed it. You have two different ways to use digital signatures to sign Office documents. You can either:

- Add an invisible digital signature to a document or
- Add visible signature lines to a document to capture one or more digital signatures.

Attach a Digital Signature

> ***Digital signature*** is an electronic stamp that displays information about a person or organization.

When you need to confirm the authenticity of a document you can attach a digital signature. ***Digital signatures*** are electronic stamps that display information about the person or organization that obtained the certification. You can obtain a digital certificate from a certification authority such as VeriSign by completing an application and paying a fee. Some companies have in-house security administrators who issue their own digital signatures by using tools such as Microsoft Certificate Server.

If you want to create your own digital certificate for personal use, you can do so by using the *Selfcert.exe* application included with Microsoft Office. This certification is unauthenticated but exposes you to how digital signatures work. When you sign your document, you are validating its contents and the document remains signed until it is modified. Therefore, signing a document and attaching the signature should be the last action you take before you distribute it. Adding a digital signature causes the document to be marked as final, so it also becomes a read-only document.

To attach a digital signature, you must first save the document, and then click the Office Button. Point to Prepare, and then click Add a Digital Signature. Your signature stamp will attach automatically, as shown in Figure 7.16, but you can change the stamp if more than one certificate is available. You can also type in the purpose for signing the document, although it is not required.

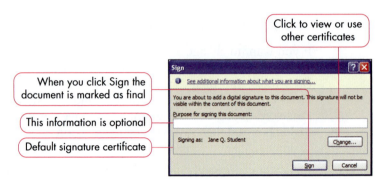

Figure 7.16 Add a Digital Signature

You can also view and remove a digital signature from a signed document. Click the Office Button, point to Prepare, and then click View Signatures to display the Signatures task pane, which lists all signatures attached to the document. In the Signatures task pane, you can click on a particular signature to view a menu that includes Signature Details and Remove Signature. When all signatures are removed, the document is no longer marked as final and all formatting commands are available.

Add a Signature Line in a Document

The *signature line* enables the user of the document to digitally sign the document.

New to Office 2007 is the ability to insert a signature line into a document. The *signature line* enables individuals and companies to distribute and collect signatures, and then process forms or documents electronically without the need to print and fax. The digital signatures, especially if verified by a certifying authority, provide an authentic record of the signer and allow the document to be verified in the future.

When the document opens and the signature line displays, users can type a signature, select a digital image of a signature, or write a signature if they use a tablet PC. After the user inserts his or her signature using one of the options listed above, a digital signature tag is attached to the document to authenticate the identity of the signer and the document becomes read-only to prevent modifications to the content.

To insert a signature line, click the Insert tab, click the Signature Line down arrow in the Text group, and then click Microsoft Office Signature Line. Click OK to the Microsoft Office Word dialog box if it displays. The Signature Setup dialog box displays, as shown in Figure 7.17, and prompts you to enter information about the signer. You can enter the expected signer's name, title, e-mail address, and any additional instructions you want to display near the signature line. You can even allow signers to add comments to the document and attach the current date to the document when they sign.

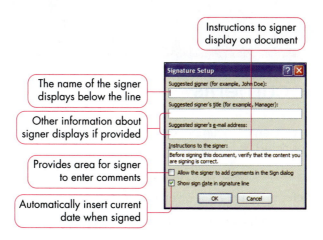

Instructions to signer display on document

The name of the signer displays below the line

Other information about signer displays if provided

Provides area for signer to enter comments

Automatically insert current date when signed

Figure 7.17 Insert a Signature Line

Hands-On Exercises

2 | Protecting Documents

Skills covered: 1. Set a Password to Open a Document and Mark as Final **2.** Set Formatting Restrictions **3.** Set Editing Restrictions **4.** Set Exceptions for Restricted Documents **5.** Attach a Digital Signature to a Document **6.** Insert a Signature Line in a Document

Step 1 **Set a Password to Open a Document and Mark as Final**	Refer to Figure 7.18 as you complete Step 1.

a. Open the document *chap7_ho2_case*.

This is a legal document that needs to be password-protected until all modifications have been finalized.

b. Click the **Office Button**, and then click **Save As**. Click **Tools**, and then click **General Options**, as shown in Figure 7.18.

The General Options dialog box displays; this is where you set passwords to open and modify a document.

c. Type **Chap7_ho2_case** in the **Password to open** box.

The password you enter contains a combination of upper- and lowercase letters, numbers, and special characters, which is recommended by security experts. Passwords are case-sensitive, meaning they must match upper- and lowercase letters perfectly. For that reason, you must pay special attention to capitalization when setting and using passwords to protect a document.

d. Click **OK**. In the Confirm Password dialog box, type **Chap7_ho2_case** in the **Reenter password to open** box, and then click **OK**.

TROUBLESHOOTING: Because passwords are case-sensitive, if you do not type the same password using the same capitalization, an error message appears stating you have not typed the same password. Click OK to close the message box, delete the passwords in the password dialog box, and type the passwords again.

e. Type **chap7_ho2_case1_solution** in the **File name** box in the Save As dialog box, and then click **Save**.

You might prefer to click on the end of the file name and add *1_solution* if you do not want to retype the whole file name.

f. Click the **Office Button**, point to **Prepare**, and then click **Mark as Final**. Click **OK** on all Microsoft Office Word dialog boxes.

Two dialog boxes might display after you mark the document as final. The first informs you the document will be marked as final and then saved. The second dialog box informs you that the document has been marked as final and all editing marks are disabled.

g. Close the document.

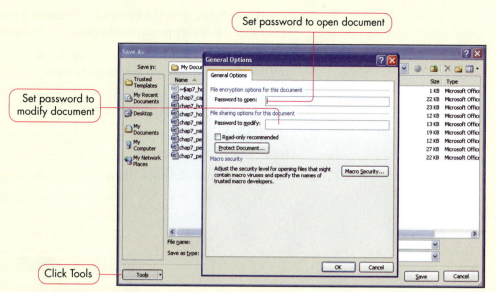

Set password to open document

Set password to modify document

Click Tools

Figure 7.18 Display the General Options Dialog Box to Set a Password

TIP Don't Show This Message Again

If a Microsoft Office Word dialog box displays Don't show this message again, you can click the option so the dialog box will not display in the future. However, if you work in a lab environment, you should ask for instructor permission before changing a setting such as this.

Step 2
Set Formatting Restrictions

Refer to Figure 7.19 as you complete Step 2.

a. Open the document *chap7_ho2_case* and save it as **chap7_ho2_case2_solution**.

b. Click the **Review tab**, click **Protect Document**, and then click **Restrict Formatting and Editing**, if necessary, to display the task pane.

The Restrict Formatting and Editing task pane displays on the right side of the screen.

c. Click **Limit formatting to a selection of styles** on the task pane. Click **Settings** to display the Formatting Restrictions dialog box, as shown in Figure 7.19.

In this dialog box, you can enable users to apply styles of your choice.

d. Click **None**.

Notice that the check marks beside each style disappear. If you click OK, none of the styles can be used in this document. Next, you re-select the styles.

e. Click **All**, and then click **OK**. Click **No** to the Microsoft Office Word dialog box that asks if you want to remove styles that are not allowed.

The user can now apply all styles. However, they cannot modify the styles.

f. Click **Yes, Start Enforcing Protection** on the Restrict Formatting and Editing task pane.

The Start Enforcing Protection dialog box opens. Use this dialog box to set a password required to remove formatting restrictions.

g. Type **Chap7_ho2_2** in the **Enter new password (optional)** box. Retype the password in the **Reenter password to confirm** box, and then click **OK**.

Most commands on the Home tab are dimmed, indicating that the document is restricted against most formatting changes.

h. Press **Ctrl+Home** to move the insertion point to the beginning of the document. Click **Heading 2** from the **Styles gallery**.

Word enables you to apply a different style; however, you cannot change character or font attributes, paragraph alignment, and so on.

i. Save the document. Leave it open for the next step.

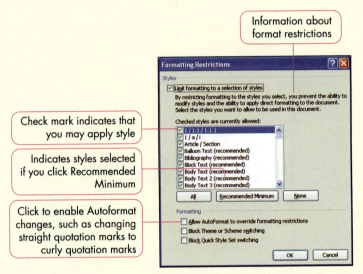

Figure 7.19 The Formatting Restrictions Dialog Box

Step 3
Set Editing Restrictions

Refer to Figure 7.20 as you complete Step 3.

a. In the *chap7_ho2_case2_solution* document, click **Stop Protection** on the Restrict Formatting and Editing task pane, type **Chap7_ho2_2** in the Unprotect Document dialog box, and click **OK**.

The formatting restriction is removed so that users may use all format options on the document.

TROUBLESHOOTING: If the Restrict Formatting and Editing task pane does not display, click the **Review tab** and click **Protect Document.** You might also need to click **Restrict Formatting and Editing** to display the task pane.

b. Click **Allow only this type of editing in the document** in the *Editing restrictions* section.

The *Editing restrictions* drop-down arrow is available so that you can specify the type of editing to restrict. Furthermore, an *Exceptions (optional)* section appears on the task pane so that you can apply exceptions to the editing restrictions, as shown in Figure 7.20.

c. Click the **Editing restrictions** drop-down arrow and click **Comments**.

d. Click **Yes, Start Enforcing Protection**. Type **Chap7_ho2_3** in the **Enter new password (optional)** box. Retype the password in the **Reenter password to confirm** box. Click **OK**.

Users are now restricted from editing the document content. They can only insert comments.

e. Press **Ctrl+Home** to move the insertion point to the beginning of the document, if necessary. Select the title *Table of Authorities*, and click **Delete**.

You cannot delete the text. The status bar displays the message *This modification is not allowed because the selection is locked*. The Restrict Formatting and Editing task pane now displays buttons to show document regions you can edit. However, because you restricted editing to comments only, no regions are available for editing.

f. Click the **Review tab**, click **New Comment**, and type **Double-check the last reference in this table**.

You can insert a comment, and the comment balloon appears on the side of the text.

g. Save the document as **chap7_ho2_case3_solution**. Leave it open for the next step.

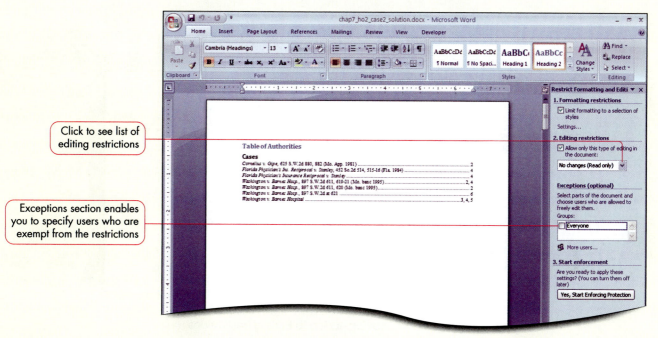

Click to see list of editing restrictions

Exceptions section enables you to specify users who are exempt from the restrictions

Figure 7.20 Editing Restrictions

Step 4
Set Exceptions for Restricted Documents

Refer to Figure 7.21 as you complete Step 4.

a. In the *chap7_ho2_case3_solution* document, display the *Restrict Formatting and Editing* task pane, if necessary. Click **Stop Protection**. Type **Chap7_ho2_3** in the *Password* box, and then click **OK**.

b. Make sure the first two boxes on the task pane contain check marks. Select the heading, **Table of Authorities**.

You want to set a user exception to allow all users to edit this heading.

c. In the *Exceptions (optional)* section of the Restrict Formatting and Editing task pane, click **Everyone**. Deselect the text.

The heading you selected appears with a light gray background, indicating that the user exception is applied to it, as shown in Figure 7.21.

d. Click **Yes, Start Enforcing Protection**. Type **Chap7_ho2_4** in the *Enter new password* box. Retype the password in the *Reenter password* box. Click **OK**.

e. Press **Ctrl+Home** to move the insertion point to the beginning of the document, if necessary. Select the information in the Table of Authorities, but do not select the heading itself, and click **Delete**.

You cannot delete the text because it is protected against editing.

f. Click the heading, *Table of Authorities*, click the **Home** tab, then click **Title** from the Styles gallery.

Word enables this editing because you are a part of *Everyone* included in the user exception for the heading. The task pane provides information on whether you can edit the current region.

g. Save the document as **chap7_ho2_case4_solution**. Leave it open for the next step.

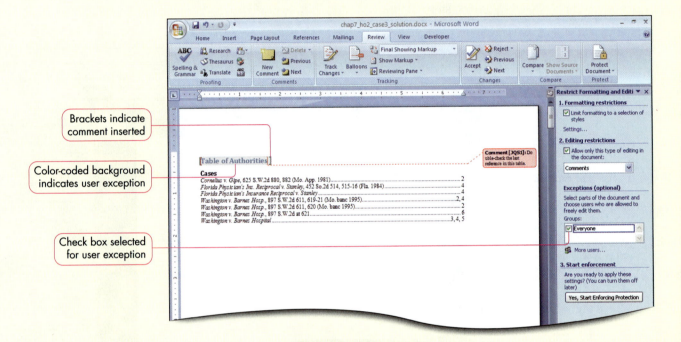

Figure 7.21 Set Exception to Editing Restrictions

Step 5

Attach a Digital Signature to a Document

Refer to Figure 7.22 as you complete Step 5.

a. Use the Windows search feature to search for the SELFCERT.EXE file and double-click it.

The SELFCERT.EXE file should be located in the C:\Program Files\Microsoft Office\Office12 folder. The Create Digital Certificate dialog box opens and provides information about the self-certification program.

TROUBLESHOOTING: If you cannot find the SELFCERT.EXE file, or if your lab computer will not allow you to install the program, continue to read over the steps in this activity so that you can see how digital signatures work.

b. Type your name in the *Your Certificate's Name* box, and then click **OK**.

A message box appears, stating that you successfully created a certificate. Although your certificate is unauthorized, you can still use it to practice working with digital certificates.

c. Click **OK** to close the message box. Close the Restrict Formatting and Editing task pane.

d. Maximize the Word application window. Save the document *chap7_ho2_case4_solution* as **chap7_ho2_case5_solution**.

e. Click the **Office Button**, point to **Prepare**, and then click **Add a Digital Signature**. Click **OK** to the Microsoft Office Word dialog box, if necessary.

The Sign dialog box displays. Your name displays at the bottom of the window because you recently created a digital signature.

TROUBLESHOOTING: If your name does not display in the Sign dialog box, click **Change** to display the Select Certificate dialog box. Click your name from the Issued to column, and then click **OK**.

f. Type **To verify contents** in the Purpose for signing this document box. Click **Sign** to close the Sign dialog box. Click **OK** to close the Signature Confirmation dialog box, if necessary.

The signature stamp displays in the status bar, as shown in Figure 7.22. The Signatures pane displays on the right side of the document, and the formatting commands are grayed out on the Ribbon because the document has been marked as read-only.

g. Close the document.

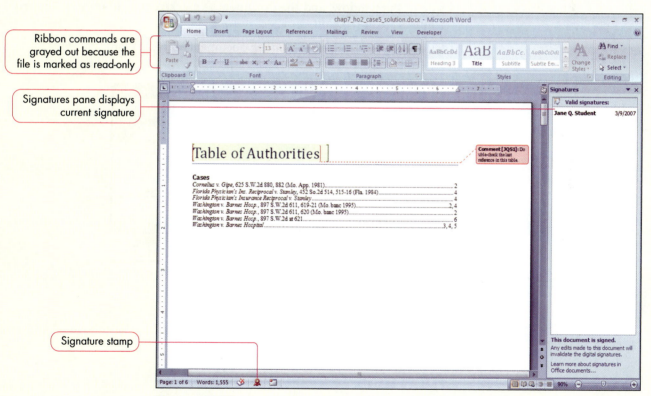

Figure 7.22 View a Document with a Digital Signature

Step 6
Insert a Signature Line in a Document

Refer to Figure 7.23 as you complete Step 6.

a. Open the document *chap7_ho2_case* and save it as **chap7_ho2_case6_solution**.

b. Press **Ctrl+End** to move the insertion point to the end of the document. Press **Enter** two times.

c. Click the **Insert tab**, and then click **Signature Line**. Click **OK** in the Microsoft Office Word dialog box, if necessary.

The Signature Setup dialog box displays.

d. Type **Clark Griswald** in the Suggested signer box. Type **Attorney at Law** in the Suggested signer's title box. Type **CGriswald@GriswaldLaw.org** in the Suggested signer's e-mail address box. Click **OK**.

The signature line displays in the document, as well as the signer's information that you entered in the Signature Setup dialog box.

e. Click **OK** to the Microsoft Office Word dialog box, if necessary. Double-click the signature line to display the Sign dialog box. Type **Clark Griswald** in the Type your name below or click Select Image to select a picture to use as your signature box, as shown in Figure 7.23, and then click **Sign**. Click **OK** in the Signature Confirmation dialog box, if necessary.

The name displays above the signature line, and the date displays in the upper-right corner of the signature line box. The Signatures pane displays on the right side of the window, and the document is marked as read-only and formatting features are grayed out.

f. Close the *chap7_ho2_case6_solution* document and exit Word.

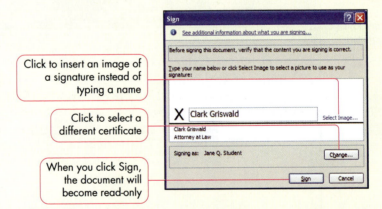

Figure 7.23 Signing on a Signature Line

Introduction to Macros

Have you ever pulled down the same menus and clicked the same sequence of commands over and over? If you find yourself performing repetitive tasks, whether in one document or in a series of documents, you should consider using macros. A *macro* is a set of instructions (that is, a program) that executes a specific task. Using a macro in Word is like recording your favorite television show: You turn on the recorder, tape the show, and then play the show over and over again as often as you want.

New to Office 2007 is the ability to save documents with macros automatically enabled or disabled. By default, Word documents with the .docx extension automatically disable any macros the file might contain. If you store a macro in a document, save it as a *Macro-Enabled Document*, which adds the extension .docm to the file, storing VBA macro code in the document to allow execution of a macro.

In this lesson, you record a macro that sets basic formats for a short business letter. Specifically, you widen the margins, apply Center vertical alignment, and apply Justify horizontal alignment. You then open an existing letter and run the macro so that it applies those format changes.

> A *macro* is a set of instructions that executes a specific task.

> A *Macro-Enabled Document* contains and allows execution of a macro.

Recording a Macro

> The process of creating a macro is called *record macro*.

The process of creating a macro is called *record macro*. When you record a macro, Word records a series of keystrokes and command selections and converts the tasks into coded statements. Before recording a macro, you should decide what you want to accomplish (such as formatting a letter) and then plan exactly what commands and tasks to include (such as margins, alignment, tabs, and so on). Furthermore, you should practice completing the tasks and commands, and make notes of the sequence of steps to perform. Doing so helps you record the macro successfully the first time.

The macro commands are located on two tabs: the View tab and the Developer tab. You can start recording a macro by clicking Macros, then Record Macro in the View tab. On the Developer tab, you click Record Macro in the Code group. The Record Macro dialog box opens so that you can name the macro, as shown in Figure 7.24. You have the option of assigning the macro to a button, which can be assigned to the Quick Access Toolbar so that it is readily available, or you can assign a keystroke combination that runs the macro. If you do not choose either option, the macro is only available in the Macros dialog box. You also have the choice of storing a macro in a particular file, so that it can only be executed when that file is open, or you can store macros in the normal template so that they can run in all files.

When you close the Record Macro dialog box, Word records everything—every keystroke and click of the mouse. For this reason, you do not want to perform any unnecessary actions while recording a macro. For example, if you press Ctrl+Home to correct a mistake while recording the macro, Word records the command to move the insertion point to the beginning of the document. This is problematic if you run the macro in an existing document and the macro inserts or formats text in the wrong location.

Type macro name

You can assign the macro to a toolbar or a keyboard shortcut

Type a description of the macro

You can save the macro in this document only or in the normal template where it is available in all documents

Figure 7.24 The Record Macro Dialog Box

You can type text to include in a macro. If you want the macro text to contain character attributes, such as bold or font color, you should turn on the attribute before typing that particular text, type the text, and then turn off that attribute. While recording a macro, Word does not let you click and drag to select text to be able to apply formatting. If you already typed text and want to add an attribute while recording, you can select the text by pressing Shift and an arrow key. You can then apply the attribute you want to the selected text.

Edit a Macro

Visual Basic for Applications (VBA) is a programming language that is built into Microsoft Office.

Macro instructions are written in *Visual Basic for Applications (VBA)*, a programming language that is built into Microsoft Office. Fortunately, however, you don't have to be a programmer to use VBA. Instead, the macro recorder within Word records your actions, which are then translated automatically into VBA. If you need to edit a macro, you can edit the statements after they have been recorded by opening the Visual Basic editor. The Developer tab includes the Visual Basic command, which opens the Visual Basic editor and displays the macro contents as programming statements, a series of code written in a specific syntax created by a particular programming language, such as Visual Basic. Each programming statement performs a specific task, such as setting a margin. Figure 7.25 displays the macro you create in Hands-On Exercise 3.

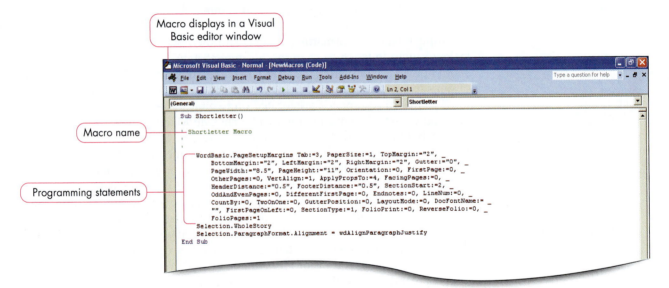

Figure 7.25 The Programming Statements of a Macro

It is helpful to have some knowledge of the Visual Basic programming language and how it works. When possible, you can make minor adjustments to improve the speed and efficiency of the macro. Every time you choose a dialog box option for a macro, the macro recorder records all dialog box settings, even those you do not change, such as the default bottom margin.

When you record macros, Word saves them in the Normal template by default so that you can use them with other documents. Within the Normal template, macros are stored in a macro project called NewMacros, which is a collection of macros you create. You can copy a macro project to another template or document. To copy the NewMacros project to another template or document, click the Developer tab, and then click Macros. Click Organizer within the Macros dialog box. Specify the destination document or template in the list box on the left side of the dialog box, click NewMacros in the *In Normal.dotm* list box, and click Copy. Use Help for more specific information on using the Organizer dialog box.

If you no longer need the macros, you can delete them from within the Macros dialog box. Select the name of the macro you want to delete and click Delete. Follow the onscreen prompts.

Security Risks of Macros

Because macros are coded in a Visual Basic application, they are essentially programs. As a program that executes commands, a macro has the potential to include code that imposes harmful viruses onto your computer. Microsoft Office includes a Trust Center to help protect users from unsafe macros. The Trust Center checks for the following scenarios before enabling a macro:

- The macro is signed by the developer using a digital signature.
- The digital signature is valid.
- The digital signature is not expired.
- The certificate associated with the digital signature was issued by a known certificate authority.
- The person who signed the macro is a trusted publisher.

If the Trust Center does not find any of these scenarios, the macro is automatically disabled and a message displays to inform you of the potential risk. You can edit the settings on your PC according to your preference for security. The following reference table describes the Settings from the Trust Center in the Word Options dialog box.

Macro Security Settings | Reference

Macro Setting	Description
Disable all macros without notification.	If you do not trust macros, click this option. All macros and security alerts about macros are disabled.
Disable all macros with notification.	This is the default setting. All macros are disabled, but it alerts you when a document contains a macro. This alert enables you to decide whether to allow a macro to run.
Disable all macros except digitally signed macros.	This setting works similarly to Disable all macros with notification; however, it enables macros to run if they are digitally signed by a trusted publisher. If you have not included the publisher in your trusted list, you will be alerted about the macro. The alert enables you to allow a macro or to include a publisher in your trusted list. All unsigned macros are disabled and you will not see an alert.
Enable all macros (not recommended; potentially dangerous code can run).	This setting enables all macros to run regardless of their authenticity or signature. This option is not recommended because it exposes your computer to potential attacks by viruses.
Trust access to the VBA project object model.	This setting is for use by developers only.

To change the macro security settings, click the Office Button, click Word Options, click Trust Center, click Trust Center Settings, and then click Macro Settings, if necessary. Alternately, if the Developer tab is available you can click Macro Security to display the Trust Center dialog box and view the settings. When you change the settings in the Trust Center, they are only valid for the program you are currently using, such as Microsoft Word.

If you open a document that contains macros and a security warning displays the message *Macros have been disabled*, you can click the Options button and display the Microsoft Office Security Options dialog box. From there, click Enable this content, and then click OK to return to the document and use any macros that were stored within the document.

Running a Macro

The process of playing back or using a macro is called **run macro**.

The process of playing back or using a macro is called ***run macro***. When you run a macro, Word processes the series of commands and keystrokes saved in the macro. Running a macro is faster than manually choosing each command when you need to use a series of commands frequently. To open the Macros dialog box, you have three options:

• You can display the Developer tab and click Macros.

• You can display the View tab and click Macros, View Macros.

• You can press Alt+F8.

With the Macros dialog box open, as shown in Figure 7.26, you can run, edit, or delete a macro.

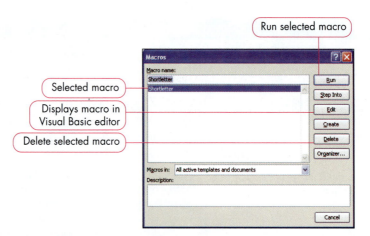

Figure 7.26 Play a Macro

If your macro includes a command that types text, that text takes on the current document's formats when you run the macro. If you specially formatted the text while recording a macro, that special format is retained when you run the macro, regardless of the document's other formats.

Hands-On Exercises

3 | Using Macros

Skills covered: 1. Record a Macro **2.** Play a Macro **3.** Modify a Macro **4.** Run an Edited Macro

---

Step 1
Record a Macro

Refer to Figure 7.27 as you complete Step 1.

a. Open a blank document.

b. Click the **Developer tab**, then click **Record Macro** in the Code group.

The Record Macro dialog box displays so that you can name the macro before you record it. The macro name can consist of up to 80 characters, but no spaces.

TROUBLESHOOTING: If the Developer tab does not display, click the **Office Button**, click **Word Options**, then click the **Popular** section, if necessary. Click **Show Developer tab in the Ribbon**, and then click **OK**.

c. Type **Shortletter** in the *Macro name* box.

You want to provide a short description in addition to your name and the current date.

d. Click at the beginning of the *Description* box and type **Formats short letters**. Click **OK** to start recording.

Word assigns the macro name you entered. You see Stop Recording and Pause Recording display in the Code group of the Developer tab. The mouse pointer looks like an arrow with an attached recorder. A square button displays on the status bar, as shown in Figure 7.27; if you click it, the macro will stop recording.

e. Click the **Page Layout tab**. Click **Margins**, and then click **Custom Margins**. Click in the Top margin box and type **2**. Press **Tab** two times, type **2** in the Left margin box, and then press **Tab** and type **2** in the Right margin box.

You change the margins for the Top, Left, and Right, but not the bottom.

f. Click the **Layout** tab on the Page Setup dialog box, and click the **Vertical alignment** drop-down arrow. Click **Center**, and then click **OK** to close the Page Setup dialog box.

Now, you want to be able to apply the Justify horizontal alignment to an existing document. To format existing text, you need to select the text while the macro is on.

TROUBLESHOOTING: If you click something unintentionally or decide you are too far off track for the macro, click Stop Recording. Repeat the steps to begin recording again. You can use the same macro name and description; allow the new macro to overwrite the first attempt when prompted to replace it.

g. Press **Ctrl+A** to select everything in the document. Click the **Home tab** and click **Justify** in the Paragraph group.

Because you are working in a blank document, the paragraph mark is the only thing that is selected. If you are not viewing formatting marks, you will not even see the paragraph mark.

h. Click the **Developer tab**, and then click **Stop Recording**.

You can also click the gray square button in the Status bar to stop recording a macro.

i. Close the document without saving it.

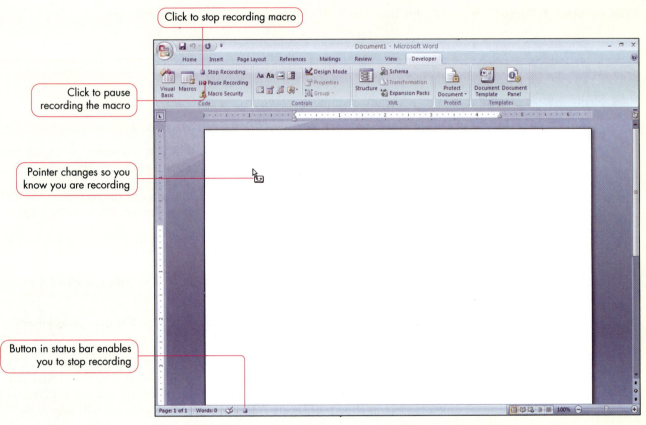

Figure 7.27 Recording a Macro

Refer to Figure 7.28 as you complete Step 2.

a. Open the document *chap7_ho3_cover*. Click the **Office Button**, and then click **Save As**. Click the **Save as type drop-down arrow**, and then click **Word Macro-Enabled Document (*.docm)**. Type **chap7_ho3_cover_solution** in the File name box, and then click **Save**.

This letter contains the 1.25" top and bottom margins, Top vertical alignment, and Left horizontal alignment. You want to run the macro to set margins and apply alignment settings.

TIP   Make a Backup

To avoid destroying a document due to macro problems, you should save the document prior to running a macro. If the macro does not provide the desired results, you can close the document and open the original document again.

b. Click the **Developer tab**, then click **Macros**.

The macros dialog box displays and the Shortletter macro is the only macro available to run.

c. Click **Shortletter**, if necessary, and then click **Run**.

TROUBLESHOOTING: The macro security level is too high if you receive a message stating that macros are disabled. A high security level protects you from running a macro that contains a virus. To disable this security so the macro can run, click **Macro Security** on the **Developer tab**, click **Enable all macros (not recommended; potentially dangerous code can run)**, and then click **OK**. Be sure to reset the security to Disable all macros with notification after completing this exercise.

d. Deselect the text and change the zoom to 75%.

Word runs the macro and sets 2" top, left, and right margins; selects Center vertical alignment; and selects Justify horizontal alignment (see Figure 7.28).

e. Save the document.

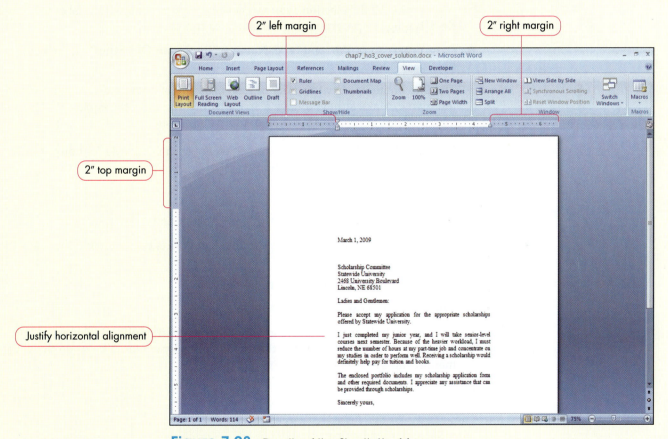

Figure 7.28 Results of the Shortletter Macro

Step 3

Modify a Macro

Refer to Figure 7.29 as you complete Step 3.

a. Press **Alt+F8** to display the Macros dialog box. Select **Shortletter** in the Macro name list, and then click **Edit**.

The Visual Basic Editor opens so that you can edit the programming statements. You will modify the TopMargin statement. It is causing the vertical alignment to be off-center because the top margin is 2" and the bottom margin is 1".

b. Delete the number 2 at the end of the statement *TopMargin: ="2"* and type **1**, as shown in Figure 7.29.

TROUBLESHOOTING: Do not delete any other part of the TopMargin statement or any other statements. If you do, the macro may not run correctly. If you accidentally delete programming statements, refer to Figure 7.25 to retype them, and then edit the TopMargin statement again.

The TopMargin statement now sets a 1" top margin. When you run this macro on a document, the document will be centered on the page because the top and bottom margins are identical and the vertical alignment is set to center.

c. Scroll to the bottom of the macro commands and click at the end of the second statement from the bottom, after *wdAlignParagraphJustify*.

You want to add a programming statement to apply Bookman Old Style font to selected text. The first line of the statement indicates that you are working with font attributes.

d. Press **Enter** and type **With Selection.Font** on the blank line.

After typing With Selection., you might see a popup menu with a list of methods. Keep typing the programming statement to complete it.

e. Press **Enter**, press **Tab**, and type **.Name = "Bookman Old Style"** on the blank line.

The line immediately after *With Selection.Font* must contain a command for the font name. Make sure you have a space before and after the equal sign (=), and make sure you type the quotation marks as indicated.

TROUBLESHOOTING: If you do not have Bookman Old Style font on your computer, choose another serif font name.

f. Press **Enter**.

g. Press **Shift+Tab** and type **End With** on the blank line.

Pressing Shift+Tab outdents the next line. *End With* is the command that ends the programming statement.

h. Click **Save Normal** on the toolbar.

i. Click **File, Close and Return to Microsoft Word**.

You are ready to run the macro again to make sure it applies Bookman Old Style font to document text and that the text is vertically centered between the 1" top margin and the 1" bottom margin.

j. Save the document.

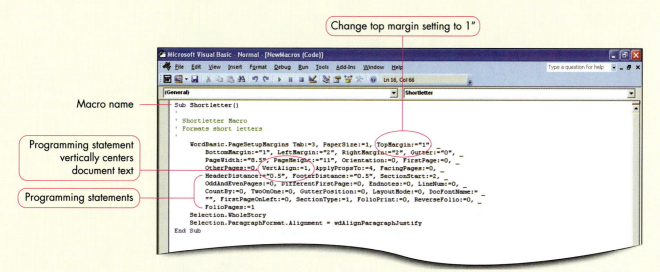

Figure 7.29 The Macro Code

Labels in figure:
- Change top margin setting to 1"
- Macro name
- Programming statement vertically centers document text
- Programming statements

```
Sub Shortletter()
'
' Shortletter Macro
' Formats short letters
'
    WordBasic.PageSetupMargins Tab:=3, PaperSize:=1, TopMargin:="1" _
        BottomMargin:="1", LeftMargin:="2", RightMargin:="2", Gutter:="0", _
        PageWidth:="8.5", PageHeight:="11", Orientation:=0, FirstPage:=0, _
        OtherPages:=0, VertAlign:=1, ApplyPropsTo:=4, FacingPages:=0, _
        HeaderDistance:="0.5", FooterDistance:="0.5", SectionStart:=2, _
        OddAndEvenPages:=0, DifferentFirstPage:=0, Endnotes:=0, LineNum:=0, _
        CountBy:=0, TwoOnOne:=0, GutterPosition:=0, LayoutMode:=0, DocFontName:= _
        "", FirstPageOnLeft:=0, SectionType:=1, FolioPrint:=0, ReverseFolio:=0, _
        FolioPages:=1
    Selection.WholeStory
    Selection.ParagraphFormat.Alignment = wdAlignParagraphJustify
End Sub
```

Step 4
Run an Edited Macro

Refer to Figure 7.30 as you complete Step 4.

a. Click the **View tab**, click **Macros**, and then click **View Macros**.

The Macros dialog box displays so that you can run a macro.

b. Click **Shortletter** in the *Macro name* box, and then click **Run**.

c. Deselect the text and change the zoom to view the whole page.

After you run the macro, the document is vertically centered, and the text is formatted with Bookman Old Style font, as shown in Figure 7.30.

d. Close the *chap7_ho3_cover_solution* document and exit Word.

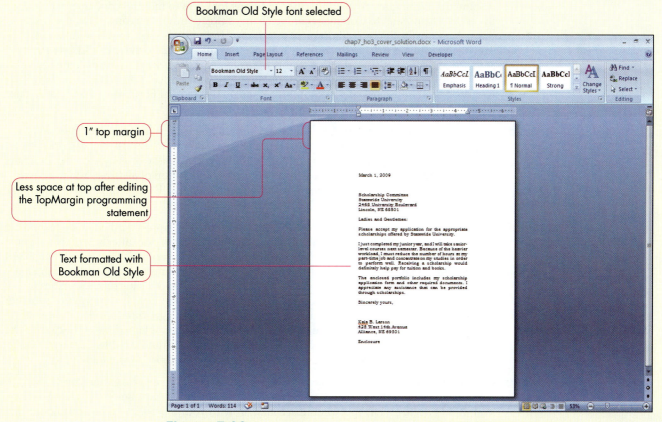

Labels in figure:
- Bookman Old Style font selected
- 1" top margin
- Less space at top after editing the TopMargin programming statement
- Text formatted with Bookman Old Style

Figure 7.30 Document After Running Edited Macro

Summary

1. **Create an electronic form.** In Microsoft Word you can create a form template, a document that defines the standard layout, structure, and formatting of a form. You can save the form as a Word document or a Word template. A form includes controls that enable the user to enter data in specific places.

2. **Insert form controls.** If you want users to fill out a form electronically, you must insert form controls, also called form fields, into the form template. Form controls help the user complete a form by displaying prompts such as drop-down lists and text boxes. A text content control is the most common and is used to enter any type of text into a form. A check box form field, as the name implies, consists of a box, which is checked or clear. A drop-down list enables the user to choose from one of several existing entries. The Date Picker displays a calendar that the user can navigate and click rather than typing in a date.

3. **Protect a form.** After you create a form, you can apply protection that prevents any modification except data entry. You must turn off the Design Mode before you protect a document. If you want to protect specific form controls without limiting access to the rest of the document, use the Group command on the Developer tab. After you group controls, click the Properties command and select a locking option.

4. **Mark a document as final.** The Mark as Final command enables you to create a read-only file, and the status property is set to Final. This is a helpful command for communicating with other people that the document is not a draft but a completed and final version. Mark as Final is a toggle setting, and anyone can remove the status from the document as easily as it is set.

5. **Set formatting restrictions.** In addition to restricting character formats, Word can also prevent users from changing the formats for font, paragraph, column, drop caps, bullets and numbering, and tabs. To set formatting restrictions on a document, click Protect Document on the Review tab, and then click Limit formatting to a selection of styles. Click Settings to display the Formatting Restrictions dialog box, where you specify exactly which formatting options to disable.

6. **Set editing restrictions.** When you set formatting restrictions, Word does not prevent users from changing content in a document. You might also want to set editing restrictions on particular documents. Editing restrictions specify conditions for users to modify a document. If you set the editing restriction to Comments or No changes (Read only), you can specify user exceptions. A user exception is an individual or group of individuals who are allowed to edit all or specific parts of a restricted document. You must install a special service to add users in the Add Users dialog box. Information Rights Management (IRM) services are designed to help you control who can access documents containing sensitive or confidential information. To remove editing restrictions, click Stop Protection on the Restrict Formatting and Editing task pane.

7. **Set passwords to open a document.** Setting passwords is one way to secure a document. When you assign a password to the document, only those who know the password can open the document. You can set a password with up to 15 characters. Passwords may consist of letters, numbers, and symbols; a good password will use a combination of all three. You may even use a combination of upper- and lowercase characters, such as EW3_proj_2. Users who do not know the password can open the document in Read Only mode.

8. **Use Digital signatures to authenticate documents.** Word uses Microsoft Authenticode technology to enable you to digitally sign a file by using a digital certificate—an attachment to a file or e-mail that guarantees the authenticity of the file, provides a verifiable signature, or enables encryption. You have two different ways to use digital signatures to sign Office documents. You can add an invisible digital signature to a document or add visible signature lines to a document to capture one or more digital signatures. When you need to confirm the authenticity of a document, you can attach a digital signature. Digital signatures are electronic stamps that display information about the person or organization that obtained the certification. The signature line enables individuals and companies to distribute and collect signatures, and then process forms or documents electronically without the need to print and fax.

9. **Record a macro.** When you create a macro, Word records a series of keystrokes and command selections and converts the tasks into specifically coded statements. Before recording a macro, you should decide what you want to accomplish with your macro, and then you should plan

...continued on Next Page

exactly which commands and tasks to include. When you start the macro, you can save it in the current document only or you can save it to the Normal template, where it will be available in all documents.

10. **Run a macro.** The process of playing back or using a macro is called run macro. When you run a macro, Word processes the series of commands and keystrokes saved in the macro. When you need to use a series of commands frequently, running a macro is faster than manually choosing each command. Furthermore, you can assign a keyboard shortcut to run a macro or edit the code to modify a macro.

Key Terms

Multiple Choice

1. Which of the following is true regarding password protection?

   (a) All documents are automatically saved with a default password.

   (b) The password assigned to a document should use a combination of upper- and lowercase letters, numbers, and special characters.

   (c) A password must be set on a document that is restricted from editing.

   (d) A password cannot be changed after it has been established.

2. When you create a form template that will be broadly distributed outside your organization, you should do all of the following except:

   (a) Insert form controls where needed.

   (b) Protect the template using Restrict Formatting and Editing features.

   (c) Save the template with a .dotx extension.

   (d) Set a password to protect the template.

3. Which form control will enable a user to choose from a list of options?

   (a) Combo Box

   (b) Check Box

   (c) Date Picker

   (d) Text

4. Which form control enables you to perform mathematical calculations in a form field?

   (a) Combo Box

   (b) Check Box

   (c) Date Picker

   (d) Text

5. Which of the following is not true about protecting a form?

   (a) The Restrict Formatting and Editing task pane enables you to prevent users from modifying the content of a form.

   (b) The Restrict Formatting and Editing task pane enables you to prevent users from modifying the styles used in a form.

   (c) If you forget the password that protects a form, you can recover it by running a macro.

   (d) You can specify certain individuals who are exempt from the formatting and editing restrictions placed on a form.

6. Which of the following can you use to authenticate the contents of a document?

   (a) Password

   (b) Digital signature

   (c) Macro

   (d) Form control

7. If you allow formatting restrictions on a document, which of the following modifications can take place?

   (a) Change line spacing

   (b) Increase font size

   (c) Modify the Heading 2 style

   (d) Delete a paragraph

8. How can you tell if a document has been digitally signed?

   (a) An icon that looks like a certificate displays on the status bar.

   (b) You must open the Add Digital Signature dialog box.

   (c) A message appears when you open the document.

   (d) A signature line is at the bottom of the document.

9. Which of the following is not an editing restriction you can apply to a document?

   (a) No changes (Read only)

   (b) Tracked changes

   (c) Digital signature

   (d) Filling in forms

10. What is the default location for a macro created in Microsoft Word?

    (a) In the Normal template, where it is available to every Word document

    (b) In the document in which it was created, where it is available only to that document

    (c) In the Macros folder on your hard drive

    (d) In the Office folder on your hard drive

11. Which of the following best describes the recording and execution of a macro?

    (a) A macro is recorded once and executed once.

    (b) A macro is recorded once and executed many times.

    (c) A macro is recorded many times and executed many times.

    (d) A macro is recorded many times and executed once.

12. What service must be installed before you can allow user exceptions on a document that has been protected from editing?

    (a) Trust Center

    (b) Microsoft Authenticode Technology

    (c) Visual Basic for Applications (VBA)

    (d) Information Rights Management (IRM)

13. Which of the following is the least appropriate advice to give to someone who wants to learn how to create and run macros?

    (a) Decide what you want the macro to accomplish.

    (b) Make a list of the sequence of tasks you want to perform prior to recording the macro.

    (c) Change your macro security settings to *Enable all macros* all the time.

    (d) Practice completing the steps before actually recording the macro.

14. Before you can insert form controls into a form or display the Visual Basic editor to modify macros, what tab must you display in the Ribbon?

    (a) View

    (b) Review

    (c) Developer

    (d) Add-Ins

15. Which statement is not true about a signature line?

    (a) If you specify a name and e-mail address of the signer, they do not display with the signature line.

    (b) You can insert a digital image of a signature on the line.

    (c) If you specify instructions for the signer, they display along with the signature line.

    (d) You can have the date inserted automatically when a signature is inserted on the line.

1 Science Fair Volunteer Request Form

The Regional Science Fair will occur on the campus of Missouri State University in the spring, and students from schools across the southwest portion of the state compete in areas such as physics, chemistry, environment, meteorology, and astronomy. You have been asked to serve as the volunteer coordinator this year; a job that is responsible for recruiting students, citizens, and parents to help during the event. Volunteers are needed to help set up, assist judges, run errands for event coordinators, and break down and clean up the facility. You decide to create a form that all volunteers can quickly fill out and submit to schedule their time. Because the form is created in Word, it can be e-mailed back to you, and then you can create a master list of volunteers.

a. Open the *chap7_pe1_volunteer* document and save it as **chap7_pe1_volunteer_solution**.

b. Click the **Office Button**, click **Word Options**, click **Popular**, if necessary, and then click **Show Developer tab in the Ribbon**, if necessary. Click **OK**.

c. Click in the table cell across from *NAME* (where the first row and second column meet). Click the **Developer tab**, and then click **Text** in the Controls group.

d. Click the **down arrow key** to move the insertion point to the cell opposite *PHONE NUMBER*. Click **Text** in the Controls group.

e. Click the **down arrow key** to move the insertion point to the cell opposite *DATE YOU CAN HELP*. Click **Drop-Down List** in the Controls group.

f. Click the **down arrow key** to move the insertion point to the cell opposite *START TIME*. Click **Combo Box** in the Controls group.

g. Click **Design Mode** in the Controls group so you can modify the properties of the form controls.

h. Click the Text control that displays opposite *NAME* in the table, and then click **Properties** in the Controls group. In the Title box, type **Name**. Click **OK**. Click the Text control that displays opposite *PHONE NUMBER* in the table, and then click **Properties** in the Controls group. In the Title box, type **Phone**. Click **OK**.

i. Click the Drop-Down List control opposite *DATE YOU CAN HELP*, and then click **Properties** in the Controls group. Type **Date** in the Title box. Click **Add**, then type **April 17** in the Display name box. Click **OK**. Click **Add**, then type **April 18** in the Display name box. Click **OK**. Click **OK** to close the Content Control Properties dialog box.

j. Right-click the Combo Box control opposite *START TIME*, and then click **Properties**. Type **Start** in the Title box. Click **Add** and type **7:00 am** in the Display name box. Repeat this process to add each hour from 8:00 am to 12:00 noon. Click **OK** to close the Content Control Properties dialog box.

k. Click the **Content Control tag** for the Start combo box and press **Ctrl+C** to copy the control, as shown in Figure 7.31. Click in the cell opposite *END TIME* and press **Ctrl+V** to paste the control.

l. Click the tab on the control you just pasted and click **Properties**. Double-click *Start* in the Title box and type **End**. Press **Tab** and type **End** in the Tag box. Click **7:00 am** in the Drop-Down List Properties section and click **Remove**. Click **Add**, type **1:00 pm** in the Display Name box, and then click **OK**. Click **OK** to close the Content Control Properties dialog box.

m. Scroll down to the bottom of the document. Replace the text ****Enter your name here**** with your name. Type your e-mail in the last line. Click **Design Mode**.

n. Click the **Developer** tab, if necessary. Click **Protect Document**, click **Restrict Formatting and Editing**, if necessary, click **Allow only this type of editing in the document**, and then click **Filling in forms** from the drop-down list. Click **Yes, Start Enforcing Protection**.

o. Type **chap7_pe1** in the Enter new password box. Retype the password, and then click **OK**. Save the document.

...continued on Next Page

p. Enter the following information into the controls in the table:

Name	John Sabella
Phone number	(417) 555-5551
Date you can help	April 17
Start time	8:00 am
End time	11:00 am

q. Save the form as **chap7_pe1_volunteerJohn_solution**. Close the document.

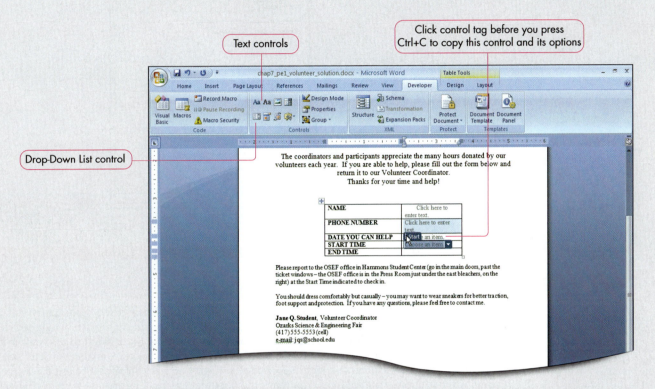

Figure 7.31 Copy a Form Control

2 Change Document Protection

Your coworker wrote the first draft of a report about water conservation in your area of the state. She wants to be sure that no other person in the department can open or modify the document while it is in development. She sent it to you, and now you must make modifications. But first, you must enter the passwords she uses to protect the document, and then you must remove the document protection so you can edit it.

a. Open the *chap7_pe2_water* document, then type **Chap7_pe2** in each of the Password dialog boxes. Save the document as **chap7_pe2_water_solution**.

b. Click the **Office Button**, click **Word Options**, click **Popular**, and then click **Show Developer tab in the Ribbon**, if necessary. Click **OK**.

c. Click the **Developer Tab**, click **Protect Document**, and then click **Stop Protection** in the Restrict Formatting and Editing task pane. Type **Chap7_pe2** in the Password dialog box when prompted. Click **Limit formatting to a selection of styles** to remove the formatting restriction. Click **Allow only this type of editing in the document** to remove the editing restriction.

...continued on Next Page

d. Click the **Office Button**, click **Save As**, click **Tools**, and click **General Options**.

e. Replace the Password to open with **Chap7_rpt**. Press **Tab** to select the password to modify. Press **Delete** to remove the password, as shown in Figure 7.32, and then click **OK**. Type **Chap7_rpt** in the Confirm Password dialog box, and then click **OK**. Click **Save** in the Save As dialog box.

f. Click the **Office Button**, point to **Prepare**, and then click **Add a Digital Signature**. Click **OK** to any Microsoft Office Word dialog boxes. Type **First draft edits complete** in the Purpose for signing this document box, and then click **Sign**. Click **OK** to close the Signature Confirmation dialog box.

g. Close the Signatures task pane and close the document.

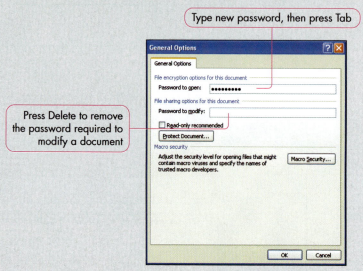

Figure 7.32 Change the Password to Open a Document

3 White Glove Cleaners

You are the Marketing Manager for White Glove Cleaners, a small but growing company that offers a residential and commercial cleaning service. When potential customers are contacted they receive a printed document that describes the cleaning services. You recently decided to update the document so it looks more professional and draws attention to key services. You also want to include a signature line where clients can sign before they return it and set an appointment for a free estimate. After you make the changes, you mark the document as final to prevent further changes.

a. Open the document *chap7_pe3_cleaners*. Click the **Office Button**, and then click **Save As**. Click the **Save as type drop-down arrow**, and then click **Word Macro-Enabled Document (*.docm)**. Type **chap7_pe3_cleaners_solution** in the File name box, and then click **Save**.

b. Click the **Office Button**, click **Word Options**, click **Popular**, if necessary, and then click **Show Developer tab in the Ribbon**, if necessary. Click **OK**.

c. Click on the left side of the heading *Standard Services* on the first page. Click the **View tab**, click **Macros**, and click **Record Macro**. In the Macro name box, type **reverse**. Click **Keyboard** to display the Customize Keyboard dialog box. Press **Alt**, and while holding it down, press **R** to assign the keystroke combination to the macro. Click the **Save changes in drop-down arrow**, click **chap7_pe3_cleaners_solution.docm**, and then click **Assign**, as shown in Figure 7.33. Click **Close** to return to the document, where the macro recording symbol displays with the pointer.

d. Click the **Home tab**, click the **Border** arrow, and click **Borders and Shading**. Click the **Shading** tab, click the **Style** down arrow, click **Solid (100%)**, and then click **OK**. Click the **Stop recording** button on the status bar.

e. Click on the left side of the heading *Special Cleaning* on the second page. Press **Alt+R** to run the macro and apply the reverse effect to the heading. Run the macro on the headings *Personnel* and *Cleaning Charges*.

f. Press **Ctrl+End** to move the insertion point to the bottom of the document. Click the **Insert tab**, click **Signature Line**, and click **OK** to any Microsoft Office Word dialog box.

...continued on Next Page

g. In the Suggested signer box, type **Sign your name here**, and then click **OK** to insert the signature line in the document.

h. Click the **Office Button**, point to **Prepare**, and then click **Mark as Final**. Click **OK** to all Microsoft Office Word dialog boxes that explain the document will be marked as final and saved. Select the address for White Glove cleaners and press **Delete**. Because the document is marked as final it is also protected from any changes, and you cannot delete the address.

i. Close the document.

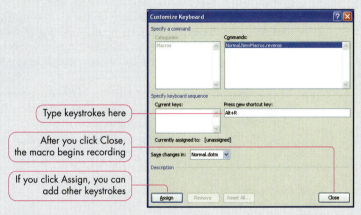

Figure 7.33 Run a Macro Using a Keystroke Combination

4 Add Form Controls to Cleaning Services Document

The sales representative for White Glove Cleaners informs you that he would like to see the cleaning services document modified again so it can be used as a form. He would like to be able to check off the services that a customer is most interested in contracting from your company. In addition to using a printed form, he indicates that he also communicates with several clients electronically, so he needs an electronic version of the document as well. And he wants it certified to assure the clients that the document is authentic. You make the necessary modifications by replacing the bullets with check boxes and adding form controls at the bottom where clients can type their name and address. You protect the form so the clients can only enter their information in the form, and you finish up by adding a digital signature.

a. Open the *chap7_pe3_cleaners_solution.docm* document and save it as **chap7_pe4_cleaners_solution.docm.** Click **Options**, which displays next to the *Security Warning* above the document, click **Enable this content** in the Microsoft Office Security Options dialog box, and then click **OK**.

b. Click the **Office Button**, point to **Prepare**, and then click **Mark as Final** to remove all editing restrictions.

c. Position the pointer on the left side of the word *Sweep* that displays in the first bullet list under the Entryway paragraph. Click the **Developer tab**, click **Record Macro**, type **checkbox** in the Macro name box, click the **Store macro in drop-down arrow**, click **chap7_pe4_cleaners_solution.docm (document)**, and then click **Keyboard**. Press and hold down **Alt** and then press **C**. Click the **Save changes in drop-down arrow**, click **chap7_pe4_cleaners_solution.docm**, click **Assign**, and then click **Close**.

d. Click the **Home tab**, click the **Bullets** down arrow, and click **None**. Click the **Developer tab**, click **Legacy Tools** in the Controls group, and then click **Check Box Form Field**. Press **Tab**, and then click **Stop Recording** in the Code group on the Developer tab.

e. Press the **down arrow key** on the keyboard to move the insertion point to the next bullet list item that starts *Shine both sides*. Press **Alt+C** to run the macro and replace the bullet with a check box. You adjust the alignment of the check box in the next step.

f. Click the **Developer tab**, if necessary, and click **Macros**. Click **checkbox** (or click project. NewMacros.checkbox if necessary), and then click **Edit**. Press **Ctrl+End** to move to the

...continued on Next Page

bottom of the window and view the programming statements for the check box macro, as shown in Figure 7.34. Select the third statement, *Selection.TypeText Text:=vbTab* and press **Delete**. Double-click the upper-left corner to close the window.

g. Select the check box and white space that precedes the first bullet item (*Sweep*) and press **Delete**. Press **Alt+C** to replay the macro, which removes the space between the check box and the service description. Run the macro on each bullet list item in the document.

h. Move the insertion point to the right side of *Name* in the *Client Information* section. Click the **Developer tab**, click **Legacy Tools**, and click **Text Form Field** in the Controls group. Add a Text Form Field for each of the remaining client information items.

i. Click **Design Mode**, if necessary, to toggle the setting off. Click **Protect Document**, and then click **Restrict Formatting and Editing**, if necessary. Click **Limit formatting to a selection of styles**, and then click **Settings**. Click **None**, and then click **OK**. Click **No** to the Microsoft Office Word dialog box that asks if you want to remove styles that are not allowed.

j. Click **Allow only this type of editing in the document**, and then click **Filling in forms** from the drop-down list. Click **Yes, Start Enforcing Protection**. Click **OK** to close the Start Enforcing Protection dialog box.

k. Close the Restrict Formatting and Editing task pane. Save and close the document.

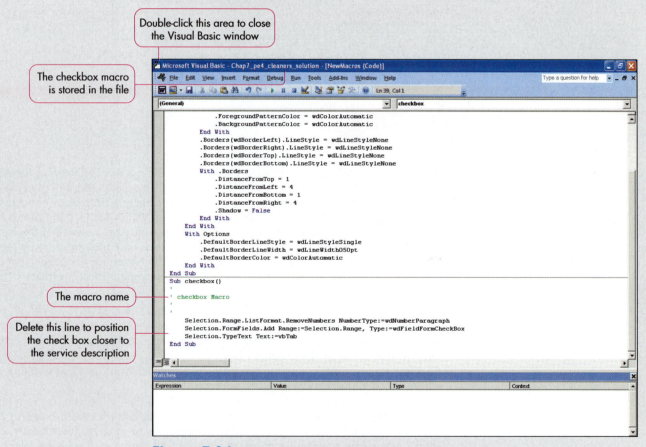

Figure 7.34 Edit the Check Box Macro

Mid-Level Exercises

1 Create a Fax Form Template

You work for a title company, which administers the process of closing on real estate property. Because you often need to send and receive documents and other information to clients prior to their appointments, you use a common form for company correspondence, including faxes. You designed a fax cover sheet last year, and now you want to improve the usefulness of that form by creating a form that enables you and other office personnel to quickly enter information about the sender as well as the recipient. Four staff members send faxes, so you decide to add their names to a drop-down list that will save typing. They can send the form from their computer, so using drop-down lists and menus works perfectly and saves a lot of paper.

a. Open the *chap7_mid1_fax.dotx* document and save it as **chap7_mid1_fax_solution.dotx**.

b. Display the **Developer tab**, if necessary.

c. Delete the asterisk (*) beside the *Date* label in the upper-right corner of the template. Replace it with the **Date Picker** control.

d. Delete the asterisk (*) beside the *From* label in the template. Replace it with a **Drop-Down List** control. The Title of the control should display **Select sender**. The drop-down list should be populated with the following names: **Deborah Ellis, Laura Jackson, Sara Emmerton**, and **Cora Besabe**.

e. Delete the asterisk (*) beside the *To, Phone, Fax*, and *Company Name* labels in the template. Replace each with a **Text** control. Insert a Text control in the Comments area.

f. Insert **Check Box Form Fields** beside each action that displays along the bottom of the fax form. The check box for *For Review* should be checked by default.

g. Protect the document; allow users only to fill in forms. Save and close the template.

h. Open the template you just created and save it as a Word document named **chap7_mid1_completefax_solution**.

i. Select today's date from the Date Picker control. Select **Cora Besabe** as the sender of the fax. Type the following next to the appropriate fields for a recipient:

To:	Phillip McCart
Phone:	(479) 555-9999
Fax:	(479) 555-9998
Company Name:	Standard Programming, Inc.

j. In the comment area, type **Please bring the attached forms when you arrive for your appointment to close on the Odom building next Friday.**

k. Mark the document as final, and then close the document.

2 Certify Science Fair Results

After the Regional Science Fair is held on the campus of Missouri State University, the director of the event must document the winners and distribute the awards in each category of the competition. The director's assistant has created an initial list of the winners in the Senior Division and has applied several layers of protection, including a password that you must enter to make modifications. You will open the document, make any necessary changes, and then protect the document again. All participants will receive the results via e-mail, and the document should be certifiable for accuracy. You

...continued on Next Page

do not want to assign a password to open the document, as that is not appropriate when distributing a public record, but you can use your knowledge of other forms of document protection so that it will be recognized as the official results, which cannot be altered.

a. Open the *chap7_mid2_results* document, then type **Chap7_mid2** as the password to modify the document. Save it as **chap7_mid2_results_solution**.

b. Remove any formatting and editing protection that is applied to the document so you can make the following changes.

c. The name of the Second Alternate is incorrect. Correct it to display **Sydni Michelle Sanders**.

d. Change the main heading of the document to use the Title style. Decrease the font size to 20, center the heading, and insert a line break so *Senior Division* appears on the first line and the remaining title displays below it.

e. Set editing restrictions so the document is read-only and no changes are allowed.

f. Remove the password necessary to modify the document.

g. Add a digital signature to the document. The purpose for signing the document should be stated as **The Official Results of Regional Science Fair**.

h. Close the document.

3 Use Macros to Automate Changes

Your company, Computer Training Concepts, was recently purchased by a larger organization and the new owner is considering a new name for the organization. His first choice for a new name is *Computer Training Solutions*. The new CEO asked you to automate the process of changing the name of the company on all documentation and correspondence. As company documents are used, modifications to reflect the new name should take place. You decide to create a macro that will quickly search each document and replace the old name with the new name. You are also directed to change the appearance of the new name so it is more distinguishable in the documents.

a. Open the *chap7_mid3_training* document and save it as a Macro-Enabled document named **chap7_mid3_training_solution**.

b. Create a macro named **ReplaceName** and save it in the **chap7_mid3_training_solution** file. Use the keystroke combination **Alt+R** to run the macro and save changes to the macro in **chap7_mid3_training_solution.docm**.

c. Activate the Find and Replace command. Find occurrences of *Computer Training Concepts*, and then replace them with **Computer Training Solutions**. Change the font attributes of Computer Training Solutions to bold and italic.

d. Replace all occurrences and close the Find and Replace dialog box. Stop recording the macro.

e. Edit the header in each section by replacing the text *Student's Name* with your name.

f. Save the document so that it requires a password to modify it. Set the password to modify as **Chap7_mid3**.

g. The CEO decides the new name should be Digital Training Solutions. Edit the macro to change the *.Text* statement to use **Computer Training Solutions** and change the *.Replacement.Text* statement to use **Digital Training Solutions**. Save and close the macro, and then run it to make the new corrections. Pay special attention to all the locations in the document where the company name displays, including headers and footers.

h. At the end of the document, insert a Signature Line. The name that displays beneath the line is **Scott Davidson** and his title is **CEO**.

i. Save and close the document.

Capstone Exercise

Many professionals have a job that requires travel. In most organizations, individuals must pay for all travel-related expenses and then submit a form in order to receive reimbursement. The form details every expense—from food to hotel to airfare—and at the end of the form the total of all expenses is calculated. The company you work for has a travel reimbursement form that all employees must print, fill in, and then submit via interoffice mail. You are responsible for converting that form so that it can be completed online and e-mailed to the accounting office.

Create a Macro That Inserts Text Controls

The travel expense form will require several text controls to enter information such as name, department, and phone number. To expedite the process of inserting text controls, you create a macro that inserts the field as soon as you press a keyboard combination.

a. Open the file *chap7_cap_travel*. The password to open is **Chap7_cap** and the password to modify is **2Travel**.

b. Remove the Mark as Final setting and save the file as a Macro-Enabled Document named **chap7_cap_travel_solution**.

c. Display the Developer tab, if necessary. Create a macro named **TextControl**. Store it in the **chap7_cap_travel_solution** document. Assign the macro to the keyboard combination **Alt+L** and save changes to the macro in **chap7_cap_travel_solution**.

d. The macro should click the **Developer tab** and click the **Text** control. It should then click **Properties** and click **Content control cannot be deleted**. Close the Content Control Properties dialog box and stop the macro.

e. Deselect the control, and then press **Alt+L** to confirm that the macro runs correctly. Delete the text control if it displays in an inappropriate location in the document. Switch to Design Mode to delete the control, if necessary.

Insert Text and Date Controls on a Form

The Word document you opened in the last steps is the basis for the printed travel reimbursement form. You decide to keep the basic outline of the document and add form controls for users to enter their personal information. The document contains asterisks to mark the location where you want to enter the personal information, so you will delete the asterisks before you insert form controls.

a. Delete the asterisks and then use the TextControl macro to insert text controls on the right side of *Name, Office Phone, Department,* and *Purpose of Trip.*

b. Insert Date Picker controls on the right side of *Request Date, Departure Date,* and *Return Date.*

c. Save the document.

Insert Controls That Compute Totals

The actual expenses are entered in a table in the document that sorts by category such as transportation, accommodations, and meals. Some expenses, such as Personal Car, might require a calculation of miles driven multiplied by the reimbursement amount per mile. After all information is entered in the table, a grand total is calculated by adding all the expenses. You decide to use legacy text fields in the table, which allow calculations.

a. Within the table, insert legacy text form fields with Number formats for each expense category that prompt for amounts in the second and third columns. Assign bookmark names to the fields you insert in the second and third columns, such as ToAirport (for the shuttle expense to the airport), DriveMiles (for number of miles driven), and Brkdays (for number of days you ate breakfast on the trip).

b. When you insert the form field for Personal Car Mileage, use **.485** as the default entry, because this is the current mileage allowance.

c. Edit fields in the second and third columns to provide a note (click the Add Help Text button inside the Text Form Field Options dialog box) on the status bar to tell the user what to do (such as *Enter number of miles driven* or *Enter mileage allowance*).

d. For the fourth column, insert number-formatted text form fields for items that do not require a calculation. Apply Currency number format and set the fields to calculate upon exiting.

e. For rows that have number formatted text form fields in the second and third columns, insert a text form field in the fourth column that calculates the total amount. For example, use =Brkdays*Brkamt to calculate the total amount spent for breakfasts during a trip. Notice that some fields will add the results from columns 2 and 3, and others will multiply them.

f. Insert text form fields in the first column below the *Other Expenses* category. Insert calculating fields in the last column with Currency format.

g. Insert a calculation field in the last cell with this formula: =SUM(D2:D17).

h. Set right alignment on the text and fields in the second, third, and fourth columns.

i. Save the document.

Capstone Exercise Continued...

Protect the Form

To make a true digital form, you wisely decide to add a line for a signature and then protect the document so users can only enter information in the control field areas. You remove all passwords, and then you certify the form for authenticity by attaching a digital signature.

a. Insert a Signature Line at the bottom of the document.

b. Remove the passwords that are required to open and modify the document.

c. Restrict formatting and restrict the type of editing to Filling in forms. Enforce the protection without setting passwords.

d. Close all panes and close the document.

Fill Out a Travel Expense Form

Now it is time to test the travel expense reimbursement form. You recently completed a trip to visit a client and will use that information to complete the form.

a. Open the travel reimbursement form and save it as a Word document named **chap7_cap_reimburse_solution**. Click Yes to save it as a macro-free document.

b. Use information from the table below to complete the form. The total expenses should total $830.00.

c. After you complete the form, attach a digital signature.

d. Save and close the document.

Form Control	Your information
Name	Enter your name
Office phone	(555) 555-0001
Department	Sales—Western Division
Request Date	Today's date
Purpose of trip	Client meeting
Departure Date	September 19, 2009
Return Date	September 21, 2009
Shuttle to airport	25
Airfare	375
Hotel	2 nights @ 125
Breakfast	3 days @ 10
Lunch	3 days @ 15
Dinner	3 days @ 35

Mini Cases

Use the rubric following the case as a guide to evaluate your work, but keep in mind that your instructor may impose additional grading criteria or use a different standard to judge your work.

Creating Your Own Form

GENERAL CASE

You have just been hired as manager of a new tuxedo rental company named Black Tie, Incorporated. You need to hire employees, but you do not yet have an application form. Create an application form that potential employees can fill out onscreen. Provide a place for personal information, education and training, employment history, and references. Include any other information you think is necessary. Be sure to add default text for each field to indicate what the user should insert into the field. Protect the form and then save the form template as **chap7_mc1_tuxedo_solution**. Open the template, enter data as if you were applying for a position, and save the document as **chap7_mc1_tuxapp_solution.docx**.

Performance Elements	Exceeds Expectations	Meets Expectations	Below Expectations
Layout	Form layout is appropriate for job application, collecting all information that is required of an applicant.	Form layout is mostly appropriate for job application and collects some information that is required of an applicant.	Form layout is not appropriate for job application and does not collect information that is required of an applicant.
Mechanics	Appropriate form fields are used in job application, and field properties are set to maximize efficiency in form.	Form fields used are adequate for use, but not most appropriate, in job application, and field properties are not completely set to maximize efficiency in form.	Appropriate form fields are not used in job application, and field properties are not set to maximize efficiency in form.
Visual aspects	Form layout is professional and intuitive. Detailed descriptions are used to identify information in form field.	Form layout is adequate but not intuitive. Brief descriptions are used to identify information in form field.	Form layout is not professional and not intuitive. Descriptions that identify information in form fields are omitted.

So Many Features to Choose From

RESEARCH CASE

In this chapter, you learned the benefit of using macros to perform a repetitive task. Other features in Word also help you with a repetitive task. Which feature should you use for a particular task? Take this opportunity to create a chart that lists the features and tools in Word such as macros, Format Painter, and Building Blocks, and then compare each feature. Consider a scenario that would require the use of each feature and why you would use one instead of the other. Use Microsoft Office Word Help to learn more about each feature, if necessary. Save your work as **chap7_mc2_features_solution**.

Performance Elements	Exceeds Expectations	Meets Expectations	Below Expectations
Creativity	Student compares at least four Word features that are used to assist with repetitive tasks.	Student compares three Word features used to assist with repetitive tasks.	Student compares fewer than three Word features that are used to assist with repetitive tasks.
Accuracy	Student demonstrates complete understanding of all features compared.	Student demonstrates partial understanding of features compared.	Student does not demonstrate understanding of features compared.
Mastery	Student provides accurate assessment of the situation in which the feature would be the best tool for the job.	Student provides assessment of the situation in which the feature could be used, but it is not the best tool for the job.	Student does not provide assessment of the situation or does not demonstrate understanding of when a tool is best suited for a situation.

Calculating Form Fields

A colleague wants to use a form as a purchase order for his small company. He created the form, but it does not work as he expected. The calculating fields do not function properly, the customer information does not appear as a form field, and to top it off, he's no longer able to type anything into his form. His frustration has forced him to call you and ask for advice on solving his problems. Your task is to troubleshoot the form and make corrections or additions that will turn it into a functioning and professional-looking electronic form that is suitable for use. Open the file *chap7_mc3_problem.dotx* and save it as **chap7_mc3_problem_solution.dotx**. Determine the reason why the form fields are not calculating, make corrections to fix the problem, add any other form features that would make this a true digital form, and save and then test the form.

Performance Elements	Exceeds Expectations	Meets Expectations	Below Expectations
Form field calculations	Student determines reason for miscalculations and updates form fields to correct.	Student determines reason for miscalculations but does not update form fields to correct.	Student does not determine reason for miscalculations and does not update form fields to correct.
Form protection	Student determines form protection error and makes appropriate correction.	Student determines form protection error but does not make appropriate correction.	Student does not determine form protection error and does not make appropriate correction.
Presentation	Student modifies all form properties to display appropriate form fields.	Student modifies some form properties to display appropriate form fields.	Student does not modify form properties to display appropriate form fields.

Word and the Internet

Web Pages, XML, and Blogs

Objectives

After you read this chapter, you will be able to:

1. Build a Web page **(page 473)**.

2. Apply themes and background color to a Web page **(page 475)**.

3. Insert hyperlinks in a Web page **(page 476)**.

4. Insert bookmarks in a Web page **(page 477)**.

5. Preview a Web page **(page 478)**.

6. Publish a Web page **(page 479)**.

7. Understand XML **(page 486)**.

8. Attach an XML schema **(page 486)**.

9. Create a blog post **(page 497)**.

10. Use the Research task pane **(page 499)**.

Hands-On Exercises

Exercises	Skills Covered
1. CREATING A WEB PAGE (page 480) **Open:** chap8_ho1_default.docx **Save as:** default.htm **Open:** chap8_ho1_products.docx **Save as:** products.htm **Open:** chap8_ho1_contact.docx **Save as:** contact_info.htm	• Save Documents as Web Pages • Add a Theme and Background • Insert and Link to Bookmarks • Insert Hyperlinks and Clip Art • Preview the Web Page
2. WORKING WITH XML (page 492) **Open:** chap8_ho2_costumes.docx chap8_ho2_schema.xsd **Save as:** chap8_ho2_costumes_solution.docx, chap8_ho2_costumes_solution.xml, and chap8_ho2_costumes_solution.mht	• Add an XML Schema • Tag Text with XML Elements • Set XML Options and Validate Tagged Text • Save as a Web Page
3. CREATING A BLOG POST (page 501) **Open:** New Blog Post document **Save as:** chap8_ho3_blog_solution.docx	• Set Up a Blog Account • Write a Blog Entry and Use the Research Task Pane • Publish a Blog Post

CASE STUDY

High School Reunion Web Site

Jerri Reed was the senior class secretary when she went to Fayetteville High School. As the time is fast approaching for her five-year reunion, she is considering ways to promote the reunion in an effort to increase attendance. Several of the reunion committee members are suggesting that she post a Web page to announce the event.

Jerri agrees that a Web page would be effective and decides to create three pages. The first page will be a home page and will advertise the reunion. It will include links to the other two pages. The second

page will include the schedule of events for the reunion and might also have hyperlinks to other pages or Web sites. She will include a detailed list of events, which will make the page long, so she decides to include navigational tools to help users find information easily. The third page will list any "missing" classmates. The information on the missing classmates page should be formatted in XML so the names can be used in other applications such as Excel or Access.

After she plans this Web site, Jerri decides to write an entry in her blog about it. She starts the blog entry and saves it as a Word document until she can finish and post it later—after the reunion committee meeting she is about to miss.

Your Assignment

- Read the chapter, paying special attention to sections that describe how to create Web pages, format data as XML, and create blog posts.
- Put yourself in Jerri's place and create a folder named *Reunion* to store the Web pages. Create a home page named *chap8_case_default* and create links to the other pages, which are provided as *chap8_case_schedule* and *chap8_case_missing*. Save the files as Web page files named **chap8_case_schedule_solution.htm** and **chap8_case_missing_solution.htm**, respectively.
- Format all pages with a theme and background, and include links to the other Web pages.
- Use the *chap8_case_schema* file to format the information on the missing classmates page using XML tags. Save a copy of the **chap8_case_missing_solution** file in XML format.
- Create a blog post and save it as a Word document named **chap8_case_blog_solution**.

Web Pages

For most students, the Internet is as much a part of their education as books and teachers. The ***Internet*** is a network of networks that connects computers anywhere in the world. It is easy to connect your computer to the Internet, and that connection enables you to view an abundance of information about every imaginable topic.

The ***World Wide Web*** (WWW or, simply, the Web) is a very large subset of the Internet, consisting of those computers that store a special type of document known as a ***Web page***. Any document that displays on the WWW is a Web page. Web pages may be self-contained and might provide all the information you need about a topic, or they may offer links to other Web pages. And therein lies the fascination of the Web—you simply click on link after link to go effortlessly from one document or resource to the next.

In this section, you will learn to create a Web page. You will format the page, add hyperlinks and bookmarks, and then save the document as a Web page.

> The ***Internet*** is a network of networks that connects computers anywhere in the world.
>
> The ***World Wide Web (WWW)*** is a very large subset of the Internet that stores Web page documents.
>
> A ***Web page*** is any document that displays on the World Wide Web.

Building a Web Page

> Sooner or later, anyone who cruises the World Wide Web wonders if he or she can create a home page or a Web site of his or her own. Word provides all the tools necessary to create a basic Web page.

Sooner or later, anyone who cruises the World Wide Web wonders if he or she can create a home page or a Web site of his or her own. Word provides all the tools necessary to create a basic Web page. You can use tables to organize and lay out the page elements, clip art and pictures to enhance the page with visual elements, bulleted and numbered lists to organize information on the page, WordArt for text, and so on. You can use Word to create a more advanced Web page; however, if your Web page design is complex, you will want to use a Web development and design program, such as Microsoft Expression.

Web pages are developed in a special language called ***HyperText Markup Language (HTML)***. Initially, the only way to create a Web page was to learn HTML, which consists of a set of codes (or tags) that are assigned to the content and describe how the document is to appear when viewed in a Web browser such as Internet Explorer.

> ***HyperText Markup Language (HTML)*** uses codes to describe how a document appears when viewed in a Web browser.

Microsoft Office simplifies the process because you can create the document in Word, then simply save it as a Web page. Microsoft Word converts the document and generates the HTML code for you. You can continue to enter text or change the formatting just as you can with an ordinary document. Figure 8.1 shows a Web page you will create in the next hands-on exercise, and Figure 8.2 displays the HTML code for that page.

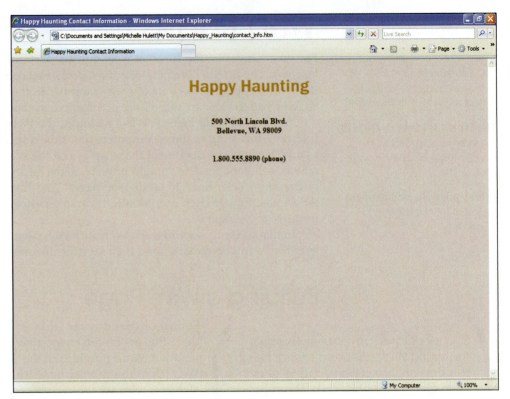

Figure 8.1 A Halloween Costume Shop Web Page

Code specifies how to format the contents

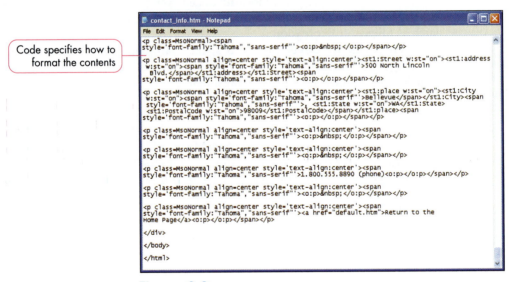

Figure 8.2 The HTML Code for the Web Page

When you create a document in Word, you can display it in Web Layout view. This particular view enables you to continue using regular Word formatting features while displaying the document as it will appear in a Web browser. After you create and format documents, you can save them as Web pages. From within the Save As dialog box, click the Save as type arrow and choose an appropriate Web format. Table 8.1 lists and describes the three Web file types.

Table 8.1 Options for Saving Web Pages

File Type	Description
Single File Web Page (*.mht; *.mhtml)	Save entire Web site files, including graphics, into one file so that you can send it to someone.
Web Page (*.htm; *.html)	Create and edit Web page documents and use regular Word editing tools. Keep saving in this format until you are done.
Web Page, Filtered (*.htm; *.html)	Save the final Web page in this format to reduce file size and reduce Word editing options. Upload this file to a Web server.

Applying Themes and Background Color to a Web Page

Web pages are more interesting when you add design elements such as background images, bullets, numbering, lines, and other graphical features. They also display better when colors and fonts are coordinated among the design elements. You can use the Word themes while developing a Web page, which enables you to coordinate colors and fonts. To make sure themes are as effective as possible, you should format your document by using Word heading styles, such as Heading 1.

Themes assign colors to the elements on the page, such as fonts, numbers, and horizontal lines, which enable you to emphasize key information. However, the theme does not automatically add a background to the Web page. A ***background*** is a color, design, image, or watermark that appears behind text in a document or on a Web page. A colored background adds visual enhancement to the Web page. You can use the Page Color command on the Page Layout tab to quickly add color to the page. If a theme is selected, the Page Color palette automatically displays colors that coordinate with the theme, as shown in Figure 8.3.

A ***background*** is a color, design, image, or watermark that appears behind text in a document or on a Web page.

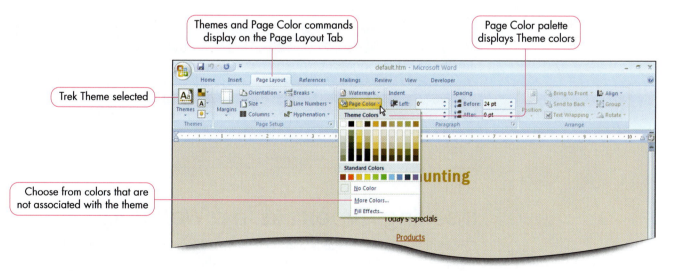

Themes and Page Color commands display on the Page Layout Tab

Page Color palette displays Theme colors

Trek Theme selected

Choose from colors that are not associated with the theme

Figure 8.3 Apply a Theme and Background Color to a Web Page

A **watermark** is text or a graphic that displays behind text.

A **watermark** is text or a graphic that displays behind text. They are often used to display a very light, washed out logo for a company; they are also frequently used to indicate the status of a document, such as DRAFT. Watermarks do not display on a document that is saved as a Web page, nor will they display in Web layout view.

If you prefer to customize the background color, design, or image, you can click the Page Color command on the Page Layout tab, and then select from the commands that display below the theme color gallery. The More Colors command displays the Colors dialog box, which enables you to choose from the standard colors or to mix a custom color. The Fill Effects command that displays when you click Page Color enables you to apply a gradient, texture, pattern, or picture background. Figure 8.4 shows the Gradient tab of the Fill Effects dialog box, where you can select a gradient design to display on the background of your Web page.

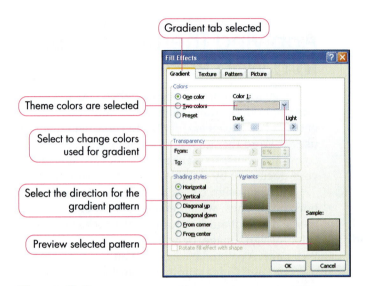

Figure 8.4 Apply a Color Gradient Background to a Web Page

Inserting Hyperlinks in a Web Page

One benefit of a Web page is that it contains references, called hyperlinks, to other Web pages. **Hyperlinks** are electronic markers that, when clicked, move the insertion point to a different location within the same document, open another document, or display a different Web page in a Web browser. Hyperlinks can lead you to Web pages stored on different computers that may be located anywhere in the world.

A **hyperlink** is an electronic marker that points to a different location or displays a different Web page.

Hyperlinks can be assigned to text or graphics. For example, consider a Web page you might create to document your visit to several national parks. You will display several pictures of the beautiful scenery and provide a summary of the trip. In your summary, you might mention a particular lodge where you spent a few nights, so you create a hyperlink from your Web page to the home page of the lodge.

Anyone who reads your page can click on the name of the lodge and then be directed to the Web site, where they can inquire about reservations for themselves. Additionally, you might want to create a link to a particular park from a picture that was taken there. You can select the picture and assign a hyperlink that, when clicked, will direct the reader to the Web site for that national park.

To create a hyperlink in your document, select the text or picture and then click Hyperlink in the Links group on the Insert tab. From the Insert Hyperlink dialog box, you can specify several types of hyperlinks:

- You can link to another Web page by typing the address (or URL).
- You can link to another place within the same document.
- You can link to an e-mail address, which opens a new e-mail message when clicked.

When you point to a hyperlink in a Word document, you see a ScreenTip that directs you to press Ctrl+Click to follow the link, which is not the way you use hyperlinks in a Web Page. However, this gives you more control over the link from a development standpoint because you are able to select the link and make changes

TIP   Hyperlink Colors

When you apply a hyperlink to text in a Web page, the text displays in a color that coordinates with the theme in use, often the Office default theme. After you click the hyperlink, the color of the text changes to the theme or default color for the followed link.

without it quickly directing you to a new page. If you right-click a hyperlink in a Word document, you will see several options for working with the hyperlink, including Edit Hyperlink (which opens the Edit Hyperlink dialog box), Copy Hyperlink, and Remove Hyperlink (which removes the link but does not remove the text or graphic).

Inserting Bookmarks in a Web Page

Some Web pages are very lengthy and require the viewer to scroll a great deal to view all the contents on the page. You can help the viewer to return to the top, bottom, or other location in that page by inserting bookmarks. A bookmark is an electronic marker for a specific location in a document, enabling the user to go to that location quickly. A hyperlink takes you to a different page, and can even take you to a specific location on a page, but the location must be identified somehow so the hyperlink knows exactly where to go; a bookmark provides that identification. Bookmarks are helpful in long documents because they enable you to move easily from one place to another within that document, without having to manually scroll. They are often used on FAQ (Frequently Asked Questions) Web pages, which list several questions and their answers. Consider the FAQ page in Figure 8.5. A bookmark was created for each question and answer set, so that when you click the question at the top of the page, you immediately move to that question and answer set further down the page. Additionally, the placement of a bookmark at the top of the page enables the user to click a link at the conclusion of each question to return them to the top of the page and the list of questions. Creating a bookmark and linking to it is a two-step process. You first create the bookmark(s) throughout the document, and then you insert a hyperlink that links to that bookmark. A bookmark for the top of the page is created automatically, so you do not have to create that one manually.

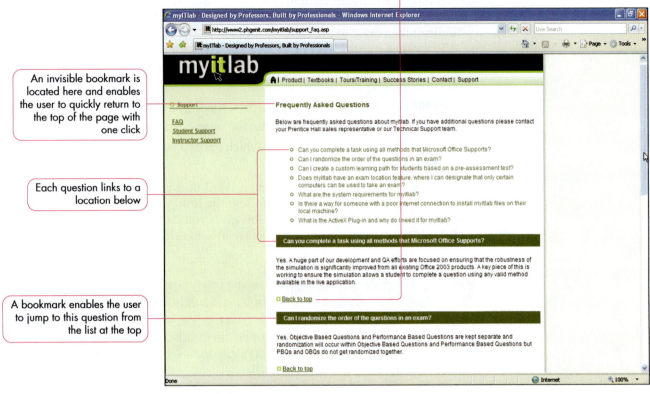

Click here to use the hyperlink that returns you to the bookmark at the top of the page

An invisible bookmark is located here and enables the user to quickly return to the top of the page with one click

Each question links to a location below

A bookmark enables the user to jump to this question from the list at the top

Figure 8.5 Using Bookmarks

TIP Bookmark Names

Spaces are not allowed in bookmark names. You can use a combination of capital and lowercase letters, numbers, and the underscore character, but you cannot begin the name of a bookmark with a number. You should create descriptive names so you can identify the bookmark easily when you create a hyperlink to it. For example, a bookmark to question #1 in a FAQ listing might be Q1.

Previewing a Web Page

After finalizing pages for a Web site, you save the document(s) as described earlier. The Web Layout view gives you a very accurate representation of how the page will look when published. You can also preview the page in an actual Web browser before you upload and publish it so that you can confirm it contains the content and is formatted to your specifications. Word contains a Web Page Preview command that must be added to the Quick Access Toolbar (QAT) before you use it. Click Customize Quick Access Toolbar, click More Commands (which opens the Word Options dialog box), click the drop-down arrow for Choose commands from, and then click Commands Not in the Ribbon. Scroll to the bottom of the list, click Web Page Preview, click Add, and then click OK. The icon for Web Page Preview displays in the QAT. When you click Web Page Preview in the QAT, the document opens in an Internet Explorer window, as shown in Figure 8.6.

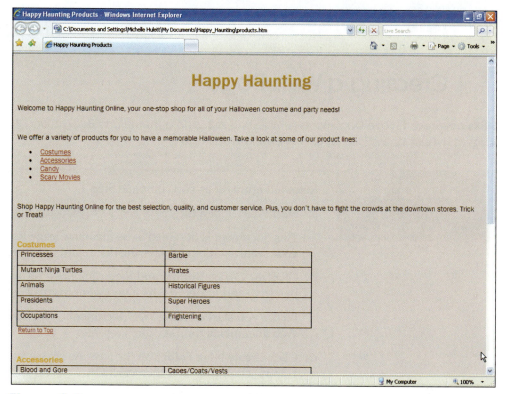

Figure 8.6 Preview a Web Page in Internet Explorer

You can also open the page from within Internet Explorer, or the browser of your choice, when Word is not active. Choose File, Open, click the Browse button, select the folder where the page is stored, select the file name of your Web page, click Open, and then click OK.

Publishing a Web Page

A **Web server** is a computer system that hosts pages for viewing by anyone with an Internet connection.

File Transfer Protocol (FTP) is a process that uploads files from a PC to a server or from a server to a PC.

You can easily save the pages to your local computer, where the default storage location is the My Web Sites folder in My Documents. However, to view the pages on the Internet you must save or publish to a **Web server**, which is a computer system that hosts pages so that they are available for viewing by anyone who has an Internet connection. You will need additional information from your instructor about how to obtain an account on a Web server at your school, if available, as well as how to upload the pages from your PC to the server. The most common method of uploading Web pages to the server is by using **File Transfer Protocol (FTP)**, a process that uploads files from a PC to a server or from a server to a PC.

Hands-On Exercises

1 | Creating a Web Page

Skills covered: 1. Save Documents as Web Pages **2.** Add a Theme and Background **3.** Insert and Link to Bookmarks **4.** Insert Hyperlinks and Clip Art **5.** Preview the Web Page

---

Step 1
Save Documents as Web Pages

Refer to Figure 8.7 as you complete Step 1.

a. Start Word. Open the *chap8_ho1_default* document.

This document is designed to be the home page for the Web site. In the next step, you create a folder and save the document in that folder.

b. Click the **Office Button**, and then click **Save As**. In the Save in box, navigate to the drive and folder in which you want to create a Web folder.

Before you start creating Web documents, you need to create a folder to store all Web documents for a specific Web site.

c. Click **Create New Folder** on the Save As dialog box toolbar, type **Happy_Haunting**, and then click **OK**.

d. Type **default** in the File name box.

> **TIP** Naming a Web Site Home Page
>
> A Web site's home page is typically saved as default.html or index.html so that it loads automatically when people type the main URL in a Web browser address box.

e. Click the **Save as type drop-down arrow** and click **Web Page (*.htm; *.html)**.

When you choose one of the three Web options, the Save As dialog box displays the Page title text area and the Change Title button.

f. Click **Change Title** to display the Set Page Title dialog box, as shown in Figure 8.7.

In this dialog box, you can edit the Web page title—the text that appears on the Web browser's title bar when the Web page displays.

g. Type **Online** in the Page title text box following the text *Happy Haunting*, and then click **OK**. Click **Save**.

The page displays in Web Layout view.

h. Open the Word documents listed below, and then save each as a Web page in the *Happy_Haunting* folder. Assign new file names and Web page titles using the information in the following table.

Open This File	Save As	Web Page Title
chap8_ho1_products	products	Happy Haunting Products
chap8_ho1_contact	contact_info	Happy Haunting Contact Information

The *Happy_Haunting* folder now contains three Web pages that you use to complete your Web site.

i. Leave each document open for the next step.

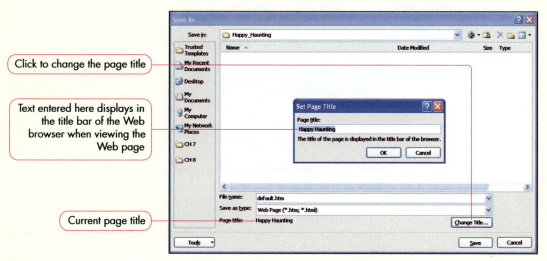

Click to change the page title

Text entered here displays in the title bar of the Web browser when viewing the Web page

Current page title

Figure 8.7 The Set Page Title Dialog Box

Step 2
Add a Theme and Background

Refer to Figure 8.8 as you complete Step 2.

a. Click the **View tab**, click **Switch Windows** in the Window group, and click **default.htm** from the list of open files.

b. Click the **Page Layout tab**, click **Themes** in the Themes group, and then click **Trek**.

The *Happy Haunting* title and the three items below it display in colors represented in the Trek theme.

TROUBLESHOOTING: If the colors do not change, the text may not be formatted with a style. You can assign a style to the text from the Home tab.

c. Click **Page Color** in the Page Background group. Click **Brown, Accent 3, Lighter 60%**, which displays in the seventh column, as shown in Figure 8.8.

You applied a light background color to the default page that covers the entire page.

d. Click **Save** in the Quick Access Toolbar to save the changes to the default.htm document.

e. Press **Alt+Tab** repeatedly until the *contact_info.htm* document displays. Repeat Steps b and c to apply the theme and background color to the page. Click **Save** on the Quick Access Toolbar to save the changes.

f. Press **Alt+Tab** repeatedly until the *products.htm* document displays. Repeat Steps b and c to apply the theme and background color to the page. Click **Save** on the Quick Access Toolbar to save the changes.

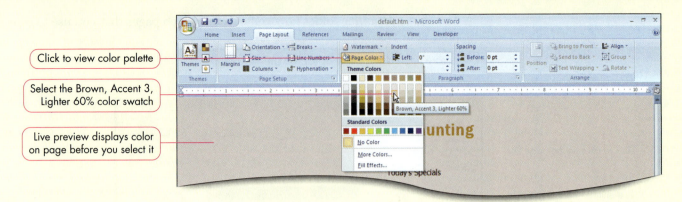

Figure 8.8 Select a Background Color for a Web Page

<table>
<tr>
<td>

Step 3
Insert and Link to Bookmarks

</td>
<td>

Refer to Figure 8.9 as you complete Step 3.

a. Click to place the insertion point on the left side of the word *Costumes*, which displays as a heading for the table that describes the variety of costumes that sell on the Happy Haunting Web site.

b. Click the **Insert tab**, click **Bookmark** in the Links group, type **costumes** in the Bookmark name text box, and then click **Add**.

c. Repeat Step b to create bookmarks at the beginning of the *Accessories*, *Candy*, and *Scary Movies* headings that display down the page. The bookmarks should be named **accessories**, **candy**, and **movies**.

> **TROUBLESHOOTING:** If you insert a bookmark in the wrong location or name it incorrectly, click **Bookmark** on the **Insert tab**, select the incorrect bookmark from the list that displays in the Bookmark name list box, and then click **Delete**. You can re-create the bookmark to meet your specifications, if necessary.

d. Press **Ctrl+Home** to view the top of the page. Select **Costumes** in the bullet list, and then click **Hyperlink** from the Links group on the Insert tab.

The Insert Hyperlink dialog box displays. You will select the bookmark to create a link from the word Costumes to the location in the document where the costume varieties display.

e. Click **Place in This Document** in the *Link to* panel of the Insert Hyperlink dialog box. If necessary, click the **plus sign** next to *Bookmarks*. Click **costumes**, as shown in Figure 8.9, and then click **OK**.

The Costumes bullet displays as a hyperlink, and the text color changes to red.

f. Hover your mouse over the *Costumes* hyperlink and view the ScreenTip that displays the name of the bookmark and *Ctrl+Click to follow link*. Press **Ctrl** and click the link to move the insertion point to the listing of costumes.

The page scrolls so the heading *Costumes* displays near the top of the screen, and the insertion point moves as well. This simplifies navigation on the page.

g. Repeat Steps d and e to create hyperlinks from each bullet list item to the corresponding bookmarks for *accessories*, *candy*, and *movies*.

</td>
</tr>
</table>

h. Select the text *Return to Top* that displays below the costumes table. Click **Hyperlink** in the Insert tab, click **Top of the Document** that displays at the very top of the *Select a place in this document* list, and then click **OK**.

This bookmark to the top of the page is created automatically when you save the document as a Web page. When you click this link, the page scrolls to the very top and displays the page heading. This enables you to view the bullet list containing links to other products, and after you create links to each product, you can quickly navigate among the different items on this page.

i. Repeat Step h to create a hyperlink from each occurrence of *Return to Top* that displays below each product table.

j. Save the Web page.

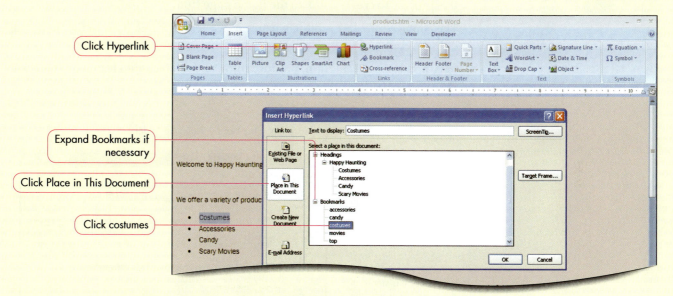

Figure 8.9 Insert a Bookmark Hyperlink on a Web Page

Step 4
Insert Hyperlinks and Clip Art

Refer to Figure 8.10 as you complete Step 4.

a. Click **default.htm - Microsoft Word** on the task bar to display the default Web page. Select **Products**, and then click **Hyperlink** in the Links group on the Insert tab.

b. Click **Existing File or Web Page** in the *Link to* panel of the Insert Hyperlink dialog box. Scroll, if necessary, and click the file **products.htm**, as shown in Figure 8.10. Click **OK**.

By creating this link, the Products page displays when you click *Products* on the home page.

c. Repeat Step b to create a hyperlink from *About Us* on the default page to the contact_info page.

TROUBLESHOOTING: If your link does not work properly, right-click the hyperlink and select from several options, including Edit Hyperlink, which displays the Edit Hyperlink dialog box and enables you to revise the link. *Remove Hyperlink* also displays when you right-click a hyperlink, and this enables you to remove the hyperlink completely.

d. Press **Ctrl+Home** to move the insertion point to the top of the page. Click **Clip Art** in the Illustrations group on the Insert tab. Type **pumpkin** in the **Search for box** in the Clip Art task pane. Click **Go** to begin the search.

e. Click a pumpkin image in the Clip Art task pane to insert it into the default page. Click **Text Wrapping** in the Arrange group on the Format tab, and then click **Square**. Move the Clip Art to the bottom right of the screen.

> **TROUBLESHOOTING:** Insert a hard line return after the *About Us* link, if necessary, to provide room at the bottom of the page to locate the Clip Art object.

f. Close the Clip Art task pane and save the document.

g. Click **contact_info.htm - Microsoft Word** on the task bar to display the contact_info Web page. Press **Ctrl+End**, and then press **Enter**. Type **Return to the Home Page**. Select the text you just typed, and then click **Center** on the Mini toolbar. Click the **Insert tab**, click **Hyperlink** in the Links group, click **default.htm**, and then click **OK**. Click **Save** on the Quick Access Toolbar. Repeat this process to create a link to the home page from the Products Web page.

The contact_info and products pages now include a link back to the home page of the Web site.

h. Save and close default.htm, products.htm, and contact_info.htm, and then exit Word.

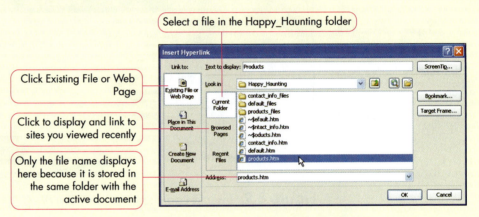

Figure 8.10 Insert a Hyperlink to the Products Web Page

Step 5
Preview the Web Page

Refer to Figure 8.11 as you complete Step 5.

a. Start Internet Explorer.

b. Click **File, Open** to display the Open dialog box. Click the **Browse** button, locate the *Happy_Haunting* folder, and then double-click the default page. Click **OK** in the Open dialog box to display the home page.

> **TROUBLESHOOTING:** If the menu bar does not display in Internet Explorer, right-click anywhere in the toolbar area and click **Menu Bar**. You can use this same procedure to remove the toolbar also. If you do not want to display the menu bar, press **Alt+F** to display the menu on a temporary basis.

You should see the Web page. Look closely at the components of the URL in the address bar, reading from right to left. You are viewing the *default.htm* document, which is stored in the *Happy_Haunting* folder, which is contained within the *Exploring Word* folder. The document is stored on drive C; that is, you are viewing the site locally, as opposed to seeing it on the Web.

c. Click the **Products** link to test it and make sure it works properly. Click the hyperlinks on the Products page to navigate from top to bottom and then back to top.

d. Click **Return to the Home Page**. Click the **About Us** link on the home page to display the contact_info page.

e. Exit Internet Explorer.

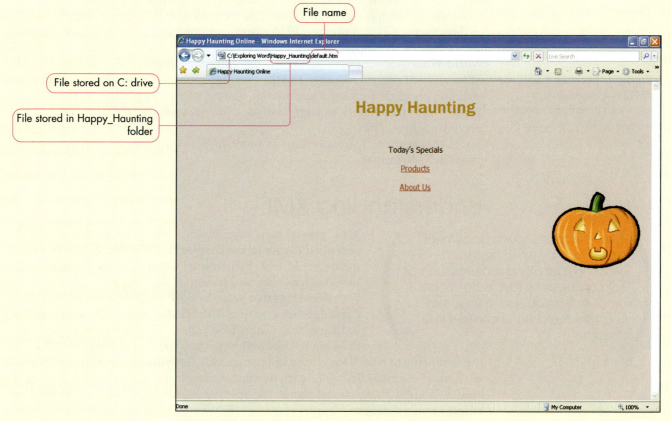

Figure 8.11 Preview a Web Page in the Browser

eXtensible Markup Language (XML)

Electronic communication and data sharing are common, if not critical, today. People create electronic documents and distribute them all over the world using many types of devices such as cell phones, PDAs, and computers. Unfortunately, some documents may be incompatible with the receiver's system and software. Therefore, the World Wide Web Consortium (W3C) developed a programming language called *eXtensible Markup Language (XML)* that describes a document's content while enabling people to exchange information among various applications. The ability to apply XML functionality to your Word documents increases the usefulness of your documents to others.

eXtensible Markup Language (XML) is a language that describes a document's content and enables easy exchange of data.

In this section, you learn how content in Word documents is processed and saved in XML format.

Understanding XML

> HTML describes how a document should look by using tags that describe formatting features such as bold and indent. XML is data about data—it lets you define tags that describe the data or content in a document.

XML goes a step beyond the code generated by HTML as described earlier in the chapter; HTML describes how a document should look by using tags that describe formatting features such as bold and indent. XML is data about data—it lets you define tags that describe the data or content in a document. Consider this example: The HTML code "<B>John Doe</B>" indicates that "John Doe" should appear in boldface, but it does not tell us anything more. You do not know that "John" is the first name or that "Doe" is the last name. XML lets you define your own tags; for example, "<name><first>John</first><last>Doe</last></name>." By tagging the content as first name or last name, the specific information can be extracted and entered into a database.

The major advantage of XML file formatting is that it is not constrained to a particular platform, operating system, hardware configuration, or software application. All Word 2007 documents are automatically stored in XML, which includes XML functionality, so that you can easily share information with others. After you create XML documents in Word, database administrators can extract XML data and then import the data into a database, which in turn can be used to create brochures, catalogs, correspondence, and Web pages.

Attaching an XML Schema

An *XML schema* is a file that defines the structure and organization of content within an XML document.

Before saving a document in XML format you must attach an XML schema to it. An *XML schema* is a file that defines the structure and organization of content within an XML document. For example, a schema can specify the number of characters allowed for a book title or dictate a range of acceptable values to be entered by a user. It is vaguely similar to a Word template in respect to being attached to a file and controlling the document. Whereas a template contains styles that dictate the formatting of a document, an XML schema dictates the structure of content in a document. Typically, the Information Technology (IT) department studies routine document creation and usage, analyzes how document content is stored and used, develops schemas for these types of documents, and makes the schemas available for end users. Figure 8.12 shows a schema that you attach to an existing document.

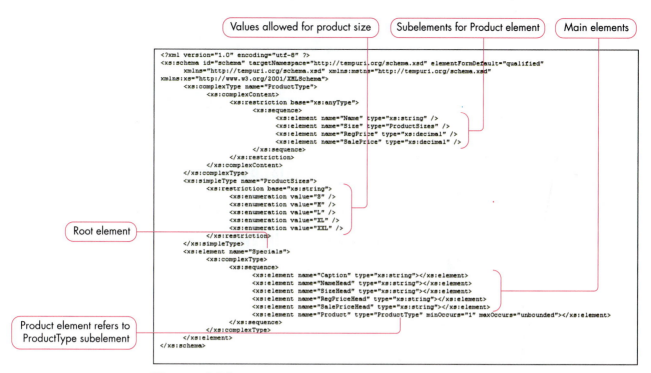

Figure 8.12 XML Schema

To add a schema, display the Developer tab, and then in the XML group click Schema, which displays the Templates and Add-ins dialog box. Click the XML Schema tab to view options for adding a schema. When you add a schema, you make it available to new and existing documents. However, you must attach the schema to be able to tag a document. This process is similar to attaching templates: the Templates tab of the Templates and Add-ins dialog box contains available templates, but you must attach a template to a document to include its functionality. After attaching a schema to your document, you apply tags to the document text. A *tag* is a marker that indicates the beginning or end of particular content within a document. The tag enables the transferability of data in such a way that other applications can import the tagged data. Figure 8.13 shows tags applied to text within a table.

A *tag* is a marker that indicates the beginning or end of particular content within a document.

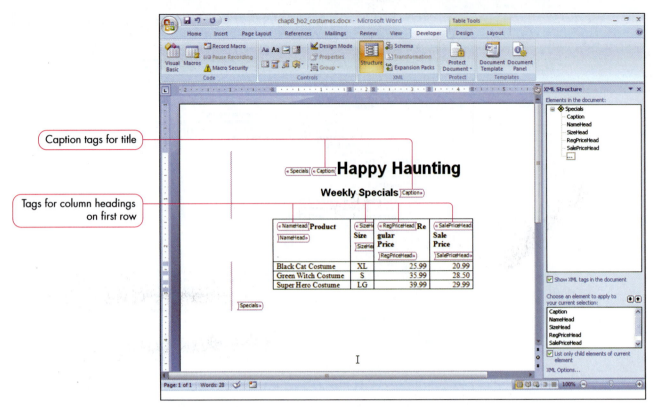

Figure 8.13 XML Tags Applied to Data in a Document

You can add more than one schema to a particular document. To add more schemas, use the same process as you did for the first schema. Each schema you add is listed in the Available XML schemas list box in the Templates and Add-ins dialog box. When you add schemas, they are available for any document. You can click the check box next to the schema you want to attach to another document. Word alerts you to any conflicts that arise when you attach multiple schemas.

If you no longer want a schema attached to a document, you can deselect the schema's check box in the Available XML schemas list box in the Templates and Add-ins dialog box. This process does not delete the schema but removes it from the current document. If a conflict prevents you from using a particular schema because of the presence of another, you can delete the schema from the Schema Library and remove it completely.

TIP XML Files

Office 2007 uses XML format by default. The XML schemas and tags are compatible with those generated by Office 2003. However, Office 2007 splits the XML output into numerous files (for example, fonts are defined in a separate document, as are document styles) that are zipped together in a .docx file.

Tag Text with XML Elements

An **element** is a descriptive name that identifies a piece of data.

After you add a schema to a document, the XML Structure task pane opens on the right side of the screen and displays elements defined by the attached schema. An **element** is a descriptive name that identifies a piece of data. It is similar to how a field name identifies data within an Access database table. For example, the field name *FirstName* identifies the data as a person's first name. One advantage of XML is its self-documenting characteristic. This means that developers can assign their own descriptive element names. These names should clearly indicate the specific types of data to be tagged in a document. You must use the schema's elements to tag the content within your document so that the association of tags and content will be available when you save the document in XML format. When you first attach a schema to a document, the XML Structure task pane displays only one element. This initial element is the **root element** that contains more specific elements defined by the schema. Your first step is to apply the root element to the entire document or to a particular section within the document. After you apply the root element, you then apply individual elements to specific data within the document, as shown in Figure 8.14.

A **root element** is the initial element that contains specific elements defined by the schema.

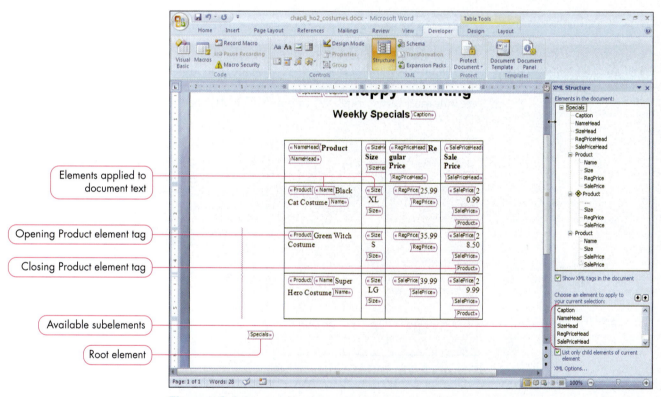

Figure 8.14 View Elements and Subelements

Work with Elements

You can display or hide XML tags while working in the document. Click the Show XML tags in the document check box on the XML Structure task pane or press Ctrl+Shift+X.

You can copy or move an element within an XML document. First, select the opening and closing element tags for a particular element. Then, use the Copy or Cut command to copy or cut, respectively, the selected element to the Clipboard. Finally, position the insertion point where you want the element and use the Paste command.

If you want to delete an element without deleting the text, right-click on either the opening or closing tag in the document window or right-click on the correct Element in the document list box in the XML Structure task pane and choose Remove tag from the shortcut menu. The menu command displays the specific element name, such as Remove Size tag. If you apply the wrong element to text, you can change the element tag. You must first remove the existing tag. After removing that tag, select the text and apply the tag for the element that corresponds with the type of selected text.

Choose Default Save Options

You can further define XML settings through the XML Options dialog box. You can control how XML documents save, validate, and appear onscreen. Figure 8.15 shows the XML Options dialog box. The settings you apply in the XML Options dialog box are automatically applied when you save XML documents.

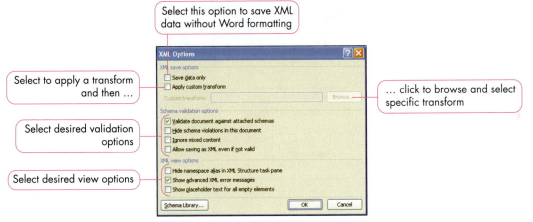

Figure 8.15 The XML Options Dialog Box

When you select the Save data only option in the XML Options dialog box, Word saves only the XML data. All formatting and WordML tags are discarded. This option is appropriate when you want to save the XML data to import into another XML application. However, you should save one version of the document with formatting in case you want to modify or use the original document.

Click the Apply custom transform check box in the XML Options dialog box if you want to apply a *transform*—a file that converts XML documents into another type of formatted language, such as HTML. In other words, transforms specify how XML documents should be formatted and how they should display. After selecting

A *transform* is a file that converts XML documents into another type of formatted language, such as HTML.

the Apply custom transform check box, click the Browse button to select the transform file to apply. If you want to include the data in a Web page, you might use a transform to convert it to HTML format so it will insert easily into your page.

The Schema validation options section controls how Word checks the accuracy of the XML tags that you apply. **_Schema validation_** is the process of examining the content and tags against the schema to ensure that tags are correctly applied to the document content and that the content conforms to any schema requirements. For example, if you apply a numeric tag to a string of text, a validation error occurs. Additionally, the schema validation might allow only certain values for an element, such as the sizes *S*, *M*, *L*, and *XL*. Word flags validation errors in two ways: (1) a purple wavy line in the left margin area, and (2) an error symbol in the XML Structure task pane next to the element that contains the validation problem. The XML view options section enables you to control the namespace alias listing in the XML Structure task pane, advanced error messages, and the placeholder text view.

If you enforce validation, Word does not save an XML document that contains validation errors. Therefore, if you are working on a complicated XML document that will take some time to finish, you can select the *Allow saving as XML even if not valid* check box. This option enables you to save the XML document even though it might contain validation errors. However, you should deselect this check box after correcting validation errors before you publish the final XML document.

You can directly open an XML file that you saved in Word in other programs, such as Excel or Access. The program that you use to open the XML document recognizes the document's structure and displays it in a particular format.

Schema validation is the process of examining the content and tags against the schema to ensure accuracy and conformity.

Hands-On Exercises

2 | Working with XML

Skills covered: 1. Add an XML Schema **2.** Tag Text with XML Elements **3.** Set XML Options and Validate Tagged Text **4.** Save as a Web Page

Step 1
Add an XML Schema

Refer to Figure 8.16 as you complete Step 1.

a. Start Word. Click the **Office button**, click **Word Options**, click **Show Developer tab in the Ribbon**, if necessary, and then click **OK**.

The Developer tab contains commands for working with XML documents, but the tab does not display automatically. Use this same procedure to remove the tab if you do not wish for it to display when you are not working with the commands it provides.

b. Click the **Developer tab**, click **Schema**, click **Schema Library** in the XML Schema tab, click any schema listed in the Select a schema section, and click **Delete Schema**. After all schemas are deleted, click **OK**. Click **OK** to close the Templates and Add-ins dialog box.

Removing any and all schemas previously used will prevent error messages from displaying and will enable you to complete the remaining steps. Because the schemas you use in this chapter have similar design characteristics, you cannot add more than one at a time to the schema library.

c. Open the file *chap8_ho2_costumes* and save it as **chap8_ho2_costumes_solution** in the *Happy_Haunting* folder.

d. Click the **Developer tab** and click **Schema**. Click **Add Schema** and browse to the folder that contains files for this project, select *chap8_ho2_schema.xsd*, and then click **Open**.

TROUBLESHOOTING: If you do not see the file name extensions, you need to activate them through Windows. Click the **Start** button and choose **My Computer**. From within My Computer, choose **Tools**, and then **Folder Options**. Click the **View tab**, deselect the *Hide extensions for known file types* check box, and then click **OK**. Close the My Computer window.

e. Type **Products** in the *Alias* box and click **OK** to close the Schema Settings dialog box.

The *chap8_ho2_schema.xsd* schema, identified by the *Products* alias, is automatically attached to the current document (see Figure 8.16). It is also available to attach to other documents in the future. If you open another document, the schema is available but not attached. You can attach the schema to other documents by clicking its check box.

f. Click **OK** to close the Templates and Add-ins dialog box.

The XML Structure task pane displays on the right side of the screen. This task pane helps guide you through the process of preparing an XML document.

TROUBLESHOOTING: If you do not see the XML Structure task pane, click **Structure** in the XML group on the Developer tab.

g. Save the document.

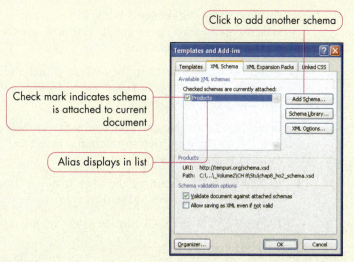

Figure 8.16 XML Schema Attached to a Document

Refer to Figure 8.17 as you complete Step 2.

a. Click **Specials** in the *Choose an element to apply to your current selection* list box. Click **Apply to Entire Document** in the dialog box.

You applied the *Specials* root element to the entire document. Word inserts the root element opening tag at the beginning of the document and the closing tag at the end of the document. The XML Structure task pane now displays a list of available elements to apply within the root element.

b. Click **Show XML tags in the document**, which displays in the XML Structure task pane, if necessary, to view the tags as you add them to the document.

c. Select the *Happy Haunting* and *Weekly Specials* titles and click the **Caption element** in the *Choose an element to apply to your current selection* list at the bottom of the XML Structure task pane.

You tagged the *Happy Haunting* and *Weekly Specials* titles with the *Caption* XML element.

d. Select the *Product* column heading text in the first cell of the table and click the **NameHead element** at the bottom of the XML Structure task pane.

e. Repeat Step d to apply the remaining three elements as itemized in the following table:

Column Heading	Element
Size	SizeHead
Regular Price	RegPriceHead
Sale Price	SalePriceHead

f. Select all cells on the second row of the table—the row containing details about the Black Cat Costume—and click **Product** in the *Choose an element to apply to your current selection* list box at the bottom of the XML Structure task pane.

The *Product* element contains subelements. When you apply an element that contains subelements, the *Choose an element to apply to your current selection* list box displays those subelements while the insertion point is located within the area to which you applied the element. You now see the following subelements: *Name, Size, RegPrice,* and *SalePrice.*

g. Select *Black Cat Costume* in the table and click the **Name subelement** in the *Choose an element to apply to your current selection* list box at the bottom of the XML Structure task pane.

h. Select *XL* in the table and choose the **Size subelement**. Select *25.99* in the table and choose the **RegPrice subelement**. Select *20.99* in the table and choose the **SalePrice subelement**.

i. Repeat Steps f–h, adapting the steps to apply the *Product* element and the respective subelements to the remaining two rows of the table.

Figure 8.17 shows the document after you tag it with the schema's elements.

j. Save the document.

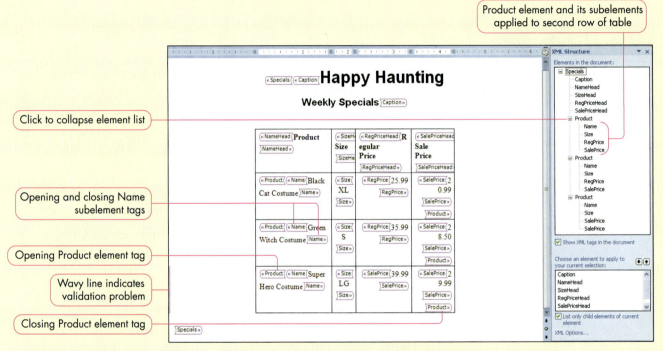

Figure 8.17 Tags Attached to Schema Elements

Refer to Figure 8.18 as you complete Step 3.

Step 3

Set XML Options and Validate Tagged Text

a. Click **XML Options** at the bottom of the XML Structure task pane.

TROUBLESHOOTING: If you closed the document at the end of step 2, the XML Structure task pane might not display when you open the document again. To display it, click the **Developer tab** and click **Structure** in the XML group.

b. Click **Show advanced XML error messages**, if it is not already selected.

When the *Show advanced XML error messages* check box is selected, Word displays more descriptive information about any validation errors when you position the mouse pointer over the error symbol in the XML Structure task pane.

c. Click **Show placeholder text for all empty elements**, if it is not already selected.

When the *Show placeholder text for all empty elements* check box is selected, Word displays the placeholder text attribute if a tagged element does not contain any text.

d. Click **Validate document against attached schemas**, if it is not already selected, and then click **OK**.

The *Validate document against attached schemas* option ensures that you correctly applied XML tags to your document. Currently, a wavy vertical purple line appears in the left margin by the last table row. Furthermore, you might see a yellow diamond with an X next to the *Size* element name in the task pane.

e. Right-click the **Size subelement** name for the third product in the XML Structure task pane.

Word displays an advanced error message, indicating specific values—*S, M, L, XL, XXL*—that are allowed for the *Size* subelement (see Figure 8.18).

f. Delete the letter *G* in *LG* for the last size in the table.

After you correct the validation error, the wavy purple line disappears.

g. Save the document.

h. Click the **Office Button**, and then click **Save As**. Click the **Save as type drop-down arrow**, click **Word XML Document (*.xml)**, and then click **Save**. Leave the document open for the next step.

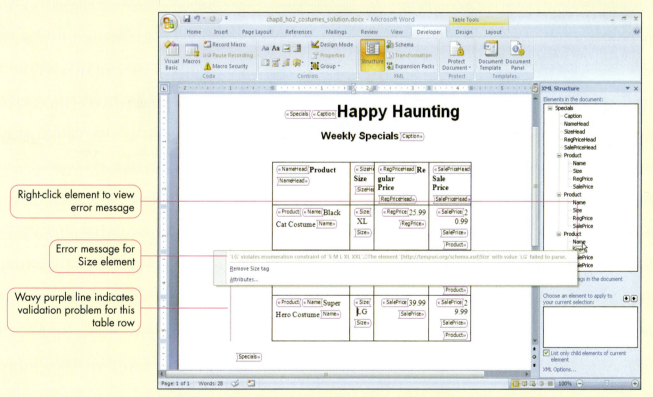

Figure 8.18 View an Error Message for an Element

Refer to Figure 8.19 as you complete Step 4.

a. Click the **Developer tab** and click **Structure**, if necessary, to display the XML Structure task pane.

b. Click **Show XML tags in the document** to hide the tags from the data in the table. Click **Structure** in the Developer tab to close the XML Structure task pane.

c. Click the **Page Layout tab**, click **Themes**, and then click **Trek**. Click **Page Color**, and then click **Brown, Accent 3, Lighter 60%**.

d. Click the **Office Button**, and then click **Save As**. Click the **Save as type drop-down arrow** and click **Single File Web Page (*.mht; *.mhtml)**. Click **Save**.

The title bar displays the file with the Web page extension, as shown in Figure 8.19. You can now create a link to this page from the home page you created in Hands-On Exercise Step 1.

e. Close the *chap8_ho2_costumes_solution.mht* document and exit Word.

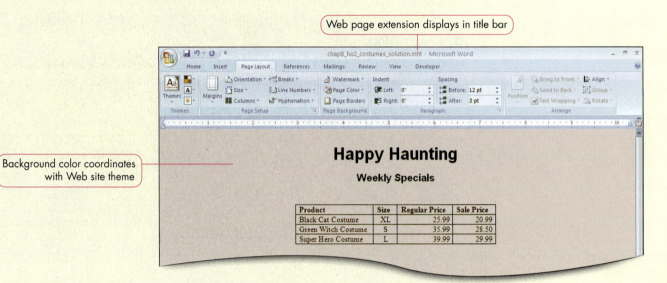

Figure 8.19 Save an XML File as a Web Page

Blogs

A **blog** is the frequent, chronological publication of personal thoughts.

Everyone has the ability to post information on the Internet about themselves, their thoughts, their interests, or simply whatever they want to make public. The frequent, chronological publication of personal thoughts and Web links is called a **blog**. The term *blog* is derived from the words *Web log*, which refers to publishing personal information on the Web. Blogs can provide a vehicle to display the works of current or future journalists and authors, or they can simply reflect the emotions and ideas of an individual for a particular point in time.

In this section, you will learn how to create and publish a blog from Word. You will also learn how to perform research from within Word.

Creating a Blog Post

> One of the most exciting features of Word 2007 is the New blog post template. This feature benefits people who are accustomed to working in Word, but who also publish blogs on a frequent basis.

One of the most exciting features of Word 2007 is the New blog post template. This feature benefits people who are accustomed to working in Word, but who also publish blogs on a frequent basis. When you open the New blog post template the window looks different because the seven tabs in the ribbon that you are accustomed to viewing are replaced with only two tabs that will provide commands you need to complete the blog post. The Blog Post tab contains commands you use to format text, but also commands that enable you to publish your blog directly to the host server for your blog, as shown in Figure 8.20. The Insert tab displays commands for items you might include in your blog, such as tables, illustrations, hyperlinks, WordArt, and symbols.

Only two tabs display with commands for creating and publishing a blog post

Click to upload blog to your blog service provider

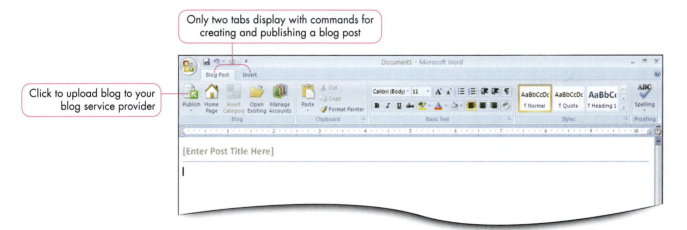

Figure 8.20 A New Blog Post Window

You can publish your blog posts by using one of several blog service providers. To learn about and find service providers, visit the Microsoft Office Marketplace, perform an Internet search, or ask your friends which service they use. Word supports several service providers, such as

- Windows Live Spaces
- Microsoft Windows SharePoint blog
- Community Server
- WordPress
- Blogger
- TypePad

You must have an established blog account with a provider before you can register and publish blogs directly from Word. Click Manage Accounts in the Blog group on the Blog Post tab, and then click New in the Blog Accounts dialog box to view the New Blog Account dialog box. From this dialog box, the blog registration wizard prompts you for the service provider information and then configures Word to enable you to post your blog directly from Word. If you use a different service, you can click Manage Accounts, click New, click Other in the Blog drop-down list, click Next, and then enter the account information, your user name, and your password. You can register several blog accounts in Word 2007. After they are registered, you can use the Manage Accounts command to change, delete, and set one account as your default blog location.

Some blogs include pictures. Even though they display with the blog post, pictures are stored in a file separate from the blog text. The file that stores the blog text includes a link to the path where the picture is stored. Your blog service provider might supply storage space for images or you might have a completely different service provider for images. In the New Account dialog box, you can click Picture Options and specify the picture provider location where you store your images that display with the blog.

Anatomy of a Blog | Reference

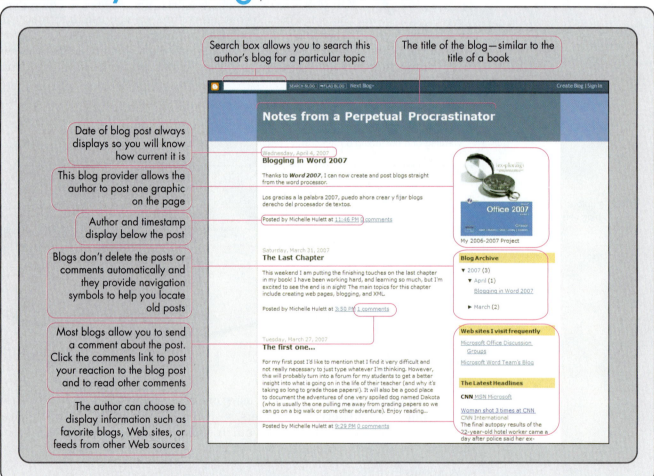

Using the Research Task Pane

The ***Research command*** enables you to conduct research investigations to find information.

The ***Research command*** enables you to conduct research investigations to find information. You can use it to look up definitions of words, identify synonyms, read encyclopedia articles, and find language translation services. In addition, you can find information through an MSN Search, identify fee-based research sites, and look up business and financial information, such as an organization's revenue or Web site address. When you insert research findings into your documents, be sure to include the proper citations.

To use the Research command, click the Review tab, and then click Research. The Research task pane displays, and you can customize the options to expand or narrow your search criteria. If you do not have a live Internet connection, your results are not as comprehensive. Figure 8.21 displays the criteria to search the Encarta Encyclopedia online for information about the topic *blogging*.

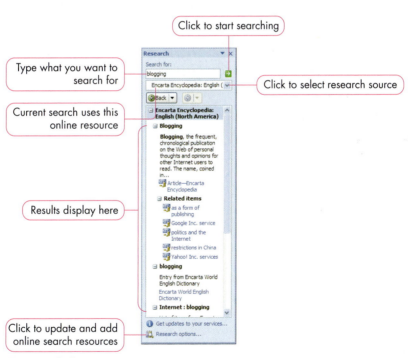

Figure 8.21 The Research Task Pane

The Research tool provides access to valuable search engines. You can quickly change the type of source to search if your initial query does not provide the information or details you need. Click the Encarta Encyclopedia drop-down arrow and Word displays a list of research sources to choose from (see Figure 8.22). The default, All Reference Books, performs an extensive search through all sources. Your list may vary based on how Office 2007 was installed on your computer and based on previous use of the Reference tool.

Figure 8.22 Research Sources

Hands-On Exercises

3 | Creating a Blog Post

Skills covered: 1. Set Up a Blog Account **2.** Write a Blog Entry and Use the Research Task Pane **3.** Publish a Blog Post

Step 1 Set Up a Blog Account	Refer to Figure 8.23 as you complete Step 1.

a. Start Word. Click the **Office Button**, click **New**, and then double-click **New blog post**. If the Register a Blog Account dialog box displays, click **Register Later**.

A new document opens and the Ribbon contains only two tabs: Blog Post and Insert. You might see more tabs if you install programs that create their own tabs. A placeholder prompts you to type the title of your post and the insertion point is below the horizontal line, ready for you to create your post.

b. Click **Manage Accounts** in the Blog group on the Blog Post tab. Click **New**.

c. Click the **Blog drop-down arrow** in the New Blog Account dialog box. Click **Blogger**, as shown in Figure 8.23, and then click **Next**.

If you have a different blog service provider, you should select that provider from the drop-down arrow and enter your personal identification and password in the next step. If you do not have an account with a blog service provider, read through these steps, and then continue with the next exercise.

d. Enter your blog service user name in the *User Name* box. Enter your blog service password in the *Password* box. Click **OK**.

e. Click **OK** when the Picture Options dialog box displays.

If you have a picture provider, you can click the Picture Provider drop-down arrow and select My own server. After you choose that option, boxes display where you type the Web address (URL) for the location where you upload your pictures and where the pictures are stored. In this exercise, we will not specify a picture provider.

f. Click **Yes** to the Microsoft Office Word dialog box that tells you there is a possibility the information you send to your blog service provider could be seen by other people.

The information that passes from Word to your blog service provider is not encrypted, and that does provide the possibility of information being intercepted; however, that possibility is very small.

g. Click **OK** to the Microsoft Office Word dialog box that indicates your account registration was successful.

When you register a blog service successfully, the service will display in the Blog Accounts dialog box.

h. Click **Close** in the Blog Accounts dialog box.

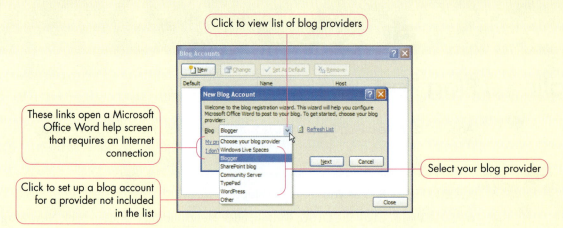

Click to view list of blog providers

These links open a Microsoft Office Word help screen that requires an Internet connection

Click to set up a blog account for a provider not included in the list

Select your blog provider

Figure 8.23 The New Blog Account Dialog Box

Step 2
Write a Blog Entry and Use the Research Task Pane

Refer to Figure 8.24 as you complete Step 2.

a. Type the following text at the insertion point: **Thanks to Word 2007, I can now create and post blogs straight from the word processor.** Select the text *Word 2007* and use the Mini toolbar to apply bold and italic formatting.

b. Click the placeholder *Enter Post Title Here* and insert the text **Blogging in Word 2007.**

c. Click the **Spelling arrow** in the Proofing group on the Blog Post tab. Click **Research** to display the Research task pane.

d. Select the entire sentence you typed in the blog and press **Ctrl+C** to copy it to the Clipboard. Click to position the insertion point in the *Search for* box on the Research task pane, replacing any previous search criteria, and then press **Ctrl+V** to insert the sentence.

e. Click the drop-down arrow located just below the Search for text box, which displays a list of sources, and select **Translation**. Click the **To drop-down arrow** and click **Spanish (International Sort)**. Click **Start searching**.

The program returns with a Spanish version of the sentence, as seen in Figure 8.24. You can copy and paste the sentence into your document, if you choose. You can also change the Translation options to use a different language.

TROUBLESHOOTING: If you click the green button with a white arrow that displays within the Translation area of the Research task pane, a Translate Whole Document dialog box displays. If you click **Yes** to the dialog box, a separate Internet Explorer window opens to display the translation. If you click **No**, it displays *No results were found*. Click the **Start searching arrow** at the top of the Research task pane for best results.

f. Select the translated text that displays under WorldLingo and press **CTRL+C** to copy it to the Clipboard. Click to position the insertion point at the end of the sentence in the blog, press **Enter** to move to the beginning of the next line, and then press **Ctrl+V** to paste the Spanish version of the text into the blog.

TROUBLESHOOTING: If you do not have an active Internet connection, the translation may not work. If you do not have an Internet connection, skip this step and proceed with the next step.

g. Click the **Office Button**, click **Save As**, and type **chap8_ho3_blog_solution** in the *File name* box. Click **Save** to keep a copy of the post until you are ready to publish.

h. Click **X** in the upper right corner of the Research task pane to close it.

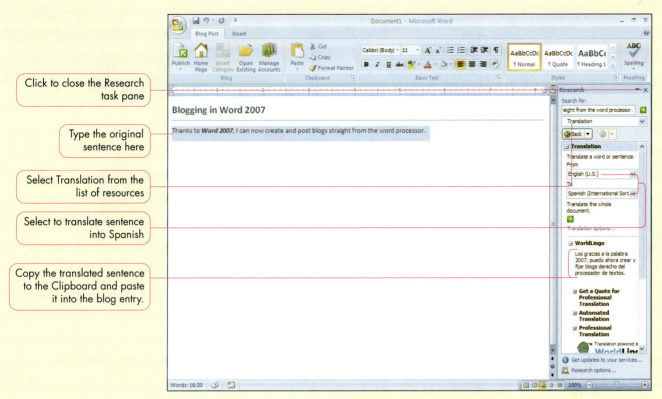

Click to close the Research task pane

Type the original sentence here

Select Translation from the list of resources

Select to translate sentence into Spanish

Copy the translated sentence to the Clipboard and paste it into the blog entry.

Figure 8.24 Translating a Sentence from English to Spanish

Step 3
Publish a Blog Post

Refer to Figure 8.25 as you complete Step 3.

a. Click **Publish** in the Blog group on the Blog Post tab.

b. Type your user name and password in the appropriate text boxes in the Connect to dialog box.

The dialog box displays the name of your blog. You can click **Remember Password** if you want to avoid typing the password each time you post to the blog server.

c. Click **OK** to save and post the blog. Click **Yes** in the Microsoft Office Word dialog box that tells you there is a possibility the information you send to your blog service provider could be seen by other people. Click **Don't show this message again** if you want to avoid clicking *Yes* at this dialog box each time you post a blog.

d. Click **Home Page** on the Blog Post tab to display your blog in a separate Internet Explorer window, as seen in Figure 8.25.

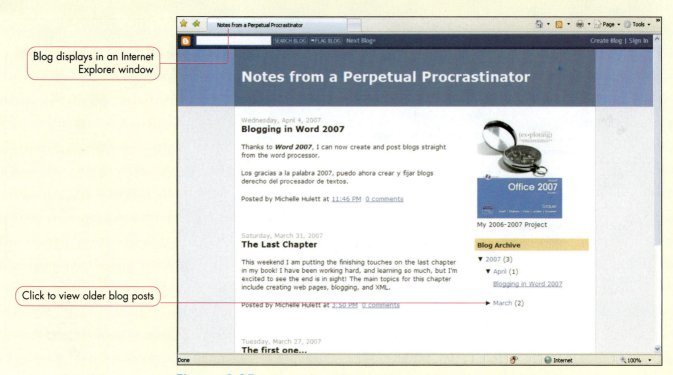

Blog displays in an Internet Explorer window

Click to view older blog posts

Figure 8.25 View a Blog in Internet Explorer

Summary

1. **Build a Web page.** Word provides all the tools necessary to create a basic Web page. You can use tables to organize and lay out the page elements, clip art and pictures to enhance the page with visual elements, bullet and numbered lists to organize information on the page, WordArt for text, and so on. Microsoft Word converts the document and generates the HTML codes for you. Web pages are developed in a special language called HyperText Markup Language (HTML).

2. **Apply themes and background color to a Web page.** Web pages are more interesting when you add design elements such as background images, bullets, numbering, lines, and other graphical features. You can use the Word themes while developing a Web page, which enables you to coordinate colors and fonts. A colored background adds visual enhancement to the Web page. You can choose from the standard palette of colors or mix a custom color. The Fill Effects command enables you to apply a gradient, texture, pattern, or picture background.

3. **Insert hyperlinks in a Web page.** Hyperlinks are electronic markers that, when clicked, move the insertion point to a different location within the same document, open another document, or display a different Web page in a Web browser. Hyperlinks can be assigned to text or graphics.

4. **Insert bookmarks in a Web page.** Some Web pages are very lengthy and require the viewer to scroll a great deal to view all the contents on the page. A bookmark is an electronic marker for a specific location in a document, enabling the user to go to that location quickly. Bookmarks are helpful in long documents because they enable you to move easily from one place to another within that document, without having to manually scroll.

5. **Preview a Web page.** As you prepare a Web page, the Web Layout view gives you a very accurate representation of how the page will look when published. You can also preview the page in an actual Web browser before you upload and publish it so that you can confirm it contains the correct content and is formatted to your specifications.

6. **Publish a Web page.** To view the pages on the Internet, you must save or publish them to a Web server, which is a computer system that hosts pages so that they are available for viewing by anyone who has an Internet connection.

7. **Understand XML.** XML goes a step beyond the code generated by HTML, which describes how a document should look by using tags that describe formatting features such as bold and indent. XML is data about data—it lets you define tags that describe the data or content in a document. The major advantage of XML file formatting is that it is not constrained to a particular platform, operating system, hardware configuration, or software application. After you create XML documents in Word, database administrators can extract XML data and then import the data into a database, which in turn can be used to create brochures, catalogs, correspondence, or Web pages.

8. **Attach an XML schema.** Before saving a document in XML format, you must attach an XML schema to it. An XML schema is a file that defines the structure and organization of content within an XML document. The XML schema specifies the type and location of content within the document. A tag is a marker that indicates the beginning or end of particular content within a document. The tag enables the transferability of data in such a way that other applications can import the tagged data. You can add more than one schema to a particular document. However, Word will alert you if the schemas conflict with each other in terms of tagging content.

9. **Create a blog post.** One of the most exciting features of Word 2007 is the New blog post template. This feature benefits people who are accustomed to working in Word, but who also publish blogs on a frequent basis. You can publish your blog posts by using one of several blog service providers. You must have an established blog account with a provider before you can register and publish blogs directly from Word.

10. **Use the Research task pane.** The Research command enables you to conduct research investigations to find information. You can use it to look up definitions of words, identify synonyms, read encyclopedia articles, and find language translation services.

Key Terms

Multiple Choice

1. Which background option enables you to apply settings for a gradient background?
   (a) More Color
   (b) Theme
   (c) Pattern
   (d) Fill Effects

2. While you are creating and editing documents that will be part of a Web site, you should save them in which format?
   (a) XML
   (b) Web page
   (c) Compatibility Mode
   (d) Text

3. Which of the following is not a legitimate object to use in a hyperlink?
   (a) Schema
   (b) E-mail address
   (c) Web page
   (d) Bookmark

4. What is the advantage of applying a theme to a Web page?
   (a) It adds a background color automatically.
   (b) It cannot be removed after you apply it.
   (c) It applies a uniform design to the links and other objects in a document.
   (d) It is automatically applied to each additional Web page you create.

5. If you view a Web page and hyperlinks display in two different colors, what is the most likely explanation?
   (a) A different theme was applied to each hyperlink.
   (b) One of the hyperlinks is invalid.
   (c) One of the hyperlinks was previously visited.
   (d) One of the hyperlinks is a bookmark.

6. Which program enables you to publish your Web pages to a Web server?
   (a) HTML
   (b) FTP
   (c) XML
   (d) Internet Explorer

7. Which of the following is not a format used to save documents as Web pages?
   (a) Web Template
   (b) Single File Web Page
   (c) Web Page
   (d) Web Page, Filtered

8. What information is relayed to the Web browser by HTML tags?
   (a) How to categorize the data on the Web page
   (b) How to save the information on the Web page
   (c) How to transfer the data to a Web server
   (d) How to format the information on the Web page

9. What type of file should you attach to a document in order to apply XML tags?
   (a) XML
   (b) XML Library
   (c) XML transform
   (d) XML schema

10. What term refers to a descriptive name assigned to a schema?
    (a) Alias
    (b) Schema Library
    (c) XML transform
    (d) Element

11. Which feature enables users to manage schemas and solutions?
    (a) Alias
    (b) Schema Library
    (c) XML transform
    (d) Element

12. After attaching an XML schema to a document, what must you apply before applying other tags?
    (a) Subelement
    (b) Root element
    (c) Alias
    (d) Element

13. What type of Web site enables you to view the frequent, chronological publication of personal thoughts?
    (a) Search engine
    (b) FTP
    (c) Web server
    (d) Blog

Multiple Choice Continued...

14. What feature enables you to look up a company's Web site address without leaving Word?

   (a) XML

   (b) Research

   (c) Blog template

   (d) Theme

15. What feature should you change in order to display information about your Web site at the top of the Internet Explorer window?

   (a) XML element

   (b) File name

   (c) Page title

   (d) Document theme

Tom Margavio owns a large real estate company in New Orleans. The real estate company offers a comprehensive list of services beyond the standard commercial and residential real estate sales and listings, including management of retirement community and commercial properties. Although the company is profitable, Tom realizes it should post information about the organization and its services on a Web site. He prefers to establish a very simple Web site in the beginning, and then contract a Web site development professional if the site generates enough response. Tom takes the following steps to turn a few basic Word documents into Web pages:

a. Start Word. Open the *chap8_pe1_default* document.

b. Click the **Office Button**, and then click **Save As**. In the Save As dialog box, navigate to the drive and folder in which you want to create a Web folder.

c. Click **Create New Folder** on the Save As dialog box toolbar, type **Real_Estate**, and then click **OK**.

d. Type **chap8_pe1_default_solution** in the File name text box. Click the **Save as type drop-down arrow** and click **Web Page (*.htm; *.html)**.

e. Click **Change Title** to display the Set Page Title dialog box. Type **Tom Margavio Real Estate** in the *Page title* box, and then click **OK**. Click **Save**.

f. Open the Word documents listed below, and then save each as a Web page in the *Real_Estate* folder. Assign new file names and Web page titles using the information in the following table.

Open This File	Save As	Web Page Title
chap8_pe1_services	chap8_pe1_services_solution	Tom Margavio Real Estate Services
chap8_pe1_contact	chap8_pe1_contact_solution	Tom Margavio Real Estate Contact Information
chap8_pe1_listings	chap8_pe1_listings_solution	Tom Margavio Real Estate Listings

g. Press **Alt+Tab** as needed to display *chap8_pe1_default_solution*, select *Real Estate Services*, and then click **Hyperlink** in the Links group on the Insert tab.

h. Click **Existing File or Web Page** in the *Link to* panel of the Insert Hyperlink dialog box, if necessary. Scroll, if necessary, and click the file *chap8_pe1_services_solution.htm*, and then click **OK**.

i. Repeat Step h to create a hyperlink from *About Us* on the default page to *chap8_pe1_contact_solution.htm*, and then create a hyperlink from *Today's Listings* to *chap8_pe1_listings_solution.htm*. Compare your Web page to Figure 8.26.

j. Save *chap8_pe1_default_solution*. Leave each document open for the next exercise.

...continued on Next Page

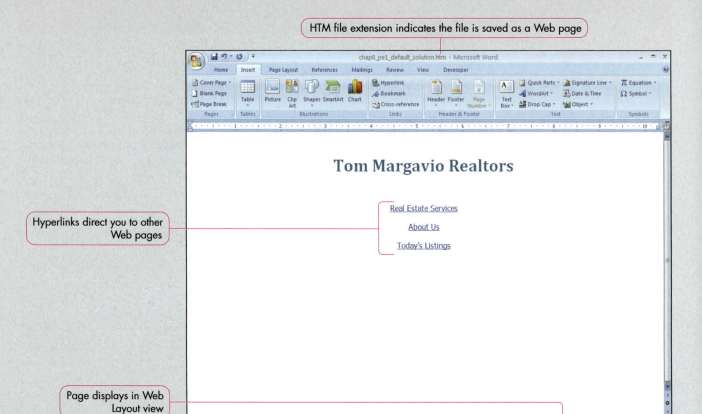

Figure 8.26 A Simple Home Page for Tom Margavio Realtors

2 Enhancements to the Real Estate Agency Web Site

Rebecca Mitchell is a summer intern at Tom Margavio Realty and offers suggestions to help Tom enhance the Web pages he created to promote the agency. Rebecca decides the pages need more color, so she suggests the use of a theme and a background image on each page. She also suggests the use of bookmarks on the services page to improve navigation between information on that page. Based on Rebecca's suggestions, Tom takes the following steps to enhance the Web pages.

a. Click the **View tab**, click **Switch Windows**, and click **chap8_pe1_default_ solution.htm** from the list of open files, if necessary.

b. Click the **Page Layout tab**, click **Themes** in the Themes group, and then click **Module**.

c. Click **Page Color** in the Page Background group. Click **Fill Effects** to display the Fill Effects dialog box, and then click the **Gradient tab**, if necessary.

d. Click **Two colors** in the Colors section. Click the **Color 1 drop-down arrow** and select **Gold, Accent 1, Lighter 80%** in the 5th column. Click the **Color 2 drop-down arrow** and select **Gold, Accent 1, Lighter 60%** in the 5th column.

e. Click **Horizontal** in the *Shading styles* section. In the *Variants* section, click the square in the upper right corner, as shown in Figure 8.27. Click **OK** to apply the background.

f. Press **Ctrl+S** to save the changes to the *chap8_pe1_default_solution* document.

g. Repeat Steps b through f to apply the theme and background color to the remaining pages.

h. Click the **View tab**, click **Switch Windows**, and click **chap8_pe1_services_ solution.htm** from the list of open files. Press **Ctrl+Home** to move the insertion point to the beginning of the document, if necessary.

i. Click to place the insertion point on the left side of the word *Residential*, which displays as a heading for the paragraph that describes that service. Click the **Insert tab**, click **Bookmark**, type **res** in the *Bookmark name* box, and then click **Add**.

...continued on Next Page

j. Repeat Step i to create bookmarks at the beginning of the *Retirement Communities*, *Multi-Family*, and *Commercial* headings that display down the page. The bookmarks should be named **retire**, **multi**, and **com**.

k. Press **Ctrl+Home** to view the top of the page. Select *Residential* in the bullet list, and then click **Hyperlink** from the Links group on the Insert tab. Click **Place in This Document** in the *Link to* panel of the Insert Hyperlink dialog box. If necessary, click the **plus sign** next to *Bookmarks*. Click **res**, and then click **OK**.

l. Repeat Step k to create hyperlinks from each bullet list item to the corresponding bookmarks for *Retirement Communities, Multi-Family*, and *Commercial*.

m. Select the text *Return to Top* that displays below each paragraph that describes one of the services. Click **Hyperlink** in the Insert tab, click **Top of the Document**, which displays at the very top of the *Select a place in this document* list, and then click **OK**.

n. Repeat Step m to create a hyperlink from each occurrence of *Return to Top* that displays throughout the document.

o. Save *chap8_pe1_services_solution*. Leave each document open for the next exercise.

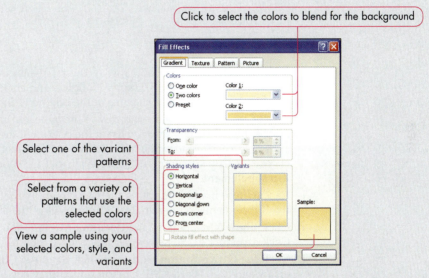

Figure 8.27   Use Fill Effects to Create a Page Background

3 Add XML to a Web Page

Rebecca Mitchell, a summer intern at Tom Margavio Realty, has been evaluating the progress of the Web pages Tom is creating to promote the agency. Her previous suggestions were well received and easy to implement, and now she has one last recommendation. Rebecca understands the importance of sharing information among staff and providing an efficient way to create, label, and use information. She conveys to Tom the benefit of using XML to label the real estate listings because the listings are often shared and communicated among the staff and clients of the company. Tom decides to let Rebecca develop a schema and apply the XML tags to the page that displays the current listings. Rebecca takes the following steps to create information that is easy to use between programs.

a. Click the **View tab**, click **Switch Windows**, and click **chap8_pe1_listings_ solution.htm** from the list of open files.

b. Click the **Developer tab** and click **Schema**. Click **Schema Library**, click **Products** from the *Select a schema* list, and click **Delete Schema**. Click **Yes** in the Schema Library dialog box to continue.

c. Click **Add Schema**, browse to the folder that contains files for this project, select *chap8_pe3_propertyschema.xsd*, and then click **Open**. Type **Real Estate** in the *Alias* box and click **OK** to close the Schema Settings dialog box. Click **OK** to close the Templates

...continued on Next Page

and Add-ins dialog box. Select *Real Estate* in the *Checked schemas are currently attached* section of the Templates and Add-ins dialog box, and then click **OK**.

d. Click **Property** in the *Choose an element to apply to your current selection* list box. Click **Apply to Entire Document**, as shown in Figure 8.28. If necessary, click **Show XML tags in the document** in the XML Structure task pane.

e. Select the *Listings for Tom Margavio Realtors* title and click the **Caption element** in the *Choose an element to apply to your current selection* list at the bottom of the XML Structure task pane.

f. Select the *Type of Property* column heading text in the first cell of the table and click the **TypeHead element** at the bottom of the XML Structure task pane.

g. Repeat Step e to apply the remaining three elements as itemized in the following table.

Column Heading	Element
Address	StreetHead
City	CityHead
Zip Code	ZipHead

h. Select all cells on the second row of the table—the row containing details about the commercial property on S. Happy Hollow—and click **Product** in the *Choose an element to apply to your current selection* list at the bottom of the XML Structure task pane.

i. Select *Commercial* in the second row of the table and click **Type** in the *Choose an element to apply to your current selection* list at the bottom of the XML Structure task pane. Select *1234 S. Happy Hollow* in the table and click the **Street subelement**. Select *Warsaw* and choose the **City subelement**. Select *65355* in the second row of the table and choose the **Zip subelement**.

j. Repeat Steps h and i, adapting the steps to apply the Product element and the respective subelements to the remaining three rows of the table.

k. Click **Show XML tags in the document** to hide the tags from the data in the table. Click **Structure** in the Developer tab to close the XML Structure task pane.

l. Click the **Office Button**, and then click **Save As**. Click the **Save as type drop-down arrow** and click **Word XML Document (.xml)**. Click **Save**.

m. Close all documents.

n. Start Internet Explorer. Press **Alt+F** to display the File menu, and then click **Open** to display the Open dialog box. Click **Browse**, locate the *Real_Estate* folder, then double-click **chap_pe1_default_solution.htm**. Click **OK** on the Open dialog box to display the home page in the browser.

o. Click each link on the default page to view the other pages. Press **Backspace** on each page to return to the default page. After you view each page, close Internet Explorer.

...continued on Next Page

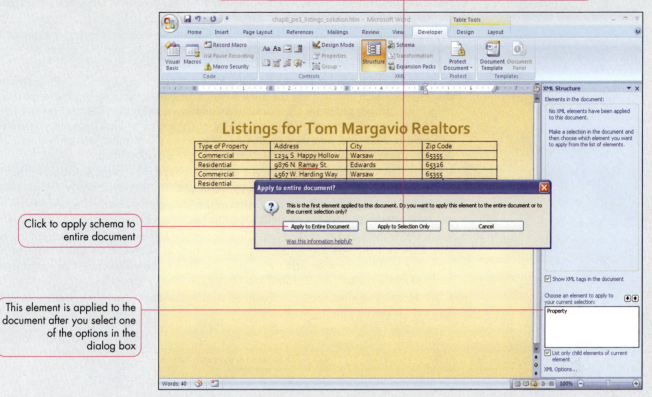

Figure 8.28 Apply Schema Element to Document

4 Create a Blog

Suad Makic is participating in a study abroad program at Missouri State University this fall and will spend the semester in Spain. He is excited about the opportunities to learn about a different country, the people, the language, and the culture. He is also very happy that he will not have classes on Friday, so he can travel and see as much of the country as possible. His parents are nervous about his time away and want him to write home as much as possible. His friends are also eager to hear about his experiences. Suad decides the most convenient and efficient way to communicate with everyone is to post blog entries as often as possible. He can use Word 2007 on his laptop, which he will have with him most of the time, to quickly write and post the blog entries. Follow these steps, as recommended by Suad, to set up a blog account and prepare the first entry. Suad also adds fun facts about Spain in his post, which he gathers from the Research task pane in Word.

a. Start Word. Click the **Office Button**, click **New**, and then double-click **New blog post**. If the Register a Blog Account dialog box displays, click **Register Later**.

b. Click **Manage Accounts** in the Blog group on the Blog Post tab. Click **New**. Click the **Blog drop-down arrow** in the New Blog Account dialog box. Click **Blogger**, and then click **Next**.

c. Enter your blog service user name in the User Name text box. Enter your blog service password in the Password text box. Click **OK**. Click **OK** when the Picture Options dialog box displays.

d. Click **Yes** in the Microsoft Office Word dialog box that tells you there is a possibility the information you send to your blog service provider could be seen by other people.

e. Click **OK** in the Microsoft Office Word dialog box that indicates your account registration was successful. Click **Close** in the Blog Accounts dialog box.

f. Type the following text at the insertion point: **Information about my upcoming travels will be chronicled here. I leave on August 20.**

...continued on Next Page

g. Click the placeholder *Enter Post Title Here* and insert the text **Next Stop—Spain**.

h. Click the **Spelling arrow** in the Proofing group on the Blog Post tab. Click **Research** to display the Research task pane.

i. Type **population of Spain** in the *Search for* box in the Research task pane, and then click the drop-down arrow that displays a list of sources, located just below the *Search for* box, and select *HighBeam Research*.

j. Scroll down the results that display in the Research task pane and notice the dates that display with each article. Find the most recent article that also displays the population. Select the number given for the population, as shown in Figure 8.29, and press **Ctrl+C** to copy it to the Clipboard. Click in the blog entry and type **Fast fact: the population of Spain in 2004 was**, and then press **Ctrl+V** to paste the number into your post. Click **X** in the upper right corner of the Research task pane to close it.

k. Click the **Office Button**, click **Save** As, and type **chap8_pe4_blog_solution** in the File name text box. Click **Save** to keep a copy of the post until you are ready to publish.

l. If you have a blog account, click **Publish** in the Blog group on the Blog Post tab. Type your user name and password in the appropriate boxes in the Connect to dialog box.

m. Click **OK** to save and post the blog. Click **Yes** in the Microsoft Office Word dialog box that tells you there is a possibility the information you send to your blog service provider could be seen by other people. Click **Don't show this message again** if you want to avoid clicking *Yes* at this dialog box each time you post a blog.

n. Click **Home Page** on the Blog Post tab to display the blog in a separate Internet Explorer window.

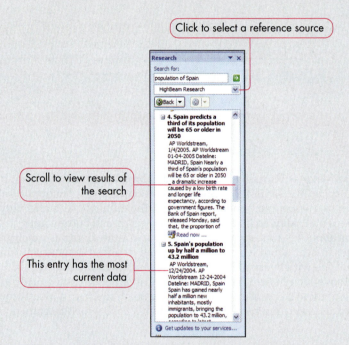

Figure 8.29 Find Information Using the Research Task Pane

Mid-Level Exercises

1 Departmental Policy Web Page

You are a part-time student assistant for the Management Information Systems department at your college. The department faculty created a document of standard policies that they want to make available on the college Web site. The department chair assigns you the job of formatting the document so that it will be easy to view and navigate as a Web page. She mentioned that a Web page that contains a lot of text should be easy to navigate and allow the user to jump to particular sections in the document. You decide the use of bookmarks and hyperlinks will be the perfect tool for this job. You also have some ideas about how to format it using colors and themes.

a. Open the *chap8_mid1_policies* document. Save the document as a Single File Web page (*.mht; *.mhtml) using the name **chap8_mid1_policies_solution**.

b. Change the Page title to *MIS Policies for Faculty and Students*.

c. Apply the **Metro theme** to the page.

d. Apply a background to the page using the Pattern fill effects. Select the **light horizontal** pattern and use **Teal, Accent 6, Lighter 40%** as the Foreground color, and **Teal, Accent 6, Lighter 80%** as the Background color.

e. Below the subheading *Standard Departmental Policies* create a list of the headings that appear above the policies. Apply the **Names** style to the list of policy headings. Create bookmarks for each policy, and then insert a hyperlink from each item in the list to the bookmark below.

f. Insert appropriate text or graphics throughout the page that link to the bookmark at the top of the page.

g. Insert a clip art graphic of a computer or student and display it near the top of the page.

h. Make any adjustments to font style, character spacing, or other formatting changes as you see fit to create a professional Web page. Save and close the document.

2 FlyRight Airways Home Page

The marketing manager at a fledgling airline company is hosting a competition, which awards a prize to the employee who designs the best home page for their Web site. A document that provides a description of the company is given to each person, and the information in that page should display in the final version. You take the following steps to develop the page you will submit.

a. Open the *chap8_mid2_airline* document. Save the document as a Single File Web page (*.mht; *.mhtml) using the name **chap8_mid2_airline_solution**.

b. Change the Page title to **Take off with FlyRight Airways**.

c. Apply the **Origin theme** to the page. Apply the **Intense Quote style** to the Company Name that displays at the top of the document and increase the font size to 20. Use a different style if you do not find *Intense Quote* on your list of Styles.

d. Select the text *Click here to contact us* that displays near the top of the document. Insert a hyperlink that links to the e-mail address *help@flyrightairways.org* and that contains the subject *Request for information*.

e. Apply a background color to the page. Use a **Gradient fill effect** that uses two colors, **Light Yellow, Accent 4, Lighter 40%** for the first color and **Light Yellow, Accent 4, Darker 25%** for the second color. Use a **Diagonal down shading style** and select **variant effect** in the upper right corner.

...continued on Next Page

f. Use the Research task pane to find information, including Web sites, for the companies mentioned in the last paragraph. Create hyperlinks to those companies (Boeing and FlyteComm) after you find their Web site addresses. The last Web site enables you to track a flight from takeoff to landing.

g. Save and close the document. Start Windows Explorer, then go to the folder containing your Web page and double-click the file you just created. Internet Explorer will start automatically because your document was saved as a Web page. Look carefully at the Address bar and note the local address, as opposed to a Web address.

3 Flight Schedules for FlyRight Airways

The president of FlyRight Airways was pleased with the selection of a Web page to display on the company Web site. However, he directs the Marketing Manager to add a page that will list the current flight schedule. This schedule can change frequently, so it should be formatted in such a way that information can be easily transferred between the company flight database and a Web page. You are the resident XML expert, so the Marketing Manager asks you to take the following steps to create an efficient solution for displaying flight schedules on their Web site.

a. Open the *chap8_mid3_flights* document.

b. Delete any unused schemas, if necessary, and then attach the schema *chap8_mid3_schema.xsd*. The schema alias should be *Fly*. Select the whole document and apply the **Flights element**. Apply the **Caption subelement** to the title of the page. Attach the appropriate subelements to the heading and data in the table.

c. Check the cities listed in the destination column and make adjustments to comply with any schema restrictions for that field.

d. Save your changes as an XML document named **chap8_mid3_flights_solution.xml**. Do not show XML tags in the document, and then close the XML Structure pane.

e. Save the page as a single-page Web page named **chap8_mid3_flights.mht**. Change the Page title to **Flight Schedules**. Apply the **Origin theme** to the page. Add the same background color that you used for the home page: a **Gradient fill effect** that uses two colors, **Light Yellow, Accent 4, Lighter 40%** for the first color and **Light Yellow, Accent 4, Darker 25%** for the second color. Use a **Diagonal down shading style** and select **variant effect** in the upper right corner. Center the flight schedule table on the page. Save the document.

f. Open the *chap8_mid2_airline_solution* Web page from the previous exercise. At the bottom of the home page, add a link to the schedules page. Save the updated document as **chap8_mid3_airline_solution.mht**.

g. View your updated home page in an Internet Explorer window. Test the hyperlink to the flight schedule page.

h. Save and close all documents.

Capstone Exercise

Heavenly Scents Candle Company is a family-owned business that manufactures and sells candles. So far, this company has relied on telephone and fax orders. Because of your extensive experience with Word 2007, the company president hired you to create a Web site.

Attach XML Schema to Product Information

You spoke with the database manager about exchanging product information between the database and your Web pages. He suggested you attach an XML schema and properly format any pages that contain product information. You also save the page as an XML document.

a. Open the file named *chap8_cap_order*.

b. Display the Developer tab, if necessary, and then display the XML Structure task pane.

c. Delete any schemas currently in the Schema Library, and then attach the schema in *chap8_cap_schema.xsd*. Give the schema an alias of *Candles*.

d. Assign the **Candles element** to the table only. Assign the appropriate elements to the column headings in the table, and then assign the appropriate subelements to each product.

e. Verify that all product descriptions comply with schema restrictions and make changes as necessary.

f. Hide the XML tags in the document and close the XML Structure task pane.

g. Create a folder named *Candles*. Save the file as a Word XML Document named **chap8_cap_order_solution** in the *Candles* folder.

Design a Set of Web Pages

You need to convert existing documents to Web pages for Heavenly Scents. But before you save them as Web pages, you redesign the pages to incorporate visual enhancements, such as color and graphics.

a. Open the documents *chap8_cap_default* and *chap8_cap_products*.

b. Display the default document, which will become the home page of the Web site. Create a background color that uses the **Bouquet Texture fill effect**. Apply the **Verve theme**. Increase font sizes of headings as necessary.

c. Insert Clip art of a candle and display it on the right side of the home page. Use picture format tools to resize the picture to two inches tall and apply the **Soft Edge Oval effect**. If you do not have access to the Internet, use your judgment on the image you use and use the picture format tools that would be most appropriate for that image.

d. Save this document in the *Candles* folder as a Web Page (*.htm, *.html) named **chap8_cap_default_solution**.

e. Display the products document. Apply the **Verve theme** and **Bouquet Texture fill effect** to the document. Save this document in the *Candles* folder as a Web Page (*.htm, *.html) named **chap8_cap_products_solution**.

f. Display the order document, which is in XML format, and change to Web Layout view. Apply the **Verve theme** and **Bouquet Texture fill effect** to the document. Center the text that is currently left justified. Save this document in the *Candles* folder as a Web Page (*.htm, *.html) named **chap8_cap_order_solution** and change the Page title to *Heavenly Scents Ordering Information*.

g. Leave all documents open for the next phase of development.

Add Navigation Elements to Web Pages

Your pages are looking good. Now you want to add the ability to navigate within a long page and also to navigate easily between the pages.

a. Display the home page. Type **View Our Products** and **Ordering Information** on the bottom of the default page. Create hyperlinks to the Products and Order Web pages from these lines of text.

b. Display the Products page. Create the following bookmarks in the appropriate places that correspond with the information on the page: *standard, exotic, sizes, descriptions*.

c. Create a list near the top of the page for the categories that display down the page. Create a hyperlink from each item on the list to the appropriate bookmark.

d. At the end of each category, create a *Back to Top* hyperlink that will use a bookmark to navigate back to the top of the document.

e. At the bottom of the page, type **HOME** and create a hyperlink to the default page. Save the page.

f. Display the order page. Type **HOME** at the bottom of the page and create a hyperlink to the default page. Save the page.

Document Progress in a Blog Post

The president of Heavenly Scents Candle Company is a strong proponent of documentation. She would like to know how much time you spent on this project and what resources you used. She advocates a casual workplace, so she recommended you just post a blog on the company server so she can read it later. You start the blog and then find the server is down for maintenance, so you save your work and post it at a later time.

a. Open a new blog post document.

b. The title of the blog post is *Preparing the Company Web Site*. Type the following sentence for the post: **I used Word 2007 to design the Web site. Features such as background color, themes, hyperlinks, and bookmarks made the process easy.**

c. Save the blog post in the *Candles* folder as **chap8_cap_blog_solution**.

d. Save and close all files.

Mini Cases

Use the rubric following the case as a guide to evaluate your work, but keep in mind that your instructor may impose additional grading criteria or use a different standard to judge your work.

Create Your Own Design

GENERAL CASE

After you complete the Capstone exercise, you decide you have better ideas for the design of the Web site. You now have the opportunity to implement those ideas and modify the Heavenly Scents Candle Web site. Open the three solution files from the capstone exercise, *chap8_cap_default_solution.htm*, *chap8_cap_order_solution.htm*, and *chap8_cap_products_solution.htm*, and save them as **chap8_mc1_default_solution.htm**, **chap8_mc1_order_solution.htm**, and **chap8_mid1_products_solution.htm**, respectively. Use formatting tools discussed in this chapter, but also use any of the formatting and layout tools you are familiar with in Word, such as tables (to lay out and position text and graphics), text boxes and shape tools (to create buttons), and WordArt. Be sure you change the hyperlinks to reflect the new files so that all the links work correctly.

Performance Elements	Exceeds Expectations	Meets Expectations	Below Expectations
Visual aspects	Background and theme colors are coordinated, appealing, and enhance the design of the Web site.	Background and theme colors are coordinated, but are distracting to the topic.	Background and theme colors do not coordinate and are distracting to the topic.
Mechanics	All hyperlinks and bookmarks work correctly.	No more than two hyperlinks or bookmarks work incorrectly.	More than three hyperlinks or bookmarks work incorrectly.
Initiative	Used more than three formatting and layout tools that were not discussed in this chapter but that are appropriate to use in the Web page design.	Used up to two formatting and layout tools that were not discussed in this chapter but that are appropriate to use in the Web page design.	Did not use formatting and layout tools that were not discussed in this chapter but that are appropriate to use in the Web page design.

Track Your Investments

RESEARCH CASE

As soon as you graduate from school, you will begin saving for retirement. You can start tracking stock prices now to determine which companies you might invest in later. Create a table in Word that lists company names in the first row and that has a date listed in the first column. Use the Research pane to look up stock prices for several weeks to see how the company stocks perform. Save the document in XML format, so you can later import the results into an Excel worksheet and graph the change over time. Name your file **chap8_mc2_stocks_solution**.

Performance Elements	Exceeds Expectations	Meets Expectations	Below Expectations
Organization	Data are organized, easy to understand, and saved in XML format.	Data are somewhat organized, easy to understand, and saved as a Word 2007 document.	Data are not organized, are difficult to understand, and are saved as a Word 2007 document.
Research subjects	Data table includes at least five different company stocks that were tracked for at least seven days.	Data table includes at least three different company stocks that were tracked for at least three days.	Data table includes fewer than three different company stocks that were tracked for fewer than three days.

Modify a Schema

DISASTER RECOVERY

A schema is necessary to tag elements of data so they can be used in other applications. Typically an IT department develops the schemas used by its organization. However, with a basic schema in place, you can modify the code for use in a different scenario. The schemas used in this chapter are all very similar but include subtle changes that make them appropriate for the exercise. Open the file *chap8_mc3_schema.xsd* in Notepad (or WordPad) and save it as **chap8_mc3_schema_solution.xsd**. Use your critical thinking skills to modify the code in the schema so that it will be appropriate to use with the data in *chap8_mc3_construction.docx*. Test your schema by attaching it to the data file, and then tag the data in that file with the appropriate elements and subelements. Save the results as an XML file with the name **chap8_mc3_construction_solution.xml**.

Performance Elements	Exceeds Expectations	Meets Expectations	Below Expectations
Mechanics	Schema was modified to include all data objects in the chap8_mc3_construction document.	Schema was modified, but did not include all data objects in the chap8_mc3_construction document.	Schema was not modified and did not include all data objects in the chap8_mc3_construction document.
Application	Schema was applied to data file and zero errors displayed.	Schema was applied to data file and fewer than two errors displayed.	Schema was applied to data file and more than two errors displayed.

Glossary

All key terms appearing in this book (in bold italic) are listed alphabetically in this Glossary for easy reference. If you want to learn more about a feature or concept, use the Index to find the term's other significant occurrences.

ActiveX controls Form elements that work in a Word 2007 document or template.

Ascending order A feature that arranges that arranges data in alphabetical or sequential order from lowest to highest.

AutoFormat A feature that evaluates an entire document, determines how each paragraph is used, then it applies an appropriate style to each paragraph.

Automatic replacement Makes a substitution automatically.

AutoText A feature that substitutes a predefined item for specific text but only when you initiate it.

Background A color, design, image, or watermark that appears behind text in a document or on a Web page.

Bar tab Tab that inserts a vertical bar at the tab setting; useful as a separator for text printed on the same line.

Bibliography A list of works cited or consulted by an author in their work and should be included with the published work.

Blog The frequent, chronological publication of personal thoughts.

Bookmark An electronic marker for a specific location in a document.

Border A line that surrounds a paragraph, a page, a table, or an image, similar to how a picture frame surrounds a photograph or piece of art.

Brightness The ratio between lightness and darkness of an image.

Building Blocks Document components used frequently such as disclaimees, company address, or names.

Bulleted list Itemizes and separates paragraph text to increase readability.

Caption A descriptive title for an image, a figure, or a table.

Case-insensitive search Finds a word regardless of any capitalization used.

Case-sensitive search Matches not only the text but also the use of upper- and lowercase letters.

Cell The intersection of a column and row in a table or in an Excel spreadsheet.

Cell margin The amount of space between data and the cell border in a table.

Center tab Sets the middle point of the text you type; whatever you type will be centered on that tab setting.

Change Case Feature that enables you to change capitalization of text to all capital letters, all lowercase letters, sentence case, or toggle case.

Character spacing The horizontal space between characters.

Character style Stores character formatting (font, size, and style) and affects only the selected text.

Check box form field Consists of a box that is checked or not.

Citation A note recognizing a source of information or a quoted passage.

Clip art A graphical image, illustration, drawing, or sketch.

Clipboard A memory location that holds up to 24 items for you to paste into the current document, another file, or another application.

Column Formats a section of a document into side-by-side vertical blocks in which the text flows down the first column and then continues at the top of the next column.

Column width The horizontal space or width of a column in a table or in a spreadsheet.

Combine Feature that incorporates all changes from multiple documents into a new document.

Command An icon on the Quick Access Toolbar or in a group on the Ribbon that you click to perform a task. A command can also appear as text on a menu or within a dialog box.

Comment A private note, annotation, or additional information to the author, another reader, or to yourself.

Compare Feature that evaluates the contents of two or more documents and displays markup balloons that show the differences between the documents.

Compatibility Checker Looks for features that are not supported by previous versions of Word, Excel, PowerPoint, or Access.

Compress The process of reducing the file size of an object.

Contextual tab A specialty tab that appears on the Ribbon only when certain types of objects are being edited.

Contrast The difference between the darkest and lightest areas of a image.

Copy The process of making a duplicate copy of the text or object leaving the original intact.

Copyright The legal protection afforded to a written or artistic work.

Crop or Cropping Process of reducing an image size by eliminating unwanted portions of an image.

Cross-reference A note that refers you to another location for more information about a topic.

Current List Includes all citation sources you use in the current document.

Curriculum vitae (CV) Similar to a resume, a document that displays accomplishments, education, and job history.

Cut Process of removing the original text or an object from its current location.

Data source A listing of information.

Database table A collection of related records that contain fields to organize data.

Date Picker Displays a calendar that you can select a date by clicking rather than typing in a date.

Decimal tab Marks where numbers align on a decimal point as you type.

Descending order Arranges data in alphabetical or sequential order from highest to lowest.

Design Mode Enables you to view and modify control fields.

Desktop Publishing The merger of text with graphics to produce a professional-looking document.

Dialog box A window that provides an interface for you to select commands.

Dialog Box Launcher A small icon that, when clicked, opens a related dialog box.

Digital certificate An attachment to a file that guarantees the authenticity of the file, provides a verifiable signature, or enables encryption.

Digital signature An electronic stamp that displays information about the person or organization that obtained the certification.

Document Information panel Provides descriptive information about a document, such as a title, subject, author, keywords, and comments.

Document Inspector Checks for and removes different kinds of hidden and personal information from a document.

Document Map A pane that lists the structure of headings in your document.

Document theme A set of coordinating fonts, colors, and special effects that give a stylish and professional look.

Draft view Shows a simplified work area, removing white space and other elements from view.

Drawing Canvas A frame-like area that helps you keep parts of your drawing together.

Drop cap A large capital letter at the beginning of a paragraph.

Drop-down list Enables you to choose from one of several existing entries.

Duplex printer A printing device that prints on both sides of the page.

Editing restrictions Specify limits for users to modify a document.

Element A descriptive name that identifies a piece of data in an XML document.

Embedding Pulls an object into a document where you can edit it without changing the source.

Endnote A citation that appears at the end of a document.

Enhanced ScreenTip Displays the name and brief description of a command when you rest the pointer on a command.

eXtensible Markup Language (XML) Describes a document's content and enables easy exchange of data.

Field A single piece of data used in a source document, such as last name.

File Transfer Protocol (FTP) A process that uploads files from a PC to a server, or from a server to a PC.

Fill The interior space of an object.

Filter Specifies criteria for including records that meet certain conditions.

Final Showing Markup A view that displays inserted text in the body of the document and shows deleted text in a balloon.

Find Locates a word or group of words in a file.

First line indent Marks the location to indent only the first line in a paragraph.

Font A complete set of characters—upper- and lowercase letters, numbers, punctuation marks, and special symbols with the same design.

Footer Information printed at the bottom of document pages.

Footnote A citation that appears at the bottom of a page.

Form A document designed for collecting data for a specific situation.

Form controls Helps you to complete a form by displaying prompts such as drop-down lists and text boxes.

Form letters Letters with standard information that you personalize with recipient information. You might print or e-mail these to many people.

Form template A document that defines the standard layout, structure, and formatting of a form.

Format Painter Feature that enables you to copy existing text formats to other text to ensure consistency.

Formatting restrictions Restrictive option that does not allow others to modify formatting or styles in a document.

Formatting text The process of changing the appearance of an individual letter, a word, or selected text.

Full Screen Reading view A viewing format that eliminates tabs and makes it easier to read your document.

Gallery Displays a set of predefined options that can be clicked to apply to an object or to text.

Go To Moves the insertion point to a specific location in the file.

Grid An underlying, but invisible, set of horizontal and vertical lines that determine the placement of major elements.

Group Categories that organize similar commands together within each tab on the Ribbon.

Grouping The process of combining objects so they appear as a single object.

Hanging indent Aligns the first line of a paragraph at the left margin and indents the remaining lines.

Hard page break Forces the next part of a document to begin on a new page.

Hard return Created when you press Enter to move the insertion point to a new line.

Header Information printed at the top of document pages.

Header row The first row in a data source.

Hidden text Document text that does not appear onscreen.

Highlighter Background color used to mark text that you want to stand out or locate easily.

Horizontal alignment The placement of text between the left and right margins.

Hyperlinks Electronic markers that point to a different location or display a different Web page.

HyperText Markup Language (HTML) Uses codes to describe how a document appears when viewed in a Web browser.

Index An alphabetical listing of topics covered in a document, along with the page numbers where the topic is discussed.

Information Rights Management (IRM) Services designed to help you control who can access documents.

Insert The process of adding text in a document, spreadsheet cell, database object, or presentation slide.

Insertion point The blinking vertical line in the document, cell, slide show, or database table designating the current location where text you type displays.

Internet A network of networks that connects computers anywhere in the world.

Kerning Automatically adjusts spacing between characters to achieve a more evenly spaced appearance.

Key Tip The letter or number that displays over each feature on the Ribbon and Quick Access Toolbar and is the keyboard equivalent that you press. Press Alt by itself to display Key Tips.

Landscape orientation Page orientation is wider than it is long, resembling a landscape scene.

Layering The process of placing one shape on top of another.

Leader character Typically dots or hyphens that connect two items, to draw the reader's eye across the page.

Left tab Sets the start position on the left so as you type, text moves to the right of the tab setting.

Legacy form fields Form elements that can be used in Word 2007 and also in previous versions of Word.

Line spacing The vertical space between the lines in a paragraph and between paragraphs.

Linking Inserts an object from another program, but retains a connection to the original data.

Live Preview A feature that provides a preview of how a gallery option will affect the current text or object when the mouse pointer hovers over the gallery option.

Macro Small program that automates tasks in a file.

Macro-enabled document A document that contains and allows execution of a macro.

Mail merge A process that combines content from a main document and a data source.

Main document Contains the information that stays the same for all recipients.

Manual duplex Operation that enables you to print on both sides of the paper by printing first on one side and then on the other.

Margin The amount of white space around the top, bottom, left, and right edges the page.

Mark as Final Creates a read-only file and also sets the property to Final on the status bar.

Markup balloon Colored circles that contain comments, insertions, and deletions in the margin with a line drawn to where the insertion point was in the document prior to inserting the comment or editing the document.

Master document A document that acts like a binder for managing smaller documents.

Master List A database of all citation sources created in Word on a particular computer.

Masthead The identifying information at the top of a newsletter or other periodical.

Merge fields Serve as placeholders for the variable data that will be inserted into the main document during the mail merge.

Microsoft Clip Organizer Catalogs pictures, sounds, and movies stored on your hard drive.

Microsoft WordArt An application within Microsoft Office that creates decorative text that can be used to add interest to a document.

Mini toolbar A semitransparent toolbar of often-used font, indent, and bullet commands that displays when you position the mouse over selected text and disappears when you move the mouse away from the selected text.

Monospaced typeface Uses the same amount of horizontal space for every character.

Multilevel list Extends a numbered list to several levels, and is updated automatically when topics are added or deleted.

Nonbreaking hyphen Keeps text on both sides of the hyphen together, thus preventing the hyphenated word from becoming separated at the hyphen.

Nonbreaking space A special character that keeps two or more words together.

Normal template The framework that defines the default page settings.

Numbered list Sequences and prioritizes the items in a list and is automatically updated to accommodate additions or deletions.

Object Linking and Embedding (OLE) A technology that enables you to insert objects or information into different applications.

Office Button Icon that, when clicked, displays the Office menu.

Office menu List of commands (such as New, Open, Save, Save As, Print, and Options) that work with an entire file or with the specific Microsoft Office program.

Original Showing Markup A view that shows deleted text within the body of the document (with a line through the deleted text) and displays inserted text in a balloon to the right of the actual document.

Orphan The first line of a paragraph appearing by itself at the bottom of a page.

Outline view Displays varying amounts of detail; a structural view of a document that can be collapsed or expanded as necessary.

Overtype mode Replaces the existing text with text you type character by character.

Paragraph spacing The amount of space before or after a paragraph.

Paragraph style Stores paragraph formatting such as alignment, line spacing, indents, as well as the font, size, and style of the text in the paragraph.

Password A security feature required to gain access to a restricted document.

Paste Places the cut or copied text or object in the new location.

Picture style A gallery that contains preformatted options that can be applied to a graphical object.

Placeholder A field or block of text used to determine the position of objects in a document.

Plagiarism The act of using and documenting the ideas or writings of another as one's own.

Portrait orientation Page orientation is longer than it is wide—like the portrait of a person.

Position Raises or lowers text from the baseline without creating superscript or subscript size.

Presentation graphics software A computer application, such as Microsoft PowerPoint, that is used primarily to create electronic slide shows.

Print Layout view The default view that closely resembles the printed document.

Proportional typeface Allocates horizontal space to the character.

Pull quote A phrase or sentence taken from an article to emphasize a key point.

Quick Access Toolbar A customizable row of buttons for frequently used commands, such as Save and Undo.

Quick Style A combination of different formatting options available in the Quick Styles gallery.

Record A group of related fields.

Record macro The process of creating a macro.

Redo Command that reinstates or reserves an action per-formed by the Undo command.

Regrouping The process of grouping objects together again.

Relational database software A computer application, such as Microsoft Access, that is used to store data and convert it into information.

Repeat The Repeat command duplicates the last action you performed.

Replace The process of finding and replacing a word or group of words with other text.

Research command A command that enables you to conduct research investigations to find information.

Reverse The technique that uses light text on a dark background.

Reviewing Pane A window that displays all comments and editorial changes made to the main document.

Revision mark Indicates where text is added, deleted, or formatted while the Track Changes feature is active.

Ribbon The Microsoft Office 2007 GUI command center that organizes commands into related tabs and groups.

Right tab Sets the start position on the right so as you type, text moves to the left of that tab setting and aligns on the right.

Root element The initial element that contains specific elements defined by an XML schema.

Row height The vertical space from the top to the bottom of a row in a table or in a spreadsheet.

Run macro The process of playing back or using a macro.

Sans serif typeface A typeface that does not contain thin lines on characters.

Scale or scaling Increases or decreases text or a graphic as a percentage of its size.

Schema validation The process of examining the content and tags against the schema to ensure accuracy and conformity.

Section break A marker that divides a document into sections thereby allowing different formatting in each section.

Selective replacement Option that enables you to decide whether to replace text and which text to replace.

Serif typeface A typeface that contains a thin line or extension at the top and bottom of the primary strokes on characters.

Shading A background color that appears behind text in a paragraph, a page, a table, or a spreadsheet cell.

Shape A geometric or nongeometric object, such as a circle or an arrow.

Shortcut menu A list of commands that appears when you right-click an item or screen element.

Show Markup Enables you to view document revisions by reviewer; it also allows you to choose which type of revisions you want to view such as comments, insertions and deletions, or formatting changes.

Show/Hide feature Reveals where formatting marks such as spaces, tabs, and returns are used in the document.

Sidebar Supplementary text that appears on the side of the featured information.

Signature line Enables you to digitally sign the document.

Sizing handle The small circles and squares that appear around a selected object and enable you to adjust the height and width of a selected object.

SmartArt A diagram that presents information visually to effectively communicate a message.

Soft page break Inserted when text fills an entire page then continues on the next page.

Soft return Created by the word processor as it wraps text to a new line.

Sorting Listing records in a specific sequence, such as alphabetically by last name or rearranging data based on certain criteria.

Spelling and Grammar Feature that attempts to catch mistakes in spelling, punctuation, writing style, and word usage by comparing strings of text within a document to a series of predefined rules.

Spreadsheet software A computer application, such as Microsoft Excel, that is used to build and manipulate electronic spreadsheets.

Status bar The horizontal bar at the bottom of a Microsoft Office application that displays summary information about the selected window or object and contains View buttons and the Zoom slider. The Word status bar displays the page number and total words, while the Excel status bar displays the average, count, and sum of values in a selected range. The PowerPoint status bar displays the slide number and the Design Theme name.

Style A set of formatting options you apply to characters or paragraphs.

Subdocument A smaller document that is a part of a master document.

Synchronous scrolling Enables you to scroll through documents at the same time in Side by Side view.

Tab A marker that specifies the position for aligning text and add organization to a document.

Table A series of rows and columns that organize data effectively.

Table alignment The position of a table between the left and right document margins.

Table of authorities Used in legal documents to reference cases, and other documents referred to in a legal brief.

Table of contents Lists headings in the order they appear in a document and the page numbers where the entries begin.

Table of figures A list of the captions in a document.

Table style An option that contains borders, shading, font sizes, and other attributes that enhance readability of a table.

Tag A marker that indicates the beginning or end of particular content within a document.

Template A file that incorporates a theme, a layout, and content that can be modified.

Text box A graphical object that contains text.

Text content control Used to enter any type of text into a form.

Text direction The degree of rotation in which text displays.

Text pane A special pane that opens up for entering text when a SmartArt diagram is selected.

Text wrapping style The way text wraps around an image.

Theme colors Represent the current text and background, accent, and hyperlinks.

Theme effects Include lines and fill effects.

Theme fonts Contain a heading and body text font.

Thumbnail A miniature display of an image, page, or slide.

Title bar The shaded bar at the top of every window; often displays the program name and filename.

Toggle switch Causes the computer to alternate between two states. For example, you can toggle between the Insert mode and the Overtype mode.

Track Changes Monitors all additions, deletions, and formatting changes you make in a document.

Transform A file that converts XML documents into another type of formatted language, such as HTML.

Type style The characteristic applied to a font, such as bold.

Typeface A complete set of characters—upper- and lowercase letters, numbers, punctuation marks, and special symbols.

Typography The arrangement and appearance of printed matter.

Undo Command cancels your last one or more operations.

Ungrouping Breaks a combined single object into individual objects.

User exception An individual or group that is allowed to edit a restricted document.

User interface The meeting point between computer software and the person using it.

View Side by Side Enables you to display two documents on the same screen.

Virus checker Software that scans files for a hidden program that can damage your computer.

Visual Basic for Applications (VBA) A programming language that is built into Microsoft Office.

Watermark Text or a graphic that displays behind text.

Web Layout view View to display how a document will look when posted on the Web.

Web page Any document that displays on the World Wide Web.

Web server A computer system that hosts pages for viewing by anyone with an Internet connection.

Widow The last line of a paragraph appearing by itself at the top of a page.

Wizard A tool that makes a process easier by asking a series of questions, then creating a document structure based on your answers.

Word processing software A computer application, such as Microsoft Word, that is used primarily with text to create, edit, and format documents.

Word wrap The feature that automatically moves words to the next line if they do not fit on the current line.

World Wide Web (WWW) A very large subset of the Internet that stores Web page documents.

XML schema A file that defines the structure and organization of content within an XML document.

Zoom slider Enables you to increase or decrease the magnification of the file onscreen.

Multiple Choice Answer Keys

Office Fundamentals, Chapter 1
1. b
2. c
3. d
4. a
5. d
6. c
7. b
8. c
9. d
10. a
11. c
12. d
13. c
14. a
15. d

Word 2007, Chapter 1
1. c
2. b
3. a
4. c
5. b
6. a
7. c
8. d
9. b
10. c
11. d
12. d
13. b
14. a
15. c
16. d

Word 2007, Chapter 2
1. d
2. c
3. b
4. a
5. d
6. d
7. d
8. d
9. d
10. d
11. b
12. d
13. c
14. d
15. c
16. a
17. b
18. a
19. a

Word 2007, Chapter 3
1. d
2. a
3. a
4. d
5. c
6. b
7. a
8. d
9. a
10. d
11. b
12. b
13. d
14. b
15. a
16. c
17. d

Word 2007, Chapter 4
1. c
2. d
3. b
4. a
5. c
6. b
7. c
8. c
9. a
10. d
11. b
12. a
13. d
14. a
15. b

Word 2007, Chapter 5
1. c
2. b
3. d
4. d
5. b
6. c
7. c
8. d
9. a
10. a
11. d
12. b
13. c
14. a
15. b

Word 2007, Chapter 6

1. d
2. b
3. a
4. c
5. c
6. b
7. a
8. d
9. d
10. a
11. b
12. b
13. d
14. b
15. c

Word 2007, Chapter 8

1. d
2. b
3. a
4. c
5. c
6. b
7. a
8. d
9. d
10. a
11. b
12. b
13. d
14. b
15. c

Word 2007, Chapter 7

1. b
2. d
3. a
4. d
5. c
6. b
7. d
8. a
9. c
10. a
11. b
12. d
13. c
14. c
15. a

Index

Quick Access Toolbar (QAT), 4, 5, 53, 72
  adding commands to, 108, 109, 113
  customizing of, 5
Quick Parts gallery, 77
Quick Print, 107, 116
Quick Print feature, 27
Quick Print option, 107, 116
Quick Styles, 382, 383, 402
  gallery, 382, 402

R

Radial diagram, 409
  exercise, 409–410
Read only restriction, 434
Real Estate Agency Web site exercise, 509–512
  enhancements in, 510–511
  XML in, 511–513
Real Estate appraisal case study, 418
Recent Documents list
  keeping files on, 21
  opening of files with, 20–21
Recipe book exercise, 305
Recipient list, 328, 330–331, 347. *See also*
    Data sources
  creation of, 336–337
Record(s), 347. *See also* Data sources
  definition of, 330
  sorting of, in data sources, 331–332, 347,
    352–353
Record macro(s), 447–448, 456–457
  dialog box, 447
  exercise with, 451–452
Redo button, 39
Redo command, 39, 53
Reference pages, 159. *See also* Indexes;
    Table of contents
  application of style for, 173
  completed document for, 178
  exercises for, 173–178
  index creation in, 171, 175–178
  table of contents insertion in, 174
Reference resources, 277–282
  additional, 287–291
  exercises for, 283–286
References tab, 73
Regional Science Fair exercise, 465–466
Regrouping, 386
Reject/accept changes, in documents, 255,
    261–262
Relational database software, 3
  Access as, 3
  characteristics of, 3
Repetitive tasks, macros and, 469. *See also*
    Macros
Replace command, 36
Replace/find commands, 94–95, 101,
    102, 116
Replacement
  automatic, 94
  selective, 94
  of text, 38, 53
Research command, 499, 505
Research sources, Encarta Encyclopedia
    online and, 499, 500
Research task pane, 43, 505
  blog post and, 502, 505
  exercise with, 514
  usage of, 499, 500
Research tools, 43, 50–51, 53
Resources, Word 2007, 109
Restrict Formatting and Editing task pane,
    422, 423
Restrictions
  editing, 434–435, 442–443, 443–444, 456
  formatting, 433–434, 441–442, 456
  user exceptions from, 434–435
Resume exercise, 241

Resume templates, 314–316, 347
  basic, 315
  downloading of, 315, 319
  Equity, 314, 317, 347
  exercise with, 318–320
  job specific, 315
  Median, 314, 317, 318, 347
  online, 315, 319
  Oriel, 314, 317, 347
  Origin, 314, 317, 347
  reference list, 317
  situation specific, 315
  Urban, 314, 317, 347
  various career fields, 315, 316
Returns
  hard, 75
  soft, 75
Reveal formatting pane, 162
Reverse, 363, 402
  newsletter creation and, 372, 373
Review tab, 74
Reviewing, of documents, 299–300
Reviewing Pane, 252–253
Revision Marks, 254
Ribbons, 4, 6–8, 53. *See also* Table Tools
    Design ribbon; Table Tools Layout
    ribbon
  components of, 7
  definition of, 6
  hiding of, 7
  PowerPoint with, 7
  use of Excel, 13, 14
Rich text control, 421
Right alignment, 148, 149
Right tabs, 143
Root elements, 489
Rotation
  of graphical objects, 387, 402–403
  of images, 224
Row(s), in tables, 199
  height changes in, 199, 203, 204
  insertion/deletion of, 198, 202, 215
Row height, 199, 203
  adjustment of, 204
Rows & Columns group, 200
Ruler, 155
  horizontal, 72
  indents and, 155
  vertical, 72
Run macros, 450, 457
  keystroke combination and, 463

S

Sans serif typeface, 133
Save As command, 21, 22, 53
  activation of, 22
  Office menu and, 23
Save As dialog box, 82
  Excel, 22
Save commands, 21, 22, 53
  characteristics of, 22
Save/save as function, 81–82, 116
  compatible formats and, 104–105, 112
  customization of, 109
Saving, of files, 18, 21–24, 53
  Access and, 24
Scale, 135–136, 136, 222
Scaling. *See* Scale
Schema, XML, 486–487, 492, 493, 505
  modification of, 519
Schema validation, 491, 495
Science fair volunteers
  exercise, 356
  request form, 460–461
Scroll bars
  horizontal, 75
  vertical, 72, 75

Scrolling, keyboard shortcuts for, 75–76
Searches. *See also* Find and Replace
    commands
  case-insensitive, 94, 95
  case-sensitive, 94, 95
Section breaks, 157–158
  creation of, 92–93, 99, 115
Section level, 92
  paragraph level *v.,* 151
Select Table dialog box, 343
Selective replacement, 94
Serif typeface, 133
Servers, Web, 479
Set Page Title dialog box, 480, 481
Shading, 145–146, 156, 179, 365
  cells with, 205, 207, 214
  newsletter creation and, 375, 376
Shadow, 135, 384
  images with, 224
Shapes, 377, 402. *See also* Graphical objects;
    specific shapes
  categories of, 377
  command, 377
  definition of, 377
  fill options for, 383, 384
  gallery, 377, 378
  insertion of, 378, 402
Shortcuts. *See also* Keyboard shortcuts
  moving/copying of text with, 35
Shortletter macro, 453
Show Markup features, 253
Show/Hide feature, 76, 115
Shrink Font command, 46
Side by side viewing, of documents,
    263–264, 271–272, 295
Sidebars, 364, 402
Sidewalk café exercise, 305–306
Signature lines, 438–439, 456
  exercise with, 446
  signing on, 446
Single file Web pages, 475
Situation specific resume templates, 315
Sizing handles, 221
Small caps, 135
SmartArt
  definition of, 378
  diagram, 379
  format options for, 380
  gallery, 379
  insertion of, 378–380, 391–392, 402
Soft page breaks, 88, 89
Soft returns, 75
Software applications
  Access, 3
  Excel, 3
  Office 2007, 3
  PowerPoint, 3
  presentation graphics, 3
  relational database, 3
  spreadsheet, 3
  virus checker, 23
  Word, 3
  word processing, 3
Sorting feature, 207, 209–210
  ascending order in, 209
  descending order in, 209
  tables with, 207, 209, 210–211,
    217, 232
Source(s), research, 295
  creation of, 277–278, 283
  searching for, 278, 283
  sharing of, 278
Source documents, 347. *See also* Main
    documents
Source Manager dialog box, 278, 279
Spaces
  nonbreaking, 137–138, 140–141, 179
  regular, 139